# HIGH-SPEED NETWORKING TECHNOLOGY

## An Introductory Survey

HARRY J.R. DUTTON ▪ PETER LENHARD

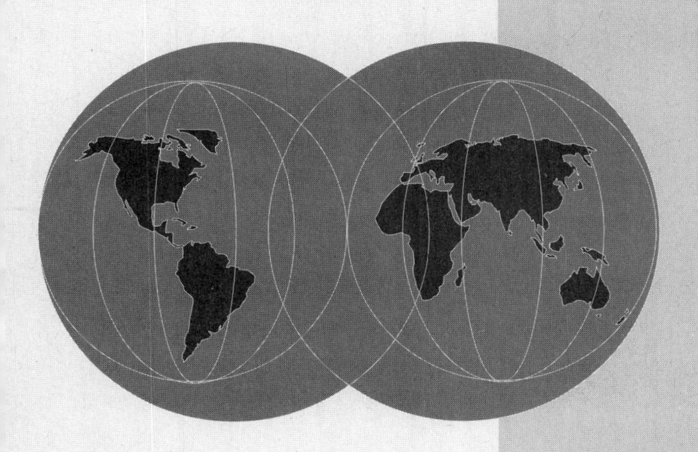

IBM

PRENTICE HALL PTR, UPPER SADDLE RIVER, NEW JERSEY 07458

**Third Edition**



For information about redbooks:

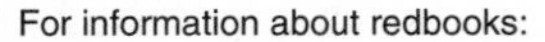

http://www.redbooks.ibm.com/redbooks

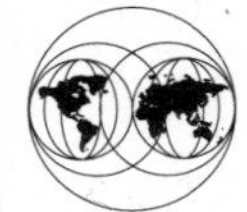

Send comments to:
redbooks@vnet.ibm.com

Published by

Prentice Hall PTR
Prentice-Hall, Inc.
A Simon & Schuster Company
Upper Saddle River, NJ 07458

The publisher offers discounts on this book when ordered in bulk quantities. For more information, contact

Corporate Sales Department,
Prentice Hall PTR
One Lake Street
Upper Saddle River, NJ 07458
Phone: 800-382-3419; FAX: 201-236-714
E-mail (Internet): corpsales@prenhall.com

*For book and bookstore information*

**http://www.prenhall.com**

Printed in the United States of America

10 9 8 7 6 5 4 3 2 1

ISBN 0-13-242421-5

Prentice-Hall International (UK) Limited, *London*
Prentice-Hall of Australia Pty. Limited, *Sydney*
Prentice-Hall Canada Inc., *Toronto*
Prentice-Hall Hispanoamericana, S.A., *Mexico*
Prentice-Hall of India Private Limited, *New Delhi*
Prentice-Hall of Japan, Inc., *Tokyo*
Simon & Schuster Asia Pte. Ltd., *Singapore*
Editora Prentice-Hall do Brasil, Ltda., *Rio de Janeiro*

# Contents

# Figures

# Tables

# Preface

This publication presents a broad overview of the emerging technology of very-high-speed communications. It is written at the "technical conceptual" level with some areas of greater detail. It was written for computer professionals who have some understanding of communications (but who do not necessarily consider themselves experts).

The primary topics of the book are:

- The Principles of High-Speed Networking
- Fiber Optical Technology and Optical Networks
- Local Area Networks (Token-Ring, FDDI, MetaRing, CRMA, Radio LANs)
- Metropolitan Area Networks (DQDB/SMDS)
- High-Speed Packet Switches (frame relay, Paris, plaNET)
- High-Speed Cell Switching (ATM)

This publication is designed to assist the reader in understanding the wider issues relating to the interconnection of IBM products. Detailed information about IBM products is given here incidental to objectives of the book, and while every effort has been made to ensure accuracy, such information should not be considered authoritative. Authoritative information about IBM products is contained in the official manuals for the product concerned.

# Audience

This publication is primarily intended for people who have an interest in the fields of data communications or voice networking. Such people will often be:

**Technical planners** in user organizations who wish to broaden their understanding of high-speed communications and the direction product development in the industry is taking.

**IBM systems engineers** evaluating the potential of different systems approaches may find the information helpful in understanding the emerging high-speed technologies.

## Structure

The book is organized as follows:

**Chapter 1, "Introduction"**

This chapter presents a broad outline of the topics dealt with in detail later in the book.

**Chapter 2, "A Review of Digital Transmission Technology"**

This chapter discusses digital transmission over copper wire. Starting with the concept of sending a digital signal along a wire it describes:

- The problems of transmission over electrical wires.
- The methods that have been developed to cope with these problems.
- The line code structures that are used in the more significant modern digital systems.
- How the problems associated with data transmission in the public network (subscriber loop) and LAN environments are addressed and solved.

**Chapter 3, "High Speed on the Subscriber Loop (HDSL and ADSL)"**

Research aimed at using the standard copper wire connection from a private home to the local telephone exchange for television and video traffic has been intense in the last few years. This has been motivated by competition within the industry. This research has been much more successful than anyone had foreseen and both ADSL and HDSL technologies look certain to boom in the immediate future.

**Chapter 4, "An Introduction to Fiber Optical Technology"**

This chapter presents a general introduction to fiber optic technology.

**Chapter 5, "Traffic Characteristics"**

High-speed networks will be used for many purposes. The traditional interactive data traffic will of course be important but voice, image, and video will be carried in the new networks.

But these new types of traffic (new to packet networks) have completely different characteristics and requirements from traditional data.

The characteristics of voice, image, and video traffic are examined and compared to those of traditional data traffic.

**Chapter 6, "Principles of High-Speed Networks"**

This chapter outlines the broad principles that must be followed in building a high-speed network (one that is able to take full advantage of high speed). The principles are discussed in relation to those used by traditional packet networks.

### Chapter 7, "Private Networks in the High-Speed Environment"

This short discussion emphasizes the problem of building many communications networks "on top of one another". At the present time there is little alternative to this approach, but for practical high-speed networking in the future a fully integrated approach will offer significant advantages.

### Chapter 8, "High-Speed Time Division Multiplexing Systems"

Time Division Multiplexing (TDM) is an important way of dividing a fast communications channel into many slower ones. It can be "inefficient" in the sense that it wastes capacity but it is simple and cost effective. If high-speed data transmission is low in cost, then perhaps TDM systems are the way to share the capacity.

Integrated Services Digital Network (ISDN) is a TDM method of access to a public network. The basics of ISDN are described.

Sonet and Synchronous Digital Hierarchy are very important protocols for sharing very high-speed optical trunks. While currently these interfaces are not available to the end user (they are internal to the PTT), it is likely that they will be made available in the near future. These protocols are described in concept.

### Chapter 9, "Cell-Based Systems (ATM)"

Cell relay systems are almost universally regarded as the long term future of data (and voice communications). Broadband ISDN is being developed as a cell relay system.

The concepts of cell relay are described and an overview of Broadband ISDN presented.

### Chapter 10, "High-Speed Circuit-Switching Systems"

In the enthusiasm surrounding high-speed cell networking, simple circuit switched approaches are often forgotten. Circuit switching can operate well at high speed (especially over short distances). The IBM ESCON Channel architecture is described as an example of a high-speed circuit switched system.

### Chapter 11, "High-Speed Packet Networking"

The technique of packet networking, familiar to all because of its use in SNA and in X.25 needs to be updated to operate at the very high speeds becoming available.

The concept of frame switching is introduced because, although it is not a high-speed technology, it illustrates a packet network approach to the transport of link level frames.

Frame relay is then described and positioned as an important technology for the here and now.

Paris is an IBM experimental networking technology designed for operation at very high speeds. Paris is described as an example of the direction research is taking.

**Chapter 12, "plaNET/Orbit - A Gigabit Prototype Network"**

The IBM plaNET project is producing prototype equipment for very high-speed networks. This equipment is in use for a number of "trial" high-speed networking projects, the most well known being the US Government sponsored "Aurora" project.

**Chapter 13, "Shared Media Systems (LANs and MANs)"**

This chapter deals with local area networks and metropolitan area networks (LANs and MANs). After an overview of available LAN technologies the chapter details what happens to various LAN systems as speed is increased. Token-ring continues to operate but becomes less and less efficient. FDDI is better (and designed to run on optical media) but it too starts to degrade at speeds in the gigabit region.

DQDB is the telephone industry's first LAN protocol. It is the basis for several operational MAN systems and for the user to public network interface called "Switched Multi-Megabit Data Service" (SMDS). DQDB also has problems with efficiency and fairness at high speeds.

**Chapter 14, "Radio LAN Technology"**

This chapter overviews the technology of indoor radio and its application to wireless LAN systems.

**Chapter 15, "The Frontiers of LAN Research"**

There is an enormous amount of research going on around the world aimed at inventing a LAN protocol that will be optimal in the speed range above about one gigabit per second. Two IBM research project LAN prototypes (MetaRing and CRMA) and a further proposal, which integrates the desirable features of both (CRMA-II), are discussed.

**Chapter 16, "Lightwave Networks"**

Until very recently the use of fiber optics in communications has been limited to replacing electronic links with optical ones. Network designs have remained the same (albeit with some accommodation for the higher speeds involved). Recently researchers have begun to report trials of a new kind of network that uses passive optical components rather than electronic ones. An outline of this technology is presented in this chapter.

**Chapter 17, "LAN Hub Development"**

An alternative to the very high-speed LAN is a local cell or packet switch. Many people believe that this technology will make very high-speed LANs redundant. This chapter overviews the issue of high-speed LANs versus LAN hubs.

**Appendix A, "Review of Basic Principles"**

This appendix is a review of the basic principles involved in multiplexing (or sharing) a link or switching device. It is included as background for readers who may be unfamiliar with this area.

**Appendix B, "Transmitting Information by Modulating a Carrier"**

This material provides some elementary background to the discussion on indoor radio for readers who may not have studied the subject before.

**Appendix C, "Queueing Theory"**

Queueing theory is the basis of network design and also the basis for understanding much of the discussion in this book. This appendix presents the important results of queueing theory and discusses its impact on high-speed protocols.

**Appendix D, "Getting the Language into Synch"**

One problem in developing a book such as this is the inconsistency in language between different groups in the EDP and communications industries. This apppendix deals with words related to the word "synchronous" in order that the reader may understand the usage in the body of the text.

## Comments on the Third Edition

By January 1995, early commercial ATM systems were available. The current state of the art for speed on wide area optical fiber is 3.6 Gbps. Optical networking continues to progress and early field trials of equipment are in progress.

The changes in this edition from the Second Edition are as follows:

**Chapter 2, "A Review of Digital Transmission Technology"** has been expanded to cover the new transmission protocols used in high-speed Ethernet, FDDI on UTP and 100VG AnyNet.

**Chapter 9, "Cell-Based Systems (ATM)"** has been replaced with an expanded treatment of ATM. This reflects the current strong focus on ATM within the industry.

**Chapter 13, "Shared Media Systems (LANs and MANs)"** has been updated to include more detail on 100 Mbps Ethernet, FDDI over UTP-5 and 100VG AnyNet.

**Chapter 16, "Lightwave Networks"** has new material covering recent research field trials of optical networking equipment.

Miscellaneous small changes have been made throughout.

As technology develops it is expected that this book will be updated and new editions produced. Comments from readers are an enormous help. Please, if you have any comment at all, send in the reader's comment form.

## Comments on the Second Edition

In the relatively short time (18 months) between the first edition of this book and the second edition, there were significant advances in every area of basic transmission technology. In addition, some development directions that were very active in 1991 looked somewhat less promising by 1993.

- In fiber optics, researchers believed that passive optical networks of 1000 devices each operating at 2 Gbps simultaneously would be built commercially.
- In copper wire transmission, substantial progress had been made in increasing the speed possible on the "subscriber loop".
- Indoor radio technology had begun to produce a new generation of "wireless LANs".

At the time of the first edition, one big question was about very fast LANs. The rationale went as follows *"If we can build LANs at 1 Gbps for much the same cost as FDDI (this is true) then why would users not prefer them to FDDI?"* By the second edition (1993), there was some question about the economic justification for very fast LANs (even FDDI). Many people believed a fast packet switch approach would provide higher throughput at a lower cost. (See Chapter 17, "LAN Hub Development" on page 17-1.)

The year and a half between editions saw an unprecedented acceleration in the development of ATM. In 1991, ATM looked to be something that would be available in about the year 2000. By 1993, ATM looked like it might become available as early as 1995 (some early products were available already). This prediction held true.

# Special Notices

This publication is intended to help both customers and IBM systems engineers to understand the principles of high-speed communications. The information in this publication is not intended as the specification of any programming interface provided by any IBM product. See the publications section of the applicable IBM Programming Announcement for the specific product for more information about which publications are considered to be product documentation.

References in this publication to IBM products, programs or services do not imply that IBM intends to make these available in all countries in which IBM operates. Any reference to an IBM product, program, or service is not intended to state or imply that only IBM's product, program, or service may be used. Any functionally equivalent program that does not infringe any of IBM's intellectual property rights may be used instead of the IBM product, program or service.

Information in this book was developed in conjunction with use of the equipment specified, and is limited in application to those specific hardware and software products and levels.

IBM may have patents or pending patent applications covering subject matter in this document. The furnishing of this document does not give you any license to these patents. You can send license inquiries, in writing, to the IBM Director of Licensing, IBM Corporation, 500 Columbus Avenue, Thornwood, NY 10594, USA.

The information contained in this document has not been submitted to any formal IBM test and is distributed AS IS. The use of this information or the implementation of any of these techniques is a customer responsibility and depends on the customer's ability to evaluate and integrate them into the customer's operational environment. While each item may have been reviewed by IBM for accuracy in a specific situation, there is no guarantee that the same or similar results will be obtained elsewhere. Customers attempting to adapt these techniques to their own environments do so at their own risk.

The following document contains examples of data and reports used in daily business operations. To illustrate them as completely as possible, the examples contain the names of individuals, companies, brands, and products. All of these names are fictitious and any similarity to the names and addresses used by an actual business enterprise is entirely coincidental.

The following terms are trademarks of the International Business Machines Corporation in the United States and/or other countries:

| | |
|---|---|
| AnyNet | APPN |
| AS/400 | ESCON |
| IBM | Micro Channel |
| NetView | Nways |
| PAL | Personal System/2 |
| PS/2 | Quiet |
| RISC System/6000 | RS/6000 |
| Series/1 | System/36 |
| System/370 | XT |
| 400 | 9076 SP1 |

The following terms are trademarks of other companies:

| | |
|---|---|
| Altair | Motorola Corporation |
| AMI | American Megatrends, Incorporated |
| AT&T | American Telephone and Telegraph Company |
| Bell | AT&T Bell Laboratories Incorporated |
| Crosstalk | Digital Communications Associates, Incorporated |
| DCE | The Open Software Foundation |
| DECnet | Digital Equipment Corporation |
| Interlink | Interlink Technologies, Incorporated |
| isoENET | National Semiconductor Corporation |
| Lambdanet | Bell Communications Research |
| Metro | Lotus Development Corporation |
| Microsoft | Microsoft Corporation |
| Motorola | Motorola, Incorporated |
| National Semiconductor | National Semiconductor Corporation |
| QPSX | QPSX Communications, Inc. |
| SNS SNA/Gateway | Interlink Computer Sciences,Inc. |
| WaveLAN | NCR Corporation |
| X/Open | X/Open Company Limited |
| 386 | Intel Corporation |

Windows is a trademark of Microsoft Corporation.

PC Direct is a trademark of Ziff Communications Company and is used by IBM Corporation under license.

UNIX is a registered trademark in the United States and other countries licensed exclusively through X/Open Company Limited.

C-bus is a trademark of Corollary, Inc.

Other company, product, and service names may be trademarks or service marks of others.

# Acknowledgments

The author of this document is:

**Harry J.R. Dutton**
IBM Australia

The project leader was:

**Peter Lenhard**
IBM International Technical Support Organization
Raleigh Center

This publication is the result of a residency conducted at the International Technical Support Organization, Raleigh Center.

Thanks go to the following people for assistance in obtaining information, comments and review:

| | |
|---|---|
| **Harman R. van As** | IBM Research Division,<br>IBM Zurich Research Laboratory, Ruschlikon, Switzerland. |
| **Frederic Bauchot** | IBM Advanced Telecommunications Systems,<br>La Gaude, France. |
| **John Creigh** | IBM Network Systems Division,<br>Raleigh, North Carolina. |
| **Michel Demange** | IBM Advanced Telecommunications Systems,<br>La Gaude, France. |
| **Joel Frigon** | IBM Advanced Telecommunications Systems,<br>Research Triangle Park, North Carolina. |
| **Neville Golding** | IBM Network Systems Division,<br>Research Triangle Park, North Carolina. |
| **David R. Irvin** | IBM US Telecommunications Center,<br>Research Triangle Park, North Carolina. |
| **Raif O. Onvural** | IBM Advanced Telecommunications Systems,<br>Raleigh, North Carolina. |
| **Peter Russell** | IBM United Kingdom Limited. |
| **Ian Shields** | IBM Network Systems Division<br>Raleigh, North Carolina. |

**Pitro Zafiropulo** IBM Research Division,
IBM Zurich Research Laboratory, Ruschlikon, Switzerland.

**Readers of the previous editions**

A special thanks to the many readers who sent in helpful suggestions and comments about the previous editions. Every comment contributed to improving the quality.

# Chapter 1. Introduction

The phrase "high-speed communication" is a relative term. It seems not long ago (1970) that a 4,800 bits per second leased line was considered very high in speed. By 1991, 2 Mbps wide area links and LANs using speeds of 10 and 16 Mbps had become universal. By the mid-1990s very much higher speeds (hundreds of megabits per second) are common.

The networking techniques and technologies currently in use are unable to operate efficiently at the newly available higher speeds. This publication describes the new approaches that are required to enable efficient use of the new high speeds. So rather than defining "high speed" to mean any particular speed, for the purposes of this document "high speed" is held to mean "any speed that requires the use of new networking techniques for efficient operation". In practice this dividing line is somewhere around 100 Mbps for LANs and about 35 Mbps for wide area communications.

## 1.1 Yet Another Revolution?

The 1990s have been a period of very rapid change in the field of data communications. Over the years the word "revolution" has been used so frequently in the EDP industry that when a genuine revolution comes along we are robbed of the right word to describe it. But "revolution" is the right word this time.

Since the inception of data communications in the late 1950s, techniques have steadily improved, link speeds have progressively become faster, and equipment cost has gradually declined. In general terms, it seems that the industry has progressed in price/performance measures by about 20% per annum compound. But now the cost of long communications lines is scheduled to reduce not by a few percent but by perhaps 100 or even 1000 times over a very few years!

The main causes of this are:

- The universal use of digital technologies within public telecommunications networks.
- The maturing of fiber optical transmission within public network facilities.

Both digital and fiber technologies have been in use for some years, but they have formed only a small proportion of public networks - digital "islands" in an analog "sea." But the real benefits of digital transmission can only be realized when circuits are fully digital from end-to-end and when the digital network is available everywhere. In many western countries that time has arrived.

The consensus among economists in the industry seems to be that bandwidth cost (though not price, yet) is reducing at a compound rate of 80% per annum. Most agree that these enormous cost savings will be passed on to end users (indeed this is already happening) but it will take some time for the full effect to be felt. This is because it is extremely difficult for any industry to manage change at anything like the rate now being experienced.

## 1.2 User Demand

Abundant, cheap communications means that many potential applications that were not possible before because of cost are now becoming very attractive. There are four generic requirements being expressed by users in relation to the new technologies:

1. To implement new data applications using graphics and image processing, etc.

2. To do existing applications in better ways.

   For example instead of using coded commands and responses (such as are typical of banking and airline applications), users would like fast response full-screen applications so that staff do not need the specialized skills that previous systems demanded.

3. To rationalize the many disparate networks that major users have.

   Many users have SNA, DECnet, TCP/IP and X.25 data networks as well as logical networks of FAX machines and a voice network. For management reasons (and for cost optimization, though this is becoming less and less of a factor) users want to have only one network to handle all traffic.

4. Integration of voice, video, and data.

   Most large users have a voice network and a separate data network, and for cost and manageability reasons would like to integrate these. In addition there is the future possibility of voice and data integrated applications.

   Many users see video as an important opportunity and would like to be able to handle this traffic.

## 1.3 The New Environment

**Bandwidth Cost**

The cost of transmitting "x" bits per second continues to reduce exponentially.

**Attachment Cost**

The cost of connecting a link (be it copper wire or optical fiber) from a user's location to the public network continues to *increase* with inflation. Having any connection at all involves "digging up the road" and this cost continues to rise.

Today's technology enables us to use a single connection for many different things simultaneously and to use significantly higher transmission rates, but the cost of having a single connection is increasing.

## Error Rates

Error rates on communication links have improved dramatically. On an analog telephone line with a modem, a typical rate might have been $10^{-5}$ - or one error in every 100,000 bits transmitted. On a fiber connection this rate may be as low as $10^{-11}$ - a million times better!

## Error Characteristics

The kinds of errors have changed also. On a digital connection errors tend to occur in bursts, whereas on an analog line they usually occur as single or double bit errors.

## Propagation Delay

At 80% of the speed of light, the speed of message propagation on a communication line hasn't changed.

## Storage Effect

At very high speeds long communication lines store a large amount of data. For example, a link from New York to Los Angeles involves a delay of roughly 20 milliseconds. At the 100 Mbps speed of FDDI this means that two million bits are in transit at any time *in each direction*. So the link has approximately half a million bytes stored in transit.

This has a critical effect on the efficiency of most current link protocols.

## Computer Technology

Computers continue to become faster and lower in cost at an approximate rate of 30% per annum compounded. However, this is not as simple as it sounds - some things (for example the cost of main storage) have reduced faster than others (for example the costs of power supplies, screens, and keyboards).

Data links are now considerably faster than most computers that attach to them. In the past, the communications line was the limiting factor and most computer devices were easily able to load the link at perhaps 95% of its capacity. Today, very few computer devices are capable of sustaining a continuous transfer rate of anything like the speed of a fast fiber link.

The "state of the art" in public network fiber facilities today is a transmission rate of 2.4 Gbps, but rates of many times this are functioning in laboratories.

## 1.4 The Traditional Packet Data Network

It is the general consensus in the industry that the structures and protocols associated with the traditional packet network are obsolete in the new technological (and economic) environment. For the purpose of this discussion the wide area networking parts of "subarea" SNA and of APPN can be included among the plethora of "X.25" based packet switching networks.

### 1.4.1 Objectives

It is important to consider first the aims underlying the architecture of the traditional packet network.

1. The most obvious objective is to save cost on expensive, low-speed communication lines by statistically multiplexing many connections onto the same line. This is really to say that money is saved on the lines by spending money on networking equipment (nodes).

   For example, in SNA there are extensive flow and congestion controls which when combined with the use of priority mechanisms enable the operation of links at utilizations above 90%. These controls have a significant cost in hardware and software which is incurred in order to save the very high cost of links.

   As cost of long line bandwidth decreases there is less and less to be gained from optimization of this resource.

2. Provide a multiplexed interface to end-user equipment so that an end user can have simultaneous connections with many different destinations over a single physical interface to the network.

3. Provide multiple paths through the network to enable recovery should a single link or node become unavailable.

### 1.4.2 Internal Network Operation

There seems to be as many different ways of constructing a packet network as there are suppliers of such networks. The only feature that the commodity "X.25 networks" have in common is their interface to the end user - internally they differ radically from one another. Even in SNA, the internal operation of subarea networks and of APPN are very different from one another. That said, there are many common features.

**Hop-by-Hop Error Recovery**

Links between network nodes use protocols such as SDLC or LAPB which detect errors and cause retransmission of error frames.

### Implicit Rate Control

Because the data link is far slower than any computer device (the end-user devices and the network nodes could handle all of the data that any link was capable of transmitting) the link provides implicit control over the rate at which data can be delivered to the network. (This is separate from the explicit controls contained in the link control.)

### Software Routing

Software is used for handling the logic of link control, for making routing decisions on arriving data packets, and for manipulating queues.

### Connection Orientation

Most (but not all) networks are based on the concept of an end-to-end connection passing through a set of network nodes. In X.25 these are called virtual circuits, and in SNA there are routes and sessions. Within "intermediate nodes" a record is typically kept of each connection and this record is used by the software to determine the destination to which each individual packet must be directed.

### Throughput

Based on the available link speeds in the 1970s and 1980s the fastest available packet switching nodes have maximum throughput rates of a few thousand packets per second.

### Network Stability

In SNA and APPN (though not by any means in all packet networks) there is an objective to make the network as stable internally as possible, thereby removing the need for attaching devices to operate stabilizing protocols.

In SNA there is no end-to-end error recovery protocol across the network.[1] In the environment of the 1970s and early 1980s this would have involved crippling extra cost (storage, instruction cycles and messages) in every attaching device. Instead, extra cost was incurred within the network nodes because there are very few network nodes compared to the number of attaching devices and the total system cost to the end user was minimized.

With recent advances in microprocessors and reductions in the cost of slow-speed memories (DRAMs), the cost of operating a stabilizing protocol within attaching equipment (or at the endpoints of the network) has reduced considerably.

---

[1] That is, there is no ISO "layer 4 class 4" protocol.

## Packet Size

Blocks of user data offered for transmission vary widely in size. If these blocks are broken up into many short "packets", then the transit delay for the whole block across the network will be considerably shorter. This is because when a block is broken up into many short packets, each packet can be processed by the network separately and the first few packets of a block may be received at the destination before the last packet is transmitted by the source.

Limiting all data traffic to a small maximum length also has the effect of smoothing out queueing delays in intermediate nodes and thus providing a much more even transit delay characteristic than is possible if blocks are allowed to be any length. There are other benefits to short packets; for example, it is easier to manage a pool of fixed length buffers in an intermediate node if it is known that each packet will fit in just one buffer. Furthermore, if packets are short and delivered at a constant, relatively even rate, then the amount of storage needed in the node buffer pool is minimized.

Also, on the relatively slow, high error rate analog links of the past, a short packet size often resulted in the best data throughput, because when a block was found to be in error then there was less data that had to be retransmitted.

However, there is a big problem with short packet sizes. It is a characteristic of the architecture of traditional packet switching nodes that switching a packet takes a certain amount of time (or number of instructions) *regardless* of the length of the packet! That is, a 1000-byte block requires (almost) the same node resource to switch as does a 100-byte block. So if you break a 1000-byte packet up into 10, 100-byte packets then you multiply the load on an intermediate switching node by 10! This effect wasn't too critical when nodes were very fast and links were very slow. Today, when links are very fast and nodes are (relatively) slow this characteristic is the most significant limitation on network throughput.

It should be pointed out that SNA networks do not break data up into short blocks for internal transport. At the boundary of the network there is a function (segmentation) which breaks long data blocks up into "segments" suitable to fit in the short buffers available in some early devices. In addition, there is a function (chaining) which enables the user to break up very large blocks (say above 4000 bytes) into shorter ones if needed, but in general, data blocks are sent within an SNA network as single, whole, blocks.

## Congestion Control

Every professional involved in data communication knows (or should know) the mathematics of the single server queue. Whenever you have a resource that is used for a variable length of time by many requesters (more or less) at random, then the service any particular requester will get is determined by a highly predictable but very unexpected result. (This applies to people queueing for a supermarket checkout just as much as messages queuing for transmission on a link.)

As the utilization of the server gets higher the length of the queue increases. If requests arrive at random, then at 70% utilization the average queue length will be about 3. As utilization of the resource approaches 100% then the length of the queue tends towards infinity!

Nodes, links and buffer pools within communication networks are servers, and messages within the network are requesters.

The short result of the above is that, unless there is strict control of data flow and congestion within, the network will not operate reliably. (Since a network with an average utilization of 10% may still have peaks where utilization of some resources exceeds 90%, this applies to all traditional networks.) In SNA there are extensive flow and congestion control mechanisms. In an environment of very high bandwidth cost, this is justified because these control mechanisms enable the use of much higher resource utilizations.

When bandwidth cost becomes very low, then some people argue that there will be no need for congestion control at all (for example if no resource is ever utilized at above 30%, then it is hard to see the need for expensive control mechanisms). It is the view of this author that congestion and flow control mechanisms will still be needed in the very fast network environment but that these protocols will be very different from those in operation in today's networks.

## 1.5 Is a Network Still Needed?

If the purpose of a network is to save money by optimizing the use of high-cost, low-speed transmission links, then if the transmission links are low-cost, high-capacity why have a network at all?

In practice, there are many other reasons to build a network:

- The reason that bandwidth costs so little is that individual links can be very fast. In a practical situation this means that single links need to be shared among many users.
- Users with many locations and devices typically need a single device to communicate with multiple other devices simultaneously. Without a network there would have to be a point-to-point link from each device to each other device that it needed to communicate with. This means that each device would need a large number of connections - all of which add to the cost. With a network each device needs only one connection.

- For reliability reasons we often need multiple routes to be available between end-using devices (in case one "goes down", etc.).

The network is still very necessary. The question is really whether "packet" networks (or cell-based networks) are justified when "Time Division Multiplexing (TDM) " networks may end up as more cost effective.

There is a question about who should own the network. A typical user may well buy a virtual network of point-to-point links from the PTT (telephone company), but the PTT will provide these links by deriving TDM channels from its own wideband trunks. From the user point of view they don't really have a network, but from the PTT viewpoint this is a very important case of networking.

## 1.6 Alternative Networking Technologies

Within the industry there is considerable debate over the best way to satisfy the user requirements outlined above (integration of data, voice, video, image, etc.). The only point of general agreement is that conventional data networking techniques are inadequate. Digital high-speed networking techniques may be summarized as follows:

**Frequency Division Multiplexing (FDM)**

FDM is an analog technique and is obsolete in the context of modern high-speed communications. But techniques very similar to FDM are being researched for sharing fiber optical links. In the context of fiber optics this is called Wavelength Division Multiplexing (WDM). Since wavelength is just the inverse of frequency (times some constant) the principles are very much the same.

**Time Division Multiplexing (TDM)**

If transmission bandwidth is to be very low in cost, then why spend money on expensive packet switching nodes. Why not use a simple time division multiplexing scheme for sharing the physical links and tolerate the "inefficiency" in link utilization? Intelligent TDMs will be needed to set up and clear down connections and to provide a multiplexed connection to the end user, but the cost of these may be considerably lower than the packet node alternative.

Within public communications networks there are new multiplexing standards called SDH (Synchronous Digital Hierarchy) and Sonet (Synchronous Optical Network). These provide standards for a significant simplification of the multiplexing techniques of the past (the "multiplex mountain"). See 8.2, "SDH and Sonet" on page 8-16.

### Fast Packet Switching, Frame Switching, Frame Relay

As explained above under "packet switching", every time a block of data is broken up into smaller packets or cells, the overhead incurred to process it within the network is increased.

> One of the aims of the new high-speed network architectures is to mitigate this characteristic such that throughput in bytes per second is constant regardless of the frame size used. However, disassembling a logical record into a stream of cells and reassembling at the other end incurs overhead in the end nodes, and there is additional overhead in end-to-end protocols for sending many blocks when one would do.

The conclusion to be reached from this is that data should be sent through the network as variable length frames. The principles of fast packet switching are:

1. Simplify the link protocols by removing the error recovery mechanism. That is, check for errors and throw away any error data but do nothing else (rely on network end-to-end protocols for data integrity). This is acceptable since the new digital links have far fewer errors than previous analog links.

2. Design the network such that all of the link control and switching functions can be performed in hardware logic. Software-based switching systems cannot match the speed of the new links.

There is an international standard for "frame relay" called CCITT I.122 (see 11.1, "Frame Relay" on page 11-4). A rather different system being prototyped by IBM research is called "Paris" (see 11.2, "Packetized Automatic Routing Integrated System (Paris)" on page 11-16).

### Cell Relay

The big problem with supporting voice and video traffic within a data network is that of providing a constant, regular, delivery rate. Packet networks tend to take data delivered to them at an even rate and deliver it to the other end of the network in bursts.[2] It helps a lot in the network if all data is sent in very short packets or "cells". In addition the transit delay for a block of data through a wide area network is significantly shorter if it is broken up into many smaller blocks.

There is a standardized system for cell switching called "ATM" (Asynchronous Transfer Mode) which provides for the transport of very short (53-byte) cells through a Sonet (SDH) based network.

---

2 There are techniques to help overcome this problem, however.

The IEEE 802.6 standard for metropolitan area subnetworks uses a cell-based transfer mechanism.

### LAN Bridges and Routers

Local area networks (LANs) are the most popular way of interconnecting devices within an office or workgroup. Many organizations have large numbers of LANs in geographically dispersed locations. The challenge is to interconnect these LANs with each other and with large corporate database servers.

LAN bridges and routers are a very popular technology for achieving this interconnection. The problem is that it is very difficult to control congestion in this environment. Also, neither of the popular LAN architectures (Ethernet and token-ring) can provide sufficient regularity in packet delivery to make them usable for voice or video traffic. FDDI-II (Fiber Distributed Data Interface - 2) is a LAN architecture designed to integrate voice with data traffic. See 13.6, “Fiber Distributed Data Interface (FDDI)” on page 13-31.

A remote LAN bridge that has several links to other bridges (the multilink bridge) is logically the same thing as a frame switch with a LAN gateway attached. Most proposed frame switch architectures handle LAN bridging as a part of the switch.

### Metropolitan Area Networks

A MAN is just like a very large LAN (really a set of linked LANs) that covers a city or a whole country. (There are many MAN trials going on in various parts of the world but the first fully commercial service has been introduced in Australia where a country-wide MAN called “Fastpac” has “universal availability” over an area of three million square miles!)

MANs are different from LANs. In a LAN network, data from one user passes along the cable and is accessible by other users on the LAN. In a MAN environment this is unacceptable. The MAN bus or ring must pass through PTT premises only. End users are attached on point-to-point links to nodes on the MAN bus. Data not belonging to a particular user is not permitted to pass through that user's premises.

MAN networks as seen by the end user are thus not very different from high-speed packet networks. However, LANs and MANs are “connectionless” - the network as such does not know about the existence of logical connections between end users and does not administer them. Thus each packet or frame sent to the network carries the full network address of its destination. Most packet networks (fast or slow) recognize and use connections such as sessions or virtual circuits.

It should be noted that there is no necessary relationship (except convenience) between the internal protocol of the MAN and the protocol used on the access link to the end user. These will often be quite different.

## 1.7 Traditional End-User Devices

The common data processing terminal devices used in the 1970s and 1980s were all designed to be optimal in the cost environment of those times. The IBM 3270 display subsystem is an excellent example. One of the key factors in the 3270 design was the assumption that "high-speed" communication meant 4,800 bits per second! In addition, multidrop connection was considered vital because of the high cost of long lines. This determined the design of the formatted data stream, the method of interaction with a host user program, and the assumed characteristics of user transactions.

What really happened was we decided to spend money on the device to save money on communications. Today an optimal solution may well be very different from traditional devices.

## 1.8 Traditional End-User Systems

In the end analysis, the application being performed is the reason for existence of the whole system. There are many ways of performing the same application on a computer system, but when most applications were designed this design and conception was done in a technological environment very different from that of today. The cost of communication is only one factor here; there is also the cost of disk storage, the cost of executing instructions, etc.

One very broad example would be the question of whether "distributed processing" is justified. Of course, there are many reasons for distributed processing, but one key reason quoted in the past was to minimize communication cost (which was very high). With communication cost declining, it is no longer the driving force for distributed processing that it was in the past. Other things, such as ease of system operation and management, become very much more significant.

Another question entirely in application design is the amount of interaction between the end user and the processor. In the past we tried to minimize the amount of data sent - today that is perhaps not the most sensible thing to do. There is no reason today that a host processor should not operate with a remote screen keyboard device in the same way that a personal computer operates with its screen keyboard - and with the same (effectively instantaneous) response characteristics.

Of course the possibilities in application design that are opened up by high-speed communication are the real reason to be interested in such communication in the first place.

There are so many new techniques available in image and in interactive video that the application possibilities are endless.

# Chapter 2. A Review of Digital Transmission Technology

Over the last 20 years, the continued development of digital technologies over copper wire and of fiber optics[1] have together provided a significant increase in available bandwidth for communication. In the case of digital transmission, existing wires can be used to carry vastly increased amounts of information for little increase (often a decrease) in cost.

Among all that has been written about these technologies, the important facts to be remembered are:

1. Any (standard) telephone twisted pair of copper wires can carry data at a speed of 2 million bits per second (2 Mbps) in one direction.[2] Newer techniques (see Chapter 3, "High Speed on the Subscriber Loop (HDSL and ADSL)" on page 3-1) are able to extend this to an amazing 6 Mbps over distances of up to three miles or 2 Mbps FDX over the same distance (without using repeaters).
2. A standard telephone channel is 64 Kbps (thousand bits per second).
3. Two pairs of copper wires that currently carry only one call each now have the ability to carry 30 calls. (There are methods of voice compression that will double this at the least and potentially multiply it by 16, that is, 512 simultaneous voice calls on a single copper wire pair.)
4. A single optical fiber as currently being installed by the telephone companies is run at 2.4 Gbps or 3.6 Gbps. At 2.4 Gbps, around 32,000 uncompressed telephone calls can be simultaneously handled by a single fiber WITHOUT the help of any of the available compression techniques. It is important to note that a single fiber can only be used in one direction at a time, so that two fibers are needed. In 1995 optical multiplexors are becoming available which will handle 20 1-Gbps channels on a single fiber. Researchers tell us that it would be possible, in 1995, to construct an optical multiplexor for 1000 2-Gbps channels *using off-the-shelf components*. However, this is not attractive, since it costs less to put multiple fibers into a single

[1] The use of a light beam to transmit information (speech) was first demonstrated by Alexander Graham Bell in the year 1880. It took 100 years and the advent of glass fiber transmission for the idea to become practical.

[2] The actual speed that can be achieved here is variable depending on such things as the length of wire and the environment in which it is installed. Over very short distances (up to 45 meters), TTP (telephone twisted pair) can be used at 4 Mbps (it is used in this way by the IBM Local Area Network). **All numeric examples used in this book are intended only to illustrate concepts and therefore must NOT be construed to be exact.**

cable. The common optical cable being used between exchanges in the United States has 24 fibers in the cable.

Many, if not most, EDP communications specialists were unprepared for these new technologies. This comes about because of the development of data communications using telephone channels. EDP specialists became accustomed to the assumed characteristics of the telecommunications environment. It was thought by many that these characteristics were "laws of nature" and would remain true forever. It was quite a surprise to discover that far from being laws of nature, the characteristics of telecommunications channels could benefit from technological advance just as EDP systems could.

In the "early days" of data communications (the early 1960s), data signaling was done at what is now regarded as very low speed, 100 to 300 bits per second. In many countries when the PTT was asked for a leased line between two locations it was able to provide "copper wire all the way." Thus data was signaled in a very simple way. A one bit was a positive voltage (such as +50 volts ) and a zero bit was a negative voltage (such as -20 volts). This is much the same way as "telegraph" and "telex" equipment have operated since their inception.

Then two things happened. The first was that data communication requirements increased (users were finding applications for many more terminals) and terminal designs became more sophisticated. This resulted in a requirement for faster transmission. The second was that PTTs found themselves unable to provide end-to-end copper wire as they had in the past, and telephone channels had to be used. Most PTTs used interexchange "carrier systems" that used "frequency division multiplexing" between exchanges. Data users were given these channels and had to find ways of using them for data.

The important characteristic of these "multiplexed telephone channels" is that while they will pass alternating current between about 200 and 3,400 cycles, they will not pass direct current. So the old methods of direct current signaling would not work any more. (It is also worth noting that more modern telephone exchange switches were developed that used switching techniques that also limited bandwidth and would not pass direct current.) A device called a MODEM (MOdulator-DEModulator) was developed to send bits as a sequence of audio tones. In its simplest form a modem might signal a zero bit by sending a 1,200-cycle tone and a one bit by sending a 700-cycle tone.

Modem technology developed very quickly indeed and today modems have become sophisticated, complex, and expensive devices. Sending 9600 bps through a telephone channel relies on many different techniques of "modulation" (variation of the signal to encode information) and the achievement borders on the theoretical limits of a telephone channel. In general, it is necessary to (very carefully) "condition"[3] lines for this kind of modem and the line cannot actually be "switched" through an exchange. The line is simply a sequence of wires and frequency multiplexed channels from one end to the other. With a telephone channel, 9,600 bps has been the limit. (Newer techniques can increase this to an amazing 16,800 bps.) Wider channels and higher speeds were obtained by combining several voice channels into one within the exchange such that the new channel has a "wider" carrying capacity. This is quite expensive.

Many people assumed that because of the need to limit the "bandwidth" within the telephone system, there was something that meant the ordinary copper wire twisted pairs played a part in this limitation. Expected problems included radio frequency emissions and "print through" of signals in one wire onto adjacent wires in the same cable by inductive coupling.

In fact, these, while always a consideration, were never the limiting factor. New technology has enabled the sending of data in just the way that it was in the early 1960s: a current in one direction for a one bit and in the opposite direction for a zero bit. (More accurately, changes in amplitude and polarity of voltage are used.) The techniques involved in digital baseband transmission are more complex but the principle is the same, and there is no need for the complex and expensive modem nor for "conditioning" the wires in the circuit.

## 2.1 Electrical Transmission

As noted in the introduction, digital information can be transmitted over copper wires by encoding the information quite directly as changes of voltage on the wire. This is called "baseband" transmission and should be contrasted with "broadband" transmission where a carrier signal is "modulated" with the digital information[4] (as for example in a modem).

The methods of encoding the information in the baseband technique are often grouped under the heading "Pulse Amplitude Modulation" (PAM).[5] When analog information (for example voice or video) is converted to digital form for transmission the most common

[3] Conditioning involves careful selection of appropriate wire pairs and inserting tuned inductors (coils) at intervals along the circuit to mitigate the effect of capacitance between the conductors.

[4] A brief introduction to the concepts involved is given in Appendix B, "Transmitting Information by Modulating a Carrier" on page B-1.

[5] Strictly, the word "modulation" means imposing changes onto a "carrier" signal in order to transmit information. In baseband transmission there is no carrier signal to be modulated; the digital bit stream is placed directly on the wire (or fiber). Nevertheless, most authors use the term modulation to describe the coding of a baseband digital signal.

technique is called "Pulse Code Modulation" (PCM). PCM-coded voice is almost always transmitted on a wire (baseband) using PAM.

High-speed digital bit streams can, of course, be sent by modulation of a high frequency (radio frequency) signal and this is sometimes done (such as in a broadband LAN) but this is relatively expensive compared to the simpler baseband method. In this chapter, only digital baseband PAM transmission is discussed.

The objective of data transmission is to transfer a block of data (or a continuous stream of bits) from one device to another over a single pair of wires. Because there are only two wires (and we are describing baseband transmission) transmission must take place one bit (or perhaps a small group of bits) at a time.

From the perspective of the transmission system we may insist that the device present a stream of bits for transmission. The problem, then is to transmit that bit stream unchanged from A to B.

## 2.1.1 Non-Return to Zero (NRZ) Coding

If the bit stream is to be sent as changes of voltage on a wire, then the simplest coding possible is NRZ. As illustrated in Figure 2-1, here a one bit is represented as a + voltage (or current in one direction) and a zero bit is represented as a - voltage (or current in the opposite direction).[6]

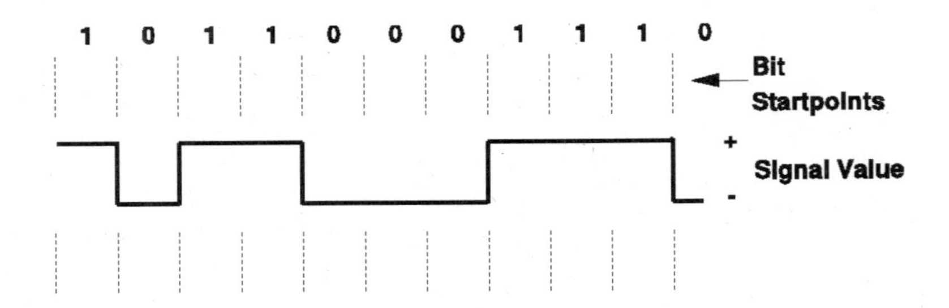


*Figure 2-1. NRZ Coding*

This method of coding is used for short distance digital links such as between a data terminal device and a modem (the RS-232 or V.24 interface uses NRZ coding).

6 In fact, there is a simpler way of representing the information. A one bit might be the presence of a voltage and a zero bit the absence of a voltage. (Early Morse code systems did use the absence of a voltage to delimit the start and end of each "dot" or "dash".) This technique is not used in modern digital signaling techniques because it is "unbalanced". The need for direct current (DC) balancing in digital codes is discussed later.

If a transmitter places a stream of bits on a wire using the NRZ coding technique, how can it be received? This is the core of the problem. Transmission is easy, but re-creating the original bit stream at a receiver can be quite difficult.

On the surface it looks simple. All the receiver has to do is look at its input stream at the middle of every bit time and the state of the voltage on the line will determine whether the bit is a zero or a one.

But there are two important problems:

1. There is no timing information presented to the receiver to say just where the middle of each bit is.

   The receiver must determine where a bit starts and then use its own oscillator (clock) to work out where to sample the input bit stream. But there is no economical way of ensuring that the receiver clock is running at exactly the same rate as the transmitter clock. That is, oscillators can be routinely manufactured to a tolerance of .005% but this is not close enough.

2. The signal will be changed (distorted) during its passage over the wire. See Figure 2-20 on page 2-41.

The signal will have started off as a sharp "square wave" at the transmitter and will be decidedly fuzzy when it gets to the receiver. The signal will no longer be just a positive or negative voltage. Instead, the voltage will change from one state to the other, "slowly" passing through every intermediate voltage state on the way.

The receiver must now do two things:

1. Decide what line state is a zero and what state is a one.

   A simple receiver might just say "any positive voltage represents a one and any negative voltage a zero". This will be adequate in many situations, but this is by no means adequate in all situations, as will be seen later.

2. Decide where bits begin and end.

   As a zero bit changes to a one bit the voltage will rise (perhaps quite slowly) from one state to the other. Where does one bit end and the next begin.

3. Decide where a new bit begins and an old one ends even if the line state does not change!

   When one bit is the same as the one before then the receiver must decide when one bit has finished and another begun. Of course, in data, it is very common for long strings of ones and zeros to appear, so the receiver must be able to distinguish between bits even when the line state hasn't changed for many bit times.

   With simple NRZ coding this is impossible, and something must be done to the bit string to ensure that long strings of zeros or ones can't occur.

A simple receiver might operate in the following way:

1. Sample the line at defined intervals faster than the known bit rate on the line (say seven times for every bit).

   When there is no data being sent, the line is usually kept in the one state.

2. When a state change is detected, this could be the start of a bit. Start a timer (usually a counter) to wait for half a bit time.

3. When the timer expires, look at the line. If it is the same as before then receive the bit. If not then the previous state change detected was noise - go back to 1 (looking for the start of a bit).

4. Set the timer for one full bit time.

5. Monitor the line for a change of state. If a change is detected before the timer expires, then go back to step 2.

6. When the timer expires, receive the bit.

7. Go to step 4.

In the jargon the above algorithm is called a "Digital Phase Locked Loop" (DPLL). Consider what's happening here:

- The receiver is using the change of state from one bit to another to define the beginning of a bit (and the end of the last).
- When there are no changes, the receiver's clock is used to decide where the bits are.
- Whenever there is a state change, the receiver re-aligns its notion of where the bits are.

Successful operation is clearly dependent on:

- How good the receiver is at deciding when a state change on the line has occurred. (Since this is often gradual voltage change rather than an abrupt one, this is a judgement call on the part of the receiver.)
- How accurate the receiver's clock is in relation to the transmitters.
- How many times per bit the stream is sampled.

  Some practical systems in the past have used as few as five samples per bit time. The IBM 3705 communications controller (when receiving bits without an accompanying timing signal) sampled the stream 64 times per bit.

  Today's systems, using a dedicated chip for each line, often sample the line at the full clock frequency of the chip. The more frequent the sampling, the more accurate will be the result.

The above technique (the DPLL) is very simple and can be implemented very economically in hardware. But it is also very rough.

*Notice here that the bit stream has been recovered successfully but the exact timing of the received bit stream has not. This doesn't matter in the example, since the objective was to transfer a stream of bits, not synchronize timing. Later however, there will be situations where accurate recovered timing is critical to system operation.*

Frequent state transitions are needed within the bit stream for the algorithm to operate successfully. The maximum number of bits without a transition is determined by the quality of the transmission line and the complexity of the receiver. Typical values for the maximum length of strings of ones or zeros in practical systems are between 3 and 6 bits.

## 2.1.2 Non-Return to Zero Inverted (NRZI) Coding

In order to ensure enough transitions in the data for the receiver to operate stably, a coding called Non-Return to Zero Inverted (NRZI) is often used. In NRZI coding, a zero bit is represented as a change of state on the line and a one bit as the absence of a change of state. This is illustrated in Figure 2-2.

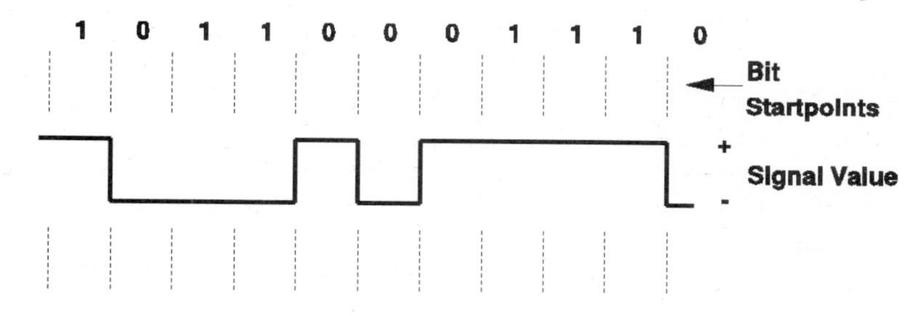


***Figure* 2-2.** *NRZI Coding*

This algorithm will obviously ensure that strings of zero bits do not cause a problem. But what of strings of one bits? Strings of one bits are normally prevented by insisting that the bit stream fed to the transmitter may not contain long strings of one bits. This can be achieved in many ways:

- By using a "higher layer" protocol (such as SDLC/HDLC) that breaks up strings of one bits for its own purposes. The HDLC family of protocols for example insert a zero bit unconditionally after every string of 5 consecutive ones (except for a delimiter or abort sequence).
- By using a code translation that represents (say) 4 data bits as 5 real bits. Code combinations which would result in insufficient numbers of transitions are not used. This is the system used in FDDI (see 13.6.5.2, "Data Encoding" on page 13-41) for example. Code conversion from 4-bit "nibbles" to 5-bit "symbols" is performed before NRZI conversion for fairly obvious reasons.

### 2.1.3 Coupling to a Line

While the above coding schemes are used in many practical situations (such as between a modem and a data processing device) they will not work properly over any significant distance using electrical baseband signaling. (They work well on optical links, however.)

It seems obvious, but it must not be forgotten, that when devices are connected together using electric wire there is an electrical connection between them. If that connection consists of direct connections of components to the wire there are several potential problems.

- Both the signaling wires and the grounds (earths) must be electrically connected to one another. If the devices are powered from different supplies (or the powering is through a different route),[7] then a "ground loop" can be set up.

  Most people have observed a ground loop. In home stereo equipment using a record turntable, if the turntable is earthed and if it is plugged into a different power point from the amplifier to which it is connected, then you often get a loud "hum" at the line frequency (50 or 60 cycles). The hum is caused by a power flow through the earth path and the power supplies.

  Ground loops can be a source of significant interference and can cause overload on attaching components.

- If the connection is over a distance of a few kilometers or more (such as in the "subscriber loop" connection of an end user to a telephone exchange) it is not uncommon for there to be a difference of up to 3 volts in the earth potential at the two locations. This can have all kinds of undesirable effects.

- It is not good safety practice to connect the internal circuitry of any device to a transmission line. In the event of a power supply malfunction, it may be possible to get the main's voltage on the line.

  This does not help other equipment connected to the line and could leave a lasting impression on any technician who happened to be working on the line at the time.

So, it is normal practice to isolate the line from the equipment by using either a capacitor or a transformer. There are other reasons for using reactive coupling:

- A transformer coupling matches the impedance of the transmission line to the device and prevents reflection of echoes back down the line.
- The received pulses are reshaped and smoothed in preparation for reception.
- The transformer filters out many forms of line noise.
- Neither a capacitor nor a transformer will allow direct current (DC) to pass.

---

[7] More accurately, if there is any resistance in the connection between the grounds - there usually is.

This means that the line is intentionally isolated from the user equipment. It becomes possible to put an intentional direct current onto the line. For example, in basic rate ISDN, a direct current is used on the same line as the signal to provide power for simple receivers. Also, in token-ring systems, a "phantom voltage" is generated in the attaching adapter and is used to signal the wiring concentrator that this device should be connected to the ring.

Transformer coupling is generally used in high-speed digital baseband transmission systems. There are other advantages to transformer coupling:

- If the code is designed carefully, the transmission leads can be reversed (swapped) at the connection to the device without affecting its ability to correctly interpret the signal.
- Interference caused by "crosstalk" (the acquisition of a signal through inductive and capacitive coupling from other wires in the same cable) usually affects each signal wire equally. The fact that crosstalk signals tend to be equal on both wires means that when they are put through the transformer coupling they tend to cancel one another out.

  The net is that crosstalk interference is greatly reduced.

## 2.1.4 DC Balancing

If we consider "baseband" transmission using a simple transmission code such as NRZI, bits are represented directly as voltage states on the line. Depending on the bit stream being transmitted with NRZI, it is possible that the line may spend on average more time in one voltage state than the other. If the line was connected to a capacitor then the capacitor would develop a charge (although slowly). However, the line itself has capacitance and thus it can develop a constant DC voltage across it.

Thus, any transmission code that can cause the line to spend more time in one state than the other has a direct current (DC) component and is said to be unbalanced. The presence of a DC component causes the transmission line and the coupling device to distort the signal. This phenomenon is technically called "baseline wander" and the effect is to increase the interference caused by one pulse with a subsequent pulse on the line. (See "Intersymbol Interference" on page 2-43.)

A DC balanced code causes the line to spend an equal amount of time in each state. Thus on average there is no DC component and the above problems are avoided. In addition DC balancing simplifies transmit level control, receiver gain, and receiver equalization.

Both the NRZ and NRZI codes described above are unbalanced in this way and so are unsuitable for high-speed digital transmission *on electrical media* (its fine on optical media).[8] So we need a different kind of code.

## 2.1.5 Pseudoternary Coding

Pseudoternary coding is the simplest DC balanced code and is used at the "S" and "T" interfaces in Basic Rate ISDN. As illustrated in Figure 2-3, this code uses three line states (hence the name) to represent two binary conditions:

- A one bit is represented by no voltage present on the line.
- A zero bit is represented by either a positive or a negative pulse.

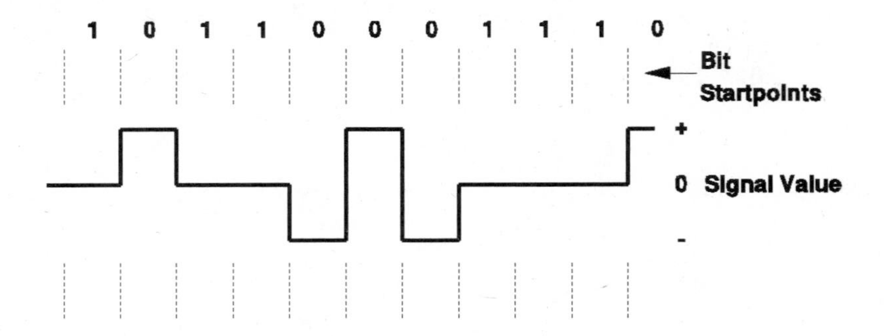


*Figure 2-3. ISDN_BR Pseudoternary Coding Example*

Pulses representing zero bits must strictly alternate in state. Successive zero pulses (regardless of how many one bits are in between) must be of opposite states. Hence the coding is DC balanced. If they are the same state, then this is regarded as a code violation.

The properties of this code are used in an elegant and innovative way by the Basic Rate ISDN "S" interface. See the discussion in 8.1.3.3, "The ISDN Basic Rate Passive Bus ("S" Interface)" on page 8-7.

The drawback of using this code compared to NRZI is that (other things being equal) it requires 3 dB more transmitter power than NRZI. It also requires the receiver to recognize three states rather than just a transition - this means a slightly more complex receiver

---

[8] The suggestion of DC balancing on a fiber seems absurd. However, this is not always so. Optical transmissions are sent and received electronically. It is often advantageous to have an AC coupled front-end stage to a high gain receiver. So some systems do balance the number of ones and zeros sent to give a DC balance to the electrical coupling stage in the receiver.

is required. Notice also that it is the one bit that is represented as null voltage and the zero that is a voltage rather than the opposite.

Of course, the synchronization problem discussed above is still present. A long string of one bits will cause the receiver to lose synchronization with the transmitter. (This problem is overcome in ISDN_BR by the regular occurrence of zero bits in the framing structure, the relatively slow speed of the interface (144 Kbps), and the use of a much better timing recovery system than the simplistic DPLL described earlier.)

#### 2.1.5.1 Alternate Mark Inversion

Pseudoternary code is also called "AMI" for Alternate Mark Inversion or "Bipolar" code. The only difference between AMI and the form of pseudoternary used in ISDN_BR is that the representation of the one and zero states are reversed. Thus in AMI, a no voltage state is interpreted as a zero bit and alternating voltage pulses are interpreted as ones. Of course, this is just a convention and makes no real difference at all. ISDN_BR reverses the convention for an excellent reason related to the operation of the "passive bus". See 8.1.3, "ISDN Basic Rate" on page 8-3.

### 2.1.6 Timing Recovery

There are many situations where a receiver needs to recover a very precise timing from the received bit stream *in addition* to just reconstructing the bit stream. This situation happens very frequently:

- In ISDN_BR a frame generated by the DTE must be in very nearly exact synchronization with the framing sent from the DCE to the DTE.
- In P_ISDN a similar but a little less critical requirement exists.
- In token-ring, the all important ring delay characteristic is minimized by maintaining only minimal (two bits)[9] buffering in each ring station. This requires that the outgoing bit stream from a station be precisely synchronized with the received bit stream (to avoid the need for elastic buffers in the ring station).

In order to recover precise timing not only must there be a good coding structure with many transitions, but the receiver must use a much more sophisticated device than a DPLL to recover the timing. This device is an (analog) phase locked loop.

#### 2.1.6.1 Phase Locked Loops (PLLs)

Earlier in this section (page 2-6) the concept of a simple "digital phase locked loop" was introduced. While DPLLs have a great advantage in simplicity and cost they suffer from three major deficiencies:

---

[9] In the current IBM token-ring adapter this is actually 2 and a half bits or 5 bps. However, in principle it is possible to cut this down to one and a half bits.

- Even at quite slow speeds they cannot recover a good enough quality clocking signal for most applications where timing recovery is important.
- As link speed is increased, they become less and less effective. This is due to the fact, alluded to earlier in this book, that circuit speeds have not increased in the same ratio as have communication speeds.

  A DPLL needs to sample the incoming bit stream many times per bit. With a link speed of 2,400 bits per second this isn't very difficult to do even by programming. But at multi-megabit speeds it becomes more and more costly and then (as speed becomes too great), impossible.
- As digital signals increase in speed (where speed begins to be limited by circuit characteristics), they start behaving more like waveforms and less like "square waves" and the simplistic DPLL technique becomes less appropriate.

What is needed is a continuous-time, analog PLL that is illustrated in Figure 2-4

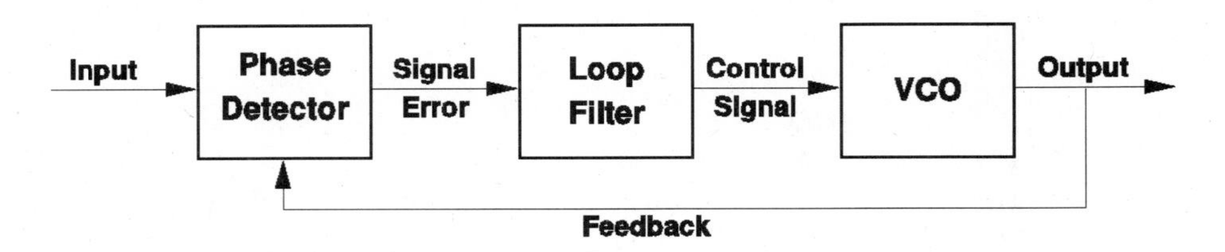


*Figure 2-4. Operating Principle of a Continuous (Analog) PLL*

The concept is very simple. The VCO is a Voltage Controlled Oscillator and is the key to the operation.

- The VCO is designed to produce a clock frequency close to the frequency being received.
- Output of the VCO is fed to a comparison device (here called a phase detector) which matches the input signal to the VCO output.
- The phase detector produces a voltage output which represents the difference between the input signal and the output signal.

  (In principle, this device is a lot like the tuner on an AM radio.)
- The voltage output is then used to control (change) the frequency of the VCO.

Properly designed, the output signal will be very close indeed to the timing and phase of the input signal. There are two (almost conflicting) uses for the PLL output:

1. Recovering the bit stream (that is, providing the necessary timing to determine where one bit starts and another one ends).

2. Recovering the (average) timing (that is, providing a stable timing source at exactly the same rate as the timing of the input bit stream).

Many bit streams have a nearly exact overall timing but have slight variations between the timings of individual bits.

The net of the above is that quite often we need two PLLs: one to recover the bit stream and the other to recover a precise clock (illustrated in Figure 2-5). This is the case in most primary rate ISDN chip sets.

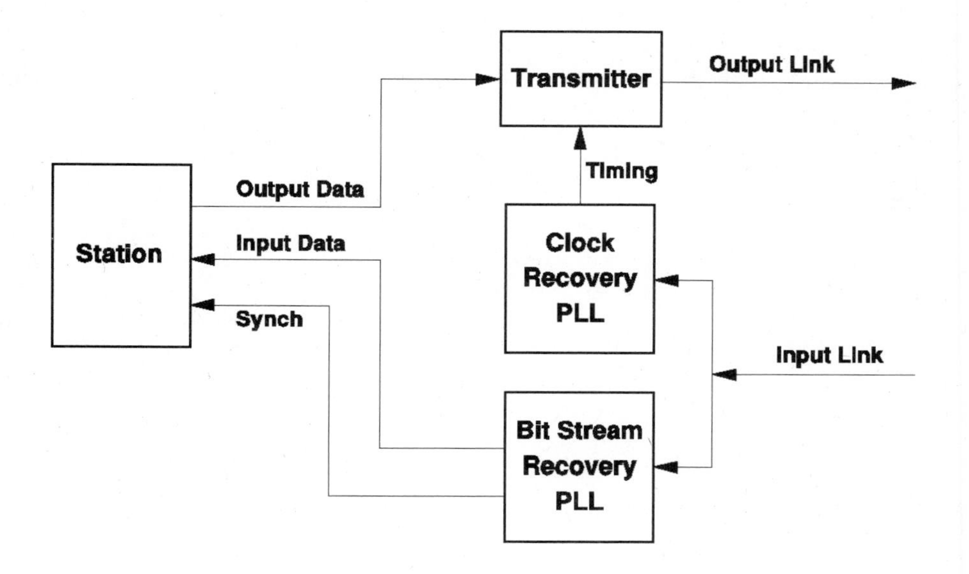


***Figure 2-5.*** *Clock Recovery in Primary Rate ISDN.* Two PLLs are used because of the different requirements of bit stream recovery and clock recovery.

PLL design is extremely complex and regarded by many digital design engineers as something akin to black magic. It seems ironic that the heart of a modern digital communications system should be an analog device.

PLL quality is extremely important to the correct operation of many (if not most) modern digital systems. The basic rate ISDN "passive bus" and the token-ring LAN are prime examples.

### 2.1.6.2 Jitter

Jitter is the generic term given to the difference between the (notional) "correct" timing of a received bit and the timing as detected by the PLL. It is impossible for this timing to be exact because of the nature of the operation being performed. Some bits will be detected slightly early and others slightly late. This means that the detected timing will vary more or less randomly by a small amount either side of the correct timing - hence the name "jitter". It doesn't matter if all bits are detected early (or late) provided it is by the same amount - delay is not jitter. Jitter is a random variation in the timing either side of what is correct.

Jitter is minimized if both the received signal and the PLL are of high quality. But although you can minimize jitter, you can never quite get rid of it altogether.

Jitter can have many sources, such as distortion in the transmission channel or just the method of operation of a digital PLL. Sometimes these small differences do not make any kind of difference. In other cases, such as in the IBM Token-Ring, jitter accumulates from one station to another and ultimately can result in the loss or corruption of data. It is jitter accumulation that restricts the maximum number of devices on a token-ring to 260.

#### 2.1.6.3 Repeaters

The ability to use repeaters is one of the principal reasons that digital transmission is so effective.

As it travels along a wire, any electrical signal is changed (distorted) by the conditions it encounters along its path. It also becomes weaker over distance due to energy loss (from resistance and inductance) in the cable. After a certain distance it is necessary to boost the signal.

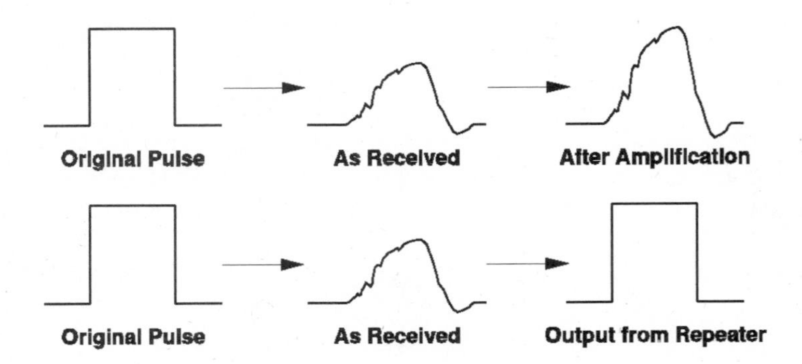


*Figure 2-6. Function of a Repeater*

The signal can be boosted by simply amplifying it. This makes the signal stronger, *but* (as is shown in the first example of Figure 2-6) it amplifies a distorted signal. As the signal progresses further down the cable, it becomes more distorted and all the distortions add up and are included in the received signal at the other end of the cable. Analog transmission systems must not allow the signal to become too weak anywhere along their path. This is because we need to keep a good ratio of the signal strength to noise on the circuit. Some noise sources such as crosstalk and impulse noise have the same real level regardless of the signal strength. If we let the signal strength drop too much the effect of noise increases.

In the digital world things are different. A signal is received and (provided it can be understood at all) it is reconstructed in the repeater. A new signal is passed on (as is shown in the second example of Figure 2-6 on page 2-14) which is completely free from any distortion that was present when the signal was received at the repeater.

The result of this is that repeaters can be placed at intervals such that the signal is still understandable but can be considerably weaker than would be needed were the signal to be amplified. This means that repeaters can be spaced further apart than can amplifiers and also that the signal received at the far end of the cable is an exact copy of what was transmitted with no errors or distortion at all.

## 2.1.7 Manchester Encoding

Manchester encoding is used in baseband Ethernet LANs both on coaxial cable and on unshielded twisted pair. The basic principle is that, instead of a particular line state being used to signal the value of a bit, the direction of change in line state signals the bit value. A zero bit is signaled by a transition from a line state of one to a line state of zero in the *middle* of the bit time. A one bit is signaled by a transition from the zero state to the one state. If we are to transmit two bits which are the same in succession (such as 11 or 00), then we have to make another transition in the link at the beginning of the bit time to prepare ourselves to make the transition in the right direction. That is, if we signal a one by going from a line state of zero to a state of one, then before we can signal the next one bit we need to get the line back to the state of zero. This is shown in Figure 2-7.

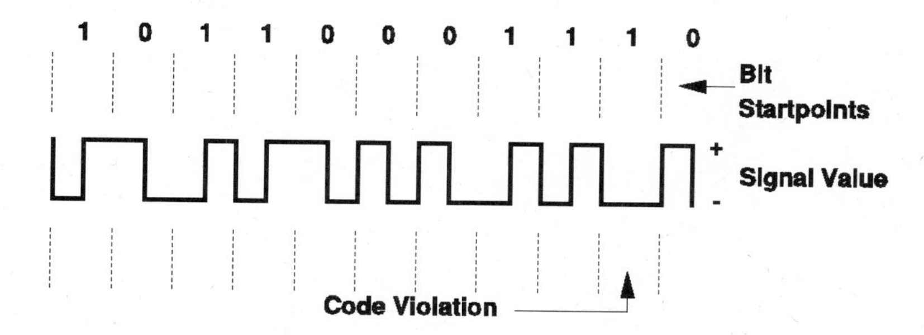


***Figure 2-7.*** *Manchester Encoding.* A zero bit is signaled by a transition from a line state of one to a line state of zero in the *middle* of the bit time. A one bit is signaled by a transition from the zero state to the one state. There may or may not be a transition at the beginning of the bit time. The absence of a transition at the middle of the bit time constitutes a “code violation”.

Because it is the *change* in signal level that is used to communicate the value of a bit rather than the amplitude of the signal, the signal level itself is relatively unimportant. In principle, Manchester Code could work over a significant DC signal. For example if the signal varied between +2 and +4 volts, then this would be just as good as a signal that varied between -1 and +1 volts. The receiver only has to detect the signal's *direction* of change rather than the signal level itself.

As noted above, Manchester Code is used in Ethernet LANs. In that context the primary purpose is to allow easy detection of collisions. When two Manchester Coded signals collide on a LAN, then the value of the resulting signal is the **OR** of the input signals (not the arithmetic sum as one might expect). This is not clean and neat because the two colliding signals will *not* be synchronized with one another in any way. The resulting signal will almost always *not* be DC balanced (the probability of a DC balanced result is very low indeed). Thus when two signals collide you get a momentary loss of DC balance on the LAN cable. It is this transient DC component that signals the sending workstation that there has been a collision. This is a particularly elegant, simple, and very effective way of detecting collisions. However it means that Ethernet is very sensitive to low frequency interference on the LAN cable. A low frequency signal (such as might be induced in a UTP cable running near a power cable) will be seen by Ethernet equipment as a succession of collisions.

As will be seen later, a closely similar code (Differential Manchester) is used on token-ring LANs but there it is used for its property of having at least one line state change per bit making possible the recovery of a very stable timing signal. Ethernet does not need accurate timing recovery.

One practical problem of Manchester Code is that it is polarity sensitive. That is, if the (two) wires carrying the signal are swapped for any reason, then a one bit will be interpreted as a zero and a zero bit as a one. Differential Manchester Coding was invented as an improvement that removes the sensitivity to polarity.

## 2.1.8 Differential Manchester Coding

Differential Manchester[10] (illustrated in Figure 2-8) is the electrical level coding used in the IBM Token-Ring LAN.

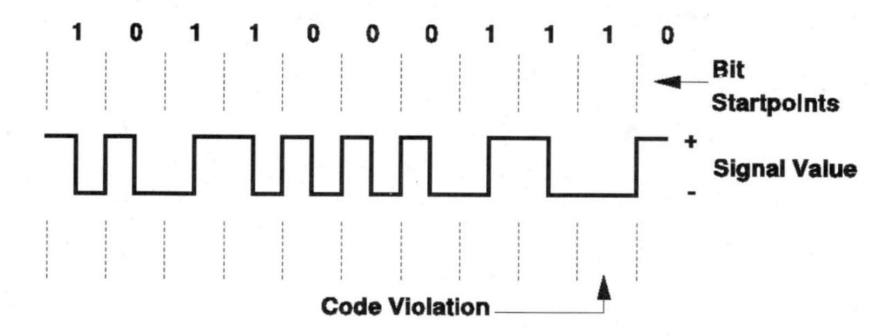


***Figure 2-8.*** *Differential Manchester Coding Example.* The presence or absence of a transition **at the bit start point** determines whether the bit is a one or a zero. A one bit is signaled by the absence of a transition and a zero bit by the presence of a transition. A code violation occurs when the signal state does not change at the middle of a bit time.

The most significant factor in the choice of this code for the IBM Token-Ring LAN was the desire to minimize the "ring latency" (the time it takes for something to travel around the ring). The mechanism used to achieve this is to minimize necessary buffering (delay) in each attaching ring station. (Current IBM token-ring adapters contain 1½ bits of delay.) To do this you need to eliminate the "elastic buffer" which would be required if each station had an independent clock. If we want to eliminate this elastic buffer and its concomitant delay, then each station's transmitter must run at *exactly the same rate* as the rate at which data is being received. The problem here is that tiny variations introduced into the timing by each station "add up" as the signal passes around the ring through multiple stations. This means that each station must be able to derive a highly accurate timing source from its received data stream. To enable the receiver's PLL[11] to derive the most accurate clock possible you need a code with many transitions in it. Hence the choice of Differential Manchester Code.

The next significant desire was to minimize the cost of each attaching adapter, although function should not be sacrificed purely for cost saving. (It was felt that as chip technology improved over the years the initial high cost of TRN chip sets would reduce significantly - and this has indeed happened.)

---

[10] Differential Manchester coding is a member of a class of codes called "biphase modulated codes"

[11] See 2.1.6.1, "Phase Locked Loops (PLLs)" on page 2-11.

The desired speed range of around 10 Mbps (in 1981) dictated the use of shielded cable. The shielded twisted pair that was decided upon for transmission can easily handle signals of several hundred Mbps, so there was no advantage to be gained from limiting the baud rate (signaling frequency).

Differential Manchester intentionally uses a high baud rate in order to minimize the cost of the adapter and the amount of buffering required in each ring station.

The baud rate is twice the bit rate. On a 4 Mbps token-ring the "baud rate" (that is the number of state changes on the line) is 8 megahertz. A 16 Mbps token-ring runs at 32 megabaud (16 megahertz). Some people consider this a waste of bandwidth, since there are codes in use that allow up to 6 bits for each state change.[12] FDDI, for example, uses a 4B/5B code that allows 100 Mbps to be sent on the line as 125 megabaud.

Differential Manchester coding provides an elegant way of satisfying the requirements:

1. Because it provides at least one state transition per bit, a receiver can derive a very stable timing source from the received bit stream with minimal circuitry. This means that the station can be a simple repeater with minimal buffering (one bit only) and hence minimal delay.

   Had it not been possible to derive such a stable timing source, the alternative was to use a structure like the one used in FDDI. This would mean a separate transmit oscillator with an elastic buffer in each station - a solution which adds to both the node delay and the cost.

2. The built-in DC balanced characteristic of the code means that there is no data code translation required before transmission. In addition it means that additional DC balance bits are not required to be added to the data - as is required in some other codes.

3. The stability of the derived timing minimizes "phase jitter" and thus allows more stations to be connected to a single ring segment.

4. A code violation is used as a frame delimiter and thus no special delimiting function is needed in the data.

5. Because the modulation technique has such a large amount of redundancy, if a link error occurs it is very likely that a code violation will result. This provides an elementary form of error detection.

---

[12] In an analog carrier system where available bandwidth is severely restricted, then perhaps the word "waste" would be justified. In a baseband LAN environment where the signal is the only one on the wire, this is difficult to call waste, since were it not used for this purpose, the additional capability of the wire would be unused.

6. In token-ring, if power is removed from a station while the station is plugged into the ring then there is a problem. The ring will cease to function because it is no longer complete. To prevent this from happening the "Ring-Wiring-Concentrator" (or hub) detects the loss of power from a ring station and switches the inactive station out of the ring. To do this a "phantom voltage" (a DC voltage of about 5 volts) is emitted by each active adapter. This DC voltage holds open a relay which keeps the station in the ring.

   For this to work, the line code must be insensitive to absolute voltage level and able to operate in the presence of DC. This is another property of both Manchester and Differential Manchester codes.

## 2.1.9 High-Speed Digital Coding (Block Codes)

In the above discussion of pseudoternary (AMI) codes it was seen that AMI codes are DC balanced and are relatively simple to implement. However, they suffer from the problem that long strings of zeros do not cause any transitions and so there is no way for a receiver to recover either the bits or the timing.

We need to do something to the bit stream to add transitions without destroying the advantages of the code. There are many things that could be done, such as bit-stuffing (as in SDLC/HDLC) or 4B/5B code translation (as in FDDI), but these techniques add overhead in the form of extra bits to the stream.[13]

The general solution adopted here is to replace a fixed-length string of zeros with a different string (one containing transitions). But of course, if that is done using valid bit combinations, when such a string is received, the receiver has no way of knowing whether the string is a substitution or not. The answer is to make use of the redundancy of the AMI code by introducing (hitherto illegal) signal combinations called code violations.

As illustrated in Figure 2-9 on page 2-20, a code violation is where there are two successive voltage pulses of the same polarity. The code violation breaks the rule that alternate voltage pulses (representing ones) must have opposite polarity.

In order to introduce the necessary transitions the general technique is to replace a string of k bits with a predetermined (unique) bit pattern, also k bits long, but including a code violation or two to ensure its uniqueness.

[13] Bit stuffing has another much worse effect: it adds a variable number of bits to the frame, destroying the strict frame synchronization required for TDM systems.

Problem solved - but what about DC balancing? Code violations by definition introduce an unbalanced DC component. Depending on the code used, the polarity of the code violations alternates in order to achieve an overall balance.

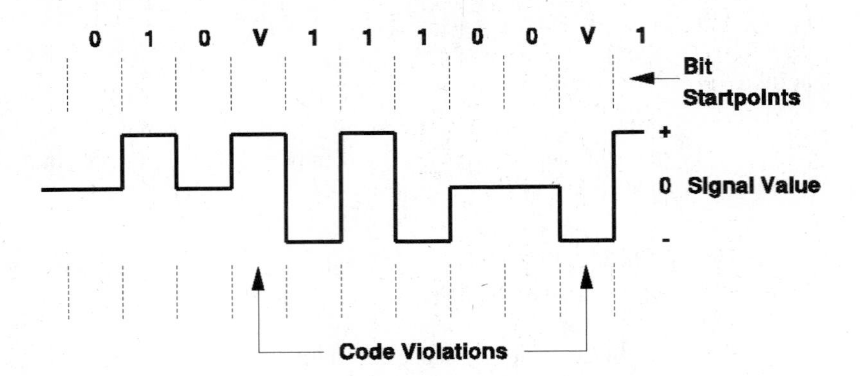


*Figure 2-9. Code Violation in AMI Coding.* A violation is a bipolar pulse of the same polarity as the preceding bipolar pulse.

There are many suggested codes. BkZS, HDBk and kBnT are names of families of codes (k=3, 4, 5... n= 2, 3..) which have great academic interest, but two members of these families are very important commercially. These are HDB3 and B8ZS because they are used by primary rate ISDN.

## 2.1.10 High Density Bipolar Three Zeros (HDB3) Coding

This code is used for 2 Mbps "E1" transmission outside the US and is defined by the CCITT recommendation G.703. It is the code used in Primary Rate ISDN at the 2 Mbps access speed.

The basic concept is to replace strings of four zero bits[14] with a string of three zeros and a code violation.[15]

```
0000 is replaced by 000V  (V = a code violation)
```

But the code violation destroys the very thing that we are using the AMI code for - its DC balanced nature. Using the above rule, a long string of zeros would be replaced with:

```
000V000V000V...
```

---

14 The size of the bit string replaced, in this case 4 bits is the "k" in the name of the code plus one. Thus in HDB3, k=3 and the number of bits replaced is k+1=4.

15 The + or - suffixes attached to the B and V notations in the figure denote the polarity of the pulse.

Each code violation pulse would have to have the same polarity; otherwise, it would be a one bit - not a code violation. Even short strings of zeros within arbitrary data would cause an unbalance as the polarity of the preceding one bit would not be predictable or controllable.

What is needed is to organize things so that successive code violations are of alternating polarity. This can be done by using a different substitute string beginning with a phony "one" bit. This phony one bit is a valid bipolar pulse which could represent a one bit, but in this context (followed two bits later by a violation) is interpreted as a zero.

```
0000 can be replaced by B00V (B = a valid bipolar pulse)
```

The whole is organized so that the polarity of code violations alternates. The code word transmitted when a string of four zeros is detected is then chosen to make the number of "B"s between successive "V"s odd.

The rule is simple: if the polarity of the last violation is the same as that of the most recent one bit, then send the string B00V (that is, invert the polarity of the violation); if the polarities are different, send 000V. This rule is summarized as follows:

| | | Polarity of last Code Violation | |
|---|---|---|---|
| | | + | - |
| Polarity of preceding one bit | + | B-00V- | 000V+ |
| | - | 000V- | B+00V+ |

The + and - signs denote the polarity of the preceding pulse.

The result can be seen in Figure 2-10. Reading the bit stream from left to right, the first pattern is B-00V- (indicating that the previous violation must have been positive). The next violation is 000V+ and is of opposite polarity.

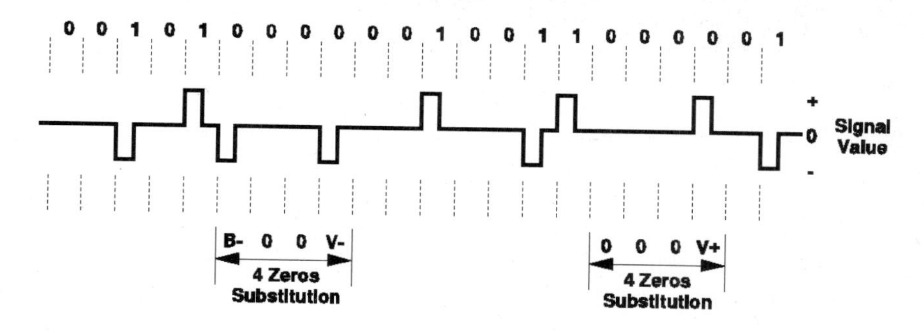


*Figure 2-10. Zeros Substitution in HDB3*

### 2.1.10.1 The Duty Cycle

In Figure 2-10 on page 2-21, the pulses were represented as only being in either + or - state for one half of one bit time. In this case the code is said to have a 50% duty cycle.[16] This is commonly done in digital codes for two reasons:

1. It reduces "intersymbol interference", that is, the distortion of one pulse by the preceding pulse. The line is allowed to settle to a zero state before the next bit time.
2. It means that only half the transmitter power is required compared to the power needed for transmitting for the full bit time.

The cost is that the nominal bandwidth occupied is increased (not a problem in most baseband environments) and that a slightly more precise receiver is needed.

## 2.1.11 Bipolar with Eight Zeros Substitution (B8ZS) Coding

This code is used for the 1.544 Mbps US primary rate ISDN access link.

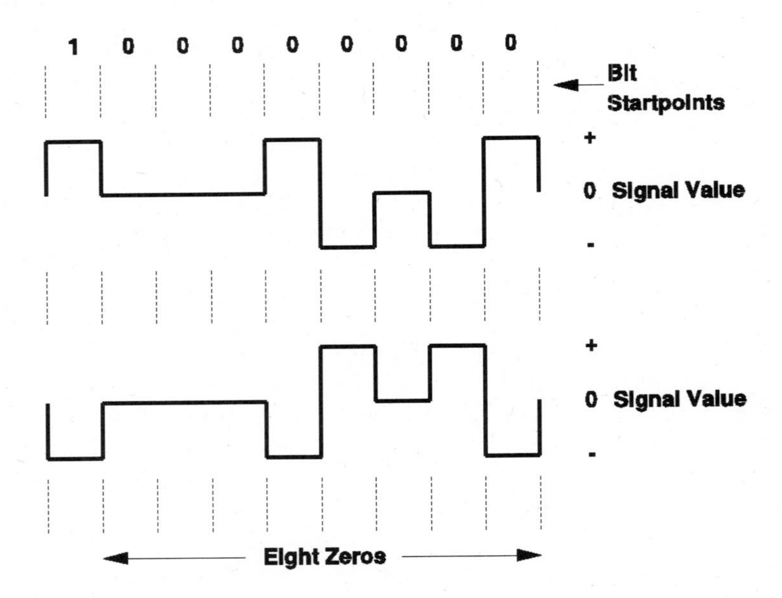


*Figure 2-11. B8ZS Substitutions.* Either of two alternative strings are used depending on the polarity of the preceding one bit.

16 This is sometimes referred to as "half bauded coding".

In principle, this is the same as HDB3, in the sense that a predetermined pulse string replaces a string of zeros. In this case, the string is 8 bits long and, like HDB3, may be anywhere in the transmitted data block - it is not confined to byte boundaries. This means that in B8ZS the maximum length of a string of zeros (after substitution) is 7. In HDB3 the maximum number of consecutive zeros allowed in the substituted string is 3.

Because the substitution is of eight zero bits, there is room in the string for more than one code violation and a couple of valid bipolar pulses thrown in. The substituted string is <000VB0VB>. As is illustrated in Figure 2-11 on page 2-22, there are two strings. Selection of one to be used depends on the polarity of the preceding one bit (you have to create a violation).

Note that because both strings are themselves DC balanced, multiple repetitions of the same string are possible.

### 2.1.12 4-Binary 3-Ternary (4B3T) Code

This code is another ternary code designed to be used in an environment where bandwidth is somewhat limited. In the codes discussed above, a two-state binary bit was mapped into a three-state ternary code. This gave a number of advantages in error detection and simplicity in the receiver, but there are some occasions where bandwidth limitation, while not severe, still must be considered.

One such environment is the "U" interface of basic rate ISDN. As discussed in 8.1.3, "ISDN Basic Rate" on page 8-3, this interface is *not* internationally standardized. Different countries adopt different techniques. 4B3T code is used in Germany.

The problem here is full-duplex transmission over a two-wire line. (A very good trick by any test!) The challenge is to get high quality transmission between the PTT exchange and the end user *at very low cost.*

Four binary bits (as a group) are transmitted as three ternary states (also as a group); thus, there is a 25% reduction in the baud rate of the line compared with AMI codes. This helps noise immunity, but at the cost of complicating the receiver. In the ISDN_BR environment this means that 160 Kbps is transmitted as 120 kbaud.

Four binary bits represent 16 different combinations. Three ternary digits represent 27 combinations. What happens is that we map groups of four binary bits to a group of three ternary bits (hence the name of the code).

It is not quite as simple as a one-to-one mapping. Some care is needed in choosing the mappings. There are still the twin problems of getting enough transitions and making sure the code is DC balanced. The trick is that some code blocks (strings of three ternary digits) have two different (logically opposite) representations. In Table 2-1 on page 2-24 ternary line states are represented by +, - or 0.

| *Table 2-1. Principle of 4B3T Code* | | | |
|---|---|---|---|
| | Ternary String | | |
| Binary String | Mode 1 | Mode 2 | Digital Sum |
| 0000 | +0- | +0- | 0 |
| ... | ... | ... | ... |
| 0011 | +-0 | +-0 | 0 |
| 0100 | ++0 | --0 | ±2 |
| ... | ... | ... | ... |
| 0111 | +++ | --- | ±3 |
| ... | ... | ... | ... |
| 1100 | 00+ | 00- | ±1 |
| ... | ... | ... | ... |
| Unused | 000 | 000 | 0 |

Notice the two modes. Ternary strings that are DC balanced in themselves (such as the +-0 string) represent the same binary block in either mode. Ternary blocks that are not DC balanced have two representations (one with positive DC bias and its inverse with negative bias). The amount of bias is noted in the table.

What happens is that the sender keeps track of the RDS (Running Digital Sum) of the block being transmitted. When the sum is positive, the next code word sent is from the Mode 2 column; if the sum is negative, the next code word sent is from the Mode 1 column. The receiver doesn't care about digital sums; it just takes the next group of three states and translates it into the appropriate four bits. The combination of 000 is not used because a string of consecutive groups would not contain any transitions (the strings of --- and +++ are possible because they alternate with each other if the combination 01110111 occurs in the data).

The code achieves a statistical DC balance rather than a balance in each transmitted symbol. This has been found to help in self-cancellation of echoes and ISI but it is not as good as DC balancing within each symbol.

### 2.1.13 8-Binary 6-Ternary (8B6T) Code

This code is similar in principle to the 4B3T code described above. 8B6T code is used in 100BaseFX (100 Megabit Ethernet on 4 pairs of UTP-3). In that environment three pairs are used for data with each pair carrying 33.333 Mbps of data. In Table 2-2 on page 2-25 ternary line states are represented by +, - or 0.

*Table 2-2. Examples of 8B6T Encodings*

| Data Byte (Hex) | Ternary String |
|---|---|
| 00 | +-00+- |
| ... | ... |
| 0A | 1+0+-0 |
| 0B | +0-+-0 |
| ... | ... |
| 46 | +0+-00 |
| 47 | 0++-00 |
| ... | ... |
| 90 | +-+--+ |
| 91 | ++--+- |
| ... | ... |
| SOSA | +-+-+- |
| SOSB | -+-+-+ |
| ... | ... |
| EOP1 | ++++++ |
| ... | ... |
| EOP5 | --0000 |
| ... | ... |
| bad-code | ---+++ |
| zero-code | 000000 |

DC balancing is used with this code and is achieved in a similar (although perhaps simpler) way as with 4B3T above.

- Each code group has a DC balance value of either 0 or 1. Zero implies that the code group is balanced within itself and therefore this group has no effect on the overall balance.
- When the data stream is transmitted, the transmitter keeps track of the current DC balance state.
- After a code group with weight 1 has been transmitted, then the next code group of weight 1 to be transmitted is sent as its arithmetic complement. Since this is a ternary code + becomes -, - becomes + and 0 stays the same. A complementary code group has a weight of -1.
- Thus the transmitted data stream never gets more than a weight of 1 out of balance.

## 2.1.14 4 out of 5 (4B/5B) Block Code

This form of block coding has been used widely in fiber optical protocols but has only recently begun to be used in copper wire communication systems (mainly where these are derived from optical ones). The difference between this form of coding and the various AMI derived codes discussed above is that here we take a group of data bits and send it as a larger group of signal bits. A group of data bits is taken together and translated into another bit pattern before transmission on the line. Typical block-coded protocols either code 4-bit groups into 5-bit groups (4 of 5 coding) or 8-bit groups into 10-bit groups (8 of 10 code).

The 100 Mbps FDDI protocol is a good example:

***Table 2-3.*** *4B/5B Coding as Used with 100 Mbps PMD.* Four-bit groups are sent as 5-bit combinations to ensure there are at least two transitions per group.

| Symbol Type | Symbol | Code Group | Meaning |
|---|---|---|---|
| Line State Symbols | I | 11111 | Idle |
| | H | 00100 | Halt |
| | Q | 00000 | Quiet |
| Starting Delimiter | J | 11000 | First Byte of SD |
| | K | 10001 | Second Byte of SD |
| Control Indicators | R | 00111 | Logical Zero (Reset) |
| | S | 11001 | Logical One (Set) |
| Ending Delimiter | T | 01101 | Terminates Data Stream |
| Data Symbols | 0 | 11110 | B′ 0000′ (X′ 0′ ) |
| | 1 | 01001 | B′ 0001′ (X′ 1′ ) |
| | | ... | ... |
| | | ... | ... |
| | | ... | ... |
| | 9 | 10011 | B′ 1001′ (X′ 9′ ) |
| | A | 10110 | B′ 1010′ (X′ A′ ) |
| | B | 10111 | B′ 1011′ (X′ B′ ) |
| | C | 11010 | B′ 1100′ (X′ C′ ) |
| | D | 11011 | B′ 1101′ (X′ D′ ) |
| | E | 11100 | B′ 1110′ (X′ E′ ) |
| | F | 11101 | B′ 1111′ (X′ F′ ) |
| Invalid Symbols | V | 00001 | Invalid |
| | V | 00010 | ... |
| | | ... | ... |

Each 4 data bits are encoded as a 5-bit group for transmission or reception. This means that the 100 Mbps data rate is actually 125 Mbps when observed on the physical link.[17] Table 2-3 shows the coding used. This provides:

- Simplification of timing recovery by providing a guaranteed rate of transitions in the data. Only code combinations with at least two transitions per group are valid.
- Transparency and framing. Additional unique code combinations (5-bit codes that do not correspond to any data group) are available. These are used to provide transparency by signaling the beginning and end of a block and to provide an easy way of determining byte alignment.
- Circuitry simplification. One of the principal reasons for using a block code is to save cost in circuitry. If bits are processed at the line rate, then our circuits must be able to operate at that rate. High-speed logic is significantly more expensive than slower-speed logic. A block code allows us to minimize the amount of serial processing required - after a block (byte or half-byte) is received in serial it is then processed as a single parallel group.

  For example in FDDI, bits are sent/received at 125 Mbaud, formed into 5-bit groups, translated into 4-bit groups and then processed as "nibbles" (half bytes) at 25 MHz. In the early days of FDDI, this meant that you could build the serial part in expensive bipolar chip technology but do most of the real processing in the much lower cost CMOS technology. (Now, you can do both in CMOS but the principle remains.)

#### 2.1.14.1 Other xB/yB Codes (8B/10B and 5B/6B)

4B/5B code is only one of a family of codes that operate in much the same manner for much the same purposes. Two such codes also in current use are:

1. 8B/10B code used in the IBM ESCON fiber optical channel protocol and in some ATM protocols
2. 5B/6B used in the 100VG AnyNet 100 Mbps LAN protocol

While the principles and many of the reasons for using xB/yB codes remain, they are often different in detail. When 5B/6B code is used with FDDI on copper there is a need for DC balancing. Since you cannot DC balance each sextet and you cannot guarantee the order of sextets such that there is a balance, then another mechanism must be employed. In this case we use two different code tables with different balance characteristics and switch between code tables so as to provide overall balance.

---

[17] It is incorrect to say that the link is operating at 125 Mbps because the rate of actual bit transport is 100 Mbps. The correct term for the line rate is "baud". A baud is a change in the line state. You could say (with equal truth) that the line is operating at 125 Mbaud or at 25 Mbaud (you could consider each 5-bit group to be a "symbol").

***Table 2-4.*** *Partial State Machine for 5B/6B Encoding Used with 100VG AnyNet.* Five-bit groups are sent as 6-bit combinations. There are two output tables and two states to allow for DC balancing.

| Input Quintet | State 1 Output Sextet | State 1 Next State | State 2 Output Sextet | State 2 Next State |
|---|---|---|---|---|
| 00000 | 001100 | 2 | 110011 | 1 |
| 00011 | 001101 | 1 | 001101 | 2 |
| 00111 | 001011 | 1 | 001011 | 2 |
| 01100 | 101000 | 2 | 010111 | 1 |
| 10101 | 011000 | 2 | 100111 | 1 |
| 11101 | 010011 | 1 | 010011 | 2 |
| 11110 | 010010 | 2 | 101101 | 1 |

Table 2-4 shows a few of the code combinations for 5B/6B code as it is used in 100VG AnyNet. This is the transmit state machine.

- There are two states. Operation commences in State 1.
- In State 1 the output table contains sextets of either weight 2 (sextet contains 2 1′s and 4 0′s) or weight 3 (3 1′s and 3 0′s).
- In State 2 the output table contains sextets of weight 3 or weight 4 (4 1′s and 2 0′s).
- The coding scheme sends codes from either table to ensure that DC balance is maintained.

Operation proceeds as follows:

1. At the beginning of a block of data the system is in State 1.
2. When an input quintet (for example 000000) is received the appropriate output sextet (in this case 001100) is transmitted and then the system goes to state 2 (selected from the Next State column).
3. If we now receive the quintet 11101 we are in state 2 so we transmit 010011 and stay in state 2.
4. If the next quintet is 01100 then we will transmit 010111 and go to state 1.

The receive process is the inverse of the above. This ensures that the system is never more than 2 bits away from an exact DC balance.

### 2.1.15 Multi-Level Codes

Multi-level codes are not often used in digital baseband transmission because they complicate the design of the receiver (that is, add to cost). They do however, use less bandwidth (this just means that the pulses are longer) than binary or ternary codes and are attractive in a bandwidth-limited environment.

In a traditional multi-level code, we use multiple signal levels to represent *more than 1 bit* per signal level. For example a simple system might send two bits per level such as:

00 = 2 volts
01 = 1 volt
10 = -1 volt
11 = -2 volts

Thus in this case, 1 baud = 2 bits. This achieves a slower signaling rate (and therefore uses less bandwidth) at the cost of a more expensive receiver and more sensitivity to some kinds of noise. In compensation, there is reduced sensitivity to other kinds of noise (impulse noise). This is a baseband form of amplitude modulation (AM). We are directly modulating a voltage (or a current) without the presence of a carrier. The more usual broadband kind of AM is discussed in Appendix B, "Transmitting Information by Modulating a Carrier" on page B-1.

#### 2.1.15.1 Carrierless AM/PM (CAP)

Quadrature Amplitude Modulation (see Appendix B, "Transmitting Information by Modulating a Carrier" on page B-1) is a very common way of carrying information when a carrier signal is present. We modulate the amplitude of the carrier and also its phase (its position in time relative to a constant signal). Just as we can use AM without a carrier, in a baseband way, we can also use QAM without a carrier. This is called carrierless AM/PM or CAP. In practice CAP is a complex partial response code and detailed description is outside our scope here, but in first principles it is simply baseband QAM.

#### 2.1.15.2 2-Binary 1-Quaternary (2B1Q) Code

An important example of a multi-level code is the 2-binary 1-quaternary (2B1Q) code used in the US for the ISDN_BR "U" interface. As mentioned above, this is a two-wire full-duplex environment. This code is important because (in the US) the U interface is available for the direct attachment of end-user equipment. This means that many manufacturers will build equipment using this code directly.

As shown in Figure 2-12 on page 2-30, the 2B1Q code uses 4 line states to represent 2 bits. In the ISDN_BR environment this means that the 160 Kbps "U" interface signal is sent at 80 kbaud. In ISDN_BR PAM (Pulse Amplitude Modulation) is used to carry the 2B1Q signal. This is just ordinary baseband digital signaling *but* the receiver must now be able to distinguish the amplitude of the pulses (not just the polarity). There are four voltage states with each state representing 2 bits.

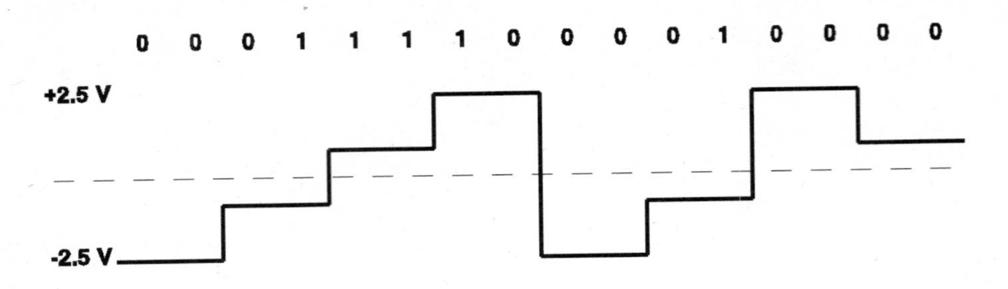


*Figure 2-12. 2-Binary 1-Quaternary Code*

Another point to note is that this code is *not* DC balanced! Further it does not inherently contain sufficient transitions to recover a good clock. For example the sequences:

`00000000 or 0101010101 or 1010101010 or 11111111`

all result in an unchanging line state leaving nothing for the receiver to synchronize on.

To overcome this difficulty, data is "scrambled" (converted by a procedure that ensures pseudo randomness in the data) before transmission and "unscrambled" after it is received.

### 2.1.15.3 Multi-Level Transmit - 3 Levels (MLT-3)

MLT-3 is an interesting coding because it is different in principle from the traditional concept of multi-level coding. It should be thought of as very similar in principle to NRZI coding (see 2.1.2, "Non-Return to Zero Inverted (NRZI) Coding" on page 2-7) but employing three signal levels instead of two.

MLT-3 is used in some LAN systems (FDDI over UTP-5 for example) to reduce the required bandwidth but it signals at 1 baud per bit. The principle is illustrated in Figure 2-13.

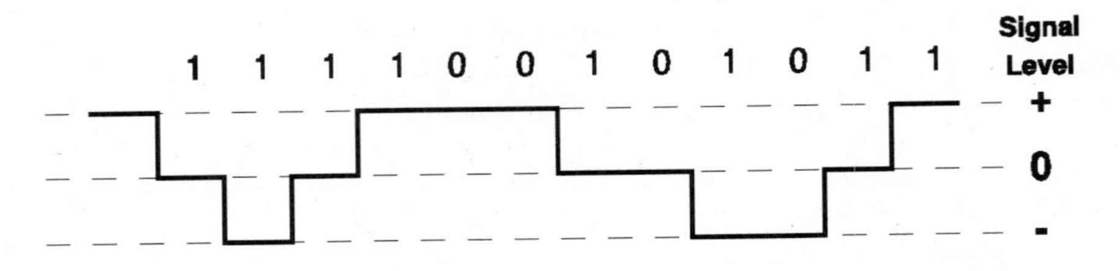


*Figure 2-13. MLT-3 Coding*

Similar to NRZI encoding, a zero bit is signaled by no change in the line status from the previous bit. A one bit is signaled by a transition. There are three signal levels here instead of two. The rules of MLT-3 are simple:

1. A one bit is signaled by a change in line state from the previous bit.
2. A zero bit is signaled by the absence of a change in line state.
3. When the line is in the zero state the next state change (to signal the next one bit) *must* be to the opposite state from the immediately preceding state. Thus if the line was in the -1 state and a one bit was signaled by moving to the zero state then the next one bit is signaled by moving to the +1 state.

This code is not of itself DC balanced, but can come "close enough" when using scrambled input data.

The reason this code is used is that the signal "uses less bandwidth" than does ordinary NRZI code. This means that the signal energy is concentrated at lower frequencies than NRZI while retaining a relatively simple transceiver structure. (See 2.2.2, "The Characteristics of a Baseband Signal" on page 2-36.) One consequence of this is that FDDI can run over UTP-5 using MLT-3 where it cannot run over UTP-5 using NRZI code (the immediate problem is excessive EMS when using NRZI).

### 2.1.16 Using Multiple Codings

Block codes perform logical functions that duplicate many of the functions of line codes. For example delimiting the start and end of a data block in token-ring is performed using a code violation in the Differential Manchester code where in FDDI the beginning and end of blocks are delimited by special 5-bit groups that have no data bit representation.

Nevertheless, block codes do not perform all of the functions of line coding. When block coding is used, it is usual to also use a line coding scheme appropriate to the particular physical medium in use. Thus in FDDI, the data is first block coded and then coded again in a manner appropriate to the physical medium. When transmission is on fiber (or in some cases STP) NRZI coding is used as well. When transmission is on UTP-5, then MLT-3 coding is used in addition to the block code.

### 2.1.17 Scrambling a.k.a. Enciphering

Scrambling is a process of randomization performed on the data stream usually immediately before transmission. Until recently, scrambling has not been used in traditional LAN environments but it is commonly used in wide area transmission systems. Recently, it has been incorporated in the ATM25 (25 Mbps over UTP-3), FDDI over UTP-5 and 100VG AnyNet specifications.

The purpose of scrambling is to provide better signal power characteristics; *it is not a form of security protection.* However, scrambling is also called ciphering[18] or enciphering[19] in some contexts such as IEEE standards documents. The use of this term suggests that data security is an objective. This is not so - the terms are interchangable in the context of transmission protocols.

The bit stream to be transmitted is EORed with a well known "pseudo-random" bit stream. On receipt the randomized bit stream is EORed again with the same randomized stream that generated it to recover the original data stream.

Implementations vary but the pseudo-random bit stream is usually reasonably short and the method of generation is defined in the applicable standard. Of course, a key question is the synchronization of transmitter and receiver scramblers as the process requires exact synchronization or the output will be garbage.

For example, scrambling is used in the proposed 25.6 Mbps ATM link access protocol (ATM25). This protocol is similar at the signal level to standard token-ring and so a comparison of the two spectra is really a comparison of an unscrambled versus a scrambled signal.

Figure 2-14 on page 2-33 shows the frequency spectra of the unscrambled token-ring signal and the scrambled ATM25 signal. In this figure both signals have been filtered for transmission on UTP-3 (thus high-frequency components of the signal have been removed).

In the unscrambled (token-ring) case, there are some strong peaks in the frequency spectrum (18 dB above the curve trend) but in the scrambled (ATM) case these peaks are gone. This means that the transmitted power is more evenly distributed over the transmitted frequencies and a better-quality signal results.

---

[18] American

[19] English

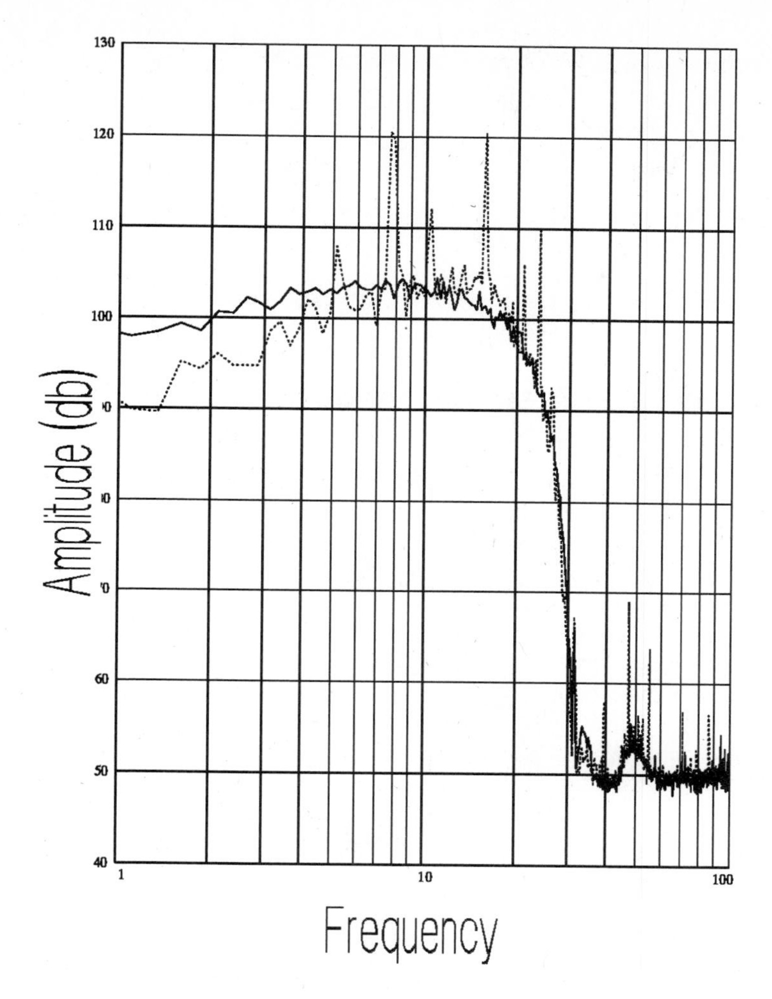


***Figure 2-14.*** *Frequency Spectra of Scrambled and Unscrambled Signals.* The dotted line in the graph shows token-ring 16 Mbps (unscrambled) and the unbroken line shows ATM25 (scrambled) protocol. The ATM25 signal is a better signal because of the absence of peaks in the spectrum.

## 2.2 Practical Transmission

There are two important environments where baseband digital transmission is used. These are:

1. The connection between an end user (such as a private home) and the local telephone exchange. This is called the "subscriber loop".
2. Local area networks.

These environments are very different but nevertheless share many common characteristics.

### 2.2.1 Types of Transmission Media

In digital baseband communication the medium is always a pair of wires (or rather, two conductors). There are five configurations which will be discussed more fully later:

**Open Wire**

Open wire is the historic form of telephone transmission. Two wires are kept apart by some four feet and strung on "telephone poles".

This transmission medium is all but extinct. But it is still the best from the perspective of sending analog voice signals over a distance. It has much lower losses and distortion than other methods. For example, in the past it was common to have a telephone subscriber loop of up to 70 kilometers or so without amplification. Sadly, it is now impractical in most situations.

**Twisted Pair**

Two wires are held together by twisting them and are insulated with either paper or plastic. There are many types and grades of twisted pair cables. The most common type is used by telephone companies for the "subscriber loop" (see 2.2.4, "The Subscriber Loop" on page 2-44) and is called "telephone twisted pair" (TTP).

Twisted pair is also very popular in some quarters for LAN cabling but (depending on the grade and quality of the particular cable) can have significant limitations in that environment. See 2.3, "LAN Cabling with Unshielded Twisted Pair" on page 2-49.

**Shielded Twisted Pair**

This is the best medium for digital baseband communication and is used for many LAN installations. It consists of multiple twisted pairs of wires in a single cable within which each pair is surrounded by a conductive shield. The whole cable is surrounded by an earthed, metal mesh shield. This works well for digital baseband transmission at speeds up to 300 megabaud and beyond.

The IBM specification for shielded twisted pair is called "Type One Cable" and is shown in Figure 2-15 on page 2-35.

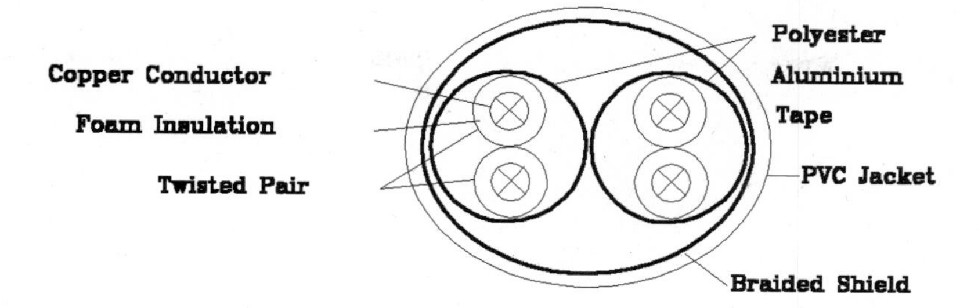


***Figure 2-15.*** *IBM Type 1 Shielded Twisted Pair.* Each of two twisted pairs is shielded from the other by an earthed polyester aluminum tape shield. The whole is further shielded in copper braid.

### Screened Twisted Pair

Screened twisted pair is the case where multiple twisted pairs are bound together in the same cable but are not shielded from one another. However, the whole cable is surrounded with a (braided) metal mesh shield.

### Coaxial Cable

Coaxial cable consists of a single conductor running down the center of an earthed cylindrical metal mesh shield. The conductor is usually separated from the shield by a continuous plastic insulator.[20] Coax is an "unbalanced" medium and is commonly used more for analog than for digital communications. (Cable TV is typically reticulated on coaxial cables.)

For digital communication it is used:

- In "Token Bus" (broadband) LANs where digital information is sent on an analog carrier.
- In the public telephone network for exchange-to-exchange communication. Digital information is again sent on an analog carrier.
- In some situations for baseband transmission over short distances, such as in the IBM 3270 controller to device link.

---

[20] Coaxial cables used for long-line telephone transmission in the past did not have a continuous plastic insulator but rather small plastic insulators spaced at regular intervals. This type of cable has many better characteristics than the ones with continuous plastic, but is very hard to bend around corners and to join.

## 2.2.2 The Characteristics of a Baseband Signal

In order to understand the way in which a signal is carried on a particular medium, it is important to understand the characteristics of the signal itself.

Take a simple "square-wave" signal such as the one illustrated in Figure 2-16. Fourier theory shows that this square pulse can be broken up into a "spectrum" of sinusoidal[21] waves. When such a square pulse is transmitted through a communication channel it behaves *exactly* as though each frequency component (sine wave) was independent and separate from the other components of the signal.

This means that once we know how a particular transmission channel or medium behaves over a range of frequencies, we can predict *exactly* how any given signal will behave when transmitted through that channel.

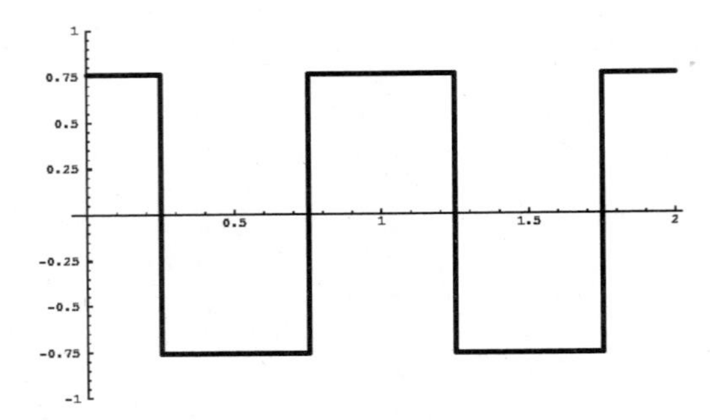


***Figure 2-16.*** *A Square Pulse*

Figure 2-16 shows a typical square-wave signal. Figure 2-17 on page 2-38 shows how it may be synthesized by successive addition of sinusoidal waves of higher and higher frequencies. The series represented by Figure 2-17 on page 2-38 is as follows:

$$\cos(2\pi \times t) - \frac{1}{3}\cos(2\pi \times 3t) + \frac{1}{5}\cos(2\pi \times 5t) - \frac{1}{7}\cos(2\pi \times 7t) + \ldots + \frac{1}{13}\cos(2\pi \times 13t) \qquad [1]$$

There are several important things to notice here:

1. The frequency of each sine wave present is an integer multiple of the lowest frequency present. This follows from the fact that we are dealing with a repeating (or periodic) signal.

---

21 The same shape as a sine wave. For example, the cosine function describes a wave exactly the same shape as the sine function but shifted by $\pi/2$ in phase.

2. Not all possible frequencies are present (or rather that some have a zero amplitude!)

3. The amount (amplitude) of each frequency present is specified by the coefficient of each series term. In this case the coefficients are:

$$1, 0, \quad -\frac{1}{3}, 0, \quad \frac{1}{5}, 0, \quad -\frac{1}{7}, \quad ...$$

   Note that the third and seventh terms have a negative sign. This does not mean a negative amplitude (whatever that may be) but rather a phase shift of $\pi$(radians). In the figure, the waveforms with a negative sign start below the x-axis, whereas waveforms with a positive sign start above (reflecting the phase shift).

4. The lowest frequency sine wave has the same period of repetition as the square pulse under study.

5. The sine waves in the series have successively smaller amplitudes as the frequency is increased. This is not true of all signals but is a characteristic of a square pulse.[22]

6. As more terms are added to the series, the shape of the pulse becomes more and more square, but some rather large "ears" have developed. These ears are an artificial result of the way we do the mathematics (called *Gibbs effect*) - they are *not* present in the real signal.

7. In this example, as higher frequencies are added to the sum they make less and less difference to the pulse shape and mainly contribute to making the corners squarer.

[22] $\sin(x) = \cos(x + \pi/2)$

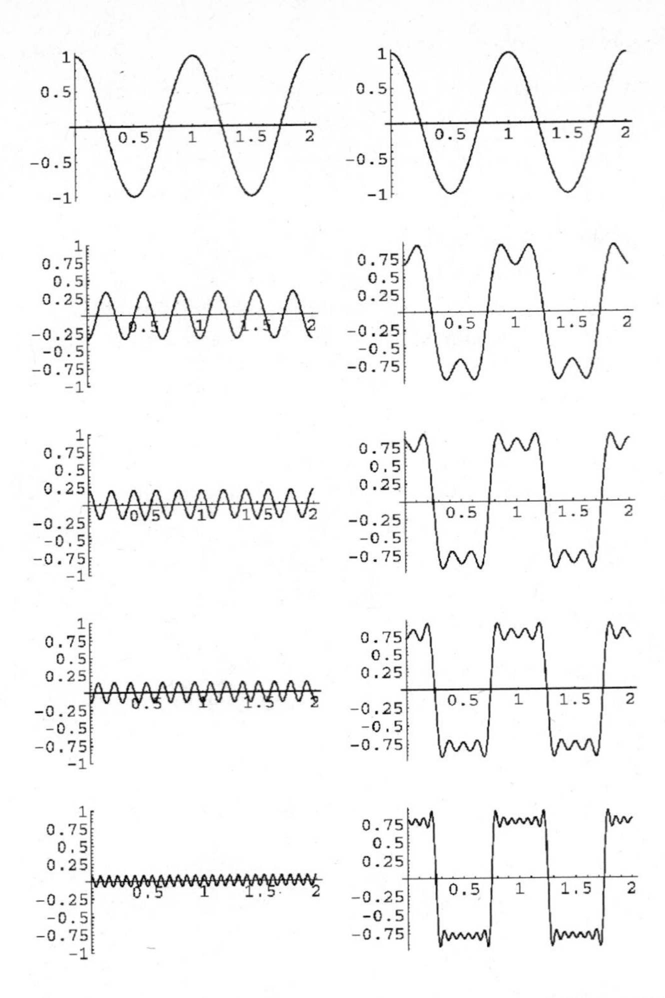


***Figure 2-17. Composition of a Square Pulse as the Sum of Sinusoidal Waves.*** The left-hand column shows each new wave as it is added to the summation. The right-hand column shows the progressive total as each new wave is added. Note that only the first, third, fifth, seventh and thirteenth harmonics are shown. For reasons of space the seventh, ninth and eleventh terms have been omitted from the figure, although they are present in the final summation waveform in the lower right-hand corner.

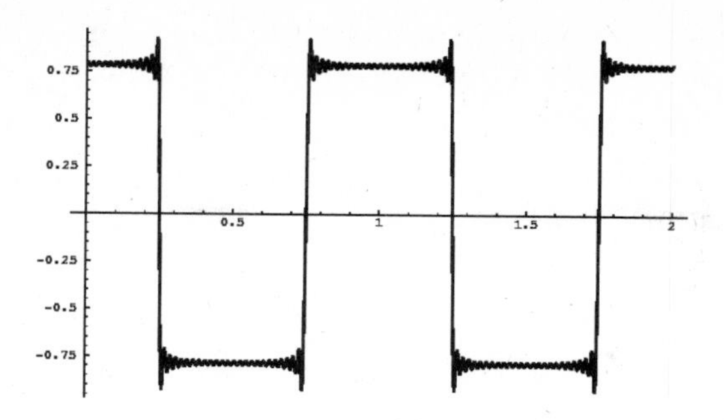


***Figure 2-18.*** *The Same Pulse as before including 50 (25 Non-Zero) Terms*

Consider sending a simple NRZ signal (say) a one bit is represented by +1 volt and a zero bit by -1 volt. If we now send a bit stream of 01010101... we will get the square wave shown earlier (Figure 2-16 on page 2-36). We can make the following observations:

1. Each bit is represented by one state change of the line. That is, 1 bit equals 1 baud.
2. The repetition frequency is *half* of the bit rate. That is, the lowest frequency sine wave present in the signal represents two bit times. So, 1 hertz = 2 baud (= 2 bits).
3. So, if the bit rate was 10 Mbps then the lowest frequency present would be *5 MHz*.
4. Again, if the bit rate is 10 Mbps (5 MHz) then there are frequency components in the signal of 5, 15, 25, 35... MHz.
5. So, if we were to send this signal over a communications channel that was limited to 10 MHz, then we would put the square wave in at one end and get a perfect sine wave out the other (all of the higher frequency components having been removed). This would be somewhat inconvenient if our receiver was expecting a square pulse! It is obvious that the closer that a received pulse edge approaches a square shape then the easier it will be to receive. In addition the received timing (important in some situations) will become more and more accurate as the pulse approaches a square shape.
6. There are many simplifications here. The signal actually varies (if it did not it could not carry information). Using the above example, if we sent the signal 00110011... we would get a frequency spectrum of precisely half of the one we got above. **When the signal is carrying information (varying) there will be many frequencies present and these will be changing.** These are usually expressed as a *spectrum* of frequencies.

There are two critical points that emerge from the above discussion:

1. **Square-wave signals have significant frequency components of many times the frequency of the square wave itself.**

2. **The various frequency components of a signal bear a critical relationship to one another in terms of amplitude and phase. If this relationship is disturbed, then the signal will be distorted.**

   This can be illustrated by considering the square pulse of Figure 2-17 on page 2-38. In this figure, the right-hand lower diagram shows the summation of the first thirteen terms. If we introduce some phase distortion by delaying the third, fifth and seventh terms by $\pi/2$ we get the pulse shown in Figure 2-19.

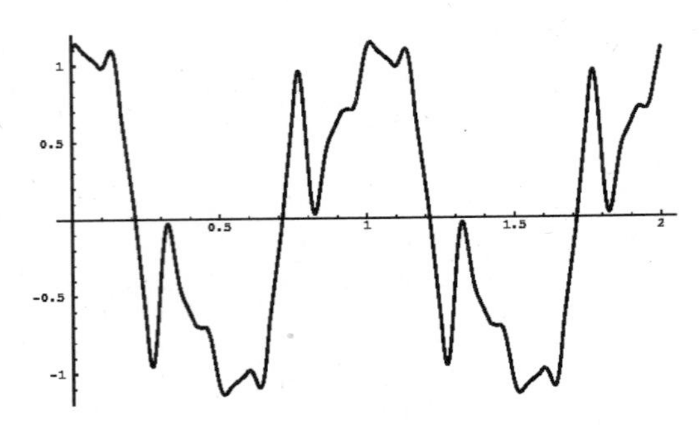


***Figure 2-19.*** *The Effect of Phase Distortion on the Thirteen-Term Summation.* The third, fifth and seventh terms have been delayed by $\pi/2$.

It is clear that the above signal would provide considerable trouble to a simple digital phase locked loop (PLL) detector! (See 2.1.6.1, "Phase Locked Loops (PLLs)" on page 2-11.) This is severe (and unrealistic) distortion; nevertheless, given the right kind of preprocessing, such signals can be handled in the real world.

## 2.2.3 Characteristics of Cables

Specific cable configurations vary enormously in their ability to carry a signal, in their usefulness for a particular situation, and in their cost. Nevertheless they all share a common set of characteristics:

**Resistance**

All wire has resistance to the flow of electrical current and this is one factor in limiting the distance over which a signal may travel. The thicker the wire, the less resistance. While it reduces the signal (and also the noise) resistance does not cause distortion of the signal.

A typical resistance value for 20 gauge (.8118 mm) wire at 70 deg F is 10 ohms per thousand feet. For 26 gauge (.4094 mm) wire this figure is 40 ohms per thousand feet.

### Leakage

This is caused by conduction between the wires through the "insulator". This is another source of signal loss.

### Inductance

Current flowing in a wire always produces a magnetic field around the wire. This field changes with the flow of current. These changes in magnetic field absorb power at some times and replace it back into the circuit at other times. This causes distortion of the digital signal. (Inductance is not all bad, since it tends to compensate for distortion caused by capacitance effects.)

### Capacitance

Capacitance is the effect caused by electrostatic attraction between opposite charges in conductors which are physically close to one another. Like inductance, capacitance takes power from the circuit at some times and discharges it back into the circuit at other times - causing distortion. However, it is extremely important to understand that capacitance and inductance work in different (in simple terms, opposite) ways.

Capacitance is most influenced by the distance between conductors and the material between them. This material is called the "dielectric". Other things being equal, if wires are separated by air the capacitance is about half of what it would be if the wires were separated by PVC. This is the reason that many cables use plastic foam for an insulator.

In all cable situations *except* the "open wire" case, capacitance is "large" and is considered the major factor limiting a cable's ability to carry a signal.

The above factors (inductance and capacitance) can be lumped together into a single characteristic called "impedance". Impedance is defined as the ratio of voltage over current at any point on the line and is a constant for a particular cable.

A normal transmission channel will change any digital pulse sent along it (see Figure 2-20).

***Figure 2-20.*** *Distortion of a Digital Pulse by a Transmission Channel.* Both of the illustrated alternatives are perfectly normal pulse shapes after transmission down a good transmission channel.

#### 2.2.3.1 Impairments in Transmission Channels

**Thermal Noise**

Heat (at any temperature) causes electrons to "bounce around" at random. This causes small random variations in the signal and is usually called background noise.

**Physical Environment**

Cable characteristics can vary significantly with temperature, sometimes in the space of an hour or so. Other environmental factors such as the presence of moisture can also change the transmission characteristics of the cable.

**Impulse Noise**

When wires (such as regular telephone twisted pairs) pass through a telephone exchange or pass close to other wires they can pick up short transient voltages (impulses) from the other wires in the same cable. This is caused by unintended capacitive and inductive coupling with the other wires in the cable.

In some telephone environments the major source of impulse noise is the relatively high voltage pulses (up to 50 volts) used for dialing in old style (step-by-step) telephone exchanges. Some telephone environments use as many as 2,000 twisted pairs in the same cable.

In the telephone subscriber loop environment, impulse noise takes the form of "spikes" of between 10 μsec and 50 μsec in duration.

In the LAN environment, impulse noise can arise if an (unshielded) twisted pair passes close (in the same duct) to normal electrical power wiring. Whenever a high current device (such as a motor) is switched on there is a current surge on the wire. Through stray coupling, a power surge can cause impulse noise on nearby communications cabling.

**Reflected Signals**

If a signal traveling on a wire encounters a change in the impedance of the circuit, part of the signal is reflected back towards the sender. Of course, as it travels back to the sender, it could be reflected back in the original direction of travel if it encounters another change in impedance.

Reflected signals (sometimes called echoes) can cause a problem in a unidirectional environment because they can be reflected back from the transmitter end, but this is not always very serious.

The real problem comes when a two-wire line is used for full-duplex communication (such as at the ISDN_BR "U" interface). Here reflections can cause serious interference with a signal going in the other direction.

Impedance changes over the route of a circuit can have a number of causes, such as a change in the gauge or type of wire used in the circuit or even a badly made connection. However, the worst impedance mismatches are commonly caused by the presence of a "bridged tap". A bridged tap is simply where another wire (pair of wires) is connected to the link but its other end is not connected to anything. Bridged taps are quite common in some telephone environments.

### Intersymbol Interference

Intersymbol interference takes place when a particular line state being transmitted is influenced by a previous line state. This is usually a result of the characteristics of the circuit causing the signal to be "smeared" so that the end of one symbol (bit or group of bits) overlaps with the start of the next.

### Crosstalk

Crosstalk is when a signal from one pair of wires appears on another pair of wires in the same cable - through reactive (capacitive or inductive) coupling effects. In telephone subscriber loop situations, crosstalk increases very rapidly when the signal frequency gets above 100 kHz. One effect of crosstalk is to place an unwanted signal on a wire pair, thus interfering with the intended signal. Another effect of crosstalk is that it causes loss of signal strength (attenuation) in the pair causing the interference.

There are two kinds of crosstalk which can have different amounts of significance in different situations. These are called "Near End Crosstalk" (NEXT) and "Far End Crosstalk" (FEXT).

The most common type of NEXT occurs when the signal transmitted from a device interferes with the signal in the other direction being received by that device. This can be a problem in the LAN environment using unshielded cable, since the transmit pair and the receive pair are bound closely together in the cable.

Another type of NEXT is interference from any transmitter at the same end of the cable as the receiver being interfered with. (This is common in the telephone situation where there can be hundreds of wire pairs in the same cable.)

FEXT is caused by interference from transmissions by other devices at the far end of the cable. In most (though not all) digital signaling situations, FEXT is not a significant problem (because it happens at the transmitter end of a cable where the signal is strong relative to the interference).

### Other Interference Sources

Wires in unshielded cables can pick up signals from many sources other than other pairs in the same cable. This is mainly from inductive coupling. Most of the time this is not too much of a problem since in a balanced wire pair you tend to get the same effect on both wires and the induced currents cancel each other out. However, sometimes you can get severe interference that will prevent use of the wire for communications.

A common example is where unshielded cable intended for LAN use is run close to fluorescent lights. The induced current can be so great as to prevent operation of the LAN. (Occasionally this means that newly installed LAN cable must be removed and replaced.)

If one wire of the wire pair is earthed the effect of stray inductive couplings is increased because the induced currents no longer cancel one another out.

### 2.2.4 The Subscriber Loop

The subscriber loop is the two-wire connection between the telephone exchange and customer premises. This environment was designed for analog telephone connection and it poses some severe problems for digital communication. Nevertheless, it is of immense economic importance.

In the US there is something of the order of 80 million subscriber loop connections. To replace them (meaning digging up the road to install new ones) would cost something like $1,500 per connection on average. A way of making more productive use of them (such as in ISDN_BR) could provide a large economic benefit. Even selection of "good" wire pairs to use for a special purpose or the conditioning of a nominated pair is a very labor intensive procedure and is to be avoided if possible.

There are wide differences between countries (and even within individual countries) in the characteristics of this wiring.

**Maximum Length**

One of the most important criteria is the length of the wire. The maximum length varies in different countries but is usually from four to eight kilometers.

**Wire Thickness**

All gauges of wire have been used, from 16 gauge (1.291 mm) to 26 gauge (.405 mm). The smaller gauges are typically used for short distances so that it is rare to find 26 gauge wire longer than 2½ kilometers (a little more than 8000 feet).

**Material**

Most installed wire is copper but some aluminum wire is in use.

**Insulation**

The majority of this cable uses tightly wound paper insulation, but recent installations in most countries tend to use plastic.

### Twists in Cable

Telephone wire is twisted essentially to keep the two wires of a pair together when they are bundled in a cable with up to 1000 other pairs. Twists do, however, help by adding a small inductive component to the cable characteristic.

The number of twists per meter is different for different pairs in the same cable. (This is deliberately done to minimize crosstalk interference.) Also, the uniformity of twists is not generally well controlled. These have the effect of causing small irregularities in impedance, which can cause reflections and signal loss due to radiation, etc.

### Different Gauges on the Same Connection

It is quite common to have different gauges of wire used on the same connection. Any change in the characteristics of the wire causes an impedance mismatch and can be a source of reflections.

### Bridged Taps

The worst feature of all in typical subscriber loops is the bridged tap.[23] This is just a piece of wire (twisted pair) connected to the line at one end, but only with the other end left unconnected. In other words, the circuit between the end user and the exchange has another (unconnected) wire joined to it somewhere along its path. This happens routinely when field technicians attach a user to a line without removing the wires that attached previous users.

In practical situations subscriber loops with as many as six bridged taps have been reported.

Bridged taps cause a large impedance mismatch (reflect a large amount of the signal) and radiate energy (causing loss of signal strength and potential problems with radio frequency emission).

### Loading Coils

On typical telephone twisted pair cable, the effects of capacitance between the two conductors dominates the characteristics of the circuit and limits the transmission distance. For many years it has been a practice to counteract some of the effect of capacitance by adding inductance to the circuit. This was done (especially over longer distances) by the insertion of "loading coils" into the loop.

It is estimated that up to 25% of the subscriber loops in the US have loading coils in the circuit.

---

[23] In some contexts bridged taps are called "stubs".

There is no available digital transmission technique which will work in the presence of loading coils. They need to be removed if the circuit is to be used for digital transmission.

### Phase Distortion

Depending on the frequency, the phase of the signal is distorted by a different amount. Several effects cause this. A delay of a constant amount of time causes a different phase shift depending on the frequency. (This is called "envelope delay".) The reactance of the line has different effects depending on the frequency being transmitted.

### Attenuation

The signal is attenuated (reduced in strength) selectively depending on its frequency. Attenuation increases rapidly with frequency. See Figure 2-21.

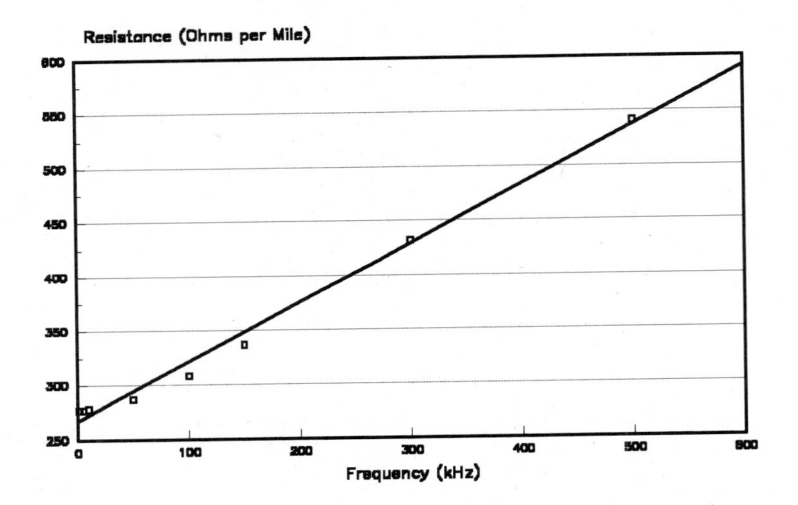


*Figure* ***2-21.*** *Resistance Variation with Frequency on a Typical TTP Connection*

This is a problem when using TTP for digital baseband transmission because a square-pulse signal has (sine wave) frequency components of many times that of the fundamental frequency. If higher-frequency components are attenuated, then the shape of the square pulse is distorted.

### Variation in Pair Quality

In a real system the characteristics of a particular pair can vary quite significantly from the characteristics of a different pair *in the same cable!* This can mean that to run a system using ISDN Primary Rate (HDB3 coding at 2 Mbps) the pairs to be used must be carefully selected.

One of the objectives of recently developed systems (such as HDSL - see 3.1.1, "High-Speed Digital Subscriber Line (HDSL)" on page 3-1) is to eliminate the need for pair selection, since this imposes a high installation cost on the system.

### 2.2.5 Echo Cancellation

As mentioned previously in this discussion, echoes are a significant source of interference. This is particularly true wherever bidirectional transmission takes place on two wires (such as in the subscriber loop).

In the traditional analog telephone environment, two-wire transmission is used from the subscriber to the nearest exchange and "four wire" (true full-duplex) transmission is used between exchanges. In this traditional environment, echoes can be a major source of annoyance to telephone users.

An historic way of handling echoes was to use "echo suppressors". An echo suppressor is a device that detects transmission in one direction (such as someone speaking) and suppresses *all* transmissions arriving from the opposite direction. Sometimes in circuits with long delays (such as in satellite circuits) echo suppressors are used at both ends. Of course, echo suppressors are useless for full-duplex transmission, since they prevent it. Even in voice applications, echo suppressors have problems because they "clip" speech when both parties attempt to speak at the same time, and they tend to suppress low level speech as well.

A better way of handling echoes is to use an echo canceller. The basic principle of echo cancellation is shown in Figure 2-22.

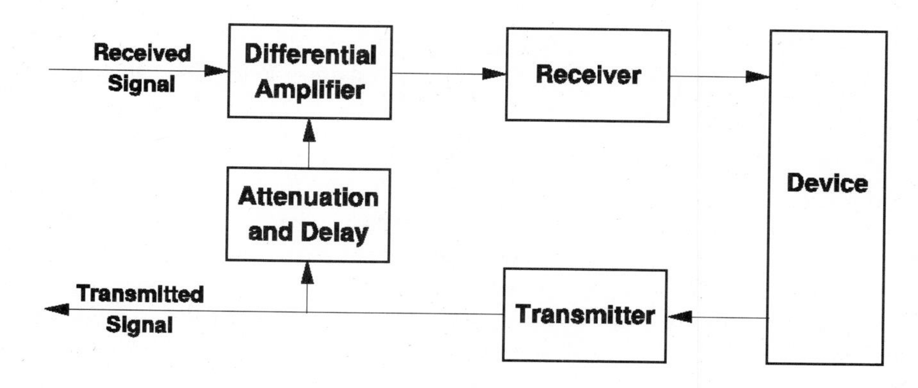


***Figure 2-22.*** *Concept of an Echo Canceller*

The concept behind an echo canceller is that as a signal is transmitted, it is copied and put into a variable delay mechanism. The delayed signal is then reduced and subtracted from the signal being received in a differential amplifier. If the delay and signal levels are set correctly, then this device will effectively remove strong echoes. Echo cancellers may be analog or digital in nature. This device is, however, only effective at removing echoes from a single source. If (as is typical) there are many echoes the device will only remove one of them.

When transmitting full-duplex onto a two-wire line there is a much larger potential problem than echo. It is the full signal from the transmitter. After all, the output from the transmitter is connected to the same two wires as the receiver. This problem is solved by using a device called a Hybrid Balanced Network. As illustrated in Figure 2-23, this is simply a number of inductive couplings organized so that the transmitter signal is cancelled out (subtracted from the signal) before the signal reaches the receiver. This technique has been used historically to split the signal from a two-wire subscriber loop onto a four-wire trunk circuit. The problem with this is that it is difficult in practice to match impedances exactly and so some of the transmitter's signal does reach the receiver (a form of near end crosstalk).

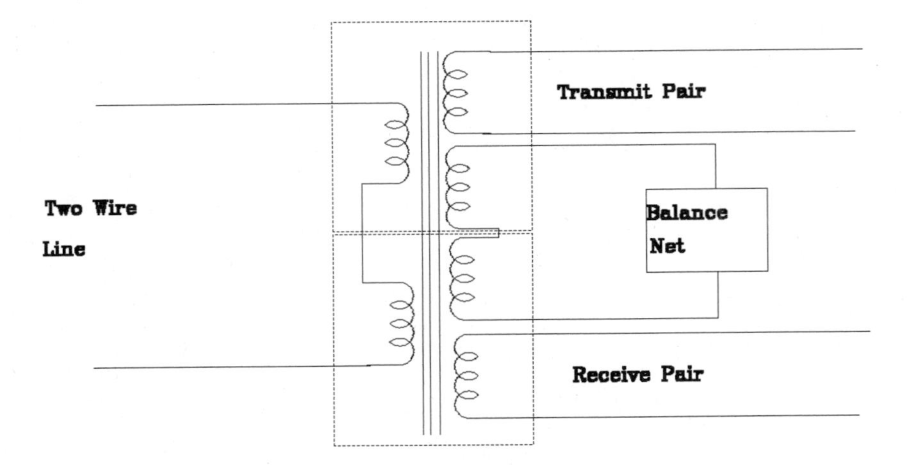


***Figure 2-23. Hybrid Balanced Network.*** This device is used to convert a signal from two-wire to four-wire operation. Two transformers each consisting of at least three tightly coupled windings and an impedance balancing network are used. The balance network is adjusted to match the impedance of whatever device is connected to the two-wire line. With careful impedance matching, the device can reduce the level of the transmitted signal reaching the received pair by as much as 50 dB.

In recent times devices called "adaptive filters" have become practical with improvements in VLSI technology. An adaptive filter automatically adjusts itself to its environment.[24] Echo cancellers can't handle interference that is systematic but not an echo (such as crosstalk from adjacent circuits), nor can they handle the effects of impulse noise or (for that matter) multiple echoes. Adaptive filters can do a very good job of cleaning up a signal when transmitting full-duplex on a two-wire line.

Of course, echo cancellers can be digital and adaptive also, so that they can adjust automatically to the characteristics of the circuit they are attached to.

A practical system will then use:

1. An analog hybrid to connect to the line.
2. Analog filters for both transmit and receive to clean up the signal a bit.
3. A digital adaptive echo canceller.
4. A digital adaptive filter.

In conjunction with an appropriate line code, this system can process full-duplex data at rates up to about 200 Kbps, and half-duplex at rates in excess of 1.8 Mbps over distances of up to 12 kilometers without the need for repeaters.

## 2.3 LAN Cabling with Unshielded Twisted Pair

### 2.3.1 The FCC versus the Laws of Physics

The two fundamental issues in telecommunications copper cable choice are easy to express. First of all, cable utility is fundamentally limited by the laws of physics. The second fundamental limitation is that a premise's wiring must meet the laws of man, notably regulatory requirements governing radiation of electronic signals into the environment. These two sets of laws often interact in ways that are disturbing to the transmission engineer. In other words, not everything that is possible in the realm of physical law is permitted by regulatory law.

All other things being equal, we know that as data rate increases the drive distance available on copper wire decreases approximately proportionally to the square roots of the data rates. So a 16 Mbps signal can travel only one-half of the distance of a 4 Mbps signal using a copper wire with constant specifications. However, all other things are almost never equal among signaling methods of devices using different protocols, implementations, or data rates. All of these considerations are further complicated by the fact that increasing data rates cause increasing radiation. The regulatory agencies reasonably

[24] An excellent account of adaptive filtering in the loop plant is given in *Waring D.L et. al. 1991*.

set an absolute standard for radiation emission that does not vary with the data rate of the signal.

### 2.3.2 UTP for 16 Mbps Token-Ring

It is possible to run token-ring transmission protocols without change to the Differential Manchester coding over good-quality telephone twisted pair (IBM Type 3 media).[25] This cable produces a high level of crosstalk and high attenuation that together degrade the signal and place severe restrictions on both drive distance and number of stations attached.

By careful design of filters to reduce high-frequency components (to solve EMC and interference problems) 16 Mbps transmission is possible in a single ring of up to 72 devices with lobe cables that do not exceed 30 meters. This very restrictive solution can be improved by using an active repeater in the hub that utilizes equalization and linear amplification to offset the degradation associated with transmission on UTP.

Using high-grade UTP (class 5) you can achieve a significant improvement in drive distance and number of stations attached over that possible with standard UTP. The situation may be improved still further by using an active hub module. This provides lobe lengths of up to 100 meters in a 72-station ring.

However, this does not solve all the problems of UTP. As far as the issue of electromagnetic compatibility (EMC) is concerned, neither of these choices offers the protection provided by shielded twisted pair (STP) by the mere existence of the shielding. In order to prevent unacceptable levels of EMC, radiation filters are needed at every station and the cost of these must be considered in the overall network media cost. In addition, when using UTP, impulse noise and crosstalk from nearby cables can be a source of significant performance degradation. (Do *not* route UTP cable close to the power cables in an elevator well!)

### 2.3.3 UTP at 100 Mbps in the LAN

It is common parlance in the industry to refer to a cable as having a capacity of x Mbps - as though this was some inherent capability of the cable itself or of the cabling system. Nothing could be further from reality. The data throughput of a particular cable depends on many things, but primarily on how the signal is to be transmitted (the transmission coding).

If we take a very good transmission environment (such as STP) and use only a small fraction of the available bandwidth we can send a very simple signal, use low-cost transceivers and have effective communication. Such is the case with token-ring (either

---

25 Similar to the EIA-568 Commercial Building Telecommunications Wiring Standard.

4 or 16 Mbps) on the STP medium. However, when the bandwidth of the medium is limited and there are other factors (such as noise and EMC emissions), then we have a very different story.

When considering data transfer at 100 Mbps, UTP must be considered a constrained medium whichever way you look at it. (Class 5 is significantly better than class 3 but they are both constrained.) Most of the factors constraining a transmission medium have been discussed earlier in this chapter. In summary, these are:

**Transmission Characteristics of the Cable Itself**

This is the effect of resistance, inductance and capacitance in the cable and connectors. The higher the frequency of the signal, the more it will be attenuated.

**Emission of Unwanted Interference from the Cable (EMC)**

The higher the frequency components in the signal, the more EMC will be generated.

**Noise**

Noise comes from crosstalk (other wire pairs in the same cable) and through electromagnetic coupling to the external environment.

If we sent a 100 Mbps signal on UTP coded in any simple way (NRZ, NRZI or even Manchester) then the system would not meet our requirements. Either there would be too much distortion introduced by the cable or too much EMC generated or the maximum drive distance would be too short for practical usage.

The combined effects of cable characteristics and EMC potential limit the usable bandwidth of UTP-3 cable to around 30 MHz and UTP-5 to about 70 MHz. Therefore, to get UTP to handle data at 100 Mbps we have to resort to more complex methods.

**FDDI over UTP-5**

This is now standardized and uses MLT-3 coding described in 2.1.15.3, "Multi-Level Transmit - 3 Levels (MLT-3)" on page 2-30.

**100 Mbps Ethernet (100BaseTX) over UTP-5**

This protocol uses two pairs of wire (one in each direction) in a UTP-5 cable. The same coding scheme as FDDI over UTP-5 (MLT-3) is used.

**100 Mbps Ethernet (100BaseT4) over UTP-3 Using Four Pairs**

The first thing to be said about this protocol is that it does *not* send 100 Mbps over a single pair of UTP-3 wires. A typical UTP-3 cable contains four pairs of wires. The protocol sends data on *three pairs in parallel* and the data rate on each pair is 33.3 Mbps. The fourth pair is used for collision detection. One restriction is that if there are more than four pairs in the UTP cable then those additional pairs *may not be used for any purpose* (this is to cut down on noise due to crosstalk). This is discussed further in 13.3.1.1, "100VG AnyNet Transmission Protocol on UTP-3" on page 13-21.

### 100 Mbps Ethernet over UTP-3 Using Two Pairs (100BaseT2)

This is a strong requirement that is under discussion in the IEEE standards committee. A number of proposals exist but the problem is complex and a resolution is expected to take some time.

### 100VG AnyNet

This protocol again uses all four pairs in the UTP-3 cable but is quite different from 100BaseT4. It is described in 13.3, "100VG AnyNet - IEEE 802.12 (100BaseVG)" on page 13-19.

***Table 2-5.*** *Summary of LAN Protocol Characteristics*

| LAN Protocol | Cable | Data Rate | Data Rate per Pair | Symbol Rate Mbaud | Encoding Scheme | Bits per Baud | Levels |
|---|---|---|---|---|---|---|---|
| Ethernet IEEE 802.3 | UTP-3 | 10 | 10 | 20 | Manchester | 1/2 | 2 |
| Token-Ring IEEE 802.5 | UTP-3 | 16 | 16 | 32 | Differential Manchester | 1/2 | 2 |
| FDDI | MM-Fiber | 100 | 100 | 125 | 4B/5B | 4/5 | 2 |
| FDDI | STP | 100 | 100 | 125 | 4B/5B | 4/5 | 2 |
| FDDI | UTP-5 | 100 | 100 | 125 | 4B/5B MLT-3 | 4/5 | 3 |
| 100VG AnyNet IEEE 802.12 | UTP-3 4 pairs | 100 | 25 | 30 | 5B/6B | 5/6 | 2 |
| 100Base-FX | MM-Fiber | 100 | 100 | 125 | 4B/5B | 4/5 | 2 |
| 100Base-TX | UTP-5 | 100 | 100 | 125 | 4B/5B MLT-3 | 4/5 | 2 |
| 100Base-T4 | UTP-3 4 pairs | 100 | 33.33 | 25 | 8B6T | 8/6 | 3 |
| 100BaseT2 | UTP-3 2 pairs | 100 | 100 | ? | Undecided | ? | ? |

# Chapter 3. High Speed on the Subscriber Loop (HDSL and ADSL)

Many people think that because the use of fiber optics is growing very rapidly that there is no progress being made in digital transmission on copper media. Nothing could be further from the truth.

Better circuitry (higher density, higher speed, lower cost) enables us to use much more sophisticated techniques for digital transmission than have been possible in the past. As mentioned above, there are vast numbers of copper "subscriber loops" installed around the world and there is a big incentive to get better use out of them.

In the previous chapter, and later in 8.1.3, "ISDN Basic Rate" on page 8-3, the principles of basic rate ISDN are discussed. This was an enormously successful research effort, so much so that the American National Standards Institute (committee T1.E1.4) is working on two projects aimed at increasing the link speeds even further.

These projects are:

1. Asymmetric Digital Subscriber Line (ADSL).

   This project is aimed at producing a standard for use of a two-wire subscriber loop for 1.544 Mbps in one direction with a much slower (say 64 Kbps) channel in the opposite direction. Many potential services, for example image retrieval, do not require high speed in both directions.

2. High-Speed Digital Subscriber Lines (HDSL).

   This project is examining a number of alternative architectures for full-duplex transmission on *unconditioned* subscriber loop connections at speeds up to 1.544 Mbps.

This is a considerable challenge! The unshielded telephone twisted pair of the subscriber loop has many impairments and as the transmission rate increases, the losses on the line increase exponentially. The subscriber loop is a very limited channel. Existing "T1 and E1" circuits use selected pairs in one direction only (two pairs are used) and they are amplified every mile.

### 3.1.1 High-Speed Digital Subscriber Line (HDSL)

There are four HDSL loop architectures under consideration:

**Dual Duplex (Two-Pair Full-Duplex)**

Two subscriber loops are used (that is, four wires) to carry a data rate of 1.544 Mbps. This is not the same as existing T1s because it is proposed to use unconditioned loops without repeaters.

Each wire pair carries 784 Kbps full-duplex using an echo-cancelled hybrid transmission method similar to that used for ISDN_BR.

**Dual Simplex (Two-Pair Simplex)**

Two pairs are used as above, but each pair carries a full 1.544 Mbps signal in one direction only.

**One-Pair 1.5 Mbps Full-Duplex**

Full-duplex T1 over a single unconditioned subscriber loop pair. This is listed "for further study" (for now, it is too difficult).

**Provisioned Single-Loop 768 Kbps Transport**

This is really like a half of the dual-duplex case, although that it will probably be quite different in detailed operation. The user interface is proposed to be standard T1 but with 12 channels disabled. That is, a 24-slot T1 frame with 12 of the slots disabled and filled with idle characters.

The following three approaches to transmission were considered by the ANSI committee:

**2B1Q Line Code**

In principle this is the same technique as is used for the US version of basic rate ISDN, although it is a little different in detail. 2B1Q line code as described in 2.1.15.2, "2-Binary 1-Quaternary (2B1Q) Code" on page 2-29, is used in conjunction with advanced echo cancellation and adaptive filtering techniques (see 2.2.5, "Echo Cancellation" on page 2-47).

**Carrierless AM/PM (CAP)**

This architecture has been suggested for the "dual-duplex" configuration.

The dual-duplex configuration is attractive because by splitting the signal over two parallel subscriber loops and running the links (loops) in a coordinated way, you can cancel a significant proportion of the NEXT.

**Multicarrier (Discrete Multitone - DMT)**

DMT is described in the following section, and several papers on HDSL and ADSL are referenced in the bibliography.

ANSI has formally endorsed 2B1Q as the transmission standard for HDSL. However, standardization in this area is unusual (the ISDN "U" interface transmission technique is not a formal standard) because most standards bodies have considered it inappropriate in an area where technology is evolving so rapidly. Recently, it has been realized that DMT is a superior transmission technique and it seems likely that a (non-standardized) form of HDSL using DMT technology will become available as well.

### 3.1.2 Asymmetric Digital Subscriber Lines (ADSL)

As the name suggests, ADSL provides a connection between a customer premises and the local telephone exchange with *different* data rates in each direction.

The primary reason for ADSL is for the distribution of video and image-based services to private homes and small businesses over existing copper wire local loops.

ADSL is a developing standard. The initial proposal was to provide a 1.5 Mbps connection from the exchange to the end user with a 64 Kbps connection from the end user to the exchange. An important point is that this is in addition to the "regular" analog voice connection over *the same* pair of wires.

When ADSL was first proposed as a standards project, the objective looked attainable but very difficult. Recent research results, however, have proven that DMT transmission can achieve a much greater throughput than the original objective. On good quality loops a data rate of 6 Mbps in one direction is possible (and this has been demonstrated in field trials). Simultaneously with this, a data rate of 384 Kbps has been demonstrated in the other direction.

The form of ADSL currently undergoing field trials gives 1.544 Mbps downstream, 64 Kbps upstream plus simultaneous analog voice. The system is arranged so that the analog voice transmission can still continue even if the ADSL NTUs (Network Terminating Units) are powered off.

Figure 3-1 on page 3-4 gives an overview of possible extended ADSL function.[1] There are four "channels":

1. A downstream channel of from 1.544 Mbps to 6.3 Mbps, depending on the line quality. This could be presented to the end user as multiple T1s, Multiple E1s or a mixture - depending on the desired function.
2. A multipurpose channel. Depending on the desired function this could be (bi-directional) Basic Rate ISDN or a single upstream channel of from 64 to 384 Kbps.
3. A control channel is present at the upstream unit to allow control and maintenance diagnostic information to be accessed.
4. The analog voice channel is separated from the ADSL transmission by the use of passive filters external to the ADSL transceivers.

---

[1] The exact detail is still under consideration by ANSI.

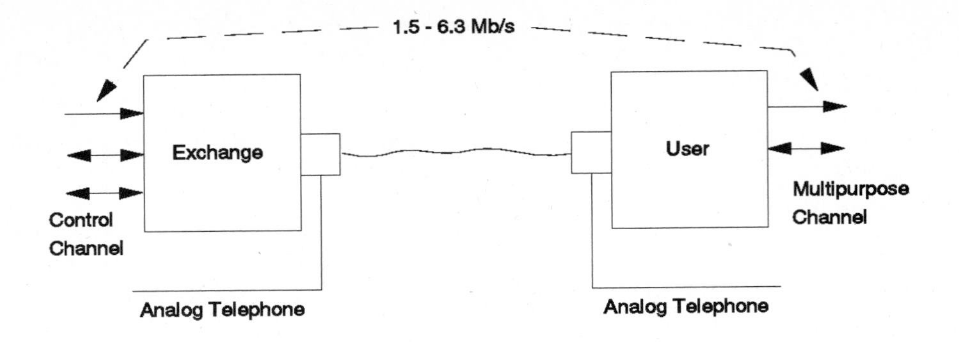


*Figure 3-1. Overview of the ADSL System*

Figure 3-2 shows how ADSL uses the available bandwidth. The baseband part (up to 10 kHz) is occupied by analog voice. Upstream and downstream parts of the transmission use different frequencies in order to avoid the need for echo cancellation.

It is expected that the final version of ADSL will extend the downstream channel frequency band down to 10 kHz overlapping with the upstream channel frequency. The system requires complex echo cancellation in order to make this possible but it is predicted that this function can be incorporated in the same chip that performs all the other ADSL functions. Hence the cost of the additional bandwidth capability is minimal.

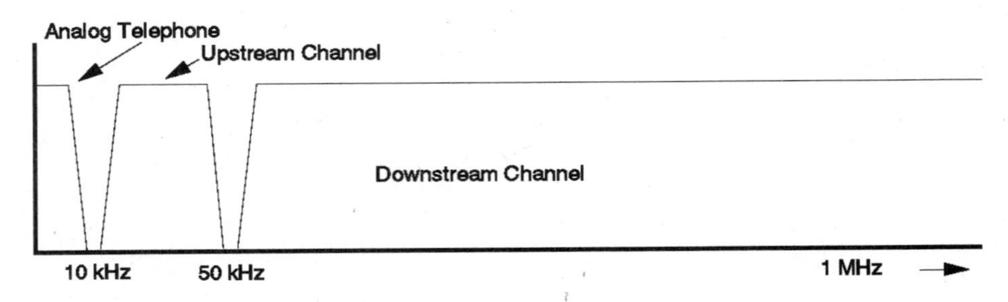


*Figure 3-2. Frequency Spectrum Use of ADSL (Initial Version)*

## 3.2 Discrete Multitone Transmission (DMT)

Discrete Multitone Transmission[2] is the transmission technique selected by ANSI for ADSL discussed in 3.1.2, “Asymmetric Digital Subscriber Lines (ADSL)” on page 3-3. It was also one of the alternatives considered for HDSL. The objective is to get the highest possible data transfer rate over existing TTP (telephone twisted pair) “tails”[3] (the connection from the end user to the exchange).

The concept involved in DMT is not new, but its practical implementation has had to wait for cost-effective hardware technology to become available. Digital Signal Processing now provides such cost-effective technology.

**Note:** The details of DMT presented in the following discussion are as they were proposed for use with HDSL. The details of ADSL implementation are slightly different. (Mainly, the symbol rate in HDSL is 2000 baud - or one block every 500 μsec. In ADSL it is 4000 baud - or one block every 250 μsec.)

### 3.2.1 The Problem

Telephone subscriber loop circuits were designed to handle a single analog voice transmission in the environment of a public telephone network. This they do very well. However, they are a very restricted and noisy medium when it comes to high speed digital transmission. This is discussed in 2.2.4, “The Subscriber Loop” on page 2-44 and may be summarized as follows:

1. Signal attenuation varies dramatically with frequency - the higher frequencies are strongly attenuated in comparison to the lower ones.
2. Crosstalk effects increase significantly as the signal frequency gets above about 100 kHz.
3. Over the typical four kilometer distance the usable bandwidth range is from zero to about five hundred kilohertz. (Some loops give adequate performance up to 1.1 MHz.)
4. There are many different types of noise present that affect different parts of the usable frequency range in different ways.
5. The amount and type of signal distortion imposed by the medium (the wire) varies with the frequency of the signal.

---

[2] The concept of DMT was pioneered by A. Peled and A Ruiz of IBM Research (see Peled and Ruiz, 1980). However, most of the current research work relating to the use of DMT for HDSL and ADSL was done by Amati Communications Corporation and Stanford University. Thanks are due to Amati for providing much of the DMT information presented here.

[3] Also called “subscriber loops”

When sending a coherent signal (whether it is digital baseband or modulations on a carrier) across this type of transmission channel, impairments that are present in the band affect the whole signal. Thus the “trick” of designing a transmission scheme is to pick a scheme that avoids or minimizes the problems inherent in the channel.

### 3.2.2 Basic Principle

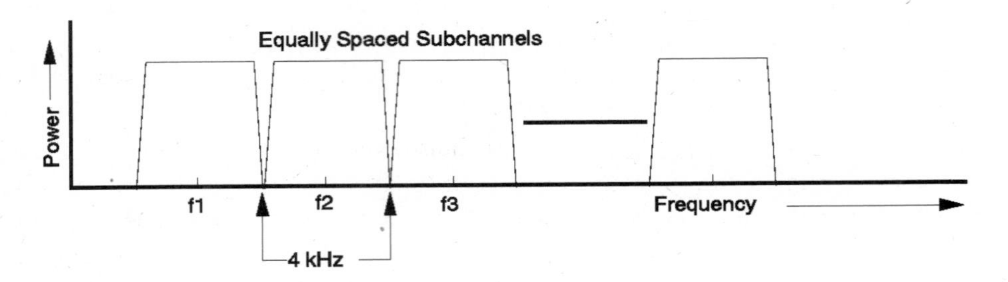


***Figure 3-3.*** *Frequency Division Multiplexing in DMT*

The basic principle of DMT is to break up the transmission channel into many (narrower) subchannels by Frequency Division Multiplexing (FDM).

**At first sight this seems absurd!**

- Shannon's laws tell us that if we break up a channel into two narrower ones then the best we can hope for is that the sum of the two narrower ones, might equal what we could do before the channel was split - and probably we would do much worse!
- If we use FDM to break up a wider channel into many narrow ones, then the total will usually be reduced significantly by the need to have “guard bands” (gaps of unused frequency space) between the subchannels to prevent them from interfering with one another. This means that the total usable bandwidth is reduced by the amount allocated to the guard bands.

**The fact is, however, that the scheme is far from absurd! DMT is the best transmission scheme yet developed for the telephone subscriber loop environment.** This comes about for a number of reasons:

1. If we treat the available bandwidth as a single channel and send any kind of signal over it, impairments in one part of the channel affect the whole signal. If we break up the channel into many narrower subchannels, then different impairments and channel characteristics will apply to each subchannel. In other words, different subchannels will have different levels of quality. We now have an opportunity to optimize each subchannel individually. For example, the high attenuation that affects subchannels in the higher parts of the frequency range will not affect the subchan-

nels in the lower parts of the range. Different types of noise will affect some subchannels without affecting others.

Shannon's laws are still unbroken - they assume that impairments in a channel uniformly affect all frequencies over the width of the channel. But this is not the case here.

2. If a coherent (single carrier) signal is used, then equalization in the receiver amplifies much of the unwanted noise. By equalizing each subchannel individually we don't have as much problem with noise.

3. The "symbol period" on each subchannel is very long compared with what it would be for a single carrier signal. In the system described here each signal state is held for a period of 500 μsec. This means that noise events (which are typically only 30 to 50 μsec long in the subscriber loop environment), have little effect on reception of the signal.

4. "Guard bands" are not needed. Guard bands are usually needed in FDM transmission, because each signal is separately generated and the signals are later combined in some way. Guard bands are needed because each frequency cannot be precisely specified or controlled (in relation to the others).

   But in this case all the channels are being generated by the same transmitter and so their interrelationships are stable in respect to each other because they are controlled by the same clock. In practical terms, DMT is performed by digital signal processing and frequencies are combined digitally (mathematically). Guard bands are no longer needed.

The *essential* point of this process is that each subchannel is operated at one of a number of potential bit rates depending on its quality. *Different subchannels run at different bit rates.* After all, some sub-bands will have a very high quality (low attenuation, little noise) while others will have a lower quality - this is the reason we split the band up in the first place. The procedure would be much less valuable if all subchannels had to operate at the speed of the slowest![4]

There are two cost factors to be overcome:

1. The adapter (transmitter and receiver) requires a signal processor capable of around three million floating point instructions per second for each direction (transmit and receive). This means that the adapter cost will be relatively high (compared to a Basic Rate ISDN adapter, for example). However, implementation of full HDSL transceivers on a single chip is planned, in which case the cost should be very reasonable.

4 Although there is some improvement due to improved noise rejection.

2. There is a delay inherent in the adapter caused by the time needed to receive the block, process and transmit it. However, in the HDSL application this delay is likely to be only a few milliseconds.

### 3.2.3 The Transmitter

A DMT transmitter using digital signal processing for HDSL is illustrated in Figure 3-4. The principle is as follows:

1. The available bandwidth is split into 256 FDM subchannels of 4 kHz each.
2. Subchannels are operated at different bit rates from one another depending on the characteristics of the particular part of the frequency band that the subchannel is allocated to.
3. Transmission takes place one "block" at a time. There are 400 bits in each block and each block is transmitted in 500 µsec.

   If we consider each "block" as a distinct line state of itself then it is valid to say that transmission rate (symbol rate) is 2000 baud.
4. Each sub-band is 2 kHz wide so the total bandwidth (potentially) used is 512 kHz.
5. Each signal uses Quadrature Amplitude Modulation (QAM) and may potentially carry 0, 1, 2, or 3 bits per block. Fractions of a bit cannot be carried - a bit time cannot extend past the end of the current block. (Some subchannels may not be good enough to carry any data at all.)
6. "Trellis Coding" of the bit stream is used. This uses redundant signal states to improve the performance of the receiver (detector). Sixteen signal states are used to encode a maximum of 3 bits. This is a 2 to 1 redundancy but more than pays for itself in improved noise rejection in the receiver.

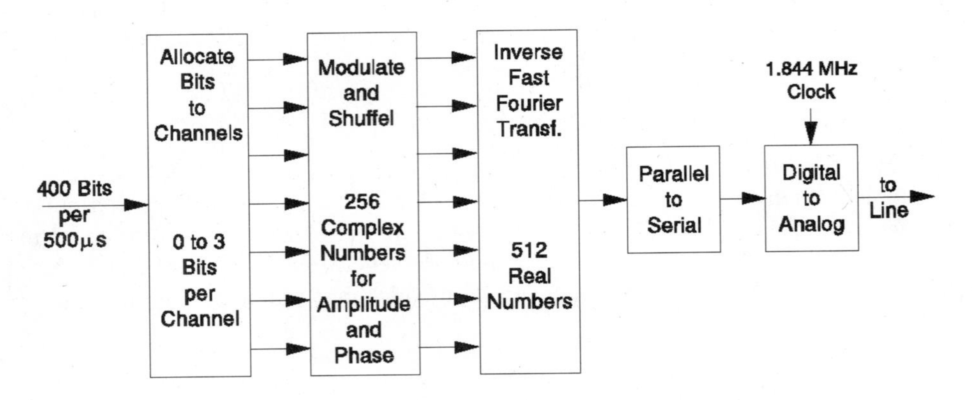


*Figure 3-4. DMT Transmitter (Schematic)*

At initialization there is a protocol between sender and receiver which determines the characteristics of each subchannel and its optimal bit rate. Thus the system must have a bidirectional capability in order for feedback to be sent from the receiver to the transmitter.

At intervals during operation these characteristics need to be updated because characteristics vary over time. For example, the resistance of telephone wire varies significantly with daytime temperature.

The system is capable of being used for 768 Kbps full-duplex over two wires or for 1.544 Mbps FDX over four wires. Operation takes place as follows:

1. A block of 400 bits arrives at the transmitter and the bits are allocated to subchannels according to the previously agreed subchannel capacities. Any integer number of bits from zero (for a very bad subchannel) to three (for a very good one) is possible.

2. For each individual subchannel, the bits to be transmitted are *digitally* modulated. A version of Quadrature Amplitude modulation is used. That is, there are four possible phase states and four possible amplitude states. This allows for 16 signal states and potentially 4 bits may be transmitted per signal period (per symbol).[5] However, the redundancy used in the Trellis Coding system reduces this to 3 bits per symbol.

   The previous state of the subchannel (amplitude and phase state) is of course known. A scheme known as "Trellis Coding" is used to encode the bits to be transmitted on this subchannel. The output of this process is a single complex number (per subchannel), which specifies the amplitude and phase to be maintained on this subchannel for the next 500 µsec.

3. The amplitude and phase of the signal in each subchannel are maintained constant for the entire duration of a block (500 µsec). There can be no further modulation.

4. The result of the encoding process is a set of 256 complex numbers that specify the amplitude and phase for each subchannel for the next 500 µsec.

5. The 256 complex numbers are digitally (numerically) processed through an Inverse Fast Fourier Transform. This produces 512 real numbers which specify consecutive voltage levels to be used to transmit the signal.

6. A preamble is added to the beginning of the block to enable the receiver to recognize the boundary between blocks easily.

7. These 512 (real) numbers are then fed in sequence to a digital-to-analog converter which transmits the signal.

---

[5] The technology allows for the number of signal states to be different on different subchannels. A maximum of 2048 signal states yielding a capacity of up to 11 bits per subchannel (10 bits with Trellis Coding) is possible.

### 3.2.4 The Receiver

A (much simplified) diagram of the receiver is shown below:

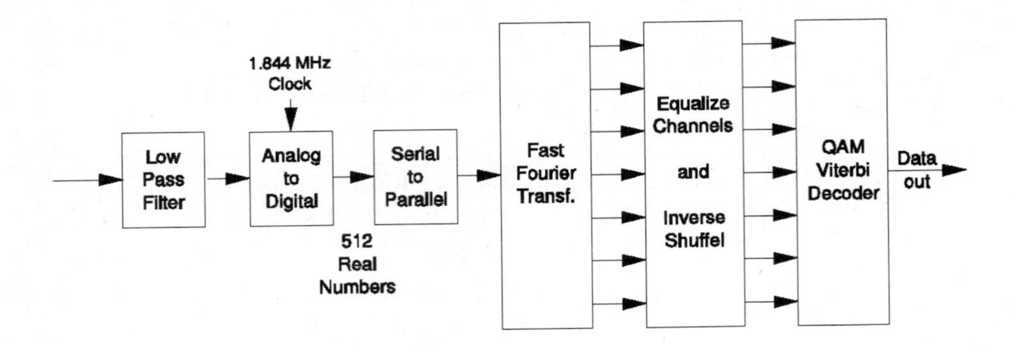


*Figure 3-5. DMT Receiver Schematic*

Operation takes place as follows:

1. The received signal is passed through an analog low pass filter to remove any frequencies above 512 kHz. Since no frequency component above 512 kHz was transmitted, these must be caused by noise. If these were not filtered out, their presence would cause "aliasing" later in the FFT processing.

2. The signal is sampled at a rate of twice the maximum frequency. This results in a continuous stream of real numbers representing signal amplitudes.

3. The "cyclic prefix" is used to identify (synchronize) the beginning of a block and then discarded.

4. The 512 real numbers representing the received block are passed in parallel (once every 500 µsec) to the Fast Fourier Transform processor.

5. The FFT processing results in 256 complex numbers (pairs of values) which represent the amplitude and phase of the signal as received on each channel.

6. The subchannels are then equalized, decoded and converted to a serial bit stream of 768 Kbps of data and 16 Kbps of control information.

7. In the "two-wire full-duplex" configuration an echo cancellation device will typically be situated at the line side of the receiver.

8. In the case of Trellis Coding being used at the transmitter (as in this system), the signal decoding takes place using a "Viterbi Decoder". (This makes use of the redundant code states in the Trellis Code to provide better noise rejection - however, it causes additional delay in end-to-end data transfer.)

**The use of Fourier Techniques in DMT**

A Discrete Fourier Transform (DFT) is a numerical technique that takes a set of numbers representing successive samples of an input signal and produces another set of (complex) numbers representing the amplitudes and phases of the sine waves that go to make up the signal. The *Inverse* Discrete Fourier Transform (IDFT) does just the opposite. It takes a set of complex numbers representing the amplitudes and phases of a set of sine waves and produces a set of (real) numbers describing the signal.

The Fast Fourier Transform (FFT) is just a computer algorithm for performing the DFT quickly. The IFFT is a computer algorithm for performing the IDFT quickly.

In DMT transmission, the FFT and its inverse are used in an unusual way. The IFFT is being used to produce a frequency multiplexed signal, and the FFT is used to decode that signal back into its original components.

### 3.2.5 Characteristics

DMT has a number of important characteristics that make it optimal in the subscriber loop environment.

**Noise Rejection**

The most significant characteristic of DMT transmission is its excellent noise rejection. The biggest problem in the subscriber loop environment is impulse noise. These impulses are typically around 30 μsec in duration but vary from about 10 μsec to 50 μsec. Because each signal period is 500 μsec, each impulse noise event is a relatively small part of the signal period. When it is processed by the Fourier transform at the receiver, the impulse has a relatively small effect on the output.

**Power Control**

The signal amplitude of each subchannel can be separately controlled simply by multiplying the amplitude/phase number by a constant before sending it to the IFFT. So power can be adjusted dynamically to suit the subchannel.

**Line Quality Monitoring**

When the system is started, the medium is analyzed at each of its subchannels to determine subchannel quality and calculate what bit rate to use on this subchannel. During operation, quality is monitored and this information can be used for predictive maintenance, etc.

# Chapter 4. An Introduction to Fiber Optical Technology

The use of light to send messages is not new. Fires were used for signaling in biblical times, smoke signals have been used for thousands of years and flashing lights have been used to communicate between warships at sea since the days of Lord Nelson.

But the idea of using a glass fiber to carry an optical signal originated with Alexander Graham Bell. But Bell's idea had to wait some 80 years for better glasses and low-cost electronics for it to become useful in practical situations.

Over the decade of the 1980s optical communication in the public communication networks developed from the status of a curiosity into being the dominant technology.

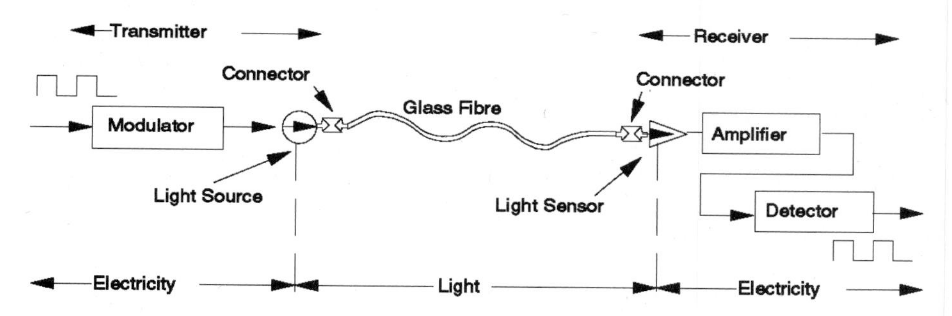


***Figure 4-1.*** *Optical Transmission - Schematic*

## 4.1.1 Concept

The basic components of an optical communication system are shown in Figure 4-1, above.

- A serial bit stream in electrical form is presented to a modulator, which encodes the data appropriately for fiber transmission.
- A light source (laser or Light Emitting Diode - LED) is driven by the modulator and the light focused into the fiber.
- The light travels down the fiber (during which time it may experience dispersion and loss of strength).
- At the receiver end the light is fed to a detector and converted to electrical form.

- The signal is then amplified and fed to another detector, which isolates the individual state changes and their timing. It then decodes the sequence of state changes and reconstructs the original bit stream.[1]
- The timed bit stream so received may then be fed to a using device.

Optical communication has many well-known advantages:

**Weight and Size**

Fiber cable is significantly smaller and lighter than electrical cables to do the same job. In the wide area environment a large coaxial cable system can easily involve a cable of several inches in diameter and weighing many pounds per foot. A fiber cable to do the same job could be less than one half an inch in diameter and weigh a few ounces per foot.

This means that the cost of laying the cable is dramatically reduced.

**Material Cost**

Fiber cable costs significantly less than copper cable for the same transmission capacity.

**Information Capacity**

The data rate of systems in use in 1995 is generally 150 or 620 Mbps on a single (unidirectional) fiber. This is because these systems were installed in past years. The usual rate for new systems is 2.4 Gbps or even 3.6 Gbps. This is very high in digital transmission terms.

In telephone transmission terms the very best coaxial cable systems give about 2,000 analog voice circuits. A 150 Mbps fiber connection gives just over 2,000 digital telephone (64 Kbps) connections. But the 150 Mbps fiber is at a very early stage in the development of fiber optical systems. The coaxial cable system with which it is being compared is much more costly and has been developed to its fullest extent.

Fiber technology is in its infancy. Researchers have trial systems in operation that work at speeds of 12 Gbps. By sending many ("wavelength division multiplexed") channels on a single fiber, we can increase this capacity perhaps a thousand fold. Some authors suggest that we could today (with today's level of technology), send 1000 2 Gbps channels on a single pair of fibers. This is about 30 million *uncompressed* telephone calls (at 64 Kbps per channel). Thirty million calls is about the maximum number of calls in progress in the world at

---

1 This overview is deliberately simplified. There are many ways to modulate the transmission and the details will vary from this example but the general principle remains unchanged.

any particular moment in time. That is to say, we could carry the world's peak telephone traffic over one pair of fibers.[2]

### No Electrical Connection

This is an obvious point but nevertheless a very important one. Electrical connections have problems.

- In electrical systems there is always the possibility of "ground loops" causing a serious problem, especially in the LAN or computer channel environment. When you communicate electrically you often have to connect the grounds to one another or at least go to a lot of trouble to avoid making this connection. This is discussed in 2.1.3, "Coupling to a Line" on page 2-8.
- Optical connection is very safe. Electrical connections always have to be protected from high voltages because of the danger to people touching the wire.
- In some tropical regions of the world, lightning poses a severe hazard even to buried telephone cables! Of course, optical fiber isn't subject to lightning problems but it must be remembered that sometimes optical cables carry wires within them for strengthening or to power repeaters. These wires can be a target for lightning.

### No Electromagnetic Interference

Because the connection is not electrical, you can neither pick up nor create electrical interference (the major source of noise). This is one reason that optical communication has so few errors. There are very few sources of things that can distort or interfere with the signal.

In a building this means that fiber cables can be placed almost anywhere electrical cables would have problems, (for example near a lift motor or in a cable duct with heavy power cables). In an industrial plant such as a steel mill, this gives much greater flexibility in cabling than previously available.

In the wide area networking environment there is much greater flexibility in route selection. Cables may be located near water or power lines without risk to people or equipment.

### Distances between Repeaters

As a signal travels along a communication line it loses strength (is attenuated) and picks up noise. The traditional way to regenerate the signal restoring its

[2] Practical fiber systems don't attempt to do this because it costs less to put multiple fibers in a cable than to use sophisticated multiplexing technology.

power and removing the noise is to use a repeater. These are discussed later in 4.1.7, "Repeaters" on page 4-25.[3] (Indeed it is the use of repeaters to remove noise that gives digital transmission its high quality.)

In long-line transmission cables now in use by the telephone companies, the repeater spacing is typically 24 miles. This compares with 8 miles for the previous coaxial cable electrical technology. The number of required repeaters and their spacing is a major factor in system cost.

Some recently installed systems (1995) have spacings of up to 70 miles.[4]

**Open Ended Capacity**

The data transmission speed of installed fiber may be changed (increased) whenever a new technology becomes available. All that must be done is change the equipment at either end and change the repeaters.

**Better Security**

It is possible to tap fiber optical cable. But it is very difficult to do and the additional loss caused by the tap is relatively easy to detect. There is an interruption to service while the tap is inserted and this can alert operational staff to the situation. In addition, there are fewer access points where an intruder can gain the kind of access to a fiber cable necessary to insert a tap.

Insertion of active taps where the intruder actually inserts a signal is even more difficult.

*However, there are some limitations:*

**Joining Cables**

The best way of joining cables is to use "fusion splicing". This is where fiber ends are fused to one another by melting the glass. Making such splices in a way that will ensure minimal loss of signal is a skilled task that requires precision equipment. It is particularly difficult to do outdoors in very low temperatures, such as in the North American or European winter.

In the early days of fiber optical systems (the early 1980s) connectors which allowed cables to be plugged and unplugged were unreliable and caused a large amount of signal loss (as much as 3 dB per connector). Of course, the larger the core diameter of the fiber, the easier it is to make a low-loss connector. In the last few years connector systems for fibers with thicker cores ("multimode fibers") have improved to the point where the use of a large number of connec-

---

[3] Repeaters have been in use for many years in digital electronic connections.

[4] As will be seen later, optical amplifiers are replacing repeaters as the technology of choice in long-line communications.

tors in a LAN system can be very reliable. Typical connector loss for an "SC" coupler (a popular modern type) using 62.5 micron fiber is around .3 dB. It is not this good with single-mode fibers of small core diameter.

One of the major system costs is the cost of coupling a fiber to an integrated light source (laser or LED) or detector on a chip. This is done during manufacture and is called "pigtailing". Although the cost of optical transceivers has decreased rapidly in the last few years, these are still twice the cost (or more) of the same transceivers using electrical connection. For example the current market price of FDDI adapters operating over a copper medium is around half that of the same adapter using fiber. The cost difference is in the optical transceivers and the pigtailing.

**Bending Cables**

As light travels along the fiber, it is reflected from the interface between the core and cladding whenever it strays from the path straight down the center. When the fiber is bent, the light only stays in the fiber because of this reflection. But the reflection only works if the angle of incidence is relatively low. If you bend the fiber too much the light escapes.

The amount of allowable bending is specific to particular cables because it depends on the difference in refractive index, between core and cladding. The bigger the difference in refractive index, the tighter the allowable bend radius. There is a tradeoff here because there are many other reasons that we would like to keep this difference as small as possible.

**Few Stable Standards Yet**

This is nobody's fault. Development is happening so quickly, and getting worldwide agreement to a standard is necessarily so slow that standards setting just can't keep up. Things are improving considerably and very quickly, however. Cable sizes and types are converging toward a few choices, although the way they are used is still changing almost daily.

There are now firm standards for optical link connections in LAN protocols (token-ring, Ethernet and FDDI), SDH (for the wide area) and in ATM for both the LAN and the wide area.

**Optics for Transmission Only**

Until very recently there was no available optical amplifier. The signal had to be converted to electrical form and put through a complex repeater in order to boost its strength. Recently, optical amplifiers have emerged and look set to solve this problem (see 4.1.8, "Optical Amplifiers" on page 4-25).

However, optical logic processing and/or switching systems seem to be a few years off yet.

### Gamma Radiation

Gamma radiation comes from space and is always present. It can be thought of as a high-energy X-ray. Gamma radiation can cause some types of glass to emit light (causing interference) and also gamma radiation can cause glass to discolor and hence attenuate the signal. In normal situations these effects are minimal. However, fibers are probably not the transmission medium of choice inside a nuclear reactor or on a long-distance space probe. (A glass beaker placed inside a nuclear reactor for even a few hours comes out black in color and quite opaque.)

### Electrical Fields

Very high-voltage electrical fields also affect some glasses in the same way as gamma rays. One proposed route for fiber communication cables is wrapped around high-voltage electrical cables on transmission towers. This actually works quite well where the electrical cables are only of 30 000 volts or below. Above that (most major transmission systems are many times above that), the glass tends to emit light and discolor. Nevertheless, this is a field of current research - to produce a glass that will be unaffected by such fields. It is a reasonable expectation that this will be achieved within a very few years.

Some electricity companies are carrying fibers with their high voltage distribution systems by placing the fiber *inside* the earth wire (typically a 1 inch thick copper cable with steel casing). This works well, but long-distance high-voltage distribution systems usually don't have earth wires.

### Sharks Eat the Cable(?)

In the 1980s there was an incident where a new undersea fiber cable was broken on the ocean floor. Publicity surrounding the event suggested that the cable was attacked and eaten by sharks. It wasn't just the press; this was a serious claim. It was claimed that there was something in the chemical composition of the cable sheathing that was attractive to sharks!

Other people have dismissed this claim as a joke and suggest that the cable was badly laid and rubbed against rocks. Nevertheless, the story has passed into the folklore of fiber optical communication and some people genuinely believe that sharks eat optical fiber cable.

### Gophers Really Do Eat the Cable

Gophers are a real problem for fiber cables in the United States. There is actually a standardized test which involves placing a cable in a gopher enclosure (conducted by a nature and wildlife organization) for a fixed, specified length of time.

Most people evaluate the advantages as overwhelming the disadvantages for most environments. But advantages and disadvantages need to be considered in the context of the environment in which the system is to be used. The types of fiber systems appropriate for the LAN environment are quite different from those that are optimal in the wide area world. This will be shown in the remainder of this chapter.

### 4.1.2 Transmitting Light through a Fiber

When light is transmitted down a fiber, the most important consideration is "what kind of light?" The electromagnetic radiation that we call light exists at many wavelengths.[5] These wavelengths go from invisible infrared through the visible spectrum to invisible ultraviolet. Because of the attenuation characteristics of fiber, we are only interested in infrared "light" for communication applications. This light is always invisible, since the wavelengths used are always longer than the visible limit of 730 nanometers (nm).

If a short pulse of light from a source such as a laser or an LED is sent down a narrow fiber, it will be changed (degraded) by its passage down the fiber. It will emerge (depending on the distance) much weaker, lengthened in time ("smeared out"), and distorted in other ways. The reasons for this are as follows:

**Attenuation**

The pulse will be weaker because all glass absorbs light. The rate at which light is absorbed is dependent on the wavelength of the light and the characteristics of the particular glass. Typical absorption characteristics of fiber for varying wavelengths of light are illustrated in Figure 4-2 on page 4-10.

**Polarization**

Conventional communication optical fiber is cylindrically symmetric. Light travelling down such a fiber is changed in polarization. (In current optical communication systems this does not matter but in future systems it may become a critical issue.)

**Dispersion**

Dispersion is when a pulse of light is spread out during transmission on the fiber. A short pulse becomes longer and ultimately joins with the pulse behind, making recovery of a reliable bit stream impossible. There are many kinds of dispersion, each of which works in a different way, but the most important three are discussed below:

1. Material dispersion (chromatic dispersion)

   Both lasers and LEDs produce a range of optical wavelengths (a band of light) rather than a single narrow wavelength. The fiber has different refractive index characteristics at different wavelengths and therefore each

---

5 Another way of saying this is that light has many frequencies or colors.

wavelength will travel at a different speed in the fiber. Thus, some wavelengths arrive before others and a signal pulse disperses (or smears out).

2. Modal dispersion

   When using multimode fiber, the light is able to take many different paths or "modes" as it travels within the fiber. This is shown in Figure 4-4 on page 4-12 under the heading "Multimode Step Index". The distance traveled by light in each mode is *different* from the distance travelled in other modes. When a pulse is sent, parts of that pulse (rays or quanta) take many different modes (usually all available modes). Therefore, some components of the pulse will arrive before others. The difference between the arrival time of light taking the shortest mode versus the longest obviously gets greater as the distance gets greater.

3. Waveguide dispersion

   Waveguide dispersion is a very complex effect and is caused by the shape and index profile of the core. However, this can be controlled by careful design and, in fact, waveguide dispersion can be used to counteract material dispersion as will be seen later.

**Modal Noise**

Modal noise is a phenomenon in multimode fiber. It occurs when a connector doesn't make a completely accurate join and some of the propagation modes are lost. This causes a loss in signal quality (and some quantity) and is thus described as "noise".

None of these effects are helpful to engineers wishing to transmit information over long distances on a fiber. But much can be done about it.

1. Lasers transmit light at one wavelength only.[6] Furthermore, the light rays are parallel with one another and in phase. Light Emitting Diodes (LEDs) that emit light within only a very narrow range of frequencies can be constructed. So the problem of dispersion due to the presence of multiple wavelengths is lessened.

2. If you make the fiber thin enough, the light will have only one possible path - straight down the middle. Light can't disperse over multiple paths because there is only one path. This kind of fiber is called monomode or single-mode fiber and is discussed in 4.1.2.3, "Fiber Geometry" on page 4-12.

3. The wavelength of light used in a particular application should be carefully chosen, giving consideration to the different attenuation characteristics of fiber at different wavelengths.

---

[6] This is not exactly true. Lasers built for communications typically transmit a narrow range of different wavelengths. This is discussed in 4.1.3, "Light Sources" on page 4-14.

4. Types of dispersion that depend on wavelength can of course be minimized by minimizing the linewidth of the light source (but this tends to add cost).
5. Material dispersion and waveguide dispersion are both dependent on wavelength. Waveguide dispersion can be controlled (in the design of the fiber) to act in the opposite direction from material dispersion. This more or less happens naturally at 1300 nm[7] but can be adjusted to produce a dispersion minimum in the 1500 nm band.

**The Design Problem**

It is clear from the above that the design of a fiber optical transmission system is dominated by two factors:

1. Signal level (or signal strength). The important aspects here are transmitter power, attenuation in the transmission system, and receiver sensitivity.
2. The control of dispersion.

The important features of any fiber transmission system are:

1. The characteristics of the fiber itself: its thickness, its refractive index, its absorption spectrum, its geometry.
2. The wavelength of light used.
3. The characteristics of the device used to create the light (laser or LED). Most important here is the frequency range (or "spectral linewidth") of the light produced.
4. The type and characteristics of the device used to detect the light.
5. How the signal is modulated (systematically changed to encode a signal). This is most important. There are many potential ways to do this and these will be discussed later.

#### 4.1.2.1 Absorption Characteristics of Glasses

Figure 4-2 on page 4-10 and Figure 4-3 on page 4-11 show the absorption spectrum of two glasses in the infrared range. Light becomes invisible (infrared) at wavelengths longer than 730 nanometers (nm).

**Note:** 1 nm = 10 (Angstrom)

---

[7] This is a result of the core size and refractive index, and achieving this balance at 1300 nm was one reason for the choice of core size and RI. 1300 nm was a good wavelength because in the early 1980s GaAs lasers were relatively easy to make compared to longer-wavelength types.

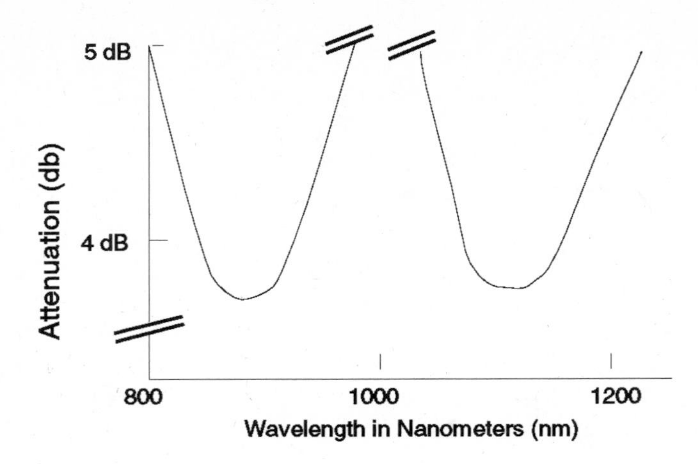


***Figure 4-2.*** *Typical Fiber Infrared Absorption Spectrum.* The curve represents the characteristics of silicon dioxide ($SiO_2$) glass.

There are a wide range of glasses available and characteristics vary depending on their chemical composition. Over the past few years the transmission properties of glass have been improved considerably. In 1970 the "ballpark" attenuation of a silicon fiber was 20 dB/km. By 1980 research had improved this to 1 dB/km. In 1990 the figure was 0.2 dB/km. As the figures show, absorption varies considerably with frequency and the two curves show just how different the characteristics of different glasses can be.

Most of the absorption in fiber is caused by light being scattered by minute variations (less than 1/10th of the wavelength) in the density or composition of the glass. This is called "Rayleigh scatter". Rayleigh scatter is also the reason that the sky is blue.

Some of the dopants (intentional impurities) added to the glass to modify the refractive index of the fiber have the unwanted side effect of significantly increasing the absorption. This is why single-mode fiber has typically lower absorption than multimode - single-mode fiber has less dopant. The conclusion that can be drawn from the absorption spectrum is that some wavelengths will be significantly better for transmission purposes than others. For ordinary silica glass the wavelengths of 850 nm and 1100 nm look attractive. For the better-quality, germanium-dioxide-rich glass, wavelengths of around 1300 nm and 1550 nm are better. All this depends on finding light sources that will operate in the way we need at these wavelengths.

The wavelength used is an extremely important defining characteristic of the optical system.

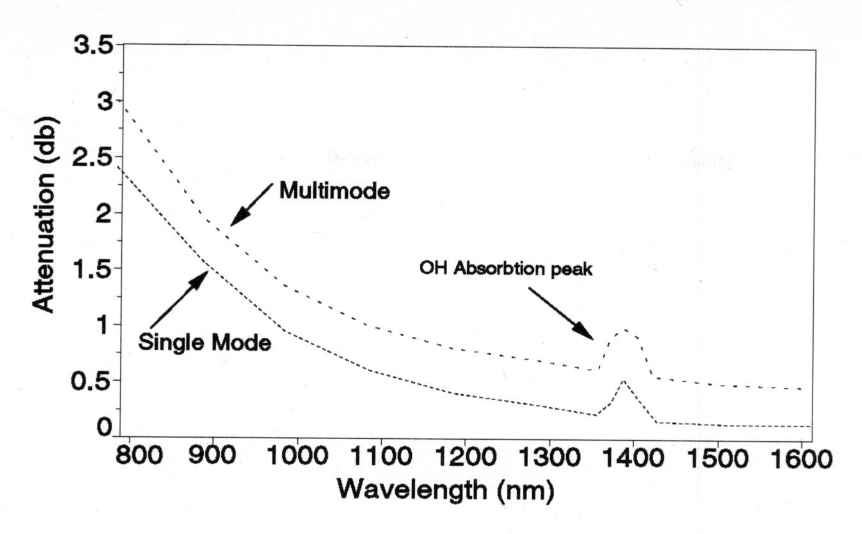


***Figure 4-3.*** *Typical Fiber Infrared Absorption Spectrum.* The curve shows the characteristics for a glass made from silicon dioxide with about 4% of germanium dioxide ($GeO_2$) added. The peak at around 1400 nm is due to the effects of traces of water in the glass.

### 4.1.2.2 Transmission Capacity

The potential transmission capacity of optical fiber is enormous. Looking again at Figure 4-2 on page 4-10 there are two very low-loss regions available in the absorption spectrum of $GeO_2$ glass. The first is about 100 nm wide and ranges from 1250 nm to 1350 nm (loss of about .4 dB per km) the second is around 150 nm wide and ranges from 1450 nm to 1600 nm (loss of about .2 dB per km). The loss peaks at 1250 and 1400 nm are due to traces of water in the glass. The useful range is therefore around 250 nm.

Expressed in terms of analog bandwidth, a 1 nm wide waveband at 1500 nm has a bandwidth of about 130 GHz. A 1 nm wide waveband at 1300 nm has a bandwidth of 160 GHz. In total, this gives a usable range of about 30 Terra Hertz ($3 \times 10^{13}$ Hz).

Capacity depends on the modulation technique used. In the electronic world we are used to getting a digital bandwidth of up to 6 bits per Hz of analog bandwidth. In the optical world, that objective is a long way off (and a trifle unnecessary). But assuming that a modulation technique resulting in one bit per Hz of analog bandwidth is available, then we can expect a digital bandwidth of $3 \times 10^{13}$ bits per second.

Current technology limits electronic systems to a rate of about 2 Gbps, although higher speeds are being experimented with in research. (Current practical fiber systems are limited to this speed because of the speed of the electronics needed for transmission and reception.)

The above suggests that, even if fiber quality is not improved, we could get 10,000 times greater throughput from a single fiber than the current practical limit.

#### 4.1.2.3 Fiber Geometry

In Figure 4-4, the top part of the picture shows the operation of "multimode" fiber. There are two different parts to the fiber. In the figure, there is a core of 50 microns (μm) in diameter and a cladding of 125 μm in diameter. (Fiber size is normally quoted as the core diameter followed by the cladding diameter. Thus the fiber in the figure is identified as 50/125.) The cladding surrounds the core. The cladding glass has a different (lower) refractive index than that of the core, and the boundary forms a mirror.

> *This is the effect you see when looking upward from underwater. Except for the part immediately above, the junction of the water and the air appears silver like a mirror.*

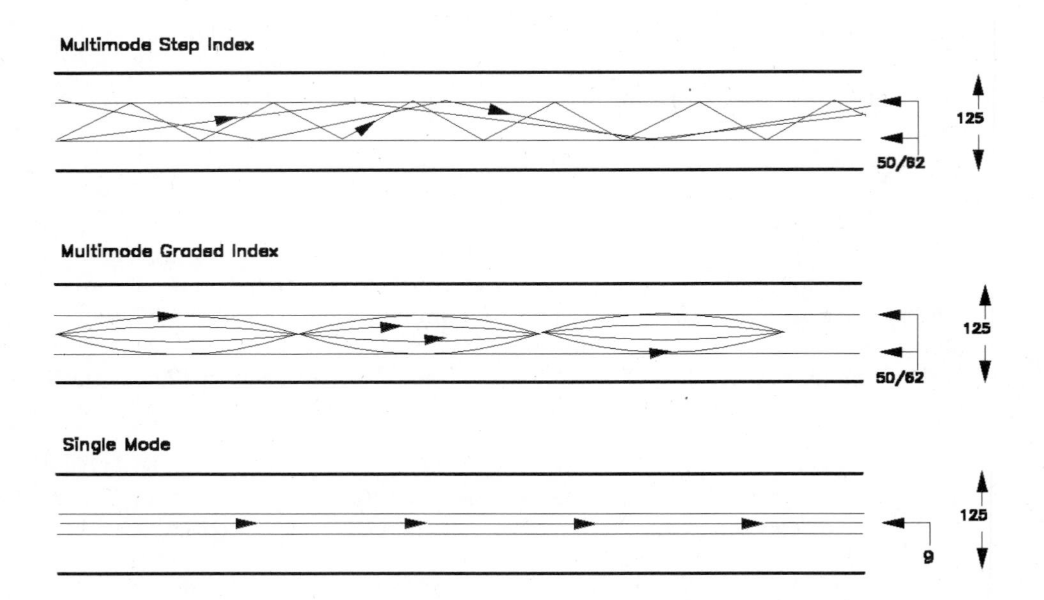


***Figure 4-4.*** *Fiber Types*

Light is transmitted (with very low loss) down the fiber by reflection from the mirror boundary between the core and the cladding.

## Multimode Fiber

The expectation of many people is that if you shine a light down a fiber, then the light will enter the fiber at an infinitely large number of angles and propagate by internal reflection over an infinite number of possible paths. This is not true. What happens is that there is only a finite number of possible paths for the light to take. These paths are called "modes" and identify the general characteristic of the light transmission system being used. Fiber that has a core diameter large enough for the light used to find multiple paths is called "multimode" fiber. (For a fiber with a core diameter of 62.5 microns using light of wavelength 1300 nm, the number of modes is around 228.)

The problem with multimode operation is that some of the paths taken by particular modes are longer than other paths. This means that light will arrive at different times according to the path taken. Therefore the pulse tends to disperse (spread out) as it travels through the fiber. This effect is one cause of "inter-symbol interference". This restricts the distance that a pulse can be usefully sent over multimode fiber.

## Multimode Graded Index Fiber

One way around the problem of multimode fiber is to do something to the glass such that the refractive index of the core changes gradually, so that light travelling down the center of the fiber effectively travels more slowly than light that is bouncing around. This system causes the light to travel in a wave-like motion such that light in different modes travels in glass of different refractive index. This means that light that travels the longest distance goes faster. The net is that the light stays together as it travels through the fiber and allows transmission for longer distances than does regular multimode transmission. This type of fiber is called "Graded Index" fiber. Within a GI fiber light typically travels in up to 800 modes.

Note that the refractive index of the core is the thing that is graded. There is still a cladding of lower refractive index than the outer part of the core.

## Single-Mode Fiber

If the fiber core is very narrow compared to the wavelength of the light in use then the light cannot travel in different modes and thus the fiber is called "single-mode" or "monomode". It seems obvious that the longer the wavelength of light in use, the larger the diameter of fiber we can use and still have light travel in a single mode. The core diameter used in a typical monomode fiber is nine microns.

It is not quite as simple as this in practice. A significant proportion (up to 20%) of the light in a single-mode fiber actually travels down the cladding. For this reason the "apparent diameter" of the core (the region in which most of the light travels) is somewhat wider than the core itself. Thus the region in which light travels in a single-mode fiber is often called the "mode field" and the mode field diameter is quoted instead of the core diameter. Depending on the relative refractive indices of core and cladding, the mode field varies in diameter.

Core diameter is a compromise. We can't make the core too narrow because of losses at bends in the fiber. As the core diameter decreases compared to the wavelength (the core gets narrower or the wavelength gets longer), the minimum radius that we can bend the fiber (without loss) increases. If a bend is too sharp, the light just comes out of the core into the outer parts of the cladding and is lost.

You can make fiber single-mode by:

- Making the core thin enough.
- Making the index difference between core and cladding small enough.
- Using a longer wavelength.

Single-mode fiber usually has significantly lower attenuation than multimode (about half). This has nothing to do with fiber geometry or manufacture. Single-mode fibers have a significantly smaller difference in refractive index between core and cladding. This means that less dopant is needed to modify the refractive index. Dopant is a major source of attenuation.

When light is introduced to the end of a fiber there is a critical angle of acceptance. Light entering at a greater angle passes into the cladding and is lost. At a smaller angle the light travels down the fiber. If this is considered in three dimensions, a cone is formed around the end of the fiber within which all rays are contained. The sine of this angle is called the "numerical aperture" and is one of the important characteristics of a given fiber.

The big problem with fiber is joining it. The narrower the fiber, the harder it is to join and the harder it is to build connectors. Connectors are needed in things like patch cables or plugs and sockets. Single-mode fiber has a core diameter of 4 to 10 μm (8 μm is typical). Multimode fiber can have many core diameters but in the last few years the core diameter of 62.5 μm in the US and 50 μm outside the US has become predominant. However, the use of 62.5 μm fiber outside the US is gaining popularity - mainly due to the availability of equipment (designed for the US) that uses this type of fiber.

### 4.1.3 Light Sources

There are two kinds of devices that are used as light sources: lasers and LEDs (Light Emitting Diodes).

#### 4.1.3.1 Lasers

Laser stands for Light Amplification by the Stimulated Emission of Radiation. Lasers produce far and away the best kind of light for optical communication.

- Laser light is single-wavelength only. This is related to the molecular characteristics of the material being used in the laser. It is formed in parallel beams and is in a single phase. That is, it is "coherent".

  This is not exactly true for communication lasers. See the discussion under "Linewidth" below.

- Lasers can be controlled very precisely (the record is a pulse length of 0.5 femto seconds[8]).
- Lasers can produce relatively high power. In communication applications, lasers of power up to 20 milliwatts are available.
- Because laser light is produced in parallel beams, a high percentage (50% to 80%) can be transferred into the fiber.
- Most laser systems use a monitor diode to detect back facet power for automatic power control. This can be used for diagnostic purposes.

There are disadvantages, however:

- Lasers have been quite expensive by comparison with LEDs. (Recent development has helped this a lot.) The main problem that causes lasers to have a high cost is temperature control required to maintain a stable lasing threshold.
- The wavelength that a laser produces is a characteristic of the material used to build the laser and of its physical construction. You can't just say "I want a laser on x wavelength", or rather you can say it all you like. Lasers have to be individually designed for each wavelength they are going to use.

  Tunable lasers exist and are beginning to become commercially available but the available tuning range is quite narrow.

- Amplitude modulation using an analog signal is difficult because laser output signal power is generally non-linear with input signal power. That is, the variations in the light produced do not match the amplitude variations of the source signal.

**Technical Parameters:** Researchers have developed a multitude (perhaps a hundred or so) of different types of communication lasers. The important features of communication lasers are as follows:

**Linewidth**

It is a fact that most lasers do *not* produce a single wavelength of light. They produce instead a range of wavelengths. This range of wavelengths is called the "spectral linewidth" of the laser.

---

[8] $10^{-15}$ seconds.

This seems to contradict the basic principle of laser operation. However, it is not so. In a semiconductor laser, a mirrored cavity is used to build up the light. By mechanical necessity, the cavity is long enough for several wavelengths to be produced.

Typically there will be around 8 "modes"[9] and the spectral linewidth is around 6 to 8 nm. It is interesting that these different wavelengths (modes) are not produced simultaneously - or rather their strength varies widely. What happens is that the laser will produce one dominant mode, perhaps for as short a time as a few nanoseconds, and then switch to a different mode and then to another, etc. The total power output of the laser does not vary - just the form of the output.

The most common communication laser is called the "Fabry-Perot" laser. In many situations this type of laser gives good service. However, because it produces a relatively wide linewidth, it is not considered suitable for applications requiring extended distances, coherent reception, or wavelength multiplexing.

The Fabry-Perot laser can be modified by placing something in the cavity that will disperse unwanted frequencies before they reach the lasing threshold. There are a number of alternatives, but a common way is to place a diffraction grating within the cavity. When this is done, the laser can produce a very narrow spectral linewidth (typically today .2 to .3 nm). Lasers using this principle are called Distributed Feedback (DFB) or Distributed Bragg Reflector (DBR) lasers.

Other lasers use a cavity external to the device itself - these are called "external cavity lasers". This allows a long cavity, and if you put a diffraction grating on one of the end mirrors you can get a very narrow linewidth indeed. (The record here is a linewidth of 10 MHz using a 20 cm (yes) long external cavity.)

Linewidth is very important because:

1. The wider the spectrum of the light source, the more dispersion the signal will suffer when travelling on the fiber. (This is not too bad for lasers when compared with LEDs, but is still an issue.)

2. In a Wavelength Division Multiplexing (WDM) system it is desirable to pack the channels as closely together as possible in order to maximize the number of channels. The narrower the linewidth the more channels you can have.

3. You can't use frequency or phase modulation techniques or coherent detection methods unless the linewidth (expressed as occupied bandwidth)

9 So named because each frequency resonates on a different path within the cavity.

is significantly less than the bandwidth of the modulating signal. (100 to 1 is a good ratio.)

### Power

The theory tells us that in an optical receiver of a given type you need a certain amount of power per bit transmitted. If you have a working system and want to double the bit rate you must double the power (or double the receiver sensitivity). But transmitters have limits to their power[10] and receivers have limits to their sensitivity. Of course, you can get a higher bit rate by reducing the attenuation (by shortening the distance between stations) thereby increasing the signal power at the receiver.

Signal power, more than fiber capacity is the limiting factor in an optical communication system.

### Operating Wavelength (or Range)

Of course, lasers must be able to operate on wavelengths appropriate to the system being designed.

### Frequency (Wavelength) Stability

In a single-channel system using incoherent detection, a bit of instability (wander) in the laser wavelength doesn't matter too much. However, if the system is using WDM techniques, each laser must keep within its allocated band and wander matters a lot.

Fabry-Perot lasers vary an enormous .4 nm per degree Celsius of temperature variation. Most of the single-mode lasers are significantly better than this, but temperature control is critical.

When most lasers are modulated by OOK (turning them on and off) they produce a "chirp" at the beginning of each pulse (this is a transient frequency shift of as much as several gigahertz). This is a problem in WDM systems and ones using coherent receivers. This is caused by instantaneous heating effects - after all, the energy ("light") produced is infrared (heat).

### Switching Time and Modulation

Of course, a fundamental operational characteristic of any laser is which modulation techniques are possible and how fast they can operate. In general, all lasers can be modulated by OOK (on/off keying) and some by FSK (frequency shift keying). Other modulation techniques require an external modulator to be placed into the light beam after it is generated.

---

[10] Often we want to limit the power somewhat artificially to stay within eye safety limits for example.

### Tuning Range and Speed

In many proposed WDM systems, transmitters, and/or receivers need to be switched between different wavelengths (channels). There are many techniques for doing this. In general, the faster the device can switch, the narrower will be the range of channels over which it can switch.

Another point is that tunable lasers are seldom capable of continuous tuning over an unbroken range of wavelengths. When they are tuned they "jump" from one wavelength to another (corresponding to the resonance modes of the laser cavity).

**Modes**

In optics, a mode is a path that light may take through a system. Thus multimode fiber is fiber that allows for multiple paths. A multimode laser is one that allows multiple paths within its cavity and hence produces light of multiple wavelengths. Such lasers do not produce multiple wavelengths simultaneously. Rather, the laser will switch from one mode to another very quickly (sometimes spending only a few picoseconds in any particular mode) apparently at random during sending a single pulse.

Thus the word "mode" relates to the path on which light is travelling at a particular instant in time. Light produced in a "multimode laser" is *not* "multimode light". Light produced by a "multimode laser" travels in a single mode along a single mode fiber perfectly well.

## 4.1.3.2 Light Emitting Diodes (LEDs)

- LEDs are very low in cost (perhaps 1/10th to 1/100th that of a laser).
- The maximum light output has typically been a lot lower than a laser (about 100 microwatts). However, recently a new class of LEDs, with output of up to 75 milliwatts, has become available.
- LEDs do not produce a single light frequency but rather a band of frequencies. The range (or band) of frequencies produced is called the "spectral linewidth" and is typically about .05 of the wavelength (50 to 100 nm).

  The linewidth can be reduced (and dispersion reduced) by using selective filters to produce a narrow band of wavelengths. However, this reduces the power of the signal too.
- The light produced is neither directional nor coherent. This means that you need a lens to focus the light onto the end of a fiber. LEDs are not suitable for use with single-mode fiber for this reason (it is too hard to get the light into the narrow core).
- LEDs cannot produce pulses short enough to be used at gigabit speeds. However, systems using LEDs operate quite well at speeds of up to around 300 Mbps.

### 4.1.4 Light Detectors

A number of different kinds of devices are used for light detection.

**PIN Diodes**

PIN diodes convert light directly to electric current. An ideal PIN diode can convert one photon to one electron of current. (Surprisingly, real devices get very close to this ideal.) This means that the current output from a PIN diode is very small and an external amplifier is needed before the signal can be dealt with by a receiver.

**Avalanche Photo Diodes (APDs)**

APDs use a similar principle to the old "photomultiplier" tubes used in nuclear radiation detection.

1. A single photon acting on the device releases a single electron.
2. This electron is accelerated through an electrostatic field until it strikes a target material.
3. This collision releases multiple electrons.
4. These electrons are then themselves accelerated through the field until they strike another target.
5. This releases more electrons and the process is repeated until the electrons finally hit a collector element.

Thus, through several stages, one photon has resulted in a current of many electrons. APDs typically have an internal amplification of between 10 and 100 times.

The multiplication effect means that an APD can be very sensitive. The negative side is that APDs are inherently noisy as the multiplier effect applies to all free electrons including those made free by ambient heat. In most long-distance, wide-area applications the internal gain is more important than other factors, and the APD is the usual device used in long-distance applications.

**Phototransistors**

Phototransistors are amplifiers where the amplification is controlled by the amount of light striking the device. These are much lower in noise and have a higher output than APDs, but are less responsive than either APDs or PIN diodes.

Phototransistors are occasionally built as part of an integrated circuit. In this configuration they are referred to as "Integrated Preamplifier Detectors" (IPDs).

#### 4.1.4.1 Coherent Detectors

It almost goes without saying that the output of the detectors discussed above is *not* at the frequency (wavelength) of light (the electronics would not go that fast). What you get is electrical pulses (hopefully) similar to the modulations in the original signal.

> This is just like the operation of a "crystal set". A crystal set uses a tunable resonant circuit to select the frequency and then the output is fed to a simple half wave rectifier (the crystal). The output is just the original signal rectified.

This, very simple, method of detection is called "incoherent detection".

Most electronic radio receivers use a quite different method called "heterodyne detection". In the optical world heterodyne detection is called "coherent detection". (In electronics the word coherent is used in a much narrower sense. It is reserved for systems where the detector "locks on" to the phase of the received signal.)

Optical coherent detection (as illustrated in Figure 4-5 on page 4-21) has two major advantages over incoherent detection:

1. Receivers can be significantly more sensitive than incoherent ones (by 15 to 20 dB). In general this is true of systems reported in the research literature.

   However, some researchers (Green 1992) claim that incoherent detectors built with an optical preamplifier can be just as sensitive and are a lot less complex.

2. In WDM systems, where there are many channels packed closely together, coherent detection allows a much better rejection of interference from adjacent channels. (This allows channels to be packed more closely together.)

In addition, there are some other advantages, such as better noise rejection.

Optical coherent detection systems can be used for all the possible types of modulation (ASK, FSK, PSK, PolSK); however, they require a linewidth significantly less than the bandwidth of the modulating signal. This means that you can't use coherent detectors with LED transmitters (or with unmodified Fabry-Perot lasers). Also, they will not work in the presence of any significant level of frequency chirp. Thus, if ASK (OOK) is used, you either have to do something to the transmitter to minimize chirp or you should use a fixed laser with an external modulator.

***The principle of coherent detection is relatively simple:*** When two signals (electrical, optical, sound, etc.) of nearly the same frequency are mixed, then additional frequencies representing the sum and difference of the two original signals are generated.

> *We use this principle when tuning musical instruments. When two instruments play the same note slightly out of tune with one another, you can hear a rapid variation in loudness of the combined sound. This variation is the "difference frequency." (Sometimes, unkindly, said to sound "like a nanny goat".) As the instruments are*

*adjusted towards one another and the difference is only a few Hz then you can count the cycles.*

An optical coherent receiver does exactly this.

- A local light source (called the local oscillator - LO) is used to generate a frequency very close to the frequency of the signal carrier.
- The two signals are mixed together.
- They are then fed to a detector.

  If detectors were infinitely fast, and if electronic signals could approach the frequency of light then you would need to put a low pass filter in front of the detector. In this case you don't. The detector will pass only the "difference frequency" because it isn't fast enough to detect anything else!

- What you have now is a difference frequency in electronic form which contains all the modulations of the original signal.
- The signal is now amplified through a number of stages.
- The amplified signal can now be processed (filtered, detected) by any of the established techniques of electronics.

You can "tune" the receiver to almost any frequency by varying the LO frequency. Of course, feedback in various forms is necessary to make a system like this stable. The system is illustrated in Figure 4-5.

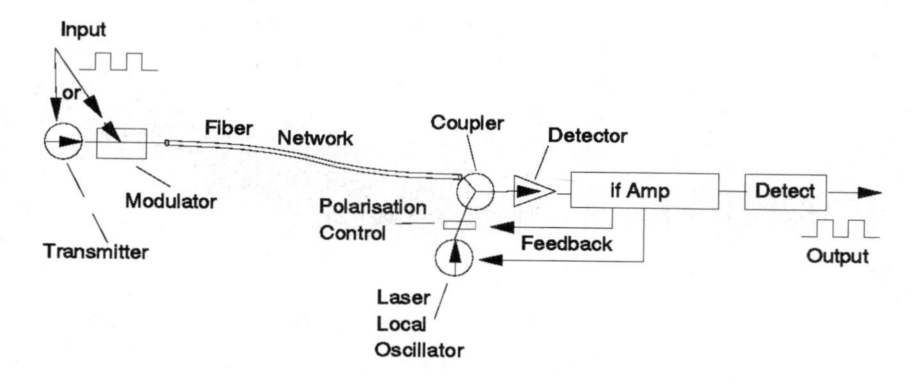


***Figure 4-5.*** *An Optical Transmission System Using Coherent Detection*

There are two significant problems with coherent reception, both of which can be solved, but at a cost:

1. Optical coherent receivers are highly polarization sensitive *and* standard single-mode optical fiber does not respect polarization. However, polarization changes

slowly and in single-channel systems it can be compensated for. In multichannel WDM systems, acquiring the polarization of a channel quickly after tuning is quite a challenge. (However in a WDM system, if we used fiber that retained polarization, we could put alternate channels at orthogonal polarizations and pack the channels even more closely together.)

Various solutions (including using two detectors with orthogonal polarization) have been suggested - but this would significantly increase the cost of such a device.

2. Stabilization of the frequencies of both transmitter and receiver within close tolerances is very difficult.

Prototype coherent receivers have been available in laboratories since the middle of the 1980s and have been used in many experiments. However, to the knowledge of the author, coherent receivers are not yet available in any commercial system.

### 4.1.5 Filters

In current optical systems, filters are seldom used or needed. They are sometimes used in front of an LED to narrow the linewidth before transmission, but in few other roles.

In proposed future WDM networks, filters will be very important for many uses:

- A filter placed in front of an incoherent receiver can be used to select a particular signal from many arriving signals.
- WDM networks are proposed which use filters to control which path through a network a signal will take.

There are many filtering principles proposed and many different types of devices have been built in laboratories.

One of the simplest is the Fabry-Perot filter. This consists of a cavity bounded on each end by a half-silvered mirror.[11]

- Light is directed onto the outside of one of the mirrors.
- Some is reflected and some enters the cavity.
- When it reaches the opposite mirror some passes out and some is reflected back.
- This continues to happen with new light entering the cavity at the same rate as light leaves it.

---

11 This is really an optical version of the electronic "tapped delay line", "transversal" filter or Standing Acoustic Wave (SAW) filter. In the digital signal processing world this is done with a shift register. This is the physical realization of the mathematical process of determination of a single term in a Fourier series.

If you arrange the cavity to be exactly the right size, interference patterns develop which cancel unwanted wavelengths. The device can be tuned quite quickly by attaching one of the mirrors to a piezo-electric device (you can get accuracy here to less than the diameter of an atom!).

There is an ingenious variation of the Fabry-Perot filter. Two pieces of fiber are used with their ends polished and silvered. The ends are placed precisely opposite one another with a measured gap (this is the hard part). This avoids the cost of getting the light into and out of a "regular" FP filter - because it arrives and leaves on its own fiber.

There are many kinds of active, tunable filters which will be important in WDM networks. These, like lasers, have the characteristic that the wider the tuning range, the slower the tuning time.

### 4.1.6 Making the Light Carry a Signal

In order to make light carry a signal, you have to introduce systematic variations (modulation) in the light to represent the signal. Then, when the light is received you must decode it in such a way as to reconstruct the original signal.

#### 4.1.6.1 On-Off Keying (OOK)

All current optical transmission systems encode the signal as a sequence of light pulses in a binary form. This is called "on-off keying" (OOK).

Sometimes this is described as amplitude modulation, comparing it to AM radio. In fact, the technique is nothing like AM radio.[12] But an AM radio carries an analog signal. The amplitude of the signal is continuously varied and the receiver recovers the signal from the variations. But in an optical system, it is much more like a very simple form of digital baseband transmission in the electronic world. The signal is there or it isn't; beyond this the amplitude of the signal doesn't matter.

In fairness, you can call OOK a special case of amplitude shift keying (ASK) in which a number of discrete signal amplitude levels are used to carry a digital signal.

Most digital communication systems using fiber optics use NRZI encoding. This means that when you have a transition from light to no light or from no light to light, a "1" bit is signaled. When there are two successive pulses of light or two successive periods of dark then a zero bit is signaled. This is discussed in 2.1.2, "Non-Return to Zero Inverted (NRZI) Coding" on page 2-7.

---

[12] It is possible to modulate a laser signal in exactly the same way as regular AM radio. In fact, there are numerous commercial systems doing just this. They just vary the amplitude of the optical signal in exactly the same way as we vary the amplitude of the RF carrier in AM radio.

#### 4.1.6.2 Frequency Shift Keying (FSK)

It is difficult to modulate the frequency of a laser and for this reason FM optical systems are not yet in general use. However, Distributed Bragg Reflector lasers are becoming commercially available. These can be frequency modulated by varying the bias current. For FSK (or any system using coherent detection) to work, the laser linewidth has to be considerably narrower than the signal bandwidth. As discussed above, coherent detection has a major advantage. The receiver "locks on" to the signal and is able to detect signals many times lower in amplitude than simple detectors can use. This translates to greater distances between repeaters and lower-cost systems. In addition, FSK promises much higher data rates than the pulse systems currently in use.

#### 4.1.6.3 Phase Shift Keying (PSK)

You can't control the phase of a laser's output signal directly and so you can't get a laser to produce phase-modulated light. However, a signal can be modulated in phase by placing a modulation device in the lightpath between the laser and the fiber. Phase modulation has similar advantages to FSK. At this time PSK is being done in the laboratory but there are no available commercial devices.

#### 4.1.6.4 Polarity Modulation (PolSK)

Lasers produce linearly polarized light. Coherent detectors are very strongly polarization sensitive (it is one of the big problems). Another modulation dimension can be achieved (potentially) by introducing polarization changes. Unfortunately, current fiber changes the polarization of light during transit - but there are techniques to overcome this.

This is not an available technique (not even in the lab) but feasibility studies are being undertaken to determine if PolSK could be productively used for fiber communications.

#### 4.1.6.5 Directional Transmission

It is "possible" to use a single fiber for transmission in two directions at once. With very complex electronics it may even be possible to use the same light wavelength at least over short distances. But this is all far too much trouble. Tapping a fiber in such a way as to allow a receiver and a transmitter access to the fiber simultaneously is difficult and there is significant loss in the received signal. Experimental systems have been constructed that do this using a different wavelength in each direction.

In practical fiber optical transmission systems, fiber is a unidirectional medium. Two fibers are needed for bidirectional transmission. Given the size of a single fiber and the number of fibers that can conveniently be integrated into a cable, this looks certain to be the predominant mode of operation for the foreseeable future.

## 4.1.7 Repeaters

Until the commercial availability of optical amplifiers in 1992, the only way to boost an optical signal was to convert it to electrical form, amplify or regenerate it, and then convert it to optical form again. See 4.1.8, "Optical Amplifiers."

Boosting the signal electrically either involves a simple amplifier or a more complex repeater. An amplifier just takes whatever signal it receives and makes it bigger. This includes the noise and whatever dispersion of the signal that has already taken place. However, amplifiers are simpler, cheaper, and not sensitive to the coding used on the fiber. They did not become commercially available until 1992 and are only now beginning to be used in new systems (especially undersea systems).

Repeaters have been the method of choice for boosting an optical signal. (Electronic repeaters were discussed in 2.1.6.3, "Repeaters" on page 2-14.) A repeater is a full receiver which reconstructs the bit stream and its timing. This bit stream and its timing are used to drive a transmitter. This means that the repeated signal has all dispersion and noise removed. However, repeaters are more complex and more costly than simple amplifiers. Repeaters are very inflexible. They have to be constructed for exactly the wavelength, protocol, and speed of the signal being carried.

They can't handle multiple wavelengths. In order to carry different wavelengths on the same fiber, the wavelengths must be separated (with a diffraction grating or a prism) at each repeater and the separate signals separately repeated and then recombined. This process is mechanically complex and requires a separate repeater for each wavelength. Repeaters that handle multiple wavelengths are therefore costly to build and to maintain.

In multimode systems, where dispersion is the main distance limiting factor, electronic repeaters will continue to be the major way of boosting a signal. In single-mode systems over long distances where dispersion isn't a problem, optical amplifiers are rapidly replacing repeaters as the device of choice.

## 4.1.8 Optical Amplifiers

In all optical cable systems installed up to 1991, the signal was regenerated (about every 50 kilometers) by using a repeater.[13] Repeaters receive the old signal, retrieve the digital bit stream, and then generate a new one. Thus, noise and distortion picked up along the transmission path are completely removed by a repeater, whereas, when an amplifier is used, these components are amplified along with the signal.

Repeaters are a problem in an optical system. The optical signal must be converted to electrical form, passed through the repeater, and then converted to optical form again.

[13] Repeaters in electrical communication systems are discussed in 2.1.6.3, "Repeaters" on page 2-14.

The repeater is complex and subject to failure. Also, optical systems suffer from far fewer sources of signal interference, noise, and distortion than do electrical ones. When a signal on a single-mode fiber arrives at its destination it is a lot weaker, but for practical purposes the signal is unchanged. (There will be some dispersion, but this can be controlled.) So a device which just amplifies the signal will do just as well (or better) than a repeater.

In the late 1980s a number of researchers around the world succeeded in developing an optical amplifier which is now firmly established as the preferred option over repeaters. This device amplifies the signal *without* the need to convert the signal to electrical form - it is a completely optical device. (although, it is electrically powered.)

This is very significant because the amplifier is much less prone to failure than an electrical repeater, operates at almost any speed, and is not dependent on the digital characteristics (such as the code structure) in the signal. It should also cost significantly less. Many people believe that this device has begun a "new generation" in optical systems.

The device itself is illustrated below:

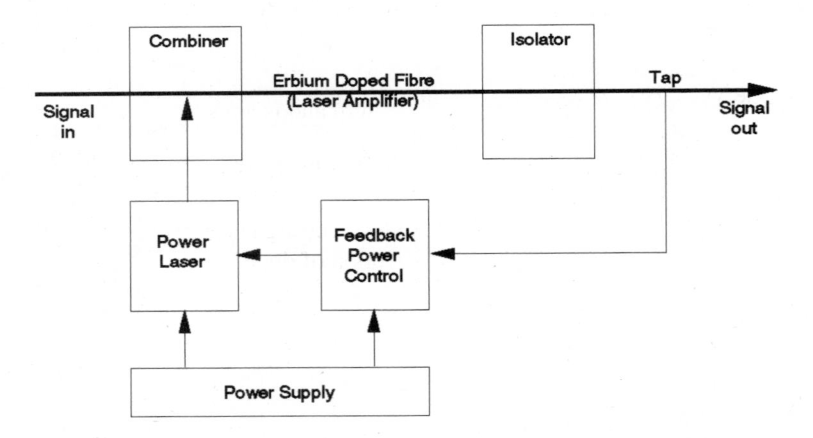


***Figure 4-6.*** *Erbium Doped Optical Fiber Amplifier.* Although the device is powered electrically, the amplification process is totally optical and takes place within a short section of rare earth doped, single-mode fiber.

The amplifier itself is simply a short (a few feet) section of fiber which has a controlled amount of a rare earth element (Erbium) added to the glass. This section of fiber is, itself, a laser.

The principle involved here is just the principle of a laser and is very simple. Atoms of Erbium are able to exist in several energy states (these relate to the alternative orbits which electrons may have around the nucleus). When an Erbium atom is in a high-energy state, a photon of light will stimulate it to give up some of its energy (also in the form of light) and return to a lower-energy (more stable) state. This is called "stimulated emission". "Laser" after all is an acronym for "Light Amplification by the Stimulated Emission of Radiation".

To make the principle work, you need a way of getting the Erbium atoms up to the excited state. The laser diode in the diagram generates a high-powered (10 milliwatt) beam of light at a frequency such that the Erbium atoms will absorb it and jump to their excited state. (Light at 980 or 1,480 nanometer wavelengths will do this quite nicely.) So, a (relatively) high-powered beam of light is mixed with the input signal. (The input signal and the excitation light must of course be at significantly different wavelengths.) This high-powered light beam excites the Erbium atoms to their higher-energy state. When the photons belonging to the signal (at a different wavelength which is not absorbed by Erbium) meet the excited Erbium atoms, the Erbium atoms give up some of their energy to the signal and return to their lower-energy state.[14] A significant point is that the Erbium gives up its energy in *exactly* the same phase and direction as the signal being amplified, so the signal is amplified along its direction of travel only. (This is not unusual - when an atom "lasers" it always gives up its energy in the same direction and phase as the incoming light. That is just the way lasers work.)

> The significant thing here is that Erbium *only* absorbs light (and jumps to a higher-energy state) if that light is at one of a very specific set of wavelengths. Light at other wavelengths takes energy from the Erbium and is amplified.

So the device works this way. A constant beam of light (feedback controlled) at the right frequency to excite Erbium atoms is mixed with the input signal. This beam of light constantly keeps the Erbium atoms in an excited state. The signal light picks up energy from excited Erbium atoms as it passes through the section of doped fiber.

The optical amplifier has the following advantages:

- It is significantly simpler than a repeater and will have a much longer mean time to failure.
- It is significantly lower in cost than a repeater.
- It will operate at almost any speed.
- It can be made physically small enough to fit on a printed circuit card.
- It will produce a gain in optical signal of about 25 dB.

[14] This doesn't happen for all wavelengths of signal light. There is a range of wavelengths approximately 24 nm wide that is amplified.

- It will amplify many different wavelengths simultaneously (with some small limitations).
- It doesn't need to understand the digital coding. Both amplitude (pulse) modulated and coherent (frequency modulated) light are amplified.

  This means that if amplifiers are installed in a long undersea cable for example, at some later time the transmission technique used on the cable may be changed without affecting the amplifiers.
- There is effectively no delay in the amplifier. The delay is only the time it takes for the signal to propagate through a few feet of single-mode fiber.

There are of course some limitations:

- The amplifier itself adds some noise (and it amplifies the noise received with the signal). This is trivial compared to noise in electrical environments but light detectors designed for the fiber environment have not been designed with much provision for noise in the signal.
- At present time, fiber-based amplifiers do not operate over the entire range of wavelengths of interest. The current range is about 24 nm (or about 3,000 GHz).
- Amplifiers (like their electrical counterparts) can saturate. That is, if the incoming signal is just too big, the amplifier will put out its full power but that will not be enough (this would "clip" all the amplitude peaks).
- If there are multiple wavelength division multiplexed channels on a single fiber then amplifiers can introduce crosstalk. That is, there is interference with a signal on one wavelength by a signal on another.

  This is only a problem where the amplifiers are operated near power saturation. It happens when the total power available is not enough to amplify all channels - the effect on an increase in signal on one channel is felt as a decrease in amplification on the other channels.

  In addition, at this stage of development amplifiers give different amounts of gain at different wavelengths. If a number of WDM channels are present then some are amplified more than others. This could be a problem in long links with many stages of amplification. Also, if the signal has a relatively large linewidth then the signal will be distorted by the amplifier (but this may not matter).
- Amplifiers do not recreate pulses. In fact they don't know about pulses - they just amplify whatever happens to arrive. In themselves, amplifiers do not create dispersion but if pulses arrive that are dispersed, then these will be amplified, dispersion and all. This means that amplifiers will not be very useful in situations where the signal is subject to dispersion.
- In many systems, amplifiers must be placed closer together than repeaters. The signal cannot be allowed to become too weak before reamplification. In current

systems, this results in the need to space amplifiers roughly every 30 kilometers where repeaters would be placed about every 50 kilometers.

Researchers have reported experimental results showing successful (simulated) transmission at 2.4 Gbps over a distance of 21 000 kilometers and higher speeds over shorter distances.

Other types of optical amplifiers (solid-state ones) exist but are still in the research stage.

#### 4.1.8.1 Signal Mixing Devices

In any optical network it is necessary to combine signals and to split them multiple ways. Such devices are in common use. 1x2, 2x2, and 2x1 couplers are commercially available. Furthermore they have very low loss. Of course, they do have some loss.

In proposed WDM network designs, there is often the need for a "reflective star" (a device that accepts many input signals, mixes them, and then splits the combined signal in as many directions as there were inputs). In laboratories these have been built of many 2x2 couplers cascaded together. Many researchers feel that this becomes impractical for devices larger than 100x100. New devices have been designed to perform the "star" function in a single device. These are called "wavelength flattened fused fiber arrays". So far these have not become commercial, but to realize WDM LANs stars of up to 1000x1000 will be necessary.

### 4.1.9 Fiber Cables

As we have seen, fibers themselves are generally 125 µm in diameter (very small indeed). Cables carrying fibers vary widely in their characteristics. One typical indoor/outdoor cable is shown in cross-section below:

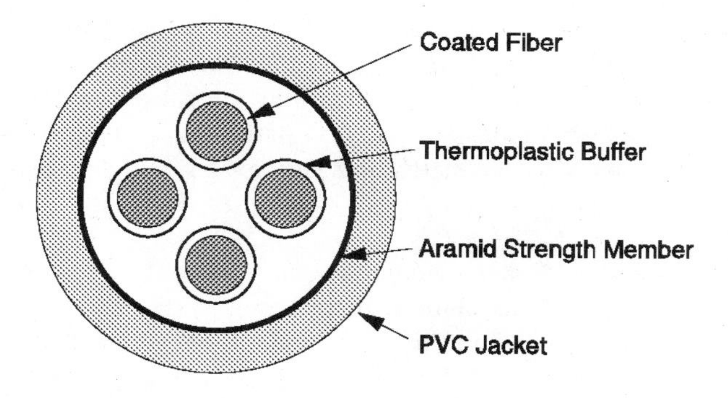


***Figure 4-7.*** *Typical Fiber Cable*

Fiber cables are made to suit the application they are to perform and there are hundreds, perhaps thousands of types. The kinds of variations you see between cables are as follows:

- Number of fibers in a single cable. This typically ranges from two to around 100. Outdoor telephone company single-mode fiber cables tend to have about 30 fibers in the single cable. Multiple cables are usually installed on routes where 30 fibers isn't enough.
- Strength members. Many cables, particularly for outdoor applications have steel wire at the core to provide strength.
- The optical characteristics of the fiber itself. Single-mode or multimode, loss in dB per km, susceptibility to temperature changes, etc.
- Electrical wire. In some cable situations it is necessary to power repeaters over long distances. One example of this is in submarine cables. Electrical power cabling is often included to deliver power to the repeaters.
- Water proofing. It sounds illogical, but water proofing is often more important in the fiber optical environment than it is in the electrical world! Glass immersed in water gradually picks up hydroxyl ions. As mentioned earlier, the presence of hydroxyl ions greatly increases the absorption of light. In addition, the presence of water causes micro cracking in the glass and these cause scattering of the light. The "net" is that water is the worst enemy of an optical fiber system.
- Sheathing. In many environments vermin (rats, etc.) do chew cable (they usually find electrical cable unpleasant but fiber is less so). Appropriate protective sheathing is very important in some applications (such as LAN cabling).

#### 4.1.9.1 Joining Fiber Cables

The diameter of the core in an optical fiber is very small and any irregularity (such as a join) can result in significant loss of power. To get the maximum light transfer from the cut end of one fiber into another, both ends must be cut precisely square and polished flat. They must then be butted together so that there is minimal air (or water) between the butted ends and these ends must match up nearly exactly. In a practical situation outside the laboratory this is very difficult to do.

In the early days of optical data communication (1983), IBM specified an optical cable for future use which was 100/140 μm in diameter. The 100 micron core is very wide and is certainly not the best size for communication. However, at the time it was the best specification for making joints in the field. (This specification is still supported by some systems - including FDDI.)

A cable join is a type of weld. The cable ends are cut, polished, butted up to one another and fused by heat. (Incidentally, with some silica fibers you need quite a high temperature - much higher than the melting point of ordinary soda glass.) In practice, a light loss of only .1 dB is the current budget for power loss in a single-mode fiber join. But it should be realized that .1 dB is the total loss of one kilometer of cable.

In data communication situations it is highly desirable to be able to change configurations easily. This means that we want to plug a cable into a wall socket and to conveniently join sections of cable. Connectors to do this exist. They hold the fiber ends in exact position and butt them together under soft pressure to obtain a good connection. But this all depends on the precision to which connectors can be machined. Most mechanical devices are machined to tolerances much greater than the width of a fiber - so connectors are difficult to manufacture and hard to fit. This all results in a relatively high cost.

Today's connectors are very efficient with typical "off-the-shelf" connectors measuring losses of around .3 dB. However, most manufacturers still suggest planning for a loss of 1 dB per connector.

In the situation where two fibers of different diameters are being joined with a connector, than a lot of light is usually lost. This is a common situation, for example, in the IBM ESCON channel system where fibers with a 62.5 µm core can be connected to fibers with a 50 µm core. Loss of light in this situation (about 3 dB) is unavoidable.

## 4.1.10 Transmission System Characteristics

The characteristics of various transmission systems are summarized in Table 4-1.

***Table 4-1.*** *Optical Fiber State of the Art*

| Medium | Source | Technology | Status | Speed | Distance | Product |
|---|---|---|---|---|---|---|
| Copper | | | in use | 2 Mbps | 2 km | 4 M |
| Multimode | LED | 802.5 | | 32 Mbps | 2 km | 64 M |
| Monomode | | FDDI | | 100 Mbps | 2 km | 200 M |
| | Laser | Long Distance | | 2.4 Gbps | 100 km | 240 G |
| | | Amplitude Modulation | in Lab | 8 Gbps | 100 km | 800 G |
| | | Coherent | | 400 Mbps | 370 km | 150 G |
| | | Solitons | | 2 Gbps | 4000 km | 8 T |

A universally accepted measure of the capability of a transmission technology is the product of the maximum distance between repeaters and the speed of transmission. In electrical systems (such as on the subscriber loop) maximum achievable speed multiplied by the maximum distance at this speed yields a good rule of thumb constant. It is not quite so constant in optical systems, but nevertheless the speed × distance product is a useful guide to the capability of a technology.

*Table 4-2. Signal Loss in Various Materials*

| Material | Attenuation | Repeater Spacing Max. 35 dB |
|---|---|---|
| Coaxial Cable | 25 dB/km | 1.5 km |
| Telephone Twisted Pair | 12 - 18 dB/km | 2 - 3 km |
| Window Glass | 5 dB/km | 7 m |
| Silica - Installed | 0.3 - 3 dB/km | 10 - 100 km |
| Silica - Development | 0.16 dB/km | 250 km |
| Halide - Research | 0.01 dB/km | 3500 km |

Table 4-2 shows the attenuation characteristics of various transmission media and the maximum spacing of repeaters available on that medium. Of course, this is very conceptual. Special coaxial cable systems exist with repeater spacings of 12 kilometers. In Chapter 3, "High Speed on the Subscriber Loop (HDSL and ADSL)" on page 3-1, we discussed systems capable of operating at very high speed over telephone twisted pairs for distances of four to six kilometers without repeaters. Nevertheless, the advantage of fiber transmission is obvious.

## 4.1.11 Optical System Engineering

Putting components (fibers, connectors, lasers, detectors, etc.) together, so that the whole will function as a communication system with desirable characteristics, is no small task.

As mentioned before the two critical factors are:

1. Dispersion
2. Attenuation

Other critical factors are the cost of components and the cost of putting them together. The more complex they are, the more they cost.

### 4.1.11.1 Dispersion

Dispersion broadens a pulse by an amount unrelated to the length of the pulse. Dispersion becomes a problem for a receiver when it exceeds about 20% of the pulse length. Thus, if a pulse at 200 Mbps is dispersed on a given link by 15% then the system will probably work. If the data rate is doubled to 400 Mbps the dispersion will be 30% and the system will probably not work. Hence *the higher the data rate, the more important the control of dispersion becomes.*

- There is no *modal dispersion* in single-mode fiber but in the multimode situation modal dispersion is very significant (even in graded index fibers).
- *Material dispersion* is significant in both types of fiber.

- *Waveguide dispersion* is significant in both MM and SM fibers but dominates in the SM case because there is no modal dispersion here.

Waveguide dispersion can be manipulated so that it acts in the *opposite direction* (has the opposite sign) to material dispersion. Single-mode fibers (for wide-area applications) of the late 1980s were adjusted such that the two forms of dispersion cancelled each other out at a wavelength of 1320 nm. For this reason, the 1300 nm, band was widely used for long distance communication links at that time.[15] However, the attenuation in the 1300 nm band is more than twice that of attenuation in the 1500 nm band. Worse, EDFAs (Erbium Doped Fiber Amplifiers) only work in the 1500 nm band, so if we want to use amplifiers, then we must use 1500 nm.[16]

**Calculating Dispersion**

Waveguide dispersion is usually quoted in ps per nm per km at a given wavelength. At 1500 nm a typical dispersion figure is 14 ps/nm/km. That is, a pulse (regardless of its length) will disperse by 14 picoseconds per nanometer of spectral linewidth per kilometer of distance travelled in the fiber. So, in a typical single-mode fiber using a laser with a linewidth of 6 nm over a distance of 10 km we have:

$$Dispersion = 14\text{ps/nm/km} \times 6nm \times 10km = 840ps$$

At 1 Gbps a pulse is 1 ns long. So if we tried to send data over the above link at 1 Gbps then we would get 84% dispersion - that is, the system would not work. (20% is a good guideline for the acceptable limit.) But it would probably work quite well at a data rate of 200 Mbps (a pulse length of 5 ns).

But a narrow-linewidth laser might have a linewidth of 300 MHz and modulating it at 1 Gbps will add 2 GHz. 2,300 MHz is just less than .02 nm (at 1500 nm). So now:

$$Dispersion = 14\text{ps/nm/km} \times .02nm \times 10km = 2.8ps$$

So in this example, dispersion just ceased to be a problem.

We can do many things to the fiber to reduce waveguide dispersion (such as varying the refractive indices of core and cladding and changing the geometry of the fiber) and it is now possible (indeed standard practice) to balance the two forms of dispersion at 1500 nm. Another way of minimizing dispersion (both material and waveguide) is to use a

[15] And that 1300 nm GaAs (Gallium Arsenide) lasers were easily available.

[16] Recently researchers have succeeded in building Praseodymium doped fiber amplifiers which operate in the 1300 nm band but these are inferior to the Erbium doped ones and are not yet commercially available. Nevertheless a gain of 23 dB at 1310 nm has been reported in the literature.

narrow linewidth laser. These techniques combined have meant that almost all new long distance single-mode systems are being installed at 1500 nm.

One important fact to remember is that modulation broadens the bandwidth of the signal (adds to the unmodulated linewidth). But again, this is trivial in current systems.

#### 4.1.11.2 Maximum Propagation Distance due to Dispersion on Multimode Fiber

On multimode fiber, modal dispersion usually dominates the other forms of dispersion, so these can be safely ignored in most cases. Fiber manufacturers do *not* quote dispersion on MM fiber in the same way as they do for single-mode fiber.

MM fiber is normally quoted as a bandwidth figure per kilometer. A good GI MM fiber would be 500 Mhz per kilometer. This means that an *analog sine wave signal* of 500 Mhz can be expected to travel 1 km without significant dispersion. To go 2 km, you would have to reduce the signal frequency to 250 Mhz.

There is one subtlety. That is, the bandwidth×distance product is not really a constant for all lengths of fiber. There is a parameter called the "cutback gamma" which is used to give the real variation of bandwidth versus distance. The problem arises when you use short pieces of fiber to measure the bandwidth and attempt to extrapolate to long distances. You end up predicting a bandwidth that is too low. Conversely if you measure the bandwidth at really long distances (which is what the fiber manufacturers do) and try to extrapolate back to short distances you will predict a bandwidth that is actually much higher than it is in reality. The simple formula is that BW is proportional to 1/length. The refined formula is BW is proportional to 1/(length**gamma).[17] Typical numbers for gamma are about 0.7-0.8.

To take proper account of this, many fiber suppliers give a table of available bandwidth for each of many typical distances.

The critical issue is to look at what *bandwidth the signal requires.* Remember that the cable is being quoted as an *analog* bandwidth and the signal is a digital "baseband" signal. The correct thing to do here is to find the bandwidth requirement of the signal you are using. What some people assume is that for NRZ data you need a bandwidth that is 0.5 of the data frequency. So, FDDI would be 1/2 of 125 Mbaud = 62.5 Mhz.

This is not a very accurate way because it ignores the difference between the frequency requirements of the pulsed (square wave) signal and the sine wave analog signal which the cable was measured. The requirement here is determined by the characteristics of the

[17] Here ** is used to mean "raised to the power of".

receiver. For FDDI a practical system might require 0.8 of the data frequency (baud rate) as a rule of thumb. It is conceivable that a system might require up to 3 times the baud rate but this seems quite unlikely.

Another issue here is the spectral linewidth. Using a spectral linewidth of 50 nm, this is not a problem since modal dispersion dominates, but if the linewidth is very wide then material dispersion should be taken into account. For a 170nm linewidth LED then a material dispersion constant of 6 or 8ps/(km×nm) for the 1.3μm LED would be a good rule of thumb. The 170nm spectral width will end up dominating the fiber bandwidth. If you use 6ps/(km×nm) and assume that the 500Mhz×km number from the fiber manufacturers is strictly modal dispersion and does not include chromatic dispersion, then your fiber ends up at 326MHz×km for your 170nm wide LED. A 2 km distance would then have about 163 MHz and will easily support 125 Mbaud data without any penalties.

#### 4.1.11.3 Attenuation Budgets

Attenuation of both multimode and single-mode fiber is generally linear with distance. The amount of signal loss due to cable attenuation is just the attenuation per kilometer (*at the signal wavelength*) multiplied by the distance. To determine the maximum distance you can send a signal (leaving out the effects of dispersion), all you need to do is to add up all the sources of attenuation along the way and then compare it with the "link budget". The link budget is the difference between the transmitter power and the sensitivity of the receiver.

Thus, if you have a transmitter of power -10 dBm and a receiver that requires a signal of power -20 dBm (minimum) then you have 10 db of link budget. So you might allow:

- 10 connectors at .3 db per connector = 3 db
- 2 km of cable at 2 db per km (at 1300 nm) = 4 db
- Contingency of (say) 2 db for deterioration due to aging over the life of the system.

This leaves us with a total of 9 db system loss. This is within our link budget and so we would expect such a system to have sufficient power. Dispersion is a different matter and may (or may not) provide a more restrictive limitation than the link budget.

### 4.1.12 Fiber Optics in Different Environments

Optical systems are built to be optimal for the particular environment in which that system is to be deployed. The point here is that the local data communications environment and the wide area telecommunications environment are very different in their character and requirements. Hence we might expect that the systems built for each environment will themselves be different.

### Wide Area Telecommunications Systems

In the wide area environment, carrying very high capacity over long distances is the primary requirement. There are relatively few sources and receivers and few connectors. There is very little need to change a system once it is installed.

- Cable cost is very important (though the cost of burying it in the ground is many times higher than that of the cable itself).
- The cost of transmitters, receivers, repeaters, connectors, etc., is much less important because that cost is only a tiny proportion of the total.
- High power is very important to achieve maximum distance between repeaters.
- Component reliability is also very important because these systems are typically multiplexed and a single failure affects many users.

### Local Area Data Communications Systems

The most important thing about this kind of system is its need for flexibility.

- The cost of transmitters and receivers, etc., is most critical (because there are a large number of these and they form a large proportion of the total).
- Cable cost is still important but much less so than in the wide area environment. Compared to electrical cables, fiber cables are much easier to install around a building (they are lighter and more flexible).
- The critical thing in this environment is joining the cable and the performance of connectors and patch cables.
- High power is important so that losses incurred in connectors and patch cables can be accommodated.
- Reliability is also very important because a single failure can disrupt the entire system.

So, in both types of application it is important to have high power and reliability. These requirements lead to different system choices:

- For wide area telecommunications, single-mode fiber and long-wavelength lasers constitute the system parameters of choice. In the 1980s, this meant 1300 nm wavelength lasers were predominant. In the 1990s, these have been replaced by 1500 nm systems (in new plant) almost universally. The remaining 1300 nm systems exist because the fiber that was installed has its dispersion minimum at 1300 nm and changing to 1500 would have meant digging up the ground and replacing the fiber. Recently, however, there has been the invention of a device which can selectively correct wavelength-dependent dispersion effects and can be used to equalize a fiber designed for 1300 nm to 1500 nm.

- For Local Data Communications, the choice is for shortwave lasers (or LEDs) and multimode fibers. In the 1980s, this meant wavelengths in the 850 nm range, but in the 1990s, there has been a general move to 1300 nm (still with LED transmitters and MM fiber). FDDI and the new ATM local area connections have been standardized at 1300 nm.

  However, we are about to witness a switch back to shorter wavelengths for short-distance, high-speed connections. "CD lasers" are the kind of lasers used in compact disk players and laser printers, etc. These lasers are very low-cost (less than US $10) and are made by some 20 or so manufacturers. Total industry volume of these lasers is about 4 million per year (1995). These operate typically between 800 and 850 nm (for the CD player application, the shorter the wavelength the better). The new standardized fiber channel (for interconnecting computers within a machine room) allows for transmission at 1 Gbps over a few hundred meters using these lasers. There is a current proposal to use these lasers at 622 Mbps for ATM local area connections (up to 300 meters).

#### 4.1.12.1 Custom Engineering or Commodity

Another big difference between the wide area environment and the local area environment is the ability to "engineer" optimized solutions for a given situation.

In the WAN, when a user (almost always a telephone company) wants to install a link, then they do a full study of the characteristics of the link involved, design and analyze a solution, and custom-build it. This is easily justified by the fact that the cost of installing links of this kind is very high.

In the local area world, the user typically wants to install a system which works with "off-the-shelf" components. This means, that you need a very few "rules-of-thumb" for interconnection of standardized components. In this situation components are over-specified to allow for extreme situations. For example, using FDDI (100 Mbps) over MM fiber (62.5 micron GI) the standard says that the maximum distance allowed is 2 kilometers. In fact, if you use good-quality cable and not too many connectors you can go to 5 kilometers safely with most available equipment. But suppliers generally will not warrant their equipment for use outside the guidelines inherent in the standard. This is because the cost of people to do optimal design exceeds the amount saved through optimization.

Optical engineering is significantly more complex than this short chapter might suggest - designing optimal networks outside of manufacturers′ guidelines is a highly skilled job. Be warned.

### 4.1.13 Future Developments

### 4.1.13.1 Wavelength Division Multiplexing (WDM)

This is the basis for new "all optical" high-speed networks. It is discussed in Chapter 16, "Lightwave Networks" on page 16-1. In 1995 IBM announced its first product to use WDM principles. This product (MuxMaster) is described in 16.3.4, "Wavelength Selective Networks" on page 16-24.

### 4.1.13.2 Solitons

Some researchers (Mollenauer, 1991) are working on a novel method of propagating pulses in a fiber without dispersion. The word "soliton" is a contraction of the phrase "solitary solution" because the phenomenon represents a single solution to the propagation equation. The effect works this way:

- The presence of light *changes* (decreases) the refractive index of glass (very slightly).
- Light travels faster in glass of a lower refractive index.
- If you have a pulse of sufficient intensity and short-enough duration[18] the faster (high-frequency components) at the beginning of the pulse are slowed down a bit and the slower (low-frequency components) in the back are speeded up.
- Thus, if the pulse length and the intensity are right, the pulse will stay together without dispersion over quite a long distance.[19] Note, it still suffers attenuation and therefore requires amplification to retain its peculiar non-dispersive characteristics.

Making the system work involves using amplifiers at regular intervals and working with a signal which is significantly more intense than typical existing systems.

Nevertheless, solitons offer a prospect of virtually error-free transmission over very long distances (although amplified along the way) at speeds of up to 5 Gbps.

This technology has not yet reached the level of laboratory prototype, but the technology looks very attractive for long-distance links in the future.

### 4.1.13.3 Better Fiber Manufacture

Figure 4-2 on page 4-10 shows the infrared absorption characteristics of two typical commercial fibers. The lower (better) curve shows a very pronounced absorption peak at about 1450 nm because of the presence of hydroxyl ions (water). This curve relates to fiber produced by a process called "Modified Chemical Vapor Deposition" (MCVD).

---

[18] 30 to 50 picoseconds - or about a centimeter.

[19] Solitons can happen in other media where waves propagate such as waves in water. The *Scientific American* magazine of December 1994 has an excellent article on this subject.

There is a much better manufacturing process available called "Vapor-Phase Axial Deposition" (VAD). This process is difficult to implement in commercial manufacture. However, it produces a fiber with a significantly lower absorption than MCVD and with little or no absorption peak due to hydroxyl ions.

Over time, as manufacturing processes improve, it is expected that VAD fibers will become lower in cost and will be universally used.

#### 4.1.13.4 Optical Logic

There is very strong current research activity in the area of providing "optical computers", that is, computers where the logic is completely optical and the signal is carried optically rather than electrically. Much progress is being made, but it is generally believed that the fruit of this research is many years off yet.

### 4.1.14 Laser Safety

It is widely believed that because of their very low power communication lasers cannot ever be a safety hazard. *This is not true.* Because lasers deliver light in a concentrated (parallel, narrow-beam, in-phase) form the light produced *can* be a hazard even at the very low power used in communications.

Many factors influence the degree of hazard. Light intensity, wavelength, and exposure duration are the most obvious. The intensity of ambient light is also important. Because the pupil in the eye closes in the presence of bright sunlight, laser emissions (say from surveying instruments) viewed in bright sunlight are much less of a hazard than when the same emissions are viewed in a darkened room.

Standards organizations around the world have developed a set of safety standards and a classification mechanism for lasers so that the hazard can be controlled.

A "Class 1" laser is defined as one that "is inherently safe (so that the maximum permissible exposure level cannot be exceeded under any condition), or are safe by virtue of their engineering design". Most (but not all) communication lasers fall into this category. It is common, however, for a communication laser to have a Class 1 emission level at the point of entry to the fiber *but a much higher level once the covers are removed from the device.*

The *only* good reference is the appropriate standard itself (these have minor differences country by country). However, as a rough guide, the following are the Class 1 limits for exposure durations of up to 10 000 seconds:

**Wavelength 700 to 1050 nm.**

> $1.2 \times 10^{-4} \times C$ Watts. Where C is a correction factor depending on wavelength (varies from 1 to 5).

**Wavelength 1050 to 1400 nm.**

$6 \times 10^{-4} \times C$ Watts.

**Wavelength longer than 1400 nm.**

$7 \times 10^{-3}$ Watts.

Notice the large variation in allowable levels with wavelength.

The maximum allowable launch power for FDDI is -6 dBm at 1300 nm. This corresponds to .25 mW of power. Since the Class 1 limit at 1300 nm is .6 mW we can conclude that any FDDI transmitter that meets the FDDI specification for maximum power output also meets the Class 1 standard at launch into the fiber. (Under the covers it may not.) Another thing that should be kept in mind is that the limit at 1550 nm is significantly higher than the limit at 1300 nm. This is another advantage for longer-wavelength systems.

A careful analysis must be made of any optical fiber communication with laser power emission levels approaching 1 milliwatt or more. This is particularly true for short-wavelength diode systems, which have a lower allowable power level.

In the US, the Federal Food and Drug Administration (FDA) regulates and enforces a laser product performance standard through the Center for Devices and Radiological Health (CDRH). The standard is Part 1040.10 of Title 21, Subchapter J of the US Code of Federal Regulations. The standard applies to laser communication products as well as all other laser products. All laser products sold in the US must be certified by the manufacturer with CDRH.

Throughout the rest of the world, IEC 825 is the primary standard, and is the base document for the European Norm 60825, which is a mandatory standard for laser products in Europe. All IBM laser products are certified to IEC 825. This is the most restrictive of the current standards.

A voluntary standard in the US, ANSI/Z136.2, addresses the specific topic of the safe use of optical fiber communication systems utilizing laser diode and LED sources. It contains all the basic mathematical relations to describe what are safe levels as a function of laser (LED) wavelength, NA of multimode fibers or mode field diameters of single-mode fibers, use of optical aids or not, viewing distance, etc. The criteria document for the development of this standard is a technical paper entitled "Toward the development of laser safety standards for fiber-optic communication systems" by R.C. Petersen and D.H. Sliney (see bibliography).

As our knowledge of the safety aspects increases, it is to be expected that relevant standards committees will modify the standards in line with better knowledge. In this light, there are proposals under way in some of the committees to significantly *increase* the maximum allowed power levels. Something like this must be done with extreme care (better to err on the side of caution) but it is widely believed that the current process will result in significantly higher power levels being allowed in 1996.

# Chapter 5. Traffic Characteristics

Many organizations see the new lower communication cost structure as an opportunity for:

1. Doing old applications better.
2. Doing new applications that were not feasible (or indeed imaginable) before.

The first requirement is to integrate existing networks into a single network. The motivation for this is not only to save money on links but to provide a better networking service by integrating the many disparate networks into a single coherently managed unit.

The kinds of existing networks that users want to integrate can be summarized as follows:

- Traditional data networks
- Voice networks
- Interconnected LAN networks
- Multiprotocol networks

In addition there are opportunities for applications using:

- Image
- Full-motion video

Traditional data networks were built to handle both interactive and batch data but were not built to handle image, voice or video traffic. The new types of traffic put a completely new set of requirements onto the network.

## 5.1 The Conflicting Characteristics of Voice and Data

It is attractive to think that when voice is digitized, it then becomes in some way "the same" as data. Or it "becomes" data. Up to a point this is true, but there are many differences between traditional data traffic and digitized voice which make the integration of the two a challenging technical problem.

**Length of Connection (Call)**

Traditionally, the most important difference between voice and data has been that voice calls are (on average) around three minutes and data calls can last for many hours. Telephone exchanges have been designed to have large numbers of external lines but relatively few "paths" through the exchange for calls. So it is possible, when the exchange is busy, for calls to "block." That is, the caller is attempting to make a connection and the called interface is unused but the call cannot be made because all paths are "blocked" (in use by other calls).

Therefore, when data is passed through a traditional telephone exchange, all the paths can be used up very quickly and the rest of the exchange will become unavailable because all paths are "blocked." Modern digital PBXs have solved this problem by providing the capacity to handle more calls than there are interfaces. For example, an exchange with 500 telephones can have a maximum of 250 simultaneous calls, but an internal capacity for perhaps 400 calls. This is because the internal data path equipment in a digital PBX represents only two or three percent of the total cost of the exchange, whereas, in the past, the function accounted for perhaps 30% of the cost. Nevertheless, while this difference is solved for the time being, in the future the problem will appear again as the sharing of voice and data on the tails becomes more common. Hence, the number of connections to be made increases and the internal limitations imposed by bus speed become a factor.

## Flow Control

The bandwidth required for voice is dictated by the digitization technique and the circuit is either in use (using the full bandwidth) or not. Data can go at any speed up to the access line speed. Voice does not need (or want) flow control. (Voice must be either handled at full speed or stopped. You cannot slow it down or speed it up.) Data, on the other hand, must be controlled, since a computer has an almost infinite capacity for generating data traffic.

Data has another problem, in that a data device, such as a terminal, can and will establish a connection and use it in a very "bursty" manner. There may be minutes or hours with no traffic at all and then a few minutes of data at the maximum transmission rate. Added together statistically the traffic does *not* "average out." What happens in large data networks is that interactive traffic tends to "peak" at different times of the day, and on particular events (for example, after a computer system has been "down" and has just recovered).[1]

---

[1] Another peculiarity here is that the difference between the peaks and the troughs in data traffic becomes greater as the network gets larger. This is not due to network size per se but rather is an effect that follows from the same cause. Networks get larger because terminal costs decrease. As the cost of terminals and attachments decreases, users are able to afford many terminals for dedicated functions. An example is in the development of banking networks. In the early networks there was only one (expensive) terminal per branch and work was "queued" for it. It was in use all of the time with a dedicated operator (with others taking over during lunch). Thus there was very little variance in the traffic over time (though the mixture of transaction types changed quite radically). Now, with cheaper terminals, most bank branches have many terminals and they are operated by their direct users, not by dedicated operators. Thus, in midmorning for example, after

Voice does exist in bursts (talk spurts) also and in general only one party speaks at one time, but statistically it poses quite a different problem for a switching system than does data.

In the past, there have been several levels of flow control available to data devices. For example, link level controls (which are aimed at optimizing the use of the link and not at network flow control), and network delivery type controls (such as pacing in SNA or packet level flow control in X.25).

### Delivery Rate Control

In data networking equipment in the past, there has also been another very important control, that of the link speed itself. Most equipment is designed to handle data at whatever speed the link can deliver it (at least at the link connection level). At the "box" (communication controller, packet switch) level, the switch is never designed for every link to operate simultaneously "flat out," but any individual link attachment must have that capability. Link speed provided an implicit control of the rate at which data could be sent or received.

But the new technology allows link speeds which are very much faster than the attaching "box". For example, a link connected to a terminal (personal computer) might run at 64 Kbps but the device, while handling instantaneous transmission or reception of blocks at this speed, may not allow for aggregate data rates much faster than (say) 500 characters per second. The same device might also be connected to a local area network at 4 Mbps with the same restriction that only a few hundred characters per second can be handled by the device. The same characteristic at higher speeds applies to the data switching processor itself.

This leads to the observation that if link speed is no longer to be a flow limiting mechanism, then others (adequate ones, such as those shown in 11.2.5, "Flow and Rate Control" on page 11-23, exist) will have to be used.

### Blocking Characteristics

Data exists in discrete blocks.[2] It is transmitted through the network in blocks. The two block sizes can be different (logical blocks can either be split up or amalgamated for transport). Telephone traffic is continuous or effectively so. It can be considered as very long indeterminate length blocks but the "real time"

---

the mail arrives, there is a processing peak with every terminal in use. At other times there can be little or no traffic.

2 There is an unfortunate conflict here in the usage of the word "block." In the telephone world it describes the action of preventing a call being set up due to lack of resources. In the data world a "block" is a logical piece of data which is kept together for transport through the network.

characteristic does not allow the network to receive a burst of speech as a single block and treat it that way.

### Acceptable Transit Delay Characteristics

An acceptable network delay for even the most exacting real time data network is about 200 milliseconds (one way). More usual is a data interactive traffic delay of 500 milliseconds or so. Batch data does not have a problem with transit delays. Voice traffic, however, is marginal on a satellite where the transit delay is 250 milliseconds one way. For first quality voice, the transit delay should be no greater than 50 milliseconds.

Further, variable transit delays (variations in response time), while an annoyance in data traffic, make voice traffic impossible. Voice packets must be delivered to the receiver at a steady, uniform rate. They must not "bunch up" and get delivered in bursts (a characteristic of today's data networks).

A short interruption to the circuit (for example, caused by an airplane flying between two microwave repeaters) which could result in a one-second outage of the link will have quite different effects for voice than for data. For data, it is nearly always preferable to have a delay of a few seconds rather than losing the data. With voice, a packet that is one half a second old is just garbage. It is much better to discard delayed voice packets quickly, thus allowing the circuit to return to normal, than it is to build up a queue, particularly due to the fixed speed of the receiving (and of the transmitting) device.

### Error Control

The most important thing about data traffic is that errors must be controlled, either detected, or (preferably) detected and corrected. This correction mechanism can often only be done by context[3] (since you don't know who the sender is until you are sure there are no errors in the block), and will require retransmissions for recovery. Voice, on the other hand, cannot tolerate the time delays inherent in recoveries and does not care about occasional errors or bursts of errors. (Voice and human language are very redundant indeed.)

### Power Demands

Problems caused by fluctuations in the demand for power should not happen in modern digital systems.

Statistics shows us that when many variable (or varying) things are added up, then the mean (average) becomes more and more stable (has less and less variation). For example, in voice calls if one takes the power demands on a trunk

---

[3] At the link level, the sender is always known regardless of the content of the block. Later when released from the context of the link, the only identification for the block is the routing information within the block itself.

amplifier for a large number of calls, then the requirement is very stable indeed and well known. The dynamics of speech, when added up over many calls, produces remarkably stable system demands.

When data is used instead of voice, many things change. Call duration is usually cited (data calls are generally much longer than voice) but there are other problems. When modems are used for data communication over a telephone channel there are no "gaps between words." The modem produces a constant, high-level signal. If too many modem calls happen to be multiplexed on a single interexchange (frequency division) trunk, then the additional electrical power required by the multiplexors and amplifiers can be so great as to cause the device to fail. (Power supplies are designed to supply only enough power for voice calls.) This restriction will go away with the advent of digital systems, but it was the cause of PTT hesitancy about allowing modems to be connected arbitrarily around the telephone system without consideration of their effects on that system.

### Volume of Data

If telephone calls are to be regarded as 64 Kbps full-duplex, then not even the largest organization transmits enough data to be more than 20 percent of its telephone traffic. Most organizations transmit less than five percent, and of all the communications traffic carried over public communication lines perhaps one or two percent is data. This is very important since anything that is done in the system to accommodate data traffic, if it adds cost to the voice part of the system, will be very hard to justify because of the large cost added to the total system for small benefit.

It is perfectly true that data traffic is growing rapidly and voice traffic is not, but there is a very long way to go, particularly in that the number of interfaces to the public networks being used for voice versus the number of interfaces being used for data is a more important criteria than the number of bits sent. This ratio of the number of interfaces is even more biased in the direction of voice traffic.

### Balanced Traffic

Most voice calls involve a two-way conversation (although that some people talk more than others!). This means that for voice transmission, the traffic is usually reasonably well balanced.

Not so for data. Even without the obvious example of file transfer (which is one way), traditional (IBM 3270 style) interactive data traffic involves very short (perhaps 30 to 50 bytes) input and large output (typically 500 bytes but often 2000 bytes or more). In graphics applications, the unbalance is even greater than this.

### Echo Cancellation

In traditional (analog) voice systems, the problem of suppressing echoes is extremely important. In a digital full-duplex system, it would seem that echos were no longer a consideration.

This is not completely true. Some echoes can be generated within a telephone handset and though this is a small problem compared with the problems of the past, it must still be considered. In a system where voice is packetized, the size of the packet determines the length of time that it takes to fill a packet before transmission (64 Kbps equals one byte per 125 μsec). As the delay in the circuit increases, then so does the problem caused by echoes.

These facts have fueled a debate over the optimal packet size for packetized voice. Some people contend that a packet of around 80 bytes or so will produce problems with echoes where packet sizes of 32 bytes will not. (This is because of the time needed to assemble a packet.)

There is a significant problem with echoes in the situation of a digital full-duplex backbone network with analog subscriber loops. As noted in 2.2.4, "The Subscriber Loop" on page 2-44, these loops can generate large echoes and this will be a problem if the network delay exceeds about 40 milliseconds.

## 5.2 Characteristics of Image Traffic

Image traffic is conceptually similar to traditional data traffic with one major difference - images are very large compared to traditional character screen images.

A traditional IBM 3270 character screen showing multiple fields and many colors averages about 2,500 bytes (the screen size is 1,920 bytes but other information relating to formatting and field characteristics is present). The same screen displayed as an image could be as much as 300 KB.

Images are therefore transmitted as groups of frames or packets (in SNA, as "chains"). Response time is important but only within normal human response requirements. Less than a second is goodness; up to perhaps five seconds is tolerable; above five seconds and users become more and more seriously inconvenienced.

Nevertheless, because image traffic is typically initiated by a human operator entering some form of a transaction, display will be relatively infrequent - because systems are such that a user typically needs to spend time looking at the display before looking at the next image. In the future this may not hold true. Online books (with illustrations) for example may encourage users to "flick through" the pages looking for the information they need. "Flicking through the pages" of a book involves the consecutive display of many images perhaps a second or two apart. This could put a substantial unplanned load onto a data network.

## 5.3 Characteristics of Digital Video

At first thought, video traffic appears to share many of the characteristics of voice traffic (you set up a connection and transmit a continuous stream of data at a more or less constant rate until you no longer need the connection). In reality, while there are many similarities, transporting video in a packet network is a quite different problem from transporting voice.

Video systems display information as a sequence of still pictures called frames. Each frame consists of a number of lines of information. The two predominant broadcast television systems currently use 625 lines at 25 frames/sec (PAL) or 450 lines at 30 frames/sec (NTSC).

### Data Rate

If a PAL signal is to be digitally transmitted we could perhaps break up a line into 500 points and encode each point in 12 bits (color and intensity, etc.). This becomes quite a high transmission rate:

```
625 (lines) × 25 (per sec) ×
   500 (points) × 12 (bits) = 93,750,000 bits/sec
```

In fact, for reasonable resolution we probably don't need 500 points in each line and maybe we can code each point as 8 bits, but whichever way you look at it the data rate is very high.

But this is altogether the wrong way to look at video. Over history we have broadcast video (a PAL signal requires about seven MHz bandwidth) over a fixed rate channel. Every point in the picture was sent (although via analog transmission) in every frame. **But the information content of a video frame is inherently variable.** The point about video is that the majority of frames are little different from the frame before. If a still picture is transmitted through a video system, all we need to transmit is the first frame and then the information content of each subsequent frame is *one* bit. This bit says that this frame is the same as the one before!

If a video picture is taken of a scene such as a room, then only a data rate of 1 bit per frame is necessary to maintain the picture (that is, 25 bps for PAL). As soon as a person enters and walks across the room then there is much more information required in the transmission. But even then much of the picture area will remain unaffected. If the camera is "panned" across the room, then each frame is different from the one before *but* all that has happened is that the picture has moved. Most pixels (picture elements - bit positions) move by the same amount and perhaps we don't need to retransmit the whole thing.

There are many examples, including the typical head and shoulders picture of a person speaking where most of the picture is still and only the lips are moving. But in a picture of a waterfall many pixels will be different from ones before *and* different in non-systematic ways. A video picture of a waterfall has a very high information content because it contains many non-systematic changes.

What is being discussed here is something a little different from what we traditionally regard as compression. When a still picture is examined, much of the picture area contains repetition. Any particular line (or point) will very likely have only small differences from the one either side of it. Within a line there will be many instances of repetition such as when crossing an area of uniform color and texture. There are many algorithms available to compress a single image to a much smaller amount. So, although one can look for redundancy and compress it, a still picture contains a fixed amount of information (from an information theory viewpoint). A sequence of video pictures is different in the sense that from an information theory standpoint, each frame can contain from one to perhaps a few million bits!

The net result of the above is the conclusion that video is fundamentally variable in the required rate of information transfer. It suggests that a variable rate channel (such as a packet network) may be a better medium than a fixed rate TDM channel for video traffic. Consider the figure below:

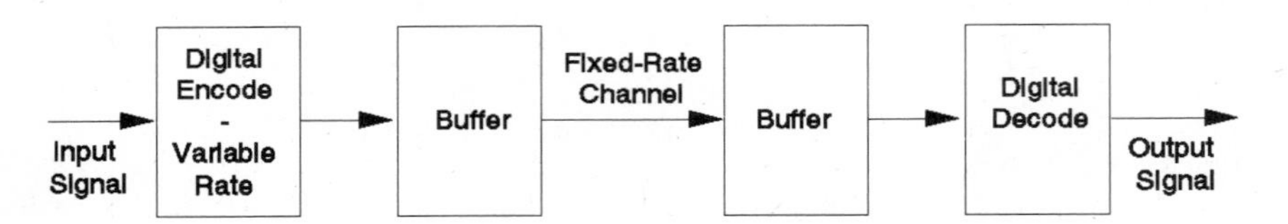


***Figure 5-1.*** *Transmitting Video over a Fixed Rate Channel*

This is typical of existing systems that transmit video over a limited digital transmission channel. Systems exist where quite good quality is achieved over a 768 Kbps digital channel. When the signal is digitally encoded and compressed, the output is a variable rate. But we need to send it down a fixed capacity channel. Sometimes (most of the time) the required data rate is much lower than the 768 Kbps provided. At other times the required data rate is much higher than the rate of the channel. To even this out a buffer is placed before the transmitter so that if/when the decoder produces too much data for the channel it will not be lost. But when the data arrives at the receiver end of the channel data may not arrive in time for the next frame, if that frame contained too much data for the channel. To solve this, a buffer is inserted in the system and a delay introduced so there will be time for irregularities in reception rate to be smoothed out before presentation to the fixed rate screen.

Buffers, however, are not infinite and if the demands of the scene are for a high data rate over an extended period of time, then data is lost when the buffers are filled up (overrun). This is seen in "full motion" video conference systems which typically operate over a limited channel. If the camera is "panned" too quickly then the movement appears jerky and erratic to the viewer (caused by the loss of data as buffers are overrun).

It is easy to see from the above example that it is quite difficult to fit video into a limited rate channel. Always remember, however, that the average rate required in the example above will be perhaps ten times less than the 768 Kbps provided and that most of the channel capacity is wasted anyway!

The extreme variation in information transfer requirement means that if a fixed rate channel able to handle the fastest rate is used then there will be a large amount of wasted capacity. If a limited channel is used then there is less (but still significant) waste of capacity but more important, there is loss of quality when a high transfer rate is used for a longer time than the buffers can hold. (Typically, existing systems buffer for a few seconds of high activity in the picture - if something such as the stereotype television car chase sequence occurs, then the system can't handle it.)

Thinking about the matter statistically, if a number of video signals were able to share the same communications resource then it is likely that when one video channel requires a high bandwidth, others will require much less. The statistics of it say that the more signals there are sharing a resource, the less variation there will be in the resource requirement.

> When there are only two users sharing, there is a reasonably high probability that there will be times when both signals will require a high transfer rate at the same time. When 50 signals share the resource there is still a finite probability that all 50 will require a high transfer rate at the same time, but that probability is tiny. This is discussed further in Appendix C, "Queueing Theory" on page C-1.

This all leads to the conclusion that high-speed packet networks and LANs are the natural medium for video transmission.

### Timing Considerations

Video traffic is like voice in one important respect - it is isochronous. Frames (or lines) are delivered to the network at a constant rate and when displayed at the other end must be displayed at the same rate. But packet networks tend to deliver data at an uneven rate (this is sometimes called "packet jitter"). Something needs to be done at the receiver end to even out the flow of packets to a constant rate. As with voice, this can be done by inserting a planned delay factor (just a queue of packets) at the receiver.

### Redundancy

Even more than voice, video is very redundant indeed. The loss or corruption of a few bits is undetectable. The loss of a few lines is not too much of a problem since if we display the line from the previous frame unchanged, most times the loss will be undetected. Even the loss of a frame or two here and there doesn't matter much because our eyes will barely notice. Of course it must be noted that when video is digitally coded and compressed, loss or corruption of packets will have a much larger effect (because the data is now a lot less redundant).

### Video Applications

Very often video applications are for one-way transmission (as in viewing television or a movie). In this case the amount of delay that we may insert into the system without detriment can be quite great (perhaps ten seconds or more).

Interactive video is a little different in that this is the "videophone" application, that is, people talking to one another accompanied by a picture. In this case, although the voice communication is logically half-duplex (that is, hopefully only one person talks at one time), the video portion is continuous. Delay is still less stringent than for voice - although the voice component has all the characteristics of regular voice (without video). It appears that synchronization of voice with the movement of lips is not too critical. Most people do not detect a difference of 120 milliseconds between the image and the sound in this situation.

### Digital Video in a Packet Network

The discussion above concluded that packet networks are a natural medium for video transmission. But certainly we don't mean "traditional" packet networks. Many, if not most, existing packet networks don't have sufficient total capacity to handle even one video signal! In order to operate properly, a packet network processing video must have a number of important characteristics:

1. Sufficient capacity. The throughput capacity of the network must be sufficient to handle several video signals together - otherwise the benefit of sharing the resource is lost.

2. End-to-end delay appropriate to the application. This varies quite a bit with the application. One-way traffic doesn't care about network delay too much. Interactive video needs a transit delay approximating that of voice (because voice accompanies it) but does not need to be exactly synchronized to the voice.

3. Minimal packet jitter. Irregularities in the rate of delivery of packets need to be smoothed out by inserting a buffer and a delay.

In addition there is the question of what to do when the network becomes congested and how to handle errors.

### Hierarchical Source Coding

All networks of finite capacity encounter congestion at various times. But with video (as with voice) you can't slow down the input rate to the network in order to control congestion (as we do in data networks) because a video frame arriving too late is simply garbage. If the network is congested the best we can do is to throw some packets away until the network returns to normal. If this happens only very infrequently, then video and voice users will not get too upset, but if it happens often then the system can become unusable.

One approach to congestion is to code the information (video or voice) into packets in such a way that the information is split up. Information essential to display of the frame is coded into a separate packet from information that merely improves the quality. This means that some packets contain essential information and others less essential information. The packets can be marked in the header so that the network will discard only non-essential packets during periods of congestion. This technique (originally invented for handling packet voice) is called "Hierarchical Source Coding" (HSC) and has the obvious advantage of allowing the system to continue basic operation during periods of congestion.

The concept is very simple. Imagine that a particular byte of encoded data represents the intensity level of a particular point on the screen. A simple HSC technique might be to take the high order four bits and send them in one packet (marked essential) and the low order four bits in a different packet (marked non-essential). In the normal case when the packets arrive at the destination the byte is reconstructed. In the case of congestion, perhaps the packet containing the less important low order bits has been discarded. The receiver would then assume the low order four bits have been lost and treat them as zeros. The result would be to give 16 levels of intensity for the particular point rather than the 256 levels that would have been available had the less important packet not been discarded. In practice, HSC techniques need to be designed in conjunction with the encoding (and compression) methods. These can be very complex indeed.

In principle, this is not too different from what we do in the analog broadcasting environment.

> Most color TV sets contain a circuit called a "color killer". When the received analog TV signal is too weak or contains too much interference, the circuit "kills" the color and displays the picture in black and white. This enables a viewer to see a picture (although a B+W one), which, if displayed in color, would not be recognizable.

In radio broadcasting of FM stereo an ingenious system is used such that two signals (left channel plus right channel and left channel minus right channel) are transmitted. The two are frequency multiplexed such that the L+R signal occupies the lower part of the frequency band and the L-R the upper part. When the signal is received strongly, the channel separation can be reconstructed by addition and subtraction of the channels. When the signal is weak, the L+R signal dominates because it occupies the lower part of the band. What you get then is only L+R (mono) reception. So when the signal is weak, you lose the stereo effect but still get a basic signal.

Hierarchical source coding may become a basic technique for processing both voice and video in packet networks.

### Error Control

The worst problem in processing video is packet jitter (erratic delays in packet delivery). Recovery from link errors by retransmission of data is not usable within a packet network containing video for this reason. The best thing to do with erred packets is to discard them immediately. Mis-routing due to errors in the destination field in the header can have catastrophic effects. Packets should have a frame check sequence field which should be checked every time the packet travels over a link and the packet discarded if an error is found.

There is a question about what to do at the receiver when an expected packet doesn't arrive due to errors or congestion in the network. It has been suggested that using a very short packet (or cell) size with an error correcting code might be a useful technique. Unfortunately, while this technique would overcome random single bit errors, etc., it is not a satisfactory way to overcome the loss of many packets in a group. This is because an error correcting code capable of recovering from this kind of situation would be so large that the overhead would be unacceptable.

The best technique for handling errors in video involves using the information from the previous frame and whatever has been received of the current frame to build an approximation of the lost information. A suitable strategy might be to just continue displaying the corresponding line from the previous frame, or if only a single line is lost, extrapolating the information from the lines on either side of the lost one.

### High-Quality Sound

High-quality sound (CD-quality stereo) involves a very high bit rate. Regular CDs use a bit rate of 4 Mbps. Encoding sound is, in principle, the same problem as for voice but with a few differences for the network:

- High-quality sound (such as a film soundtrack) is continuous - unlike voice transmission where talk exists in “spurts”.

- The data rate is much higher (but the same compression techniques that worked for voice also work here).
- Delay through the network doesn't matter as much - this depends on the requirements for the video signal the sound accompanies.
- The major requirement is that (like video and voice) high-quality sound be delivered to the network at a constant rate and played out at the receiver at a constant rate.

## 5.4 Characteristics of Multimedia Applications

Many people believe that the ability to provide a coordinated mixture of data, voice, and video services to the desktop will provide major productivity enhancements for business. Indeed some people believe that this ability is the key to a whole new way of living and working for large numbers of people, the final removal of distance as an inhibitor to intellectual interaction between people. Proposed applications may be classified as follows:

- Multiparty videoconferencing
- Real-time audiovisual collaboration (one on one)
- Interactive training
- Enhanced personal videoconferencing

There are several important points to note here:

1. Communication requires a large amount of bandwidth.
2. Communication must be to each user's desktop (or home).
3. Multiple types of information are involved (voice, data, video, image).
4. The presentation of this information to the end user must be coordinated. That is, *presentation of the different forms of related information must be synchronized.*

The most important technical issues[4] for the network are:

- *Latency* is the variation in time between when the stream is transmitted and when it is presented to the end user. This is more than propagation delay because of the need for buffering, etc., at the end user device.
- *Jitter* is variation in latency over time. This causes erratic presentation of information to the end user.
- *Skew* is the difference in time of presentation to the end user of related things (such as a video of someone speaking and the related sound).

---

[4] See "Multimedia Networking Performance Requirements" by James D. Russell in the Bibliography.

- *Overrun and Underrun* are perhaps not predominantly network issues. This is where the video or voice signal is generated at a different rate from the rate at which it is played out. In the case of overrun, information is generated faster than it can be displayed and at some point information must be discarded. Underrun is where the playout rate is greater than the rate of signal generation and therefore "glitches" will occur when data must be presented but none is there. To an extent, depending on the application, a good system can mask the effects of overrun and underrun.

The importance of each of these factors varies with the application but skew is both the most important for the application and the greatest challenge for the network (and incidentally for the workstation itself).

**Interactive Applications**

Applications such as video conferencing (personal or group) have the same requirements as regular voice. That is, a maximum latency of about 150 ms is tolerable.

Jitter must be contained to within limits that the system can remove without the user knowing (perhaps 20 ms is tolerable).

Skew (between audio and video) should be such that the audio is between 20 ms ahead and 120 ms behind the video.

**One-Way Video Distribution**

In this application a delay of several seconds between sender and receiver is quite acceptable in many situations. This largely depends on whether the user expects to watch a two-hour movie or a 20-second animated segment in a training application. The delay really only matters because it is the time between the user requesting the information and when it starts being presented. For a movie, perhaps 30 seconds would be tolerable; for a short segment, one second is perhaps the limit.

Jitter and skew, however, have the same limits as the interactive applications above.

**Audio with Image Applications**

These are applications such as illustrated lectures and voice annotated text where still images are annotated by voice commentary. Depending on the application, latency may need to be less than 500 ms (between the request for the next image and its presentation) but the skew (audio behind the image) could be perhaps as long as a second or so.

These requirements place a significant demand on the network as discussed above. You need:

1. Adequate (high) data rates (to keep latency low and to allow sufficient capacity to service the application)
2. Low latency
3. Very low jitter
4. Very low skew
5. End-to-end control through propagation of a stable clock

All of this must be delivered to the workplace (desk or home)!

# Chapter 6. Principles of High-Speed Networks

If the user requirements outlined in the previous chapter (integration of data, voice, video, image, etc.) are to be satisfied by packet networks, then clearly a new type of packet network will be needed. Network nodes will need to handle the full data throughput capacity of the new high-speed links (one million packets per second - plus) and network architectures will need to accommodate the unique characteristics of voice and video traffic.

The requirements may be summarized as follows:

**Very High Node Throughput**

Nodes must be able to route (switch) data at the peak combined rate of all links connected to them. In corporate networks this might mean a maximum of perhaps 20 links at 155 Mbps, but this seems a little high for the decade of the 1990s. More likely would be a switch with less than 20 links where perhaps four of them are 155 Mbps and the rest might be at the "T3" rate of 45 Mbps.

But corporate private networks are one thing. Public telecommunications networks are something else. The proposal with ATM (B_ISDN) is that packet (cell) switching should become the basis of a multi-function network, which will replace the world's telephone network. To do this, a mainline trunk exchange (probably a cluster of switching nodes) would need to handle perhaps 100 links of 620 Mbps today and perhaps the same 100 links would be running at 2.4 Gbps by the time the system was built.

Using 53-byte cells, a 2.4 Gbps link can carry just less than six million cells per second *in each direction.*

The example is a little extreme but the principle is clear. We are going to need the ability to process cells at rates of well above one hundred million per second for Broadband ISDN to become a reality.

**Minimal Network Transit Time**

This is a critical requirement for voice and is discussed later in 6.2.2.2, "The Effect of End-to-End Network Delay on Voice Traffic" on page 6-13.

**Minimal Variation in Network Transit Time**

When any traffic with a constant bit rate at origin and destination travels through a network, the variations in network delay mean that a buffer somewhat larger than the largest foreseeable variation in transit time is needed. This buffer introduces a delay and for practical purposes can be considered a net addition to network transit time. This is further discussed in 6.2.2.2, “The Effect of End-to-End Network Delay on Voice Traffic” on page 6-13.

To meet the above requirements networks will need to have the following characteristics:

**Totally Hardware Controlled Switching**

There is no way that current software-based packet switched architectures can come to even one hundredth of the required throughput - even assuming much faster processors.

However, there are several hardware switching designs that will meet the required speeds at (predicted) reasonable cost.

**Suitable Network Architecture**

The network architecture must make it possible for the data switching component in a node to decide the destination to which an incoming packet should be routed *at full operating speed.*

The network architecture must provide mechanisms for the stable operation and management of the network but the data switching element must not need to get involved in extraneous protocols.

**Link Error Recovery**

Recovery from transient link errors by retransmission (for voice traffic), as is usual for data traffic, can seriously conflict with the requirement for uniform delivery rates. For voice, a delayed packet is worse than a packet in error. However, by the nature of packetization, it is necessary that packets contain a header which carries routing information (identification) so the destination switch can route it to the appropriate destination. An error in this information will cause a packet to be routed to the wrong destination *and* a packet to be lost from the correct circuit.

But these very high-speed networks are planned to operate solely over digital (preferably fiber optical) circuits. Error rates on these circuits are around ten thousand times better than they were for traditional analog data links.

For the data portion of the packet or cell, error checking and recovery can be applied on an end-to-end basis especially if the error rates experienced on links is very low.

The header portion is not so fortunate. An error in the header can cause a packet to be misrouted to the wrong destination. The network must at least check the headers.

### Packet Length

Short (less than 64 bytes), fixed-length packets or cells are an attractive option because:

1. Their fixed-length nature gives a uniform transmission time (per cell) characteristic to the queueing within a node for an outbound link. This leads to a more uniform transit-time characteristic for the whole network.
2. The shorter the cell the shorter the time needed to assemble it and hence the shorter the delay characteristic for voice.
3. Short, fixed-length cells are easy to transfer over a fixed-width processor bus, and buffering in link queues is a lot easier and requires less processor logic.

One elegant solution to both the network delay and error recovery problems would be to use very short packets (perhaps 32 bytes) of fixed length. If this is done then Error Correcting Codes (ECC) can be used as a recovery from transient link errors. Two bytes of ECC are required for every 8 bytes of data. A 32-byte packet would then have a routing header (2 or 4 bytes) included within it and one or four ECC 2-byte groups appended to it (one if it is thought necessary only to check the header, two if the data is to be error recovered also). Therefore, a packet would be either 34 or 40 bytes. (This represents an overhead on the transmission channel in the full ECC case of 20%.) It happens that the use of ECC in this way for a voice packet is considered wasteful and unnecessary. The loss of a packet or two (provided it is relatively infrequent) or the corruption of a few bits of data is not considered to be significant.

The international standard for cell size is now 48 bytes (for ATM). In ATM the header is checked for validity but the data within the cell is not (or, rather, that checking and error recovery on the data within a frame (group of cells) is left to the end-to-end protocol called the "adaptation layer").

However, there is another side. Video transmission is fine with packet sizes of over a thousand bytes. Data transmission can be achieved with low overhead if the packet size adopted is large enough to carry the largest natural data block as produced by the user's application.

The longer the packet the fewer packets per second must be switched for a given data throughput.

This subject is discussed in more detail in 6.5, "Transporting Data in Packets or Cells" on page 6-19.

### Flow Control

Control of congestion is a critical matter in any packet switching environment. Traditional techniques of flow control are not possible at very high packet rates because they require significant amounts of programmed logic to operate on every packet.

In a high-speed switch, input rate regulation and capacity reservation are the appropriate techniques. These can be agreed by the control processors when a connection is started and enforced at the entry points of the network.

This subject is discussed further in 6.1, "Control of Congestion" on page 6-6.

### Congestion Control

Congestion occurs when a node builds up too much data for its internal buffers to process. This can happen even in data networks with very detailed explicit flow controls.

One way to handle congestion is to avoid it. Good flow controls can help in avoiding congestion. Another sure way of handling congestion is to make sure that the maximum demand that can ever be placed on the network can be met at all times. This means running links and nodes at average utilizations of around 10 or 20% at the peak! But this foregoes the benefits of sharing the network.

If the network is to process variable rate data (say voice) from many thousands of users simultaneously, and if no single user can make a peak demand sufficient to be noticed, then the statistics of the situation work for us. As described in Appendix C, "Queueing Theory" on page C-1 as you add up many variable sources (that are unrelated to one another) the total becomes very stable.

Congestion becomes a problem where there are a number of sources that can individually place a significant demand on the network (such as in variable-rate video). In this case a small number of users (as few as 10 perhaps) might be able to each make peak demands simultaneously and bring the whole network to a standstill. The trick here is to avoid the situation where any single user can make a significant demand on the network.

But some types of traffic change radically over time. Data traffic peaks at different times in a business day. Batch data peaks during the night.

When congestion occurs packets must be discarded. For some data types (voice, video) coding can be such that low priority packets can be discarded with the net effect of a "graceful degradation" of the service. If these packets are marked as discardable in some way (this is a feature of both ATM and Paris), then the system can alleviate congestion by discarding these.

If congestion becomes very serious, then the network will need to discard packets not marked as discardable. The network should have a way of prioritizing traffic by service class so that an intelligent packet discard strategy may be adopted.

This packet discard strategy must be performed by the (hardware) data switching element. The discard strategy must be very simple.

### Sequential Delivery

If packets applying to one conversation are allowed to take different routes through the network (for load balancing for example) then they must be resequenced before delivery to the receiver. However, this means that each would have to carry a sequence number (more overhead) and the technique would result in "bursty" uneven delivery. To overcome this, delivery would then need to be buffered sufficiently to even out the bursts. This would add cost but more importantly it would add to the transit delay and thus degrade the quality.

In a high-speed network this means that each connection must be limited to a fixed path through the network.

### Priorities

There is no consensus yet on whether transmission priorities are relevant in a high-speed network. A transmission priority may be given to a packet and that priority enables it to "jump the queue" ahead of lower priority packets when being queued for transmission within a node.

Within a tightly controlled traditional packet networking system such as SNA, the system of priorities has worked well. It gives better response time to higher priority traffic and also enables the use of much higher resource (link and node) loadings than would be possible without them.

But at such high speed, with relatively small cells (at the speeds we are considering even a 4KB block is small - in time), many people suggest that the cost of implementing priorities may be greater than it is worth. Most studies of high-speed node technology suggest that the total switching (processing, queueing and transmission) in the kind of node under discussion will be much less than one millisecond.

Other kinds of priority are, however, considered essential. In a large network there needs to be some control and prioritization of the selection of routes through a network, depending on the required service characteristics for a particular class of service.

In addition it seems generally agreed that a service class type of priority should be used to decide which packets to discard at times of network congestion.

### End-to-End Protocols and "Adaptation"

The characteristics of a high-speed network developed thus far are such that it gives very high throughput of very short packets, but in the case of congestion or of link errors packets are discarded.

To provide a stable service, the network needs to have processing at the entry and exit points of the network. This processing will, for example, break long frames of data up into cells and reassemble at the other end. In addition, for data traffic it should implement a Frame Check Sequence (FCS) calculation to identify frames containing errors. It may also have a retransmission protocol to recover from data errors and lost packets, etc. (Or it may just signal to the user that there has been a problem and allow the user to do recovery.)

Each type of network traffic requires different adaptation layer processing.

## 6.1 Control of Congestion

The flow and congestion control mechanisms used in existing software-based packet networks are not adequate for the high-speed environment. Some types of traffic, voice or video for example, cannot have their delivery rate slowed down. You either have to process it or clear the circuit.

Also, traditional "rotating window" flow controls such as are used within traditional packet networks require complex processing in software within the network nodes. Processing in software would prevent a totally hardware-based switching operation. It thus conflicts with the need for very fast routing performed by hardware functions.

The primary method suggested for control of flows in a high-speed packet network is to control the rate of entry of packets to the network and not have controls within the network itself. In the high-speed environment, at very high loadings, when congestion does occur the network will recover by simply throwing some data away.

There are many ways to perform flow control external to the network. For example, in TCP/IP networks, the IP switches do not participate in complex congestion control procedures. Congestion control is performed through a rotating window protocol operating between end users (TCP entities). This works to a point but the network can't enforce this on the end users and it is quite possible for individual end users to adopt a non-conforming protocol (for example UTP). In addition, the protocol involves substantial overhead and has problems with fairness in certain situations. However, for data transport in high-speed networks there will be some form of rotating window end-to-end protocol which will perform a flow control function.

In the high-speed environment, an input rate control system is needed (perhaps in addition to end-to-end user flow controls) which will apply to all (data, voice, video, etc.) types of traffic.

When a circuit is set up its throughput demands are assessed by a node that allocates capacity to the individual circuit (call). These demands are things like minimum guaranteed packet throughput rate, maximum allowed peak rate, priority (if any), and loss priority (the tendency for the network to throw away the packet when congestion occurs).

The method of operation suggested is that the attaching user node should control its rate of data presentation to the network through a system called "Leaky Bucket Rate Control" and *that the network should monitor this traffic at the network entry point to make sure that the end user node does not exceed its allowance.*

In a sense, input rate control mechanisms are not new. In traditional data networks, end-user devices were connected to data switching nodes typically by 2,400 bps and 4,800 bps links. The data switching nodes themselves were connected perhaps by "fast" 64 Kbps links. The speed of the attaching links and the internal processing speed of the end-user devices themselves provided a limitation on the rate at which data could be sent to the network. In addition, these links were typically operated using "polling" link protocols. The networks could (and many did) control the rate of data input by controlling the polling process. In the emerging high-speed environment, devices are typically connected to the network through a LAN and thus there is no longer the implicit rate control provided by the slow speed of the attaching link.

#### 6.1.1.1 Leaky Bucket Rate Control

This mechanism is a control on the rate at which data may be sent into the network rather than a control of data flow through the network. Once data has entered the network there is no proposed control of flows except the implicit throughput capability of the links and nodes involved.

In concept, leaky bucket rate control operates as follows:

- A packet entering the network must pass a "gate" called the leaky bucket. This is really just a counter, which represents the number of packets that may be sent immediately on this path.
- In order for a packet to pass and enter the network the counter must be non-zero.
- The leaky bucket counter has a defined maximum value.
- The counter is incremented (by one) n times per second.
- When a packet arrives it may pass the leaky bucket if (and only if) the counter is non zero.
- When the packet passes the barrier to enter the network, the counter is decremented.
- If the packet has been delayed it will be released immediately after the counter is incremented.

Leaky bucket rate control may be operated on individual connections or it may operate on a group of connections such as all the connections on the same link or all the connections on the same virtual path (as in ATM). In addition, there may be a number of leaky buckets implemented in series to give a closer control of rates.

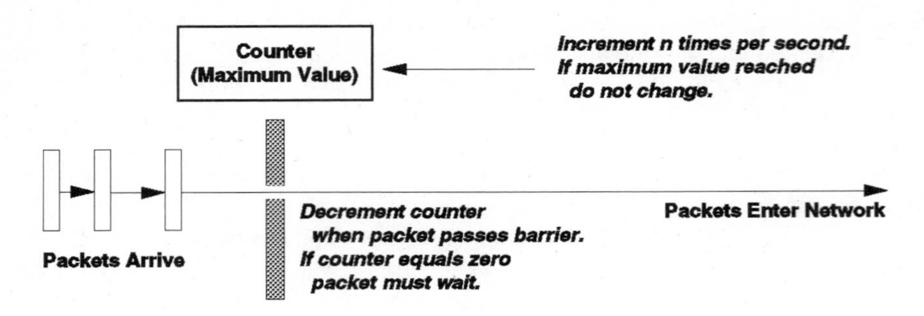


***Figure 6-1.*** *Leaky Bucket Rate Control*

In some variations of the leaky bucket scheme, there is no input queue to the leaky bucket! A packet arriving at the barrier is either allowed immediate passage or is discarded. From a network perspective it doesn't matter whether there is a queue there or not. The choice of whether or not to have queueing here depends very much on the type of traffic being carried and the design of the particular adaptation layer involved.

This scheme has the effect of limiting the packet rate to a defined average, but allowing short (definable size) bursts of packets to enter the network at maximum rate. If the node tries to send packets at a high rate for a long period of time, the rate will be equal to "n" per second. If however, there has been no traffic for a while, then the node may send at full rate until the counter reaches zero.

Paris (described in 11.2, "Packetized Automatic Routing Integrated System (Paris)" on page 11-16) uses two leaky buckets in series with the second one using a maximum bucket size of 1 but a faster clock rate. The total effect is to limit input to a defined average rate but with short bursts allowed at a defined higher rate (but still not the maximum link speed).

The scheme can be dynamic in that the maximum value of the counter and/or the rate at which the counter is incremented may be changed depending on current conditions within the network (provided that the network has some method of signaling these conditions to the end user).

Figure 6-2 on page 6-9 shows one potential configuration such that individual circuits have rate control applied to them and an aggregate rate control is applied to the total of a logical grouping of circuits. This is relatively efficient to implement in code.

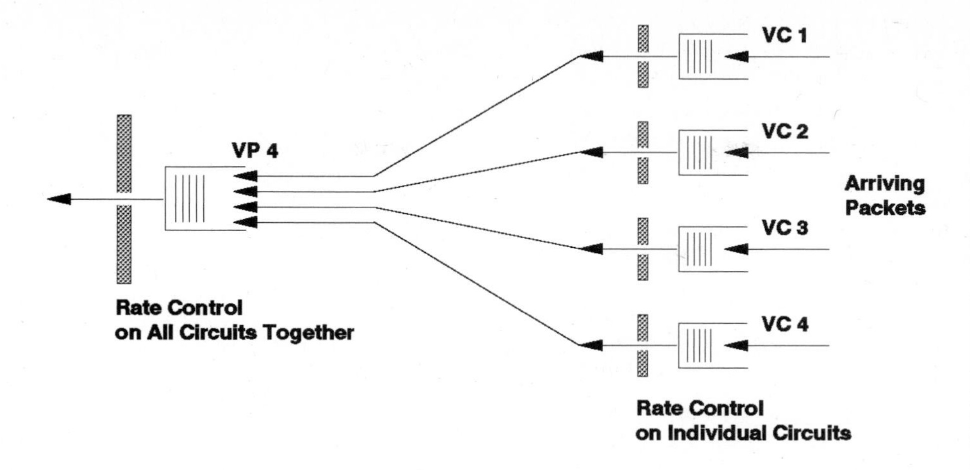


***Figure 6-2.*** *A Cascade of Leaky Buckets.* Leaky bucket rate control is applied to individual circuits and then to the total of a logical group.

## 6.1.2 Congestion Control in Cell Networks

There is a predicted problem in congestion control of ATM networks which applies (potentially at least) to all cell-based networks.

The primary characteristics which distinguish cell networks from packet networks are:

1. A cell-based network does *not* have any internal flow or congestion control. While the internal operation of packet networks is different for every network equipment maker, most implement link level error recovery and some form of internal flow control in order to avoid congestion. Some packet networks go much further and provide a fully secure internal operation.

2. Cells are typically of fixed length. If a packet (say in X.25) is not full, a short packet is sent. If there is not enough data to fill a cell, then it is padded out to full size.

3. Cells are typically (though not always) shorter than packets. The ATM cell size is 48 data bytes where the default X.25 packet size is 128 bytes. In practice, in X.25 style networks, much larger packet sizes (up to 2 KB) are often used.

It is really a matter for the "higher layer" protocols but error recovery in the cell-based network is *always* performed from end-to-end (from adaptation layer to adaptation layer). When a cell network detects an error on a link or becomes congested, the only mechanism it has for resolving the situation is to discard cells (data). For example, in a congestion situation a node might discard all the data queued for transmission on a particular link or group of links.

The problem is that cells are very short. Cells do not have the space to contain additional header overheads to enable error recovery (by retransmission) of individual cells. Error recovery is done by retransmission of whole user data blocks. For example, when a 2KB block is sent through a cell network, it is sent as 43 cells. If an individual cell is lost (or discarded by the network) then the error recovery operation is to *re-send the whole logical data block!* That is, re-send all 43 cells.

This doesn't matter too much for cells lost due to random errors on internode links (error rates are extremely low). But in the case where the network discards data due to congestion, there is a potential problem.

When a node discards, say, 1000 cells it is *extremely unlikely* that these cells will come from a small number of logical data blocks. It is very likely that the 1000 cells will be from different logical blocks of user data. If the average user data block length is 2KB (a low estimate) then the amount of data that must be re-transmitted is 43,000 cells. *So discarding 1000 cells has caused the retransmission of 43,000 cells.* But this only happens when the network is already congested!

It is quite clear that unless there are very effective protocols in place to prevent congestion and to limit the effects when congestion occurs this type of network just isn't going to work at all!

In practice there are several things that can be done:

1. If there are a very large number of end users on the network with no single user able to have a meaningful effect on the network load, then quite high link and node utilizations (perhaps 85%) can be approached *without* the danger of congestion situations happening. For example a network handling only voice traffic could process perhaps 50,000 simultaneous calls over a 1 Gbps link at a stable utilization of perhaps 95%. On the other hand, a network handling heterogeneous traffic containing a number of broadcast quality video sources may not be stable at much above 60% utilization.
2. Good input rate controls can ensure that no one user has the ability to cause disruption to the network.
3. Selective discard of low priority cells. Both voice and video traffic can be coded in such a way that cells essential to the basic signal are identified separately from those that contribute to a higher quality result (see 6.2.3.1, "Variable Rate Voice Coding" on page 6-15). If these cells are marked, the network can alleviate congestion by discarding less important information (and incidentally, information that won't be retransmitted in order to effect recovery).

But the best plan for a cell network is to operate it at utilizations such that congestion is extremely unlikely. In other words operate it at relatively low link utilizations - this costs money in terms of link capacity but may result in the lowest total cost network.

## 6.2 Transporting Voice in a Packet Network

According to the international standard, when voice is converted to digital form, the analog signal is sampled at the rate of 8,000 times per second (one sample every 125 μsec) and each sample is represented by 8 bits. This gives a constant bit rate of 64,000 bits per second.

The coding system is called "Pulse Code Modulation" (PCM). The basic concept of PCM is that each 8-bit sample is simply a coded measure of the amplitude of signal at the moment of sampling. But this can be improved upon by a system called "companding" (Compression/Expansion). It happens that the signal spends significantly more time in the lower part of the scale than it does at the peaks. So what we do is apply a non-linear coding so that the lower amplitude parts of the waveform are coded with more precision than the peaks. (In basic concept this is just like the "Dolby" system for improving the quality of tape recordings.) In practice, PCM is always encoded this way but the standard is different in different parts of the world. One system is called "μ-law" and the other "A-law".

In order to transport this across a packet network, individual samples must be assembled into packets. The principle is described below.

### 6.2.1 Basic Principle

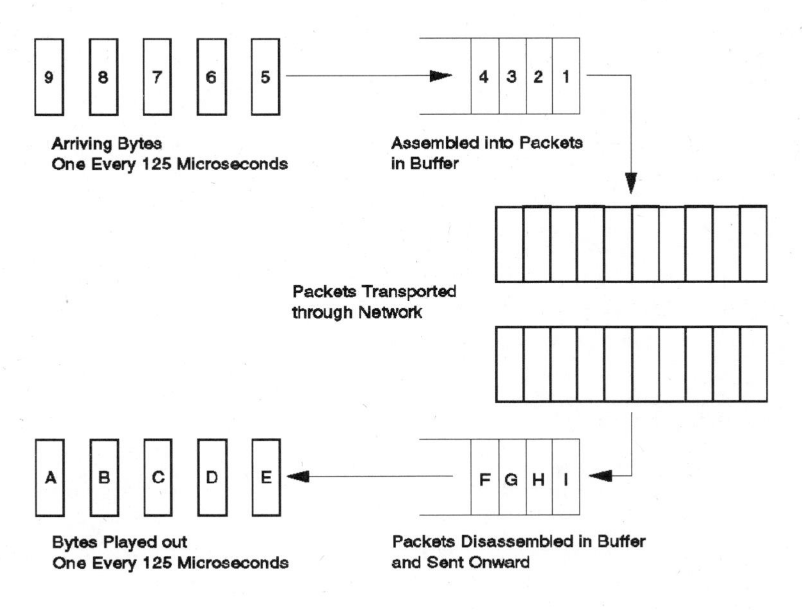


***Figure 6-3.*** *Transporting Voice over a Packet Network*

Figure 6-3 illustrates the principle of sending voice over a packet network:

1. The telephone handset generates a stream of 8-bit bytes of voice information at the rate of one every 125 μsec.
2. The digitized voice stream is received into a buffer until a block the length of a packet has been received.
3. When the packet is full it is sent into the network.
4. Once the packet is received at the other end it is disassembled and sent to the destination at the rate of one byte every 125 μsec.

A number of points should be made about this principle:

- The end-to-end delay as experienced by the end users will be the time taken to assemble a packet *plus* the transit delay through the network.
- If the network delivers packets to the destination packet disassembler at an uneven rate, then buffering will be needed at the destination to smooth out irregularities in the packet delivery rate.
- Most packet networks deliver packets at an uneven rate.
- What must happen is that when the circuit is established the receiving packet disassembler must hold the first packet for some length of time sufficient to overcome the largest possible variation in transit delay before sending anything on to the receiver.

  This increases the end-to-end delay significantly.

### 6.2.2 Transit Delay

The transit delay in a network is the time it takes a packet to travel through the network. This is made up of transmission time, propagation delay and node delay (processing and queueing delays within a node).

#### 6.2.2.1 Transit Delay Variation

The problem with most packet networks is that the transit delay varies with the instantaneous load on the network. Figure 6-4 shows the regular arrival of packets into a network and the irregular rate of delivery of those packets. As mentioned earlier, to overcome these variations in network transit time we need to have a deliberate delay at the receiver and a queue of arriving packets so that the delays are not apparent to the receiver.

There is another problem here and that is that the bit timing of the "playout" operation cannot ever be quite the same as the timing of the transmitter - unless of course, there is a universal worldwide timing reference available. In continuous transmission, there will be occasional overruns or underruns at the receiver (clock slips) due to this lack of clock synchronization.

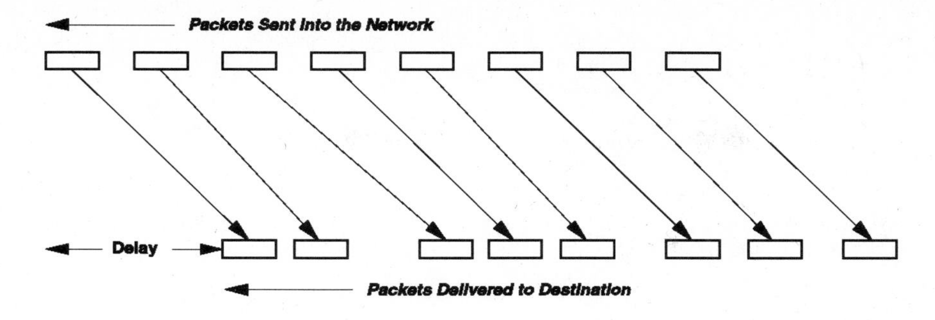


*Figure 6-4. Irregular Delivery of Voice Packets*

#### 6.2.2.2 The Effect of End-to-End Network Delay on Voice Traffic

The end-to-end delay experienced in a voice situation is made up of three components:

1. Packet Assembly Time

   The time it takes to assemble a packet or cell. Using the ATM standard 48-byte cell, we will need at least a 4-byte header (in addition to the cell header) leaving 44 bytes. At 64 Kbps (PCM code) this gives a packet assembly time of 5.5 milliseconds. For 32 Kbps the assembly time is 11 milliseconds.

   As more exotic coding schemes are employed, the packet assembly time increases as the required data rate decreases.

2. Network Transit Time

   This depends on the structure of the network but should be less than one millisecond per node traversed *plus* propagation delay at about 5.5 μsec per kilometer.

3. Delay Equalization

   This is the deliberate delay inserted immediately before the receiver in order to smooth out the effects of transit delay variation (jitter). Depending on the characteristics of the network this delay could be set somewhere between two and ten milliseconds.

The delay characteristics of the network are very important for two reasons:

1. Long transit delays cause the same effect subjectively as the well known "satellite delay". (This is 240 milliseconds one way.) Most people find holding a voice conversation over a satellite circuit difficult. The effect is one that many people never become accustomed to.

There is some argument over what is an acceptable delay. Some academics say 100 milliseconds others 150. But all agree that a one-way delay of 90 milliseconds or so causes no subjective loss of quality to most people.

2. The problem of echoes. Experience shows that when the delay is 45 milliseconds or more there is a potential problem with echoes.

   The primary source of echoes is the "hybrid" device[1] where the connection to the end user is carried over a two-wire analog circuit. Another source is reflections on the two-wire line itself.

   In the case where the connection is fully digital from one end to the other the situation is controversial. In a paper on the subject (Sriram et al. 1991) the authors argue that echo cancellation is not needed in situations where the circuit is fully digital from end to end. Other people say that there is mechanical feedback caused in some telephone handsets and that this is a source of echo that cannot be eliminated by the fully digital circuit. This is an important and unresolved issue.

   The importance rests in the fact that while echo cancellation technology is very good indeed, echo cancellers cost money.[2] In small countries where distances are short, network providers have only installed echo cancellers on international connections. A requirement for echo cancellation could add significant cost to their networks. In larger countries (such as the USA or Australia) propagation delays are so great that echo cancellation is a requirement anyway.

### 6.2.3 Voice "Compression"

There are various ways available to reduce the data rate required in a voice circuit from the 64 Kbps standard rate. A coding scheme which reduces the data rate to 32 Kbps without measurable loss of quality is called Adaptive Differential PCM (ADPCM). In concept this encodes each sample as the difference between it and the last sample, rather than as an absolute amplitude value.

There are many ways of voice compression which rely on the fact that a voice signal has considerable redundancy. (You can predict the general characteristics of the next few samples it you know the last few.)

PCM and ADPCM are very good indeed in terms of quality. It is very difficult for a listener to detect the difference between an original analog signal and one that has gone

---

1 See 2.2.5, "Echo Cancellation" on page 2-47.

2 Papers in the technical literature suggest that to build a digital echo canceller for this environment using a digital signal processor (DSP) requires a DSP of about 5 MIPS. This outweighs all the other functions performed in a digital packetizer/depacketizer (PADEP) by a ratio of five to one.

through encoding and later decoding. And because digital transmission is perfectly accurate, there is no loss in quality no matter how far the signal travels.

Nevertheless, even though we can't hear a quality loss, a small loss does take place. This was the reason that the 64 Kbps standard for digital voice was adopted in the first place. In large public networks, (such as in the USA) the transition between the existing analog system and a universal digital system was (is) expected to take a very long time. During that transition, a call through the network may go through the conversion from analog to digital and back again many times. Quality loss adds up, little by little. The standard was chosen because it was felt that there would need to be as many as *seven* conversions from analog to digital and back again along the path of some calls.

#### 6.2.3.1 Variable Rate Voice Coding

One of the ways of encoding voice looks to see when there is no actual speech and just stops sending data during the gaps.[3] This is not a new principle - it was used in the past over long distance analog circuits but is much improved using digital techniques. Speech does occur in "talk spurts" and it is half-duplex (most of the time only one person is talking). This means that about 60% of any (one-way) voice conversation consists of silence. Why transmit silence?

There are many techniques available for encoding voice in this way. In the encoded form the conversation consists of short bursts of packets. A device called a "Voice Activity Detector" (VAD) is used to turn the encoding process on or off. It also should be noted that even within a period of speech the encoded information rate is variable.

One characteristic of the VAD is that it suppresses echoes. Provided the echo is at a relatively low level, the detector will stop encoding the signal. However, this is not perfect because when both parties talk simultaneously (a not unknown phenomenon) each party could hear an echo of his/her own speech mixed up with the voice of the other speaker.

A reasonably good quality variable rate voice coding scheme should result in a peak data rate of around 20 Kbps or a little more during talk spurts and an average rate (in each direction) of around 10 Kbps.

Thus variable rate voice puts a statistical load onto the network, but variable rate coding does *not* remove the need for fast and uniform network transit delays.

#### 6.2.3.2 Encoding Priority Schemes

In 6.1, "Control of Congestion" on page 6-6, it was seen that one method of alleviating congestion is to discard packets when there is a problem. If the packets can be coded in

[3] An excellent discussion on this subject may be found in "A Blind Voice Packet Synchronization Strategy".

some way such that there are "essential" and "discardable" packets we can hope for a situation where all that happens when the network becomes congested is a graceful degradation in quality of service.

One suggested method is to code the voice packets in such a way as to put "essential" and "quality improvement" cells in different packets. This is conceptually shown in Figure 6-5. The most significant bits of each sample are placed into the same packet and the least significant bits into a different packet. The packets are marked in the header to say which packet may be discarded and which one may not.

When the packets are presented at their destination for playout (after buffering for a time), if a low priority packet is missing the decoder can extrapolate, and although the voice quality is affected the signal is still understandable.

The example shown above is intentionally very simple. In practice the coding schemes used in this way will be variable rate ones and the algorithm will be much more complex than just a selection of bits by their significance. Nevertheless, the principle is still the same.

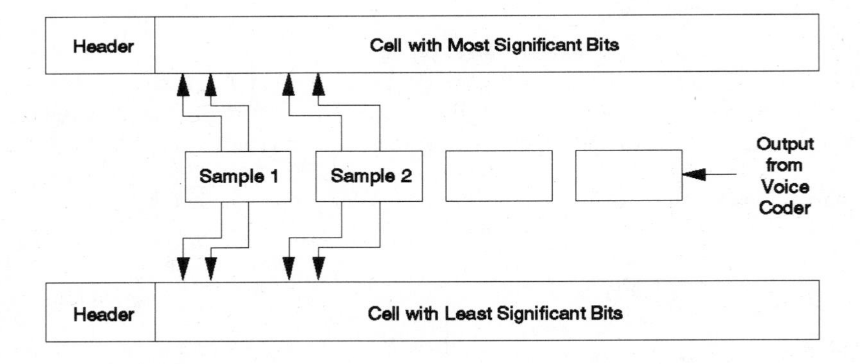


***Figure 6-5.*** *Assembly of Packets for Priority Discard Scheme*

## 6.3 Transporting Video in a Packet Network

The transmission requirements of digital video were discussed in 5.3, "Characteristics of Digital Video" on page 5-7. As far as the network is concerned video traffic is very similar to voice in the sense that both require a timing relationship to be maintained between the sender and the receiver. Packets or cells must arrive at a regular rate if the receiver is to maintain a stable picture.

There are some differences from voice, however:

- The absolute amount of bandwidth required is enormous compared with telephone quality voice transmission.
- The quality required of a video transmission varies widely with the application. Broadcast quality requires a significantly greater bandwidth than does remote education or video conference applications. Video phones require even less (as low as 128 Kbps).
- While a raw video signal is a very high constant rate, the characteristics of video make variable rate coding schemes significantly more effective than they are for voice. The problem is that the amount of variation is extreme. A still picture, properly coded, has an information content of 25 bits per second. A piece of very fast action may require an instantaneous rate of over 100 Mbps.

  Voice traffic occurs in spurts but the extremes of variation in throughput requirement are not at all the same.
- Video is much more redundant than voice and a "glitch" is perhaps less significant. A missed frame here and there will hardly be noticed.
- The natural coding of video (because of the amount of information) is in large blocks (in excess of a thousand bytes).
- Most video is not interactive. Broadcast quality video is almost never so. For one-way video we don't have the strict network delay problems that exist with voice. We can afford to have a large reassembly buffer and a playout delay of perhaps several seconds to compensate for transit delay variations in the network.
- Interactive video is usually accompanied by voice and so tighter transit delay requirements are needed, but video does not need to be exactly synchronized to the voice in any case. A 100 millisecond difference is quite acceptable. Thus we can afford a 100 ms playout buffer for video traffic even if it accompanies a voice signal.
- Encoding priority schemes such as described earlier for voice are also available for video traffic (see 6.2.3.2, "Encoding Priority Schemes" on page 6-15). This enables packets carrying "less essential" parts of the signal to be discarded by the network during periods of congestion.

The biggest problem with video is the enormous data rate that is required. If the peak data rate required by a single video user (or even a small number of users) is a significant percentage of the total capacity of the network, then there is potentially a serious congestion problem. For example, if a broadcast quality signal fully variable rate encoded required a peak data rate of 50 Mbps (even though the average might be say 10 Mbps) and the base network uses 140 Mbps internode links, (that is, a single user can take up 30% of one resource) then there is a potential congestion problem. The safe planned utilization of a network (for stable operation) in this situation might be as low as 30%.

As the number of users increases and the capacity of the network increases, the problem becomes less and less significant. One hundred broadcast-quality video users with characteristics as described above will require perhaps 1,000 Mbps *but the maximum total peak requirement might be no more than 1,200 Mbps.* In the previous example, the peak requirement of a single user was four times the average requirement. In the case of a hundred users, the peak (for practical purposes) is only 20% greater than the average. This is the result described in Appendix C.1.4, "Practical Systems" on page C-6.

## 6.4 Transporting Images

Image traffic is really not too different from traditional data traffic. Images range in size from perhaps 40 kilobytes to a few megabytes. If the user happens to be a real person at a terminal, subsecond response time is just as valuable for images as it always was for coded data transactions.

In the "paperless office" type of application, image users tend to spend more "think time" looking at the screen once it is displayed. That means that the transaction rates per terminal tend to be lower but perhaps that is because most of the experience to date is with systems that are very slow in displaying the image and the user is thereby encouraged to get all the information possible from one display before looking at the next.

In engineering graphics (CAD) applications, interaction can be as often as once a minute and the user demands subsecond response time for megabyte-sized images.

Of course, images can be compressed and ratios of four to one are about average. This reduces network load and speeds up transmission time.

Image systems are only in their infancy, but many people consider that they will become as common as interactive coded data systems are today. Storing the enormous quantity of data required is a greater problem than transmitting it (actually, transmitting it is the easy part).

An open question for the future is "what will be the effect of very high-quality displays?" It is possible today to buy color displays with a resolution of 4,000 points by 4,000 points with 256 colors and excellent quality. (The main use of these to date has been in air traffic control, military applications and in engineering design.) The picture quality is so good that it rivals a color photograph. The point here is that images with this level of resolution are many times larger (even compressed) than the typical formats of today.

If these high resolution systems become popular then there will be significantly higher requirements for the network.

## 6.5 Transporting Data in Packets or Cells

The term "packetization" refers to the process of breaking up blocks of user data into shorter blocks (called "packets") for transmission through the network.

**Packets**

The term "packet" has many different meanings and shades of meaning, depending on the context in which it is used. In recent years the term has become linked to the CCITT recommendation X.25 which specifies a data network interface. In this context a packet is a fixed maximum length (default 128 bytes) and is preceded by a packet level header which determines its routing within the network.

In the late 1960s the term "packet" came into being to denote a network in which the switching nodes stored the messages being processed in main storage instead of on magnetic disk. In the early days a "message switch" stored received data on disk before sending it on towards its destination.

In a generic sense, "packet" is often used to mean any short block of data which is part of a larger logical block.

The major advantages of breaking a block of data into packets for transmission are:

1. The transit delay through the network is much shorter than it would be if the data was transported in long blocks or "frames".
2. Queues for intermediate links within the network are more easily managed and offer a more uniform delay characteristic. See Appendix C.1.4, "Practical Systems" on page C-6. This results in less variation in the end-to-end transit time.
3. Buffer pools and I/O buffers within intermediate nodes can be smaller and are more easily managed.
4. When an error occurs on a link (whether it is an access link or a link within the network itself) then there is less data to retransmit.

There are disadvantages, however:

1. Processing time (load due to processing instructions), both in the network nodes themselves and in the attaching equipment, is greatly increased. As described elsewhere in this document, most software-driven data switching equipment takes about the same amount of processor time to switch a block regardless of the length of that block. (This is not exactly true due to the effects of I/O interference, but that is usually small.) For example if a 1 KB block is broken up into eight 128-byte packets, then the load on the network switching nodes is multiplied by eight.

The use of hardware logic for routing in cell-based switches minimizes this effect. However, even in a system where hardware-based routing is used, there is significant overhead in the end-user equipment needed for breaking the user data block up into cells and in doing "adaptation layer" processing.

2. The additional bandwidth taken up by headers. The network routing header is necessary but it takes link capacity to transmit and is an overhead. In the example above where a single block is broken into 8 smaller packets, then we have multiplied the overhead by 8. This is why packet and cell networks are designed to use very short headers. The need for very short headers is perhaps the primary reason for using connection-oriented protocols.

3. If the network is designed to do its congestion control by discarding data, and if error recovery is done by the re-transmission of whole blocks then there is a very nasty "multiplier effect" which can severely impact network performance. This is discussed in 6.1.2, "Congestion Control in Cell Networks" on page 6-9.

## 6.5.1 Transit Delay

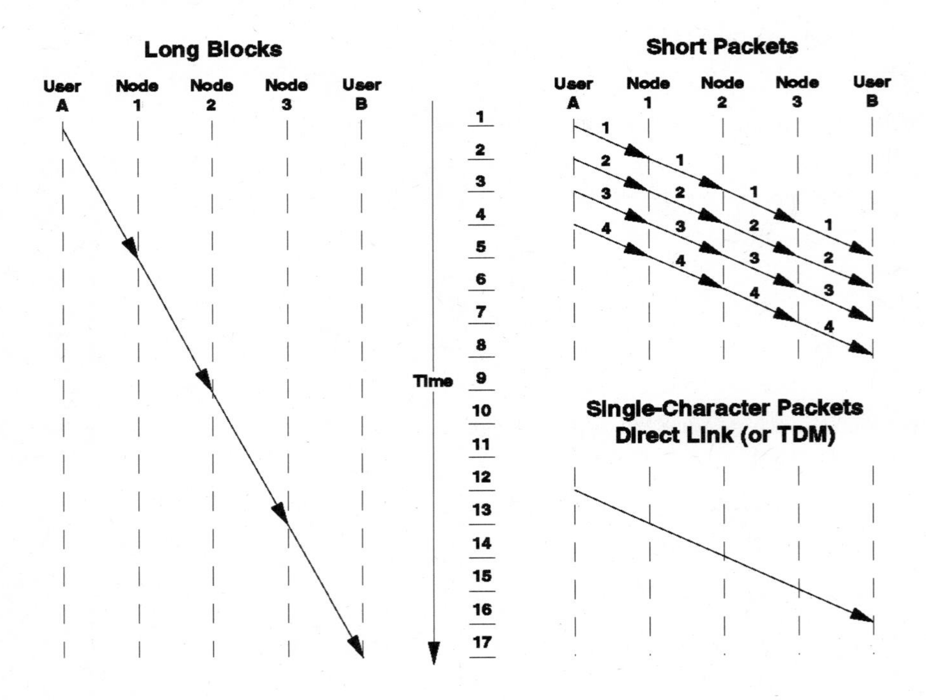


*Figure 6-6. Effect of Packetization on Transit Time through a 3-Node Network*

Assume User A in Figure 6-6 has a block of 1024 bytes to send through a 3-node network to user B. Assume also that the link speeds are the same, the nodes are infinitely fast, there is zero propagation delay, and that there is no other traffic.

- User A sends to Node 1 and takes (for our discussion purposes) 4 units of time.
- Node 1 sends to Node 2 also taking 4 units of time.
- Node 2 sends to Node 3.
- And so on until the message arrives at User B.

The total time taken has been 4 times 4 units = 16 units of time.

Now, if the 1024-byte block is broken up into four 256-byte packets, then the following scenario will occur:

- User A sends the first packet to Node 1, taking 1 unit of time.
- Node 1 sends this packet to Node 2, but while this is happening User A is sending packet 2 to node 1.
- While User A is sending the third packet, Node 1 is sending a packet to Node 2 and Node 2 is sending a packet to Node 3.
- This happens through the network until the last packet arrives at User B.

It is obvious from the diagram that sending the message as small packets has reduced the network transit time to 7 units compared with the 16 units needed without packetization. This is due to the effect of overlapping the sending of parts of the message through the network.

The section of the figure headed "Direct Link" refers to what happens in the limit as we keep reducing the packet size. When we finally get to a packet size of one character, we have a network throughput equivalent to a direct link or TDM operation of the nodes. Transit time in this case is 4 time units.

## 6.5.2 The Isochronous Debate

Multimedia systems place a unique demand on the network because they require the synchronization of various types of network traffic. These requirements were discussed in 5.4, "Characteristics of Multimedia Applications" on page 5-13. Some people believe that the only networking system that will meet the requirements of multimedia applications (at least in the immediate future) is isochronous transport. Isochronous data transfer offers the following benefits:

1. Eliminates network-induced skew and jitter.
2. Provides a stable method of clocking end-to-end.
3. Minimizes propagation delays.

But there are also disadvantages:

1. Compressed video is a variable rate data stream. When fitting a variable rate stream into a fixed rate pipe, skew and jitter are introduced by the workstations. In order to combat skew and jitter, buffers are introduced into the workstations, and these cause a significant increase in latency.

2. A fixed rate "pipe" allocates a fixed amount of capacity and for most of the time it will be not used. This is inefficient.

3. Because there is a fixed rate connection between workstations, in order to communicate with other workstations you have to have multiple connections, or a circuit-switched architecture. This significantly impacts the flexibility of the system.

In order to deliver isochronous capability to the desktop you need a TDM-based WAN and either a TDM-based LAN or a TDM-based link connection (such as ISDN_PR) to the desktop. If you are using a LAN this means the use of FDDI_II or "Isochronous Ethernet" (see 13.4, "Isochronous Ethernet" on page 13-23). Of course isochronous transport has the significant (non-technical) advantages:

1. It is well known and understood in the field.

2. It is predictable and controllable.

3. Existing WAN systems universally use isochronous approaches internally (indeed SDH is currently being installed in many countries as the primary WAN backbone).

4. Existing voice and video products are based on isochronous transport and can easily be modified to operate over an isochronous LAN architecture.

Other people, while agreeing with the requirements, believe that ATM (and even frame relay) will be able to meet the requirements even in the short term.

Fast packet networking (such as ATM) has two major advantages:

1. ATM offers a "variable bandwidth" connection through the network. This means that (provided the connection to the end user is fast enough) inherently variable rate information such as compressed video can be handled at the variable rate. So, although ATM introduces more network latency than isochronous transmission, the actual end-to-end latency can be much less (because the need for buffering in the workstations is minimized).

2. While even a well-constructed ATM network will introduce some skew and jitter in the transmission, it is believed that this can be minimized.

   It should be noted that most of the ATM UNI (user/network interface) definitions under consideration use framed data transfer at the physical layer. The aim of this is to allow for the delivery of a consistent network clock (via the frame timing) from end-to-end so that problems of underrun, overrun, and jitter are minimized.

3. Because ATM usage of bandwidth is statistical and demand-based, you don't waste capacity when there is nothing to send (someone else can use it).

4. You can have multiple virtual connections in operation simultaneously to the same workstation *without* needing to allocate fixed capacity to each. This is a much more efficient use of bandwidth.

On this one, the jury has not yet even begun to consider its verdict.

## 6.6 Connection-Oriented versus Connectionless Networks

One distinguishing characteristic of a network (or network protocol) is the presence or absence of a "connection" between the end users. When a connection is present the network is called "connection-oriented" and when there is no connection the network is called "connectionless".

After 30 years of building data networks, this is still an issue on which there is considerable disagreement and which can evoke strong feelings.

#### 6.6.1.1 Connectionless Networks

In a connectionless network, a network node does not keep any information relating to interactions currently in progress between end users of the network. Every data block transmitted must be prefixed by the full network address of both its origin and its destination.

> Sometimes (such as in the pre-1979 versions of SNA[4] ), the network address takes the form of a structured binary number, which can be used relatively easily to determine the appropriate routing for the data. Sometimes (such as in typical LAN networks), the network address has no meaningful structure that is usable for routing purposes.

Characteristics of connectionless networks are as follows:

- When a data block arrives the network node must calculate on which outbound link to send the data towards its destination. This decision may be very complex and compute intensive or very simple, depending on how much information about the destination is available within the destination address field.

---

[4] In early SNA each node had a number. When a frame was routed by a node there was a single table showing which link traffic for a given node number must be sent on. The switching node knew nothing about routes or about connections.

In the extreme case where the destination address contains no information at all about its location (as is the case with LAN addresses), the node may need to keep tables relating every known destination address to its real location in the network. This is the case with “transparent bridges” between LANs.

Usually, the destination address will be structured in some way such that it can be related to knowledge of the network's topology kept within the node. For example, the network address may contain a destination node number and the switching node may contain a network map so that it may calculate the best outbound path on which to forward the data block. This process can be very simple (such as in the first version of SNA) or very complex (such as in ARPANET or TCP/IP).

- If the network allows multiple paths to be used for individual data blocks, then blocks will arrive in a different sequence from the sequence in which they were delivered to the network.

  If blocks can be delivered out of sequence, then a much more complex end-to-end protocol will be required to resequence them before presentation to the end user.

- The header prefix required in a connectionless situation is typically much longer than for a connection-oriented network. This affects the efficiency of the network as headers take up link capacity and require transmission time. This may or may not be important, depending on the length of the data blocks being handled.
- There is no need for a connection establishment sequence for one end user to send data to another. To send data, an end user just has to put the destination address onto the front of the message and send it. This saves time and overhead.
- Implementation of flow and congestion controls in a connectionless network is much more difficult than in a connection-oriented one because individual connections (though they of course exist) are unknown by the network and thus cannot be controlled.

#### 6.6.1.2 Connection-Oriented Networks

In a connection-oriented network, once a connection is established, there is no need to place a destination address in the block header every time a data block is sent. All that is needed is an identifier to specify which connection is to be used for this block.

There are many ways of constructing connection-oriented networks. For a description of the method used in SNA APPN see 6.7.4, “Logical ID Swapping” on page 6-31.

Characteristics of connection-oriented networks are as follows:

- The connection must be established somehow. Permanent connections (such as PVCs in X.25) are typically established by a system definition procedure. Temporary connections (such as SVCs in X.25) are typically established by placing a “call”.

Setting up a call can take considerable processing overhead in network nodes and can often take a significant delay (such as five seconds).

- Congestion control is easier than for connectionless networks because network nodes can regulate the flow on individual connections.
- Data switching is usually (but not always) significantly more efficient than for connectionless networks because the onward route of the data is predetermined and therefore does not need to be calculated.
- When a link or a node becomes inoperative (goes down), connections that were passing through the affected link or node are typically lost. A new connection must be established through a different route. This takes time and usually disrupts the connection at the end-user level.

  Connectionless networks typically reroute traffic automatically around link or node failures.

#### 6.6.1.3 Connection-Oriented Connectionless Networks

In a series of token-ring LANs connected by "source routing" bridges, we see the case of a connection existing over a fixed route where the individual switches (the bridges) do not know about connections at all. This principle is described in 6.7.3.1, "Source-Routing LAN Bridges" on page 6-29.

The IBM experimental high-speed packet switch called "Paris" uses a method of switching similar to that described above for TRN bridges. (See the description in 11.2, "Packetized Automatic Routing Integrated System (Paris)" on page 11-16.) Paris is different because the data switching part has no record of the existence of connections. The routing decision is made by the switching nodes completely on information present in the header of every data message. (The control processor in each node does know about connections passing through the node's switching part, as it allocates capacity and monitors throughput for congestion control purposes.)

Connections do exist in both these systems but in either system it is only the source node that knows about it.

#### 6.6.1.4 Connections across Connectionless Networks

Consider the diagram in Figure 6-7 on page 6-26. This is an important case in practical networks.

In the example there is a connection between the two end users. This connection is known about and supported by nodes A and B, but the switching nodes in the network do *not* know that a connection exists. The end-to-end function holds the network address and the status of its partner end-to-end function and looks after data integrity and secure delivery, etc.

What exists here is really a connection-oriented network built on top of a connectionless one.

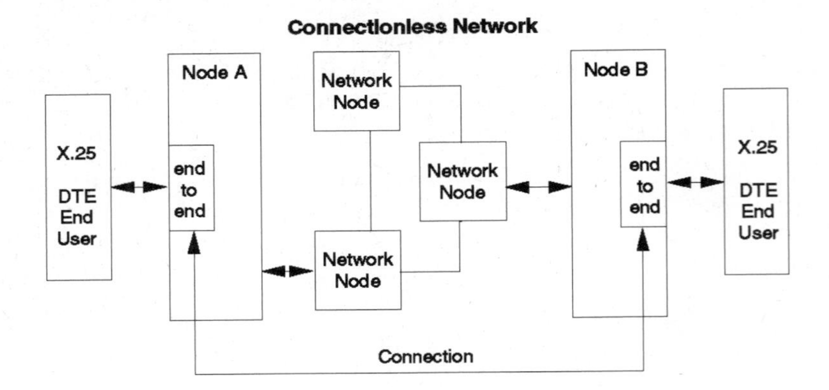


*Figure 6-7. A Connection across a Connectionless Network*

#### 6.6.1.5 A Connection Is Always Present

Well, almost. In an application sense, it is very rare for communication to take place without a connection being present logically, even if the components of the network sometimes do not know about it.

#### 6.6.1.6 Connections in SNA Networks

In SNA the only entity that can send or receive data is the logical unit (LU). Data is *always* sent from one LU to another on a connection called a "session".

But inside SNA networks sessions are handled differently:

1. In the first versions of SNA, network nodes (always IBM 3705s running the Network Control Program, NCP) selected the link on which to forward a given data block by the binary "subarea number" (really destination node number) within the destination address field of the data header.

   Since the network was (and still is) constrained to deliver data blocks in sequence, there could be one and only one possible path from any given origin node to any given destination.

2. Since about 1980, SNA "subarea" networks (networks in which the real network address is structured such that the node number is present as a subfield) have been connection-oriented. That is, there are predefined routes through the network which are known by each network node. Sessions are still unknown to the network nodes (or, more correctly, to the transmission network component of the network nodes)

but are carried on connections called virtual routes (VRs). VRs map to explicit routes (ERs). The destination subarea (node) number together with the ER number in the frame header is used to determine the routing of incoming data blocks.

The routing headers used by this form of SNA are 26 bytes long comprising origin and destination network addresses (each of 48 bits) and Explicit Route and Virtual Route numbers.

3. SNA APPN networks select a new route for each end-user session through the network. The APPN network nodes keep connection tables which record a fixed (for the duration of a session) relationship between a session identifier (called an LFSID) on one link with a session identifier on another link. For a more detailed explanation of this form of routing, see 6.7.4, "Logical ID Swapping" on page 6-31.

   This means that the routing header for SNA APPN is only 6 bytes (two of which are the LFSID).

## 6.7 Route Determination within the Network

There are two aspects to routing within a network:

1. Determining what the route for a given connection shall be.
2. Actually switching (routing) the packet within a switching node.

There are many methods of determining a route through a network. So long as this can be performed before the connection is set up (or during the connection establishment) it doesn't matter much to the switching nodes. For very high throughput, the critical item is that the switching element must be able to decide where to route an incoming packet in a few microseconds.

### 6.7.1 Fixed Route Definition

This is the method used by SNA since 1979. A set of predetermined routes are manually defined either when the system is set up or added "dynamically" (during network operation) later. Dynamic addition consists of adding a new route definition by operator command.

Frames carry a header with a route number (in the case of SNA a destination node number and a "virtual route" number). Determining a route is a very simple and fast process - all the processor has to do is compare the route number in the frame header with a routing table.

The great advantage of this technique is that it is probably the most efficient software switching technique available. It requires less processing in the switch than any other available method. The disadvantage is that determining routing tables is a difficult and complex procedure. (Complexity increases exponentially with the size of the network.)

This requires a significant amount of work from support staff. In addition it is not very flexible.

The technique is gradually being replaced by the label swapping technique (APPN) or the newer ANR technique (HPR).

### 6.7.2 Dynamic Node-by-Node Routing

In this method there is no route determined when the connection is set up. This is due to the fact that there is no connection. Each packet is sent into the network with its full destination address imbedded in the header. Each node knows the current network topology and loadings and is able to decide where and on which path the packet should be directed.

This process can be very fast (for a software technique). It is the principle behind "ARPANET" routing and that of TCP/IP. Special switches exist which use this technique and achieve throughputs of 50,000 packets per second.

But this is a software-based technique. It is very difficult to see how it could be efficiently implemented in hardware. Packet rates of millions per second are not likely to be achieved by this method any time soon.

### 6.7.3 Source Routing

Source routing is an important technique for high-speed networking because it minimizes the processing necessary for routing a packet (frame or cell) in an intermediate node. The originating node (or interfacing function) is responsible for calculating the route that a packet must take through the network.

The rationale here is that devices at the end points of the network (such as user workstations) do not have the throughput requirements of intermediate nodes but typically have significant compute power available. Thus it is considered to be more efficient (cost effective) to place the compute load related to routing in the end station.

Using the source routing technique the sending workstation appends (in the network header) an ordered list of nodes and links (a routing vector) to every packet sent. This routing vector is used by intermediate nodes to direct the packet towards its destination.

Source routing is currently used in several situations:

**Token-Ring Bridging**

> The most common use of source routing is for bridging token-rings. Here, additional logic is used in each attached workstation but the bridges are typically simple, very high in throughput, and low in cost. In contrast, "transparent

bridges" (used typically for Ethernet traffic) place significant load on the bridges but require no change to the software in the workstations.

**APPN**

While APPN uses the label swapping technique for data routing, it uses source routing for setting up connections (sessions) through the network. (The BIND command is source routed.)

**Automatic Network Routing (ANR)**

ANR has been studied in two IBM Research Projects (Paris and plaNET) and is used now in High-Performance Routing (HPR), a recent extension of APPN. (See 11.2.2, "Automatic Network Routing (ANR)" on page 11-18.)

In order to use source routing the sending node must be able to discover enough of the network topology to calculate a route. This could be done either by a discovery process (such as sending a route setup message along the physical path of a new connection) or by keeping (or having access to) an up-to-date topology database for the whole network.

A drawback of this method is that the routing vector in the packet header takes some storage and is an overhead. But this is quite small and the benefits of being able to make a fast routing decision outweigh the small increase in bandwidth overhead.

### 6.7.3.1 Source-Routing LAN Bridges

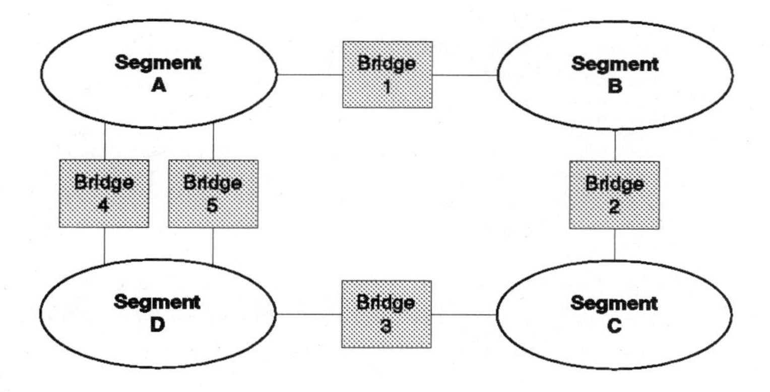


***Figure 6-8.*** *Topology of a Multisegment LAN*

Source routing is the method used in IBM Token-Ring Networks to control the route a frame travels through a multisegment LAN. Source-routing bridges put the responsibility of "navigating" through a multisegment LAN on the end stations. A route through a multisegment token-ring LAN is described by a sequence of ring and bridge numbers placed in the routing information field of a token-ring frame.[5] The routing information field in a MAC frame, if present, is part of the MAC header of a token-ring frame. The presence of routing information means the end stations are aware of, and may make decisions based upon, the routes available in a multisegment LAN. By contrast, transparent bridges take the responsibility for routing frames through a multisegment LAN, which leads to more complex bridges, and end stations that are unaware of whether they are bridged, and if they are, what route they are taking.

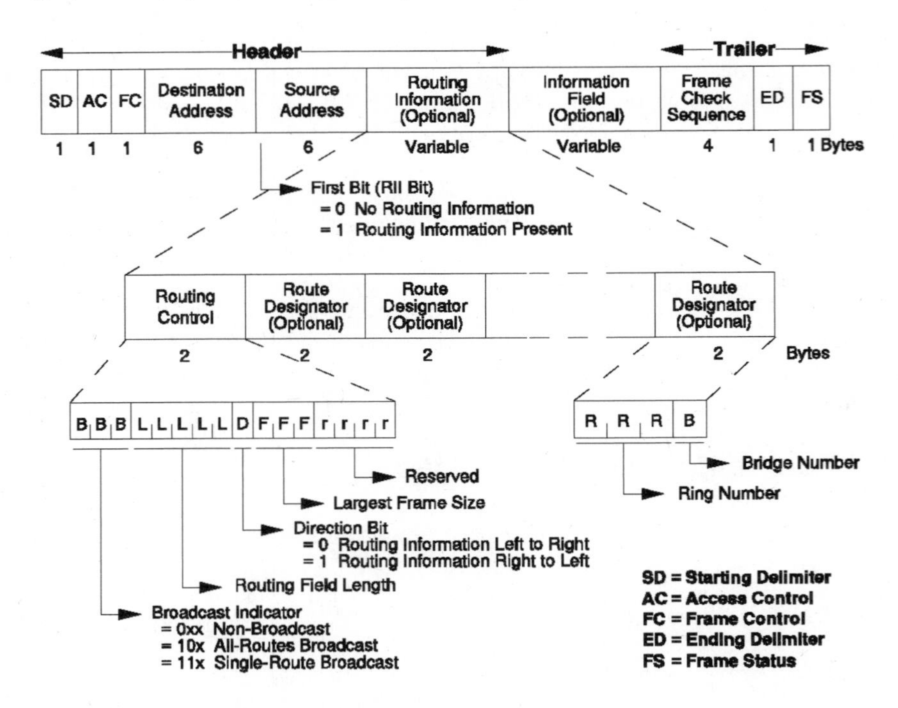


***Figure 6-9.*** *Routing Information of a Token-Ring Frame*

Figure 6-9 shows how the routing information is carried by a token-ring frame. If the Routing Information Indicator (RII) bit (the high order bit) of the source MAC address is set, then the frame contains a routing information field.[6] The routing control field contains at minimum a 2-byte control field, and optionally contains a number[7] of 2-byte route designator fields. Each route designator field contains a 3-digit ring number and a

[5] Each ring segment in a LAN has a ring number assigned when the bridges are configured. On an active ring it is held by the Ring Parameter Server management function. Bridges are also given numbers when they are configured. Together, the ring numbers and bridge numbers, known as route designators, are used to map a path through a multisegment LAN.

1-digit bridge number. Together they map out a route through a multisegment token-ring LAN. Details on the other fields in Figure 6-9 may be found in the *IBM Token-Ring Architecture Reference*.

When a frame containing a routing information indicator is sent, all bridges on the LAN segment will examine the frame. The bridge will copy a broadcast frame as long as it hasn't already been on the bridged ring segment (the ring segment attached to the other half of the bridge) and it meets the adapter's single-route broadcast frame criteria. If the frame is a non-broadcast frame, the bridge interprets any routing information either left-to-right or right-to-left, depending on the value set in the direction bit and then forwards the frame if appropriate.

The broadcast indicators in the routing control field also control the way a bridge treats the frame. The types of broadcast frames are:

**Non-Broadcast,** also known as Routed frames. The frame will travel a specific route defined in the routing information field.

**All-Routes Broadcast,** also known as General Broadcast frames. The frame will be forwarded across the bridge provided certain conditions are met.

**Single-Route Broadcast,** also known as Limited Broadcast frames. The frame will be forwarded by all bridges that are configured to forward single-route broadcast frames. If the network is configured properly, a single-route broadcast frame will appear once on each LAN segment.

Typically all-routes broadcast and single-route broadcast frames are used to discover a route during session setup. Once the route is established, non-broadcast frames are generally used.

### 6.7.4 Logical ID Swapping

Logical ID swapping is an internal network technique for routing data through a network of packet switched nodes. While the technique is widely used in existing networks and not specifically a high-speed technique, it is regarded by many as an appropriate technique for supporting high-speed networks supporting frame relay and ATM. A connection-oriented technique (see 6.6, "Connection-Oriented versus Connectionless Networks" on page 6-23), it is used widely by many different networking systems.

---

[6] The high order bit in the destination MAC address is used to indicate a group address. A group address field would be redundant in the source field because token-ring frames can only originate from a uniquely identified adapter.

[7] IBM implementation of the IEEE 802.5 standard limits the number of bridge hops to seven.

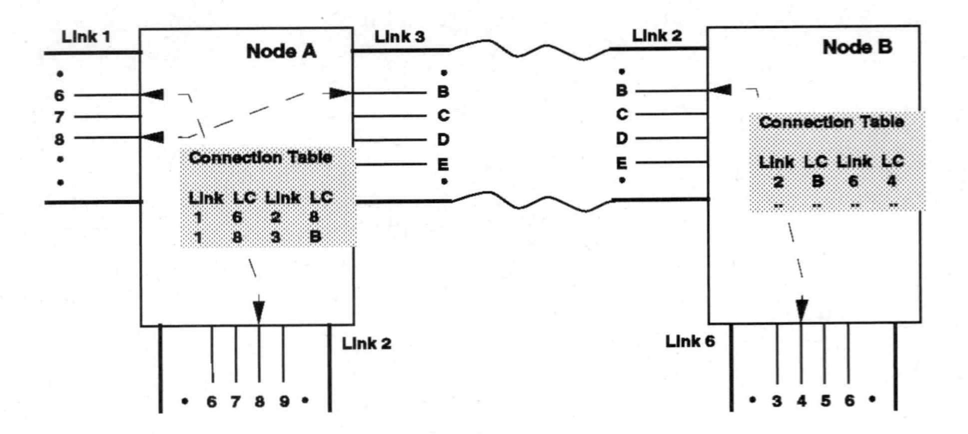


*Figure 6-10. Data Networking by Logical ID Swapping*

Notice that logical ID swapping is an *internal* process for routing packets or cells within a network. These internal network protocols are typically *not* specified by international standards.

This technique is used in IBM APPN networks and in a number of proprietary networking protocols. It may also be used in networks supporting:

- X.25
- Frame relay
- Asynchronous Transfer Mode (ATM)

Networks that use this technique typically multiplex many connections (or sessions) on a link using some form of logical "channelization". That is, each block (or frame) sent on the link has a header which includes an arbitrary number identifying which logical connection that this block (or frame) belongs to. Systems vary in the rules governing how the number is allocated and how a path through the system is defined but the principle is the same.

- In APPN, the logical channel identifier is called a Local Form Session Identifier (LFSID) and is located in the format 2 (FID_2) transmission header. The connection is called a session.
- In X.25 the logical connection is called a virtual circuit. The identifier is called a logical channel and is contained within the packet header.
- In frame relay the identifier is called the DLCI (Data Link Connection Identifier) and this is located in the address field of the link header. The connection is called a virtual link.

- In ATM the identifier is called a Virtual Channel Identifier (VCI) and it is situated in the cell header.

### 6.7.4.1 Data Transfer

In Figure 6-10 on page 6-32 there is a logical connection between an end-user system connected to link 1 (ID 8) on node A and another end-user system attached to link 6 (ID 4) on node B. In operation the procedure works as follows:[8]

1. The end-user system places data to be sent on a link to the network (in the example, link 1 on node A).
2. The user data has a header appended to it which contains a logical channel identifier (in the example, lc 6).
3. Node A receives the block and looks at the header. It finds that the received block has lc 6.
4. The node then looks at the connection table for lc 6 on link 1 (the node knows which link the data was received on).
5. The node finds that lc 6 on link 1 is connected to lc B on link 3.
6. The node then changes the lc ID within the data header from 6 to B.
7. The node then queues the data for transmission on link 3.
8. When node B receives the data it sees that it belongs to lc B. (Notice here that both nodes know the same lc number at each end of the link because it is the same link. The lc number only has meaning in the context of the single link between node A and node B.)
9. Node B then repeats the process changing the ID to “4” and sending it out on link 6.

### 6.7.4.2 Determining the Route

There are many ways of determining the route and setting up the connection tables.

- It could be done by a central node and updates sent to each node along the path when the connection is set up.
- It could be determined by the originating node (or a node providing route calculation support to the originating node). If this is done, the route can be sent out in a special message which travels along the specified route and signals the control processor in each node to set up the connection tables.

  This is exactly what happens in APPN. In APPN, when a session is set up, a routing vector is included in the connection (session) setup packet (the BIND). As the BIND

---

8 Another example in this document is ID swapping used with frame relay.

progresses through the system, each node in the path builds a connection table entry for the new session.

- It can be done in a distributed way by allowing each node that receives the setup message to calculate the next hop along the path.
- It may be predefined through a system definition process.

The point about this is that connection setup is relatively infrequent (compared to the routing of data blocks) and is not too time critical. A connection setup time of 200 milliseconds (or even a second or two) is quite tolerable in even a very high-speed network.

Of course, in most systems the tables do not exist in the form suggested in the example - they will be set up in whichever way is most efficient within the using system.

#### 6.7.4.3 Characteristics

The system has the following characteristics.

**Minimal Bandwidth Overhead**

The ID part of the header is the only essential field for this method of routing. The systems described above use between 10 and 20 bits for this field.

**Fixed Route(s)**

Frames (packets, cells, etc.) flow on the fixed predetermined route. This means that frames will (in most systems) arrive in the same sequence in which they were sent.

**Efficient Switching**

Relatively few instructions are required to perform the switching function. In order to route a packet towards its destination reference must be made to the connection tables. So whatever process performs the switching must have very fast access to the tables. In addition, when a new connection is set up or an old one is terminated the tables must be updated. (The database of network topology and loadings can, of course, be maintained quite separately.)

In a software-based system (traditional packet switch) this is no problem at all as the function that maintains the tables shares the same storage as the code that does the switching.

In a system using a hardware-based routing mechanism, this mechanism must have very fast (sub-microsecond) access to the tables. The updating function must also have access though its demands for access are not as critical (it can wait a bit).

This means that in a hardware implementation you need to have a shared set of tables that is instantly accessible to the hardware switch and also easily accessible from the control processor.

This can increase the cost of the implementation above that of the ANR technique. (See 11.2.2, "Automatic Network Routing (ANR)" on page 11-18.)

**Requires Connection Setup**

The techniques require that the connection tables be set up and maintained dynamically. This is a processing overhead in each node and makes "datagram" transport quite inefficient.

## 6.8 End-to-End Network Protocols

When you increase the speed of the links in a network or even the throughput rate of the network nodes one major factor does not change - propagation delay. (Sadly, we can't increase the speed of light - at the present level of technology anyway.)

Network layer protocols perform the following functions:

- Data error detection (if the underlying network does not detect errors in the data).
- Data error recovery by retransmission (if the underlying network does not guarantee the integrity of the data).
- Recovery from lost frames or packets.
- Packet or frame resequencing (if the underlying network does not guarantee the delivery of packets in the sequence in which they were delivered to the network).

Existing network protocols that perform the above functions are generally viewed to have too many "turnarounds" in them. This applies to OSI (layer 4), TCP (especially) and most other common end-to-end protocols. An excellent description of this problem may be found in *A Survey of Light-Weight Transport Protocols for High-Speed Networks.*

The result of this is that as we speed up the underlying packet network, application throughput (especially for interactive applications) does not improve very much in many cases. When we have a high-speed network we would like it to give better performance than traditional packet networks have delivered in the past.

Considerable work is proceeding in the research community aimed at producing an efficient end-to-end (layer four) protocol for use with high-speed networks. One such proposal is called XTP. (A good description of XTP may be found in: *The Xpress Transfer Protocol (XTP) - A Tutorial.*)

The primary object of a good network layer protocol for the high-speed environment is to minimize the number of "turnarounds" (when a sender must wait for an acknowledgment from the receiver) in the protocol. To do this the following principles may be employed:

- Optimism. Assume that the underlying node hardware and links are very reliable. Errors will occur and they must be recovered, but they will be very infrequent.
- Assume that the user (program) at the other end of the connection is there and ready to receive all that we send. Don't use a "handshaking protocol" to find out first.
- Try to put as many small packets into one block as reasonably possible (if your network can process large frames).
- Design the network protocol for fast connection setup and termination. Perhaps "piggyback" the first data packet onto the control packet that sets up the connection.
- Clearly define the interface to higher layer (session and presentation layer) functions and minimize the number of interface crossings necessary to transfer a block of data.

## 6.9 SNA in a High-Speed Network

SNA is unique in that it uses a minimal network layer protocol, preferring to put the error recovery functions into the network. At the network layer SNA assumes that the network it is running over is very stable and reliable.

When SNA networks are run "over the top" of other networks (such as X.25 or frame relay or a LAN) then we must do something to make sure that the underlying network is very reliable. (This was a design decision in the early days of SNA, to put the reliability (and its attendant cost) into the backbone part of the network and avoid the cost of providing extensive network layer function. At the time, this was optimal from a cost point of view.)

In the case of X.25, an X.25 virtual circuit is regarded as a link in SNA. But it is a special link. No end-to-end link protocol is run over it because of the cost and performance implications. This means that to run SNA over a packet network (X.25), that network must be reliable. If the network loses data on a virtual circuit and signals this to SNA, SNA will see this as the unrecoverable loss of a link and all sessions travelling on that link are immediately terminated. Application-level error recovery is then necessary in order to resume operation.

In some SNA systems there is an optional network layer protocol (called "ELLC") which does give full error recovery over an unreliable network connection. This was developed in the early days of packet networks and today these networks are generally very reliable and ELLC is considered unnecessary.

When SNA is run over a LAN network or a frame relay network, where the loss of a frame or two occasionally is a normal event, an end-to-end protocol is used to stabilize the connection. This is called IEEE 802.2 and is a "link layer" protocol as far as the ISO model is concerned. Nevertheless, when an end-to-end protocol is run across a network in order to recover from network errors, it is just an academic point to discuss which OSI layer is being obeyed. The function here is network layer class 4 regardless of how it is performed.

The big problem with running SNA over a disjoint packet network (even a LAN) is that the network management and directory functions are not integrated with those of SNA. This means that you run two networks, SNA and something else, underneath where neither network knows about or can coordinate properly with, the other.

If a fast packet switching architecture was to be fully integrated into SNA then a different structure would be possible.[9] The "transmission network" part of SNA could be replaced with a fast packet switching architecture. In addition to the minimal adaptation function, a full network layer would need to be interposed between the SNA end users and the network to maintain the stability of the service to the end user. This is exactly what is done with LAN and frame relay support now but done somewhere higher up in the protocol stack. A system like this offers the potential benefit that both the network management and directory systems of SNA, and the underlying fast packet network, could be integrated and work together providing a single unified network interface to the end user.

## 6.10 A Theoretical View

Packet switching architectures may be better understood by comparing the functions performed by the protocols against one another. ATM requires that nodes implement only the functions of the three sublayers of the physical layer. Other packet switching techniques require more complexity, as shown in the architectural model given in Figure 6-11 on page 6-38. In general the higher you go up the stack the more complex processing in a network transit node becomes.

[9] IBM has not announced any plan for doing what is suggested here. The discussion is included in order to bring into perspective the interaction of SNA with high-speed networks. IBM cannot comment on future plans.

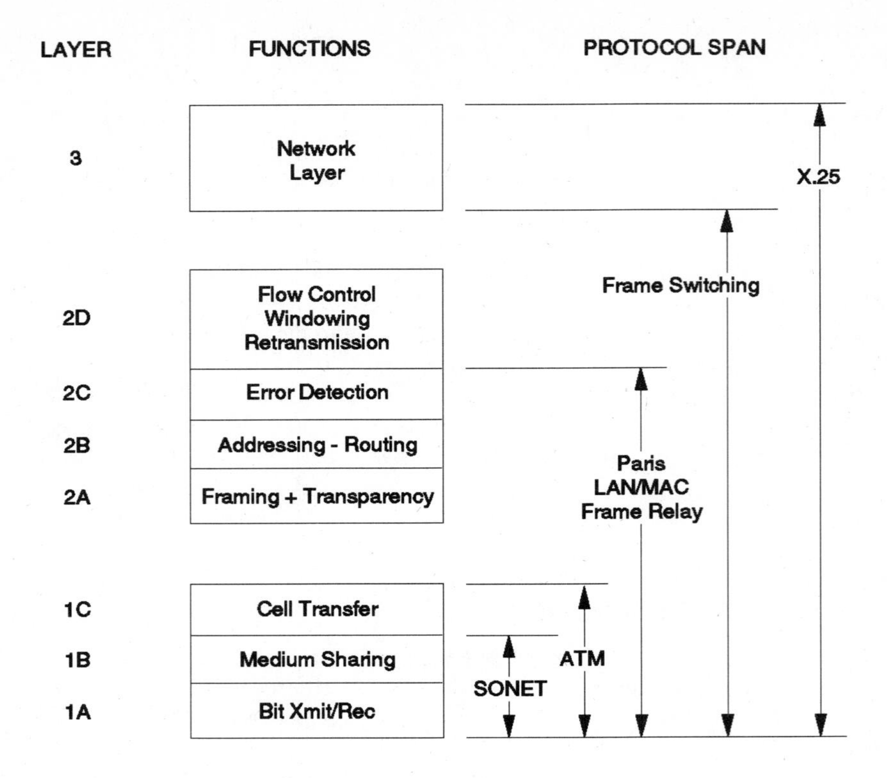


*Figure 6-11. Protocol Span of Packet Networking Techniques*

The degree of complexity can be best understood if the layer 1 and 2 functions needed in non-ATM packet service are broken up into sublayers.[10] If the functions performed by HDLC/SDLC link control are broken up in this way we get the following structure:

**Sublayer 1A**

This layer adapts to the medium characteristics, transmission coding and things like bit timing and jitter tolerance.

**Sublayer 1B**

This is the MAC function when many devices are connected to a shared medium. In SDLC link control this is the control of "multidropping"; in a LAN architecture it is the physical (but not logical) control of transmission of data onto the shared medium. In Sonet this is the TDM function.

---

[10] The sublayering concept described here is due to Vorstermans et. al. 1988. See bibliography.

**Sublayer 1C**

This is the ATM cell transfer function. It doesn't exist in traditional DLC designs.

**Sublayer 2A**

This layer builds the frame that will be passed to the physical layer. Addition of the framing flags (B'01111110') and the provision of transparency (by bit "stuffing") is done here.

**Sublayer 2B**

This function is responsible for routing the data to different destinations (that is, the address part of the header).

**Sublayer 2C**

This function provides the Frame Check Sequence (FCS) bytes at the end of the frame and is responsible for error detection.

**Sublayer 2D**

This layer handles error recovery by retransmission and link level flow control (by window rotation).

As mentioned elsewhere in this document, ATM requires that only the physical layer be implemented in network nodes.

Different networking techniques use different sublayer functions:

**X.25** requires the full implementation of all three layers: layer 1 (without the ATM sublayer), layer 2 (LAPB) and layer 3 (Packet Protocol).

**Frame Switching** requires the full implementation of layer 2 (that is, sublayers 2A, 2B, 2C, and 2D), thus including the complexity of retransmission, windowing, and flow control.

**Frame Relay, LAN/MAC and Paris** all provide much the same level of function. These require sublayers 1A (optionally 1B) along with sublayers 2A, 2B and 2C.

**ATM** (without considering the AAL) uses all three sublayers of layer 1. With the AAL it is equivalent to frame relay.

**Sonet** is a TDM system and uses only the function of the first two sublayers of layer 1.

## 6.11 Summary of Packet Network Characteristics

The following table summarizes the characteristics of the packet networking techniques described in this document and compares them with two traditional packet networking technologies (APPN and X.25).

*Table 6-1. Packet Switching Technology Comparison*

| Function | APPN | X.25 Packet Switching | Frame Relay | Cell Relay (ATM) | ANR |
|---|---|---|---|---|---|
| Throughput (typical) | 500 to 30,000 packets per second | 500 to 30,000 packets per second | 1,000 to 100,000 frames per second | 10 to 100 million cells per second | 100,000 to 500,000 frames per second |
| Access Speed | up to 2 Mbps | up to 64 Kbps | up to 2 Mbps | E3 (35 Mbps) + | E3 (35 Mbps) + |
| Packet Size | Variable | 128 bytes | Variable | 48 + 5 bytes | Variable |
| Standards Body | n/a | CCITT | CCITT and ANSI | CCITT | n/a |
| Standards Approval | n/a | 1980 | 1990 | 1992 (frame), 1996 (service) | n/a |
| Bandwidth Management | Flow Controls | Network Dependent | Network Dependent | Input Rate Control | Input Rate Control |
| Routing | Label Swap-ping | Not Specified | Not Specified | Label Swap-ping | Source |
| Error Detection | Full | Full | Full | Header Only | Full |
| Error Action | Recovery by Retrans-mission | Network Dependent | Discard Frame | Discard Cell if Bad Header | Discard Frame |
| Real Time Voice | No | No | No | Yes | Yes |
| Full Motion Video | No | No | No | Yes | Yes |
| Switched Calls | Yes | Yes | Not Yet | Yes | Yes |

# 6.12 High-Speed Packet and Cell Switching Architectures

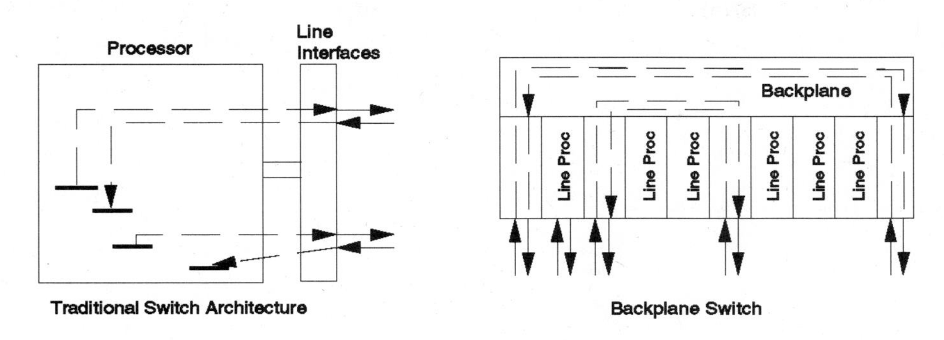


*Figure 6-12. Two Approaches to Packet Switch Design*

A major challenge in the implementation of very high-speed networks is in the design of the packet[11] switch itself. There are many possible approaches but the serial multistage design has the greater potential throughput - although there are some problems in detailed construction.

## 6.12.1 Traditional Approach

This approach is very well known and is the basis for the overwhelming number of packet switches in existence today. A single memory acts as a common area into which data is received and from which it is sent. The architecture of the IBM 3705/3725/3745 family of packet switches is a good example of the traditional approach.

There are many detailed differences in the way data is received into and transmitted out of storage. The tasks to be performed when data is received include:

1. Detection of the boundaries of characters and assembling bits into characters. Associated with this there is the task of recognizing control characters and sequences.
2. Detection and synchronization of the boundaries between blocks of data.
3. Transfer of the data and control information into the memory.
4. Processing the logic of link control.
5. Processing the switching logic.

[11] For the purposes of this discussion the word "packet" should be taken to mean "physical block of data" such that acceptable alternatives would be "cell" or "frame".

6. Processing control and management logic.

There are similar tasks to be performed when data is transmitted.

Depending on the switch design some (or all) of these functions except the switching logic, control and management can be performed outboard of the main processor. In the first IBM 3705 all these functions were performed by the controller program (even assembling bits into characters). In the most recent 3745 hardware everything up to and including the link control logic is performed outboard either in hardware or in an outboard programmable device.

### 6.12.2 Bus/Backplane Switches

In this design there are a number of separate adapter cards, each of which connects one or more external links. These cards may have completely hardware logic or contain a microprocessor and be program controlled.

All switch functions including routing are performed on each adapter card. Data transfer between adapter cards is done on a "backplane". The backplane is a parallel bus capable of transferring many bits in parallel (typically 64 or 128 bits at a time). All adapters connect to this backplane.

The backplane has a high throughput by virtue of the parallelism of data transfer. However, it has significant disadvantages.

- Total system throughput is the throughput of the backplane (because only one adapter can be sending at any one time).
- There is considerable overhead in arbitration (deciding which adapter can use the backplane next).
- Backplanes get slower and less effective the longer they are. You can't have more than a fairly small number of adapters before the whole system is slowed down.

Structures like this are also used by many devices and in general have a higher throughput possibility than memory-based switches, but they don't have sufficient potential for the job of trunkline ATM switch.

A good example of a backplane switch is the IBM plaNET switch described in Chapter 12, "plaNET/Orbit - A Gigabit Prototype Network" on page 12-1. plaNET can have a maximum number of eight adapters, each operating at just above 1.1 Gbps simultaneously.

## 6.12.3 Multistage Designs

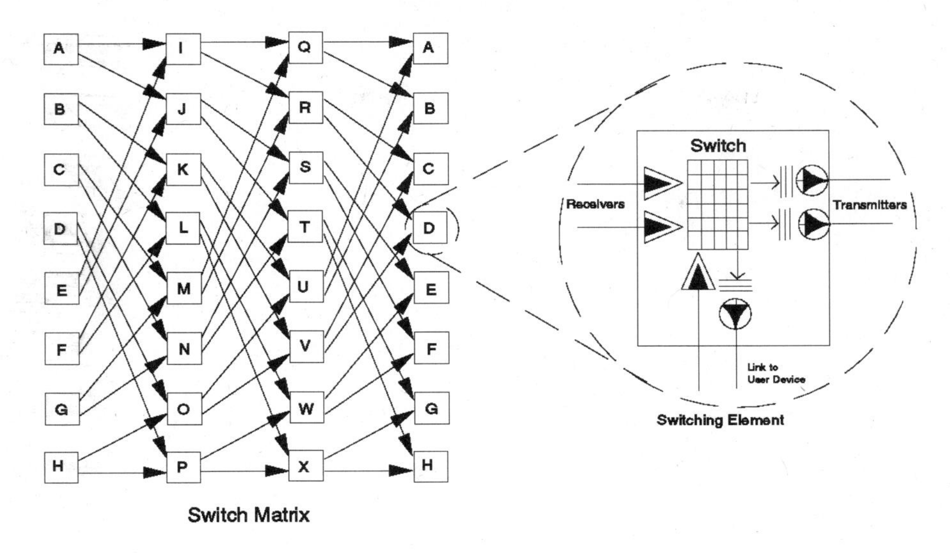


***Figure 6-13.*** *Stage-by-Stage Serial Switch (24 Ports)*

Figure 6-13 shows an example of a serial stage-by-stage packet switch. There are a few points to note about the drawing:

1. Each box in the switching matrix (on the left of the figure) represents a single switching element. Switching elements are illustrated on the right of the figure.
2. The column on the right of the switching matrix is *the same column* as the column on the left (the figure is drawn this way for ease of understanding).
3. Each switching element has a single (bidirectional) link to an attached device. These are shown on the switching element but not in the switch matrix (again to assist in readability).
4. Not shown in the figure is the *essential* control and management processor. Each switching element needs a connection to a control and management process.

### 6.12.3.1 General Principle

In the professional literature there are reported in excess of 50 different switch designs that use roughly the same general scheme. The paper by Daddis and Torng (see bibliography) classifies them into 17 categories. The figure above is, therefore, only one possibility out of very many.

The concept is as follows:

- A large switch is built up from many small, identical switching elements.
- Each switching element connects to one external link (input and output) and has at least two other inputs and two other outputs.
- The switching elements are interconnected by serial links in a structure such that data can be routed from any input to any output.
- Each switching element receives a packet in full before directing the packet to an output port.

There are many advantages to this architecture:

1. It leads to a low-cost implementation, since a single switch element (perhaps more than one) can be accommodated on a single chip. Individual switch elements are very simple.
2. Such switches are easy to build and are scalable.
3. The switch elements themselves operate only at the maximum link speed. This should be contrasted with a TDM bus style design where the circuitry must run significantly faster than the speed of individual link connections.
4. The total switch throughput is very high, since (with random traffic) the maximum system throughput is the number of stations *times* the link speed *times* two (links are FDX).

There are also disadvantages:

1. Congestion control is very difficult in the case where traffic is non-random. That is, if all traffic is to or from a small number of servers then congestion can become a real problem.
2. Traditional link control protocols such as LAPB and SDLC are very hard to implement because there would need to be link control logic at the single chip level.

#### 6.12.3.2 Architectural Issues

There are four main topics to be addressed when considering this type of switch architecture:

**Interconnection Structure**

There are many proposed alternative interconnection structures. The one illustrated in Figure 6-13 on page 6-43 is called a "self-routing interconnection network".

It is important to remember that one of the principal requirements in most networking systems (ATM, frame relay, etc.) is that packets must be delivered by the system in the same order as they were presented to the system. So the obvious operational methodology for the figure in the diagram (route an incoming packet to the other output port if the correct one is busy) is not a very good idea.

The example in the figure is an unusual one. The more usual proposal is for each switching element to have two inputs and two outputs only without the external link connection. In this case all external inputs would arrive at the left of the diagram and all outputs would leave at the right (the switch would not wrap around).

## Routing Data

Depending on how intelligent you can make the switching elements and how much interaction you want to have with the control processor, you can use almost any routing architecture here. However, there is very little time between arriving packets. If full routing tables are kept in each switching element, then they will require (potentially) a large amount of storage and continuous updating from the control processor.

One proposed method of routing within the switch itself is a simple version of ANR routing.

- When a packet arrives in a switching element *from an external link*, the global network addressing and routing system is used to determine which output port this packet should be sent to.
- A route through the switch to the destination port is then calculated for this packet. (The internal routing scheme within the switch can be completely independent from the network addressing and routing scheme.)
- The route to the destination port is simply a binary vector and it is appended to the front of the packet. (Note that this "route" is completely internal to the packet switch and is not related to the global networking scheme.)
- The packet is then sent to the next switching element.
- When the packet arrives at the next switching element the first bit (or group of bits) in the local routing vector is used to determine which output link (within this switching element) should be used (two possible links in our example).
- The switching element then removes the routing bits it used and sends the packet to the next stage.
- The next switching element does the same until the end of the route is detected.
- When a packet arrives with a routing vector indicating the end of the route, the packet is routed to the attached external link.

Another issue for the switch architecture is the handling of broadcast traffic. Some protocols (LAN emulation for example) require the ability to broadcast. A methodology is needed for the switch to handle broadcast without creating too much congestion.

### Contention Resolution and Buffering

No matter what we do there is always a probability of congestion within a packet switch. If all inputs unexpectedly decide to transfer large data files to a single output, there will be congestion and there needs to be some process to handle it.

In very high-speed switches the primary method of relieving congestion is to discard packets. Input rate controls are relied upon to adjust traffic rates to whatever the network can accommodate.

Buffering is a question which has been the subject of a considerable amount of research. Should data be buffered on input (before the switching decision is made) or on output, in both places, or not at all? (The last alternative implies routing packets back through the network on a different port if the selected output port is congested.) A consensus for buffering on output seems to have developed. However, the method of buffering is critically linked to the way other aspects of the switch operate, such as its addressing structure, its interconnection system, and its congestion control.

It is rather obvious here that short fixed-length cells are easier to handle in buffer queues than are long variable-length frames. However, cells must be routed individually, and this means that the switching elements must be able to make routing decisions at a very high rate.

Buffering in individual switch elements is subject to quite wide statistical variation. This is different from the traditional packet switch case where the variations are smoothed out because individual links share the same buffer pool. The result is that you need multiple buffers in the switching elements (just how many depends on many things).

### Control and Management Processor

The biggest problem about the control and management processor is how to connect it to the switching elements. The tempting way is through the switching fabric but that is not a good idea because a malfunction in the switching process could prevent the control processor from getting in to correct it.

A separate data flow must be constructed just for control purposes.

Control consists of keeping routing tables in switching elements up to date, monitoring congestion and collecting management information, etc.

#### 6.12.3.3 Practical Matters

As the principle is described above, each connection is a single-wire physical link. The links between the switch stages are the same as the external link connections. In practice, things need to be quite a bit different.

External links are different from internal ones because they are subject to much more distortion than inter-chip connections. There are practical problems in receiving the signal and recovering its timing on external connections that don't exist on internal ones.

The big issue is cost.

1. If you build each switch in CMOS technology then you will certainly get one (and possibly many) switch elements on the one chip. But CMOS technology has a practical maximum speed (currently around 60 MHz).
2. When the speed is increased you can use a "bipolar" technology but that is significantly less dense and therefore considerably higher in cost than CMOS.
3. Increasing the speed further, there comes a point when you need Gallium Arsenide chips. This is an order of magnitude more expensive than bipolar technology.

Cost is optimized if we keep the speed down.

External links are serial by their nature and we can't do much about that, but connections between chips on a board can be parallel (to a limit imposed by the number of wires you can attach to the chip). In practice, a multistage switch such as the one described above could be built in CMOS technology with serial internal connections up to a maximum speed of around 40 or 50 Mbps (on all links). Above that, it is much more cost effective to use parallel connections between switching elements (chips) than it is to use faster logic.

A practical architecture at (say) 1 Gbps would have separate transceiver chips for the external links. These would handle the coding and timing, etc., and would interface to the body of the switch through a parallel connection at a significantly lower clock rate than the line speed. Internal connections would all be parallel.

#### 6.12.3.4 Characteristics

Switches of this general architecture have the following characteristics:

- They are capable of very high throughput rates.
- They are very modular and scalable - as you add links the total capacity adjusts.
- They lend themselves to relatively low-cost implementation.

#### 6.12.3.5 A Practical Example

The IBM 9076 SP2 parallel supercomputing system includes a multistage switch similar in general principle to that described above. This is a system option and is called the "High Performance Switch" (HPS).

The IBM 9076 is an array of RISC System/6000 processors configured and supported such that they operate together as a single supercomputer. The HPS connects the processors together. It has the following characteristics:

- Connection to each processor (external connection) as well as connections between switching elements uses a byte wide bidirectional interface with two control wires (18 wires). Data transfer rate is 40 megabytes per second in each direction. The connection is electrical.
- Average switch latency for a 64-way switch is 500 ns.
- In principle the architecture could be extended to a switch supporting 1024 devices. In this case the latency would be increased because of the additional switching stages necessary.

# Chapter 7. Private Networks in the High-Speed Environment

Most of this publication deals with technologies for transporting information from one place to another. The effectiveness of these technologies in satisfying the needs of an organization is determined by how the technology is realized into practical systems. This chapter addresses the question of the effectiveness of isolated transmission networks in fulfilling organizational needs. The discussion applies equally to traditional packet switching networks and to new high-speed services such as ATM.

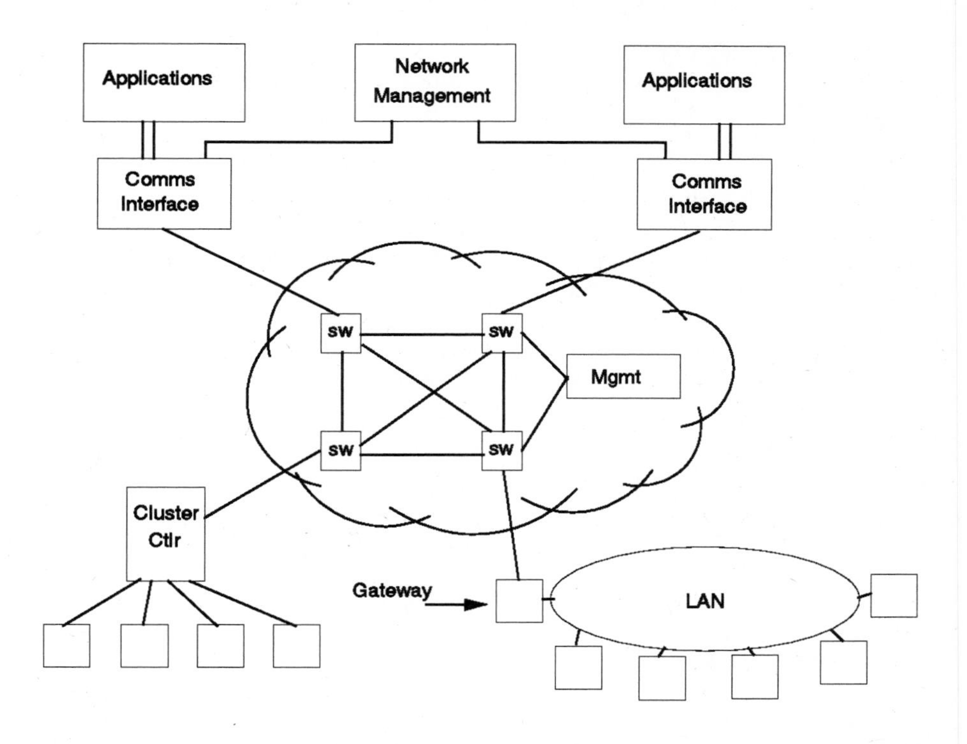


***Figure 7-1.*** *A Hierarchy of Networks.* One type of data network is built "above" the other. This could be the common case of an SNA network running "over the top" of a private "X.25 network".

From a user perspective the network connects places where data is entered or processed. That is, the users of the network are application programs within processors (people using a terminal are inevitably connected to the network through a program of some kind). These application programs exist within all kinds of processors from PCs and workstations to dedicated data processing elements such as servers and mainframes, etc. A good network should provide seamless, transparent and reliable connection between these programs. This means that from a user (organizational) perspective the interface to the network is the application program interface within a processor.

The communications carrier (PTT) view of the network is quite different. Because the PTTs provide a public, shared service the interface to it must be well defined and it must prevent users from exercising any control over (or even knowing about) the internal operation of the public network. Thus a PTT network (such as X.25 or ATM) aims to *isolate* the end users.

### 7.1.1 The Isolated Transmission Network

In the traditional "low-speed" data communications technology, so called "X.25 networks" are the classical example of a network dedicated to providing the data transmission function in isolation from all the other functions necessary in a complete desktop-to-desktop communications system.

X.25 is a network interface (there is no standard for the internal operation of an X.25 service and so real networks vary widely in their internal operation). It was designed for the use of PTTs (telecommunications carriers) as a service (user) interface to a public packet switched data network. As such it *must* isolate the end user from the internal operation of the network. That is, there must be a barrier to prevent end users from interfering with (or even knowing about) the internals of the public network. (It's hard to see how you could run a public network in any other way.)

The problem for an organization is how to build a network which will satisfy the needs of the end users in a cost-effective way.

**The thesis of this section is that while isolated transmission networks are necessary in the public network environment, there are significantly better ways available to users of private networks.**

### 7.1.2 Nested Networks

Consider Figure 7-1 on page 7-1. Here we see an isolated transmission network used within a wider private network architecture.

> In terms of the ISO model the inner network is performing the functions of layers 1 to 3 and the outer network is performing the functions of layers 4 to 6.

The inner network could be X.25, ATM, frame relay, bridge or router based. The outer network could be typically SNA, DecNet or TCP/IP among many others.

The critical issues with this structure are:

1. Adaptation cost
2. Network management cost and complexity
3. Function placement

The amount of cost associated with each of these issues varies according to the combination of inner and outer networks involved. For example, there is a lot less adaptation processing required for SNA to operate over a frame relay interface than over an X.25 one. On the other hand, an X.25 SVC is significantly easier in network management terms (less definition and less coordination required) than a frame relay permanent connection. Another example would be that a TCP/IP network will operate better over a connectionless structure than over a connection-oriented one.

#### 7.1.2.1 Adaptation

The first problem is making the outer network compatible with the data structures and formats of the inner network. This is adaptation.

Again, using SNA as an example: In order to send an SNA frame over an X.25 service the data block must be split up into packets and sent as many smaller blocks. In addition there is link error recovery and packet level flow control which must be implemented on this interface. In the technology used for this purpose, this costs significant processing power and storage. However, for an X.25 service, SNA "trusts" the network to have a very low error rate or at least notify the attached SNA devices when a packet has been lost. This works quite well in most networks.

In sending SNA over a frame relay service we don't need to packetize. But we now have to detect and request retransmission of error frames. In addition link level acknowledgments travel across the FR network and need to be processed (in X.25 these are local).

To send SNA over a connectionless environment such as a bridged LAN or a router network, we need to establish a "connection" (set of control blocks) at either end in order to integrate with the connection-oriented SNA structure.

To send SNA over ATM we will need adaptation to break a frame into cells, reassemble the cells when received, perform error recovery by re-transmission, and perform rate control at the input to the network.

The point is that whenever there is a difference between the architecture of the inner and outer networks (there almost always is) then there is additional processing and logic required for adaptation at the interface.

## 7.1.2.2 Network Management

Figure 7-2 shows the network view as seen by the network management system in the outer network. Knowledge of how wide area connections are made is not available to it. It should be noted here that there are two completely independent network management systems and two (usually different) sets of people performing network operation.

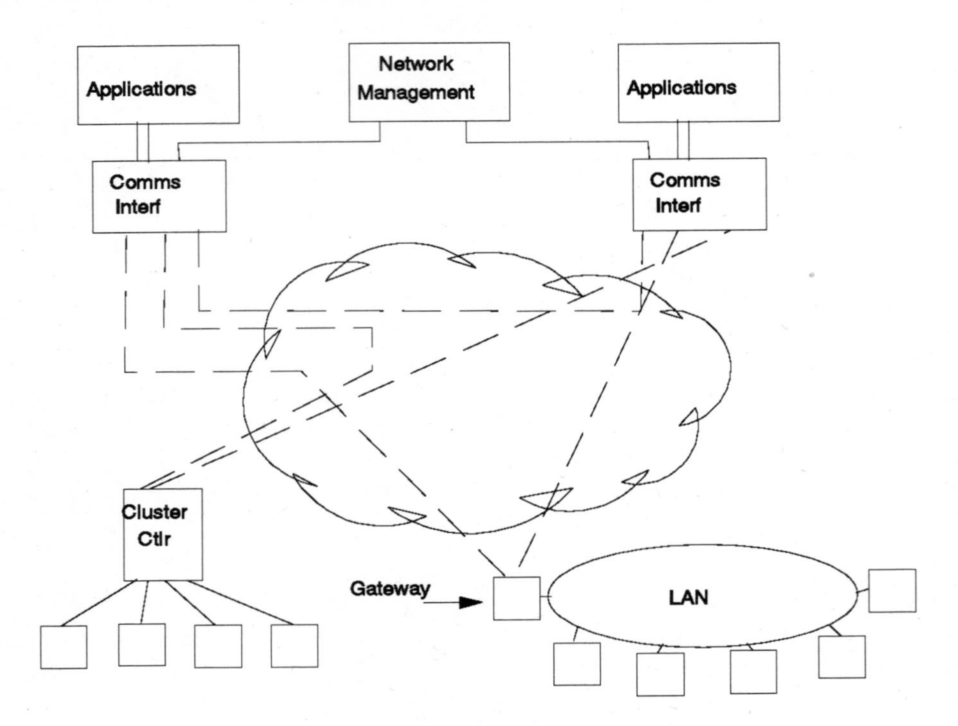


*Figure 7-2. Nested Network.* View as seen by the network management system of the outer network. The transmission (inner) network is invisible to the user (outer network).

**System Definition**

From the point of view of the outer network, the links with the transport network must be defined (usually by a hard coded SYSDEF process). The inner network must also define the interfaces to the outer one (again by hard coding) and also any permanent connections required. There will be inevitable mismatches between the two sets of definitions and this is a significant source of problems.

**Network Directory**

Each network has its own separate and isolated directory structure, although much of the information is about the same resources. In addition, the lack of integration between network directories causes a significant increase in network traffic needed to keep the separate directories up to date.

**Network Operation**

As stated above, two different sets of operational personnel are often needed - usually the skills needed are so different that the tasks cannot be performed by the same people.

**Fault Diagnosis and Fix**

When a fault occurs in one network it is often seen as a symptom in the other (especially faults in the inner network). Even if one network notifies errors to the other, the time stamps are almost never accurate and it is difficult to relate events in one part of the network with events in another part. Hence another level of difficulty is introduced in the diagnosis and fixing of faults.

#### 7.1.2.3 Function Placement

When SNA was designed, its architects took the view that the users would want to minimize the total cost of their computer systems (processors, communications, terminals, application programming). A critical design decision at the time was to place most of the function into the network switches and into the processors rather than into the end user devices. This was because an organization might have only a few processors, perhaps less than 10 network switches, but a few thousand terminals. Better to place the cost where the number of boxes (multiplier) was least.

This resulted in SNA being a very highly reliable network structure but having a relatively high cost if looked at separately from the devices connecting to it. Reduction in function within the nodes would bring a lower cost but add cost to each and every connecting device.

SNA therefore has only a minimal end-to-end network recovery function (OSI layer 4 function).

When SNA users started attaching to the first X.25 public networks, a very bad network stability problem was encountered. This was due to some early networks being designed to discard data whenever congestion or errors occurred. The designers of these networks believed that end users would implement end-to-end protocols outside the network to give it stability. SNA did not have these protocols (because of the cost tradeoff - it didn't need them). This point was covered obliquely in 7.1.2.1, "Adaptation" on page 7-3.

The above is history but the point is current. **If you design the transmission network to minimize its cost without regard to how it is to be used then you may be increasing the total system cost to the end user.**

### 7.1.3 Conclusions

From the above discussion there are two important conclusions:

**Private Network Environment**

When the same organization owns all aspects of the network, it makes sense to avoid the artificial barrier created by having a separate transmission network. A single integrated, seamless structure will be easier to manage, higher in performance, and lower in cost than a separate structure.

**Public Network**

We can't avoid having a separate transmission network when it is shared among many users. A user must simply choose the most cost effective service available (allowing for the differences in cost of the user's equipment dictated by the public network chosen). Nevertheless, when all else is equal, public facilities should be chosen to match as closely as possible the user's network. When there is a choice the simplest public offering will usually be the best (leased lines will usually be better for the user than public packet networks - in all ways except cost).

# Chapter 8. High-Speed Time Division Multiplexing Systems

## 8.1 Integrated Services Digital Network (ISDN)

Some people believe that ISDN is probably the most significant development in communications since the invention of the automatic telephone exchange.

ISDN describes and specifies a (digital) user interface to a public (digital) communications network. It *does not* describe the internal operations of the communications network - just the interfaces to it and the services that it must provide.

Much of the impetus for ISDN comes from the desire to use the installed copper wire "subscriber loop" at higher speeds, with more reliability and new services. In most countries the total value of installed copper wire subscriber loop connections represents the largest single capital asset in that country. There is an enormous potential benefit in getting better use from it.

Existing copper subscriber loops vary widely in quality and characteristics and making use of it for digital connections represents a significant technical challenge. See 2.2.4, "The Subscriber Loop" on page 2-44.

This document is not concerned with the details of narrowband ISDN. The subject is discussed because it illustrates the use of modern digital signaling techniques and TDM operation.

### 8.1.1 Types of ISDN

There are three generic types of ISDN.

**Narrowband ISDN** is the form of ISDN that is becoming widely available today. There are two forms of access (Basic Rate and Primary Rate) and the service offered is the connection of 64 Kbps channels primarily on a switched service basis. There is also a low rate "connectionless" packet switching ability available through the "D" channel.

Thus narrowband ISDN offers TDM connection of 64 Kbps channels through a switched network. Channels normally *cannot* be faster than 64 Kbps - if you use two channels this does not give a single 128 Kbps channel; it gives two, unrelated 64 Kbps channels.

Special equipment may of course be designed to synchronize multiple B channels and provide a wider single channel; indeed, there is equipment available which will do this. However, this equipment is not a part of the network.

**Wideband ISDN** is a form of ISDN where a user *is* able to access a wider synchronous data channel through using a group of adjacent slots on an ISDN Primary Rate interface. Thus if six slots are used, they may form a single, 384 Kbps data channel (this is called an H0 channel).

Some ISDN public network equipment on the market today allows this option, but most PTTs do not yet offer this as part of their ISDN service even if their equipment allows it.

**Broadband ISDN** does *not* provide high-speed synchronous channels. It is a cell-based packet switching system.

Since both narrowband and wideband ISDN offer synchronous TDM derived "clear" channels, many people assume that broadband ISDN will be similar. In fact broadband ISDN is based on "Asynchronous Transfer Mode" (ATM) cell switching[1] and works in a very different way. This is because of the problem of allocating variable bandwidths over a Time Division Multiplexed (TDM) trunk circuit as described below in 8.3, "The Bandwidth Fragmentation Problem" on page 8-22.

### 8.1.2 The ISDN Reference Model

The CCITT has defined ISDN in terms of a set of functions with fixed relationships to one another and with defined interfaces between them. These are illustrated in Figure 8-1 on page 8-3. The function being performed is digital transmission between a customer (end user) and a public telephone exchange. The functions defined are as follows:

**ET** Exchange Termination.

**LT** Line Transmission Termination. This is termination of the transmission line at the exchange. (LT and ET can be in the same physical piece of equipment.)

**NT1** Network Termination 1. This function terminates the subscriber loop transmission line and provides an interface for customer equipment. In Basic Rate ISDN, NT1 changes the transmission protocol and reformats the frame.

NT1 has a different status in the US from its status in other countries. In the US, NT1 is legally considered "customer premises equipment" (it is "like" a modem[2]). In the rest of the world, NT1 is considered service provider equipment. Thus in

1 See 9.1, "Asynchronous Transfer Mode (ATM)" on page 9-3.

2 It is nothing like a modem.

the US it is possible for the NT1 function to be integrated within end-user equipment, while in other countries it will be a separate physical box.

**NT2** Network Termination 2 is a PBX or communication controller function.

**TA** The Terminal Adapter function connects non-ISDN terminals to the ISDN network.

**TE2** Terminal Equipment 2 is just the new name for all "old style" terminals with RS-232/422/449, V.24/35 or X.21 (generically called "RVX") interfaces.

**TE1** Terminal Equipment 1 is terminal equipment designed to interface directly to the ISDN system.

**R, S, T, U, V** designate reference points where protocols are defined.

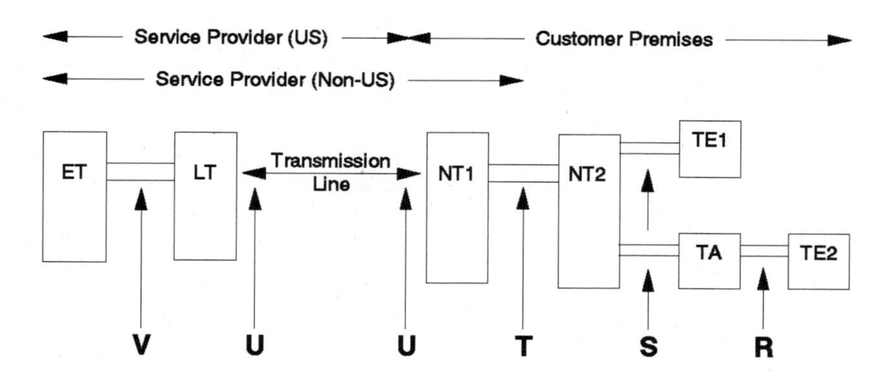


*Figure 8-1. ISDN Reference Configuration*

## 8.1.3 ISDN Basic Rate

For people hitherto unfamiliar with digital communication techniques, perhaps the most surprising thing about ISDN is its connection to the small end user (such as a small business or a private home). This "ISDN Basic Rate Interface " (BRI) uses the same twisted pair of copper wires (subscriber loop) as is currently used for a home telephone. This single pair of wires carries two (64 Kbps) B channels and a (16 Kbps) D channel.

Thus, on the same physical wire as exists today a user has two independent "telephone lines" instead of one, *plus* a limited ability to send data messages to other users without the need to use either of the two B channels.

**"B" (Bearer) Channel**

A "B channel" is 64 Kbps in both directions simultaneously (64 Kbps full-duplex). When a user places a "call" (for voice or for data) a continuous path is allocated to that call until either party "hangs up" (clears the call).

This is the principal service of (regular) ISDN. The B channel is an end-to-end "clear channel" connection (derived by TDM techniques) which may be used for voice or for data. It can be thought of in the same way as an analog telephone connection but, of course, it is digital.

**"D" Channel**

The D channel is not an "end-to-end clear channel" like the B channels. This D channel carries data in short packets and is primarily used for signaling between the user and the network (when the user "dials" a number, the number requested is carried as a packet on the D channel). The D channel can also be used for sending limited amounts of data from one end user to another through the network without using the high capacity B channels[3] (this can be useful in a number of applications).

In Basic Rate the D channel operates at 16 Kbps.

The ISDN BRI allows for up to eight physical devices to be attached simultaneously to the network by means of a "passive bus". Obviously, since there are only two B channels a maximum of two devices can use a B channel simultaneously. However, all eight devices can simultaneously share access to the D channel for low-speed data applications.

#### 8.1.3.1 The ISDN Basic Rate "U" Interface

The "U" interface is the interface between the Network Terminating Unit (NT1) on the customer's premises and the local telephone exchange.

This interface must transfer user data at a total rate of 144 Kbps full-duplex over an existing *two-wire* subscriber loop. This is a complex problem, because signals must travel in both directions over the same physical wires; and, therefore, one device receiving a signal from another device will also receive an echo of its own transmissions in the form of interference with the received signal.

As discussed in 2.2.4, "The Subscriber Loop" on page 2-44, this connection is variable in quality and has all kinds of impairments. Nevertheless, it is considered very important that the protocol should operate over *any* subscriber loop connection *without* the need to select especially good ones or to perform any "conditioning".

---

3 This is a facility that is available in some networks and not in others.

The U interface is *not* internationally standardized. The CCITT considered that technology was changing so rapidly in this area that the presence of a standard would be likely to inhibit future development. In addition, since the installed subscriber loop varies markedly in characteristics from one country to another (different average distance, different wire gauges) this was felt to be a necessary freedom. Thus in Europe, the PTT supplies the Network Terminating Unit (NT1) and is free to use any protocol on the U interface that it deems appropriate.

In the US, the situation is different. For legal reasons, all equipment on customer premises must be open to competitive supply (especially the NT1). To enable this the American National Standards Institute (ANSI) has published a standard for the BRI U interface. In the US therefore, a supplier of EDP equipment may decide to integrate the NT1 function within a terminal or a personal computer and connect to the U interface.[4] In the rest of the world suppliers of EDP equipment *must* connect to the S (or T) interface.

In practice there are three U interface standards in general use:

**US**

This country uses true full-duplex transmission over the two-wire subscriber loop. To achieve this the interface circuits must use very sophisticated adaptive echo cancellation techniques (see 2.2.5, "Echo Cancellation" on page 2-47).

The line code used is the 2B1Q code described in 2.1.15.2, "2-Binary 1-Quaternary (2B1Q) Code" on page 2-29. The data rate is 160 Kbps (144 Kbps of user data plus framing and a maintenance channel) but the signaling rate is only 80 kbaud. The line code was chosen because in the environment of an impaired transmission channel, a lower signaling rate helps with echo cancellation and makes the signal easier to receive.

The maximum practical distance over which this technique will work is about 12 kilometers.

**Germany**

In Germany,[5] true full-duplex transmission is also used. The line code is 4B3T code at a data rate of 160 Kbps and a signaling rate of 120 Kbps (see 2.1.12, "4-Binary 3-Ternary (4B3T) Code" on page 2-23).

As in the US, the receiver must use advanced adaptive echo cancellation techniques.

---

4 As of June 1995, all ISDN Basic Rate interface adapters announced by IBM use the S interface only.

5 Some other countries such as Australia also use 4B3T encoding.

The maximum distance for transmission (without special repeaters) is 4.2 kilometers using .4 mm wire and 8.0 kilometers using .6 mm wire. These maxima match the characteristics of subscriber loops in Germany.

### Other Countries (Time Compression Mode)

As stated above, country telecommunication carriers are able to decide which protocols to use on the U interface (and perhaps use many different ones).

A common protocol in use in many countries does *not* use simultaneous full-duplex bidirectional transmission. Short bursts of data are sent at a higher data rate, but in one direction at a time. This gives the effect of real full-duplex transmission, but without the complexity and cost of using adaptive echo cancellation. This technique is sometimes called “Time Compression Mode” or “Burst Mode”.

The method of operation is as follows:

- A frame of 38 bits (illustrated in Figure 8-2 on page 8-7) is transmitted from the network exactly once every 250 microseconds.
- The transmission data rate is 384 Kbps and “regular” half-bauded AMI transmission code is used (see 2.1.5.1, “Alternate Mark Inversion” on page 2-11). The signaling rate is the same as the bit rate - 384 kbaud. This means that the transmission time for a frame is 99 μsec.
- The frame carries two bytes from each B channel and four bits from the D channel. This gives each B channel an average rate of one byte every 125 μsec, which equals 8000 bytes per second or 64 Kbps. The D channel rate is 16 Kbps.
- When the NT1 receives a complete frame, it waits 5.2 μsec “guard time” (to allow reflections to dissipate a bit) and sends its frame up to the network.
- This means that the maximum time available for signal propagation is:

  $$250 - 2 \times (99 + 5.2) = 42.6\ \mu sec$$

  Since propagation must take place in both directions the maximum propagation delay in one direction is a bit less than half of this - that is, 20.8 μsec.

  Since propagation speed on most subscriber loops is between 5 μsec and 5.5 μsec per kilometer, the maximum available distance using this technique is about 4 kilometers.

The advantage of the technique is that it is simple, easy, and relatively low in cost (saves the cost of the special adaptive echo canceller chip required by the other techniques). The disadvantage is the rather short maximum distance available, though of course, you could speed up the transmission rate and get greater distances if needed.

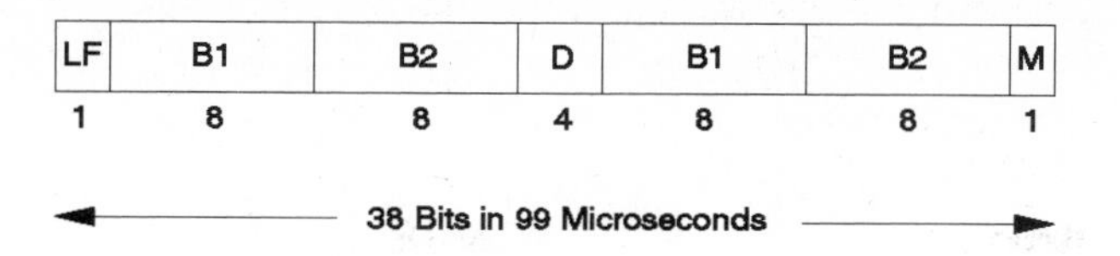


*Figure 8-2. "U" Interface Frame Structure.* The M channel is used for service and maintenance functions between the NT and the exchange.

### 8.1.3.2 Multiframing

The M channel used in Time Compression Mode (TCM) is a simple example of a "superframe" or "multiframe". Within each 38-bit TCM frame a single bit is used to provide two independent clear channels. Every second bit (the M bit in every second frame) is for a "service channel". Since the frame rate is one every 250 μsec this gives an aggregate rate for the channel of 2048 bits per second.

One bit in every four frames belongs to the "service channel". Since the frame rate is 4096 frames per second (one every 250 μsec) the service channel operates at 1024 bits per second.

Of course there is a need to identify which bit is which. To the "higher level" 38-bit frame, the M bit forms a single clear channel, but within itself it has a structure. A multi-frame begins with a code violation (that is, the M channel bit violates the code of the 38-bit frame). This delimits the beginning of the multiframe. After the code violation (CV) the next M channel bit belongs to the transparent channel, the next to the service channel, the next to the transparent channel, and then the next multiframe starts with another CV.

The concept of multiframes (frames within frames) is very important as it is used extensively within ISDN Primary Rate and Sonet/SDH.

### 8.1.3.3 The ISDN Basic Rate Passive Bus ("S" Interface)

Simple, elegant and efficient, the passive bus is an excellent example of what can be achieved with modern digital signaling technology.

Consider Figure 8-3 on page 8-8. The Network Termination Function (NT1) is here a separate physical device. NT1 operates on the U interface on its upstream side (to the exchange) using two wires. On the downstream side it must communicate with up to eight separate "terminal equipment" devices connected to the passive bus. To do this it uses the "S" interface protocol.[6]

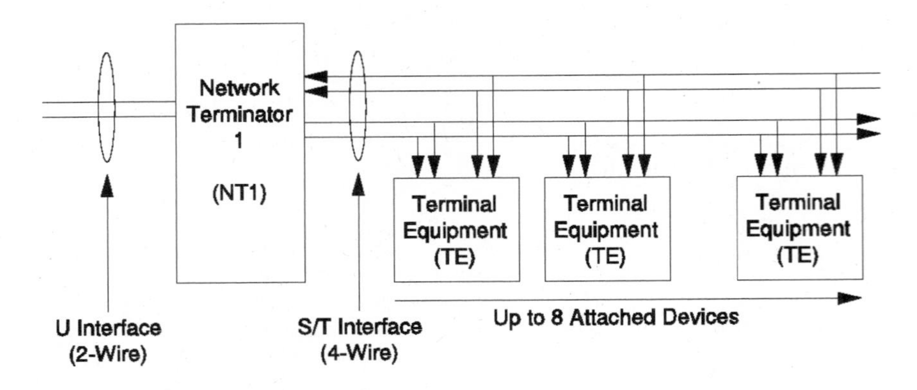


*Figure 8-3. ISDN Basic Rate Passive Bus*

The passive bus consists of just four wires connected (through a transformer) to the NT1. Two wires are used for transmission and two for reception. Up to eight TE devices are able to "plug in" to this bus and to operate independently of each other. The protocol is performed by all connecting TEs and by the NT1.

The objective is for each TE to be able to communicate with the network using either (or both) of the B channels and the D channel. Since a B channel is a clear channel (that is, the device may send any sequence of bits without restriction), only one TE may use a B channel at any one time. The D channel is a packet channel and TEs are constrained to use a rigorous protocol (called "LAPD" for Link Access Protocol D channel) for operation.

The frame formats and method of operation of the S and U interfaces are very different and this means that NT1 has quite a lot of function to perform. Nevertheless, it is important to realize that NT1 passes both the B and D channel data through to the exchange *without any form of modification or processing of the data.* NT1 does frame reformatting and electrical signal conversion only - it does not change or look at the data.

### Frame Formats

Figure 8-4 on page 8-9 shows the frame formats used on the S/T interface. The first thing to notice about these is that the formats are quite *different* depending on the direction of transmission (TE-to-NT, or NT-to-TE).

6 This same protocol is used for the "T" interface also, so it is often referred to as the S/T interface protocol.

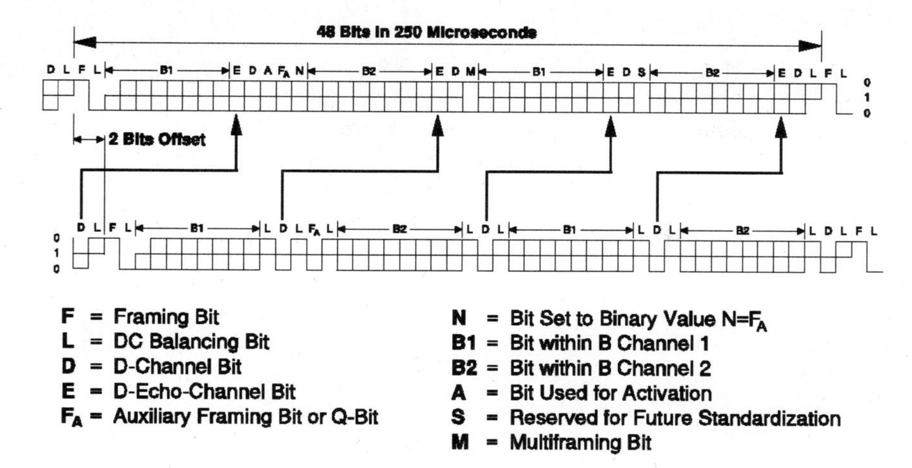


***Figure 8-4.*** *ISDN Basic Rate S/T Interface Frame Structure.* The frame format used in the TE to NT direction is different from the one used in the NT to TE direction.

### Frame Timing

Frames are sent in each direction, as nearly as possible, exactly one every 250 µsec. Since a frame is 48 bits long this means that the data rate is 192 Kbps.

Each frame contains 2 bytes from each B channel and 4 bits from the D channel. Note that these are spaced at regular intervals throughout the frame.

### Frame Generation

In the NT to TE direction (of course) the NT generates the frame and puts data in each field. TEs can access (read) any or all fields in the frame as appropriate.

In the TE to NT direction things are different. There is no single device available to generate the frame so *all TEs generate a frame and transmit it onto the bus simultaneously*.

This would normally be a formula for disaster: multiple devices writing independent information onto the same wires at the same time. However, this is not the case. The line code and the frame structure are organized so that the framing bits will be the same polarity for all TEs. Thus, provided the timing is accurate, all TEs may write the same frame to the bus at the same time.

The line code used is Pseudoternary and is described in 2.1.5, "Pseudoternary Coding" on page 2-10.

**Frame Synchronization**

Each TE derives the timing for its frame transmission from the timing of the frame it receives from the NT. The TE starts its frame transmission precisely 3 bits after it receives the start of a frame from the NT and subsequent bits are transmitted using the clock derived from the received bit stream.

There are problems here with jitter and with propagation delay. Each TE will detect the frame from the NT at a (very slightly) different time (jitter). Therefore the TEs will not transmit exactly simultaneously. This effect is minimized by requiring a very high-quality receiver.

Also, it takes time for electricity to propagate down the bus (about 5 μsec per kilometer). At 192 Kbps a bit is just over 5 μsec long. We can't do much about this! The result of the propagation delay problem is that the passive bus must limit the distance between the first TE on the bus and the last one. That is, TEs must cluster together on the bus.

For a different reason (operation of the D channel) there is a maximum distance (again due to propagation delay) between the NT and the first TE on the bus.

**TE to NT Frame**

Fields within the TE-to-NT frame may be put there by different TEs. For example, one TE may be using one B channel and another TE the second B channel. Of course, only one TE may use a B channel at any one time.

Because no TE can know what another TE is writing into the frame, each field that can be separately written has an additional DC balance bit (designated "L") to ensure the overall DC balance of the frame.

Each D channel bit has a separate DC balance bit and may be written by any TE (or all of them together).

### 8.1.3.4 Operation of the D Channel

The D channel operates quite differently from the B channels. Where the B channels are "transparent" (the TE may send or receive any arbitrary bit stream), the D channel is rigorously structured.

A TE on the D channel sends and receives short packets of data. One primary requirement is that TEs must share the D channel with some kind of fairness. Consecutive packets may belong to different TEs. All communication is from the network to/from individual TEs. There is no TE-to-TE communication possible (except through the exchange).

There is no problem with transmission from the exchange to the TE. Since there is only one device sending, it is able to intermix packets for different TEs at will. But in the other direction, multiple TEs cannot transmit data on the same channel at the same time.

This is the same situation that existed in the past with multiple terminal devices sharing a multidrop analog data link. As with analog data links in the past, the problem is how to control which device (TE) is allowed to send at a particular time. In the past "polling" was used for this purpose but with digital signaling techniques available a much more efficient technique is used.

As far as the TDM structure is concerned (that is, at the "physical layer") the D channel is a clear channel of 16 Kbps full-duplex. As frames are transmitted or received by each TE, consecutive D channel bits are treated as though there was no other information in between. A link control protocol is used between each TE (through the NT) to the exchange.

Operation of the D channel depends on the interaction of four things:

**LAPD Link Control**

LAPD is a version of the international standard HDLC. It is very similar to IBM SDLC, LAPB (the link control in X.25), and IEEE 802.2 LLC. As far as the S interface TDM structure is concerned, the important aspects are the frame structure and the address bytes.

A LAPD frame is started and ended by the binary sequence B′01111110′. This is a unique sequence, since whenever a string of five one bits appears in the data, the transmitter must unconditionally send an additional single zero bit (later removed by the receiver). So the only time a string of zeros followed by six ones occurs is when there is a frame boundary or an abort. The frame delimiter (B′01111110′) is also sometimes referred to by the letter "F".

Immediately following the frame delimiter there is a 2-byte address field. This will be discussed later but from the S bus perspective the important thing to note is that this contains a TE identifier (number) and is unique. It is the uniqueness that is important here.

**Pseudoternary Line Code**

This was discussed in 2.1.5, "Pseudoternary Coding" on page 2-10. It is important to note that to send a one bit the transmitter *does nothing*. That is, a one bit is represented by *no voltage* on the line. Zero bits are represented by alternating + or - voltages.

**The D Channel Echo**

In the NT-to-TE direction there is a channel called "D channel echo". Notice that this is in addition to the regular D channel.

The D channel echo is generated in the NT1 and has no function upstream towards the exchange. When a D channel bit is received from the TEs, it is immediately reflected back to the TEs in the echo channel. Every TE can see the status of the last D channel bit received from the TEs by the NT1.

### Timing

Two timing aspects are critical.

1. As discussed above, each TE must generate and send a frame as nearly as possible at *exactly* the same time as each other TE. This is done by synchronizing each TE's transmitter timing with its receiver and by limiting the distance between the first and the last TE on the bus.

2. A D channel bit sent in the TE-to-NT direction *must be received by its sender (on the D channel echo) before the TE sends the next D channel bit.* This characteristic is critical to the whole operation.

To receive a frame on the D channel a TE simply monitors the received D channel for a frame character followed by an address field containing its (the TE's) address. When this is detected, the TE receives the frame.

Sending a frame from the TE to the network is much more complex:

### Monitor for Idle Channel

When the TE wants to send a frame to the network (through the NT1) it first monitors the D Channel Echo for a sequence of 8 one bits. Continuous one bits denote an idle channel.

### Send Flag and Address

Once the TE sees an idle D channel, it will begin transmitting its frame upstream, one bit at a time, into the D channel bit positions of the TE-to-NT frame.

### Collision Avoidance

It may have happened that another TE was also waiting to send. If it was, it may also have started transmission into the D channel at the time of exactly the same bit as the first TE did. (This is quite a likely event.)

After each TE has sent a bit on the D channel it must wait and listen for the echo. The echo must be received before the TE is allowed to send the next bit. The Pseudoternary line code makes the bus act as a logical OR. That is, within some limitations it is *legal* for multiple TEs to send data simultaneously.

If a TE receives a zero bit on the echo channel when the last bit it sent was a one, then it must immediately terminate its transmission (before sending the next bit). The TE that sent the zero will continue to send without knowing that another TE ever tried. Since address fields are unique (they always contain a unique TE number among other things), the TE with the highest numbered address will win the contention.

**Send Data and FCS**

By the time the address field is sent the contention operation will be over and the winning TE may go on to send a single frame of data. The TE appends a Frame Check Sequence (FCS) number to the end of the data to provide an error detection mechanism but this is treated as data as far as the D channel itself is concerned (NT1 doesn't know or care).

**Monitor for Ones**

When data transmission is complete the TE will monitor the D channel echo for a sequence of 9 one bits instead of 8 before it is allowed to attempt to send another frame. If it sees 9 one bits, but has nothing to send, it will change its monitoring counter such that for subsequent blocks it will monitor for strings of eight ones again.

Another TE waiting for access to the D channel is allowed to start transmitting after only 8 one bits and will thus obtain access before the first TE has another chance.

This procedure ensures that every TE is allowed the opportunity to send at least one frame before the first TE is allowed to send the next frame.

**Priorities**

It is possible to have low priority TEs (or low priority functions within a TE) that are allocated a lower priority. In this case the TE will wait to see 10 one bits before sending and wait to see 11 one bits after sending but before sending again.

This ensures that TEs with an allocated count of 8 always have sending priority over those with a count of 10.

**Passive Bus - Theme and Variations:** Within the above mode of operation, several configurations of passive bus are possible.

**The Short Passive Bus** is between 100 and 200 meters long (depending on the cable) and allows TEs to be placed anywhere on the cable (attached via 10-meter stubs).

**The Extended Passive Bus** insists that the TEs be grouped on the cable over a distance of between 25 to 50 meters (again depending on the cable characteristics). The maximum overall length allowed from the NT is 500 meters.

**Point-to-Point Operation** is possible if only one TE is connected and in this case the length is limited by propagation delay to a maximum round-trip delay of 42 microseconds. 42 μsec is the maximum round-trip delay allowed such that the D channel echo can be received before the next D bit is sent.

Maximum length due to cable impedance is expected to be about one kilometer.

For operation on buses longer than about 200 meters, a special NT is needed which adapts for the time delay due to propagation.

**LAPD Link Control:** As mentioned above, LAPD is a member of the HDLC series of link control protocols.[7]

Each TE has at least one connection with the ISDN network. This connection is used for passing call requests and call progress information. The TE may also have other connections with services within the network. Thus, running on the same link, there are multiple TEs, each (perhaps) with multiple simultaneous connections to different points within the network. This means that there is a need to address each endpoint uniquely.

In SDLC a single "control point" (which does not have an explicit link address) identifies up to 255 secondary devices using a single-byte link address. In LAPB (X.25), communication is always between peer entities and so the link address may take only two values (X′01′ or X′03′). LAPD uses a 2-byte address which contains two fields:

1. A SAPI (Service Access Point Identifier) which represents the service or endpoint within the ISDN network.
2. A TEI (Terminal Endpoint Identifier) which identifies the TE.

Link control operation is conventional.

**ISDN Frame Relay:** Frame relay is a fast packet-switching service which was designed to be used with ISDN. In fact its definition is part of the ISDN definition - although, it is an additional "service" which may be provided by network providers. The frame relay service may be accessed through a B channel, an H channel (ISDN wideband access), or through the D channel.

The basic service of delivering low-rate packet data from one end user to another using D channel access is *not* frame relay but rather is a basic service of the ISDN network. Frame relay is more fully described in 11.1, "Frame Relay" on page 11-4.

### 8.1.4 ISDN Primary Rate Interface

Primary Rate (PRI) transmission uses two pairs of wires (subscriber loops) - one pair in each direction. Because of the use of unidirectional transmission the problem of interference due to echoes is much less. In addition, the service does not use unselected subscriber loops. Wire pairs are carefully selected for quality *and have repeaters inserted*

[7] LAPD is described in detail in *IBM ISDN Data Link Control - Architecture Reference.*

*approximately every 1.6 kilometers (1 mile).* This allows a much higher transmission rate.

Communication is always point-to-point since there may be only one device (typically a combined NT1/NT2 such as a PBX) connected to the primary rate interface.

In Europe, the transmission rate used is 2 Mbps. In the US, the speed used is 1.544 Mbps (the same as "T1"). This results in the availability of 30 B channels with one (64 Kbps) D channel in Europe with 23 B channels plus one D channel in the US. The systems are very similar and so only the European system is described here.

**Wideband Channels:** On the primary rate interface it is possible to take a group of B channels and use them as a single wideband data channel. This a feature of the ISDN definition but is implemented in only a very few real ISDN networks. An H0 channel concatenates six slots giving a single channel with an available bandwidth of 384 Kbps. There are also H11 channels (24 slots - 1536 Kbps) and H12 channels (30 slots - 1920 Kbps). H channels are end-to-end wideband transparent connections on which the user is entitled to put any data desired.

**Coding and Frame Structure:** Communication is point-to-point on four wires and so the electrical level coding and the frame structure is conventional.

In Europe the coding used is HDB3 which is described in 2.1.10, "High Density Bipolar Three Zeros (HDB3) Coding" on page 2-20.

The frame structure is shown in Figure 8-5. Slot 0 is used for framing and maintenance information. Slot 16 is a 64 Kbps D channel. All other slots may be used for B channels or as part of an H channel.

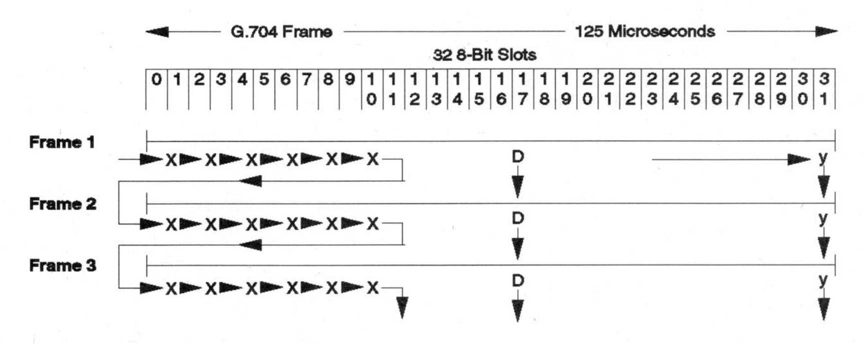


***Figure 8-5. ISDN Primary Rate Frame Structure (Europe).*** Arrows show the sequence of slot concatenation for an H0 (wideband) channel, the D channel (slot 16) and a B channel (slot 31).

## 8.2 SDH and Sonet

Sonet (Synchronous Optical Network) is a US standard for the internal operation of telephone company optical networks. It is closely related to a system called SDH (Synchronous Digital Hierarchy) adopted by the CCITT as a recommendation for the internal operation of carrier (PTT) optical networks worldwide.

Sonet and SDH are of immense importance because of the vast cost savings that they promise for public communications networks.

Traditionally, public telephone company networks have been built by using a cascade of multiplexors at each end of a high-speed connection. In physical realization, this resulted in the configuration illustrated in Figure 8-6.

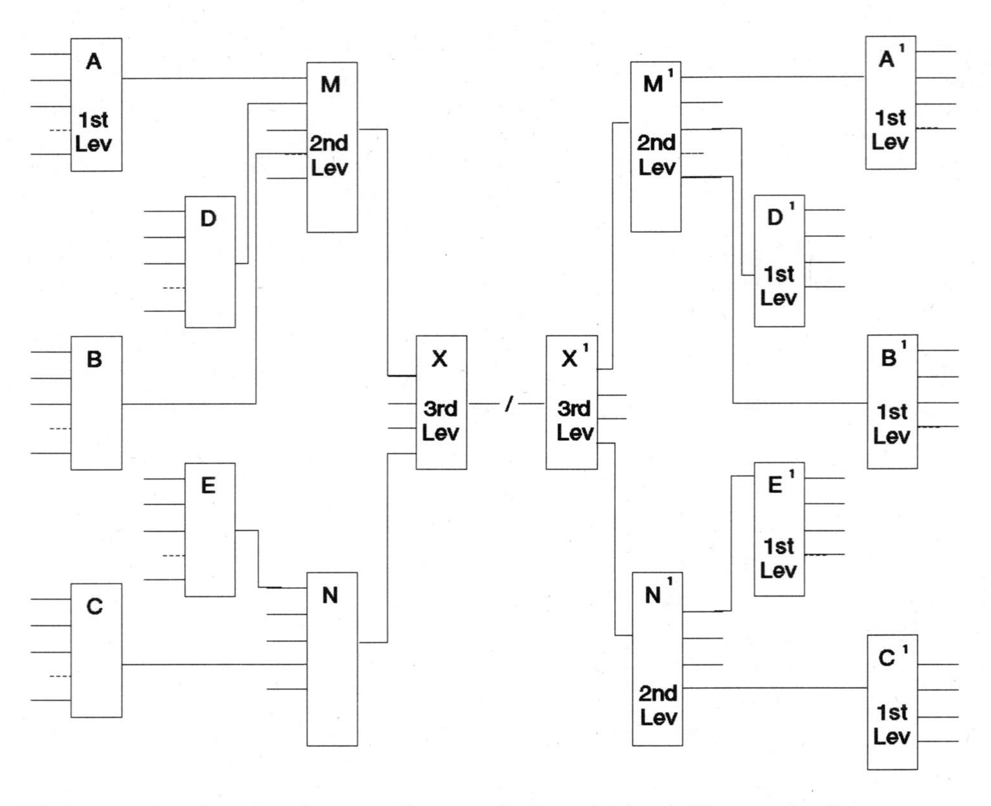


*Figure 8-6. The Multiplexor Mountain.* Each multiplexor illustrated exists as a separate physical device, although many multiplexors may be mounted together on a single rack.

In order to use a high-speed interexchange link it was necessary to multiplex a very large number of slower-speed circuits onto it in stages. The faster the link, the more stages required.

There are a number of important points to remember here:

1. The internals of this structure are proprietary. Each pair of multiplexors in the system has to be manufactured by the same supplier. In Figure 8-6 on page 8-16, the concept of multiplexor pairs is illustrated. A pair of multiplexors "see" a clear channel connection between them even though the connection might really go through several higher layer multiplexors. (In Figure 8-6 on page 8-16, multiplexors A and A′, B and B′ are multiplexor pairs.)

2. The multiplexing structure in the US is different from the structure used in Europe, and both are different from the structure used in Japan. This leads to compatibility problems when interconnecting systems between countries, and also means that equipment designed and built in one country often cannot be used in another.

3. There is an enormous cost benefit to be gained by integrating the multiplexing function with the internal functioning of the telephone exchange and hence removing the multiplexors entirely. Modern telephone exchanges are digital time-division multiplexors in themselves.

4. If access is needed to a single tributary circuit (or small group of circuits) then it is necessary to demultiplex the whole structure and then remultiplex it.

**Sonet and SDH eliminate these problems.** A single multiplexing scheme is specified that allows:

1. A standardized method of internal operation and management, so that equipment from many different manufacturers may be used productively together.

2. Multiple speeds of operation, such that as higher and higher optical speeds are introduced the system can expand gracefully to operate at the higher speeds.

3. Worldwide compatibility. A single optical multiplexing hierarchy which applies throughout the world and accommodates the existing speeds used in both Europe and the US.

4. Many levels of multiplexing and demultiplexing to be accomplished in a single step. (You do not have to demultiplex the higher levels to gain access to the lower levels.)

5. Many different payloads (different-speed channels) to be carried through the system.

6. Access to low bandwidth (T-1, E-1 style) tributaries without the need to demultiplex the whole stream.

7. Considerably better efficiency than before. For example, the floating payload feature of Sonet eliminates the need for the customary 125-μsec buffers required at crosspoints in the existing ("plesiochronous") multiplexing schemes.

## 8.2.1 Sonet Structure

The basic structure in Sonet is a frame of 810 bytes, which is sent every 125 μsec. This allows a single byte within a frame to be part of a 64-Kbps digital voice channel. Since the minimum frame size is 810 bytes, then the minimum speed at which Sonet will operate is 51.84 Mbps.

```
810 bytes × 8000 frames/sec × 8 (bits) = 51.84 Mbps
```

This basic frame is called the Synchronous Transport Signal level 1 (STS-1). It is conceptualized as containing 9 rows of 90 columns each as shown in Figure 8-7.

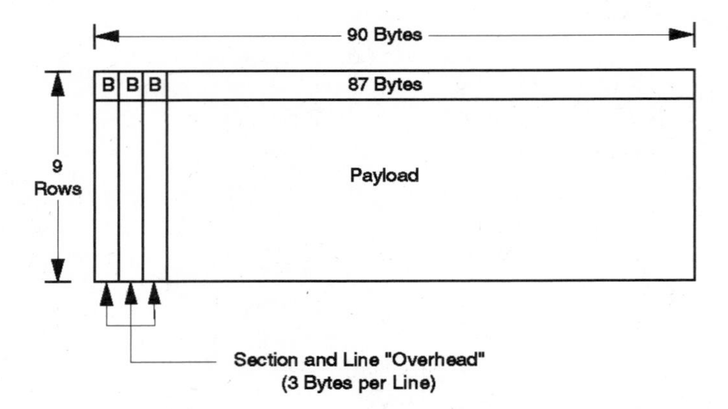


***Figure 8-7.*** *Sonet STS-1 Frame Structure.* The diagramatic representation of the frame as a square is done for ease of understanding. The 810 bytes are transmitted row by row starting from the top left of the diagram. One frame is transmitted every 125 microseconds.

- The first three columns of every row are used for administration and control of the multiplexing system. They are called "overhead" in the standard but are very necessary for the system's operation.
- The frame is transmitted row by row, from the top left of the frame to the bottom right.
- The representation of the structure as a two-dimensional frame is just a conceptual way of representing a repeating structure. In reality it is a string of bits with a defined repeating pattern.

The physical frame structure above is similar to every other TDM structure used in the telecommunications industry. The big difference is in how the "payload" is carried. The payload is a frame that "floats" within the physical frame structure. The payload envelope is illustrated in Figure 8-8 on page 8-19.

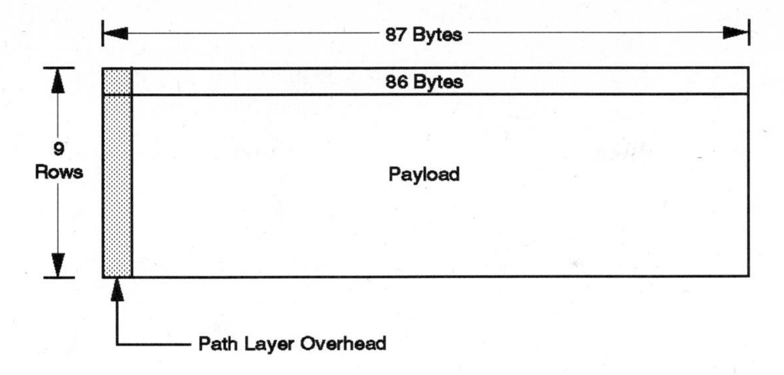


***Figure 8-8.** Sonet Synchronous Payload Envelope*

Notice that the payload envelope fits exactly within a single Sonet frame.

The payload envelope is allowed to start anywhere within the physical Sonet frame and in that case will span two consecutive physical frames. The start of the payload is pointed to by the H1 and H2 bytes within the line overhead sections.

Very small differences in the clock rates of the frame and the payload can be accommodated by temporarily incrementing or decrementing the pointer (an extra byte if needed is found by using one byte (H3) in the section header). Nevertheless, big differences in clock frequencies cannot be accommodated by this method.

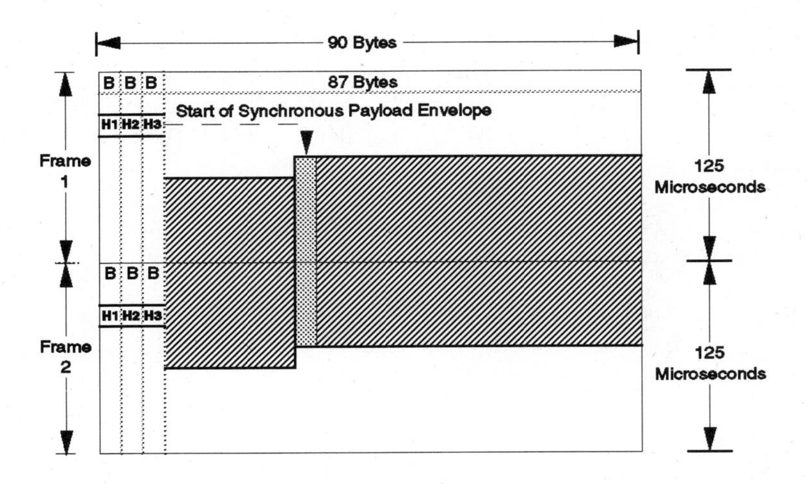


***Figure 8-9.** Synchronous Payload Envelope Floating in STS-1 Frame.* The SPE is pointed to by the H1 and H2 bytes.

Multiple STS-1 frames can be byte-multiplexed together to form higher-speed signals. When this is done they are called STS-2, STS-3, etc., where the numeral suffix indicates the number of STS-1 frames that are present (and therefore the line speed). For example STS-3 is 3 times an STS-1 or 155.52 Mbps. This multiplexing uses the method illustrated in Figure 8-10.

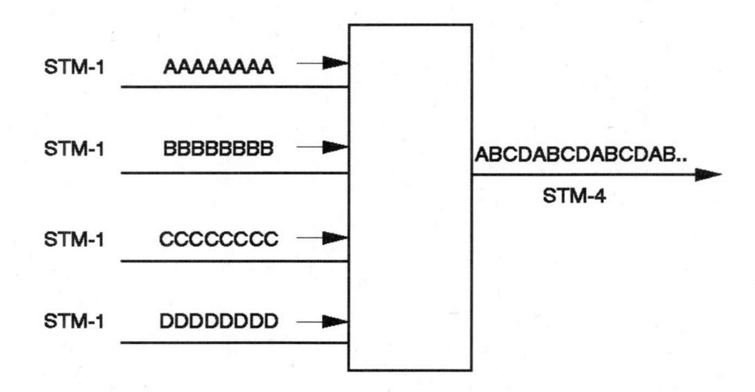


***Figure 8-10.*** *STM-1 to STM-4 Synchronous Multiplexing*

An alternative method is to phase-align the multiple STS frames and their payloads. This means that a larger payload envelope has been created. This is called "concatenation" and is indicated in the name of the signal. For example, when three STS-1s are concatenated such that the frames are phase-aligned and there is a single large payload envelope, it is called an STS-3c.

## 8.2.2 SDH

In the rest of the world, Sonet is not immediately useful because the "E-3" rate of 35 Mbps does not efficiently fit into the 50 Mbps Sonet signal. (The comparable US PDH signal, the T-3, is roughly 45 Mbps and fits nicely.)

The CCITT has defined a worldwide standard called the Synchronous Digital Hierarchy, which accommodates both Sonet and the European line speeds.

This was done by defining a basic frame that is exactly equivalent to (Sonet) STS-3c. This has a new name. It is Synchronous Transport Module level 1 or STM-1 and has a basic rate (minimum speed) of 155.52 Mbps. This is shown in Figure 8-11 on page 8-21.

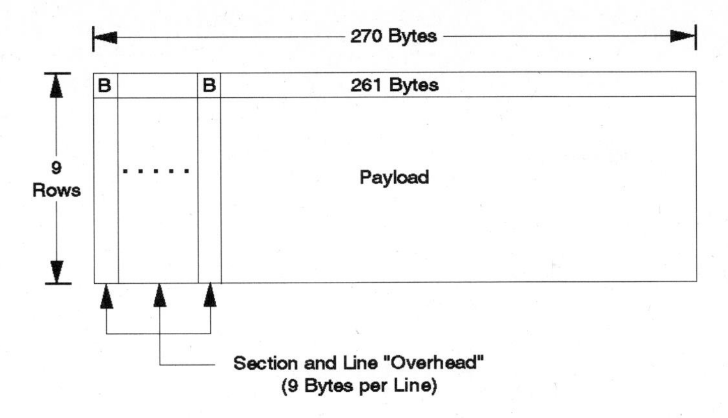


***Figure 8-11.*** *SDH Basic Frame Format*

Faster line speeds are obtained in the same way as in Sonet - by byte interleaving of multiple STM-1 frames. For this to take place (as in Sonet) the STM-1 frames must be 125-μsec frame aligned. Four STM-1 frames may be multiplexed to form an STM-4 at 622.08 Mbps. This (again like Sonet) may carry four separate payloads byte multiplexed together (see Figure 8-10 on page 8-20). Alternatively, the payloads may be concatenated (rather than interleaved) and the signal is then called STM-4c.

## 8.2.3 Tributaries

Within each payload, slower-speed channels (called tributaries) may be carried. Tributaries normally occupy a number of consecutive columns within a payload.

A US T-1 payload (1.544 Mbps) occupies three columns, a European E-1 payload (2.048 Mbps) occupies four columns. Notice that there is some wasted bandwidth here. A T-1 really only requires 24 slots and three columns gives it 27. An E-1 requires 32 slots and is given 36. This "wastage" is a very small price to pay for the enormous benefit to be achieved by being able to demultiplex a single tributary stream from within the multiplexed structure without having to demultiplex the whole stream.

The tributaries may be fixed within their virtual containers or they may float, similar to the way a virtual container floats within the physical frame. Pointers within the overhead are used to locate each virtual tributary stream.

### 8.2.4 Sonet/SDH Line Speeds and Signals

*Table 8-1. Sonet Speed Hierarchy*

| Signal Level | Bit Rate | DS-0s | DS-1s | DS-3s |
|---|---|---|---|---|
| STS-1 and OC-1 | 51.84 Mbps | 672 | 28 | 1 |
| STS-3 and OC-3 (STM-1) | 155.52 Mbps | 2,016 | 84 | 3 |
| STS-9 and OC-9 | 466.56 Mbps | 6,048 | 252 | 9 |
| STS-12 and OC-12 (STM-4) | 622.08 Mbps | 8,064 | 336 | 12 |
| STS-18 and OC-18 | 933.12 Mbps | 12,096 | 504 | 18 |
| STS-24 and OC-24 | 1244.16 Mbps | 16,128 | 672 | 24 |
| STS-36 and OC-36 | 1866.24 Mbps | 24,192 | 1008 | 36 |
| STS-48 and OC-48 (STM-16) | 2488.32 Mbps | 32,256 | 1344 | 48 |
| STS-n and OC-n (STM-n/3) | n × 51.84 Mbps | n × 672 | n × 28 | n |

### 8.2.5 Status

Sonet/SDH standards are now firm and equipment implementing them is beginning to become available. However, there are many desirable extensions that have not yet been standardized. For example, there is no generalized standard for interfacing customer premises equipment to STS-3c (STM) available as yet. The ITU-T has specified this for attachment to ATM networks and a similar specification exists in FDDI.

### 8.2.6 Conclusion

Successful specification of a system which integrates and accommodates all of the different line speeds and characteristics of US and European multiplexing hierarchies was a formidable challenge. Sonet/SDH is a complex system but it is also a very significant achievement. It is expected that equipment using SDH will become the dominant form of network multiplexing equipment within a very short time.

## 8.3 The Bandwidth Fragmentation Problem

Existing telecommunication backbone systems are almost exclusively based on TDM structures. The system is cost effective and efficient in an environment where bandwidth allocation is done in a small number of fixed amounts.

In the future, high-speed backbone wide area networks owned by the PTTs will need to become a lot more flexible. It is predicted that there will be significant demand for arbitrary amounts of bandwidth and for "variable bandwidth", such as is needed for a video signal. Many planners in the PTTs believe that TDM technology is not sufficiently flexible to satisfy this requirement. This is partly because of the perceived "waste" in using fixed rate services for variable traffic (such as interactive image, variable-rate voice or variable-rate encoded video) and partly because arbitrary variable amounts of bandwidth are very difficult to allocate in a TDM system. This latter problem is called "bandwidth fragmentation".

The problem of bandwidth fragmentation on a TDM link is exactly the same problem as storage fragmentation in main storage buffer pools within a computer system.

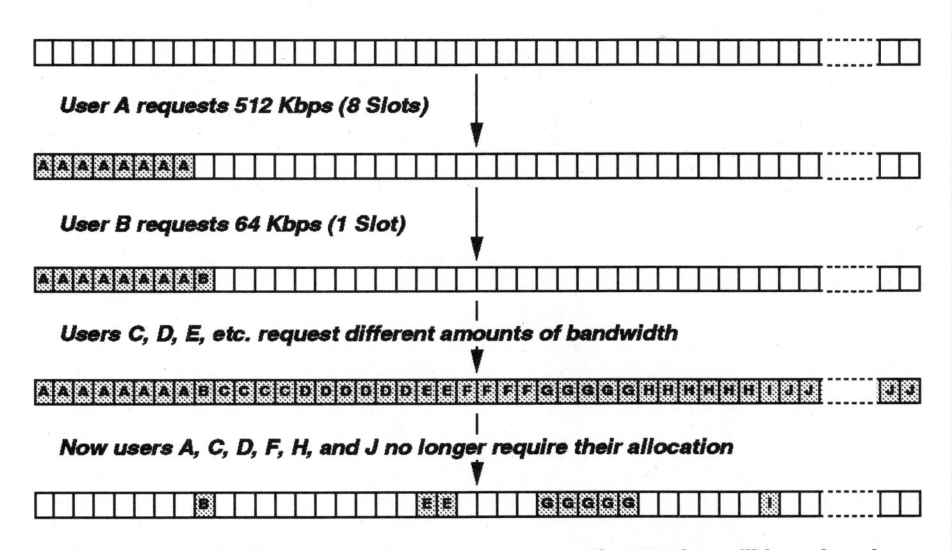


*Figure 8-12. Bandwidth Fragmentation*

For the example in Figure 8-12 assume we have a 4 Mbps link which consists of 64, 64 Kbps slots. The example is a trivial one but it illustrates the point. In computer memory variable-length buffer pools (before virtual storage fixed the problem), it was found that after operation for a long period of time perhaps only 20% of the memory would be in use and the other 80% would be broken up into fragments that were too small to use. This is a significant waste of resource. In addition, the control mechanisms needed to operate a scheme such as this would be complex and more expensive than alternative schemes based on cell multiplexing.

A mechanism like the computer's virtual storage could be used to concatenate multiple 64 Kbps channels into wider logical channels, but that requires significant hardware and will only work when communication on the link is peer-to-peer. In the new Sonet/SDH system it is possible for multiple devices to access the same link and extract groups of channels (tributaries) without the need to demultiplex the whole channel. A virtual channel allocation system would take away this ability.

This problem is the primary reason that Broadband ISDN uses a cell-based switching system.

### 8.3.1 Synchronous Transfer Mode (STM)

Synchronous Transfer Mode was a proposed TDM system for implementing Broadband ISDN. It was developed for some time by standards committees. It uses the same principles as SDH (and can be thought of as an extension of SDH). STM was abandoned in favor of the Asynchronous Transfer Mode (ATM) cell-switching approach. One of the reasons for this was the difficulty in managing bandwidth allocation (bandwidth fragmentation).

## 8.4 Plesiochronous Digital Hierarchy

PDH is the digital networking hierarchy that was used before the advent of Sonet/SDH. The link speeds are included here for reference.

***Table 8-2.*** *PDH Speed Hierarchy - USA*

| Level | Speed in Mbps | Number of Channels |
|---|---|---|
| DS-0 | 64 Kbps | 1 |
| T-1, DS-1 | 1.544 | 24 |
| T-2, DS-2 | 6.312 | 96 |
| T-3, DS-3 | 44.736 | 672 |
| T-4, DS-4 | 274.176 | 4032 |

***Table 8-3.*** *PDH Speed Hierarchy - Europe*

| Level | Speed in Mbps | Number of Channels |
|---|---|---|
| E-1 | 2.048 | 30 |
| E-2 | 8.448 | 120 |
| E-3 | 34.368 | 480 |
| E-4 | 139.264 | 1920 |
| E-5 | 564.992 | 7680 |

# Chapter 9. Cell-Based Systems (ATM)

The concept of cell switching can be thought of as either a high performance form of packet switching or as a form of statistical multiplexing performed on fixed-length blocks of data.

A cell is really not too different from a packet. A block of user data is broken up into packets or cells for transmission through the network. But there are significant differences between cell-based networks and packet networks.

1. A cell is fixed in length. In packet networks the packet size is a fixed maximum (for a given connection) but individual packets may always be shorter than the maximum. In a cell-based network cells are a fixed length, no more and no less.

2. Cells tend to be a lot shorter than packets. This is really a compromise over requirements. In the early days of X.25 many of the designers wanted a packet size of 32 bytes so that voice could be handled properly. However, the shorter the packet size, the more network overhead there is in sending a given quantity of data over a wide area network. To efficiently handle data, packets should be longer (in X.25 the default packet size supported by all networks is 128 bytes).

3. Cell-based networks do *not* use link-level error recoveries. In some networks there is an error checking mechanism that allows the network to throw away cells in error. In others, such as in ATM (described below) only the header field is checked for errors and it is left to a "higher-layer" protocol to provide a checking mechanism for the data portion of the cell if needed by the application.

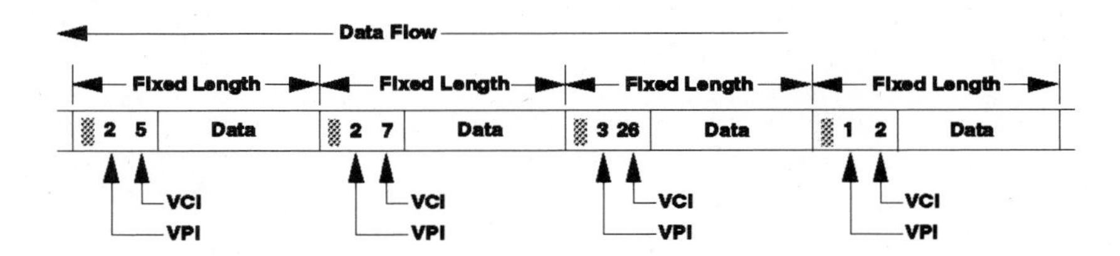


***Figure 9-1.*** *Cell Multiplexing on a Link.* Cells belonging to different logical connections (identified by the VPI and VCI) are transmitted one after the other on the link. This is not a new concept in the data switching world but it is quite different from the fixed multiplexing techniques used in the TDM approach.

Figure 9-1 shows a sequence of cells from different connections being transmitted on a link. This should be contrasted with the TDM (Time Division Multiplexing) technique, where capacity is allocated on a time slot basis regardless of whether there is data to send for that connection. Cell-based networks use extremely fast and efficient hardware-based switching nodes to give very high throughput, that is, millions of cells per second. These networks are designed to operate over very low-error-rate, very high-speed digital (preferably optical) links.

The reasons for using this architecture are:

- If we use very short fixed-length cells then it simplifies (and therefore speeds up) the switching hardware needed in nodal switches.
- The smaller the cells can be made, the shorter the transit delay through a network consisting of multiple nodes. This principle is described in 6.5, "Transporting Data in Packets or Cells" on page 6-19.
- The statistical principle of large numbers (see Appendix C.1.4, "Practical Systems" on page C-6) means that a very uniform network transit delay with low variance can be anticipated with the cell approach.
- Intermediate queues within switching nodes contain only cells of the same length. This reduces the variation in network transit delays due to irregular-length data blocks (which take irregular lengths of time to transmit) in the queues.

The reasons that cell switching had not been popular in the past are:

- High-error-rate analog links potentially cause too high an error rate to allow end-to-end recovery. In most cases, link-level error recovery is needed.
- With the software-based switching technology of the 1970s and 1980s a cell (or packet) takes the same amount of processing time in a switching node *regardless of its length.* Thus the shorter the packet or cell, the greater the cost of the processing in the intermediate switches.
- Hardware technology had not progressed to the point where total hardware switching was economically feasible (it has been technically possible for some years).
- In the older technology end-to-end error recovery processing added a very significant cost to the attaching equipment. (Significantly more storage and instruction cycles required.) This is needed with cell networks today but hardware cost has become much less and this is no longer a problem.
- The presence of link headers at the front of each cell caused a measurable overhead in link capacity. In the days when a 2,400 bps link was considered "fast" this was a significant overhead. The cost of link capacity (or bandwidth) is reducing daily and this overhead is no longer considered significant.

The cell technique is intended to provide the efficiencies inherent in packet switching without the drawbacks that this technique has had in the past. Because cells are small and uniform in size, it is thought that a uniform transit delay can be provided through quite a large network and that this can be short enough for high-quality voice operation.

## 9.1 Asynchronous Transfer Mode (ATM)

Asynchronous Transfer Mode (ATM)[1] is a new communications technology which is fundamentally and radically different from previous technologies. Its commercial availability marks what promises to be a genuine revolution in both the data communications (read computer) and telecommunications (read telephone) industries.

Around about 1988 the telecommunications (carrier) industry began to develop a concept called **Broadband Integrated Services Digital Network or B-ISDN**. This was conceived as a *carrier service* to provide high-speed communications to end users in an integrated way. The *technology* selected to deliver the B-ISDN service was/is called **Asynchronous Transfer Mode or ATM**.

ATM has expanded to cover much that is not strictly B-ISDN. B-ISDN is a carrier interface and carrier network service. ATM is a technology that may be used in many environments unrelated to carrier services. Holding long and convoluted discussions about the fine distinctions between ATM and B-ISDN is pointless in the context of understanding the technology. For most practical purposes the terms ATM and B-ISDN are interchangeable. Hence in this book we will use the term ATM almost exclusively.

In 1990 industry forecasters were saying that ATM would begin an experimental phase in 1993, have early commercial products in perhaps 1997 and that the year 2000 would be the year of the mass usage. In 1993 they said commercial products in 1994 and mass acceptance as early as 1995! Reality seems to be commercial products in 1995 and mass acceptance in 1996/1997. (Although many of the standards are not scheduled for completion until the middle of 1996!)

In the past two years an unprecedented consensus has formed throughout the communications industry that ATM will be the universal networking standard. This consensus has caused the vast bulk of development in the industry to be shifted towards ATM development. Within the last year or so some 50 organizations have either foreshadowed or announced ATM products.

The almost universal acceptance (among suppliers and developers) of ATM comes from the fact that *ATM is a compromise*:

- ATM will handle all the different kinds of communication traffic (voice, data, image, video, high-quality sound, multimedia, etc.) in an integrated way.

[1] This discussion on ATM is condensed from *Asynchronous Transfer Mode (Broadband ISDN) - Technical Overview*, IBM number GG24-4330 by the same author.

- ATM can be used in both the LAN and the WAN network environments and hence promises a seamless interworking between the two (something we have never had before).

Thus it is effective in a much wider range of communications environments than any previous technology. There are a number of other factors:

- ATM is a new technology designed to operate in the current technological environment (as distinct from older networking systems that are now obsolescent).

- ATM is a very cost-effective alternative for building a LAN system. Users can be connected to an ATM LAN system using adapters supporting the transmission speeds according to their individual bandwidth requirements.

But **ATM is a compromise**.

- ATM does not handle voice as efficiently (or as cost-effectively) as does an isochronous network.

- ATM does not handle video as easily as isochronous transfer does (although it is probably a lot more efficient).

- ATM certainly does not handle data as effectively or efficiently as a "packet transfer mode" or frame relay system.

- ATM is likely to be problematic in any high-error-rate environment (such as some slower copper wire connections).

**Nevertheless, ATM will handle all types of traffic perfectly adequately and in an integrated way**. This means that instead of having a proliferation of many specialized kinds of equipment for different functions, we can have a single type of equipment and network which will do everything. The wide range of application for ATM means that there will be very large demand for ATM products. It is widely believed that the resulting reduction in costs will more than compensate for marginal inefficiencies in handling any single type of traffic.

A number of factors led to the development of ATM:

1. The advent of very high-speed communication links (especially in the use of fiber optical connections) meant that the technological environment changed utterly. While existing networking architectures will continue to work in the new environment, their performance does not improve (they do not go any faster) when link speeds get faster. Thus a new data network architecture was needed.

2. The very real user demand for data communications services and for ever-faster services caused the carriers to look for an integrated way of supplying these services. Running separate and disparate networks is very expensive.

3. Silicon chip technology improved to the point where we can now build very fast (hardware-based) switching systems and these provide an opportunity to perform some applications significantly more efficiently (such as LAN systems).
4. The general belief that integrated packet (or cell) based switching systems will be significantly lower in cost than time division multiplexed (TDM) type systems.
5. The development (again due to improvements in silicon technology) of much faster and lower-cost computer hardware made many new applications possible that were not economically feasible before. Multimedia applications such as personal videoconferencing is one such application.

### 9.1.1 ATM Concept

The key concepts of ATM are as follows:

**Cells**

All information (voice, image, video, data, etc.) is transported through the network in very short (48 data bytes plus a 5-byte header) blocks called *cells*.

**Routing**

Information flow is along paths (called *virtual channels*) set up as a series of pointers through the network. The cell header contains an identifier that links the cell to the correct path for it to take towards its destination.

Cells on a particular virtual channel always follow the same path through the network and are delivered to the destination in the same order in which they were received.

**Hardware-Based Switching**

ATM is designed so that simple hardware-based logic elements may be employed at each node to perform the switching. On a link of 1 Gbps a new cell arrives and a cell is transmitted every .43 μsec. There is not a lot of time to decide what to do with an arriving packet.

**Adaptation**

At the edges of the network user data frames are broken up into cells. Continuous data streams such as voice and video are assembled into cells. At the destination side of the network the user data frames are reconstructed from the received cells and returned to the end user in the form (data frames, etc.) that they were delivered to the network. This adaptation function is considered part of the network but is a higher-layer function from the transport of cells.

**Error Control**

The ATM cell-switching network only checks cell headers for errors and simply discards errored cells.

The adaptation function is external to the switching network and depends somewhat on the type of traffic but for data traffic it usually checks for errors in data frames received and if one is found then it discards the whole frame.

At no time does the ATM network attempt to recover from errors by the re-transmission of information. This function is up to the end-user devices and depends on the type of traffic being carried.

**Flow Controls**

An ATM network has no internal flow controls of any kind. The required processing logic is too complex to be accommodated at the speeds involved. Instead ATM has a set of input rate controls that limit the rate of traffic delivered to the network.

Other forms of input control are under discussion in various standards bodies.

**Congestion Control**

There is only one thing an ATM network can do when a link or node becomes congested. Cells are discarded until the problem has been relieved. Some (lower-priority) cells can be marked such that they are the first to be discarded in the case of congestion.

Connection endpoints are *not notified* when cells are discarded. It is up to the adaptation function or higher-layer protocols to detect and recover from the loss of cells (if necessary and possible).

## 9.2 The Structure of an ATM Network

The conceptual structure of an ATM network is shown in Figure 9-2 on page 9-7.

**ATM Networks**

In the referenced figure there are three quite separate ATM networks - two private and one public.

Private ATM networks are sometimes called *customer premises networks* and indeed they will very often be confined to a local area such as a building or a campus. However, a private ATM network can be distributed over a wide area by the use of carrier (non-ATM) links between ATM nodes. Such links could be copper-wire leased lines, “dark” fibers[2], or Sonet/SDH[3] TDM connections.

---

2 A dark fiber is a fiber connection provided by a carrier that is not restricted just like a copper wire leased line. It is dark because there is no light in the fiber until the user puts it there.

3 See 8.2, “SDH and Sonet” on page 8-16.

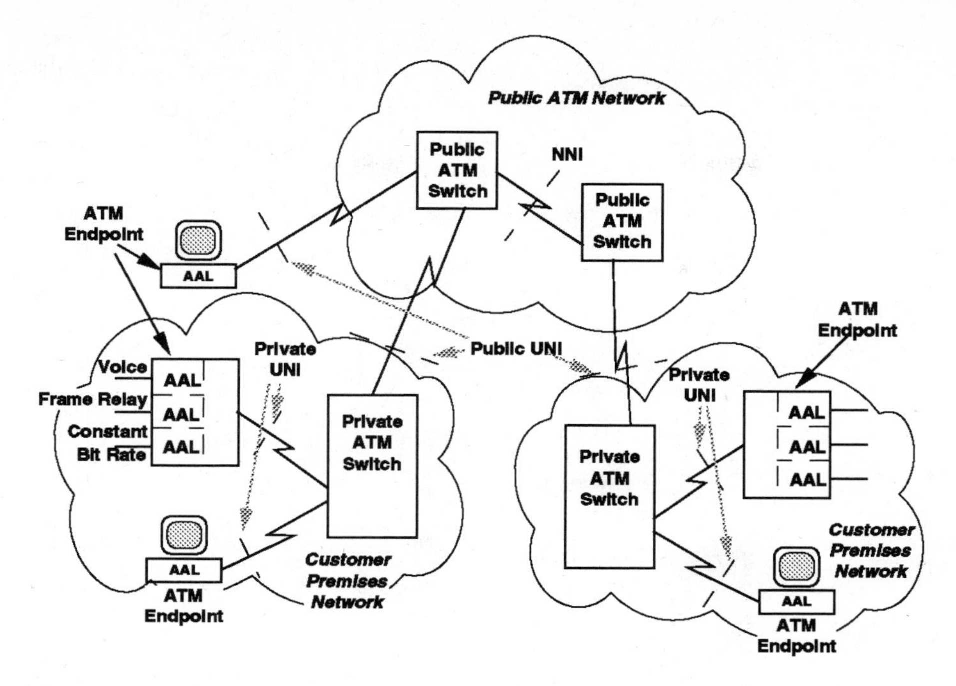


*Figure 9-2. ATM Network Structure Overview*

## ATM Switches

Four ATM switches are shown in Figure 9-2. These perform the backbone data transport within the ATM network. They are usually classified as either private ATM switches or public ATM switches. The difference between private and public ATM equipment could be trivial in some cases but will often be quite major. Public and private switches will differ in the kinds of trunks (links) supported, in accounting and control procedures and in the addressing modes supported. There is also the obvious question of size. Public network equipment will usually need much higher throughput than will private equipment.

Public ATM switches are sometimes referred to as network nodes (NNs). This is incorrect as the term network node is not defined in ATM standards - even though there is a network node interface.

Private ATM switches and networks are sometimes called customer premises nodes (CPNs) or customer premises networks. Again, this terminology, while useful, is not defined in the ATM standards.

## ATM Endpoint

The ATM endpoint is a piece of end-user equipment that interfaces to an ATM network in a native way. An endpoint sends and receives ATM cells on link connections defined by ATM standards. An endpoint (and only an endpoint) contains an ATM Adaptation Layer (AAL) function.[4]

An ATM endpoint connects to the ATM network over the user network interface (UNI).

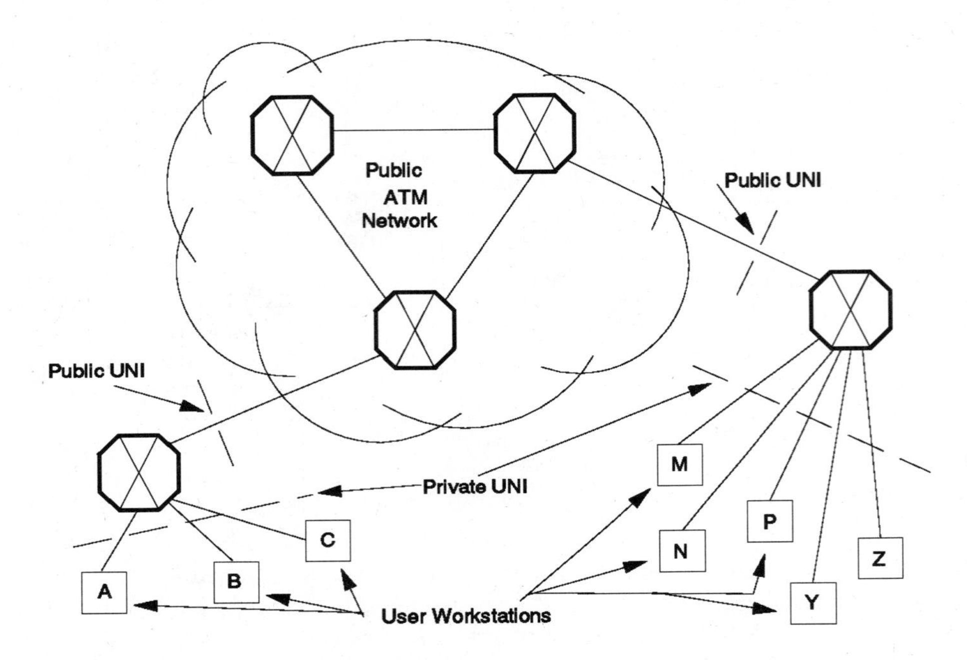


*Figure 9-3. ATM User-Network Interfaces*

## User Network Interface (UNI)

The UNI is specified exactly by the applicable standards. It is structured according to the reference model for ISDN illustrated in Figure 8-1 on page 8-3.

There are two somewhat different UNIs called *public* and *private*. The public UNI is for connection of end-user equipment to a public ATM network. The

4 However, it must be noted that ATM switches will often contain ATM endpoint functions as well as switch functions.

private UNI is for use within a single organization's premises or for a private network using lines leased from the PTT.

The major differences between the two are:

1. Some of the link types allowed at the private UNI use protocols that only work over very short distances (such as 100 meters). These would be obviously not applicable to a public network interface.

2. Public ATM networks will use E.164 addresses (similar to telephone numbers) while private networks will probably use addressing techniques derived from LANs or from OSI.

3. The public UNI is defined and controlled by the ITU-T. The private UNI is defined by the ATM Forum.

### Network Node Interface a.k.a. Network-to-Network Interface (NNI)

As shown in Figure 9-2 on page 9-7, this is the trunk connection between two ATM switches. As the standard has evolved three distinct flavors of the NNI have emerged.

1. The **NNI-ISSI** will be used to connect ATM switches within a local area and belonging to the same telephone company. In the US this equates to nodes which are in the same LATA (Local Access Transport Area).

2. The **NNI-ICI** is the intercarrier interface and will typically be used to interconnect ATM networks operated by different telephone companies. This could be the interface between the local carrier and the longline carrier (in the US) or an international connection.

3. The **Private NNI** (PNNI) allows connection of different ATM switches in a private network environment.

The differences between these interfaces is mainly one of emphasis. For example, the addressing formats used are likely to be different and you might not need accounting at a private NNI, where you certainly do need it at the NNI-ICI.

### Links

There may be one or many physical link connections between the nodes. These are shown as shaded areas in Figure 9-4 on page 9-11. The multiplexing of virtual paths and virtual channels over a physical link connection is shown in Figure 9-5 on page 9-13.

Links between nodes may be carried as clear channels such as over a direct point-to-point connection but may also be carried over a Sonet/SDH connection or over a PDH connection.

## Network Internals

In Figure 9-2 on page 9-7 the ATM public network is shown as a cloud. Representation of public networks as clouds has become traditional since the first public data network standard, X.25. One of the reasons for the cloud representation was that the standard defined only the interface to the end user and the services to be provided by the network. The internals of X.25 networks are not covered by any standard. *Things are different in ATM.* The internals of the ATM network are in the process of rigorous standardization and so while the end user may still see it as a cloud (because its internal detail will be masked from the end user) its internal protocols will be exactly understood.

## Cells

As mentioned earlier, the ATM network transports data (including voice and video) as 53-byte cells. The objective is to provide a very short, constant transit time through the network. Within the network there are no error recoveries (there is error detection for cell header information). Flow and congestion control are done not by the detailed interactive protocols of traditional data networks, but by control on the rate of admission of traffic to the network (and a strong reliance on the statistical characteristics of the traffic). When network congestion is experienced there is no alternative - cells must be discarded.

## ATM Adaptation Layers (AAL)

End users of an ATM network will be of two kinds:

- Those that interface to the ATM network directly through either the public UNI or a private UNI
- Those that do not know anything about ATM and interface using a non-ATM protocol (such as frame relay)

In either case a significant amount of logic is required *over and above what is provided by ATM* in order to use the network productively.

For all types of users there are common tasks that must be performed in order to connect to the ATM network. In its definition ATM includes processing for these common tasks. This is called the *ATM Adaptation Layer (AAL).* The AAL is the real end-user interface to ATM.

The AAL *never* interfaces to an external link or device. The AAL provides a programming interface and end users are connected to the ATM network by program functions external to ATM. The AAL only provides some common attachment functions - many protocol layers are usually required above the AAL for useful work to be performed.

Figure 9-2 on page 9-7 is perhaps a little misleading in the positioning of the AAL. End users using voice or frame relay or whatever must attach through an

AAL *but a lot more than just the AAL code is needed.* AAL just provides a more convenient, standardized way of accessing the network from a program. The program then interfaces with other external links, such as voice or frame relay or higher layers of some other communication protocol.

## 9.2.1 Virtual Channels and Virtual Routes

Perhaps the key concepts in ATM are those relating to how data is routed through the network. Figure 9-4 illustrates these concepts.

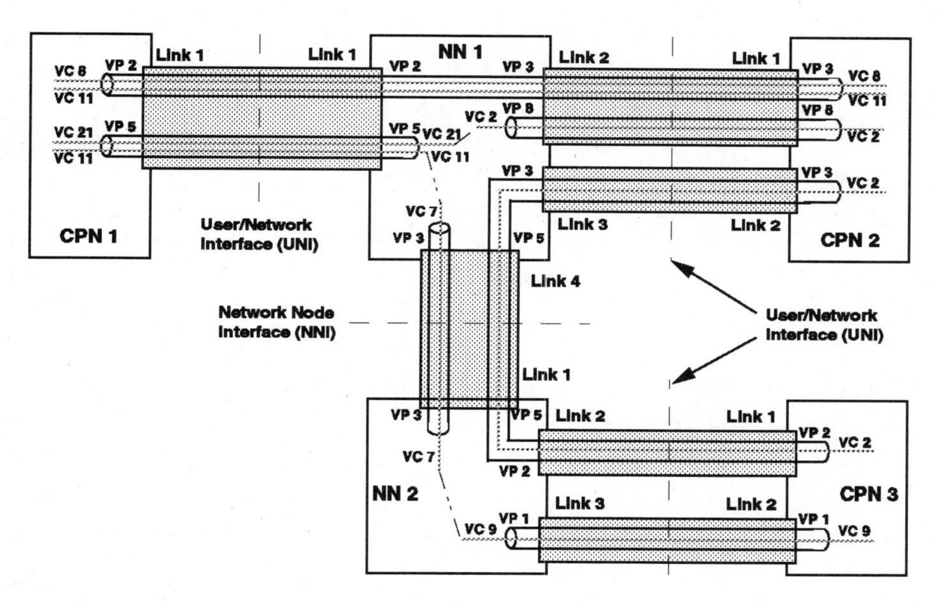


***Figure 9-4.*** *Routing Concept in an ATM Network*

**Virtual Path (VP)**

A VP is a route through the network representing a group of virtual channels (VCs). VPs may exist:

1. Between ATM endpoints (as between endpoint 1 and endpoint 2 and between endpoint 2 and endpoint 3 in Figure 9-4)
2. Between ATM switches and ATM endpoints (as between ATM switch 1 and endpoint 1, ATM switch 1 and endpoint 2 and ATM switch 2 and endpoint 3 in Figure 9-4) and
3. Between ATM switches (as between ATM switch 1 and ATM switch 2 in Figure 9-4)

A VP may be routed through an ATM switch by reference only to the VP number or it may terminate in an ATM switch. A VP entering an endpoint always terminates in that endpoint.

**Virtual Channel (VC)**

The concept of a virtual channel is defined in ATM as a unidirectional connection between end users. However, the use of the acronym VC for many other purposes in communications (such as the virtual circuit in X.25), means that its use is often confused.

**Virtual Channel Connection (VCC)**

A virtual channel connection is the end-to-end connection along which a user sends data. The concept is very close to that of a virtual circuit in X.25. The major difference is that a virtual channel connection carries data in one direction only, whereas a virtual circuit is bidirectional.

While a VCC is defined to be unidirectional, it must be noted that VCCs *always occur in pairs*. One VCC in each direction. Thus a bidirectional communication channel consists of a pair of VCCs (carried over the same route through the network).

The concepts of VC and VCC are likewise almost the same. The acronym VC is most often used in a generic context and VCC in much more specific ways.

**Virtual Channel Link (VCL)**

A virtual channel link is a separately identified data flow within a link or a virtual path. A virtual channel connection (VCC) through the network is a sequence of interconnected (concatenated) VCLs.

The relationship between links, VPs and VCs is summarized in Figure 9-5 on page 9-13.

**Links within nodes**

An ATM node may have many links attached. The maximum number of links and their addressing (numbering) within the node is *not* within the scope of the ATM standards.

**VPs within links**

Within each link there are a number of VPs. The maximum number is defined by the number of bits allocated to virtual path identifiers (VPIs) within the ATM cell header (8 or 12 bits).

**VCs within VPs**

Each VP has a number of VCs within it. The maximum number is restricted by the number of bits allocated to virtual channel identifiers (VCIs) within the cell header (16 bits).

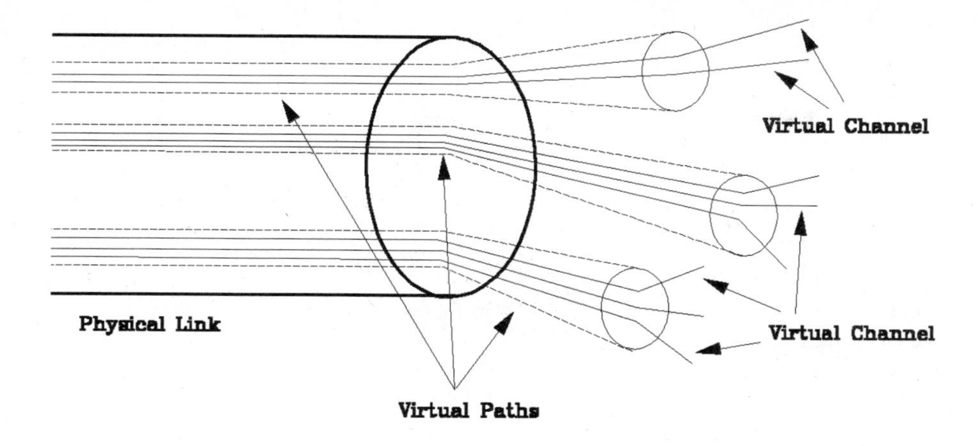


*Figure 9-5. Link, Virtual Path and Virtual Channel Relationship*

As far as the architecture of ATM is concerned, each link may have all possible VPs and each VP may have all possible VCs within it. (In practice, nodes will limit the maxima to much smaller values for practical considerations, such as table space within a node.)

It is important to note that the scope of the numbering of each entity is just within the entity above it in the hierarchy. For example, all VPs may exist on all links - so VP number 2 may exist on link number 3 and there may be a VP number 2 on link number 7 and both VPs are unrelated to one another. There could be a VC number 17 in *every* VP in a node.

**VPs and VCs are only numbers!** They identify a virtual (logical) path along which data may flow. They have *no* inherent capacity restrictions in terms of data throughput.[5] That is, dividing the link into VPs and VCs has nothing whatever to do with division of link capacity. You could saturate any link no matter what the speed with data on just one VC - even if the link had all possible VPs and VCs defined!

A good analogy is the US road system, where a single physical road can have many route numbers (sometimes up to 30 or more). The cars traveling on the road may consider themselves to be following any one of the numbered routes. But at any point in time all the cars on the road may consider themselves to be using the same route number.

---

[5] There are deliberate restrictions imposed on the rate of entry of data into the network, but this is not relevant here.

## 9.2.2 Cell Format

The cell format at the user network interface (UNI) and the network node interface (NNI) is illustrated in Figure 9-6 and Figure 9-7.

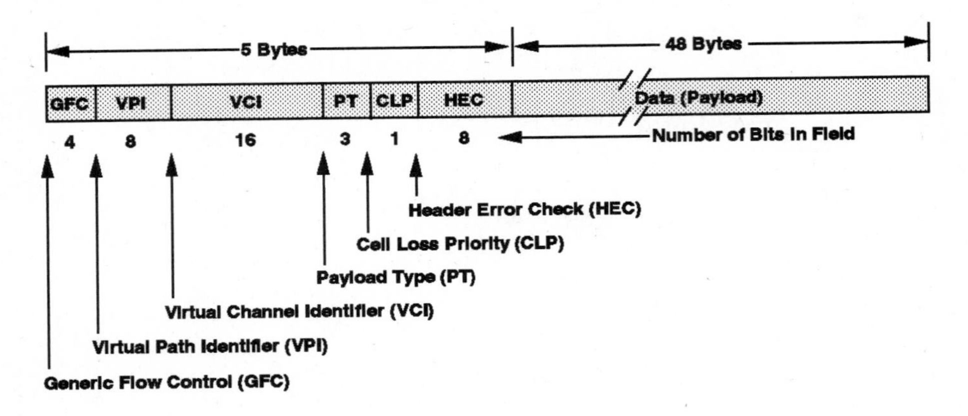


*Figure 9-6. ATM Cell Format at User Network Interface (UNI)*

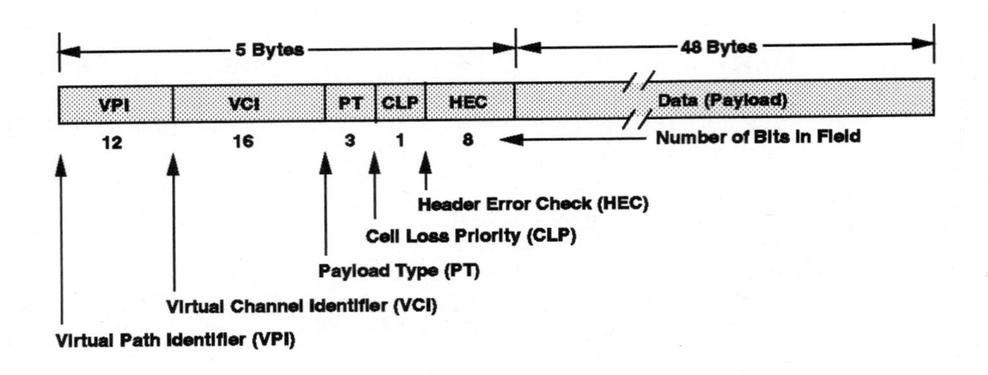


*Figure 9-7. ATM Cell Format at Network Node Interface (NNI)*

### Cell Size

An ATM cell is always 48 bytes of data with a 5-byte header; it *cannot* be longer or shorter. This cell size was determined by the CCITT (now called the ITU-T) as a compromise between voice and data requirements.

### Generic Flow Control (GFC)

At the present time, the GFC function has not been standardized. However, from the two cell headers it should be noted that the GFC field does *not* appear in the cell header on the NN interface. Therefore it is not carried through the network and has only local significance between the ATM endpoint and the ATM switch to which it is attached.

### VPI and VCI

The most important fields in the cell header are the virtual path identifier (VPI) and the virtual channel identifier (VCI). Together these identify the connection (called a virtual connection) that this cell belongs to. There is no destination network address because this would be too much of an overhead for a 48-byte cell to carry.

The VPI/VCI together are similar in function to the logical channel identifier in X.25 or the DLCI of frame relay in that they do not identify the destination address of the cell explicitly, but rather they identify a connection which leads to the desired destination.

#### Reserved Values

There are a number of reserved VPI and VCI values that are used for signaling, operation and maintenance and resource management. The range from VCI=0 to VCI=15 is reserved by the ITU-T. The range from VCI=16 to VCI=31 is reserved by the ATM Forum. This applies to VCIs within all VPs.

#### Empty Cells

A cell with both VPI and VCI values set to zero indicates that the cell is unassigned (empty). Unassigned cells are used on physical links that have framed structures (generally PDH and SDH). On these connections when there is no data to send on a link, the sender must send something so an empty cell is sent. At the receiver, these cells are immediately discarded. On links that are unframed (such as the 100 Mbps optical link derived from FDDI), the gaps between cells are filled with idles and therefore empty cells are never transmitted.

Any given ATM node may implement fewer than the possible maximum VPI and VCI numbers. In fact most nodes will do this. When a node implements less than the maximum then it must use an integral number of contiguous bits and these must be the low-order bits of the field. VC and VP values of 0 have reserved usages.

### Payload Type (PT)

Three bits are available for payload type (PT) identification, hereafter named bit0, bit1, and bit2 in the sequence of their occurrence in the 3-bit field. The first bit, bit0, determines if this cell is for a user data flow (when set 0) or for operations, administration and management (OA&M). If the cell carries user data (bit0=0) then bit1=1 means that congestion was experienced somewhere along the cell's route (bit1=0 means no congestion on the route).

Bit2 is used by higher layers. At the present time it is only specified for AAL-5 where bit2=1 means that this cell is the end of a block of user data (bit2=0 means this cell is the beginning or the middle of a block).

### Cell Loss Priority (CLP)

When set to 1 this bit indicates that the cell is of *low* priority. That is, if the system needs to discard cells to relieve congestion, then this cell should be discarded first. It is incorrect but in some publications this bit is referred to as the DE (Discard Eligibility) bit.

### Header Error Check (HEC)

This field allows the *correction* of all single-bit errors in the header part of the cell *or* for the *detection* of most single and multi-bit errors. The *or* in the previous sentence is critical. When the algorithm determines that there is an error it has no reliable way of determining whether that error is a (correctable) single-bit error or an (uncorrectable) multi-bit error.

What to do in this situation requires further study. If the overwhelming majority of errors are single bit, then it seems the best thing to do is to correct them and to tolerate the fact that some misrouting will occur on cells that really had multi-bit errors. Or you could play it safe and discard all cells where the algorithm says there is an error.

In addition to its use for error detection, it is used for determining cell boundaries on some types of physical link connection.

When the link is unsynchronized and cell boundaries are unknown (such as at initialization), the receiver will scan its input data looking for 5-byte groups such that the 5th byte is a valid HEC for the previous 4 bytes. When this condition is detected, the receiver waits for 48 bytes to go past and then tries again if the next 5 bytes received also pass the test as a valid header. This process is repeated a specified number of times. When the check is successful for the defined number of times, the receiver declares that it has obtained valid cell synchronization. The chances of invalid synchronization being gained are very low.

### 9.2.3 Network Characteristics

#### 9.2.3.1 Connection-Oriented Network

An ATM system is a connection-oriented system. There is no way to send data in an ATM network except on a pre-established connection (VCC). The system uses either call-by-call (switched circuit) setup or semi-permanent connections (set up by OA&M procedures).

#### 9.2.3.2 Connectionless Operation

There is a connectionless mode of operation defined. This operates "over the top" of the ATM network. There are one or many "connectionless servers" which are just connectionless routers within the ATM network. Each user that requires connectionless service has a connection to the connectionless server.

In this mode of operation the first cell (or cells) of a group carries the full network address of the destination within its data (payload) field. Subsequent cells belonging to the same user data block do not carry a full network address, but rather are related to the first cell by having the same VPI/VCI as it had.

In a sense connectionless operation is external to the ATM network since it operates at a layer above ATM and operates using pre-established ATM connections.

#### 9.2.3.3 Guaranteed In-Sequence Delivery

Cells delivered to the network by an ATM endpoint over a virtual connection are transferred to the partner ATM endpoint in the same sequence as they were presented to the network. This is very important, as it means that the end user (or the adaptation layer function) does not have to resequence cells that arrive out of order. But it also restricts the network to using a single path for any given virtual connection (at any particular point in time).

The payload (data) part of a cell may contain errors. Transmission errors within the data portion of the cell are *not* detected by the network (this is up to either the end-user equipment or the adaptation layer).

#### 9.2.3.4 Broadcast and Multicast

Broadcast and multicast operation is available in ATM. In reality, there is no true "send it to everyone, I don't care" form of broadcast. A broadcast is a multicast with all users connected.

Multicasting takes place over a tree structure, as illustrated in Figure 9-8 on page 9-18. Its official name is "point-to-multipoint connection".

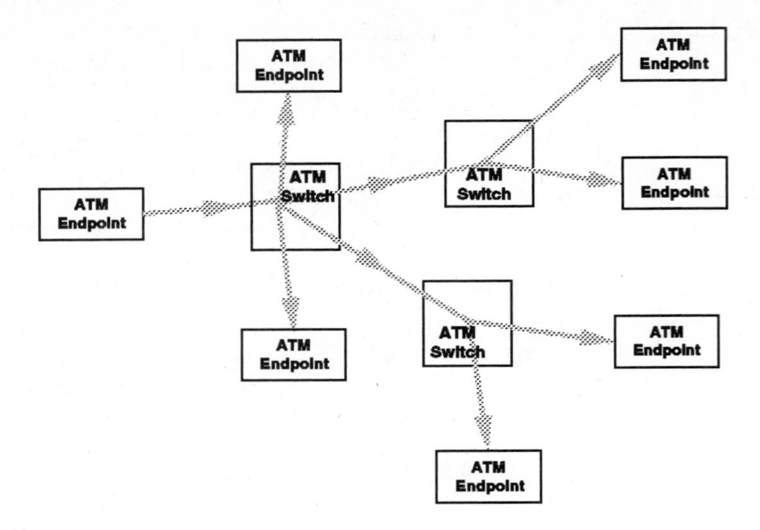


***Figure 9-8.*** *Multicast Tree*

- Communication is from the root of the tree to each leaf.
- Data may be sent from a leaf to the root[6] but there is no leaf-to-leaf communication possible over the same connection.
- For any endpoint to have the ability to send to all other endpoints in the multicast group, there must be a separate multicast tree built on which it may send data.
- Data is copied as late as possible for every outgoing link in the structure. Multiple copies of the same data *never* appear on the same link.
- The VPI/VCI is swapped at each branch point when the data is copied, and thus there is no relationship between the VPI/VCIs used on each stage of the route.

  This is mentioned to contrast the operation with an alternative that was discussed as an option. That is, if a reserved VPI/VCI was used at each endpoint, then the VPI and VPI numbers for a given broadcast tree would be the same at each endpoint. This is not how multicast works in ATM (although it is a common misunderstanding).
- Multicast trees may be set up and changed by signaling (switched setup) or defined by the network administrator (semi-permanent).

[6] This depends on which "release" or "phase" of ATM we are using. Leaf to root communication is not supported in ATM Forum phase 1.

While any-to-all multicast is not yet specified in ATM it is expected that the function will become available in the future. It is called "multipoint-to-multipoint connection".

#### 9.2.3.5 Quality of Service (QoS)

Each virtual channel connection has a given quality of service characteristic associated with it. This QoS specifies an average bandwidth as well as a maximum peak (instantaneous) allowed bandwidth. In serious overload situations, when the network cannot recover from overload by discarding only cells marked as low priority, the network can select which cells to discard depending on the QoS characteristic on the VC.

The QoS parameters defined by the ITU-T are as follows:

- Cell Transfer Delay (Network Latency)
- Cell Delay Variation (Jitter)
- Cell Transfer Capacity (Speed - average and peak allowed rates)
- Cell Error Ratio
- Cell Loss Ratio
- Cell Misinsertion Rate

A VP also has a QoS associated with it. VCs within a VP may have a lower QoS than the VP but they cannot have a higher one.

#### 9.2.3.6 Cell Discard and Loss

Cells may be lost or discarded by the network. The network does *not* detect the loss of cells and does *not* signal the end user when it has discarded cells from a particular connection.

Some variable bit rate encoding schemes for voice and for video are structured in such a way that two kinds of cells are produced:

- Essential cells which contain basic information to enable the continued function of the service,
- Optional cells which contain information that improves the quality of the service (voice or picture quality)

If the end-user equipment marks a cell as low priority, that cell will be discarded first if cells need to be discarded due to network congestion.

If discarding marked cells is insufficient to relieve the network congestion, then the network may optionally use the QoS to decide which cells to discard next. How the QoS is used to select cells to be discarded is not defined in the standards.

In this case a lower quality of service may be specified, which would allow the network to discard cells belonging to these virtual connections in situations of extreme congestion.

In cell-based networks where congestion is handled by cell discard, and recovery is accomplished by retransmission of full blocks rather than individual cells, there is a potential problem in congestion situations. See 6.1.2, "Congestion Control in Cell Networks" on page 6-9.

### 9.2.3.7 Congestion Control

There is no flow control in an ATM network of the kind that is standard in traditional packet switching networks (such as SNA). That is, windowed link protocols and procedures such as pacing cannot be efficiently performed in the high-speed environment.

In ATM when a connection is requested, the parameters of that connection (service class, requested average throughput and requested peak throughput rate) are examined and the connection is allowed only if the network has sufficient capacity to support the new connection.

This is a lot easier said than done. Any system that allocates capacity in excess of real capacity on the basis of statistical parameters allows the possibility (however remote) that by chance a situation will arise when demands on the network exceed the network resources. In this case, the network will discard cells. The first to be discarded will be arriving cells marked as lower priority in the CLP bit (cells already queued in buffers will not be discarded). After that discarding will take place by service class or randomly depending on the node's implementation.

### 9.2.3.8 Input Rate Policing

At the entry point to the network, the ATM switch monitors the rate of data arrival for a VP or a VC according to the negotiated QoS parameters for that connection. It will take action to prevent an ATM endpoint from exceeding its allowed limits.

The ATM endpoint is expected to operate a "leaky bucket" rate control scheme (see 6.1.1.1, "Leaky Bucket Rate Control" on page 6-7) to prevent it from making demands on the network in excess of its allowed capacity.

Depending on the network (and the user's subscription parameters) the network may either:

- Discard cells received in excess of the allowed maxima.
- Mark excess cells with the CLP (cell loss priority) bit to tell the network that this cell is of low priority and may be discarded if required.

Since there is no real control of flow within the network this function is very important.

Another function that is performed at the entry point to the network is collecting traffic information for billing. There is no standard as yet but it seems certain that many public networks will have a charging formula taking into account the average and maximum allowed cell rate as well as the actual traffic sent. In fact, it is quite possible that some administrations will charge only for the maximum allowed capacity and connect time (the network must provide for the capacity if the user has a circuit even if that capacity is not used). This kind of system is used in other industries. In some countries, electricity is billed for according to peak usage rate regardless of the total amount of electricity used.

#### 9.2.3.9 End-to-End Data Integrity

There is no end-to-end data integrity provided by the ATM network itself. This is the responsibility of the end-user equipment. The adaptation layer function (implemented in the ATM endpoint) provides an error checking function such that errored data is discarded but it does not provide recovery of lost data. This must be provided by the using system externally to the ATM network.

#### 9.2.3.10 Priorities

In traditional data networks connections often have priorities depending on the type of traffic and its importance. Traffic of high priority will be transmitted on any link before traffic of a lower priority. *There are no priorities of this kind in ATM.* There is no priority field (as distinct from cell loss priority) in the cell header.

### 9.2.4 Data Routing

ATM networks route data internally using a process called "logical ID swapping". This is important because the network is constrained to deliver cells on a virtual connection in the same order in which they were presented to the network. (Of course different virtual connections between the same pair of ATM endpoints may go by different routes.)

In ATM there are two IDs for each virtual connection: the VPI and the VCI. Some ATM switches may only know about and switch VPs. Other switches will know about and switch both VPs and VCs.

An ATM switch must keep a table of VPIs relating to each physical link that it has attached. This table contains a pointer to the outbound link where arriving data must be routed. If the VP terminates in the particular ATM switch, then each ATM switch must keep a table of VCs for each terminating VP. This table contains pointers for the further routing of the data. The VC may be (for example) a signaling channel and terminate in this particular ATM switch. Alternatively, the VC may be logically connected to another VC through this ATM switch in which case the ATM switch must route the data to the appropriate outbound connection (identified by the link, VPI and VCI).

When the ATM switch routes the cell onward using only the VP then the VPI number is changed. (VPIs only have meaning within the context of an individual link.) When the ATM switch routes the cell by using both the VPI and the VCI then the outgoing cell will have a different VPI and VCI.

## 9.2.5 Logical ID Swapping in ATM

The basic principles of logical ID swapping are discussed in 6.7.4, "Logical ID Swapping" on page 6-31. In ATM, two levels of logical ID (the VPI and the VCI) are used and thus logical ID swapping in ATM is a two-stage process.

The procedure is shown in Figure 9-9:

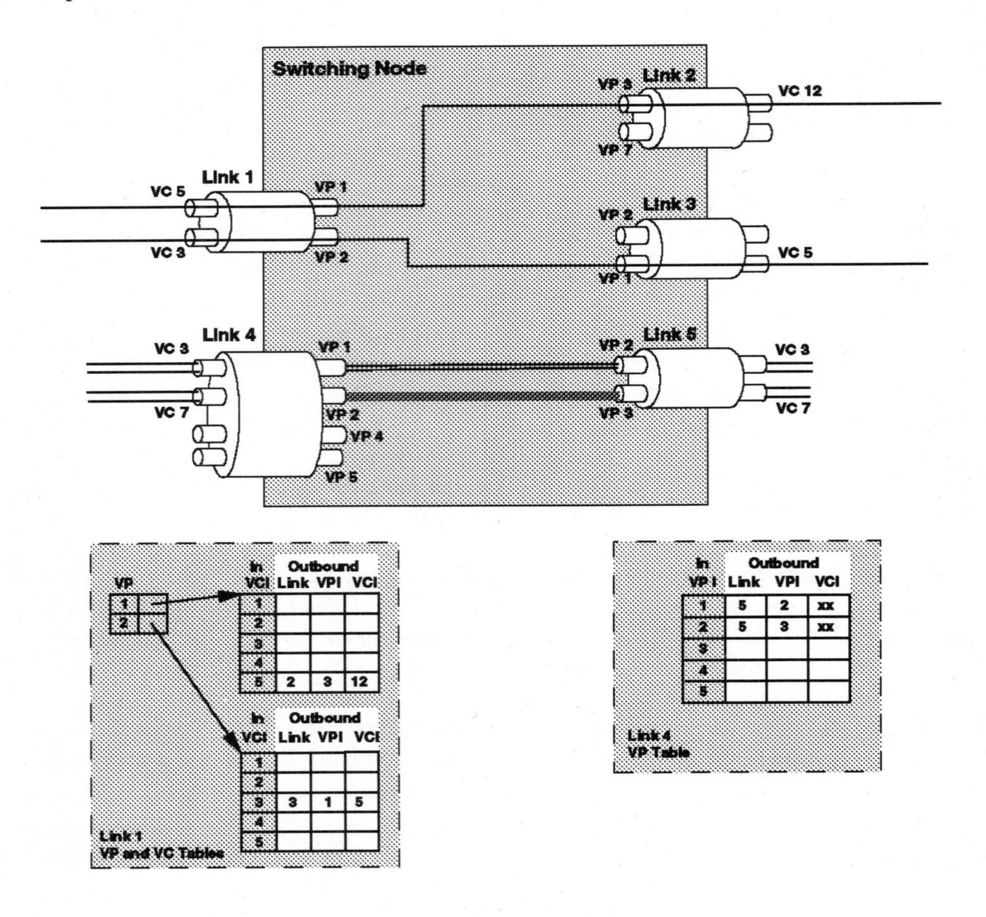


*Figure 9-9. Logical ID Swapping in ATM*

- Looking at Link 1 we see that there is a VP 1 which has a VC 5 within it.
- A connection exists between Link1/VP=1/VC=5 and Link 2/VP=3/VC=12.
- We can see that VP 1 on Link 1 terminates within this ATM switch.
- Necessary routing tables for Link 1 are shown.
  - There is a VP table with an entry for each VP on the link.
  - Because each of the two illustrated VPs on Link 1 terminate in this node the table entry for each VP is minimal. It consists only of a pointer to a VC table.
  - There is a VC table for each VP that terminates in this switch.
- When a cell arrives on Link 1 with VP=1 and VC=5 the switch first looks to the routing table for Link 1. It locates VP=1 in the VP table and uses this to find the VC table.
- The switch then looks to the VC table for the entry for VC=5.
- From the table entry it discovers that the cell is to be routed to Link 2 with VP=3 and VC=12.
- It changes the cell header to reflect the new VPI and VCI values and routes the cell to Link 2.

The case of VP switching is shown for Link 2. This case is very simple because the VCI does not change. The VP table shows an outbound link ID and a new VPI but not a VCI. The VPI is used to locate the appropriate table entry and the cell is routed accordingly (and the VPI is updated).

Since the VPI and/or VCI fields in the cell header have been changed, the HEC field in the cell header must be recalculated before the cell can be transmitted. This is because, when a cell is switched from one link to another, the VPI is *always* replaced[7] (regardless of whether the VCI is replaced or not) and the HEC is always recalculated.

It is important to note that there is a separate VP table for every inbound link and a separate VC table for each VP that terminates in this node.

Multicast and broadcast operations (described in 9.2.3.4, "Broadcast and Multicast" on page 9-17) are achieved by having multiple destination entries in the VP or VC tables. The system copies each cell once for each destination routing.

7 Although it may be replaced with the same value it had before.

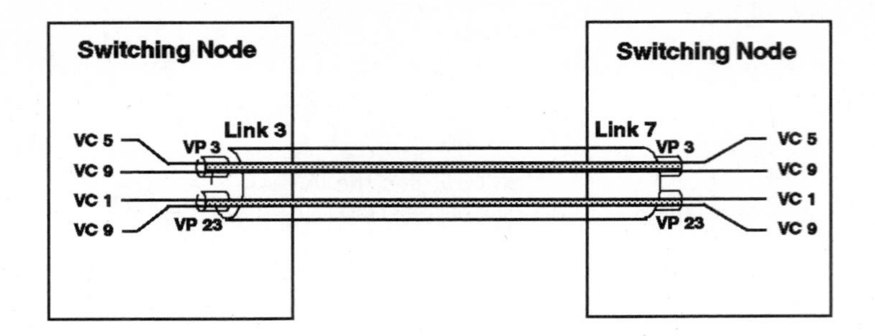


***Figure 9-10.*** *VPIs and VCIs within a Link.* VPI and VCI numbers are the same at each end of a link (because there is nothing within the link that can change them)

## 9.2.6 Some Definitions

The formal definitions of VC and VP related concepts rely on an understanding of ATM label swap routing. These are illustrated in Figure 9-11.

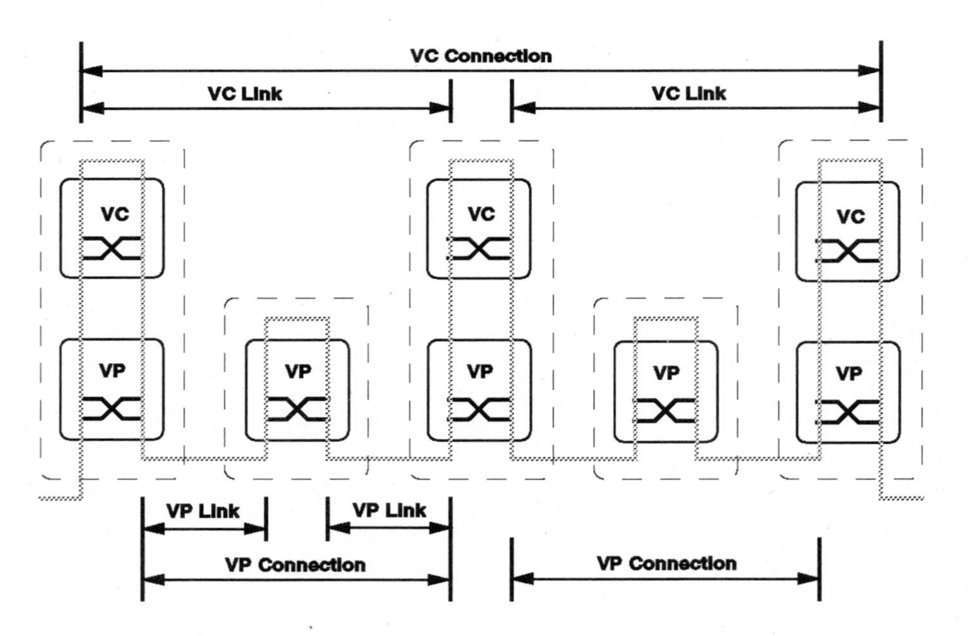


***Figure 9-11.*** *VP and VC Concepts*

Although some of these terms were introduced earlier they can now be treated with more precision.

**Virtual Channel (VC)**

The best definition of a virtual channel is "a logical association between the endpoints of a link that enables the unidirectional transfer of cells over that link".

This is not the definition used by either the ATM Forum or the ITU-T. The ATM Forum defines it as "a communication channel that provides for the sequential unidirectional transport of ATM cells". The ITU-T definition is "A concept used to describe unidirectional transport of ATM cells associated by a common unique identifier value".

Thus the Forum definition appears to equate to a VCC where the ITU-T definition equates to a VCL.

**Virtual Channel Link (VCL)**

A VCL exists from the point where a VCI value is assigned and where it is translated or terminated. Since it exists within a VP it may pass through a number of ATM switches (if the VP is switched). It is unidirectional.

**Virtual Channel Connection (VCC)**

This is a concatenation of VCLs extending from one end user to another through the ATM network. The endpoint is actually a service access point (SAP).

VCCs always exist in pairs (one for each direction).

**Virtual Channel Switch (VCS)**

This is the VC switching function shown in Figure 9-11 on page 9-24. A VCS connects VCLs together to form VCCs. To do this it terminates VPCs and translates (changes) VCI values.

**Virtual Path (VP)**

A group of virtual channels associated in such a way as the group can be switched through the network without the switching element ever knowing about the separate existence of VCs. Thus all VCs within a VP travel on the same path through the network. VCs within a VP may have lower QoS characteristics than the VP but may not have higher ones.

A VP may exist through a short sequence of nodes (for example on a backbone) or it may extend from ATM endpoint to ATM endpoint.

**Virtual Path Link (VPL)**

A VPL exists between the point where the VPI value is assigned and where it is translated or the VP is terminated. In practice this means that a VPL exists only within a point-to-point link between ATM switches. When a link arrives in an ATM node the VPI is always translated. So the VPL only extends over the range of a single inter-switch ATM link.

It should be noted that ATM links between switches can run over SDH for example and be "networked" (switched) through the SDH network. This operates at the layer below the ATM layer and is unknown to ATM.

**Virtual Path Connection (VPC)**

This is a concatenation (sequence) of VPLs that extends between virtual path terminations. This is the virtual path. It is unidirectional.

**Virtual Path Switch (VPS)**

The VPS is the processing function that connects VPLs to form VPCs. This function translates the VPI values and directs cells to the correct output link on a particular ATM switch.

**Virtual Path Terminator (VPT)**

This processing function terminates the VP and makes the VCs available for separate and independent routing.

**Virtual Path Connection Identifier (VPCI)**

This is the identifier of the VP connection returned by the network when call setup is performed. It is 16 bits long.

The VPCI is used in the signaling protocols instead of a VPI. The VPI is only unique within a single ATM link. In the case of a simple ATM concentrator device, such as that shown in Figure 9-12, multiple downstream connections are concentrated onto a single upstream connection. The upstream connection is connected at the UNI. This means that a single signaling channel at the UNI is controlling multiple downstream links. The VPCI has additional bits to allow the link to be uniquely identified.

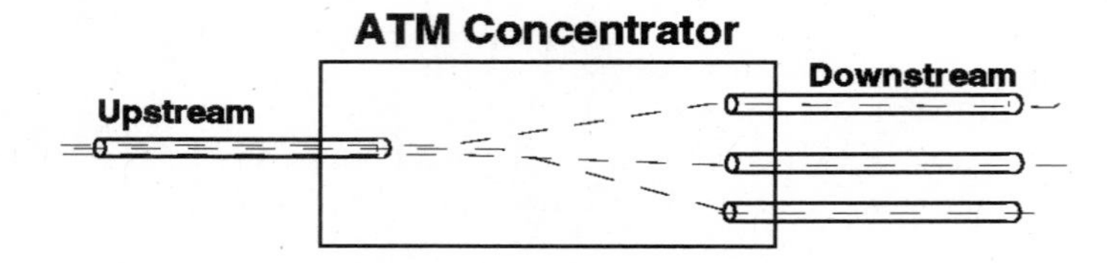


***Figure 9-12.** Simple ATM Concentrator*

In the first versions of ATM the VPI and VPCI will be "numerically equivalent".

## 9.2.7 End-User Interface

As discusser earlier, end-user equipment can attach natively to an ATM network through the well-defined user network interface (the UNI). This equipment is called an ATM endpoint. However, a real end-user application (which resides within the end-user equipment) attaches to ATM through the AAL.

Thus you could consider that there are two interfaces to an ATM network - one an equipment interface (the UNI) and the other (the real end-user program interface) through the AAL.

Figure 9-13 shows the data flow from one end user to another over an ATM network. There are several important things to notice about this structure.

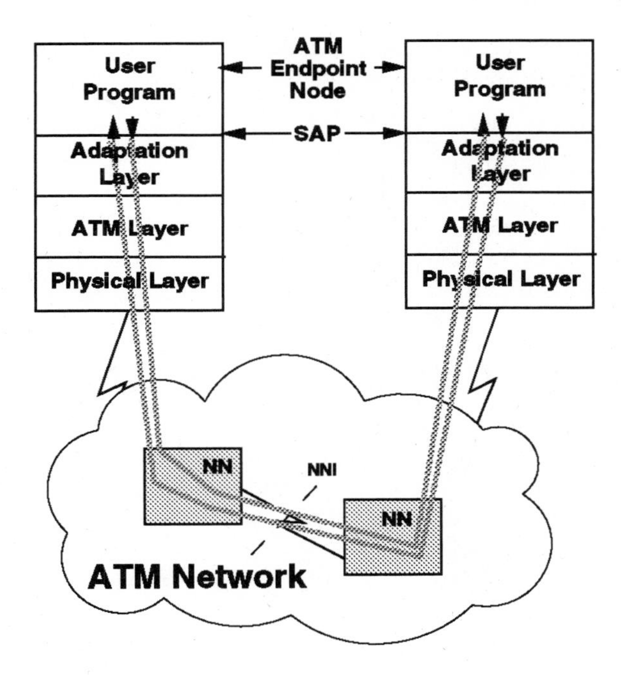


***Figure 9-13.*** *Data Flow through an ATM Network*

- Each box in the figure represents an ATM endpoint in a separate physical device.
- The *only* way to interface to ATM is through a program of some kind. That is, within the ATM endpoint, the physical layer, ATM layer and adaptation layer are rigorously defined by the ATM standards. The "primitives", which the user program uses to interface to the AAL layer (at the AAL service access point - SAP), are also rigorously defined.

  However, the ATM code can interface to *nothing* else. It forms the interface between user code and the ATM network. This means, for example, that if we want to support a voice connection there is a *program* sitting between the ATM AAL-1 (which handles constant bit rate voice) and the physical adapter that connects to one or other source of voice information. ATM does *not* connect to a voice line directly (nor to anything else).

- When a user program sends data that data is processed first by the adaptation layer, then by the ATM layer and then the physical layer takes over to send the data to the ATM network. The cells are transported by the network and then received on the other side first by the physical layer, then processed by the ATM layer and then by the receiving AAL. When all this is complete, the information (data) is passed to the receiving user program.
- The total function performed by the ATM network has been the *non-assured* transport (it might have lost some) of user information from program to program.
- The user program mentioned here is quite obviously *not* end-user code in the normal sense of the term. In order to make the network useful a very significant amount of processing (protocols, etc.) must be performed.

  Looked at from a traditional data processing viewpoint, all the ATM network has done is to replace a physical link connection with another kind of physical connection - all the higher-layer network functions must still be performed.

## 9.3 The ATM Adaptation Layer (AAL)

In order to make an ATM network practical it is necessary to adapt the internal network characteristics to those of the various traffic types that will use the network. This is the purpose of the adaptation layer.

An ATM network carries cells from one end of the network to the other. While the cell header has error checking in it (this is necessary because of the possibility of misrouting cells which had bit errors in the header), there is *no* error check on the data part of the cell. In addition, cells can be lost or discarded during transport and in error situations (this depends on the specific network equipment) could get cells out of sequence and/or duplicate cells.

The function of the adaptation layer is to provide generalized interworking across the ATM network. However, this function is very basic indeed. In the case of data, the AAL takes frames (blocks) of data delivered to it, breaks them up into cells and adds necessary header information to allow rebuilding of the original block at the receiver. This involves checking for errors. *The AAL does not do any error recovery.* In the case of data, if a frame being received has any errors at all, then it is discarded and not delivered to the receiving end. Error recovery is the responsibility of a higher-layer protocol.

For data, the adaptation layer provides the same service as the MAC layer of the LAN - the *non-assured* transport of complete blocks. Figure 9-14 on page 9-29 shows the logical structure of an ATM network.

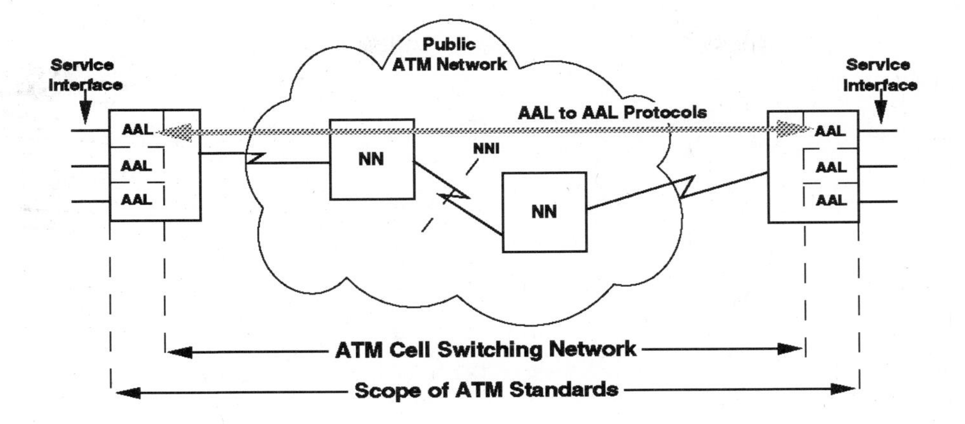


***Figure 9-14.*** *The ATM Adaptation Layer (AAL)*

## 9.3.1 Service Interface

The *service interface* is the interface to higher protocol layers and functions - that is, the service interface is the boundary of ATM. The AAL connects the service interface to the ATM cell-switching network. Note that the service interface is an *internal* interface within a device. It is specified as a series of logical primitives which will be implemented very differently in different products. The service interface definition does not include the means of physical delivery of the service primitives.

### 9.3.1.1 AAL Service Classes

The ITU-T has defined four different generic classes of network traffic that need to be treated differently by an ATM network. These classes are designated Class A to Class D. Originally, there were four different AAL types proposed - one for each traffic class. This changed during the standards definition process as the problem came to be better understood.

The four service classes are summarized in Figure 9-15 on page 9-30.

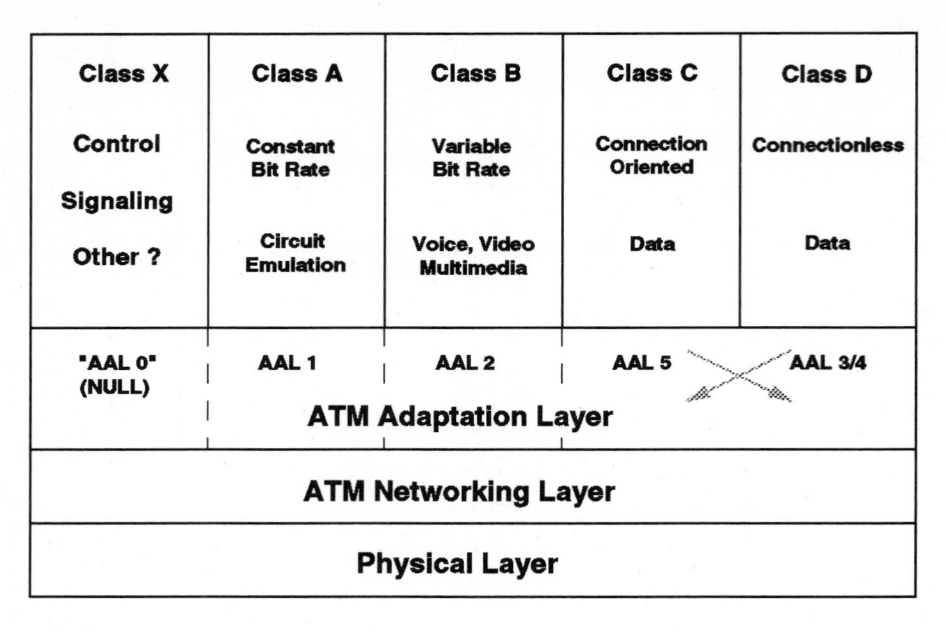


*Figure 9-15. Service Classes and AAL Types*

## Class A (Circuit Emulation)

This service emulates a leased line. It is intended for constant-rate voice and video applications, etc.

These applications have the following characteristics:

- There is a constant bit rate at source and destination.
- There is a timing relationship between source and destination.
- There is a connection between end users of the service.

The adaptation layer must perform the following functions in order to support this service:

- Segmentation and reassembly of data frames into cells
- Handling (buffering) of cell delay variations
- Detection and handling of lost, discarded, duplicated or misrouted cells
- Recovery of the source clock frequency (in a plesiochronous way)
- Detection of bit errors in the user information field

### Class B (Variable Bit Rate Services)

This is intended for voice and video traffic that is basically isochronous at the level of end-user presentation, but which may be coded as variable-rate information.

These services have a variable flow of information, need some timing relationship between the ends of the connection and are connection oriented.

The services provided by the AAL for class B are:

- Transfer of variable bit rate information between end users
- Transfer of timing between source and destination
- Indication of lost or corrupted information not recovered by the AAL itself

The requirements here are quite complex, for example:

1. Many video applications will be primarily one way and go to multiple destinations (multicast). However, typical one-way video is not too sensitive to network delay (a few seconds is fine).
2. Other video applications (such as videoconferencing) require a complex multicasting or hubbing regime. Videoconferencing requires synchronization of video and voice. It also has quite strict end-to-end delay requirements.

It is the class B traffic that produces nightmares for network engineers. High-bandwidth variable loads require complex rate control structures because of their unpredictable nature and because their data rates can often peak at a significant percentage of the network resources being used. In other words, unless your network is designed correctly class B traffic can disrupt its operation with great ease.

It should not be surprising that AAL type 2 (the AAL which provides service for class B traffic) is as yet undefined.

### Class C (Connection-Oriented Data)

This is traditional data traffic as known in an SNA or X.25 network.

These services are connection oriented and have a variable flow of information.

Two services are provided called *message mode* and *streaming mode*. Message mode provides for the transfer of single frames of user information. Streaming mode provides transport for multiple fixed-length frames of user data.

An AAL for class C must provide:

- Segmentation and reassembly of frames into cells
- Detection and signaling of errors in the data

In addition, it could provide other services such as the multiplexing and demultiplexing of multiple end-user connections onto a single ATM network connection. There is strong disagreement as to the need for this last function, however.

**Class D (Connectionless Data)**

This service has several uses in sending ad-hoc data but could be used, for example, to carry TCP/IP or LAN interconnection traffic where the protocol in use is inherently connectionless.

These services are connectionless and have a variable flow of information. It is intended to support connectionless networking protocols, such as TCP/IP and services that transfer data character by character (such as an "ASCII TWX" terminal).

Like the other three types of service, class D requires:

- Segmentation and reassembly of frames into cells
- Detection of errors in the data (but not retransmission)

In addition to these basic services class D specifies:

- Multiplexing and demultiplexing of multiple end-user data flows onto a single cross-network data flow (for single-character transmissions)
- Network layer addressing and routing

**Class X (User Defined)**

This is a connection-oriented ATM transport service where the requirements (variable or constant bit rate, traffic type and timing, etc.) are user defined. The only things that the network is involved with are the required bandwidth and QoS parameters.

Class X connections would be provided by AAL-0.

Class X is not defined in the ITU-T recommendations; it is, however, discussed in ATM Forum material.

It can be seen that the functions provided by the AAL are very basic ones. They are similar to those provided by a LAN at the MAC layer. This is the level of function provided by the AAL (although the AAL handles many types of service in addition to data). For data applications a logical link layer (such as IEEE 802.2) will still be needed for successful operation.

## 9.3.2 Structure of the AAL

There are now five different AAL types:

- AAL-0 means no AAL function is being performed. Cells are transferred between the service interface and the ATM network transparently.
- AAL-1 provides functions for service class A.
- AAL-2 provides the required functions for variable-rate services class B. As yet there are no defined standards in this area.
- AAL-3/4 provides service for both classes C and D. AALs 3 and 4 were combined during the standards definition process, when it was realized that the same process could perform both functions. It is quite complex and regarded by some as over-designed.
- AAL-5 provides functions for both classes C and D but is significantly simpler (although it is also less functional). Some people think it will be fine for class C traffic but AAL-3/4 will still be needed for connectionless traffic. Others disagree.

There is also a Signaling AAL (SAAL) defined; this adaptation layer does not provide user-to-user services but is a series of AAL functions that support signaling connections between ATM switches and/or between an ATM endpoint and an ATM switch (network).

The internal logical structure of AAL-3/4 and AAL-5 is shown in Figure 9-16. AAL-1 has a much simpler structure but the principle is the same.

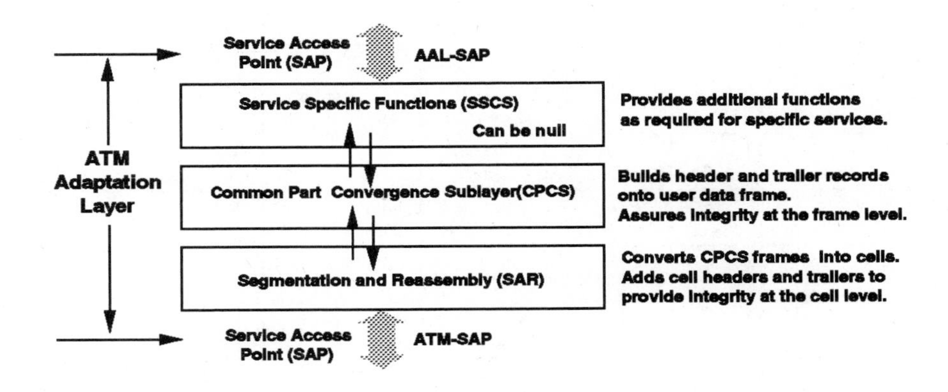


***Figure 9-16.*** *Structure of Sublayers in AAL-3/4 and AAL-5*

- Data is received in frames (for AAL-3/4 these can be up to 64 KB).

- A service-specific function may be performed here if needed to provide a more standard service interface (SAP) for common protocols. One such function already defined is for frame relay. This layer will, however, often be null.
- **CPCS** stands for Common Part Convergence Sublayer. This operates on whole frames of user data, and the exact function depends on which AAL is being used.
- **SAR** means Segmentation and Reassembly. This is the layer that takes data and builds a stream of 48-byte cells. Again functions depend on which AAL we are discussing.
- The interfaces between the sublayers shown in the figure are defined as logical primitives - they are not SAPs. This means that there is no intention to allow an external programming interface between the sublayers.

## 9.3.3 ATM Network Physical Interfaces

The following table summarizes link types that have either been accepted by standards bodies or are current proposals. Not all of these will ultimately find wide acceptance.

***Table 9-1 (Page 1 of 2).*** *ATM-UNI Interfaces*

| | Rate (Mbps) | Cell Throughput | System | Medium | WAN/LAN | Owner |
|---|---|---|---|---|---|---|
| DS-1 (T-1) | 1.544 | 1.536 | PDH | Cu | Both | ANSI |
| E-1 | 2.048 | 1.92 | PDH | Cu | Both | ETSI |
| DS-3 (T-3) | 44.736 | 40.704 | PDH | Cu | WAN | ANSI |
| E-3 | 34.368 | 33.984 | PDH | Cu | WAN | ETSI |
| E-4 | 139.264 | 138.24 | PDH | Cu | WAN | ETSI |
| SDH STM-1, Sonet STS-3c | 155.52 | 149.76 | Sonet/SDH | SM Fiber | WAN | ITU-T |
| Sonet "Lite" | 155.52 | 149.76 | Sonet/SDH | MM Fiber | LAN | Forum |
| SDH STM-4c, Sonet STS-12c | 622.08 | 599.04 | Sonet/SDH | SM Fiber | WAN | ITU-T |
| FDDI-PMD | 100 | 100 | Block Coded | MM Fiber/STP | LAN | Forum |
| Fiber Channel | 155.52 | 150.34 | Block Coded | MM Fiber | LAN | Forum |
| DXI (RVX) | 0-50 | 0-50 | Clear Channel | Cu | LAN | Forum |
| Raw Cells | 155.52 | 155.52 | Clear Channel | SM Fiber | WAN | ITU-T |
| Raw Cells | 622.08 | 622.08 | Clear Channel | SM Fiber | WAN | ITU-T |
| Raw Cells | 25.6 | 25.6 | Clear Channel | Cu UTP-3/5 | LAN | Forum |

| *Table 9-1 (Page 2 of 2). ATM-UNI Interfaces* | | | | | | |
|---|---|---|---|---|---|---|
| | **Rate (Mbps)** | **Cell Throughput** | **System** | **Medium** | **WAN/LAN** | **Owner** |
| Sonet "Lite" | 51.84<br>25.92<br>12.96 | 49.536<br>24.768<br>12.384 | Sonet Frame | Cu UTP-3/5 | LAN | Forum |
| Raw Cells | 100 | 100 | Clear Channel | Cu UTP-3 | LAN | Proposed |
| Raw Cells | 155.52 | 155.52 | Clear Channel | Cu UTP/STP | LAN | Forum |

ATM was defined to make the physical data transport function as independent as possible from the ATM switching function and the things that go on above the ATM layer. It is able to operate over a wide variety of possible physical link types. These vary in speed, medium (fiber or copper), and structure to suit the particular environment in which the link has to operate.

The main issues for ATM data transport are:

1. High speed (data rate)

   This almost goes without saying, but if the network is to be made stable by relying on the statistics of aggregated data streams, then link capacity has to be sufficient to support many simultaneous users.

2. Low latency (for some applications)

   ATM will be made to operate over a satellite connection, but the additional latency involved will make some applications (such as interactive multimedia) significantly more difficult.

3. Very low error rates

   This is key. Because of the fact that an errored cell causes retransmission of the whole data block (many cells), some people feel that ATM is likely to be unstable in high error rate situations.

There is no doubt, however, that ATM systems will be developed to run over radio media (radio LANs) and over satellite connections.

## 9.4 ATM Status

ATM is a fast developing standard. The primary body responsible for ATM standards is the International Telecommunications Union - Technical Standards Division, the ITU-T (formerly the CCITT). An organization known as the ATM Forum, which is a group made up of almost every data communications and telecommunications equipment supplier in the world, is defining "standards" (called implementation agreements) for ATM that go well beyond the development done by the ITU. Basically, the ITU is defining the WAN standards for ATM and the ATM Forum is defining the LAN (or campus area) standards. The ATM Forum was consciously set up to develop its standards very quickly and this is indeed happening.

By 1995 there were several research networks and many early commercial ATM networks in operation around the world.

Work on the standards is progressing very rapidly. The basic set of standards are now available although there are many aspects still not addressed. Nevertheless, as of January 1995 many of the standards are not very firm and many aspects could change even in quite fundamental ways.

The major obstacle to be overcome is that, as yet, there is no experience in operating cell-based switching systems for voice or video traffic. Over the years network engineers have developed an excellent body of knowledge about the behavior of circuit-switched systems carrying voice and the design parameters are very well known. (Of course there is a lot of knowledge available about packet-switching systems for data traffic and some of this knowledge has application.)

The (billion dollar) question is "what is the statistical behavior of variable rate packetized voice and video systems when operated on a large scale". Many people (perhaps the majority) believe that it will all add up statistically very nicely and stable operation of these systems will be possible with link and node utilizations as high as 80% or more. Some other people say no. They believe that the variation in the aggregate traffic load due to statistical variance could be so great as to prevent network operation at resource utilizations much above 20%. (Some speakers expressed this view at the CCITT Study Group XVIII meeting in Melbourne in December 1991.)

If network utilization can approach 80%, then the economic viability of ATM is difficult to question. At loadings of 20% the economics are problematic. Time will tell.

## 9.4.1 IBM ATM Products

IBM has announced a wide range of ATM products. These fall into two categories:

**Wide-Area ATM Products**

IBM has a series of wide-area network ATM switches called the *IBM 2220 Nways BroadBand Network Switch.* These switches optimize the use of wide-area bandwidth and are designed for the integration of voice, data, image and video traffic.

**Local Area Network Products**

IBM has developed a series of products for use in the LAN environment.

1. An ATM switch module for the IBM 8260 LAN hub.
2. Attachment blades for the IBM 8260 hub to support ATM connections.
3. An interfacing product to allow the attachment of traditional LANs (token-ring and Ethernet) to an ATM network.
4. A concentrator module to provide low-cost attachment of workstations at 25 Mbps.
5. Adapter cards to provide attachment for PCs and workstations directly to ATM networks at either 25 or 100 Mbps.

## 9.5 Practical ATM

All of the discussion in the previous section was about broadband ISDN as much as it was about ATM. ATM is the technical structure and protocols for the service called broadband ISDN. The B_ISDN service is designed as far as possible to be independent of the implementing technology.

It is hard to overestimate the importance of broadband ISDN. Broadband ISDN is proposed to be the *replacement* for all of the telephone exchanges in the world! Of course, such replacement takes a long time and enormous levels of investment. The concept will need to be proven in the field, the standards will need to be stable and properly debugged, and the benefits thoroughly proven before the required level of investment will be forthcoming.

Nevertheless, it is very widely believed in the telecommunications industry that broadband ISDN will become the worldwide telecommunications network of the next century.

### 9.5.1 ATM in the Wide Area Network

In the wide area network environment, ATM offers a number of significant benefits:

**Integration of Services**

The number of specialized services offered by carriers around the world had proliferated in the last few years. This is seen as a direct response to the proliferating needs of users. One of the benefits of ATM is the ability to satisfy most user requirements with a single service and to reduce proliferation of new kinds of networks.

**Lower Equipment and Network Cost**

It is widely believed that ATM switching equipment will cost significantly less than time-division multiplexing (TDM) equipment to do the same job.

**Appropriate Technology to the High-Speed Environment**

ATM offers a technology that can deliver service at the very high speeds now becoming available and being demanded by users.

**Bandwidth Cost Saving**

In basic economic terms, this is not (or should not be) an issue. The real cost of bandwidth is so low that the idea of spending money on equipment to save money on bandwidth seems silly. In the WAN environment for PTTs, this is indeed the case. In the LAN environment, where bandwidth really is free, this is the case for everyone.

For private network users in the real world, bandwidth cost is still very significant in many (indeed most) countries. In this case, for isochronous services, ATM can save a very significant amount of bandwidth and hence cost.

There are two quite distinct environments here:

1. The carrier environment where ATM is provided as a service to the end user.
2. The private network environment where a large organization purchases lines from a carrier (or installs them itself) and builds a private ATM network.

## 9.5.2 ATM in the LAN Environment

Many people believe that it will be the LAN environment in which ATM gets its first significant usage. There are good reasons:

**Users Need a Higher-Capacity LAN System**

Existing shared-media LANs were designed and developed in an environment where communications bandwidth (bits per second) was almost free. Compared to the internal speeds (and the possible I/O rates) of early personal computers, the LAN was very nearly infinite.

As personal computers and workstations have increased in capability there has been an attendant rise in the demand for LAN capacity. In the short term, this can be solved by re-structuring large LANs into smaller ones, bridging, routing, and the like, but the improvement in workstation capability and the increase in bandwidth demand does not look likely to slow down, especially when going into multimedia applications. A faster (higher-throughput) LAN system is needed.

### Switching versus Shared Media for the LAN Environment

Looking at Figure 9-17 and Figure 9-18, the performance advantage of a switched system over a shared-medium system is easily seen. In Figure 9-17, let us assume that we have 50 devices connected to a 10 Mbps Ethernet LAN. This is a shared-medium system. Only one station may transmit data at any one time. This means that the total *potential*[8] network throughput is 10 Mbps.

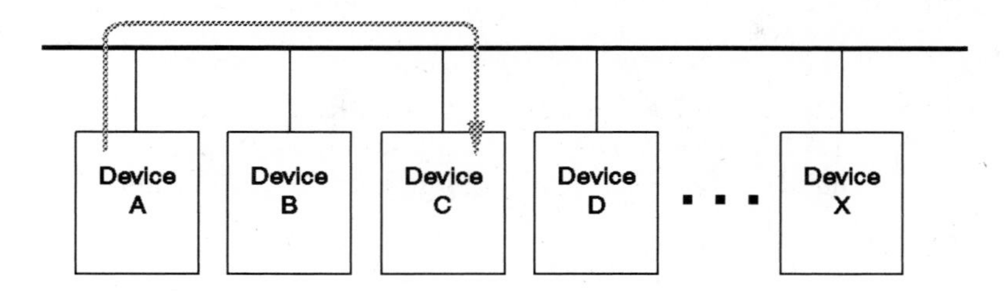


***Figure 9-17.*** *Connection to Shared Media*

In Figure 9-17, we have the same devices connected through a switch (let us assume a link speed of 10 Mbps). Each device is capable of sending at the full media speed.[9] The total *potential* network throughput here is not 10 Mbps but 50 times 10 Mbps - or 500 Mbps.

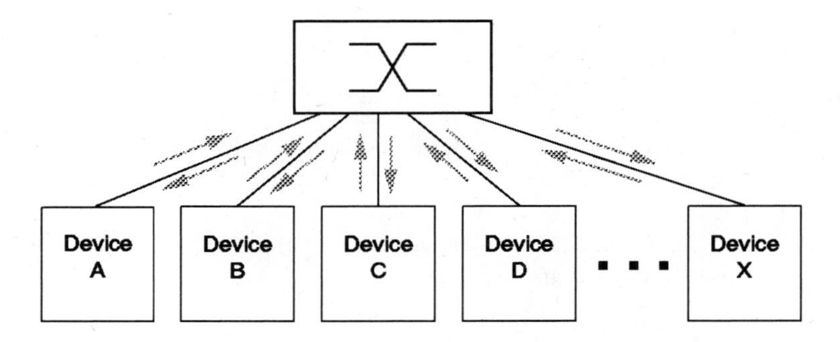


***Figure 9-18.*** *Connection to a Switch*

The difference is in the cost. The adapter cards for 50 terminals connected to an FDDI LAN (only 100 Mbps total throughput) will cost about $2,000 each or a

[8] In reality, of course, quite a lot less.

[9] In this situation, too, throughput is limited by statistical considerations.

total of $100,000. 10 Mbps adapter cards (if they existed) could cost perhaps $300 each[10] for a total of $15,000.

Of course, with ATM you need a switch, but with FDDI you need a hub. It is expected that ATM switches will cost only marginally more than FDDI hubs. Both systems need a network management workstation.

The net is that an ATM system will deliver much greater throughput than a shared-medium LAN system for a significantly lower cost.

### Security

On a shared-medium LAN, all of the data traffic passes through every workstation. In ATM, a single end-user station only receives data intended for that station. Thus users cannot "listen in" to other people's information.

### Asymmetric Bandwidth

In a LAN environment some users will require much higher data throughput than others. Servers, in particular, need much higher throughput than any of their clients. In a shared-medium system all these devices must have adapters that run at the same speed (the speed of the LAN).

In ATM, individual stations can have connections at speeds appropriate to their capability. A speed of 25 Mbps is faster than any current (ISA bus) PC. Many workstations can easily handle a throughput of 50 Mbps, and specialized servers are being built to handle total rates of a few hundred Mbps. This ultimately saves cost both in the workstations themselves and in the network switching equipment.

### ATM Supports Isochronous (Timing Dependent) Traffic

Perhaps the most discussed near-term application is for multimedia of one form or another on workstations. This usually requires video and sound as well as traditional data. The video and sound components require a system that can deliver data at a timed rate (or can adjust to one). A number of proposed LAN architectures to do this are being explored (isochronous Ethernet, FDDI-II) but ATM offers the potential to allow these applications in an integrated way.

### Reduced Need for Routers and Bridges

In an ATM environment there is still a need for routers and bridges but in some network configurations the need is significantly less, for example, where a number of different LAN protocols are used by groups of devices on a set of linked LANs. In an ATM system a number of separate virtual LANs can be set

---

10 The cost is about the same as an Ethernet adapter **plus** some hardware to convert data frames into cells and back again.

up (one for each protocol) and the need for a router is removed. The bridging function between dispersed locations is performed by ATM without the need for bridges as such. Bridges are only needed to connect between ATM-attached workstations and workstations attached to existing LANs.

#### 9.5.2.1 LAN Emulation over ATM

In order for ATM to be used as a seamless extension of an existing LAN system the concept of emulating a traditional LAN over an ATM system is being developed. This would enable:

- Use of existing LAN software systems over ATM
- The seamless integration of existing LANs with new ATM services
- The use of ATM to intelligently bridge between existing LANs

The proposals are such that the benefits of ATM can still be obtained but that ATM can be a smooth and logical growth of an existing LAN networking system.

# Chapter 10. High-Speed Circuit-Switching Systems

Circuit-switching systems (such as telephone exchanges) have been around for a long time. With the rise of packet switching technologies and the advent of LANs, many people have discounted the usefulness of circuit switching. However, fast circuit switches (both electronic and optical) are competitive with LAN and packet switch technologies as potential high-speed replacements of current LANs.

There are two quite separate aspects of circuit switching which need to be considered:

1. The speed of the switched links themselves
2. The speed at which a circuit can be set up and later cleared

If it takes a "long time" (whatever this means) to set up a circuit then the system will only be efficient for dedicated transfers of large files. If the setup time is "short" then we could perhaps make a new connection (call) for every block (or transaction) that we want to send.

There are some disadvantages of circuit switching:

**Propagation Delay**

The time needed to set up a connection (a call) and the time needed to clear it are critically dependent on the distance between connected stations. This hardly matters in a telephone system (provided it's less than a second or so) but can be critical to some proposed uses for high-speed systems.

**Bandwidth Inefficiency**

For things like large file transfer (provided the end stations can operate at full network speed), a circuit switched system can be very efficient almost regardless of the circuit setup time (because it represents only a small proportion of the total). If the circuit is held for a long time and there is only sporadic data transfer, then use of system resources will be very inefficient.

If we want to use the circuit switch as a substitute for a packet switch (that is, set up a circuit for every block of data to be transferred), then the efficiency of bandwidth occupancy will be very low. This assumes that the setup time for the circuit is high compared with the block transfer time. (Of course, bandwidth efficiency may not matter!)

**Many-to-One and Many-to-Many Capabilities Are Lost**

In a circuit-switched system you can't have multiple circuits active at the same time. This is probably the biggest problem.

 

If the system is purely for long file transfers then this capability is not needed. But if simultaneous connection is needed from multiple stations to a single device, then we have a limitation.

**Short Hold Mode**

If the system is able to set up a circuit, transfer the data, and then clear the circuit again *very quickly*, then we can establish what is effectively a packet switching system over a circuit switch. In the low-speed environment of public X.21 networks, this principle is very well established. When using an X.21 (short hold mode) system, in principle you set up a call when you want to send a block of data, and clear the call when you have finished the immediate transaction.[1] In this kind of system, typical call holding time is around five seconds, call setup time is around 150 ms, and call clear time is about 80 ms.

IBM has *standard* software for some SNA-based systems that does just this and the networks are built intentionally for this type of operation (you pay for calls in 5-second intervals). This can be a very efficient mode of operation. The way this has to work in the end devices is that the device must set up a virtual call with a partner device. When the circuit is cleared the virtual call must remain active. If it does not, then there is significant overhead incurred in the establishment of a new call for each transaction.

With the short hold principle you *can* have multiple simultaneous connections from a single station (the connections are logically simultaneous but physically distinct).

There are also a number of big advantages to circuit switched systems:

**Throughput Is Not Limited by Link Speed**

The total system throughput is the number of possible paths through the switch times the link speed. Thus if the switch allows 20 simultaneous connections at 10 Mbps then the total system throughput is 20 x 10 Mbps = 200 Mbps. The maximum throughput of a LAN is the link speed (minus an efficiency factor). Thus a circuit-switched system with attached links running at 10 Mbps can have a throughput significantly higher than that of a 100 Mbps FDDI LAN.

Depending on the internal construction of the switch, it may be possible to have half of the attached stations communicating with the other half of the stations simultaneously. In this case the system is said to be "non-blocking".

---

[1] The system decides when the transaction is finished by waiting for a defined time interval before clearing the call.

In many cases, for cost reasons, the switch will only be able to handle a finite number of connections - when this number is reached you can't have any more calls regardless of how many stations are idle and request connection.

**"Protocol Transparency"**

Except for the protocols needed to set up and clear a call, there is no limitation imposed by the system on the protocols used by the communicating stations. This gives excellent stability, as one of the major sources of network problems is protocol mismatches between the using devices and the network.

The remaining problem with circuit-switching systems is one of cost. Telephone exchanges (and PBXs) are very cost efficient because they have a fast TDM bus inside and slow interfaces to each user. The switching fabric within the box is a TDM bus. But this can only be done if the bus is many times faster than the link attachments. This is not true in a high-speed situation.

The story is the same as elsewhere. Circuitry at speeds of around 2 Gbps is extremely expensive (GaAs technology is needed). At 200 Mbps it is still costly (bipolar technology will do this but it is not very dense, so the costs tend to be high). At 10 Mbps we can use CMOS technology, which is very dense and low in cost.

At even 10 Mbps the switch needs to be a space division (or cross-point) architecture - since TDM won't work. The number of "cross connects" you need in the switch grows exponentially with the number of possible simultaneous connections and linearly with the number of attached stations. A fully non-blocking switch for a large number of devices could become quite expensive.

All that said, circuit switching can be attractive and cost competitive in a number of environments. Circuit setup time depends a lot on the attaching protocols but the IBM ESCON channels can set up a circuit in 2 μsec. Another recently announced IBM device performs this same function (in a more limited environment) in .5 μsec.

## 10.1 The IBM ESCON Channel Architecture

IBM Enterprise Systems Connection (ESCON) architecture was designed for interconnecting mainframe computers and their I/O controllers in a distributed system environment. It is optimized for this purpose and is not intended for general purpose communications in either the LAN or WAN environments. Nevertheless, it is a very advanced, high-speed, circuit-switched system and is useful as an example of what can be achieved with the circuit-switching technique.

With ESCON, users can construct distributed computer and peripheral configurations spanning quite large areas (a few kilometers). Optical connection is extremely beneficial in this environment for its high noise immunity, low error rates, high speed and, most important, electrical isolation. One of the major problems in computer cabling has been the potential for "ground loops".

The ESCON system was very well described in a special issue of the IBM Research and Development Journal (July 1992). The brief discussion here looks at ESCON as a local communications architecture. This is only a small aspect of the wider ESCON system.

The switching principle used in the IBM ESCON Director is illustrated in Figure 10-1.

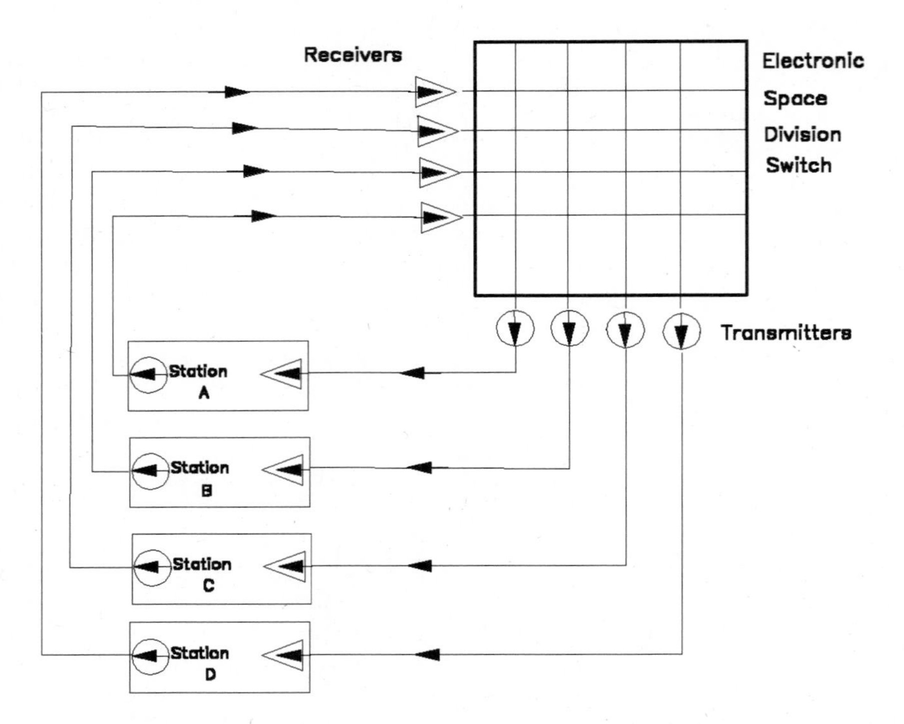


***Figure 10-1.*** *Principle of the ESCON Director (Circuit Switch).* Fiber optical links are used to connect stations to an electronic space division switch.

Conceptually, the Director is a conventional cross-point (space division) switching system (although its internal operation is far from conventional). Copper wire connections from the stations (control units and processors) have been replaced with fiber but the switch itself is electronic.

Stations, whether controllers or processors (at the switching level the distinction has no meaning), connect to the ESCON Director on optical fiber. The Director is a (very) fast circuit switch. Above the physical connection structure known by the Director there is a logical "virtual link" (channel) structure unknown to the Director.

**Data Rate - Warning**

The synchronous (user) data transfer rate of the ESCON system is 160 Mbps. The bit rate on the fiber is 200 Mbps. The difference is due to the use of 8/10 coding in the transmission.

From the point of view of a computer engineer, the speed is quoted as 200 Mbps because this is consistent with the way it is expressed in processor engineering. In communications, things are looked at differently. From the point of view of a communications engineer the rate is 160 Mbps, because that is how communications systems are usually expressed. For example, in communications engineering the FDDI data rate is always quoted as 100 Mbps where the bit rate on the fiber is actually 125 Mbps (using 4/5 coding).

In most IBM documentation on ESCON the quoted data rate is 200 Mbps because it is regarded as a channel.

#### 10.1.1.1 Method of Operation

Operation is very simple (in concept).

1. When a station is not connected to anything the Director is listening for any input.
2. When a station wants to communicate with another station it sends a connection request to the Director.
3. The Director receives the connection request and if the requested destination is not busy it makes the switched connection and passes the connection request on to the destination station.
4. From this point the Director is not involved in the communication. Data passes between connected stations freely (in synchronous mode) until either station sends a DISCONNECT request.
5. The director senses the DISCONNECT request and breaks the circuit (after the DISCONNECT has been sent on to the partner station).

The reason that ESCON works so well is the architecture of the Director itself. The Director pipelines connection and disconnection requests and can handle them at a maximum rate of one every 200 ns (that is 5 million per second). The time taken to make a switch depends on load (request rate) and number of active stations, etc., but in most situations connections are made in between 2 and 3 μsec (plus any propagation delay). A stable operation at a rate of between one and two million connections (plus disconnections) per second can be sustained.

### 10.1.1.2 Performance

Looking at this system as a form of packet switch, to transfer a block of data we must:

1. Make a connection request.
2. Send the data.
3. Make a disconnection request.

Let us assume we want to transfer a 1,000-byte block. At a data rate of 160 Mbps, a 1,000-byte block takes 50 μsec to transmit. If it takes 3 μsec to establish a connection and perhaps 2 μsec to clear it the total "overhead" is 5 μsec. This gives a total time of 55 μsec.

If the system were a real packet switch, we wouldn't have the connection establishment and clearing overheads. But a real packet switch would have to receive the data block in full, perform processing to determine the routing, and then retransmit the data towards its destination. For the 1,000-byte block above that is 50 μsec times two for transmission time plus perhaps 2 μsec for route determination within the packet switch itself. A total time of 102 μsec. In this example the circuit switch clearly outperforms the packet switching technique.[2] (In the real environment of a computer channel I/O system performance will be even better than this example suggests, because computers tend to transfer more than one block of data and control information per connection.)

### 10.1.1.3 Structure

**Optical Links**

The optical links use a wavelength of 1300 nm (dispersion minimum) over either multimode or single-mode fiber. (The single-mode option is a recently announced extension to allow for longer connection distances.) LED transmitters and PIN detectors are used at a link speed of 200 Mbaud.

Data on the link is coded using an 8/10 coding system. The data rate on the link is 160 Mbps (20 MBps). (This compares with the maximum speed of the electronic channel system of 4.5 MBps.) Conceptually this coding system is much the same as the 4/5 coding scheme used with FDDI (this is described in more detail in 13.6.5.2, "Data Encoding" on page 13-41). The reasons behind using a 10-bit code to transmit only 8 bits are:

1. Provide redundant codes to allow for data transparency (delimiters and control codes are not valid data combinations).

---

[2] The example is a little simplistic because additional end-to-end protocol exchanges are needed in the real world. However, they have the same effect on both circuit and packet switching systems, so they have been omitted.

2. Provide a balancing of the number of ones and zeros within the transmitted data stream such that the number or ones and zeros is always equal[3] (DC balancing) and no string of like bits is ever longer than five. (This latter aids in timing recovery.)
3. An additional level of error checking is obtained because errors most often cause a good data code to be changed into an invalid one.
4. Byte synchronization is implicit in the code design such that the receiver can continually monitor byte alignment and if this is lost initiate action to re-establish byte synchronization.

**Data Blocks**

Data blocks have a length which may vary from 7 bytes to 1035 bytes and contain two CRC check bytes. There is a header added to each block containing the origin and destination link identifiers and a control field. Whenever a station receives a block the CRC is checked and the block discarded if an error is found. Error recovery is done by retransmitting the affected block.

**ESCON Director**

The ESCON Director (IBM 9032 Model 1) is able to handle up to 60 connected stations at any one time and it allows for up to 30 simultaneous connections between stations (it is non-blocking). The total possible throughput of a director is therefore 30 times 160 Mbps - 4.8 Gbps.

However, it should be noted that in a large system environment most of the traffic is between channels and control units. There will also be some channel-to-channel traffic but there will be little or no control unit to control unit traffic. Thus, actual throughput depends on how you use the system.

### 10.1.1.4 IBM Single-Mode Fiber Trunk Specifications

The following are the specifications of fiber needed for single-mode operation with IBM ESCON channel devices:

| | |
|---|---|
| **Operating Wavelength** | 1270-1340 nm |
| **Mode Field Diameter** | 9± 1 μm |
| **Cable Attenuation @ 1310 nm** | 0.5 dB/km |
| **Cutoff Wavelength** | 1280 nm |
| **Zero Dispersion Wavelength** | 1310± 10 nm |

[3] DC balancing is not really needed on optical fiber in current single-channel systems like this one. However, balancing enhances the operation of the electronics at either end of the circuit.

| | |
|---|---|
| **Dispersion Slope (max)** | 0.095 ps/(nm$^2$-km) |
| **Cladding Diameter** | 125± 3 μm |
| **Core Concentricity Error** | 1.0 μm |
| **Cladding Non-Circularity (max)** | 2.0 % |

# Chapter 11. High-Speed Packet Networking

Frame switching describes a very common generic network interfacing technique. Many "X.25 networks" on the market offer an "SDLC PAD" function which is capable of switching data from an SDLC link in one part of the network to another SDLC link somewhere else in the network. The term "Frame Switching" does not describe any standardized protocol or interface at all.

The frame switching technique is not new. Nor is it a "high speed" technology. Understanding frame switching is, however, important to understanding the genesis of frame relay.

Consider two machines communicating over a point-to-point SDLC[1] link.

In the diagram, when Box A needs to send something to Box B, header and trailer information specific to the link control protocol is appended to the beginning and end of the block to be sent. This block of data is called a "frame".

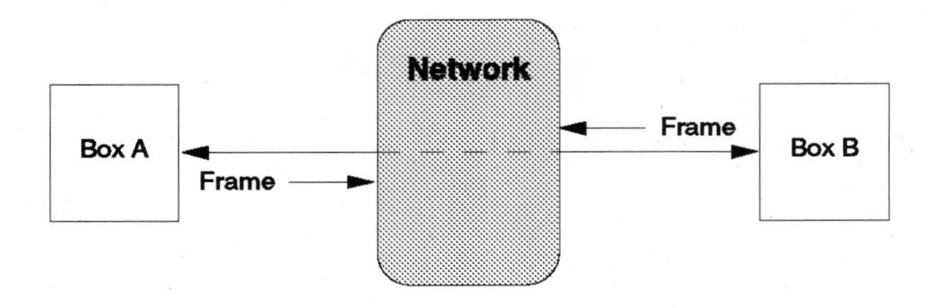


1 In principle, the link protocol used doesn't matter at all. Frame switching interfaces exist for many different types of link control, such as BSC and LAPB as well as SDLC.

In a network situation, inside the frame there will typically be a network header on the front of the user data.

If we want to place a network between boxes A and B as illustrated above, then there are many alternatives. Typically in the front of the user data message there will be a set of network protocol headers. We could:

1. Terminate the link control protocol (from Box A's perspective make the network "look like" Box B) and then use the network protocol headers to route the data to its destination. The problem with this is that the network needs to understand the network headers in the data. This is often a complex problem since there are many different network protocols in existence.

2. Take whatever is sent by Box A, put our own network headers onto the front, route it through the intermediate network and then send it on to Box B.

   This is very simple to do and satisfies many requirements but:

   - Link control protocols have very short time-outs, which can be lengthened but are a problem if the network delay is irregular.
   - Many link controls (especially SDLC) rely for their operation on regular polling. Sending polls across the network (and receiving the responses) can cause significant additional network overhead.
   - The network addresses of the communicating boxes must be prespecified to the network and must be fixed. The address in the link control header[2] can be used to identify different destinations, but this ability is very limited.

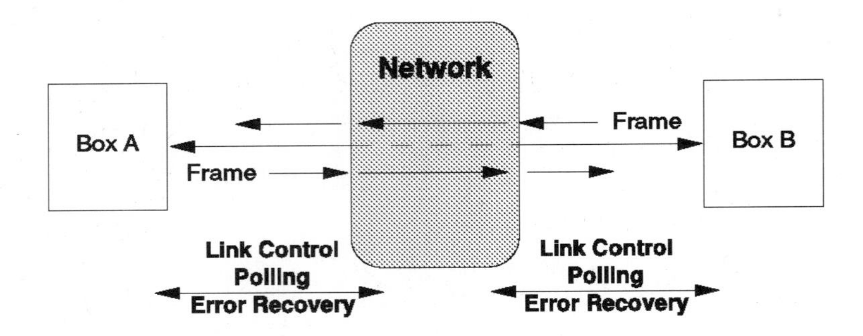


*Figure 11-1. Frame Switching.* The network viewed from Box A "looks like" Box B but polling and error recovery are handled locally and do not pass through the network.

[2] in SDLC one can address up to 255 secondary "boxes" but the control end of the link has no address - it is specified by context.

Frame switching is like alternative 2 above, but the polling function is handled locally at each end of the network. Only data and control messages are forwarded through the network. The details of how this works vary from one implementation to another. A number of characteristics should be noted:

- The link control from the user to the network is terminated in the nearest network node. This means that link time-outs are no longer a problem. Since SNA has no time-outs in its network protocols (outside the physical and link layers), SNA systems will not have any problem with time-outs. Some other protocols do rely on time-outs and can experience problems in this situation.

- Many implementations of this kind allow the end-user boxes to initialize their communications at different times. This precludes those boxes from exchanging their characteristics using XID (eXchange IDentification) protocols. It is this characteristic which prevents many networks from correctly handling SNA type 2.1 nodes. These nodes rely on XID type 3 to tell each other their characteristics and will not function correctly unless the frame switching network understands the XID protocols and properly synchronizes the initialization.

- Since the line control is terminated by the nearest network node when a frame is sent to the network, it is acknowledged immediately on receipt. If that frame is subsequently lost by the network (through a node failure, for example), the end "boxes" will "think" that the frame has been received by the destination when it really has not.[3] This is no problem for SNA (or OSI), since link control is not relied upon for network level acknowledgments (that's what layered architecture is all about). However, it is disruptive, since if a frame is lost there is no recovery and connections (sessions) running above the link layer must be terminated and restarted.

  Some older devices (predominantly BSC) actually use line control level acknowledgments to signal correct receipt of the data to the user application. (There are BSC versions of frame switching available in the marketplace.) These older devices will not function correctly over a frame switching system because data can be lost without being detected.

- There is another problem with link level switching systems (this also applies to LAN bridges and routers). The network loses the ability to distinguish between different types of traffic based on priority.

  For example, an SDLC link may carry many SNA sessions at a number of different priorities. At any point in time the link may be carrying highly critical interactive traffic or batch traffic (or a mixture). The network has no way of knowing so it must treat all traffic as a single priority.

---

3 Contrast this with the description of frame relay. In frame relay the link control operates across the network and thus can be used to recover from network losses of data.

The consequence of this is that the network is unable to load its intermediate links or nodes to utilizations much above 60% at the peak (with average utilizations of perhaps 20% to 30%). In contrast, if the network is able to distinguish between data flows based on priority, then resources can be utilized up to 60% (peak) for interactive traffic only and the remaining capacity may be used for non-critical batch traffic. (SNA networks operate this way.)

The "net" of the above is that networks that switch frames are much less efficient in their use of link bandwidth (and node cycles) than networks (like SNA) that are able to recognize priorities.

## 11.1 Frame Relay

Frame relay is a standardized technique for *interfacing* to a packet network. Standards are under development for frame relay to be used *for the internal operation* of the packet network as well as for the user interface. However, a network can be called "frame relay" if it supports FR interfaces to end users.

Frame relay originated as an optional service of ISDN. Users send frames to a network node over an ISDN B, H, or D channel and these frames are passed to another user in some other part of the network (also through a B, D, or H channel). Frame relay has, however, been implemented in few (if any) public ISDN networks. Rather, frame relay has become very important as a network interfacing technique quite independently of ISDN.

Frame relay is an interface definition. While it is possible (standards are under development) for networks to use frame relay techniques internally for transmission between network nodes, there will be many networks that do not work this way. A frame relay network is a network that allows a user to attach through a frame relay interface, and which provides the services and facilities necessary to support communication between FR interfaces.

**An interim technology?**

While frame relay should not be regarded as a true high-speed technology, it is extremely important because:

1. It can be implemented fairly easily on existing packet switching equipment.
2. It can provide an immediate throughput improvement of between two and ten to one over previous technologies *using existing equipment*.

## 11.1.1 Concept of Frame Relay

Frame relay is an exceedingly simple concept. Communicating devices interact with one another across the network transparently. That is, a network is interposed between devices communicating on a link but the devices are not aware that this has happened. In practice, it is not quite as simple as the above suggests, because a special link control protocol is used, but the principle still holds.

## 11.1.2 Basic Principles

The basic principles of frame relay are as follows:

**A virtual link (connection) exists across the network.**

This connection consists of pairing a local address (called a Data Link Connection Identifier, DLCI) on one port (link) with a local address on another port somewhere else in the network. This is *exactly* the same as the virtual circuit concept in X.25, where a VC is a pairing of logical channels on different ports across the network. See Figure 11-2.

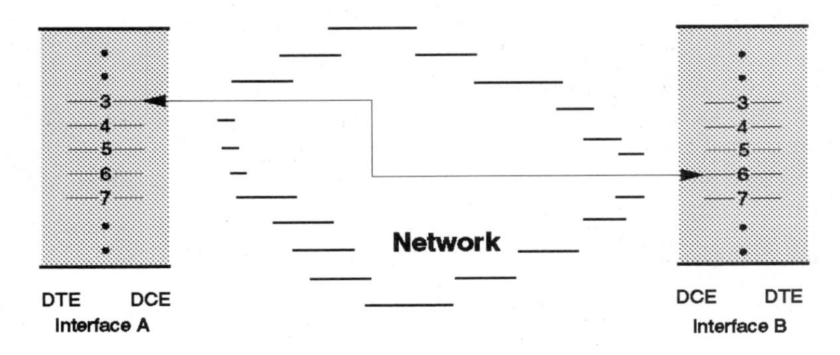


***Figure 11-2.*** *Virtual Connection.* Two DLCIs (number 3 on interface A and number 6 on interface B) are communicating with one another. This pairing of DLCIs is called a virtual connection.

The frame relay local address is just the address field in the data link frame. In frame relay this is called the Data Link Connection Identifier (DLCI).

When User A communicates with User B the link address field (DLCI) as seen by User A is "3". When User B communicates with User A it sees the connection as having DLCI 6. The network, in this case the node, has a connection table which relates DLCIs on one interface with DLCIs on another and so constructs a table of virtual connections. Each table entry must consist of <node id, link id, DLCI> because the DLCI field has meaning only in the context of a particular link.

Data delivered to the network with a given DLCI on a particular port is transported across the network and delivered to the port appropriate to this virtual connection. When the data is forwarded by the network, the DLCI is swapped. The new DLCI represents the connection on the destination port.

**Many virtual connections may share a single physical port.**

This is the central characteristic of a separate network. It is true of X.25 style networks as well. The end user "saves" the cost of all the ports that would be needed if point-to-point lines were installed.

**Every non-error frame is relayed.**

This means polls and acknowledgments (if any) are relayed. The network does not know the difference between a poll and a data frame. It is all just data to the FR network.

**Error frames are discarded.**

The FR network makes no attempt at error recovery of incorrect frames. Error recovery is the responsibility of the link control protocol.

**Frames may be up to 8,250 bytes long.**

Up to a network imposed maximum, frames may be of any length. (A minimum network capability of 262 bytes is mentioned in the standard.) Most of the announced FR networks have a maximum frame size of 2 KB. The standard allows frame lengths of up to 8 KB and it is expected that networks handling frames of this size will become available in the future.

**There is no "packetization" performed on transported frames.**

Some networks may packetize internally (though these will probably be a minority).

FR networks avoid the irregular time delays and consequent time-out problems caused by the presence of relatively long frames by using fast link connections between nodes. (See the discussion in Appendix C.1.4, "Practical Systems" on page C-6.)

**Link control operates from device to device across the FR network.**

Although the FR specification was originally related to the ISDN LAPD specification, there is no constraint on the logic of whatever link control is used. The link control must, however, use the HDLC frame format and allow for the two address bytes of FR at the start of the frame.

- The frame format is identical to that of SDLC/HDLC *except* that two address bytes are used. See Figure 11-3 on page 11-9.
- This frame format is the format used by the link control called "LAPD" on the D channel of narrowband ISDN.

- The generic frame format of the HDLC series of link controls consists of FAC (Flag followed by Address followed by Control) then data, then an FCS (Frame Check Sequence) field and another flag.

  In frame relay there are no control bytes. That is, the network does not look at the link control protocol at all.

  The beginning flag signals the start of a frame and also the start of accumulation of the Frame Check Sequence.

- Some product implementations will undoubtedly use the LAPD protocol because it is a point-to-point protocol and does not involve polling. Normal SDLC and LAPB are more difficult because they only use a single address byte and therefore a code change is required to use FR. Also, SDLC uses polling and this adds unnecessary network traffic.

  IBM SNA products use the IEEE 802.2 protocol instead of LAPD (see 11.1.7, "SNA Connections Using Frame Relay" on page 11-12). IEEE 802.2 is a link control protocol designed to operate in a LAN environment in many ways similar to the FR environment.

**A Local Management Interface (LMI) is used to access the network's management functions.**

There is a reserved link address (DLCI) which allows for communication between the attaching device and the network. This provides a mechanism for communicating the status of connections (PVCs). Initially there are three functions available:

- A query command that allows the DTE to ask the network if it is still active. This is called a "heartbeat" or a "keep alive" message.
- A query to ask the network for a list of valid DLCIs defined for this interface.
- A query to determine the status (congested or not) of each DLCI.

In the future this may be used for more extensive network management information and for setting up virtual link connections dynamically (switched virtual circuits). Attached devices are not required to use the control channel. Of course, if the LMI is not used the attached device cannot establish switched virtual circuits.

**The LMI is used to set up switched virtual connections.**

There is a method of setting up switched virtual connections in the FR standard. This involves sending a call request to the network using the Local Management Interface (LMI). Notice that this is an "out of band signaling" situation. The request to set up a connection is sent on a different DLCI (the LMI) from the one over which the connection will be made. (In X.25 a call request is placed on the logical channel which will latter carry the data.)

Most public frame relay offerings announced in the United States do not offer switched virtual connections.

**Signaling about congestion provides a flow control function.**

The network is able to signal the attached device about congestion in the network. This is done with two bits in the address section of the frame header called the "FECN" (Forward Explicit Congestion Notification) and the "BECN" (Backward Explicit Congestion Notification) bits.

When the FECN bit is set it indicates that there was congestion along its path in the direction of flow. The BECN bit indicates that there was congestion in the network for frames flowing in the opposite direction to the frame containing the notification.

Many (if not most) products that currently use FR do not make use of congestion notification. The IBM 3745 FR attachment feature does use congestion notification to control the window size used.

There is a problem here. User devices may ignore the FECN and BECN notifications and just keep sending data at maximum speed into the network. Unless the network has an internal mechanism to detect this condition (and close down the misbehaving user) congestion will be made worse. This could mean that data from well-behaved users could be discarded while the errant device just keeps on sending! Practical networks need to have an enforcement mechanism and attaching user devices are of little practical use unless they support the FECN and BECN functions.

## 11.1.3 Frame Format

The format of a frame is shown in Figure 11-3 on page 11-9. It is the same as a normal SDLC/HDLC frame *except* that it uses two address bytes and the control fields are absent.

- Looked at from a link control perspective, the DLCI field performs the same function as the SDLC address - it identifies the connection.
- The EA bits indicate whether the extended (3- or 4-byte) address options are in use.
- The DE (Discard Eligibility) bit tells the network that this frame can be discarded if network congestion becomes a problem. In transporting both video and voice traffic some coding schemes produce "essential" and "nonessential" frames. When a nonessential frame is discarded there is a degradation in quality but the connection still functions.

- The FECN and BECN bits are notifications from the network to the user equipment (DTE) that congestion exists along the path.

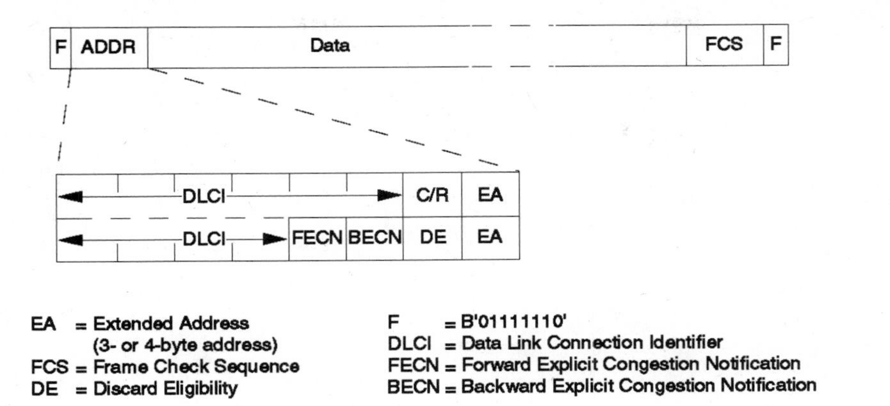


***Figure 11-3.*** *Frame Format.* Link control fields are absent since they are ignored by the network.

## 11.1.4 Operation

Frame relay is the simplest networking protocol imaginable.

1. An SDLC/HDLC type frame is sent by the end-user device to the network.
2. The network receives the frame and checks the FCS fields to determine if the frame was received correctly. If the frame was bad then it is discarded.
3. The network uses the address field to determine the destination of the data block.
4. The network uses its own internal protocols (which could be "like" frame relay or totally unlike) to route the frame to its intended destination. The destination is always another link within the FR network.
5. The network changes the address field in the frame header to the correct identifier for this connection on the destination link.
6. The network sends the frame on the destination link.
7. The frame is received by the destination end-user device.

## 11.1.5 Characteristics of a Frame Relay Network

**Lower safe link utilizations because priorities are impossible.**

While the frame relay interface realizes important performance gains because it does not know about the contents of the data, it loses the ability to prioritize *within* a single link. In SNA many sessions can be operated over a single link. These sessions may operate at different priorities and, because the network can detect the priority of each session, it is able to operate at quite high resource (switching nodes, links, etc.) utilizations.

If there are several virtual connections (or links) sharing a real link within the network, there is no way of giving the interactive traffic priority. The "net" of this is that node and link utilizations within the frame relay network cannot be as high as they could be in an SNA network for example. This means that a faster link may be needed.

**Mixture of long and short blocks causes erratic response times.**

The presence of a long frame and short frames mixed up within a network produces highly erratic response times. This is because the queuing delays have a big variation. (See the discussion in Appendix C.1.4, "Practical Systems" on page C-6.)

The solution to this is to shorten the maximum frame length. If the length of the frame in bytes is shortened then this defeats the purpose of frame relay. What can be done is to shorten the frame length *in time*. You do this by using a higher-speed link.

**Flow control is achieved by using the link control protocol across the network.**

The only available flow control is by using the link control protocol from end-to-end across the network. This means that we have lost a lot of control. To get acceptable batch throughput a large link window size will be necessary. But when the network starts to experience congestion the only control is to cut back on the window size.

The same conclusion is reached as above. The network must be fast and have a uniform delay to get acceptable throughput for batch traffic.

IBM products that use the FR interface will dynamically change the window size according to the congestion signals from the network.

**No enforcement of congestion indications.**

Although congestion within the network can be signaled to the attached device with the FECN and BECN indications there is no compulsion on the end station to take any notice. That is, devices may receive a signal from the network to say there is congestion and yet continue to send data at the maximum rate.

At this point the only thing the network can do is to start discarding data. Unless the network is very sophisticated and is able to detect rogue users, it will throw data away from all users not just the misbehaving ones.

**The frame relay advantage is in the network not on the link.**

> Frame relay gains its throughput advantage by enabling the use of simple techniques within intermediate network nodes. When two end-user devices are interconnected over a transparent data link (with no intermediate switching nodes), frame relay offers no advantage over HDLC or SDLC.

In summary a frame relay network gains efficiency by trading network complexity off against link capacity. Within a frame relay network link and node utilizations have to be kept low in order for the network to operate stably. (In contrast, SNA subarea networks use very complex mechanisms internally, but are able to operate links and nodes at very high utilizations.)

### 11.1.6 Comparison with X.25

At a functional level frame relay and X.25 are the same thing. The user has a "virtual circuit" through the network. Data is presented to the network with a header identifying the particular virtual circuit (connection) used and it is presented to the destination on the same virtual circuit (connection) - even though the identifier at each end of the VC may be different.

At a detail level they are quite different. In X.25 the basic service is a virtual call (switched virtual circuit) although permanent virtual circuits are available in some networks. frame relay is currently defined for permanent virtual circuits only; however, standards bodies are working on a definition for switched connections.

In X.25 there is a rigorous separation between the "Network Layer" (networking function) and the "Link Layer" (function of delivering packets to the network). In frame relay both functions are integrated into the same operation. Another way of saying this is to say that in X.25 networking is done at "layer 3" and that in frame relay networking is done at "layer 2".[4]

All of the above said, frame relay as an interface is much simpler than X.25 and therefore can offer higher throughput rates on the same equipment.

Some people view frame relay as the natural successor to X.25. Indeed many suppliers of X.25 network equipment are adding FR interfaces to their nodes. In the US, a number of public (X.25) network providers have announced that they will provide a frame relay service as well.

---

4 In strict terms this kind of characterization is not very helpful any more. In the OSI model, networking is done at layer 3 - therefore the layer at which we network IS layer 3. Functions of link control (layer 2) are paralleled in layer 4. There is a real need to review our paradigms in this area.

### 11.1.7 SNA Connections Using Frame Relay

The first consideration in running SNA over a frame relay network[5] is that FR is the interface to a *separate* network. At the interface between a piece of SNA equipment and a frame relay network, many virtual connections (links) are multiplexed over a single physical link. The SNA equipment must be able to multiplex many virtual links over a single real link. SNA equipment already does this for X.25 and for LAN network connections, but the FR connection is little different.

SNA connections over FR networks[6] promise to be much more stable and more efficient than similar connections over X.25 networks.

**Error Recovery**

Because there is a link control running end-to-end across the FR network, network errors will be recovered by the link control.

When SNA is used over X.25 this does not happen. An error in the network causes the catastrophic loss of all sessions using that virtual circuit.[7]

**Interface Efficiency**

Because there is no packetization or packet level protocol to perform, the FR network interface is likely to use significantly less resource within the attaching SNA product than is required to interface to X.25.

**Network Management**

FR has a signaling channel which allows the exchange of some network management information between the device and the network. X.25 has no such ability.

Nevertheless, at the current state of the definition it is not possible to provide full seamless integration of SNA network management with the management of the FR network over which it will run. The latest releases of SNA equipment, however, are able to receive the network diagnostic information from an FR network and present it to the user integrated with the rest of the network management information. Because you can't look past the interface into the FR

---

[5] **Information in this section is derived from an early SNA prototype implementation. The description is conceptual and may not accurately reflect the operational detail of any product.**

[6] It is convenient to refer to "FR networks" and to "X.25 networks" to mean "networks that support FR interfaces" and "networks that support X.25 interfaces" regardless of how they operate inside. The majority of FR networks do not use FR protocols internally.

[7] Except in the case of the IBM System/36 and IBM AS/400 which are able to use an end-to-end link protocol (called ELLC) across the X.25 network. ELLC uses the elements of procedure of LAPB as an end-to-end network protocol.

network itself, to some extent the FR network (like X.25 networks) forms a "black hole" in the SNA network management system.

**Multidrop**

Although it is not in the FR standard, there is a potential ability to use FR for limited "multidrop" connection for devices located in close physical proximity to one another. This is a real problem in X.25 since the X.25 interface is strictly point-to-point, so that if there are many devices in the same location many links to the X.25 network are necessary.

Using FR, a relatively simple "interface splitter" device could be constructed which would allow the connection of multiple FR devices to the same network link attachment.

Frame relay support in SNA is an extension of the LAN support. Figure 11-4 shows how frame relay may be situated logically in relation to the two most important LAN architectures.

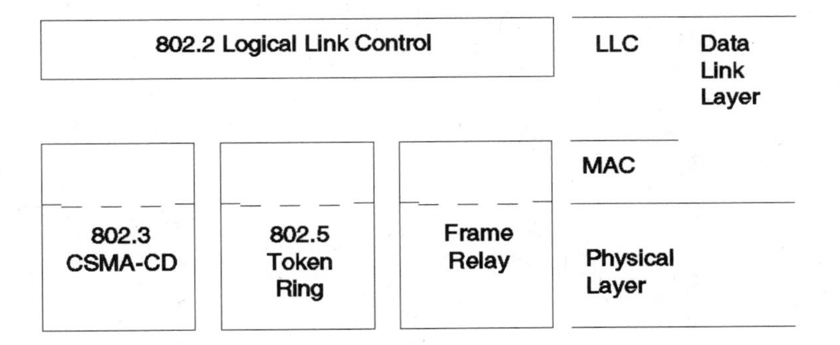


***Figure 11-4.*** *Frame Relay in Relation to IEEE Standards.* Frame relay functions as an alternative MAC layer which is used by the logical link control and medium access control functions.

There are differences of course.

1. The LAN environment at the Media Access Control level (MAC layer) is a connectionless environment. You can send data to any device at any time provided you know the correct address to send to.

   Frame relay provides connections across the network. In the early networks these connections must be predefined although later there will be an ability to set up connections on demand (switched virtual connections).

2. The LAN environment provides a broadcast function but frame relay does not.

3. A frame relay network can provide congestion information to attaching devices where a LAN typically does not.
4. The network management environment is quite different.
5. An end station in a LAN environment must support source routing protocols in order to allow communication across "source routing" bridges. In frame relay this is not needed.

These differences are either irrelevant or can be fairly easily accommodated.

Most important are the similarities:

1. Both SNA and frame relay are connection-oriented systems. When SNA uses a LAN connection it usually builds a switched connection across the LAN.
2. Both LAN and frame relay take an entire data frame and transport it to another user. The functions of framing, addressing, error detection (but not recovery) and transparency are handled by the network attachment protocol (MAC layer).
3. In both LAN and frame relay a single physical attachment to a device may contain many virtual links to other devices.

The link control protocol used across the LAN is called IEEE 802.2. This is just another link control protocol like SDLC, LAPB and LAPD (all forms of HDLC). The difference is that SDLC, LAPB and LAPD perform the functions of framing, transparency (via bit-stuffing), error detection and addressing. In the LAN environment these functions are provided by the MAC protocol and in frame relay they are provided by the frame relay link control. IEEE 802.2 is simply a link control protocol that leaves the responsibility for framing, addressing, etc., to the MAC function. Thus 802.2 provides exactly the function that is needed for frame relay. In addition 802.2 uses an addressing structure that allows multiple Service Access Points (SAPs), which provide a way of addressing multiple independent functions within a single device.

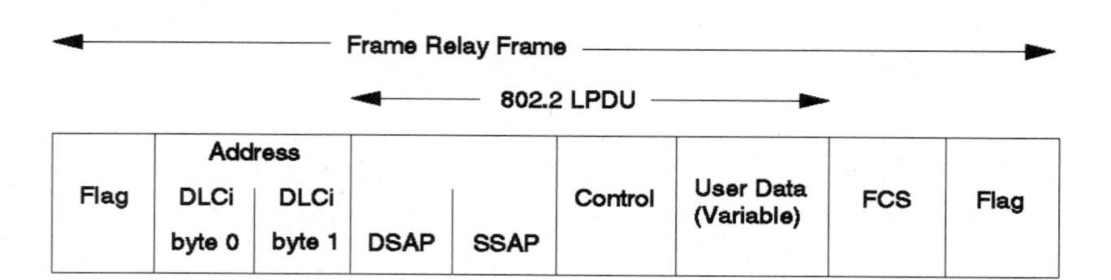


***Figure 11-5.*** *Frame Relay Format as Used in SNA.* The LPDU format is exactly the same as that used in the LAN environment.

Thus the link control used by SNA across a frame relay connection is IEEE 802.2 (the LAN link control). In addition SNA devices use the congestion information provided by the frame relay network to control the rate of data presented to the network (flow control).

The HDLC family of link controls uses a “rotating window” scheme to provide delivery confirmation. Multiple blocks may be sent before the sender must wait for an acknowledgment from the receiver. This means that several blocks may be in transit at any time, and helps compensate for propagation delays.

In IEEE 802.2 this rotating window mechanism is used for flow control across a LAN. Since most LANs contain bridges, there is a need to control the flow of data in the case where the bridge becomes congested. The mechanism is exactly suited to use across a frame relay network.

The flow control mechanism operates at the sender end only and the receiver is not involved in its operation. The transmitter is allocated a number (n) of blocks that it may send before it must wait for an acknowledgment. The receiver acknowledges blocks by number and an acknowledgment of block number 3 (for example) implies correct receipt of blocks numbered 1 and 2 (but, in practice, most receivers acknowledge every block).

When the transmitter is notified by the FR network of congestion along its forward path (by receiving the BECN bit in the header of a received frame)[8] it reduces its send window size to 1. In the uncongested state there may be n frames in the network between transmitter and receiver. When congestion is detected this is immediately reduced to 1.

As operation continues, if the transmitter has had m (an arbitrary number) responses without seeing another congestion notification, then the send window n is increased by one. This will continue to happen until the maximum transmit window size n is reached.

The described mechanism is about as much as any end-user device can do. It is really a delivery rate control. However, it must be noted that if FR networks are to give stable operation then they will need flow and congestion controls internally.

### 11.1.8 Disadvantages

As discussed above (11.1.5, “Characteristics of a Frame Relay Network” on page 11-9), faster links are required than would be needed in a better controlled network (such as an SNA network) to handle the same amount of traffic. This is partly because the network cannot know about priorities within the link and partly because of the variability in frame lengths allowed.

---

8 The transmitter's “forward” path is the “backward” path of blocks being received. Hence it is the BECN bit that a transmitter must examine.

In the environment where the cost of wide area links is dropping very quickly, this may not be important.

### 11.1.9 Frame Relay as an Internal Network Protocol

Many people assume that FR networks will use the logical ID swapping technique (described in 6.7.4, "Logical ID Swapping" on page 6-31) for internal network operation. Indeed this would be a good technique for FR since it is easy to implement on existing networking equipment.

The advantage of FR internally within the network then lies in the ability to "throw away" error frames and not handle error recoveries. This means that far fewer instructions are needed for the sending and receiving of data on intermediate links. Buffer storage requirements within intermediate nodes are reduced because there is no longer any need to hold "unacknowledged" data frames after they have been sent. Standards work is under way to specify this method of operation and the interconnections between FR nodes (using FR) within a network.

However, it seems unlikely that FR will be widely used in this way. Many people see FR as an interim technique which will give a substantial improvement in data throughput on existing equipment. In the real world, networks offering FR interfaces will also offer X.25 and perhaps LAN routing interfaces as well. These networks will continue to use their existing internal network protocols (many use TCP/IP internally).

## 11.2 Packetized Automatic Routing Integrated System (Paris)

Paris is an experimental very high-speed packet switching system developed by the IBM T.J. Watson Research Center at Yorktown Heights, New York. It was built to develop a better understanding of the principles and problems involved in high-speed packet switched communication and has been used in a number of field trials.[9]

The objectives of the Paris development were to build a system appropriate to a private backbone network supporting voice, video, data and image. Such a private network might have a relatively small number (less than 20) of 100 Mbps links around the US. (In fact the principles and technology involved here can be extended quite easily to large networks involving perhaps thousands of links and interconnections.)

[9] Paris is a research project *not* a product. Networking BroadBand Services (NBBS) architecture and its implementation in the IBM 2220 Nways BroadBand Switch has been derived from the research work done in the Paris project.

The underlying principles are those outlined in Chapter 6, "Principles of High-Speed Networks" on page 6-1. To minimize the delay in each switching node:

- Throw away error data without retry (as in frame relay). This prevents delays on links caused by retries and can be accommodated quite well by appropriate end-to-end protocols at the entry points to the network. This also minimizes buffer use in switching nodes, since data doesn't have to be stored after transmission in case a retry is needed.
- Use a protocol such that the data switching function can be performed in hardware without software involvement. This means there needs to be a new and innovative approach to flow controls.
- Use variable-length packets, because this lessens the load on the switching nodes. Statistics dictate that the maximum block size be such that its transmit time cannot have too drastic an effect on link queuing delays. See Appendix C.1.4, "Practical Systems" on page C-6. The maximum packet size allowed in Paris is 4 KB, but that is quite arbitrary and is dictated mainly by the link speed and the amount of buffer storage allocated in the switching nodes.
- Adopt a simplified priority scheme. Priorities cause extra complexity (extra delay) in switching nodes. The system aims to "guarantee" a very short nodal delay which, if achieved, makes priorities (especially for voice traffic) unnecessary. There is a very simple priority mechanism in Paris, which is discussed later.

## 11.2.1 Node Structure

Figure 11-6 is a schematic representation of the elements of a Paris network.

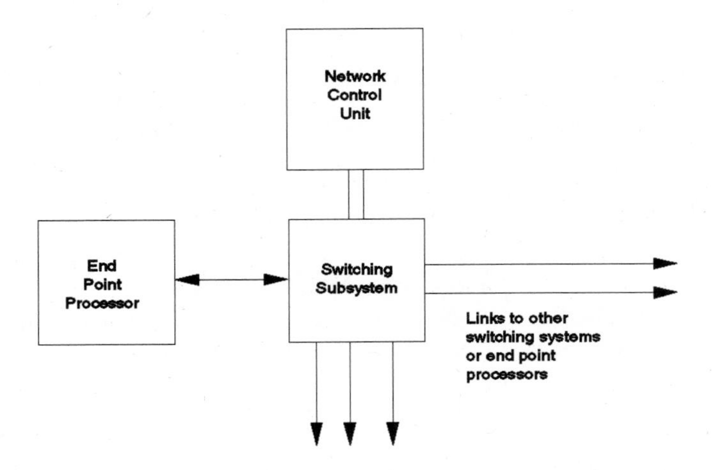


***Figure 11-6.*** *Paris Node Structure*

**Switching Node**

An intermediate switching node is comprised of a Network Control Unit closely linked to a switching subsystem.

**Network Control Unit**

This is a general purpose processor. It contains:

- A network map (topology database)
- Route selection function
- Network directory
- Capacity allocation function

**Switching Subsystem**

This is the business end of the system - the frame switch. It handles the routing and buffering of data and the priority mechanism.

**End Point Processor**

This processor links the Paris backbone network to the outside world. It must:

- Contain an interface to the switching subsystem which is able to send data blocks in the required format.
- Because every data packet sent must contain routing information, the EPP must contain either a network control function (with topology database, etc.) or a function that can obtain network topology from the nearest network control function.

Some end point functions are:

- Voice packetization and playout
- Flow control (admission rate control)
- Error recovery
- External interfaces and protocol adaptation, etc.

## 11.2.2 Automatic Network Routing (ANR)

The heart of the Paris system is the system of switching data in intermediate nodes. Switching is "connectionless". The switching subsystems process data packets without ever knowing or caring about connections. No connection information is kept in the switching subsystem.

Instead, the full route that the packet must take is included in the beginning of the packet itself.

**Note**

This is very similar in principle to the "source routing" method of interconnecting LANs. The method is also used in the connection setup process in APPN. In APPN, the session setup control message (the BIND) carries its route as a control vector within itself. Data switching in APPN is done via connection tables in each node but setting up connections is done by the routing vector method.

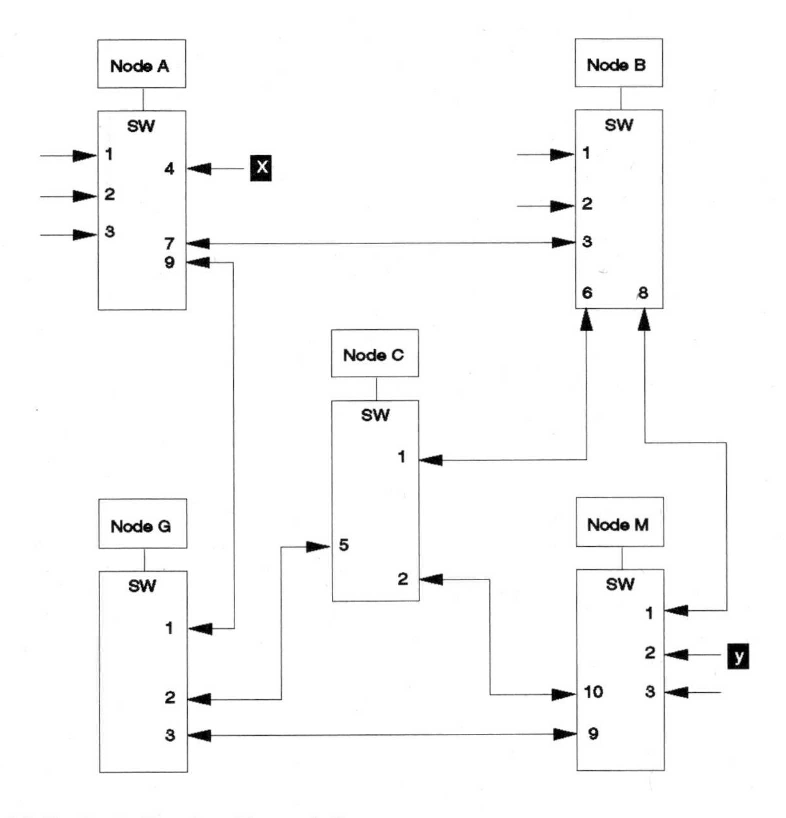


*Figure 11-7. Paris Routing Network Structure*

In Figure 11-7, imagine that we wish to send a packet into the network at point x and have the network deliver it to point y. The packet could go by several routes but one possible route is through node B. The routing vector would contain:

```
7,8,2,,,
```

- Since the packet arrives at node A there is no entry in the vector to denote node A.

- When the packet arrives at node A, node A looks at the first entry in the routing vector. That is the number 7.
- The entry "7" is removed from the routing vector.

  (This enables the next switching function to look at a constant place in the received packet for its routing information. This helps reduce the amount of logic needed in the switching hardware.)
- The packet is queued for link 7.

Notice here that there is nothing in the routing vector to specify the node name or number. The routing vector now looks like:

```
8,2,,,
```

The data arrives at node B and the process is repeated:

- The number 8 is removed from the routing vector and the packet is queued for link 8.

When the packet arrives at node M, by the same process it will be sent on link 2. Now all that is left of the routing vector are two null entries and so link 2 must be connected to an endpoint processor.

There are several possible routes for our packet:

```
7,8,2,,,
9,3,2,,,
9,2,2,2,,,
9,2,1,8,2,,,
```

Any or all of these could be used to send packets from point **x** to point **y**. The switching subsystems keep no record of connections and route data only based on the routing header.

In a practical system, there will be a Frame Check Sequence field either in the header or at the end of the data or in both. A receiving node should check the FCS field before routing the data, as an error in the header could cause misrouting of the packet.

This system places the responsibility for determining the route onto the sending system. This means that the endpoint processor must have a means of calculating an appropriate route. Hence the need for the endpoint processor to have either a continuously updated topology database or access to a network control function that has this information.

Sending data in the opposite direction is exactly the same process, except that **y** is now the origin. This shows that a real connection between two end users can take two completely different paths. In a practical system, for management and control reasons, it would probably be necessary to have data belonging to a single “call” (connection through the network) travel on the same path. There are a number of potential ways of achieving this.

Figure 11-8 shows the format of a data packet.

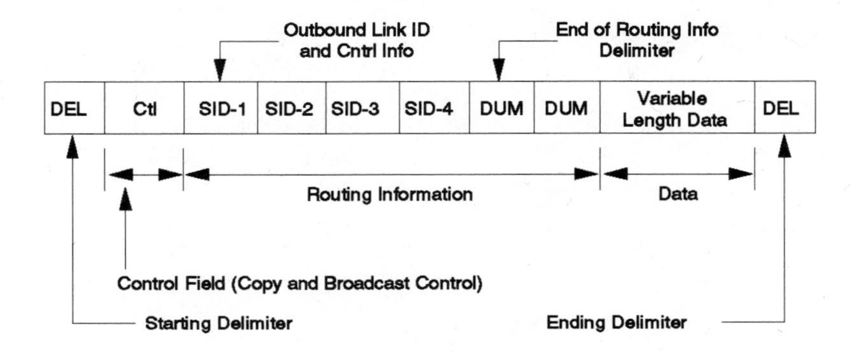


*Figure 11-8. Data Packet Format*

The “routing information” field shown contains the ordered set of links specifying the route a packet must take. Refer to Figure 11-7 on page 11-19. The numbers located within each node, adjacent to the link attachment, represent link numbers *within that node*. These are used in the following discussion.

## 11.2.3 Copy and Broadcast Functions

A number of copy and broadcast functions are possible within the system.

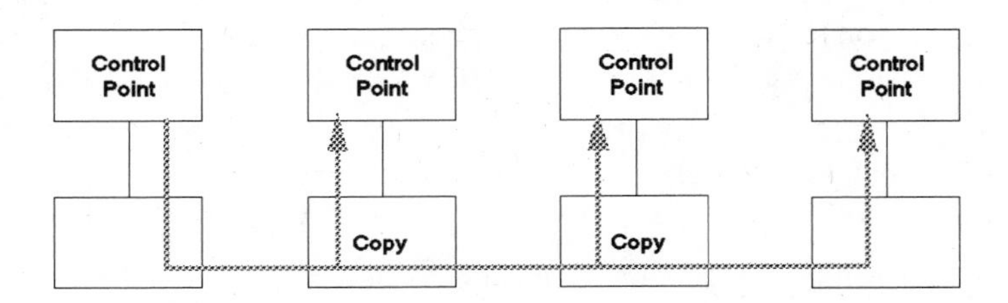


*Figure 11-9. Connection Setup Using Linear Broadcast with Copy*

**Broadcast**

In the Control field of the packet header there is a single bit which causes the switching node to send a copy of the packet onto all its outbound links (after removing the routing vector).

**Selective Broadcast**

The SID contains more information than just the identifier of the next link. It contains 4 bits of control information. One of these is for selective broadcast. When a SID is removed from the front of a packet, it is examined and if the broadcast bit is "on" the packet is routed to all outbound links on this node (except the link that the packet arrived on). It is possible to broadcast to only a subset of nodes - hence the use of the word "selective".

**Copy**

A copy bit exists in the Control field that directs every switching node along the route to send a copy of this packet to its network control processor.

**Selective Copy**

A bit to control this function is also in the SID. Selective copy copies the packet to the control processor only for selected nodes along the path.

These broadcast and copy functions are important for network control and connection setup procedures.

### 11.2.4 Connection Setup

Although the network data switching function itself does not know about connections, these are present between the end points of the network.

- When an Endpoint Processor (EPP) wants to start a connection it requests a route from the nearest Network Control Unit (NCU).

  **Note**

  The NCU keeps a full topology database of the network, which includes every link with current link utilizations. These link utilizations are continuously calculated by a monitor function within each node and when a significant change in loading occurs, the change is broadcast to every NCU in the network.

- The NCU calculates the route as a sequence of SIDs for *both* directions between the end points and sends it back to the requesting EPP.

- The EPP then sends a connection setup request frame to the desired partner EPP with the copy function set.

- The switching systems copy the request to every NCU along the desired route. Each NCU will then check to make sure that sufficient capacity is available for the desired connection.

  This is a complex decision. For a data call, the amount of required capacity will (on average) be many times less than the peak rate. The node must allocate an appropriate level of capacity based on some statistical "guess" about the characteristics of data connections. Voice and video traffic have quite different characteristics and the NCU must allocate capacity accordingly.

- For important traffic classes a second path may be precalculated so that it will be immediately available in case of failure of the primary path.
- Each NCU along the path will reserve a certain amount of bandwidth for the connection. This bandwidth reservation is repeated at intervals. If a specified time elapses and there has not been another reservation for this connection, the NCU will de-allocate the capacity.
- An NCU may disallow a connection request and notify the requesting EPP.
- The destination EPP replies (also copying each NCU along the path) using the reverse path sent to it in the connection request. This ensures that both directions of a connection take exactly the same path (same links and nodes). This is important in error recovery and management of the network.

## 11.2.5 Flow and Rate Control

The primary method of flow control in the Paris network is a "delivery rate control" system rather than a flow control mechanism. The concept is to control the rate at which packets are allowed to enter the network rather than controlling individual flows. All flow and rate control in a Paris network takes place in the EPP.

The scheme used is called "leaky bucket" rate control. In order for a packet to pass the leaky bucket, the counter must be non-zero.

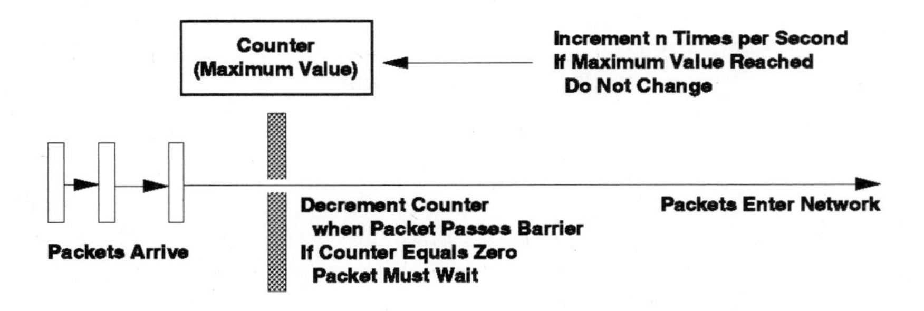


*Figure 11-10. Leaky Bucket Rate Control*

The "leaky bucket" is a counter which has a defined maximum value. This counter is incremented (by one) n times per second. When a packet arrives, it may pass the leaky bucket if (and only if) the counter is non-zero. When the packet passes the barrier to enter the network, the counter is decremented.

This scheme has the effect of limiting the packet rate to a defined average, but allowing short (definable size) bursts of packets to enter the network at maximum rate. If the node tries to send packets at a high rate for a long period of time, the rate will be equal to "n" per second. If, however, there has been no traffic for a while, then the node may send at full rate until the counter reaches zero.

Paris, in fact, uses two leaky buckets in series, with the second one using a maximum bucket size of 1 but a faster clock rate. The total effect is to limit input to a defined average rate but with short bursts allowed at a higher rate (but not the full speed of the transmission medium). The scheme is a bit conservative but allocates capacity fairly. Paris has an adaptive modification based on network congestion. It can alter the maximum rates at which the buckets "leak". The network provides feedback via a congestion stamp on the reverse path. This feedback is used to alter the rate at which the counters are incremented, and thus the rate at which packets are able to enter the network.

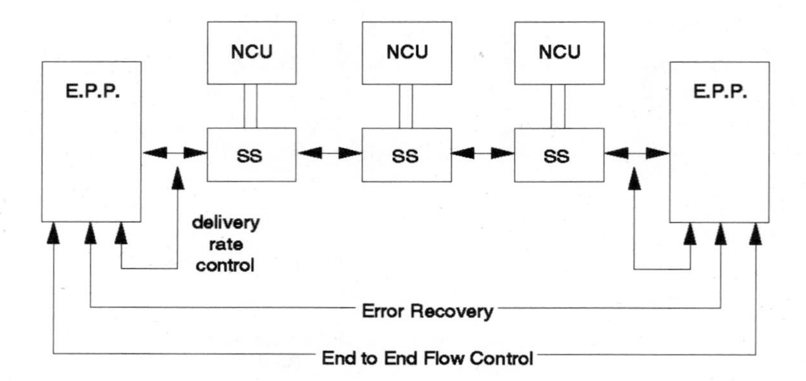


***Figure 11-11.*** *Paris Flow and Rate Control*

In addition to the delivery rate control, which restricts the rate at which data may enter the network, there are end-to-end protocols that allow for error recovery and for flow control for each individual connection.

These controls are different depending on the type of connection. For data a protocol is used that allows for error recovery by retransmission of error (or lost) packets and also provides flow control to allow for speed matching between the end users. Voice traffic does not have any retransmission for recovery from errors, but it does need a method of playout that allows for the possibility of irregular network delays and for lost packets, etc.

### 11.2.6 Interfaces

#### 11.2.6.1 Physical Interfaces

The Paris system will operate over almost any clear channel physical interface of appropriate speed. Typical connection could be through G.703 electrical interface to an optical transmitter at (say) 150 Mbps. Also possible would be connection to Sonet/SDH at a number of different rates such as STS-3c.

#### 11.2.6.2 User Data Interfaces

End-user equipment is connected to the network via an adaptation (or interfacing function). As with ATM (see 9.3, "The ATM Adaptation Layer (AAL)" on page 9-28), an adaptation layer is needed to interface and adapt the network to different kinds of user traffic. A number of different interfacing layers (or modes of operation of a common protocol) would be needed depending on the type of traffic to be handled.

Paris requires much less adaptation function than does ATM. This is because:

- Paris sends full frames (there is no need to break logical user blocks of data up into small units for transmission).
- Paris performs error detection on the data part of the frame as well as the routing header. There is no need for any additional function to provide error detection on the data.

In addition to the adaptation function there is also an interfacing function needed which converts the network interface protocol to the internal network protocol. This is not quite the same thing as adaptation.

For example, a frame relay service could be built using a Paris backbone network very easily. To use a Paris network for TCP/IP traffic requires that IP routers be built at the Paris network entry points. These routers would have to accommodate the difference between the connection-oriented nature of the Paris network and the connectionless nature of IP (this adaptation is a standard function of IP).

Handling SNA is a different matter and is discussed in 6.9, "SNA in a High-Speed Network" on page 6-36.

#### 11.2.6.3 Transporting Voice

The principles of handling voice in a high-speed packet network are discussed in 6.2, "Transporting Voice in a Packet Network" on page 6-11. These principles hold for voice transport in a Paris network. The major difference is that a packet size larger than 48 bytes may be used. This means that echo cancellation is necessary.

This is discussed fully in *A Blind Voice Packet Synchronization Strategy* (see bibliography).

### 11.2.7 Performance Characteristics

**ANR routing is easily handled in hardware.**

- All the information needed to route the data to the next link is available within the ANR field of the packet header. Data switching can be done in hardware without reference to connection tables or network topology information.
- There is no requirement for the NCU processor to keep updating tables in the switching subsystem when new connections are created or terminated.

**Switches frames not cells.**

Switching full data link frames rather than small cells has many advantages:

- Proportionally lower overheads due to packet headers.
- Lower overheads in the switching process because the switches tend to require a given amount of processing per packet regardless of packet length. This is discussed in 6.5, "Transporting Data in Packets or Cells" on page 6-19.
- Lower overheads in the endpoint processors due to segmentation and reassembly. Some segmentation is still required but that can be done relatively easily in software.
- Lower overhead in the EPPs due to simultaneous reassembly of packets from cells. If cells belonging to multiple packets were able to arrive intermixed with one another, the EPP would need to have many reassembly tasks and buffers to rebuild the packets.

**Provides selective copy and multicast.**

These abilities make the management and control functions within the network significantly more efficient than more conventional methods.

**Low overhead due to routing headers.**

Assuming a 2-byte SID in a practical network the maximum likely ANR field is 14 bytes (7 hops). (It has been shown that 5 hops is the practical maximum in most public and private large networks.) As the packet is routed through the network the size reduces as SIDs are removed. This is very small compared with existing systems - SNA subarea networks carry a 26-byte routing header (called a "FID_4 TH").

Since packets in the Paris system are full data link frames (rather than short cells), the proportion of overhead caused by the routing system is very low.

**Uses clear channel links.**

The system requires internode links that operate on "clear channels". That is, it does not need complex link connections with preformatted frames (such as G.704).

**Designed as an integrated system.**

The whole Paris system was designed to work as a whole with network control and management, user interfaces, and end-to-end protocols included as parts of an integrated whole.

A part of the aim of the research project was to demonstrate the effectiveness of designing the system as a whole rather than as a number of disjoint functions. This has been very successfully demonstrated.

The disadvantages are minimal.

**Variable length frames introduce variability into transit delays.**

This is certainly true if the link speed is low relative to the maximum packet length. On the very high-speed links to be used by Paris, this is not a concern. See Appendix C.1.4, "Practical Systems" on page C-6.

**Longer voice packets introduce the need for echo control.**

Paris uses 128-byte voice packets which require longer to assemble than would 48-byte ATM voice cells. This introduces a "propagation delay" which can increase the effect of echoes. There is no echo in a digital link. But there are echoes from analog (two-wire) tail circuits and from both analog and digital handsets. See the discussion in 6.2.2.2, "The Effect of End-to-End Network Delay on Voice Traffic" on page 6-13.

# Chapter 12. plaNET/Orbit - A Gigabit Prototype Network

An overview of the plaNET network structure is shown in Figure 12-1.

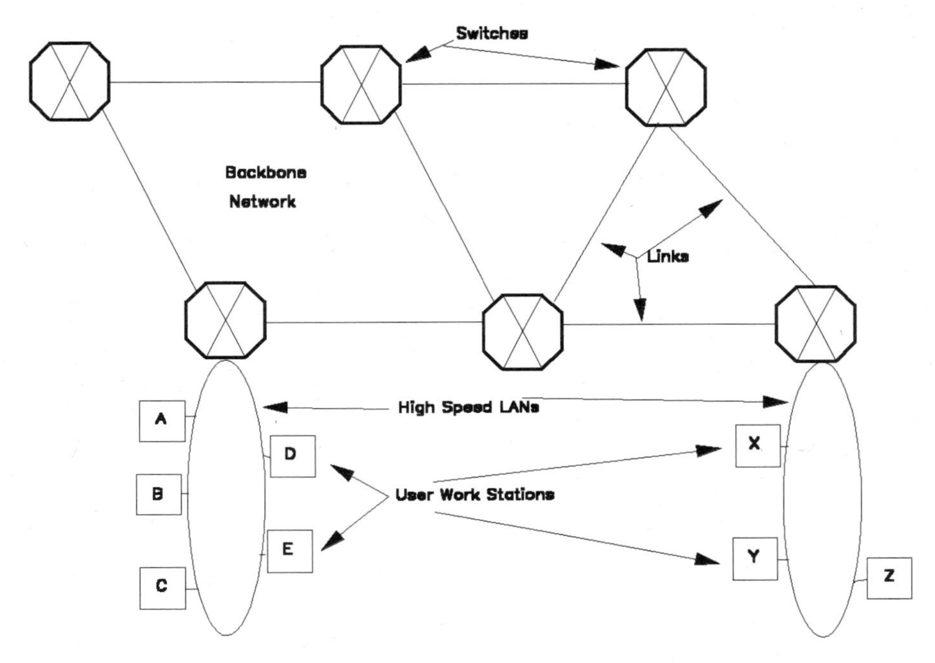


***Figure 12-1.*** *plaNET/Orbit Network Structure*

Packetized Lightweight Architecture Network (plaNET) is a networking system (architecture and devices) developed by IBM Research to investigate issues in very high-speed networking.[1] The system consists of three components:

- The network architecture itself
- Network node hardware (called a plaNET node)
- A LAN adapter and software

The plaNET system is very well described in several papers written by IBM Research, which are listed in the bibliography. Thus, it is *not* described in detail here. The fol-

1 As with other IBM Research projects, plaNET is a research prototype system, *not* a product. IBM can make no comment about possible use of plaNET technology in future IBM products.

lowing discussion uses plaNET to illustrate some of the issues surrounding the architecture of high-speed networks, and so only a few of the unique parts of plaNET are described.

### 12.1.1 Overview

The important characteristics of the system are as follows:

1. plaNET nodes attach to very high-speed (up to 1 Gbps) links.
2. Data is transported through the network either as ATM cells or as variable-length "frames". Frames and cells are intermixed on links and within switching nodes.
3. Three modes for routing data are supported:
   a. Label swapping (connection-oriented) mode - required for ATM.
   b. Automatic Network Routing (a form of source routing). This can be used for either connection-oriented or connectionless traffic.
   c. Tree routing mode.
4. A LAN system (called Orbit) is a part of plaNET. End users are always connected to the Orbit LAN and never directly to the plaNET switch.

   An end user might be a program within the Orbit LAN station (IBM RISC System/6000), in which case it is called a "native" attachment. Alternatively end users may be connected through a gateway (bridge or router function) within the Orbit LAN station.
5. The Orbit LAN is integrated with the wide area network system in a seamless way. There is no distinction between a node on the LAN and a wide area switching node. Exactly the same protocols and routing system are used for both. Thus there is no need for routers or bridges to interconnect the WAN with the LAN. This delivers a seamless, integrated connection from one end user to another regardless of where they are.

### 12.1.2 Origin

The plaNET system is an integration of concepts and techniques taken from earlier IBM Research work on the Paris system (see 11.2, "Packetized Automatic Routing Integrated System (Paris)" on page 11-16) and from ATM technology (see 9.1, "Asynchronous Transfer Mode (ATM)" on page 9-3). The Orbit LAN is a buffer insertion ring and uses the protocols described under the heading "MetaRing" (although there is a crucial difference in the structure of the LAN address). See 15.1, "MetaRing" on page 15-1.

plaNET equipment is being used in a number of high-speed network "trials" in different parts of the world.

## 12.1.3 The Concept

plaNET is conceived of as a seamless, integrated networking system which provides transparent connectivity from user desktop to user desktop across both local and wide area high-speed connections.

This is quite a different thing from the conception of a network common within the telecommunications industry. In the PTT "world" the network is seen as something that extends from one "service interface" to another service interface usually across a wide area.[2] The service interface is rigorously defined and is designed to *isolate* the end user from the network. (Because the network is provided by the PTT, and there are many end users, an end user must never be able to interfere with or even to know about the internals of the PTT network.) X.25 and ATM (B_ISDN) are just such isolating interfaces. This issue is discussed further in Chapter 7, "Private Networks in the High-Speed Environment" on page 7-1.

In the public network environment there is no realistic alternative to this conception. However, when we are building a private network there is the opportunity to do much better.

plaNET is designed to be "seamless", and "transparent" and to efficiently handle all types of network traffic.

**Variable-Length Frames and Cells Together**

plaNET transports both ATM cells and variable-length frames through the network intermixed. A cell is simply a short frame. This applies both to wide area point-to-point links and to LAN connections.

As discussed previously (see 6.5, "Transporting Data in Packets or Cells" on page 6-19), there are generally two reasons for using a cell-based network structure:

1. The switching nodes are believed to be less complex and therefore faster and lower in cost.
2. Queuing delays within the network are more uniform if fixed-length cells are used.

The construction of plaNET has proven that while the switching nodes are indeed more complex, there is very little increase in cost (because all additional functions fit on unused areas of chips that would be needed anyway). In addi-

2 That is, the network as conceived by PTTs covers only layers 1 to 3 of the ISO model. In contrast plaNET (and SNA) extends from user interface (layer 6/7) to user interface. Thus plaNET includes layers 4 to 6 which are not considered in the traditional PTT view.

tion, it is believed that switch technology is not a restriction on the system - thus there is less need to optimize. Secondly, the time distribution of queuing delays is important but at the very high speeds involved the absolute length of probable delays is very small and the variation is quite low in absolute terms. (At a speed of 1 Gbps, a 4 KB block takes only 32 μsec to transmit. The transmit times are overshadowed by the propagation delays.)

The advantages in a less complex (even null) adaptation function more than compensate for the added complexity in the switches. Since the adaptation function will normally be located within attaching devices, in a practical network of perhaps 20 switching nodes there may well be 2,000 attached devices. The cost of the adaptation function (processing speed, special chips) is multiplied by the number of devices which implement it (in this case 2,000). The cost of extra complexity in the switch is multiplied only by the number of switches (here 20). This design tradeoff comes as a result of the user-to-user view of the network itself. If you were designing only the transport network part it would be logical to minimize the cost in the switching nodes without regard to any added cost in the attachments.

### Transparency

In this context transparency is conceived of as minimizing the transformations done to the data within the network (dissection into cells, reassembly later). This is intended to maximize throughput.

### Seamlessness

By minimizing the need for an adaptation function there is less of a barrier between user applications and the network itself. That is, end user applications[3] are the best arbiters of how error recovery should be done, what should be re-transmitted, etc.

### Network Directory (Topology Database)

Every plaNET node (including Orbit stations) is known by its 48-bit network name. When a node is brought on line, its location and link attachments are automatically added to all the directories in the network. Thus when a node needs to find the location of another node there is no need to broadcast (as LAN stations do, for example). Up-to-date information is available in the directory.

It is not necessary for every Orbit station to have a full network directory and topology. Lower capability stations can access a nearby directory in another node. (This is just like the structure of APPN, where network nodes contain a

---

[3] This does not mean the user application program but rather the supporting system software.

full topology database and network directory, but end nodes, while having full function, have only local directory and topology information.)

This makes a very significant improvement in network efficiency and speed of connection setup because of the reduced number of broadcasts and the ability to get accurate topology information very quickly.

## 12.1.4 Data Routing

### Automatic Network (Source) Routing

Using ANR the sender of a data block prepends the block with the sequence of nodes and links to be traversed along the path to its destination. In order to do this the sender must have access to a database carrying an up-to-date network topology (including such things as current link loads and priorities). As the block travels through the network, each node along the path uses the first entry in the list of addresses to direct the data to its next hop and then removes the entry from the list. When the list is exhausted, you have reached the destination. This system is described in 11.2.2, "Automatic Network Routing (ANR)" on page 11-18.

Using ANR, intermediate nodes only have a minimal amount of work to do to determine where the data is to be routed. This operation is easy to perform in hardware. ANR can be used to support "connection-oriented" traffic. (The end users have a connection between them, even though the switching nodes along the path are unaware of it.[4])

ANR can also be used for sending connectionless traffic. An end user only has to ask its supporting directory for a path to the destination, prepend this to the data to be sent, then send the data. There is no network "call setup" procedure involved.

ANR has the additional capability of allowing multicasting along a route. Thus it is possible to send a frame to another user and have a copy of that frame sent to the control processor of every node along the path. (This capability is used extensively by the control functions for setting up new connections.)

### Label Swapping

The label swapping technique was discussed in 6.7.4, "Logical ID Swapping" on page 6-31. It has significant advantage in that the overhead of destination addressing carried in the header is minimized. However, a setup procedure is needed to build table entries in all the switching nodes along the path between

---

4 This is not exactly true, the capacity allocation function of nodes along the path do know about connections (in order to allocate capacity). However, there is no routing table and the switching function within each node is not aware of the connection.

users, and there is complexity added to the switch in requiring a very fast memory lookup for every data block. (This memory lookup needs to be extremely fast, and the memory must allow access from the control processor for continual updating simultaneously with access from the data switching function.)

Label swapping in plaNET is available for ATM cells or for frames. When carrying ATM cells, the ATM header size (5 bytes) is retained but the bit format is changed (bits are organized differently). This operation is performed (in hardware) at every interface between plaNET and ATM devices.

**Tree Routing**

The "tree routing" function is new in plaNET. It was not present in Paris and it does not exist in ATM. A tree is simply a structured path which is identified by a number. There may be many different trees in a system.

A tree has branches and when data arrives at a branch a copy is sent in both directions. Thus, a frame sent on a tree will arrive at all the nodes in the tree. (It is even possible to send to a tree from a node not in the tree - you use ANR to get the frame to any node having that tree defined and then the next hop is simply the tree number.)

This function is very useful when broadcasting to a defined subset of network users (like a closed user group). It would also be used in a MAN environment where end users were part of a virtual LAN. The virtual LAN would be defined as a tree and broadcasts from the LAN would be routed along it.

### 12.1.5 WAN/LAN Integration

One of the most significant features of plaNET/Orbit is its integration of LAN and WAN elements. There is no real distinction between plaNET nodes connected to the LAN (via Orbit adapters) or within the switching network itself. Thus routing of data is seamless from one end user to the other. There is no concept of router or bridge required.

Integration of WAN and LAN environments has been achieved by using the same addressing techniques (ANR, label swap, tree) with identical header formats for both environments. When data is received on a point-to-point link (such as defined in ATM) the receiver knows which node sent it. It came from the node at the other end of the link (there is only one). On a LAN there are many peer devices connected to a common medium. When a frame is sent on a LAN, usually there are the 48-bit destination and origin addresses in the header for the LAN adapters to use to decide which adapter should receive it. Using the same addressing structure as the WAN means that the usual LAN addresses are not there!

*The key to system operation is that Orbit adapters do NOT recognize their 48-bit address; they use a short form local address.* When the LAN is initialized, each Orbit station is dynamically allocated a number (6 bits). In either the label swap or ANR routing environments, Orbit stations recognize this address - not their globally known 48-bit address. Within plaNET directories, this local address of the node is stored with the global 48-bit address so that routes can be constructed.

**ANR Frames**

An ANR routing vector addressing a LAN has two entries. When an ANR frame preceded by the routing vector enters a plaNET node, the next hop address points to the LAN adapter not to the station. When the frame reaches the Orbit LAN adapter the next hop address is the address of the destination station.

Most ANR frames contain a header of some kind after the ANR fields and this header further identifies the origin and the destination.

The receiving node removes the frame from the LAN.

**Label Swap Frames**

In principle label swapping mode works much the same as ANR. There is a dynamically assigned Orbit adapter address which it recognizes as its own. In order to avoid adding extra bytes to the ATM 5-byte header, this label takes the place of some of the logical channel and path identifier bits. In fact, on the LAN you need two addresses, because there may be station-to-station traffic in addition to the plaNET node-to-station traffic and the data part of the cell cannot carry a header (it's too small). Origin and destination along with some bits for LCI/LPIs. Assuming a 6-bit node addresses, it is seen that 12 bits are available for LCI and LPI.

The receiving node removes the frame from the LAN.

**Tree Addressing**

Tree addressing is different. A station needs to recognize the tree number and receive the frame if it is a member of the particular tree. But the station must not remove the frame from the ring because other stations on this LAN may also be members of the same tree and need to receive the frame.

Trees are a form of broadcast operation. you can broadcast to all nodes by having a tree of which all nodes are members.

Tree-routed frames are removed after they have been seen by all nodes on the LAN by the "elected leader" Orbit adapter.

### 12.1.6 End-to-End Protocol

The system uses a special highly efficient end-to-end protocol called RTP (Rapid Transport Protocol). This follows the general principles outlined in 6.8, "End-to-End Network

Protocols" on page 6-35. In addition it has been designed for very efficient implementation in software.

### 12.1.7 System Components

The structure of the plaNET/Orbit system is shown in Figure 12-2.

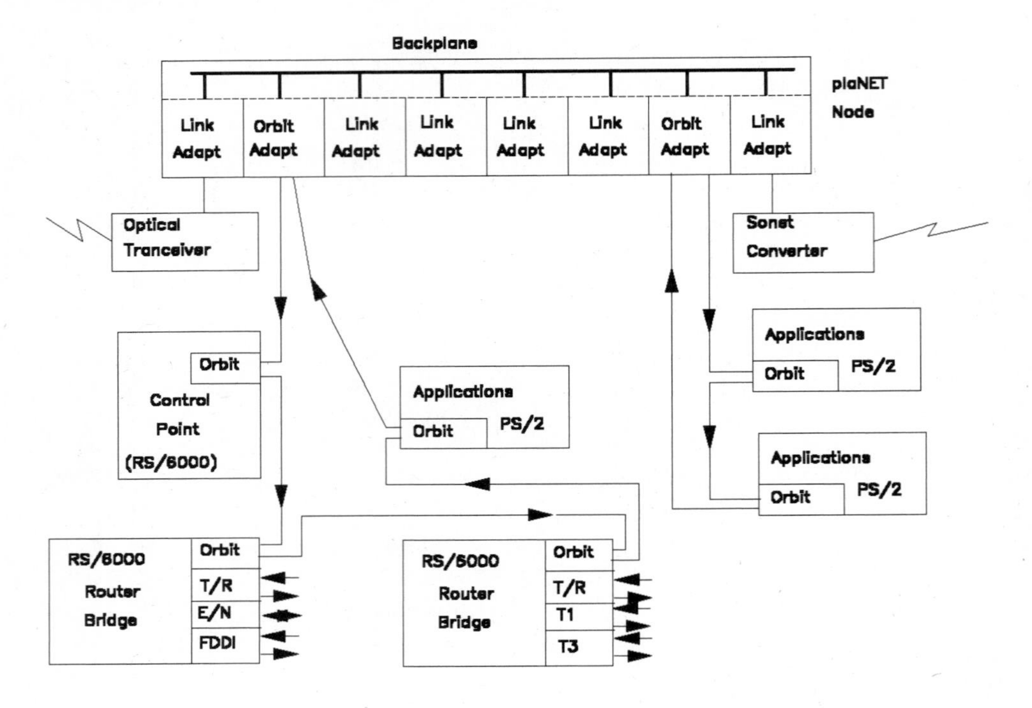


*Figure 12-2. Orbit and plaNET System Structure*

#### Switching Nodes

The switching nodes consist of a backplane and up to eight link or orbit adapters. Each link adapter may operate at any speed up to 1.1 Gbps but in practice links run at around 800 Mbps.

The backplane has an aggregate throughput limit of about 6.4 Gbps and therefore there is a very low probability of congestion. (Congestion is possible if a large number of broadcast requests are received at one time, but the probability is very low.)

Link adapters are electronic with coaxial cable interfaces. These are connected to wide area "dark" fiber or to Sonet (SDH) links by the use of external converters.

### Orbit Adapters

Orbit LANs can be dual ring, single ring, or bus in configuration. Each Orbit LAN operates at a speed of just above 1 Gbps. A plaNET node may connect up to eight Orbit LANs (but in that case could not connect to a link because of the limit of eight adapters). A special Orbit adapter was built for the IBM Micro Channel (the I/O bus in the IBM RISC System/6000, the IBM PS/2 and some models of the IBM 4300 series). The same Orbit adapter can be used in both RS/6000s and in PS/2s although different software is, of course, required.

All end users in the system are connected through Orbit LANs; thus, no link-connected end users are possible.

### RS/6000 Control Point and Management Processor

In order for a plaNET node to operate it must be supported by a control point processor. This is an application within any connected RS/6000. Since the plaNET switch is not programmable, all of the "internal control" functions required to support the node are performed here. Setting up the table entries which represent connections (for label swap routing) and allocating for requested connections (ANR mode) are among the most critical.

This processor holds a topology database which reflects the topology and status of all resources (nodes, links, LANs) within the network. It also contains up-to-date loading information for links, etc. It is connected to all other control point processors through a spanning tree structure over which it exchanges updated topology information with other nodes.

### Connecting to Other Networks

Connection to other types of networks (slower links, different LANs) is accomplished by routing (and/or bridging within an RS/6000). This is illustrated at the bottom of the diagram.

It is important to note that this function could reside within the control point processor as well as user applications for that matter.

Location of functions is a user design decision.

### Applications

Native applications reside within IBM PS/2s or RS/6000s. Other applications can be accessed through connections to other types of networks.

# Chapter 13. Shared Media Systems (LANs and MANs)

Local area networks (LANs) and metropolitan area networks (MANs) consist of a common cable to which many stations (devices) are connected. Connection is made in such a way that when any device sends, then all devices on the common medium are able to receive the transmission. This means that any device may send to any other device (or group of devices) on the cable.

This gives the very obvious benefit that each device only needs one connection to the cable in order to communicate with any other device on the cable.

> An alternative would be to have a pair of wires from each device to each other device (meaning n × (n-1)/2 connections between n devices would be needed - for 10 devices this would mean 45 separate connections).

Because the LAN is a shared medium, if two devices try to send at the same time, then (unless something is done to prevent it) they will interfere with each other and meaningful communication will be impossible. What is needed is some mechanism to either prevent devices from attempting to send at the same time, or to organize transmission in such a way that mutual interference does not result in an inability to operate.

## 13.1 Basic Principles

There are three generic ways in which the medium (cable) may be shared and this is often used to classify LANs.

**Broadband LANs**

In a broadband LAN, frequency division multiplexing is used to divide the cable into many separate channels. This principle is described further in Appendix A.1.1, "Frequency Division Multiplexing" on page A-1.

The most common example of a broadband LAN technique is in cable television, where many TV signals are multiplexed onto the same coaxial cable via frequency division multiplexing.

**Time Division Multiplexing LANs**

The method of operation of a TDM LAN is exactly the same as the method used in modern digital PBXs, except that the ring connecting the "users" is no longer enclosed within a single box but is carried around an area over some medium such as twisted pair or coaxial cable.

When one device needs to send to another, a slot is allocated (there are ways of doing this without a ring controller) and this time division slot is used to establish a slower-speed channel between the devices. This is exactly as it is done within the PBX but potentially, at least, without the controlling computer.

A very early system of this kind is the very slow speed IBM 3600/4700 B_LOOP protocol.

Another system on the market uses the standard G704 slot structure at 2 Mbps over a twisted pair. This enables the use of mass-produced, easily available chips. This method is low in cost, allows for the easy use of voice and data on the same medium, and can be made reasonably flexible. However, its use is limited to a maximum of 15 simultaneous communications over the shared ring.

Many of the new high-speed LAN protocols (FDDI_II, DQDB, etc.) which are discussed in this book have provisions to handle TDM style traffic.

**Baseband LANs**

In a baseband LAN the cable is treated as a single high-speed channel. If Box A wants to send something to Box B on the LAN, in principle all it has to do is put a destination header on the block and send it. But what if another device is already sending? This is the major problem for the LAN. It leads to several techniques (protocols) for control of access to the transmission medium.

Devices on a baseband LAN can be almost anything digital, including digitized voice, data and video, etc.

Some LANs use a baseband technique within one or a small number of frequencies on a broadband LAN (a form of sub-multiplexing discussed in Appendix A.1.4, "Sub-Multiplexing" on page A-4).

## 13.1.1 Topologies

There is an almost infinite variety of ways to connect LAN cable. The two most common types of LAN connection are illustrated in Figure 13-1 on page 13-3.

The LAN protocol used, the configuration of the cable, and the type of cable are *always* intimately related. Cables vary from two-wire twisted pair telephone cable to optical fiber and speeds vary from 1 Mbps to many gigabits per second.

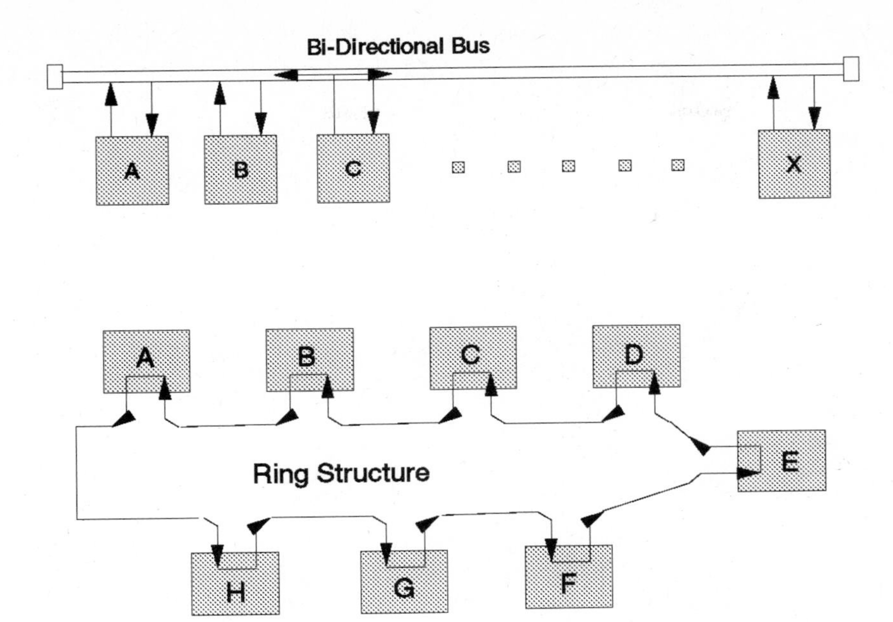


*Figure 13-1. Popular LAN Topologies*

The principle LAN configurations are:

**Rings**

A ring style LAN is one where data travels in one direction only and having passed through (or by) every node on the LAN returns to its point of origin.

Ring LANs may be wired in many ways. The ring may fan out from a hub such that, while the data path is a ring, the wiring may be a star. This is very common as it helps in fault bypass.

**Dual Rings**

Some LANs use two rings operating in opposite directions.

**Buses**

The basic idea of a bus is that data placed on it travels in both directions from its point of origin to every connected device.

**Directional Buses**

In a true bus environment, it is hard to synchronize multiple stations with one another. Many times buses are used which are unidirectional and have a head end which generates synchronization and perhaps framing. To get full data transfer capability unidirectional buses are usually used in pairs (one for each direction).

It is important to note that on a LAN, if communication is to be meaningful, all stations must use the same signaling techniques and access rules (protocols).

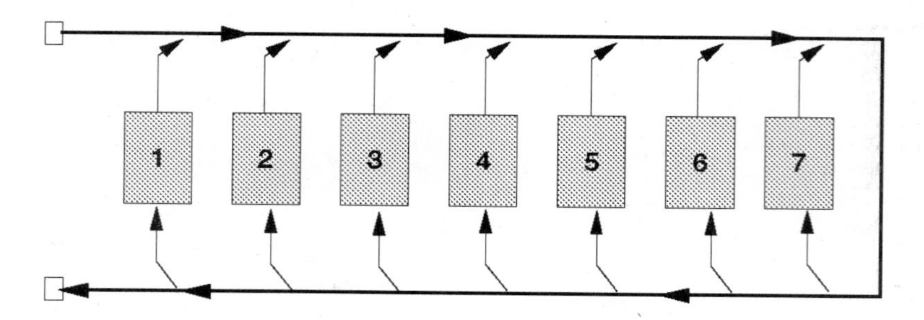


***Figure 13-2.*** *Folded Bus LAN Topology*

## 13.1.2 Access Control

The biggest problem in a LAN is deciding which device (end user) can send next. Since there are many devices connected to a single communications channel, if more than one device attempts to send, then there will be a collision and neither transmission will be successful.[1]

Figure 13-3 on page 13-5 shows a LAN with six devices (labelled A to F) attached. The arrow above each device represents the flow of data being generated by the device for transmission to some other device on the LAN. An "o" represents a block of data generated, and the numbers on the right of the diagram represent the passage of time. Thus:

1. At time 1 devices A and E generate some data to send on the LAN.
2. At time 2, device D generates a block of data to send.
3. At time 3, devices B and C generate data.

[1] There is an exception in the case of analog radio-based LANs, where the use of Frequency Modulation (FM) transmission ensures that the strongest signal is received correctly.

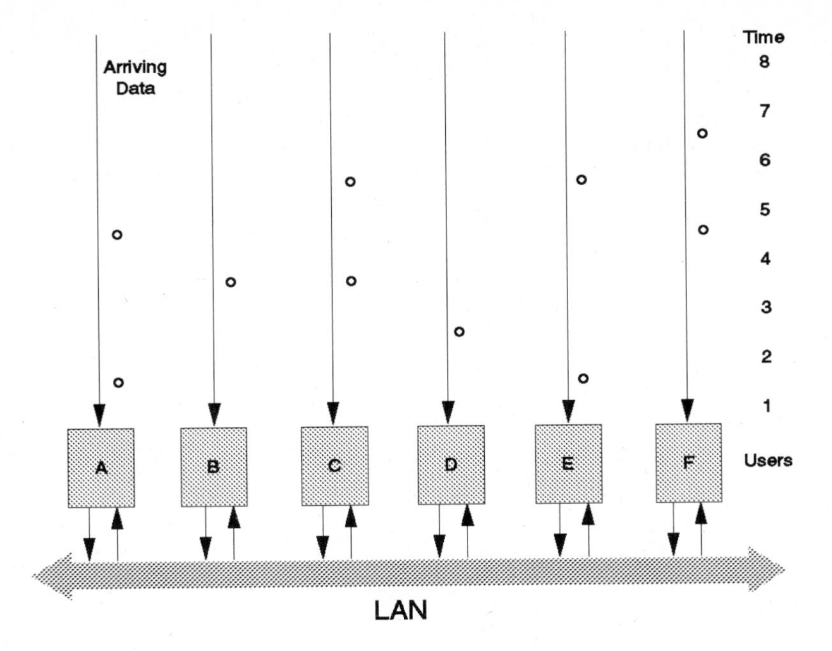


***Figure 13-3.*** *Transactions Arriving at a Hypothetical LAN.* Arrivals are separated in time and space. The problem is how to decide which device can send next.

If the system is to be satisfactory, then each user must get a "fair share" of the LAN. This is usually taken to mean that:

- Data should be sent on the LAN in the order that it "arrives" (is generated).
- No device should be able to monopolize the LAN. Every device should get equal service.
- Priority may be given to some types of traffic or user in which case higher priority traffic should receive access to the LAN before lower priority traffic.
- Within each priority level data should be sent in the order that it was generated and every device should get equal service.

Even though they are distributed over many locations separated perhaps by great distances, transactions arriving at the LAN form a *single* logical queue. The objective is to give access to the LAN to transactions in the queue in FIFO (First In First Out) order.

If each device was able to know the state of the whole queue and schedule its transmissions accordingly then the system could achieve its objective.

Unfortunately devices are separated from one another perhaps by many kilometers. Because of the geographic separation, it takes time for information to travel from one device to another. The only communication medium available to them is the LAN itself!

This, then, is the problem for any LAN system. **A LAN system aims to provide "fair" access for all attached devices but it is not possible for each device to know about the true state of the notional "global queue".**

**Fairness**

A real communication system has other things to worry about than fairness. Users are concerned with what functions a system delivers and, importantly, at what cost. The challenge in design of a LAN protocol is to deliver the optimal cost performance. Fairness and efficiency are important but the resulting system is the objective.

There are many ways of approaching the ideal of "fairness".

**SA** Send Anyway

When a device has something to send it just sends anyway without regard for any other device that may be sending.

This has never been seriously used for a cable LAN but was used in the "Aloha" system where multiple devices used a single radio channel to communicate one character at a time. Using Frequency Modulation (FM), the strongest signal will be correctly received and the weaker signal(s) will be lost.

This technique works but at very low utilizations. It requires a higher layer protocol capable of retrying if data is lost.

**Contention with Carrier Sense** (Carrier Sense Multiple Access (CSMA) with or without Collision Detection (CD))

Using this technique, before a device can send on the LAN it must "listen" to see if another device is sending. If another device is already sending, then the device must wait until the LAN becomes free. Even so, if two devices start sending at the same time there will be a collision and neither transmission will be received correctly. In CSMA/CD, devices listen to their own signal to detect collisions. When a collision occurs the devices must wait for different lengths of time before attempting to retry. This collision detection feature is present in some techniques and not in others. Either way, each user of the LAN must operate an "end-to-end" protocol for error recovery and data integrity.

In all CSMA type LANs there is a gap in time between when one device starts to send and before another potential sender can detect the condition. The longer this gap is, the higher the chance that another sender will try to send and, therefore, the higher the possibility of collision. In practice, one of the major determinants of the length of the gap is the physical length of the LAN. Thus the practical efficiency of this kind of LAN is limited greatly by the physical length of the LAN. The utilization of the carrier medium (usually a bus) is limited more by collision probabilities than by data block sizes. In some situations, 20% is considered quite good.

Performance:

- As the data transfer speed of the LAN increases, throughput does not increase at the same rate. Faster link speeds do nothing to affect the propagation delays. Thus the length of the "gaps" during which collisions can occur becomes the dominant characteristic.
- There is no way of allocating priorities.
- Fairness of access to the LAN is questionable.
- Low access delay. CSMA techniques do have the advantage that if nothing is currently happening on the LAN, a device may send immediately and doesn't have to wait (as it does in some other techniques). A disadvantage is that as LAN utilization increases, access delay becomes highly erratic and (potentially at least) unbounded.

The big advantage of CSMA techniques is one of cost:

- The hardware adapters are very simple and low in cost.
- The cables typically used are low-cost telephone twisted pair or CATV style coaxial cable.
- They usually run over bus-type networks, which use less cable than ring or star topologies.

**Token Passing** (Token-Ring, Token Bus, FDDI)

A "token" (unique header containing control information) is sent from user to user around a "ring". Only the device with the token is allowed to send at a particular instant in time. "Block" multiplexing is used and blocks are limited in length by a time delay (maximum sending time) which is user specified.

In detail, the token passing protocols differ considerably, but the performance characteristics are as follows:

- The LAN can be utilized efficiently up to quite high capacities. Utilization of 70% or even more can be achieved.
- Access is fair in the sense that all devices on the ring get an equal opportunity to use the LAN.
- It is possible to have a priority scheme such that, for example, real-time traffic can be given priority over more normal data traffic. Even packetized voice may be handled in a limited way. The problems of voice and data

mixture do not go away, but there is considerable improvement over CSMA/CD.

- Ring techniques also suit fiber optical cables since it is difficult (possible but difficult) to treat optical fiber as a bus and attach many users to the common medium. Fiber technology is, in 1995, primarily a point-to-point unidirectional technology.

- Geographic length is less of a problem and it is now possible to have practical rings thousands of miles in length. There are practical limits on the length and the number of devices imposed by imperfections in synchronization ("phase jitter", etc.) on the physical medium. On an electrical token-ring, LAN operation is considered problematic if the number of stations or repeaters goes above 250 or so.

Two problems exist with the token passing approach:

1. There is an access delay due to "ring latency" between when a device has data to send and when it may start sending *even if there is no traffic*. This is because the device must wait for a token to arrive before it is allowed to send.

2. As the data transfer speed increases so does the length of the LAN (measured in bits). That is to say, the higher the speed of the LAN, the more bits can fit on it at one time. This means that on a reasonably sized LAN there would be room for more than one frame to be present simultaneously, but that is not allowed because there is only a single token.

   The problem here is not that efficiency gets less, but that there is an opportunity to become more efficient than the protocol can take advantage of.

The biggest problem with this method has been its cost. Since the token controls everything, there must be something to control the token and, for example, to handle the condition of errors occurring which put a permanently busy token onto the ring. Since it is considered vital that there be no "ring control unit" (which is obviously capable of failure and, therefore, has to be backed up, etc.) then each device attachment must be capable of ring control. There must be a mechanism to control which device is the ring controller when the ring is started and another to ensure takeover by one and only one other device if the current controller fails. All this takes logic and the cost has been significantly higher than for the CSMA technique. Recent improvements in chip technologies have minimized this cost differential however.

**Insertion Rings** (MetaRing)

The principle of MetaRing[2] is to allow a device to send anytime provided that no data is arriving on the LAN when it starts sending. Thus, because it takes time for data to travel from one node to another, *multiple nodes can transmit at the same time.* This does not cause collisions because there is a buffering scheme that intervenes and prevents collisions from causing loss of data.

MetaRing uses two counter-rotating rings so that a control message may travel in the opposite direction to the data. This control message visits each device and essentially allocates LAN capacity (permission to send) among all the devices on the LAN.

This scheme has the following characteristics:

- As the link speed is increased and ring latency (in terms of the number of bits held on the ring at any one time) increases, the ring is able to handle more and more traffic.
- At relatively low speeds (say, 16 Mbps) the protocol could produce a ring latency that is too high for some applications, but at speeds of 100 Mbps and above this is much less of a problem.
- A fair access scheme is implemented using the control signal.
- There is very little access delay at low ring utilization.
- The technique offers significantly higher throughput than FDDI for roughly the same cost.

**Distributed Queueing** (DQDB)

The distributed queueing protocol of DQDB[3] aims to provide fairness of access by having a device keep track (as far as it can) of the state of the notional global queue and its position in that queue.

The protocol uses two slotted buses to provide communication in both directions. The protocol is described in 13.9, "DQDB/SMDS - Distributed Queue Dual Bus" on page 13-55.

The characteristics of this protocol are:

- The buses are managed in slots so that capacity may be allocated for constant rate traffic ("isochronous"- voice).

---

2 There are many kinds of insertion ring. One of the earliest was implemented on the IBM Series/1 computer in 1981. MetaRing is a highly sophisticated version of an old principle.

3 Distributed Queue Dual Bus

- Over relatively short distances the protocol provides excellent fairness of access to the buses. This breaks down a bit over longer distances at heavy loadings, but can still be very effective.
- A single node can use the entire network capacity effectively.
- Data is sent in cells of 48 data bytes.
- There is no slot reuse, so over long distances or at very high speed the maximum capacity is still only the speed of the bus.
- Both buses are used for data transport.
- There is very little access delay at low and medium LAN utilizations because data may be sent in the first free slot when there is nothing already queued downstream.

This technique is used in metropolitan area network equipment currently being installed by many PTTs. It is also the basis of the access protocol called "SMDS".

**Using a Ringmaster** (CRMA)

The CRMA protocol uses a folded bus (similar to a ring) topology, but has a ring controller node. The ring controller sends out a (preemptive) control message at short intervals. This message asks each node how much data has arrived on its queue since the last time it saw the message (cycle). Thus what it is really doing is taking a picture of the global queue at defined intervals.

This information enables the system to grant access to the LAN much more fairly than other protocols. In Figure 13-3 on page 13-5 it can be seen that data may arrive at each node in a somewhat random fashion. Protocols that grant equal access for each node (such as token passing protocols) will give access to a block of data that just arrived at a hitherto idle node *ahead* of data that may have been waiting in a queue at a busier node for some time. Thus, for example, in token-ring protocol if six blocks arrive in quick succession at node A, and then a single block arrives at node B, the block at node B will get access to the LAN before some of the blocks queued at node A.

CRMA aims to allow access to the LAN for all traffic globally in FIFO order!

The characteristics of CRMA are:

- It gives the best fairness characteristic of any of the protocols being discussed.
- It will operate at almost any speed (the higher the better).
- It does not allow spatial reuse. This means that when data is received by a node, the cell that the data has been received from (and therefore is now

logically empty) cannot be used by other stations to carry data. This is a waste of potential capacity.

- It avoids the problem of potentially high access delay due to ring latency, by suspending the cyclic protocol at very low loads and allowing a device to send immediately when data becomes available.

## 13.2 100 Megabit "Ethernet"/IEEE 802.3

When the first edition of this book was produced (in late 1991), CSMA/CD networks were deliberately left out. This was for two reasons:

1. There is an inherent performance problem in increasing the transmission speed. For reasons discussed later, increasing the transmission speed doesn't bring very much increase in throughput in CSMA/CD networks.
2. At the time, there was no serious proposal before any standards body for the introduction of such a protocol.

Since then, a number of proposals have been discussed before the IEEE 802.3 committee for the standardization of exactly this.

### 13.2.1 CSMA/CD Principle

The principles of CSMA/CD LANs are well understood and described in many textbooks. However, a short overview is presented here as background to the discussion of performance.

**Structure**

In IEEE 802.3 networks, stations are connected to a bus such as that shown in Figure 13-1 on page 13-3. Any station may transmit on the bus and the transmission propagates in both directions and is received by all other stations.

In modern 802.3 networks, the wiring is usually through a hubbing device (each station is wired point-to-point to the hub and the bus is put together by wiring within the hub).

**Frame Format**

Each transmitted frame is preceded by an 8-byte preamble used for synchronization and delimiting the start of a frame. This is followed by the header including the destination address (6 bytes), the source address (6 bytes) and a 2-byte length field. The user data may vary from 46 to 1500 bytes - if a frame is shorter than 46 data bytes it must be padded out to length. The whole is followed by a 2-byte CRC. Thus a frame on the LAN may be from 70 bytes to 1524 bytes.

**Protocol**

The CSMA/CD protocol is extremely simple.

- When a station has data to transmit, it listens to the bus to see if any other station is transmitting.
- If no other station is transmitting, the station starts its own transmission immediately.
- If another station is transmitting (the bus is busy), then the station must wait until the bus becomes free.
- As soon as the bus becomes free, the station may start its own transmission.
- Because there is a time delay for electricity to travel down the bus, two stations may start transmission simultaneously. If this happens, a collision will occur and data will be lost.
- In order to recover from the loss of data due to collisions, a transmitting station must listen to the bus while it is sending to monitor for collisions.
- On detection of a collision, the transmitting station sends a short "jamming" signal (to improve the chance that the other transmitting station will also detect the collision) and immediately stops its transmission.
- Each station (that was in the collision) now waits for a random delay before trying to transmit again.

### 13.2.2 CSMA/CD Performance

The central problem for CSMA/CD protocols is propagation delay.

- When a station starts to transmit, it takes time for the signal to propagate down the bus and for other stations to become aware that the bus is busy. During that time a second station may detect that the bus is free and start transmitting itself - causing a collision.
- When some station is transmitting (and the bus is busy), other stations may themselves acquire data for transmission. When the bus becomes free, all the stations that were waiting now try to transmit.
- However, propagation delay has the same effect at the end of a transmission as it did at the beginning. It means that stations become aware that the bus is now free at different times, depending on where they are on the bus in relation to the transmitter that has just stopped.

Propagation speed in this environment is about 5.2 μsec per kilometer (this increases slightly if there are many repeaters involved - because they buffer a few bits). If an average data block ("frame") is 1000 bits long then the average transmission time is 100 μsec (at 10 Mbps). Overall efficiency depends critically on the ratio of these two factors.

The accepted formula for the *absolute maximum* throughput on a CSMA/CD LAN is:

$$\text{Maximum Utilization} = \frac{1}{1 + 6.44\rho}$$

Where:

$$\rho = \frac{\text{end-to-end delay}}{\text{transmission time}}$$

(This formula is *not* absolutely accurate in all situations because it rests on assumptions about the statistical distribution of stations wanting to transmit. It represents the worst case.)

Applying the formula to a regular 802.3 LAN at 10 Mbps, for a block length of 1000 bits (100 μsec transmit time), and a LAN length of 2 km (a delay of 10.4 μsec), we get a maximum utilization of 58%. At 100 Mbps the maximum utilization (from the formula) is 13%. It is important to realize that these percentage figures represent a kind of 100% utilization figure. To achieve this utilization, attached stations would need to have an infinite queue length (and an infinite access delay). Thus when evaluating queueing delays we need to treat this "maximum utilization" as the media speed. (See Appendix C, "Queueing Theory" on page C-1.)

If we want a "reasonable" access delay for a station, we can look at Figure C-2 on page C-2. A queue length of two represents 70% utilization (roughly) of the LAN. This is 70% of the above maximum, *not* 70% of the medium speed.

Thus for queueing delay representing 70% utilization for the regular 802.3 case above, the maximum allowable LAN utilization is 58% x 70% or a useful maximum utilization of 40%.

Figure 13-4 on page 13-14 illustrates the above formula graphically. For a 100 Mbps speed the block size scale shown goes from 1,000 to 10,000 bits. (The maximum block length allowed on an 802.3 LAN is 1,500 bytes - 12,000 bits.) It is easy to reach conclusions from the graph:

1. At the short block lengths typical of most CSMD/CD LANs and/or at distances much greater that 200 meters, the maximum available throughput would be so low as to make the system unattractive.
2. For longer blocks (say around 1000 bytes) and for distances of less than 200 meters, then the available maximum throughput will be enough to make such a system attractive.

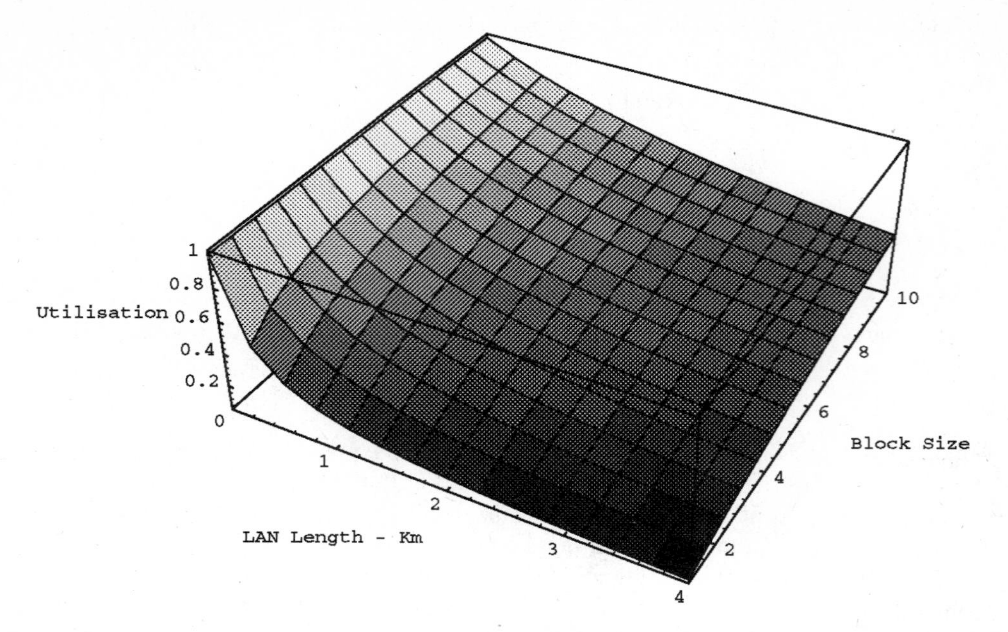


***Figure 13-4.*** *Maximum Utilization of a CSMA/CD LAN.* Block size is expressed in 10s of microseconds so at 100 Mbps the block size units represent thousands of bits.

However, this might be sufficient:

- The kinds of applications that users want 100 Mbps transfer rates for are those using image and graphics, where there is a lot of data and block sizes are long anyway.
- By using a central hub the LAN length can be limited to 200 meters and yet still cover quite a large workgroup area.

### 13.2.2.1 Why Does Ethernet Work so Well?

From the above discussion it seems clear that CSMA-CD leaves a lot to be desired as a LAN access method. Clearly, depending on traffic characteristics, it has a maximum useful throughput of between 15% and 40% of the medium speed. Further, access delay (the time it takes for a workstation to get access to the LAN) is random and unpredictable. *Yet Ethernet works. Ethernet equipment forms over 80% of all LAN equipment in existence and in the vast majority of cases it functions very well indeed. The question is why?*

Figure 13-5 on page 13-15 shows what happens as more and more load is presented to an Ethernet. By "presented" here we mean that a station on the LAN has the data and is trying to send it. Notice that when load gets too high for the LAN, instead of data continuing to be transported at some maximum figure, LAN operation collapses and nothing at all gets through! Why then does it work so well? (*and it does!*)

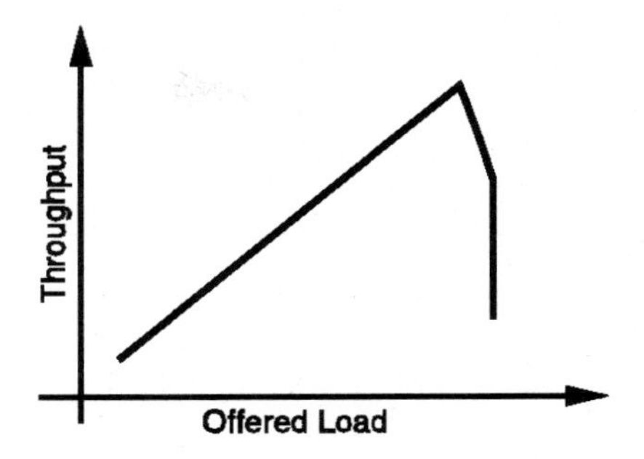


***Figure 13-5.*** *Relationship between Offered Load and Throughput on Ethernet.* As "offered load" increases so does throughput (the network handles the load) until a point is reached where too many stations are trying to send. At this point the network collapses and no traffic gets through.

There are many answers to this:

- The real problem is that the assumptions upon which Figure 13-5 is based are false. These assumptions are as follows:

  1. A large number of workstations are connected to the LAN
  2. Traffic demand from workstations is "random" in nature
  3. Traffic is any-to-any

  The fact is that very few LANs, if any, exhibit these characteristics.

- Traffic is almost never any-to-any at random. Traffic is almost always client-to-server and server-to-client. On a typical LAN with 100 workstations there will be only perhaps five servers (for example, two data servers, two print servers and a WAN gateway server).

  When a client sends a request to a data server, it must wait for the server to respond before it sends anything else. In its turn, when the server has sent one data block (out of a file of perhaps 100 data blocks) then the client must respond before the server is allowed to send the next block (to this particular client).

  This has two effects:

  1. It provides an elementary "higher-layer" flow control protocol. If the LAN becomes congested and data takes some time to get through, then the rate of requests drops correspondingly.

2. Every operation on the LAN becomes serialized to the speed of the server. If 30 clients try to get data from the server simultaneously, then the server will only be able to service these requests at the (quite limited) speed of its disk access subsystem. Indeed many servers limit the maximum number of requests that can be in progress at any one time.

   This means that the total maximum demand that can be placed on the LAN (in many situations) is the total available throughput of the servers. Even top-of-the-line (PC based) servers still cannot provide an average data rate of 10 Mbps.

- The client/server method of operation described above also has the side effect of ensuring that only a very few stations ever make simultaneous requests! Figure 13-5 on page 13-15 assumes that traffic comes from an unlimited (large) number of simultaneous requesters. With only a few simultaneous requests, you do get some throughput and the system does continue to operate without collapse.
- Perhaps one answer is that it doesn't work very well at all! In recent years, LANs have become bigger and workstations faster, so throughput has become a more and more significant problem. Large users have been continually faced with segmenting their LANs and connecting the segments together with bridges or routers to get around severe congestion problems.

Nevertheless, most practical LANs consist of perhaps five PCs sharing a printer or a dozen or so PCs sharing a file server. In these situations Ethernet is cheap, simple, and works very well indeed.

### 13.2.3 Objectives for 100 Mbps Operation

The objective of the 100 Megabit CSMA/CD development was to provide a natural growth path upward from the existing 10Base-T (10 Mbps on UTP) standard. It is felt that there is significant user demand for a simple, cost-effective upgrade path.

Several proposals were considered by the IEEE. A good solution should provide the following:

- It must be low in cost. Otherwise the user would be better off going to FDDI (on copper or fiber).
- It must preserve the existing 802.3 MAC (Medium Access Control) logic. This is needed to allow most existing software to use the system.
- It *must* use UTP (unshielded twisted pair) cabling. This is because most current 802.3 users have UTP cabling.
- It must be capable of easy migration from the existing standard. An ideal would be to have a situation like the token-ring 16/4 data rate standard.

### 13.2.4 100Base-T - 100 Megabit Ethernet Generic Baseband Operation

100Base-T is the generic name for the IEEE 802.3 standards covering operation at 100 Mbps on a baseband medium. The 100Base-T component forms the link between unique physical layers designed for different media and the existing IEEE 802.3 MAC. This satisfies all of the above objectives except for operation on two pairs of UTP-3.

This is not a big item, since all of the timings and parameters of 10 Mbps Ethernet are maintained with 100Base-T. This means that the performance characteristics (maximum utilization, etc.) are the same as for 10Base-T. The major difference is in geographic extent, where all 100Base-T devices must be located within 100 meters of a hub device. Bus connection as used in traditional Ethernet is not possible.

### 13.2.5 100Base-TX - 100 Megabit Ethernet on UTP-5

This is the same protocol as FDDI on UTP-5. The signal is coded in 4B/5B code, scrambled and coded for transmission using MLT-3 coding. The only real difference between this and FDDI is that FDDI sends and receives a continuous stream of bits/characters whereas 100Base-TX transmits/receives blocks of data. There are minor changes to the protocol to accommodate this. This is described in 13.7.2, "Twisted Pair Physical Medium Dependent (TP-PMD) - UTP-5" on page 13-46 and 2.1.15.3, "Multi-Level Transmit - 3 Levels (MLT-3)" on page 2-30.

### 13.2.6 100Base-T4 - 100 Megabit Ethernet on UTP-3 (4 Pairs)

This is what is most commonly meant when people refer to "100 Megabit Ethernet". Because of the great difficulty of getting 100 Mbps data rates over a single pair of UTP-3 this solution uses multiple pairs at a lower rate. The most common UTP-3 cable in use carries four wire pairs and all four pairs are used by 100Base-T4. The important characteristics are as follows:

- Connection of a station to the Ethernet is always point-to-point between the station and a wiring hub.
- The maximum cable distance from workstation to hub is 100 meters. (This is for signal propagation reasons as much as for timing reasons.)
- The protocol is able to operate either as 100 Mbps or standard 10Base-T Ethernet on UTP. Adapter cards are able to detect what type of hub they are connected to and to dynamically select which mode of operation to use.
- Data flow is half-duplex (just like regular Ethernet). That is, all four pairs are used by the transmitting station and FDX operation is not possible.

The protocol operates as follows:

- One pair is used for detection of the mode of operation (10/100 Mbps) and is *never* used to carry data. This pair is also used for collision detection in a similar way (by detection of DC unbalance) that is done in traditional Ethernet.
- Three pairs are used in parallel to carry the data. Each pair carries a data rate of 33.33 Mbps and thus the total data rate is 100 Mbps.
- 8B6T code (see 2.1.13, "8-Binary 6-Ternary (8B6T) Code" on page 2-24) is used for data transmission. This gives a signaling rate of 25 Mbaud and a dominant signal frequency of 12.5 MHz. This fits reasonably easily within the available bandwidth of UTP-3.
- Consecutive data bytes from the user data block are taken and sent on the three pairs in a round-robin fashion. Header and trailer sequences are added independently to the data sent on each transmission channel to facilitate synchronization and reassembly of the data block at the receiver.
- The maximum frame size is still limited to 1518 bytes as with traditional Ethernet.

### 13.2.7 100Base-T2 - 100 Megabit Ethernet on UTP-3 (2 Pairs)

This protocol would use a single pair of UTP-3 in each direction between a workstation and a hub. Various standards bodies have been trying to develop a standard for this (especially in the context of FDDI) since 1991. We seem no closer to a solution. It is an extremely difficult thing to do.

It is widely believed that 100 Mbps data rates are achievable over relatively short distances of UTP-3 (say 100 meters) but there is significant disagreement over what the best approach might be and what the adapters might end up costing. It may be that the required data rate is achievable only at the cost of using very sophisticated digital signal processing techniques.

One significant problem is that the whole reason for wanting to use two pairs (when most cables carry four at least) is so that the other pairs can be used for other purposes (such as telephone). However, use of the additional pairs for other things (especially decadic dialed telephone) introduces "crosstalk" noise into the pairs we are using for 100Base-T2. But if you can't use the additional pairs for other purposes then you might as well use the 100Base-T4 (4-pair) solution.

### 13.2.8 100Base-FX - 100 Megabit Ethernet on MM Fiber

This is another case of a standard being "re-used". 100Base-FX is the same as FDDI on MM fiber (with minor modifications to allow for the continuous nature of the FDDI stream and the burst nature of Ethernet). See 2.1.14, "4 out of 5 (4B/5B) Block Code" on page 2-26.

## 13.3 100VG AnyNet - IEEE 802.12 (100BaseVG)

At the time of writing (January 1995) the IEEE was in the final stage of adopting "100VG AnyNet" as IEEE 802.12 standard for "Demand-Priority Access Method" LANs. In January 1995, the first 100VG AnyNet products were already available commercially.

Originally conceived as one alternative for "100 Megabit Ethernet" the original proposal was expanded to allow the connection of token-ring stations as well.

This is a highly practical solution to 100 Mbps LAN networking which addresses both the performance and the cabling problems and appears to meet the objectives stated above. There are three key concepts:

1. Each station is connected in a "star" pattern from a hub. That is, each station is linked point-to-point to the hub. *But the "hub" is not a standard LAN hub - it is a fast circuit-switching device. In fact, 100VG AnyNet is not a LAN architecture at all - it is a circuit-switching architecture.*

2. It is considered too costly to run UTP cable at 100 Mbps, so the proposal uses multiple pairs, each operating at a more cost-effective speed. *The proposal suggests using four twisted pairs from the hub to each workstation, and transmitting data on all four simultaneously - each pair runs at an easy 25 Mbps data rate.* This brings a secondary advantage of eliminating any need for very high-speed logic in the adapter cards - significantly reducing the cost.

   During control and signaling states, two pairs are used in each direction, so there is a full-duplex path between the station and the hub. During data transfer all four pairs are used in one direction (half-duplex operation).

3. The LAN frame formats (either Ethernet or token-ring) are preserved. That is, only the MAC (medium access control) part of the LAN protocol changes and other parts stay the same. There is nothing in 100VG AnyNet that will map Ethernet header format to token-ring (or vice versa); therefore, when both kinds of device are connected to a common system *only* stations using the same protocol can communicate with one another.

The protocol operates (conceptually) as follows:

- When a station has some data to transmit it places a REQUEST condition onto its link with the hub. Note, the REQUEST condition is a tone signal[4] not a packet.
- When the hub decides that the station is to be serviced, it signals the station to start transmission. (At this point the hub does not know the destination of the frame it is about to receive.)
- The hub receives the first part of the frame (the header) into an elastic buffer and determines the destination station.
- The hub signals the destination station (again by tone) that data is about to arrive.
- The destination station signals the hub (by ending its transmission of idles) that it is able to receive.
- During the last three steps, the hub continues to receive data.
- The hub commences transmission to the destination station an all four pairs.
- Both stations and the hub go back to idle when the transmission is complete.

There are a number of quite significant advantages here:

1. There is no possibility of collision. The hub controls which station sends at any time.
2. We can have both priority stations and determinant (bounded) access delays. This is because the hub can decide the order and priority in which it accepts data from stations. The CSMA/CD problem of indeterminate access delay is removed. This is why the standard is named "Demand-Priority Access Method".
3. The performance problem due to propagation delays has not gone away but it has improved quite a lot - mainly by limiting the allowed distance from station to hub.

   There is a new performance issue in the question of how fast can the hub respond - this is an implementation question. The hub could end up as a (one at a time) packet switch. However, this problem is thought to be containable.
4. There are three options for transmission protocol allowed within the standard:
   - An option to use 100 ohm (voice grade) UTP-3 (because most existing cabling uses this and because the major type of existing multi-pair (bundle) cabling is UTP-3). This is done by using all four pairs in the cable in parallel to send data.
   - An option for use on multi-mode fiber (2 fibers) at 1300 nm.
   - An option for use on 150 ohm STP cable (2 pairs).

4 The "tone" signal is a simple 16-bit pattern endlessly repeated.

Operation on STP and fiber is straightforward and conventional but operation on UTP-3 was a significant challenge and so it is described in more detail below.

5. Implementation using existing software (and adapter firmware) is clearly possible since the MAC protocol is unchanged. Of course, new adapter cards must be designed for the new environment.

### 13.3.1.1 100VG AnyNet Transmission Protocol on UTP-3

This is an interesting and innovative technique which illustrates some important principles.

As mentioned above the key points of the protocol are:

- Connection of each station is point-to-point between that station and the hub.
- Data transmission uses all four wire pairs in parallel at 25 Mbps each, for a total throughput of 100 Mbps.
- Each pair uses a 5B6B encoding scheme and thus the symbol rate is 30 Mbaud.
- Thus, the fundamental frequency of the signal is 15 MHz (although many higher-frequency components are also present).
- The signal is scrambled for reasons explained in 2.1.17, "Scrambling a.k.a. Enciphering" on page 2-31.

Operation takes place as follows:

1. A MAC frame of data (including the LAN header and the FCS field) is regarded as a single stream of bits as shown in Figure 13-6.

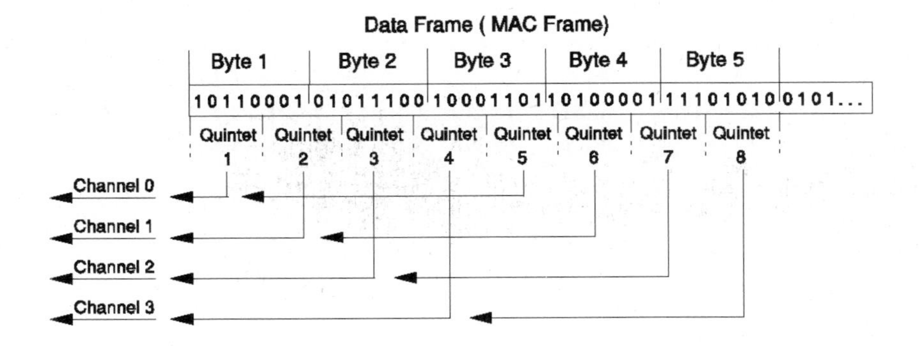


***Figure 13-6.*** *100VG Allocation of Bits to Channels*

2. The bits of the MAC frame are considered to be a stream of 5-bit quintets.

3. Quintets are allocated to transmission channels on a round-robin basis such that channel 0 is allocated quintets 1,5,9,13... Channel 1 is allocated quintets 2,6,10,14... Channels 2 and 3 are likewise allocated quintets.
4. Operation of a single channel is shown in Figure 13-7.

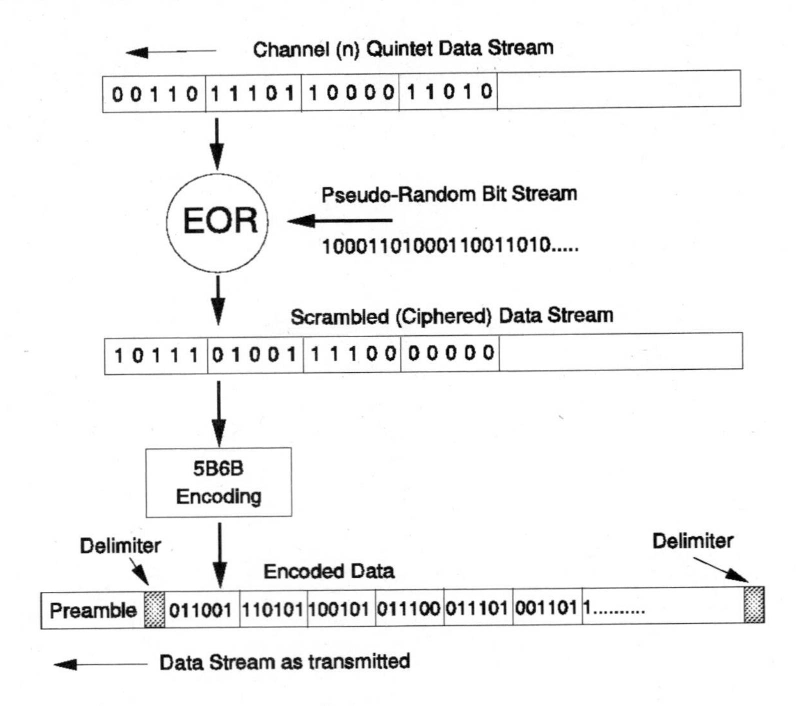


*Figure 13-7. 100VG Data Encoding and Scrambling Process (Single Channel)*

5. Quintets are taken and scrambled (as individual quintets, not as a continuous bit stream).
6. The scrambled bit stream is then encoded using a 5B/6B code. Codes of the form xB/yB are discussed in 2.1.14.1, "Other xB/yB Codes (8B/10B and 5B/6B)" on page 2-27. In this case, there is an unusual feature in that two code tables are used and their use is swapped according to the running digital sum (of zeros and ones transmitted) so as to maintain DC balance.
7. There are other conditions to be taken into account such as minor differences between cable pairs resulting in skew of the data on the cable and data blocks that are not an exact multiple of 5 bits in length. These are accommodated by sending a preamble and postamble to each block with the data portion identified by the presence of special delimiter characters. These delimiters enable the receiver to synchronize the reception of the four different data streams.

8. Reception is the inverse of the transmission process.

## 13.4 Isochronous Ethernet

A current proposal under consideration by the IEEE committee 802.9 (Multimedia Workstation) is for the standardisation of a protocol called "Isochronous Ethernet". Many people believe that isochronous communication is necessary for the multimedia workstation. See 5.4, "Characteristics of Multimedia Applications" on page 5-13 and 6.5.2, "The Isochronous Debate" on page 6-21. This technology has been demonstrated using adapter cards (called isoENET) from National Semiconductor Corporation.

The important principles are as follows:

**Network Topology**

User workstations are connected radially to a hub using UTP cable as shown in Figure 13-8.

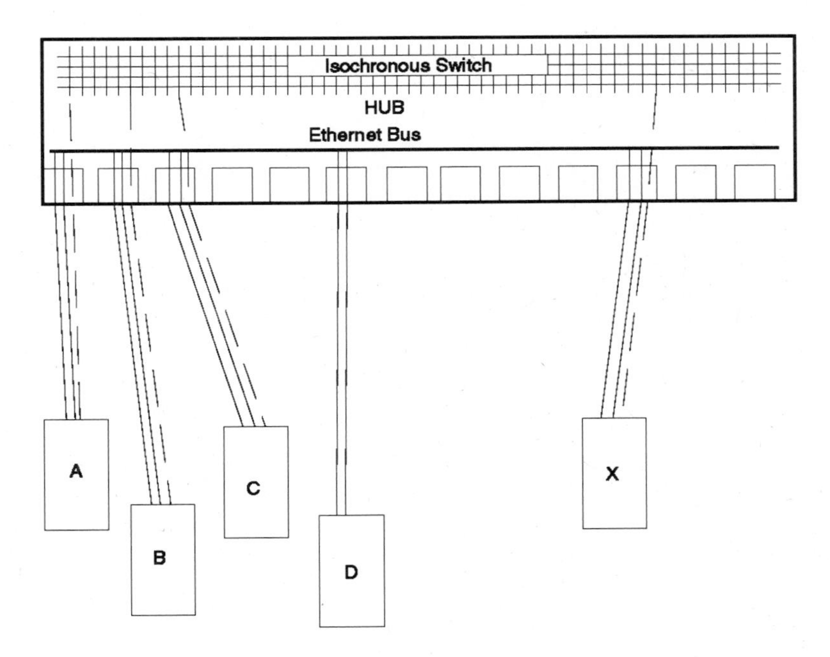


*Figure 13-8. Isochronous Ethernet Network Topology.* The dotted lines represent isochronous 6.144 Mbps isochronous channels.

### Link Encoding for Higher Speed

10BaseT Ethernet connections use Manchester Encoding for data transmission on the copper medium. This encoding scheme uses two link state changes to represent a single bit.

In Isochronous Ethernet the data encoding is changed to use 4/5 code as used in FDDI (see 13.6.5.2, "Data Encoding" on page 13-41) and the link speed is (very slightly) increased. The "raw" bit rate as seen on the link is now 20.48 Mbps.[5] This gives a data rate of 16.384 Mbps rather than 10 Mbps. The physical transmission on the link remains the same. This means that potential problems with RF emissions and the characteristics of UTP cable are minimized.

### TDM on the Link

Each individual link (between the user workstation and the hub) is time division multiplexed to give two channels. One channel operates at 10 Mbps and the other at 6.144 Mbps.

### Ethernet 10 Mbps Operation Is Unchanged

The 10 Mbps channels are connected at the hub to form an Ethernet bus and regular Ethernet operation is exactly the same as always.

### TDM Channel Operation

From a TDM standpoint, you have a hub device with a number of radially connected workstations with 6.144 Mbps dedicated links connected point-to-point to each of them. The TDM bandwidth is divided into 96 channels of 64 Kbps each. This gives 94, "B" channels, a single "D" channel and a maintenance channel. This is the same speed as an American T2 channel or an FDDI-II wideband channel.

$$6.144 \text{ Mbps} = 4 \times T1 = 3 \times E1 = 1 WBC$$

At the hub there is a switching device capable of interconnecting individual channels or groups of channels as requested by the workstations.

### Isochronous Hub Operation

Isochronous Ethernet is quite different in concept from the other isochronous LAN (FDDI-II). FDDI-II operates as a single medium with all stations sharing the isochronous capacity. Iso Ethernet (as far as isochronous operation is concerned) *is not a LAN at all.* The isochronous connections operate as point-to-point connections from workstation to switch (within the hub).

---

[5] You could call this the baud rate, but when 4/5 code is used it is probably better to say that the baud rate is 4.056 MBaud with 5-bit symbols.

This gives Iso Ethernet a much higher throughput capacity (potential) than FDDI-II. Each workstation has 96 channels dedicated from it to the switch. System capacity is 96 channels times the number of workstations (divided by two). In FDDI-II system capacity is 16 times 96 channels. Provided the switch has sufficient capacity, total system throughput of an Iso Ethernet LAN could be significantly higher than this.

**Isochronous Control**

In FDDI-II capacity is allocated by (synchronous) data messages on the synchronous part of the LAN. Iso Ethernet has a dedicated 64 Kbps "D" channel from each station to the hub. This channel is used for all control and diagnostic information related to the isochronous capability.

Thus, apart from the TDM sharing of the workstation to hub link, the isochronous and synchronous components of the LAN are totally unrelated.

The important features of Isochronous Ethernet are as follows:

1. Existing star-wired UTP cabling is used.
2. There is no change to existing Ethernet software (above the level of the I/O driver).
3. Isochronous and packet channels do not compete for link bandwidth.
4. The regular Ethernet traffic can be connected to other Ethernet segments with a repeater - there is no need for bridging.
5. New Iso Ethernet adapter cards are required for all attaching LAN stations. However, because it is star wired, the hub can have some connections using regular Ethernet and others using Iso Ethernet with both types forming part of the same synchronous LAN segment. This is shown in Figure 13-8 on page 13-23, where stations A, B, C and X are Iso Ethernet stations but station D is not. Regular Ethernet operation is possible for all stations but isochronous operation is only possible on the Iso Ethernet stations.

#### 13.4.1.1 Gateways

Of course, the system is not very useful without connection to the wide area. ISDN, T1 and E1 type connections would form modules within the hub and these would be connected to the isochronous switch. The gateway function is a part of the hub. Thus continuous isochronous channels could be constructed from any workstation through the wide area network.

## 13.5 Token-Ring

Many excellent descriptions of the detailed operation of token-ring protocol are available and so it will not be described in detail here. However, there are a number of important features of token-ring that need to be reviewed in order to understand why we need to use different protocols at very high speeds.

### Configuration

A number of devices called "stations"[6] are connected by a series of point-to-point links such that the whole forms a "ring". Data is sent in one direction only so that if station A (in Figure 13-9) sends data to station B then the data will pass through stations D, E, F, G and C *before* it is received by station B. Data links are usually electrical (although they may be optical) and the data rate is either 4 or 16 million bits per second.

A ring is usually wired in the form of a "star". A device called a Ring Wiring Concentrator (RWC), which may be active or passive, is used at the center and two pairs of wires (in the same cable) are connected (point-to-point) from the RWC to each station. This is done so that individual stations may be added to or removed from the ring conveniently.

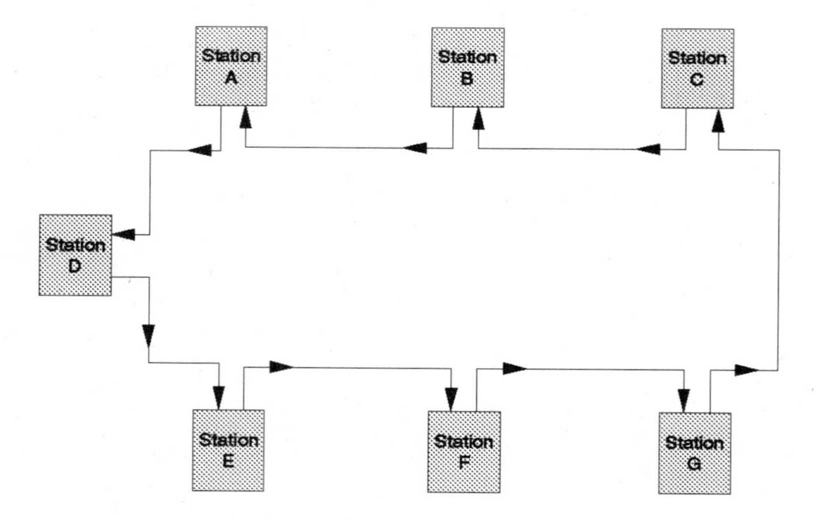


***Figure 13-9.*** *Conceptual Token-Ring Structure*

[6] Sometimes also referred to as "nodes".

The RWC has an electromechanical relay in each station connector. This relay is held open by a direct current "phantom" voltage generated by the station. If a station loses power or is unplugged, the relay closes and bypasses that particular station and its connecting cable.

### Data Transmission

Data is sent in blocks called "frames" which have a variable length and are preceded by a fixed format header. When station A wants to send data to station F it builds a header with its own address and the address of the destination (station F) in it and appends this header to the data.

When station A sends the data it *always* goes to the next station on the ring (station D) and this station repeats the data onto its outbound link.

The process proceeds around the ring until the data arrives at its destination station (F). Station F also sends the data onward around the ring but recognizes itself as the destination address. In addition to propagating the frame on the ring, station F copies the frame into its input buffers.

### Access Control

It seems obvious from the structure described above that only one station can transmit at a time. The problem is how to control (with fairness) which station has permission to send.

This problem is solved by using a special header format called a "token". The token is sent from station to station around the ring. When a station receives the token it is allowed to send one frame of up to a specified maximum size (specified as a maximum transmission time). When a station finishes sending its frame it must send a free token to allow the next station a turn at sending.

### Monitor Function

The token controls which station sends next, but what controls the token? Errors can cause tokens to be lost or permanently marked as busy. Physical breaks can occur in the ring.

A special station (called a monitor station) is needed on the ring to control the token and to continually verify proper functioning. In addition this station generates the ring timing (clock) and equalizes the accumulated timing error (jitter), etc.

In practice, *every* station has the monitor capability. When the ring starts up, one station becomes the "active monitor". This is to remove the need for special nodes which would need backup in case of failure, etc.

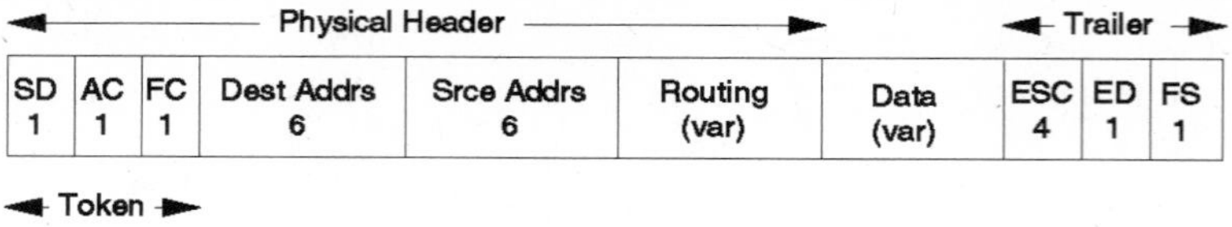

← Physical Header → ← Trailer →

| SD | AC | FC | Dest Addrs | Srce Addrs | Routing | Data | ESC | ED | FS |
|---|---|---|---|---|---|---|---|---|---|
| 1 | 1 | 1 | 6 | 6 | (var) | (var) | 4 | 1 | 1 |

← Token →

***Figure 13-10.*** *Token-Ring Frame Format.* A token consists of the SD (Start Delimiter), AC (Access Control) and FC (Frame Control) fields alone. Numbers denote the field lengths in bytes.

The concept described above is very simple but a number of things must be done to make sure that the concept works in practice:

**Minimize Delay in Each Station**

In some early LAN architectures, a whole data frame was sent from one station to another and then retransmitted. This meant that the transmit time for the frame was added to the transit time *for every station that the message passed through.* This protocol actually works quite well where there are very few (for example, four) devices in the LAN. In a LAN of perhaps 100 devices, the "staging delay" becomes critical.

One key component of TRN is its use of Differential Manchester Coding at the electrical level. This is discussed in 2.1.8, "Differential Manchester Coding" on page 2-17. Potentially, this enables a ring station to have only 1 bit of delay, but in current adapters this is 2½ bits.

The monitor station generates a clock, and every other station derives its timing from the received data stream and uses this derived timing to drive its own transmitter. This is done to avoid having a large "elastic buffer" (delay) in each node. But there is a down side. Jitter (the very small differences in timing between the "real" timing and what the receiver is able to recover - see 2.1.6.2, "Jitter" on page 2-13) adds up, and after a while (240 stations) threatens to cause the loss of data. The monitor station (but only the monitor station) indeed contains an elastic buffer to compensate for jitter around the ring.

**Structure of the Token**

With only a one-bit delay in each station, how can a station receive the token and then send data? It might repeat the token to the next station before it had the opportunity to start transmission.

The technique used here relies on the fact that the token is a very short (24 bits) fragment at the beginning of a frame header. Bit 3 of the Frame Control field determines whether this is a token or the beginning of a frame. So, when a station has something to send, it monitors for a token. When it detects the token it *changes* the token bit in the FC field to mark the token as "busy" and then appends its data.

### Removing a Frame from the Ring

An analogy that has been often used in relation to token-rings is that of a railway train. The "train" goes from station to station around the ring. But this gives very much the wrong impression.

At 4 Mbps a single bit is around 50 meters long![7] A data block of (say) 100 bytes is 800 bits or 40 kilometers long! This is much longer than most LANs - so, in fact, the beginning of a data block arrives back at the sending station (usually) long before the station has finished sending the block! If this were a railway train on a loop of track, the front of the engine would arrive back at the start before the back of the engine left (not to worry about the carriages).

> In fact, there is a real problem with small token-rings. This is that a transmitting station could potentially receive the beginning of a token before it has finished transmitting this same token. This gives logical problems in the protocol. It is avoided by having a serial elastic buffer in the active monitor station that inserts sufficient delay to ensure that no ring can be shorter than a token (24 bits).

A frame could be removed from the ring by the destination station. But, a destination station does not know that it is the destination until most of the header has already been propagated around the ring. In any case there are broadcast frames to think about where there are multiple destinations. In addition, if the frame is left on the ring, we can use a bit in the trailer (set by the receiving station) to say "frame copied" to give a basic level of assurance to the transmitting station that somebody out there received the frame.

So, the frame is removed from the ring by the sending station. In the 4 Mbps version of the IBM Token-Ring, after completing transmission of its frame, a sending station transmits idle characters until it receives the header from its transmitted frame. When it has completely received the frame header, it releases a new token onto the ring so that the next station may have an opportunity to transmit.

In summary, after completing its transmission, the sending station waits only to receive the header of the frame it just transmitted (not the whole frame) before releasing a free token. However, it will still receive and remove the entire frame it transmitted (including checking the bits in the trailer).

---

7 Electricity travels on twisted pair media at about 5 μsec per kilometer.

When the ring speed is increased from 4 Mbps to 16 Mbps several things happen:

**Data transfer is faster.**

It takes less time to transmit a frame.

**Staging delay in each node is less.**

Delay stays at 2½ bits but a bit now takes ¼ of the time.

**The speed of light (and of electricity) hasn't changed at all!**

A major component of ring latency (propagation delay) is unchanged.

**The bits are shorter.**

At 16 Mbps, a bit is 12.5 meters in length. (The railway train analogy begins to look a little more sensible!)

But (in the 4 Mbps version of the protocol) the sending station still waits until the header of the frame it has just transmitted is received before it places (releases) a new token onto the ring. The effect of this "gap time", where the transmitting station is sending idles while waiting for the header to be received, is small at 4 Mbps. At 16 Mbps the effect can be significant.

For operation at 16 Mbps, the token-ring protocol is modified such that when a station finishes transmission it will immediately send a free token. This is called "early token release".

As ring speed is increased further, the TRN principle will still operate, but throughput does not increase in the same ratio as the link speed:

**Latency**

When a station has transmitted its one frame it must send a token to let the next station have a chance. It takes time for the token to travel to another station and during this time no station can transmit - the ring is idle. As ring speed is increased the transmission time becomes shorter but this latency (between transmissions) is unchanged. This means that in percentage terms, latency becomes more significant as speed is increased.

The situation could be improved by allowing a station to send multiple frames (up to some limit) at a single visit of the token. (FDDI does just this.)

**No "Guaranteed Bandwidth"**

There is no mechanism available to guarantee a station a regular amount of service for time-critical applications.

### No "Isochronous" Traffic

Isochronous traffic (meaning non-packetized voice and video) is different from the guaranteed bandwidth real-time characteristic mentioned in the previous point. TRN does not allow this either.

### Potentially Wasted Capacity

Only one active token may be on the ring at any time. This means that only one station may transmit at any time. In the case (in the diagram above) where station E is transmitting to station F, station C might perhaps transmit to station A, thus doubling the throughput of the ring - if a protocol could be found that made this possible.

## 13.6 Fiber Distributed Data Interface (FDDI)

FDDI was developed by the American National Standards Institute (ANSI). It was originally proposed as a standard for fiber optical computer I/O channels but has become a generalized standard for operation of a LAN at 100 Mbps. The FDDI standards are now firm and there are many FDDI devices available on the market. However, mass acceptance in the marketplace has yet to happen. The important characteristics of FDDI are as follows:

### Optical LAN at 100 Mbps

FDDI is primarily intended for operation over optical fiber but recently has been proposed for operation over standard copper wire (shielded twisted pair).

### Dual Token Rings

There are two token rings operating in opposite directions. The primary ring carries data. The secondary ring is used to "wrap" the ring should the ring be broken. The secondary ring is not normally used for data traffic.

### Ring Characteristics

Using multimode optical fiber for connection, an FDDI ring (segment) may be up to 200 km in length attaching a maximum of 500 stations up to two kilometers apart.

### Frame (Packet) Switching

Like many other types of LAN (Token-Ring, Ethernet, etc.), data transfer takes place in frames or packets. In FDDI the maximum frame size is 4500 bytes. Each frame has a header which contains the physical address of the destination FDDI station.

### Guaranteed Bandwidth Availability

In addition to the "equality of access" characteristic of token-ring, FDDI offers a form of "guaranteed" bandwidth availability for "synchronous"[8] traffic.

**Token-Ring Protocol**

The ring protocol is conceptually similar to the token-ring (IEEE 802.5) LAN but differs significantly in detail. FDDI ring protocol is dependent on timers, whereas TRN operation is basically event driven.

**Ring Stations**

An FDDI station may connect to both rings or to only the primary ring. There may be a maximum of 500 stations connected to any one ring segment.

**Ring Monitor**

Like token-ring, there is a ring monitor function. But unlike token-ring, this function is performed cooperatively by all stations rather than by a single active monitor. During operation all stations monitor for errors and if any are found the finder requests re-initialization of the ring.

Different from token-ring, each station does *not* need to have the ring monitor function.

## 13.6.1 Structure

Figure 13-11 shows the basic structure of an FDDI LAN. This consists of counter-rotating rings with the primary one carrying data.

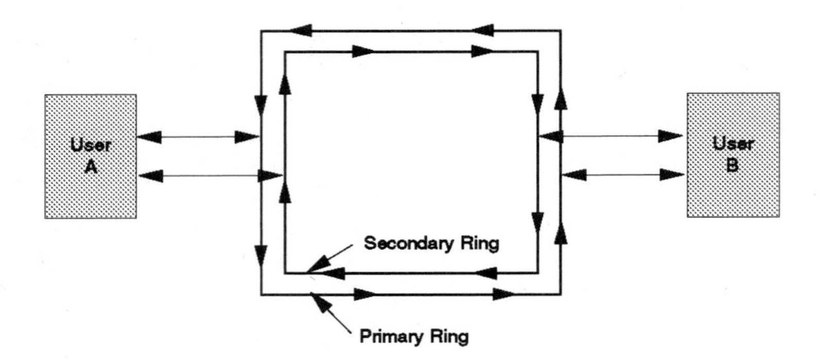


***Figure 13-11.** FDDI Basic Structure*

8 In FDDI the word "synchronous" is used to mean "traffic which has a real time requirement". That is, to transmit synchronous traffic a station must gain access to the ring and transmit its frames within a specified time period. This is *not* the usual meaning of the word synchronous. See the description in Appendix D, "Getting the Language into Synch" on page D-1.

Should there be a break in the ring, the stations can "wrap" the ring through themselves. This is shown in Figure 13-12 on page 13-33. The secondary ring is used to complete the break in the primary ring by wrapping back along the operational route.

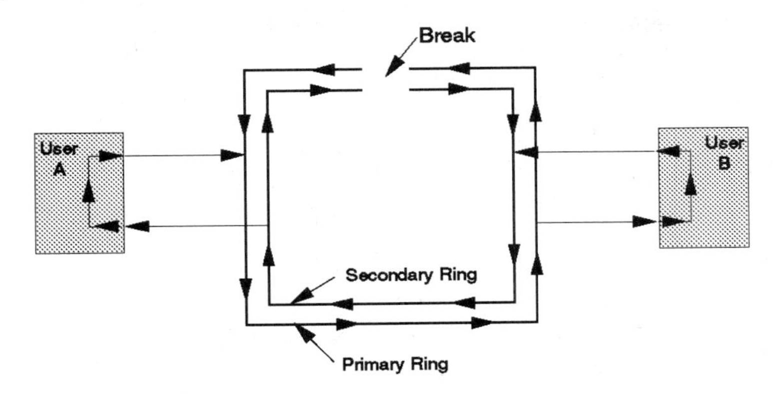


*Figure 13-12. FDDI Ring Healing*

There are two classes of station:

**Class A stations** connect to both the primary and secondary ring and have the ability to "wrap" the ring to bypass error conditions. These are sometimes called Dual Attachment Stations (DAS).

**Class B stations** connect only to the primary ring. This is to allow for lower cost (lower function) attachments. These are called Single Attachment Stations (SAS).

Figure 13-13 on page 13-34 shows class A and B stations connected to a backbone FDDI ring. In addition a Ring Wiring Concentrator (RWC) is present that allows the connection of multiple class B stations in a "star wired" configuration.

The ring wiring concentrator could be a simple device which performs only the RWC function or it could be quite complex containing a class A station with the ring monitor function as well.

Some users choose to attach some SAS stations to the secondary ring. This allows the secondary ring to be used for data transport and of course gives higher aggregate throughput. However, unless there is a bridge between primary and secondary rings, an SAS station on the primary ring cannot communicate with an SAS station on the secondary ring.

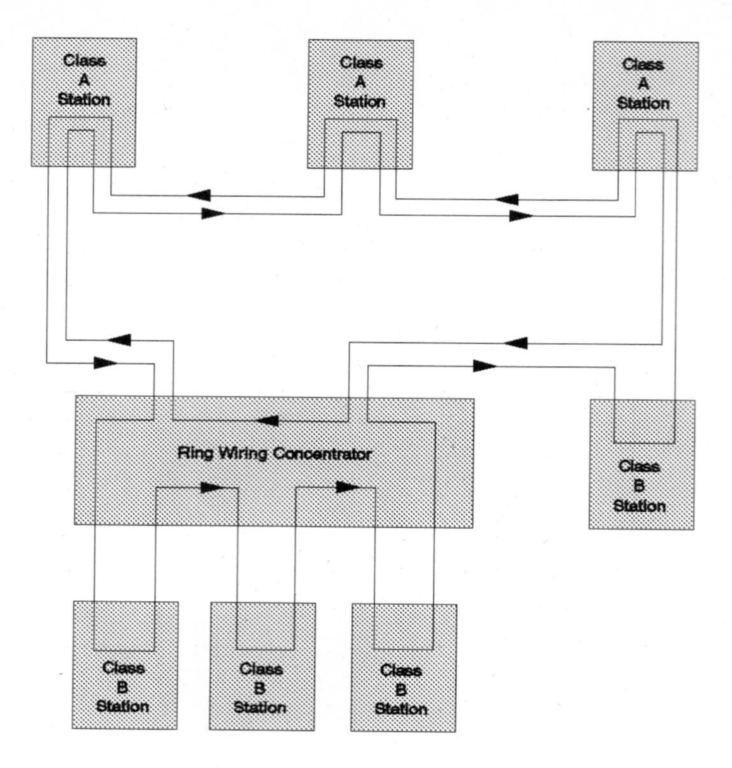


*Figure 13-13. FDDI Ring Configuration*

## 13.6.2 Access Protocol Operation

Ring access in FDDI is controlled by a special frame called a token. There is only one token present on the ring at any time. In principle when a station receives a token it has permission to send (place a frame of data onto the ring). When it finishes sending, it must place a new token back onto the ring.

FDDI is a little more complex than suggested above, due to the need to handle synchronous traffic. There are three timers kept in each ring station:

**Token Rotation Timer (TRT)**

This is the elapsed time since the station last received a token.

**Target Token Rotation Timer (TTRT)**

This is a negotiated value which is the target maximum time between opportunities to send (tokens) as seen by an individual station. TTRT has a value of between 4 milliseconds and 165 milliseconds. A recommended optimal value in many situations is 8 milliseconds.

**Token Holding Timer (THT)**

This governs the maximum amount of data that a station may send when a token is received. It is literally the maximum time allocated to the station for sending during each rotation of the token.

When a station receives a token, it compares the amount of time since it last saw the token (TRT) with the target time for the token to complete one revolution of the ring (TTRT).

- If TRT is less than the target, then the station is allowed to send multiple frames until the target time is reached. This means the ring is functioning normally.

  ```
  TTRT - TRT = THT
  ```

- If TRT is greater than TTRT, it means the ring is overloaded. The station may send "synchronous" data only.
- If TRT approaches twice TTRT, there is an error condition that must be conveyed by the ring monitor function to the LAN Manager.
- This implies that each station may observe delays to traffic and thus must be able to tolerate these delays - perhaps by buffering the data.

When a station attaches to the ring, it has a dialog with the ring monitor and it indicates its desired Token Rotation Time according to its needs for synchronous traffic. The ring monitor allocates an Operational Token Rotation Time, which is the minimum of all requested TTRT values. This then becomes the operational value for all stations on the ring, and may only be changed if a new station enters the ring, and requests a lower TTRT value.

Within the asynchronous class of service there are eight priority levels. In token-ring a token is allocated a priority using three priority bits in the token - a station with the token is allowed to send frames with the same or higher priority. In FDDI the priority mechanism uses the Token Rotation Timers rather than a specific priority field in the token.

The sending station must monitor its input side for frames that it transmitted and remove them. A receiving station only copies the data from the ring. Removal of frames from the ring is the responsibility of the sender.

When a station completes a transmission, it sends a new token onto the ring. This is called "early token release". Thus there can only be *one* station transmitting onto the ring at one time.

In summary:

- A token circulates on the ring at all times.
- Any station receiving the token has permission to transmit synchronous frames.
- If there is time left over in this rotation of the token, the station may send as much data as it likes (multiple frames) until the target token rotation time is reached.
- After transmission the station releases a new token onto the ring.
- Depending on the latency of the ring, there may be many frames on the ring at any one time but there can be only one token.
- The transmitting station has the responsibility of removing the frames it transmitted from the ring when they return to it.

### 13.6.3 Ring Initialization, Monitoring and Error Handling

In an FDDI ring there is no single "ring monitor" function such as in an IEEE 802.5 token-ring. This is because all stations on the ring perform part of the function cooperatively.

- The elastic jitter compensation buffer that exists in the active monitor of 802.5 does not exist, because every node regenerates the clock and there is no jitter propagation around the ring.
- All stations monitor the ring for the token arriving within its specified time limit.
- When the ring is initialized all stations cooperate to determine the TTRT value.
- When a break in the ring occurs all stations beacon but give way to any received beacon on their inbound side. In this way the beacon command that circulates on the ring identifies the immediate downstream neighbor of the break in the ring.

### 13.6.4 Physical Media

There are four types of media currently used for FDDI:

- Multimode fiber

  This is the originally defined mode of operation and the predominant mode of adapters on the market.

- Single Mode fiber

  This has been included in the standard by ANSI but as yet has only minor usage.

- Shielded Twisted Pair (STP) copper wire

  The use of FDDI over STP cable, while it doesn't have the electrical isolation advantages of fiber, is significantly less than the cost of using FDDI on fiber. This makes FDDI an economic alternative for the desktop workstation.

  In 1992, when a proposal was put to the ANSI committee for a standard that would work on STP but not on UTP it was rejected in favor of the (hoped for) development of a standard that would work on both types of cable. Subsequently, a group of manufacturers (including IBM), concerned that a standard that would work on UTP was some time away, announced products using a specification called "SDDI".

  The ANSI committee approved a standard which will work on STP or UTP-5. Most manufacturers are moving to use this standard instead of the previous SDDI implementation.

- Unshielded Twisted Pair-5 (UTP-5)

  There is now a standard for using FDDI over UTP-5 but ***no standard exists for operating over UTP-3***. The UTP-5 standard involves using a changed data encoding scheme from the simple encoding used on fiber.

The ANSII committee is still studying other media:

- Unshielded Twisted Pair-3 (UTP-3)

  There are many problems with the use of UTP-3 as discussed in 2.3, "LAN Cabling with Unshielded Twisted Pair" on page 2-49. Nevertheless, many users have installed low-grade Telephone Twisted Pair (TTP) cabling for Ethernet connections. Many of these users now wish to use the same cable for FDDI.

  This problem will be solved. However, the cost of necessary transceivers is still in question.

- SDH/Sonet links

  An FDDI structure could be operated over a wide area using channels derived from the public network. It has been proposed that channels derived from SDH/Sonet be used[9] to construct an FDDI ring over a wide area using public network facilities. The proposal is to map the full 125 Mbps rate into an STS-3c channel. This proposal has been accepted.

### 13.6.4.1 Media Specifications

FDDI is specified to use either single-mode or multimode fiber at a wavelength of 1,300 nanometers. The standard multimode fiber specification is 62.5/125 but the other sizes of 50/125, 85/125 and 100/140 are optional alternatives. The mode field diameter for

9 See 8.2, "SDH and Sonet" on page 8-16.

single-mode fiber is 9 microns. This means that an LED is usually used as the light source (rather than a laser) and that the detector is a PIN diode (rather than an avalanche photo diode).

The power levels are expressed in dBm.[10] Two different transmitter power ranges and two different receiver sensitivity "categories" are specified. These are:

$$\text{Transmit Power Cat. 1} = \text{From } -20\,dBm \text{ to } -14\,dBm$$

$$\text{Transmit Power Cat. 2} = \text{From } -4\,dBm \text{ to } 0\,dBm$$

$$\text{Receiver Sensitivity Cat. 1} = \text{From } -31\,dBm \text{ to } -14\,dBm$$

$$\text{Receiver Sensitivity Cat. 2} = \text{From } -37\,dBm \text{ to } -15\,dBm$$

A typical transceivers may have the following specification:

```
Input:  - 16 dBm
Output: - 27 dBm
```

(Input and output here refer to the optical cable.) What this says is that this FDDI transmitter transmits at a power level of −16 dBm and that the associated receiver is able to handle a signal of −27 dBm. In this implementation this means that you have 11 dB for loss in cables, etc. If this cable loses 3 dB per kilometer, then if devices are two kilometers apart, the cable loss will be 6 dB and there is 5 dB left over for losses in splices and connectors, etc.

In practical terms (as discussed in 4.1.9, "Fiber Cables" on page 4-29) cables vary in their losses and loss varies by temperature. Calculation of maximum allowable distance is something that needs to be done carefully, in conjunction with the cable manufacturer's specifications.

On another point of practicality, some devices on the market actually transmit at a higher power level than that specified here. In addition, it is easy to overload a PIN diode receiver if the power level is too high. This means that if FDDI stations are installed close together (for example, in the same room), attenuators may be needed in the cable to cut down the light to a level acceptable to the receiver.

[10] This is a measure of absolute power. The signal level in decibels in relation to one milliwatt. Thus 3 dBm is 3 dB above 1 milliwatt or 2 mw. -6 dBm is 6 dB below one mw or .25 mw.

### 13.6.4.2 Optical Bypass Switch

Optical bypass switches (as illustrated in Figure 13-14) may be used (either built into the station or as separate devices) to maintain connectivity of the rings when power is turned off or when the node fails.

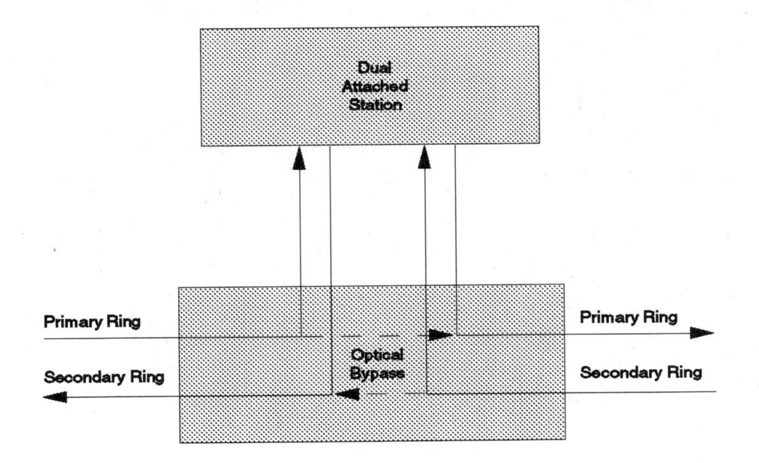


*Figure 13-14. Optical Bypass Switch*

These switches are mechanical devices (switching is mechanical but operation could be electrical) usually operating by moving a mirror. They depend on mechanical movement being precise. Since mechanical operations cannot be exactly precise, they introduce additional loss to the ring even if the station is operating correctly. This limits further the possible distance between nodes.

## 13.6.5 Physical Layer Protocol

The basic functions of the physical layer are:

1. To transport a stream of bits around the ring from one station to another.
2. Provide access to the ring for each individual station.

To do this it must:

- Construct a system of clocking and synchronization such that data may flow around the ring.
- Receive data from a station and convert it into a form suitable for transmission.
- Receive data from the ring and convert it into the form expected by the node access protocol.

- Provide a transmission system that allows the station to send and receive any arbitrary bit stream (transparency).
- Signal the station (node access protocol) at the beginning and end of every block of data.
- Keep the ring operational and synchronized even when there is no data flowing.

#### 13.6.5.1 Ring Synchronization

In FDDI, each ring segment is regarded physically as a separate point-to-point link between adjacent stations. This means that the exact timing of data received at a station *cannot* be the same as the timing of data transmitted. Since it is not possible to build (at an economic cost) oscillators that are exactly synchronized, there will be a difference between the data rate of bits received and that of bits transmitted! This is solved by the use of an "elasticity buffer" (see Figure 13-15).

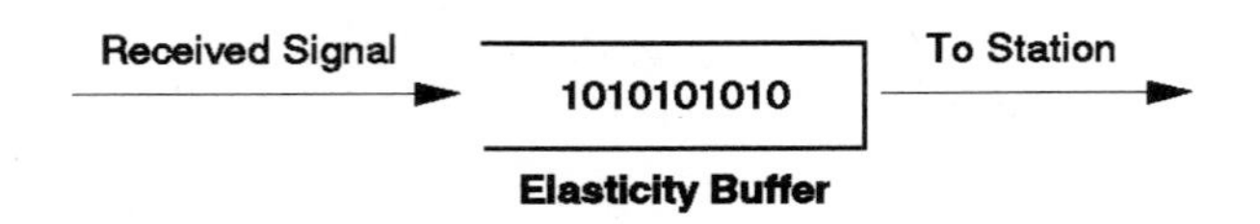


***Figure 13-15.*** *Ten-Bit Elasticity Buffer Operation*

Most of the time a station simply passes data on around the ring. The need is to pass this data with minimal delay in each station. This means that we need to start transmitting a block towards the next station *before* it is completely received. The received signal arrives at the rate of the upstream station's transmitter. When data is sent onward to the next station in the ring, it is sent at the rate of this station's local oscillator. So data is being received at a different rate from the rate that it is being transmitted!

This discrepancy is handled by placing an "elastic buffer" between the receiver and the input port to the ring station. The ring station is then clocked at the rate of its local oscillator (that is, the transmit rate).

The FDDI specification constrains the clock speed to be ± .005% of the nominal speed (125 megahertz). This means that there is a maximum difference of .01% between the speed of data received and that of data transmitted.

When a station has no data to send and is receiving idle patterns, the elasticity buffer is empty. When data begins to arrive, the first 4 bits are placed into the buffer and nothing is sent to the station. From then on, data bits are received into the buffer and passed on out of the buffer in a FIFO manner.

If the transmit clock is faster than the receive clock, then there are (on average) 4.5 bit times available in the buffer to smooth out the difference. If the receive clock is faster than the transmit clock, there are 5 bit positions in the buffer available before received bits have to be discarded.

This operation determines the maximum frame size:

```
(4.5 bits / .01%) = 45,000 bits = 9,000 symbols = 4,500 bytes
```

A 16-bit idle pattern is sent after the end of every frame (between frames) so that the receiver has time to empty its elasticity buffer if necessary before the arrival of another frame.

While this mechanism introduces additional latency into each attached station, it has the advantage that it prevents the propagation of code violations and invalid line states.

#### 13.6.5.2 Data Encoding

Each four data bits is encoded as a 5-bit group for the purposes of transport on the ring. This means that the 100 Mbps data rate is actually 125 Mbaud when observed on the ring itself. This type of encoding is discussed in 2.1.14, "4 out of 5 (4B/5B) Block Code" on page 2-26.

#### 13.6.5.3 NRZI Modulation

The bit stream resulting from the above encoding is further converted before transmission by using "Non Return to Zero Inverted" (NRZI) procedure. This adds more transitions into the data stream to further assist with timing recovery in the receiver. In NRZI procedure, a one bit causes a state change and a zero bit causes no state change.

A sequence of IDLE patterns (B′11111′) will result in a signal of 010101, thus maintaining synchronization at the receiver. Some valid data sequences (for example X′B0′ coded as B′10111 11110′) can contain up to 7 contiguous one bits. These need to have additional transitions if the receiver is to synchronize satisfactorily.

The net effect of 4B/5B encoding and NRZI conversion is that the maximum length of signal without a state change is 3 bits.

### 13.6.5.4 Physical Layer Operation

Figure 13-16 summarizes the operation of the physical layer(s) of FDDI.

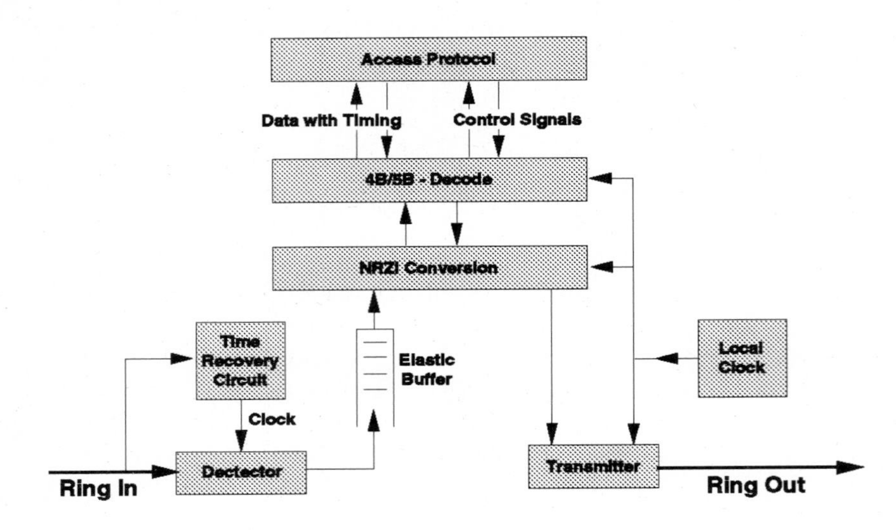


*Figure 13-16. Physical Layer Structure*

### 13.6.5.5 Physical Layer Comparison with Token-Ring

In some discussions of FDDI, a comparison is drawn with token-ring. The point made that since FDDI uses a data rate of 125 Mbps to send a data stream of 100 Mbps, and token-ring uses two signal cycles per bit (16 Mbps is sent at 32 Mbps), that therefore token-ring is somehow "inefficient" by comparison. Nothing could be further from the truth.

Because FDDI is intended primarily to operate over a multimode fiber connection, physical level operation was designed for this environment and is therefore quite different from the electrical operation of token-ring.

In the token-ring architecture, a major objective is to minimize delay in each ring station. This is achieved by having only a single bit buffer in each station for the ring as it "passes by". Operation with such a short delay requires that the output data stream be *exactly* synchronized (both in frequency and in phase) with the input data stream.

There are two problems here:

1. Simple identification and recovery of the data bits

This requires fairly simple circuitry and usually takes the form of a Digital Phase Locked Loop (DPLL).

2. Reconstructing the exact timing of the incoming bit stream

   This means that a new timing signal must be constructed as nearly as possible identical with the signal that was used to construct the received bit stream. To do this requires a very complex analog phase locked loop.

This then is one of the major reasons for using the Manchester code for TRN. Because of the guaranteed large number of state transitions in the code, the recovery of accurate timing information is much easier and the necessary circuitry is simpler and lower in cost.

On an optical link, data is sent as two states: light or no light. Recovering an accurate clock is more difficult here (especially on multimode fiber). At the speed of FDDI, there is less need to minimize buffering in the node. Also, because of the "early token release" protocol, there is much less loss of efficiency due to node delay. For these reasons, FDDI does not synchronize its output clock to its input clock. The penalty is the need to have the elastic buffer and the added node delay that that implies.

### 13.6.6 Node Structure

Figure 13-17 shows the theoretical model of FDDI compared to the IEEE LANs (token-ring, Ethernet, etc.). Their relationship to the OSI model is shown on the left.

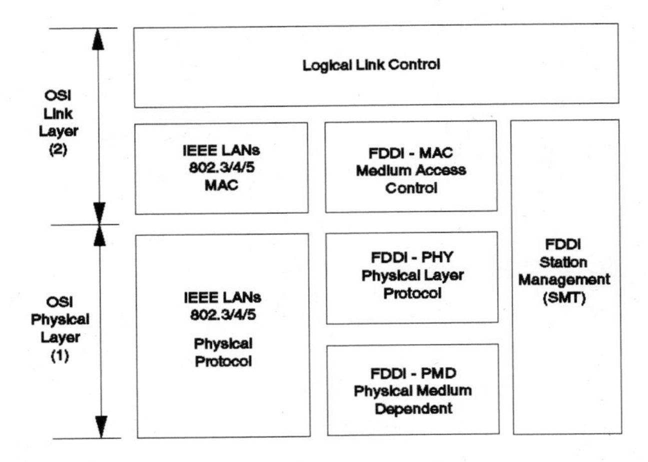


***Figure 13-17.*** *FDDI Node Model*

It is assumed by FDDI that IEEE 802.2 logical link control will be used with FDDI, but this is not mandatory.

The FDDI standard is structured in a different way from the others. Station management is not a new function. Most of its functions are performed, for example, by token-ring, but the functions are included in the physical and MAC components. Also, the physical layer is broken into two to facilitate the use of different physical media.

The functions of the defined layers are as follows:

**Physical Medium Dependent Layer (PMD)**

- Optical link parameters
- Cables and connectors
- Optical bypass switch
- Power budget

**Physical Layer Protocol (PHY)**

- Access to the ring for MAC
- Clocking, synchronization, and buffering
- Code conversion
- Ring continuity

**Media Access Control**

- Uses token and timers to determine which station may send next.
- Maintains the timers.
- Generate and verify the frame check sequence, etc.

**Station Management (SMT)**

- Ring Management (RMT)

  This function manages ring operation and monitors the token to ensure that a valid token is always circulating.

- Connection Management (CMT)

  This function establishes and maintains the physical connections and logical topology of the network.

- Operational Management

  This function monitors the timers and various parameters of the FDDI protocols and connects to an external network management function.

### 13.6.7 High-Speed Performance

Compared with the 16 Mbps token-ring, of course FDDI data transfer (at 100 Mbps) is much faster. Ring latency is, however, another matter. Propagation speed is much the same.

The delay in a TRN node is around two bits. In an FDDI node the delay will depend on the design of the particular chip set but it is difficult to see how the delay could be less than about 20 bits. This means that an FDDI ring will have a longer latency than a 16 Mbps token-ring of the same size and number of stations.

FDDI follows the same "early token release" discipline as 16 Mbps token-ring but still only one station may transmit at any time.

Token Holding Time (THT) is the critical factor. If THT is relatively short, then a station may only send a small amount of data on any visit of the token. If it is set large then a station may transmit a lot of data. Since it can take a relatively long time for the token to go from one station to another, during which no station may transmit, the longer the THT the greater the data throughput of the ring.

A short THT means that "ring latency" can be relatively short, so that the delay for a station to gain access to the ring is also short. A short THT therefore is suitable for support of real-time applications. If the THT is very short, the system gives better response time but low overall throughput. If it is set very long, then you get a high throughput but a relatively poor response time.

The key tuning parameter is the "Target Token Rotation Time" (TTRT). At ring initialization, all stations on the ring agree to the TTRT (the shortest TTRT requested by any node is adopted). Stations then attempt to meet this target by limiting their transmissions. TTRT is a parameter which may be set by system definition in each node.

Work reported by Raj Jain (referenced in the bibliography) suggests that a value of 8 milliseconds is a good compromise in most situations.

Of course, there may be only one token on the ring at any time and only one station may transmit at any time. In a long ring (a large number of stations and/or a great geographic distance), this represents some wasted potential.

## 13.7 FDDI on Copper Wire (SDDI/CDDI)

The acronym Copper Distributed Data Interface (CDDI) refers to the use of FDDI protocols over a copper-wire medium. SDDI refers to its use over shielded twisted pair (IBM Type 1 cable). Because of the ability to use existing cable, copper can be significantly more cost-effective than a fiber connection (although "not as good").

### 13.7.1 SDDI

In 1992 a group of nine suppliers (one of which was IBM) announced a specification and a series of products for the use of FDDI protocols over installed STP cable plant. Operational equipment implementing this specification first became available in 1992.

There is not much to be said conceptually about SDDI. The FDDI signal is put on the copper wire as a baseband signal *exactly* as it would have been transmitted on a fiber. There is *no* special coding or modulation or modification of the signal. A one bit is signaled as a voltage of between .35 and .7 volts and a zero bit is the absence of voltage.

Transmission distance between workstation and hub (or between two directly connected workstations) is limited to 100 meters.

This is intended for use in the single-ring configuration for the attachment of individual workstations - it is not intended for use as the dual-ring backbone. This is mainly because of the distance limitation.

### 13.7.2 Twisted Pair Physical Medium Dependent (TP-PMD) - UTP-5

This is the official standard for operation over STP or UTP-5. The important aspect of this is that MLT-3 coding is used.

The important characteristics of this operation are illustrated in Figure 13-18.

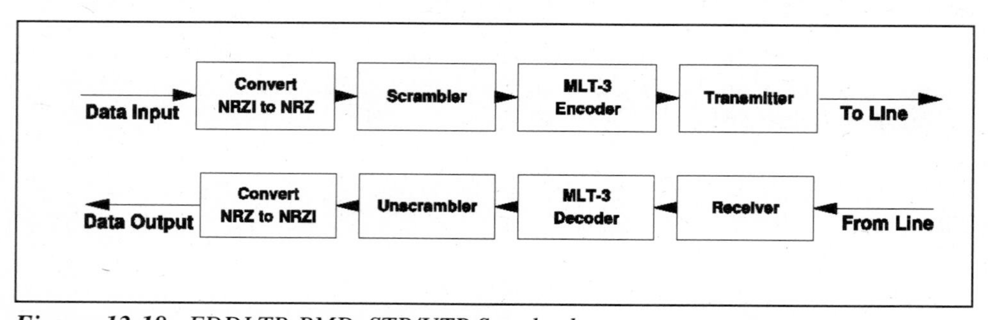


*Figure 13-18. FDDI TP-PMD, STP/UTP Standard*

1. Operation of the fiber-optic FDDI physical layer is *unchanged*. That is, the TP-PMD (Twisted Pair Physical Medium Dependent) function presents data to the FDDI physical layer and receives data from it exactly as if the data were coming-from/going-to a fiber.
2. Figure 13-16 on page 13-42 illustrates the physical layer's operation. The TP-PMD replaces only the detector and transmitter functions leaving everything else the same.
3. In the transmit direction, data is input to the PMD in the top left-hand box of Figure 13-18 on page 13-46. Notice how it was converted to NRZI and how it is immediately converted back to NRZ form.
4. The data is scrambled (randomized) to provide a more uniform transmitted spectrum. Scrambling is discussed in 2.1.17, "Scrambling a.k.a. Enciphering" on page 2-31.
5. The data is now converted to MLT-3 code (see 2.1.15.3, "Multi-Level Transmit - 3 Levels (MLT-3)" on page 2-30) and sent on the outbound link.
6. On the input side the reverse happens, but note that the input is clocked from the speed of the input line and the output is clocked from the local oscillator in the adapter (node).

## 13.7.3 CDDI on UTP-3

FDDI carried over *unshielded* twisted pair (UTP) cable is very important because of the very large amount of installed UTP cable. It is believed that a significant number of users would use FDDI on UTP cable if such a product became available.

Within the technical community (and within the standards community) it is widely accepted that transmission of FDDI protocols over distances of up to 100 meters on UTP is technically possible (there are a number of proposed techniques). There are two problems:

1. It is felt by many that sophisticated coding and signal processing techniques will probably be needed to achieve the objective.
2. Even with advanced techniques there is disagreement over whether the spurious (EMC) emission limit (imposed by law in some countries) can ever be met. Certainly, if these limits can be met without shielding then the cable installation standards will need to be tight and rigorous. (A badly installed STP system can cause excessive EMC.)

These problems can be summarized in one word - cost. The challenge is not so much building a system that will work but in building one that is cost effective.

## 13.8 FDDI-II

FDDI-II is an extension of FDDI that allows the transport of synchronized bit streams, such as traditional (not packetized) digital voice or "transparent" data traffic, across the LAN. This is called "isochronous" traffic.[11]

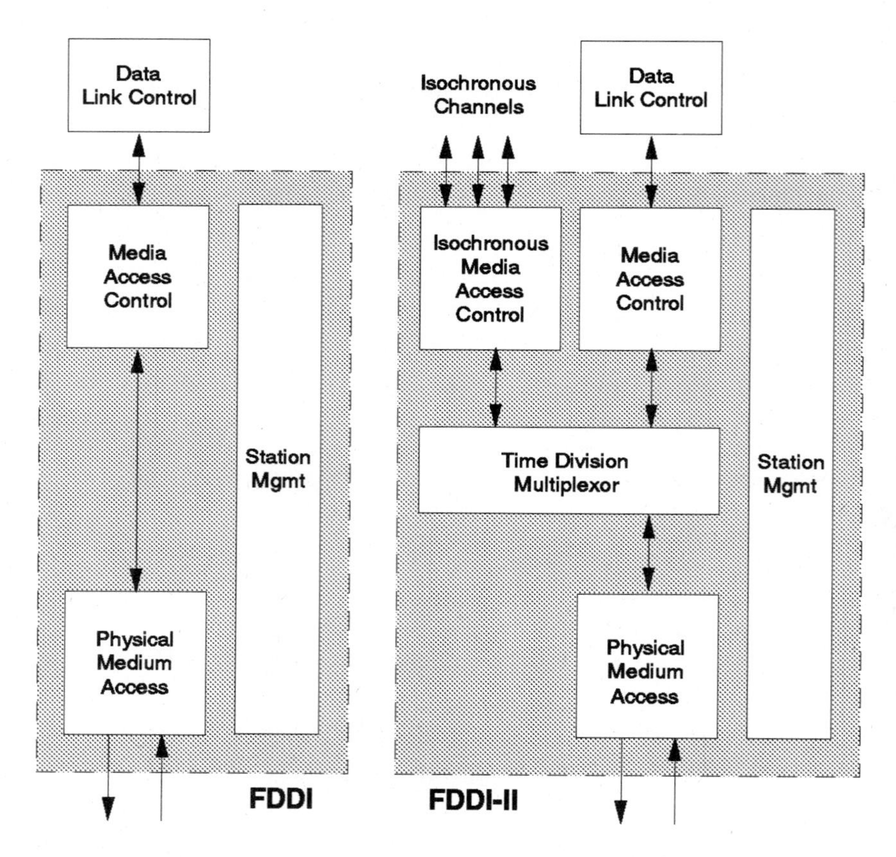


***Figure 13-19.*** *FDDI and FDDI-II Conceptual Structure.* In FDDI-II a time division multiplexor is used to divide the LAN into multiple bit streams. For data transport one of the bit streams is mediated using FDDI access control protocols unchanged.

---

[11] It is very easy to get confused here by the terminology. See Appendix D, "Getting the Language into Synch" on page D-1 for more information on the use of the words "synchronous", "isochronous", etc.

**Note:** The FDDI-II standard is still in the process of development and is not yet formally complete. While it seems unlikely that the broad concepts discussed here will change, anything is possible.

Most varieties of LAN (Ethernet, TRN, etc.) can handle voice traffic if an appropriate technique of buffering and assembly into packets is used. Regular FDDI (1) is the best at this because its timed protocol allows a station to get access at relatively regular intervals. However, these protocols are primarily data protocols and cannot provide transparent carriage for an isochronous bit stream such as unpacketized voice.

The key to understanding FDDI-II is the fact that the FDDI protocols are used *unchanged* but travel within one channel of a time division multiplexed frame. Isochronous traffic (voice, etc.) is handled by the TDM separately from the FDDI data protocol. Looked at from the viewpoint of what happens on the LAN cable itself, FDDI and FDDI-II are utterly different.

Figure 13-19 on page 13-48 shows a highly conceptualized structure of the FDDI and FDDI-II nodes. The difference is that a time division multiplexor has been placed between the FDDI media access control and the physical layer protocol. In addition, there is an "isochronous medium access control" which provides continuous data rate services.

## 13.8.1 Framing

Like most voice-oriented TDM systems (ISDN_P, DQDB, SDH/Sonet, etc.), FDDI-II uses a fixed format frame that is repeated every 125 μsec.[12] Each 125 μsec frame is called a "cycle". At 100 Mbps each cycle contains 1560 bytes plus a preamble. The ring may operate at different speeds but can only change in 6.144 Mbps increments (because of the frame structure).

Each cycle has four components:

**Preamble**

When the frame is sent by the cycle master it is preceded by five idle symbols[13] (20 bits). This is used as a buffer to account for differences in clock speeds between the received data stream and a ring station's transmitter. Subsequent stations may vary the length of the preamble. This principle is discussed more fully in 13.6.5.1, "Ring Synchronization" on page 13-40.

[12] One frame per 125 μsec equals 8000 frames per second. If a single slot is 8 bits then this gives 64 Kbps - the speed of "standard" digitized voice.

[13] Because FDDI-II uses 4/5 code for sending on the link FDDI defines fields in terms of 4-bit "symbols".

### Cycle Header

The cycle header is 12 bytes long and consists of the following fields:

- Starting Delimiter (8 bits)
- Synchronization Control (4 bits)
- Sequence Control - C2 (4 bits)

  When the ring is operating in hybrid mode every 125 μsec cycle carries a sequence number. The sequence control field indicates whether the sequence number field is valid or not.

- Cycle Sequence - CS (8 bits)

  This is just the sequence number of this cycle. During initialization, the field is used for other purposes.

- Programming Template (64 bits - 16 symbols)

  Each 4-bit symbol in the programming template corresponds to one wideband channel. Only two states are valid. One state indicates that the corresponding wideband channel is used for packet data, and the other state indicates that this WBC is in use for isochronous traffic.

- Isochronous Maintenance Channel (8 bits)

  This is a single 64 Kbps isochronous channel which is available for maintenance purposes.

### Dedicated Packet Group

Twelve bytes in each cycle are concatenated to form a single 768KB channel. This is to ensure that even if all the wideband channels are in use for isochronous traffic then there will still be some remaining capacity for data packets.

### Wideband Channels (WBC)

At 100 Mbps there are 16 wideband channels, each carrying 96 bytes in each cycle. This means that each wideband channel has an aggregate data rate of 6.144 Mbps (96 × 64 Kbps). This is the same rate as a “T2” channel in the US digital TDM hierarchy.

Each WBC may be allocated to either packet data or isochronous service. A WBC must be wholly dedicated to either mode of operation.

The WBCs and the DPG are byte interleaved with one another within the frame.

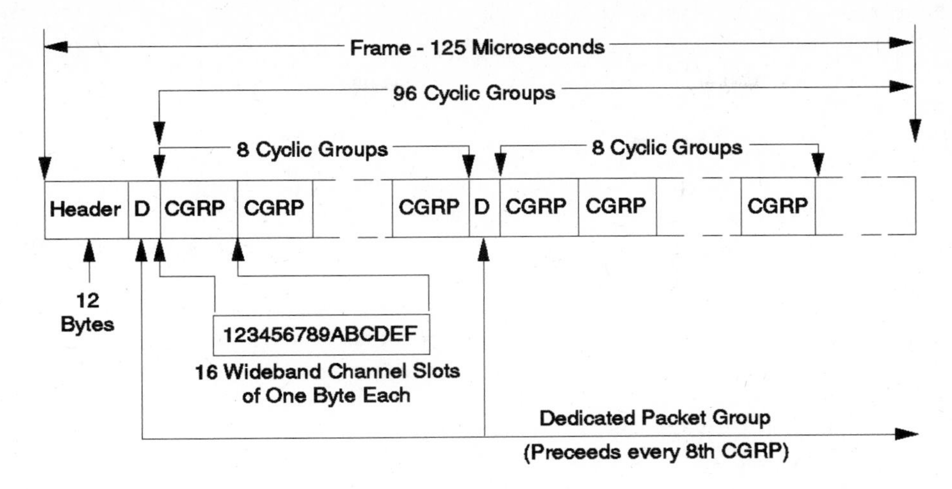


*Figure 13-20. FDDI-II TDM Frame Structure*

There is only one packet data channel. When one or more wideband channels are allocated to packet data they are concatenated with each other and with the dedicated packet group to form a single continuous bit stream. This continuous bit stream is recovered and reconstructed at every node. The FDDI protocol is used to operate this channel exactly as if it were the only bit stream on an ordinary FDDI ring. Figure 13-21 shows the packet data channel as it exists within the TDM frame. In the example four WBCs (labeled C to F) are concatenated with the DPG to form a single contiguous "clear channel".

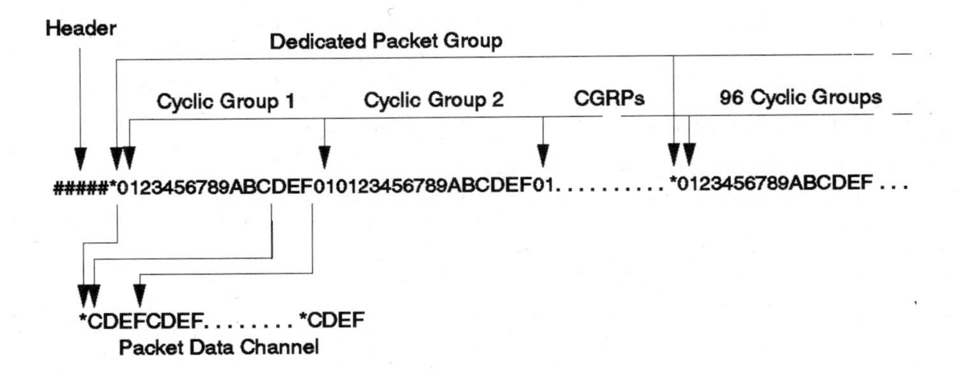


***Figure 13-21.** Derivation of Packet Data Channel from the TDM Frame.* In this example WBCs 12 to 15 (labelled C, D, E and F) are concatenated with the DPG to form the packet data channel.

Notice that each DPG contains a single byte from each WBC. So there are 96 DPGs in each frame. Because the frame rate is 8000 per second (frame is 125 μsec long), each byte represents a rate of 64 Kbps.

### 13.8.2 Cycle Master

In hybrid mode a station called the "cycle master" generates 125 μsec frames (called cycles), assures cycle integrity, and contains a latency adjustment buffer to ensure that there is always an integral multiple of cycles on the ring. A cycle master is an FDDI monitor station (and therefore it must be connected to both rings and it must contain the FDDI Monitor function) with the additional capability of generating, controlling and handling errors for the TDM mode of operation. It is not necessary for every ring station in an FDDI ring to be capable of being a monitor or a cycle master. However, for the ring to operate in hybrid mode (FDDI-II mode), every connected station must be capable of FDDI-II operation (handling the TDM frame structure). Isochronous bandwidth allocation is performed through the interaction of three logical processes.

**Synchronous Bandwidth Allocator (SBA)**

This is a function associated with the cycle master. It controls the partitioning of the TDM frames between synchronous and isochronous operation. There is one (active) SBA per FDDI-II ring.

**Wideband Channel Allocator**

This function allocates wideband channels, *not* to stations, but to channel allocators. There is only one active WBC allocator per ring (of course, normally located within the cycle master).

**Channel Allocator**

The channel allocator administers the allocation of channels to workstations. There may be more than one channel allocator in an FDDI-II ring.[14] This is to allow disjoint subsets of workstations (or functions) to have their bandwidth managed independently. However, in many implementations, it is expected that there will be only one channel allocator and it will also reside within the cycle master.

Channels are allocated to stations in groups of between 1 and 96. Channel allocators are given capacity by the WBC allocator, one WBC (96 channels) at a time.

---

[14] This is the reason we need the two functions of channel allocator and wideband channel allocator.

## 13.8.3 Operation

### Initialization

The FDDI-II ring is initialized in "basic mode". Basic mode is the name given in FDDI-II for regular FDDI. This is used to set up the timers and parameters for the FDDI data protocol.

If every active station is capable of operating in "hybrid mode" then after initialization, the ring may switch its operation to this mode. In hybrid mode the "cycle master" station creates and administers the TDM structure thus making the isochronous circuit-switched service available.

### Isochronous Bandwidth Allocation

The cycle master station may change the channel allocations (change a WBC from isochronous operation to packet mode or vice versa) at almost any time.

In order to change modes without disrupting anything, the cycle master waits until it has the token. This means that no data traffic is using the WBCs. The cycle master then changes the programming template in the cycle header to reflect the new status. Stations inspect the cycle header in each cycle to demultiplex the contents of that cycle, so the allocations change in the very next cycle.

### Allocating Isochronous Bandwidth to a Station

When a station wants to set up an isochronous circuit, its management function sends a request to a channel allocator. Operation takes place as follows:

1. The requesting station sends a control message (as a normal FDDI frame) to its associated channel allocator. This request contains the number of channels (64-Kbps slots) required as well as a minimum number of channels that would be acceptable if the full number cannot be allocated.

2. The channel allocator evaluates the request in relation to its allocation rules and decides if the station should be granted the channels.

3. The channel allocator then looks to see whether it has sufficient available channels within any of the WBCs currently allocated to it. If capacity is available (and if the request is legal) then the allocation will be made and a message sent to the requesting station granting the channels.

4. If the channel allocator does not have enough capacity available to satisfy the request, it may make a request to the WBC allocator for another WBC.

5. This request may (or may not) result in a request by the WBC allocator to the SBA to gain more isochronous capacity. (The SBA monitors the synchronous operation and will not allocate additional isochronous capacity if the synchronous channel is utilized more than a specified amount.)

When bandwidth is allocated to a station, it is the station's responsibility to notify the other stations with which it plans to communicate using the newly available isochronous channels. Station-to-station protocols using the isochronous capability are the responsibility of the stations themselves.

**Communication between Ring Stations and the Cycle Master**

Ring stations exchange control messages with the cycle master, the channel allocator, and with each other by sending packets on the packet data channel. (Hence the need for the dedicated packet group to allow some packet communication even if all the WBC capacity is allocated to isochronous traffic.)

This capability is used, for example, in the setup of an isochronous channel.

**Isochronous Data Transfer**

The cycle master may allocate part (or all) of a WBC in units of a single byte slot for use by a station.

Once capacity is allocated by the cycle master, it is the responsibility of the requesting station (and the destination station) to agree on how this capacity will be used.

**Error Processing**

Error handling for the TDM frame structure as well as for the packet channel is handled by the cycle master.

## 13.8.4 FDDI-II Gateways

Many people in the industry believe that the primary function of FDDI-II is to allow for multimedia communications. (See 6.5.2, "The Isochronous Debate" on page 6-21.) To do this you need a gateway function to connect the FDDI-II ring to wide area (ISDN, T1, E1, etc.) services. The objective is to provide isochronous connection from a workstation on an FDDI-II LAN in one location to another workstation (which may or may not be connected to FDDI-II) in a remote location.

However, an FDDI-II application could be a lot wider than multimedia. It could also be used as a transport for point-to-point T1 or E1 type connections. This raises the possibility of using FDDI-II as a private MAN. In some countries, "dark fiber" can be used over short distances (a few kilometers) without involving the PTT. Data and voice connections could be shared on the same FDDI-II LAN, thus avoiding the need for multiple cables. This would apply to any large campus area but especially in places where it is difficult or costly to lay multiple cables.

The operation of a gateway through ISDN primary rate at any isochronous speed in excess of a single 64 Kbps channel is a technical challenge. While T1, E1, and FDDI-II keep groups of 64 Kbps channels together and allow them to be used as a single wideband channel, ISDN does not. When WAN connection is through ISDN, you need some means of synchronizing data transfer on multiple channels if you want to construct channels of bandwidth greater than 64 Kbps (such as 384 Kbps).

It should be pointed out that as yet there is no standard available for the operation of FDDI-II to ISDN or FDDI-II to T1/E1 gateways.

## 13.9 DQDB/SMDS - Distributed Queue Dual Bus

DQDB protocol is the basis for the internal operation of a number of metropolitan area networks (MANs) currently being installed in many countries. It is also the basis of a proposed US standard for user access to a MAN called SMDS.

The DQDB protocol was designed to handle both isochronous (constant rate, voice) traffic and data traffic over a very high-speed optical link.

### 13.9.1 A Protocol by Any Other Name...

DQDB is also known by several different names and each has a different connotation.

**QPSX**

When the protocol was invented (by two people at the University of Western Australia) it was named QPSX (Queued Packed Synchronous eXchange). Later when a company was set up to build equipment based on the protocol, that company was called "QPSX Communications".

**DQDB**

Because the company was called QPSX, the name of the protocol was then changed to "DQDB" to avoid confusion with the company name.

**IEEE 802.6 MAN Subnetwork**

This protocol was accepted in 1990 by the Institute of Electrical and Electronic Engineers (IEEE) as a standard for metropolitan area subnetworks and numbered IEEE 802.6.

**SMDS**

"Switched Multi-Megabit Data Service" is the name given to the service based on DQDB in the United States. DQDB is used as an *access protocol* for a high-speed packet network. Minor changes were made to the IEEE 802.6 recommendation to enable it to fulfill this role.

It should be noted that networks using SMDS as their access protocol are not constrained to use 802.6 internally. Some networks will but others may work quite differently.

**CBDS**

Connectionless Broadband Data Service is the service name given to networks using QPSX equipment in Europe.

**Fastpac**

Fastpac is the service name given to the network service by Telecom Australia, which is implementing the first fully commercial (tariffed) network to use the QPSX technology in the world.

### 13.9.2 Concept

A DQDB MAN is in many ways just like any other LAN. A number of stations (nodes) are connected to a common medium which allows data to be sent from one node to another. Because of the use of a shared medium, there must be an access protocol to control when a node is allowed access.

Data is transmitted in short "segments" (cells) of 48 data bytes.[15]

Different from most LANs, it is intended for operation over a wide geographic area and at bit rates of up to 155 Mbps. Another difference from many LANs is that it is also designed to handle isochronous (for example, non-packetized voice) traffic.

### 13.9.3 Structure

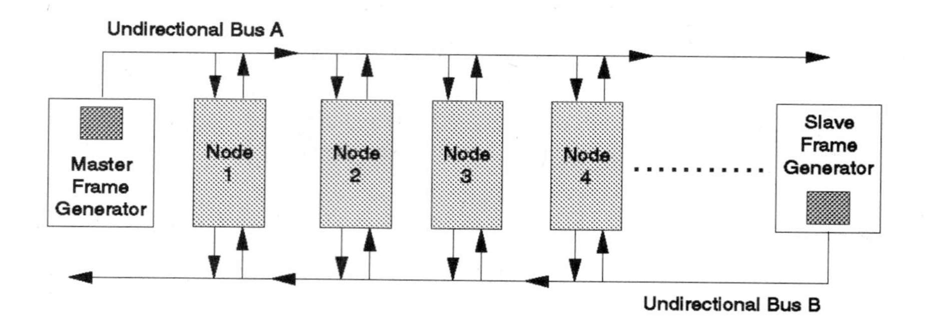


*Figure 13-22. DQDB Bus Structure*

- As shown in Figure 13-22 a DQDB network consists of two buses denoted by Bus A and Bus B in the figure.
- The two buses transport data in opposite directions.

---

[15] Notice this is the same length as for Asynchronous Transfer Mode (ATM).

- At the head end of each bus a slot generator creates a timed signal and formats it into 53-byte slots. The slot format is shown in Figure 13-23 on page 13-57.
- Each node is connected to *both* buses.
- When a node wants to transmit data, it does so into the first available empty slot traveling in the desired direction. Slot availability is determined by the Medium Access Control protocol, which all nodes must obey.

  The node must know the relative location (upstream/downstream) of the other connected nodes so that it can determine on which bus to send the data. In Figure 13-22 on page 13-56, if node 2 wants to transmit data to node 4 then it must use bus A. To send data to node 1 it would use bus B.
- Data is never removed from the bus. The buses are terminated electrically and slots "drop off the end".
- There is no scheme for reuse of slots after data has been copied from them. For example if node 1 sends data to node 2 on bus A, then potentially the slot could be reused by node 3 to send to node 4. This is not possible in DQDB at the present time.[16]

The framing structure is shown in Figure 13-23.

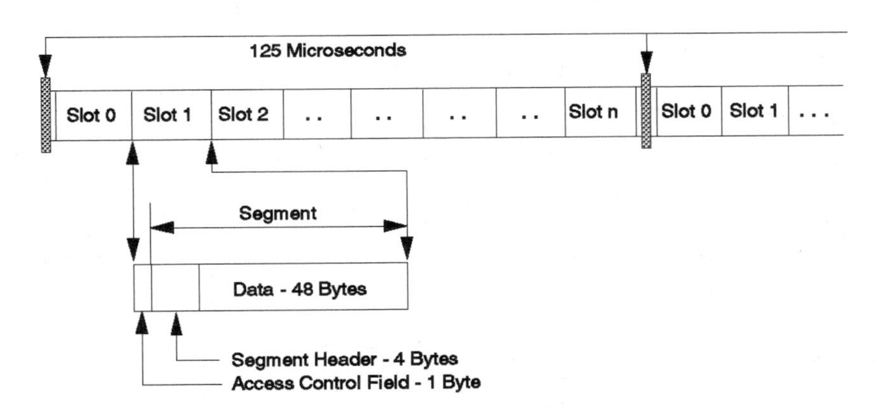


*Figure 13-23. DQDB Frame Format as Seen by the DQDB Protocol Layer.* Not shown is a 4-byte slot prefix used by the physical layer.

At the physical layer, preceding each slot there is a 4-byte field consisting of a 2-byte slot delimiter and 2 bytes of control information, which are used by the layer management

[16] An enhancement aimed at developing an "eraser node" which could allow slot reuse is under consideration by the IEEE 802.6 committee.

protocol. The slots are maintained within a 125 μsec frame structure so that isochronous services can be provided.

There are two types of slots:

**Pre-Arbitrated (PA) Slots**

These slots are assigned to a specific node by the frame generator. Thus they are called "Pre-Arbitrated". The frame generator will generate these at specified rates (for example one every 125 μsec) for use by isochronous traffic. They are ignored by the distributed queue medium access procedure.

The number and timing of these slots is variable depending on how much isochronous traffic is being carried. Remaining capacity is formatted as Queued Arbitrated (QA) slots.

**Queued Arbitrated (QA) Slots**

These slots carry normal data traffic and are allocated through the "distributed queue" MAC procedure. (In FDDI terminology this is asynchronous data traffic - DQDB does not handle synchronous traffic in the FDDI sense.)

### 13.9.4 Medium Access Control

In light load situations, or in situations where each node is unable to transmit at a rate close to that of the bus, a strategy that says "send data into the next available slot" could work quite well. In the real world a system like that would not be practical because a single upstream node (close to the frame generator) could take 100% of the bus capacity, leaving downstream nodes unable to gain access for any purpose. A means is needed to control when a node is allowed to send. This is the heart of the DQDB system. *Each node keeps track of as much of the global queue as it needs to determine its position in that queue.*[17]

The protocol works in the following way:

The protocol is full-duplex and it is also symmetric. Node access to Bus A is arbitrated (controlled) by requests flowing on Bus B. Node access to Bus B is arbitrated by requests flowing on Bus A. Both processes happen simultaneously and operate completely independently from one another.

**Considering only Bus A:**

- When a node has nothing to send, it monitors the bus to keep track of the queue of data waiting.

[17] See 13.1.2, "Access Control" on page 13-4 for an explanation of the notion of a global queue.

This is done by counting requests for slots from downstream nodes (requests flow on Bus B) and cancelling a request every time an empty slot (that would satisfy a request) passes by (on Bus A).

- If some data arrives to be sent, the node looks to see if any other node (downstream of itself) has requested, but not yet received, a slot. (How it does this will be discussed in a moment.)
- The node sends a request on Bus B to tell nodes upstream of itself that it needs a slot.
- If there are no requests pending from nodes downstream of itself, the node may send into the next empty slot that arrives on Bus A.
- If there were already pending requests from downstream, it monitors Bus A and allows sufficient empty slots to pass to fulfill all of the pending requests from downstream nodes.
- When all the requests for slots that were pending when data arrived have been satisfied, then the node is allowed to send into the next empty slot.
- Now, the node probably wants to send again and hence must have kept track of what happened on the bus while it was waiting to send the previous segment.

  A node is not allowed to make multiple requests (not allowed to have more than one request outstanding at any time).

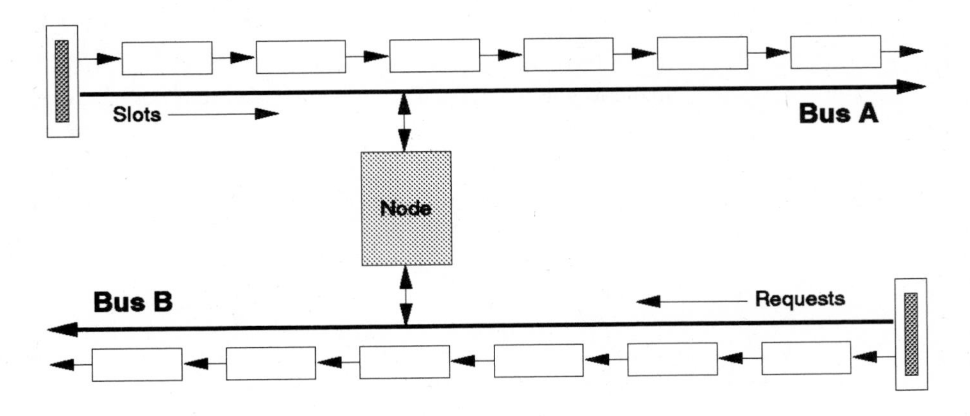


*Figure 13-24. DQDB Medium Access Principle*

To make this work, the node keeps two counters (for each bus independently).

### Request Counter

When the node has nothing to send, it monitors the bus.

- The request counter for Bus A is incremented (increased by one) every time a slot passes by on Bus B with the request bit set.
- The request counter is decremented (decreased by one) every time an empty slot passes by on Bus A.
- The request counter is *never* decremented below zero.

In this way a node knows at any instant in time, the number of pending downstream requests for slots.

### Waiting Counter

When the node wants to send and there are pending downstream requests, it must wait until sufficient empty slots have passed by to satisfy all pending downstream requests. To do this it keeps a Waiting Counter.

When the node wants to send, it:

- Copies the request count into the waiting counter.
- Sends a request upstream by setting the request bit in the next available slot on Bus B (provided it is not already set).

The request counter continues to operate normally.[18] As empty slots pass on Bus A, now both request and waiting counters are decremented as empty slots pass.

When the waiting counter reaches zero, the node may send into the next empty slot. Notice now that the request counter still contains an accurate status of requests queued from downstream.

This is ingenious. Each individual node does not (and cannot) know the true status of the global queue. All it knows is the state of requests from itself and from nodes downstream of itself. Yet, the total system will allocate slots in the exact order in which they were placed.

What the node really does is to keep track of its position in the order of requests from itself and from nodes downstream of itself on the bus.

It must be emphasized that the protocol operates separately and independently for each direction of data traffic on the buses. Thus there are two sets of counters operating completely independently for each direction of data transfer.

---

[18] The description here is conceptual. In reality the counters operate slightly differently from the way described but the net effect is the same.

This protocol when operated by all nodes on a DQDB MAN allows:

- Access in time order of access requests. Notice that this applies each time a cell (the 48-byte data part of a slot) is to be sent. A node cannot request more than one slot at a time. Once it makes a request, it must wait until that request is satisfied before it is allowed to make another request.
- Each node knows enough about the status of the global queue for the access to be functionally equivalent to the operation of a centralized queue.

#### 13.9.4.1 Priorities

There are four priorities defined in DQDB. To implement this there are three request bits in a cell header. What happens is that each node must keep three request counters. A passing slot decrements the highest priority non-zero counter. A passing request increments the request counter for the corresponding priority level *and the request counters of all lower priority levels.* High priority traffic is always sent before traffic of lower priority.[19]

### 13.9.5 Node Attachment to the Buses

In most descriptions of "QPSX protocol" or of DQDB, a diagram similar to Figure 13-25 is included.

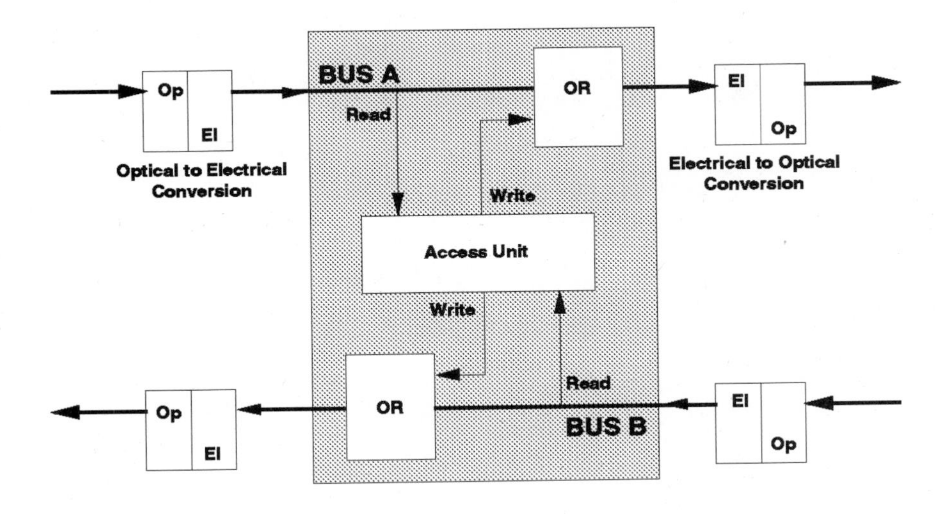


***Figure 13-25.** DQDB Node Conceptual Operation*

[19] In detail there are some problems with priorities. In the presence of "bandwidth balancing" priorities don't work and in any case, the need for priorities in this environment is questionable.

The node is described as being "external" to the buses. That is, data "passes by" the node and the node writes into empty slots using an OR function. (Slots are preformatted to all zeros and when data is written to them it is done by ORing the data onto the empty slot.) It is said that this gives better fault isolation than token-rings because node failures that don't result in a continuous write operation will not affect the operation of the bus.

This should be regarded as an objective rather than an achievement. The current state of technology makes an "OR" write to an optical bus almost impossible. The optical signal must be converted to electrical form and then decoded. Of course if power to this function is lost (or if the circuits malfunction) then the bus will fail.

A simplified node structure is shown in Figure 13-26.

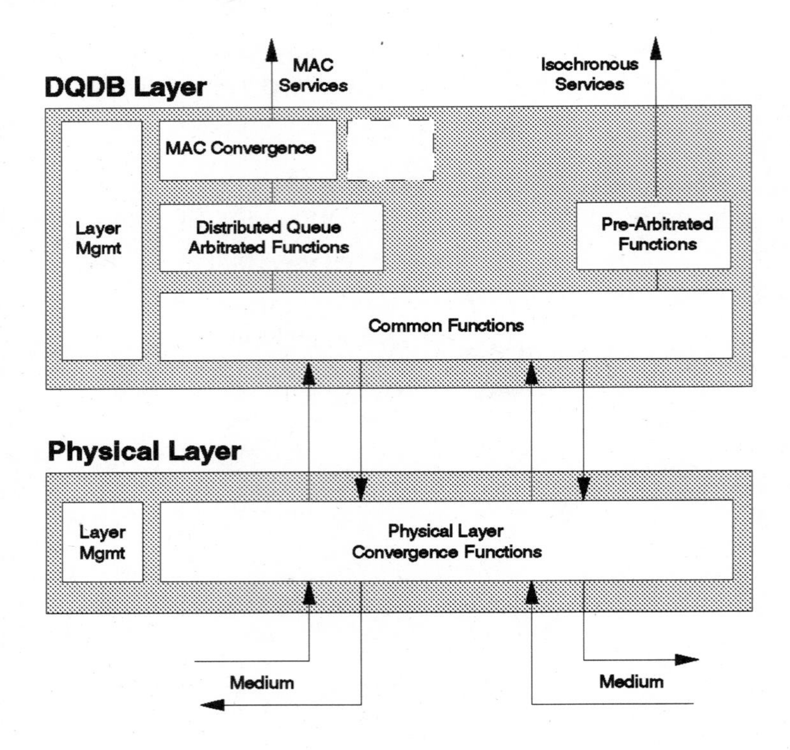


*Figure 13-26. DQDB Physical Convergence Layer*

This structure is one of the best features of DQDB. The definition allows the use of many different physical connection mechanisms and specifies rigorously the boundary between the DQDB protocol layer and the physical medium dependent layer.

Figure 13-26, which shows the OR writing to the bus, really shows the *interface* between the DQDB layer and the physical convergence layer. The physical convergence layer is different for each supported medium. Media defined so far include:

- Fiber connection at 35 and 34 Mbps
- Sonet connection at 45 Mbps
- Fiber connection at 155 Mbps
- Copper connections at T1 (1.544 Mbps) and E1 (2 Mbps) are under study.

The line codes used are different depending on the medium. For example, on optical media DQDB will use an 8B/10B code similar in principle to the 4B/5B code used in FDDI. (See 13.6.5.2, "Data Encoding" on page 13-41.) On a copper medium, a different code is used.

Also, the exact node structure with respect to link connection may be different for different media. On optical media, a node structure similar to FDDI will be used (see Figure 13-16 on page 13-42). Links between nodes are asynchronous with respect to each other. An elastic buffer is used in the node to accommodate speed differences.

On copper media, a synchronous operation of the bus (similar to token-ring) is used.

## 13.9.6 The Great Fairness Controversy

DQDB has been associated with considerable controversy due to the assertion by some people that the heart of DQDB, the media access protocol, doesn't work. Or more accurately, that DQDB doesn't provide fairness as claimed under heavy load situations.

The problem is propagation delay, not the amount of time it takes for a slot (carrying a request or data) to pass from node to node along the bus. In Figure 13-27, consider the extreme condition where propagation delay consists of five slot times between Node A and Node B.

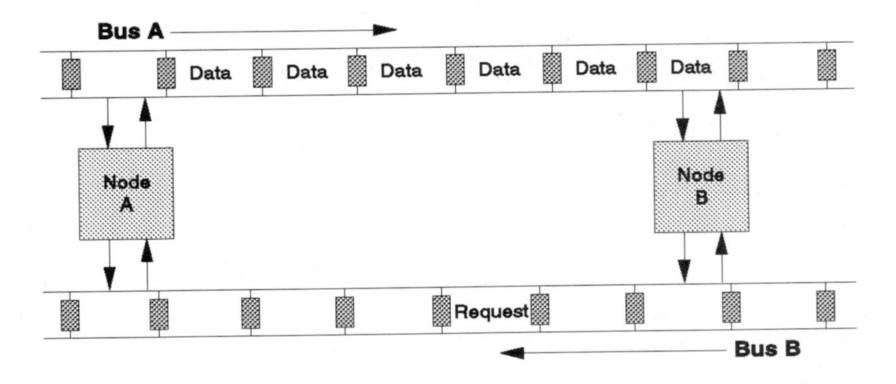


***Figure 13-27.** DQDB Fairness.* Problem is propagation delay along the bus.

- If Node A has a lot of data to send, then it may send immediately provided there are no outstanding requests.
- Let us assume that this is the case and Node A wants to send at full rate.
- Now Node B wants to send. It queues the first segment for sending and sends a request upstream. (Nodes always send a request even when the request counter is zero.)
- Node A continues to send until the request from Node B reaches it.
- When the request reaches Node A, it will dutifully allow the next slot on Bus A to pass in order to satisfy the request.
- Then Node A will continue to send into every available slot on Bus A.
- When the empty slot arrives at Node B, it will use the slot and send some data.
- Typically, Node B will then want to send another segment of data.
- To do this it must place another request.

Notice the effect: Node A is able to send 10 segments of data for every one segment that Node B can send! This is because it takes 10 segment times after Node B sends a request for a free slot to reach it.

At a transmission rate of 155 Mbps a single slot is 536 meters long! So the situation described above can be reached with a bus length of less than three kilometers. *There are many ways of describing this situation but "fair" is not one of them.*

#### 13.9.6.1 Bandwidth Balancing

The way of providing fairness is called "Bandwidth Balancing". (The problem is, objectively, not as bad as it sounds.) In bandwidth balancing, a node that is sending must allow an empty slot (that doesn't have a matching request) to pass unused at defined intervals (in fact, quite a low rate). This is done by the node entering a dummy request into its request counter for every n (specified parameter) segments it sends.

This has a much greater effect than might be thought at first. In the example above, while the situation described is happening, Node A lets another free slot pass. Node B will get a free slot, "think" it was the result of its last request, send a segment and another request. Thus Node B now has two requests in transit between itself and Node A. If/when another slot is released there will be three. What is happening is that the small number of free slots let pass by Node A satisfy requests which then generate more requests.

This solves the problem of throughput unfairness reasonably well but:

1. Bandwidth balancing does *not* work in the presence of priorities.

2. There is a relatively long "convergence time". That is, it takes some time for the node lower down the bus to get enough free slots to get to the point where the DQDB algorithm is operating as intended. This means that there is still some unfairness in the access delay.

In practical systems, at least for the moment, the nodes will not be fast enough to use every available slot anyway, so bandwidth balancing will be unnecessary in early systems.

### 13.9.7 Data Segmentation

Because data in the DQDB system is sent as very short cells (48 bytes), data blocks, which may be of any length up to about 9 KB[20], must be segmented to fit into slots.

In order to send a data block there must be a header containing, as a minimum, the origin and destination node addresses. (DQDB allows the use of either 48-bit LAN addresses - compatible with other IEEE LAN protocols, or 60-bit ISDN compatible addressing.) Of course other information is needed in the header in addition to just the addresses. A trailer containing an FCS (Frame Check Sequence field) is highly desirable.

Consider Figure 13-28. Segments are placed into cells and sent on the bus. But how can a receiver decide which ones are intended for it? The first segment of a data block has the destination node address inside it. So a receiver only has to monitor for cells containing its address to determine which cells should be received. But what about all the rest of the cells in the data block? There is no header and thus no destination LAN address.

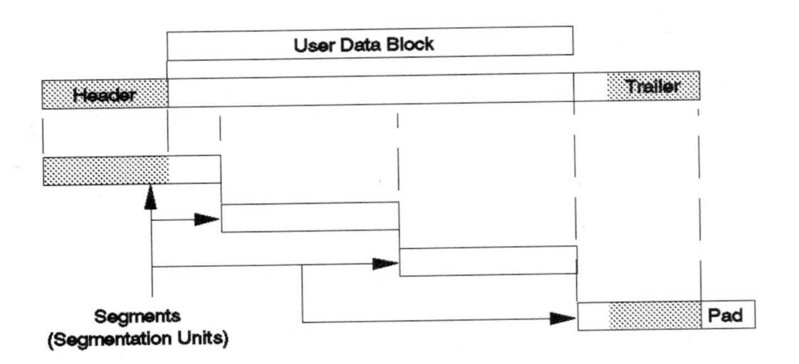


*Figure 13-28. Segmentation of a Data Block to Fit into a Slot (Cell)*

20 The currently defined maximum data block length is 9188 bytes.

Here is another unique aspect of DQDB. DQDB (like most LANs) is a "connectionless" system (see 6.6, "Connection-Oriented versus Connectionless Networks" on page 6-23) but a "connection" is established between the sending node and the receiving node for the duration of each data block. As shown in Figure 13-23 on page 13-57 the cell format contains a 5-byte header in front of the 48-byte data field. Within that header there is a 20-bit Virtual Channel Identifier (VCI) field. This VCI field is used to identify segments (after the first) of each data message.

- Each node continuously monitors passing slots for slots marked "beginning of block" containing its node address.
- When such a slot arrives, the receiving node records the VCI in that slot.
- From this point on, it will monitor passing slots and receive all those that contain a matching VCI until one is received with an end of data indication in the header.

VCIs are reused by sending nodes. Each VCI only has meaning within an individual data block, so each sending node would strictly only need one VCI. In practice, each node is allocated a few (about 4) VCIs which are cyclically reused.

There is a problem here that is not present in other LAN protocols. The node receives a block in multiple segments. What if two nodes decide to send a block of data to the same receiving node simultaneously? Segments belonging to multiple user data blocks will be received mixed up with one another. To handle this each node must have multiple receive buffers capable of holding the maximum size user data block. The receiver must be implemented in such a way as to allow multiple blocks to be reassembled simultaneously.

## 13.9.8 Cells, Slots and Segments

The following diagram summarizes the structure of a slot.

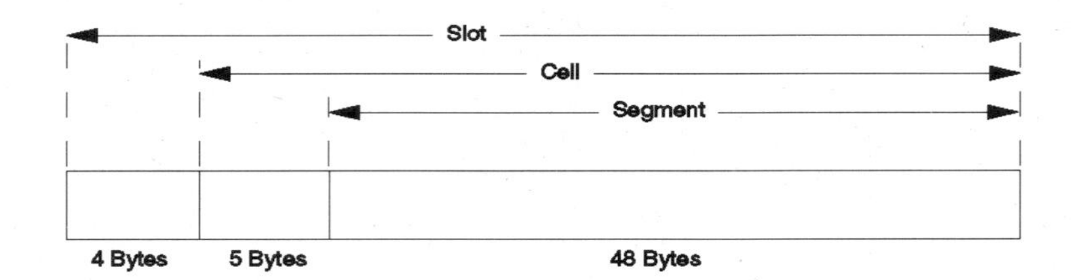


*Figure 13-29. Slot Format*

A slot is actually 57 bytes long. The slot header contains physical synchronization and maintenance information and may be different depending on the particular physical medium used.

## 13.9.9 Isochronous Service

Isochronous data must be delivered at a constant rate. Voice communication (unpacketized voice) is a typical example of isochronous service. This can also apply to digitized video of the kind that yields a continuous bit stream rather than being built into packets.

The above description related to DQDB protocol operation has nothing whatever to do with isochronous service. As mentioned earlier, there are two kinds of slots:

1. Queued Arbitrated (QA) slots
2. Pre-Arbitrated (PA) slots

Queued Arbitrated slots are managed by the DQDB protocol.

Pre-Arbitrated slots are allocated by the head of bus function (node containing the frame generator) at predetermined fixed time intervals (typically once every 125 μsec). Preformatted slots containing a flag to say they are pre-arbitrated are created by the frame generator. They are identified by the VCI (Virtual Channel Identifier) number in the slot header. Because a slot contains 48 usable bytes (every 125 μsec) a single slot identified by a single VCI gives 48, 64 Kbps channels (the same as two US T1 circuits).

Nodes may use preallocated slots in any desired way. For example, single bytes may be used to carry single voice channels, or a group of 32 contiguous bytes may be used to carry a 2 Mbps clear channel link.

Precisely how the PA capability should be used is *not* defined by the IEEE 802.6 specification.

## 13.9.10 Fault Tolerance

The primary method of recovery from link failure in a DQDB system is provided by the ability to loop the buses, as shown in Figure 13-30.

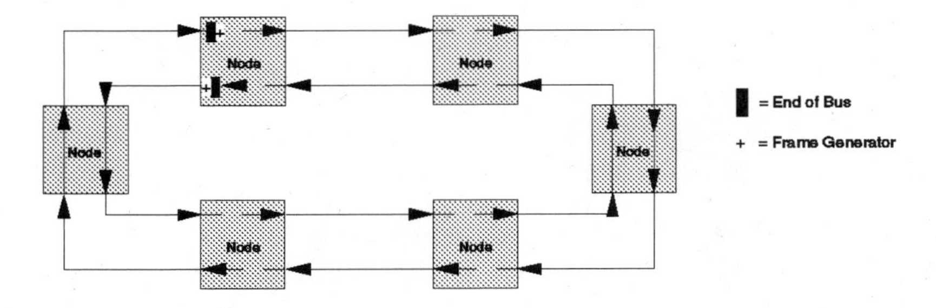


***Figure 13-30.*** *DQDB Looped Bus Configuration.* In this configuration one node doubles as the slot generator and the buses are looped into a ring configuration.

The network topology is still a dual bus but it is configured as a ring. All of the nodes are capable of being the frame generator.

Figure 13-31 shows what happens when the ring is physically broken. The original frame generator node ceases the role of frame generator and the two nodes on either side of the break in the ring take up the frame generator role.

This allows the reconfigured system to operate at full throughput regardless of the break in the ring. Other dual ring systems (such as FDDI) fall back to half capacity when there is a break in the ring - or (again like FDDI) keep a spare unused.

In addition, the "OR-WRITE" mode of attachment to the bus isolates the bus from a large proportion of potential node malfunctions.

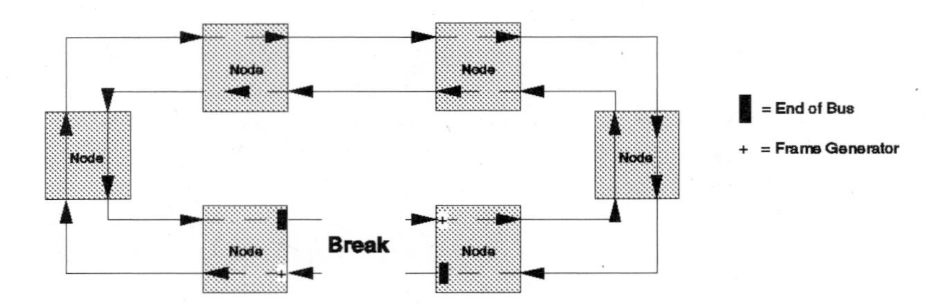


*Figure 13-31. DQDB Reconfiguration.* Each node is able to be a slot generator. Here, the bus has been broken and the two nearest nodes have taken over the role of head of bus.

## 13.9.11 Metropolitan Area Networks (MANs)

A Metropolitan Area Network is a new type of public network which will be provided by telecommunications carriers in various countries. The IEEE has named their standard 802.6 "Metropolitan Area Sub-Network". Thus DQDB is the IEEE protocol standard for metropolitan area networks.

In some ways, a MAN is just like a big LAN - that is, a LAN covering a large geographic area but there is a critical difference: *A user device must never interface directly to the MAN.* That is, the MAN must *never* pass through end user premises. The reason is obvious: data on the MAN belongs to many different organizations and (even with security precautions such as encryption) most users are not willing to have their data pass through a competitor's building. Thus, nodes which access the MAN are always on telephone company (PTT) premises. End users are connected through "access" nodes on point-to-point links.

From a user perspective the MAN is just a fast cell-switching network. The fact that a LAN-type of structure is used by the PTT is irrelevant to the user provided that the user interface stays the same.

An operational MAN is built as a series of interlinked subnetworks as shown in Figure 13-32. Interlinking between subnetworks (either locally or over remote point-to-point connections), is performed by bridges. End users (subscribers) are connected to the MAN through access nodes (gateways) over point-to-point links.

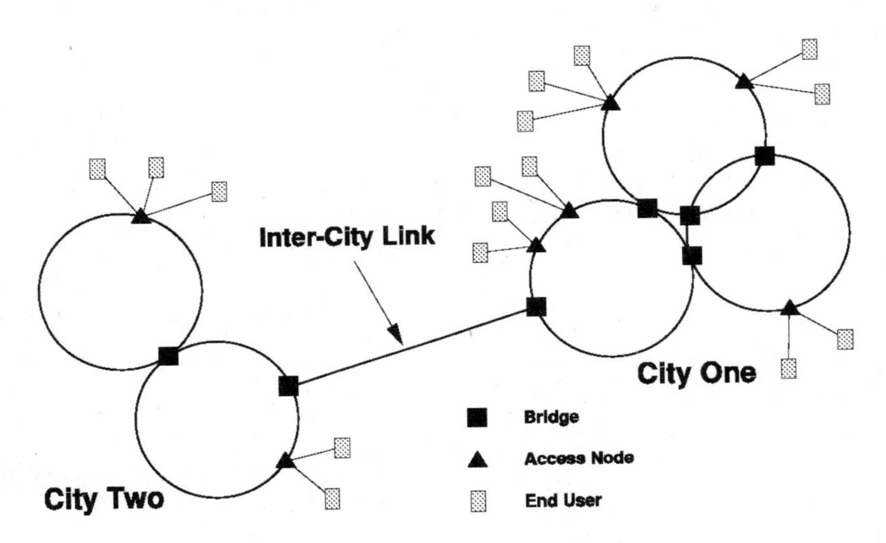


*Figure 13-32. Configuration of a Metropolitan Area Network*

Services offered by the MAN to the subscriber are the same as those offered by a LAN - although they are implemented in quite a different way.

**Send Data**

The subscriber may send data to any other subscriber anywhere on the MAN. Since other subscribers may not want to receive data from anywhere, the access nodes must provide a filter to prevent the reception of unwanted messages.

**Closed User Groups**

Each subscriber address may be a member of one or more closed user groups. A closed user group is just a filter that allows free communication within members of the group (a list of addresses) but prevents communication with addresses that are not in the group (except where specifically allowed).

**Broadcast**

Each subscriber may send a broadcast message (indeed some protocols require this ability for correct functioning). However, it would be very dangerous for a subscriber to be able to broadcast to every address on the MAN. This must be prevented. To do this means that the true "broadcast" function of the DQDB protocol cannot be accessed (even indirectly) by a subscriber.

What actually happens is that the subscriber equipment sends a broadcast message to the access node and this node replicates the message and sends a copy to each member of the appropriate closed user group. That is, although the user sends a "broadcast" it is treated by the network as a number of separate messages.

As will be seen in 13.9.11.3, "Switched Multi-Megabit Data Service (SMDS)" on page 13-74, the protocol used between the MAN and the subscriber is DQDB itself. This means that the access nodes are really a type of bridge with an active filtering function built in. Access nodes also have network management and accounting (billing) functions.

In the first MAN trial networks, the link to the end user is either T3 (45 Mbps) or E3 (35 Mbps) on fiber or T1 (1.544 Mbps) or E1 (2 Mbps) on copper. The inter-city links are either T3/E3 or 140 Mbps single-mode fiber.

### 13.9.11.1 MAN Subscriber (End-User) Interface

Figure 13-33 illustrates the end-user connection as it is foreseen in many countries. The service provided (at least initially) in many countries is the wide area interconnection of LANs.

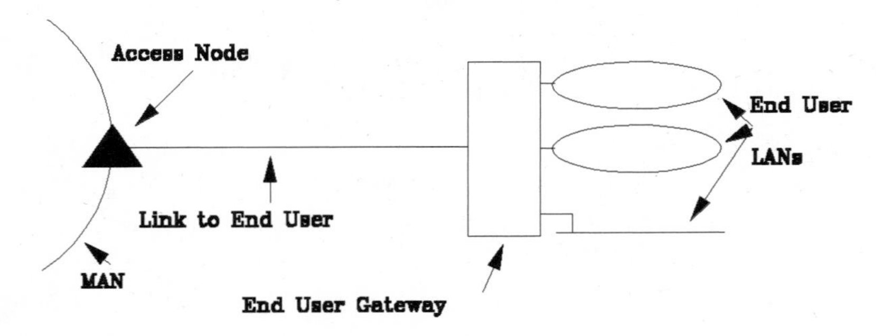


***Figure 13-33.*** *End-User Access to an IEEE 802.6 MAN*

In the US, the connection between the end user and the network is the "link to end user" as shown in Figure 13-33. This link will use the SMDS protocol and the customer (user) may purchase the end-user gateway equipment from any supplier.

Outside of the US (at least in some countries) the network supplier (PTT, telephone company) will supply the end-user gateway equipment and thus the end-user interface to the network would be the LAN interface. How this will work legally and administratively is not yet settled and further discussion is outside the scope of this document.

Using the Australian "Fastpac" network as an example, there are two accesses to the network available - a 2 Mbps (4-wire copper, E1) interface and a 35 Mbps (fiber, E3). The 2 Mbps interface is published and users may attach equipment from any supplier to this interface. The 35 Mbps interface is considered proprietary and users purchase the end-user gateway equipment as part of the network service. Different countries may adopt quite different approaches to this problem.

Another feature of MAN networks is their pricing. Since the network is shared the user will be billed for data traffic (just as with X.25). In addition, there will be a charge for link connection to the network (again just as X.25). However, since there are no virtual circuits (no connections) there can be no charge for connection holding time (a significant part of the cost in many X.25 networks). Precise prices must wait until network providers decide on their tariffs.

#### 13.9.11.2 User Interface to Fastpac

The first fully commercial (with universal service and published tariffs) MAN is being built by Telecom Australia and is called "Fastpac". One problem encountered in building the network was that there is no internationally standardized protocol available suitable for an end-user interface. At high speeds (35 Mbps) the DQDB protocol itself could be used even though that requires special hardware (interface chips).

At the slower (2 Mbps) interface speed, the need was for a *connectionless* interface that was easy for equipment suppliers to implement and nevertheless gave users full access to the network's facilities.

The solution adopted was to design a new interface constructed solely from standardized protocol elements but put together in a new way. The concept is extremely simple. The user equipment builds an IEEE 802.6 frame including the frame header and sends it to the network over an E1 (2 Mbps G.703/G.704 connection) using LAPB link control to protect against errors on the local access link.

This design is reasonably clean and uncomplicated. Logically it is very close to the structure of X.25 (although it is connectionless) and follows the OSI layering. There is very little that is new in the interface - just existing standards used together in a new way.

Diagrammatically the interface is as follows:

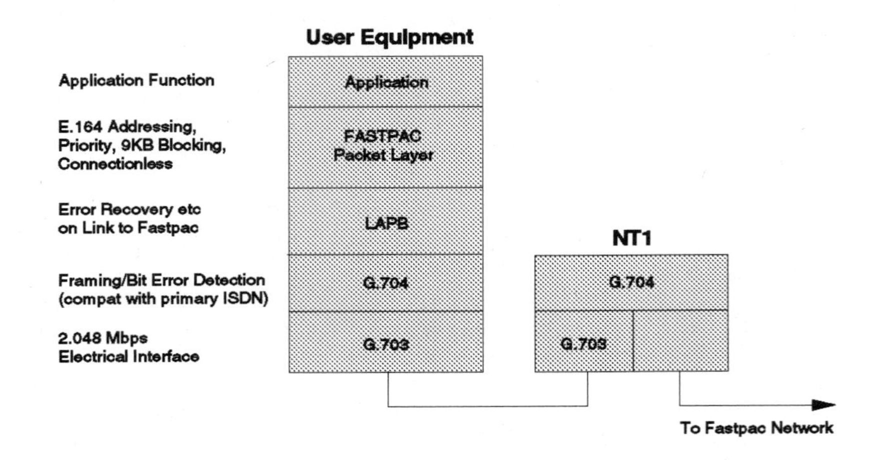


*Figure 13-34. Fastpac 2 Mbps Access Structure*

- Layer 1 (Physical Access) is done with G.703/G.704 standards.

  These are the physical layers of ISDN (primary rate access). The specification is identical to CCITT ISDN specifications at this layer.

- Layer 2 (link layer) uses LAPB link control.

  LAPB is an implementation of the international standard link control HDLC (HDLC is a superset of IBM SDLC). LAPB is the link control used in X.25 (and accepted as part of OSI).

  Note that the scope of LAPB is from the user device to the network access point - NOT across the network. That is, LAPB is used to protect the transmission of user data to/from the Fastpac network access point. LAPB is NOT used across the network (unless the end user decides to implement this as an end-user function).

  There is an additional mode allowed for HDLC where data may be sent as Unnumbered Information (UI) frames. This means that if an error occurs on the link then the data will be discarded. This is an optional mode of operation for products like LAN bridges which don't need this level of error recovery.

- Packet layer is IEEE 802.6 DQDB (Distributed Queue Dual Bus) access packet headers.

  There is no "protocol" as such implied by the use of this header. The protocol is "connectionless" and "stateless" and therefore has no responses or command sequences. There is no flow control protocol. A packet header contains the origin and destination Fastpac addresses as well as some control information indicating what the user wishes to be done with the packet (when sending) or network status conditions (when receiving).

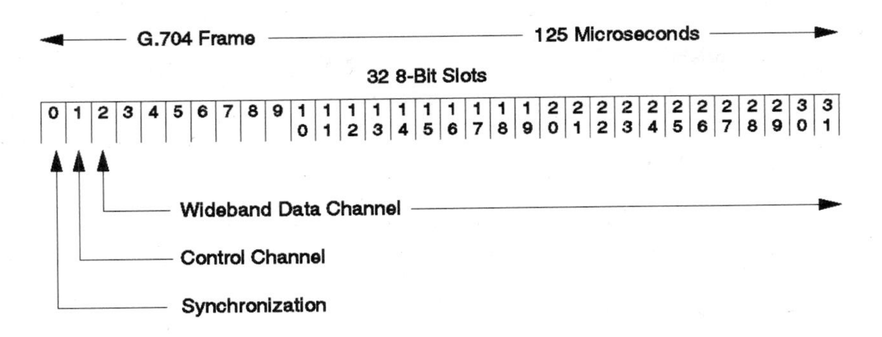


*Figure 13-35. G.704 Frame Structure as Used by Fastpac Interface*

The above structure allows a user to construct as many as 31 channels of one slot each, one channel using a concatenation (aggregation) of all 31 data slots, or any combination of slots to form any number of channels up to 31. This structure is further discussed in 8.1.4, "ISDN Primary Rate Interface" on page 8-14. Different from ISDN, where it is used as a signaling channel, slot 16 is used for data in Fastpac in the same way as any other slot.

The connection to Fastpac uses only two logical channels. The first logical channel is used for data and is made up by aggregating as many slots as needed from the G.704 frame. This is similar to the "wideband" mode of ISDN.

For example, a bandwidth of 640 Kbps could be achieved by using slots 2 to 11 from the G.704 frame. The maximum number of slots used is 30 (numbers 2 to 31). Slot 1 is used as the control channel.

At first sight this system looks ridiculous. The access from the user to the network is a point-to-point link which runs at 2 Mbps full-duplex regardless. What purpose is served by limiting the throughput of the link? This is actually very sensible. Australia is a very large geographic area (2.9 million square miles) and one objective of Fastpac is to provide service to all locations in the country. Fastpac will cover the major cities, but what about small towns a long distance from the city (as much as 1500 miles)? The structure enables the access link to be multiplexed through Telecom Australia's digital backbone network. By limiting the number of slots, Telecom can provide access to Fastpac from anywhere in a reasonably cost effective way.

### 13.9.11.3 Switched Multi-Megabit Data Service (SMDS)

SMDS is a definition of the features and functions to be offered by a high-speed public data network. Initially, the scope of such a network was defined to be within a local area (in the US this is called a LATA) but there is no reason why the service cannot be extended to cover any geographic area desired. It does define the technical interface from the customer to the PTT premises, but it does *not* define how the service is to be implemented. Figure 13-36 shows the reference configuration.

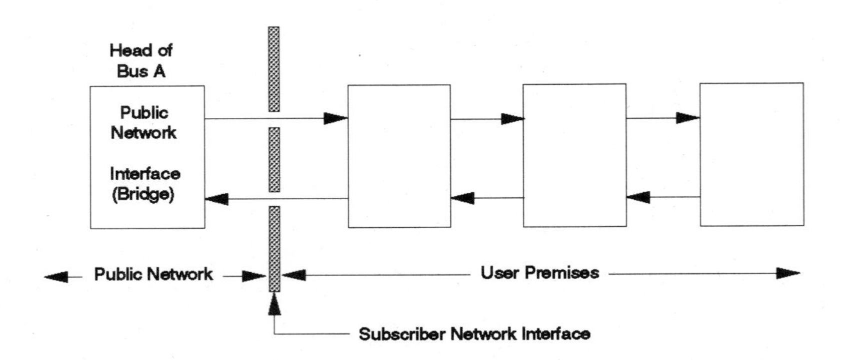


*Figure 13-36. SMDS Subscriber Network Interface*

**Reference Configuration**

The most important characteristic of the reference configuration is the interface from the user to the network. This is called the "Subscriber Network Interface" (SNI). The interface between the subscriber and the network provider is the link from the user's premises.

There may be one or many pieces of customer equipment attached to the same link. In the case where multiple customer devices are attached, these devices have concurrent access to the network over the same link.

**Interface Characteristics**

SMDS is defined to use two speeds - US "T1" (1.544 Mbps) and US "T3" (45 Mbps). The interface protocol is IEEE 802.6 (DQDB).

**Service Features**

- Connectionless Transfer

  The user sends "datagrams" to the network containing a header with both source and destination network addresses included. All data is sent this way, there is no such thing as a "virtual circuit". Datagrams may be up to 9188 bytes in length.

- Closed User Groups

  The service defines a number of features which provide much the same facilities as the "closed user group" does in an X.25 public network.

  These services are called:

  – Destination Address Screening
  – Source Address Screening
  – Source Address Validation

  These enable a user to define a list of addresses to which this address is allowed to send and from which it may receive. A user may decide that all the devices belonging to this organization may only communicate with each other, or they may be organized in groups, or some may be able to send/receive to/from any address in the public network.

- Broadcasting

  The service defines a feature called "group addressing" which allows a user to send to a group of other users. This means that users can define a set of nodes and have the services of a "virtual LAN".

- Access Classes

  Access classes are really throughput classes. The network uses a form of "leaky bucket" flow control to limit the flow of data from a user to the network. See 11.2.5, "Flow and Rate Control" on page 11-23. Different parameters for the "leaky bucket" can be specified to give different users different throughput characteristics. Presumably different throughput classes will attract different charges for network usage.

- Performance Objectives

  An important point about SMDS is that network performance objectives are stated. The initial objective is a 20 millisecond delay between users connected in the same local area.

### Conclusion

The important thing to remember about SMDS is that it is a service and an interface specification not a network architecture. There are already network providers who have announced their intention to provide SMDS services using MAN technology internally. In the future as broadband ISDN is introduced it is likely that SMDS services will become a service of a much wider broadband ISDN (ATM) public network.

# Chapter 14. Radio LAN Technology

Within the past year or so a number of manufacturers have begun to offer local area networks based on very-low-power radio communication at speeds of 1 Mbps and above.[1] Radio[2] is one way to achieve "wireless" communication. The other common method uses infrared optical broadcast.

The task of a radio LAN is the same as that of any LAN - to provide peer-to-peer communication in a local area. Ideally, it should appear to the user to be exactly the same as a wired LAN in all respects (including performance). The radio medium is different in many ways to wired media and the differences give rise to unique problems and solutions. This section will concentrate on the aspects unique to the radio medium and will discuss only in passing aspects that are held in common with wired media.

## 14.1 Characteristics of the Indoor Radio Medium

### 14.1.1 Common Medium

There is only one broadcast space. That is, in principle a radio signal transmitted anywhere in the world on a given frequency could be received anywhere else in the world (of course depending on propagation and signal strength). In practice, the strength of a radio signal decreases as the square of the distance from the transmitter (in some systems the decrease is with the fourth power of the distance!). It is this that enables us to re-use the same frequencies when transmitters are far enough apart. Contrast this with the wired environment where each pair of wires is a separate "signal space" with minimal interference.

Thus in a radio system everyone shares essentially the same space and this brings about the biggest problem - sharing the limited available bandwidth.

### 14.1.2 Multi-Path Effects

At the extremely high frequencies involved, radio waves reflect off solid objects and this means that there are many possible paths for a signal to take from transmitter to receiver. Figure 14-1 on page 14-2 shows some of them. In this case both transmitter and

---

1 Slower speed systems have been available for some years.

2 Some brief background material on sending digital data as modulations on a carrier may be found in Appendix B, "Transmitting Information by Modulating a Carrier" on page B-1.

receiver are in the same room. Part of the signal will take the obvious direct path but there are many other paths and some of the signal will follow each of these. (Reflection from the floor is especially significant.)

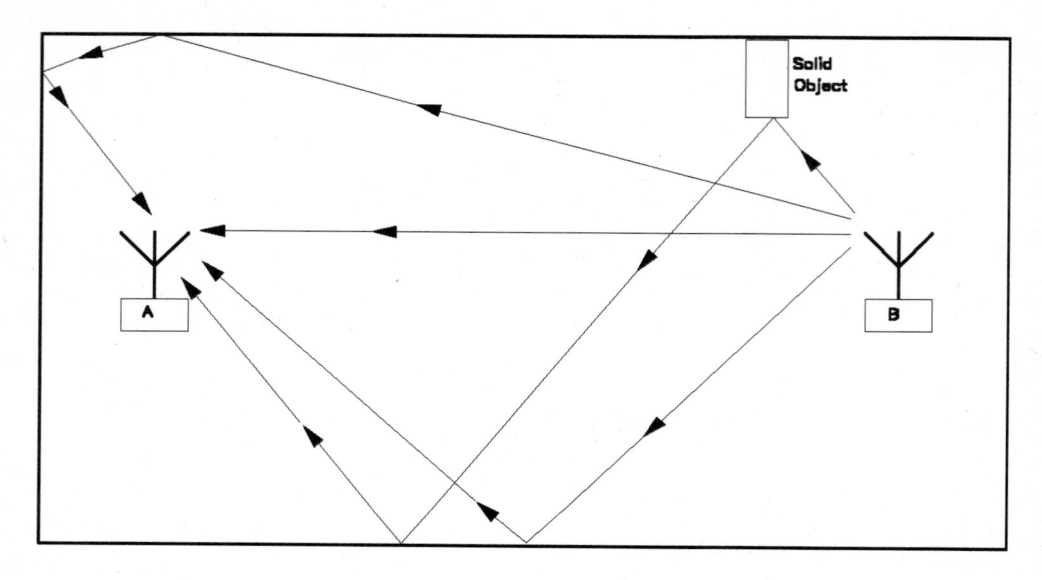


***Figure 14-1.*** *Multi-Path Effect.* The signal travels from transmitter to receiver on multiple paths and is reflected from room walls and solid objects.

This has a number of consequences.

1. To some extent the signal will travel around obstacles (and through soft ones). This is what gives radio its biggest advantage over infrared transmission in the indoor environment.

2. As shown in Figure 14-1 a signal arriving on many paths will spread out in time (because some paths are shorter than others). More accurately, many copies of the signal will arrive at the receiver slightly shifted in time.

   In the office and factory environments, studies have shown that the delay spread is typically from 30 ns to 250 ns, of course depending on the geometry of the area in question. (In the outdoor, suburban environment, delay spread is typically between .5 μsec and 3 μsec.) Delay spread has two quite different effects which must be countered.

   **Rayleigh Fading**

   When two signal components arrive after traveling different distances they add together in the receiver. If the difference in the length of the paths they traveled is an odd multiple of half the wavelength of the carrier signal, then they will cancel one another out (if it is an even multiple they will strengthen one another). At 2.4 Gbps the wavelength is 12.5 cm.

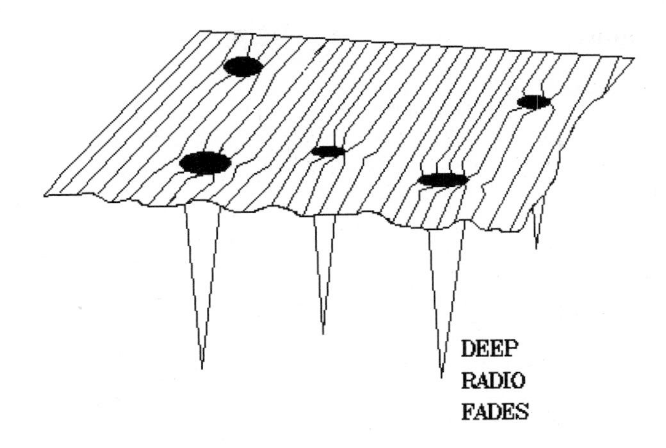


***Figure 14-2.*** *Rayleigh Fading.* The signal strength pattern in an indoor area can look like this. The strength can be relatively uniform except for small areas where the signal strength can fall to perhaps 30 dB below areas even one meter away.

In a room there can be dozens or even hundreds of possible paths and all the signals will add in quite complex ways.

The result is that in any room there will be places where little or no signal is detectable and other places, a few meters away, where the signal could be very strong. If the receiver is mobile, rapid variations in signal strength are usually observed.

### Inter-Symbol Interference

When we are digitally modulating a carrier another important consideration is the length of the symbol (the transmission state representing a bit or group of bits). If we are sending one bit per symbol and the bit rate is 1 Mbps then the "length" of a bit will be a bit less than 300 meters. In time, at 1 Mbps a bit is 1 μsec long. If the delay spread is 250 ns then each bit will be spread out to a length of 1.25 μsec and will overlap with the following bit by a quarter of its length.

This is called Inter-Symbol Interference (ISI) and has the effect of limiting the maximum data rate possible. ISI is present in most communications channels and there are good techniques for combating it (such as Adaptive Equalization). It is most severe in the radio environment.

Most people are familiar with this effect since it is the cause of "ghosts" in television reception - especially with indoor antennas.

3. When people move about the room the characteristics of the room (as far as radio propagation is concerned) change.

Overcoming multi-path effects is the most significant challenge in the design of indoor radio systems.

### 14.1.3 Intermittent Operation

In an office or factory environment people move about the area and occasionally move large objects about. This can cause intermittent interruption to the signal, rapid fading and the like.

### 14.1.4 Security

Because there are no bounds for a radio signal, it is possible for unauthorized people to receive it. This is not as serious a problem as would appear since the signal strength decreases with the fourth power of the distance from the transmitter (for systems where the antenna is close to the ground - such as indoor systems). Nevertheless it is a problem which must be addressed by any radio LAN proposal.

### 14.1.5 Bandwidth

Radio waves at frequencies above a few GHz do not bend much in the atmosphere (they travel in straight lines) and are reflected from most solid objects. Thus radio at this frequency will not normally penetrate a building even if it is present in the outdoor environment. Inside the building this means that there is a wide frequency space available which could be used for local applications with very little restriction.

### 14.1.6 Direction

In general radio waves will radiate from a transmitting antenna in all directions. By smart antenna design it is possible to direct the signal into specific directions or even into beams. In the indoor environment, however, this doesn't make a lot of difference because of the reflections at the wavelengths used.

### 14.1.7 Polarization

Radio signals are naturally polarized and in free space will maintain their polarization over long distances. However, polarization changes when a signal is reflected and effects that flow from this must be taken into consideration in the design of any indoor radio system.

### 14.1.8 Interference

Depending on which frequency band is in use there are many sources of possible interference with the signal. Some of these are from other transmitters in the same band (such as radar sets and microwave installations nearby). Electric motors, switches, and stray radiation from electronic devices are other sources of interference.

### 14.1.9 Characteristics of ISM Frequency Bands

The "ISM" (Industrial, Scientific and Medical) bands were allocated for indoor radio applications. Spread spectrum techniques *must* be used in these bands, but if transmitter power is very low (less than 1 watt), equipment does not need to be licensed in most countries. Note that there is some variation between countries on the boundaries of these bands.

***Table 14-1.*** *Indoor Radio Frequency Band Characteristics*

| | **915 MHz** | **2.4 GHz** | **5.8 GHz** | **18 GHz** |
|---|---|---|---|---|
| Frequency | 902-928 MHz | 2.4-2.48 GHz | 5.73-5.85 GHz | 18 GHz |
| Wavelength | 32.8 cm | 12.5 cm | 5.2 cm | 1.6 cm |
| Width of Band | 26 MHz | 80 MHz | 120 MHz | |
| Usage | ISM-SS | ISM-SS | ISM-SS | Narrowband |
| Range | Greatest | 95% | 80% | |
| Status | Crowded | Low Use | V Low Use | V Low Use |
| Interference | High | Low | Low | Low |

The 18 GHz band is for narrowband microwave applications and is not wide enough for spread spectrum techniques. Nevertheless, one major radio LAN system on the market uses this band.

## 14.2 Sharing the Bandwidth

With many workstations in the same area wanting to communicate a method is needed to share the bandwidth. Different LAN designs use quite different methods of operation and of bandwidth sharing. However, most use a combination of the methods outlined below:

**Frequency Division Multiplexing (FDM)**

The principle of FDM is described in A.1.1, "Frequency Division Multiplexing" on page A-1.

**Time Division Multiplexing (TDM)**

The principle of TDM is described in A.1.2, "Time Division Multiplexing" on page A-2.

**Polarization Division Multiplexing (PDM)**

Provided that polarization can be maintained, potentially we could use the direction of polarization as a multiplexing technique. In the presence of multiple reflections, however, polarization changes and is essentially unpredictable. Thus polarization is not usable as a multiplexing technique in the indoor radio environment. (In the outdoor environment polarization is widely used as a way of doubling capacity on high-speed digital microwave links.)

**Space Division Multiplexing (SDM)**

Using directional antennas and reflectors we can (roughly) shape radio signals into beams. Signals can be beamed from one location to another and the same frequency can be used for many beams between different locations. Typical outdoor microwave systems operate this way.

Channel separation is far from perfect but a radio LAN system could be built with carefully selected frequencies and directional antennae such that the same frequency is reused for many connections.

Structuring the network in a cellular fashion is also a form of SDM. This is described in 14.7.2, "Cellular Systems" on page 14-18.

**Code Division Multiplexing (CDMA)**

In a spread spectrum system (with some techniques) it is possible to transmit multiple signals at the same frequency at the same time and still separate them in the receiver. This is called CDMA and is discussed later.

## 14.3 Conventional Narrowband Radio (Microwave)

It is perfectly sensible to build a radio LAN using conventional narrowband microwave radio. The Motorola "Altair" product is an example of such a system.

There are a number of problems, however:

1. The use of microwave radio even at low power usually requires licensing of the equipment to a specific user and allocation of a unique frequency.
2. The ISM bands (by regulation) can only be used by spread spectrum systems.

## 14.4 Spread Spectrum and Code Division Multiple Access (CDMA)

The concepts of spread spectrum and of CDMA seem to contradict normal intuition. In most communications systems we try to maximize the amount of useful signal we can fit into a minimal bandwidth. In spread spectrum we try to artificially spread a signal over a bandwidth much wider than necessary. In CDMA we transmit multiple signals over the same frequency band, using the same modulation techniques at the same time! There are of course very good reasons for doing this. In a spread spectrum system we use some artificial technique to broaden the amount of bandwidth used. This has the following effects:

**Capacity Gain**

Using the Shannon-Hartly law for the capacity of a bandlimited channel it is easy to see that for a given signal power the wider the bandwidth used, the greater the channel capacity. So if we broaden the spectrum of a given signal we get an increase in channel capacity and/or an improvement in the signal-to-noise ratio.

This is true and easy to demonstrate for some systems but not for others. "Ordinary" frequency modulation (FM) systems spread the signal above the minimum theoretically needed and they get a demonstrable increase in capacity. Some techniques for spreading the spectrum achieve a significant capacity gain but others do not.

**The Shannon-Hartly Law**

The Shannon-Hartly law gives the capacity of a bandlimited communications channel in the presence of "Gaussian" noise. (Every communications channel has Gaussian noise.)

$$Capacity = B \log_2 (1 + \frac{P_S}{2 N_0 B})$$

Where P represents signal power, N noise power and B available bandwidth.

It is easy to see that with P and N held constant, capacity increases as bandwidth increases (though not quite as fast). So, for a given channel capacity, the required power decreases as utilized bandwidth increases. The wider the bandwidth the lower the power we need to use for a given capacity.

**Security**

Spread spectrum was invented by military communications people for the purpose of battlefield communications. Spread spectrum signals have an excellent rejection of intentional jamming (jammer power must be very great to be successful). In addition, the Direct Sequence (DS) technique results in a signal which is very hard to distinguish from background noise unless you know the peculiar random code sequence used to generate the signal. Thus, not only are DS signals hard to jam, they are extremely difficult to decode (unless you have the key) and quite hard to detect anyway even if all you want to know is when something is being transmitted.

**Immunity to Multipath Distortion**

Some spectrum spreading techniques have a significantly better performance in the presence of multipath spreading than any available narrowband technique. This will be discussed later.

**Interference Rejection**

Spread spectrum signals can be received even in the presence of very strong narrowband interfering signals (up to perhaps 30 dB above the wanted signal).

**Multiplexing Technique (CDMA)**

Some techniques of frequency spreading enable the transmission of many completely separate and unrelated channels *on the same frequency and at the same time as other, similar signals.*

There are two major techniques for generating SS signals:

1. Direct Sequence (DS) - also called Pseudo Noise (PN)
2. Frequency Hopping (FH)

## 14.4.1 Direct Sequence Spread Spectrum (DSSS)

Also called "Pseudo Noise" (PN), DSSS is a popular technique for spreading the spectrum. Figure 14-3 shows how the signal is generated.

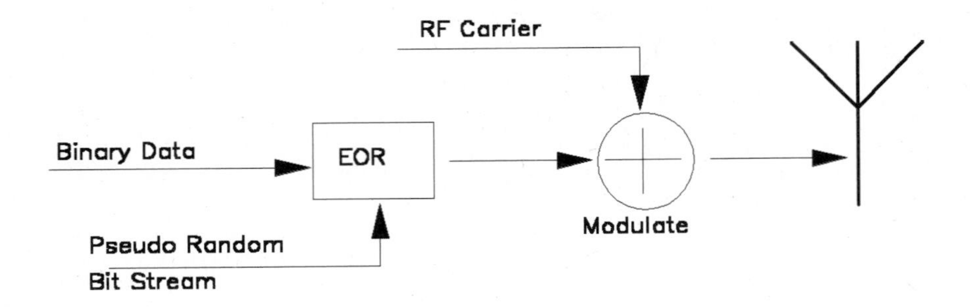


***Figure 14-3.*** *Direct Sequence Spread Spectrum Modulation - Transmitter*

1. The binary data stream (user data) is used to "modulate" a pseudo-random bit stream. The rate of this pseudo-random bit stream is much faster (from 9 to 100 times) than the user data rate. The bits of the pseudo-random stream are called *chips*. The ratio between the speed of the chip stream and the data stream is called the *spread ratio*.

2. The form of "modulation" used is typically just an EOR operation performed between the two bit streams.

3. The output of the faster bit stream is used to modulate a radio frequency (RF) carrier.

4. Any suitable modulation technique can be used but in practical systems a very simple bi-polar phase shift keying (BPSK) approach is usually adopted.

Whenever a carrier is modulated the result is a spread signal with two "sidebands" above and below the carrier frequency. These sidebands are spread over a range plus or minus the modulating frequency. The sidebands carry the information and it is common to suppress the transmission of the carrier (and sometimes one of the sidebands). It can be easily seen that the width (spread) of each sideband has been multiplied by the spread ratio.

At first sight this can be quite difficult to understand. We have spread the spectrum *but in order to do it we have increased the bit rate by exactly the signal spread ratio.* Surely the benefits of spreading the spectrum (such as the capacity gain hypothesized above) are negated by the higher bit rate?

The secret of DSSS is in the way the signal is received. The receiver knows the pseudo-random bit stream (because it has the same random number generator). Incoming signals (after synchronization) are correlated with the known pseudo-random stream. Thus the chip stream performs the function of a known waveform against which we correlate the input. (There are many ways to do this but they are outside the scope of this discussion.)

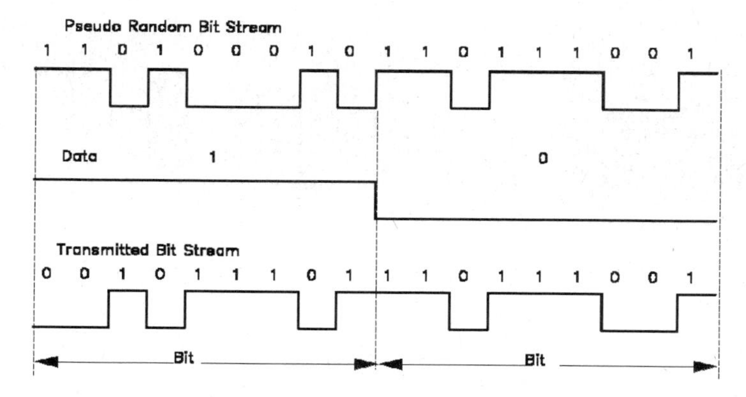


***Figure 14-4.*** *Direct Sequence Spread Spectrum Modulation.* A pseudo-random bit stream much faster (here 9 times the speed) than the data rate is EORed with the data. The resulting bit stream is then used to modulate a carrier signal. This results in a much broader signal.

DSSS has the following characteristics:

**Capacity Gain**

The capacity gain predicted by the Shannon-Hartly law is achieved. This means that for the same system characteristics, you can use a lower transmit power or a higher data rate (without increasing the transmitter power).

**Improved Resistance to Multi-Path Effects**

Above it was mentioned that the length of a data bit at 1 Mbps is about 300 meters. We can think of this as a notional "data wavelength". ISI is most difficult to suppress when the delay spread is less than this data wavelength. Because we have introduced "chipping" we can perform equalization at the chip wavelength. This chip wavelength is significantly less than the data wavelength (by the spread ratio).

It turns out that we can remove delayed signals (where the delay is longer than a chip time) very effectively using adaptive equalization. This gives extremely good compensation for ISI.

Rayleigh fading is reduced with DSSS. The location of radio fades within an area is critically dependent on the wavelength. Since the wavelength at one side of the band is different (slightly) from the wavelength at the other side, the location of radio fades is also different. The wider the bandwidth used, the less the problem with fading. This mitigates the Rayleigh fading problem somewhat but does not entirely eliminate it.

**Immunity to Narrowband Interference**

Because the energy of the data signal is spread over a wide range, the presence of a narrowband signal (even a very strong one) within the wideband range has little effect on the DSSS receiver (all it sees is a small increase in the signal-to-noise ratio.

It is even possible to transmit a DSSS signal "over the top" of a group of narrowband signals (using the same frequency space). This is seen in Figure 14-5.

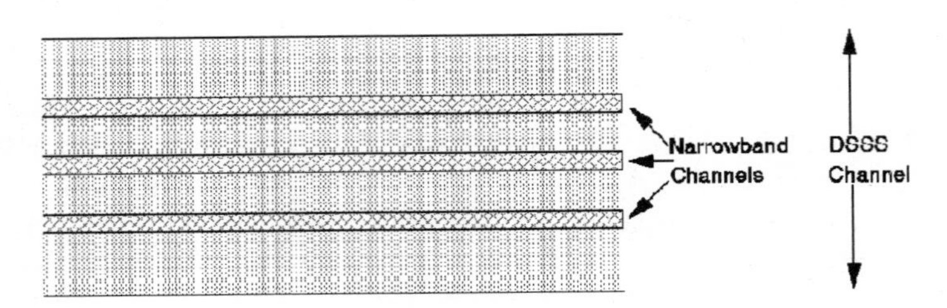


***Figure 14-5.*** *DSSS over Narrowband Channels*

The narrowband channels see the DSSS signal as an increase in noise level (which, if kept within reason will have little effect). For metropolitan area cellular radio systems, DSSS has been seriously suggested for use "overlaying" existing analog FDM cellular radio channel space.

**Security**

Because the signal is generated by a pseudo-random sequence a receiver must know the sequence or it can't receive the data. Typically such sequences are generated with shift registers with some kind of feedback applied. Unless the receiver knows the key to the random number generator it can't receive the signal.

The biggest problem with DSSS is synchronizing the receiver to the transmitter pseudo-random sequence. Acquisition of synchronization can take quite a long time. Radio LAN systems are not as sensitive (from a security point of view) as a military communication system and it is feasible to use a short, predictable, bit sequence instead of a pseudo-random one. Security is not as good (to receive it you still need a DSSS receiver but you don't need the key anymore), but synchronization can be achieved very quickly and the correlator in the receiver doesn't have to be as smart.

**Near-Far Problem**

While DSSS is extremely resistant to narrowband interference it is not very resistant to the effects of being swamped by a nearby transmitter on the same band as itself (using the whole bandwidth). A signal from a far away transmitter can be blanketed out by a nearby transmitter if the difference in signal strength at the receiver is only about 20 dB.

### 14.4.2 Code Division Multiple Access (CDMA)

The DSSS technique gives rise to a novel way of sharing the bandwidth. Multiple transmitters and receivers are able to use the same frequencies at the same time *without* interfering with each other! This is a by-product of the DSSS technique. The receiver correlates its received signal with a known (only to it) random sequence - all other signals are filtered out.

This is interesting because it is really the same process as FDM. When we receive an ordinary radio station (channels are separated by FDM), we tune to that station. The tuning process involves adjusting a resonant circuit to the frequency we want to receive. That circuit allows the selected frequency to pass and rejects all other frequencies. What we are actually doing is selecting a sinusoidal wave from among many other sinusoidal waves by selective filtering. If we consider a DSSS signal as a modulated waveform, when there are many overlapping DSSS signals then the filtering process needed to select one of them from among many is exactly the same thing as FDM frequency selection except that we have waveforms that are not sinusoidal in shape. However, the DSSS "chipping sequences" (pseudo-random number sequences) *must be orthogonal (unrelated).* Fortunately there are several good simple ways of generating orthogonal pseudo-random sequences.

For this to work, a receiving filter is needed which can select a single DSSS signal from among all the intermixed ones. In principle, you need a filter that can correlate the complex signal with a known chipping sequence (and reject all others). There are several available filtering techniques which will do just this. The usual device used for this filtering process is called a Surface Acoustic Wave (SAW) filter.

CDMA has a number of very important characteristics:

**"Statistical" Allocation of Capacity**

Any particular DSSS receiver experiences other DSSS signals as noise. This means that you can continue adding channels until the signal-to-noise ratio gets too great and you start getting bit errors. The effect is like multiplexing packets on a link. You can have many active connections and so long as the total (data traffic) stays below the channel capacity all will work well. For example, in a voice system, only about 35% of the time on a channel actually has sound (the rest of the time is gaps and listening to speech in the other direction). If you have a few hundred channels of voice over CDMA what happens is the average power is the channel limit - so you can handle many more voice connections than are possible by FDM or TDM methods.

This also applies to data traffic where the traffic is inherently bursty in nature. However, it has particular application in voice transmission because, when the system is overcommitted there is no loss in service but only a degradation in voice quality. Degradation in quality (dropping a few bits) is a serious problem for data but not for voice.

**No Guard Time or Guard Bands**

In a TDM system when multiple users share the same channel there must be a way to ensure that they don't transmit at the same time and destroy each other's signal. Since there is no really accurate way of synchronizing clocks (in the light of propagation delay) a length of time must be allowed between the end of one user's transmission and the beginning of the next. This is called "guard time". At slow data rates it is not too important but as speed gets higher it comes to dominate the system throughput. CDMA of course does not require a guard time - stations simply transmit whenever they are ready.

In FDM systems, unused frequency space is allocated between bands because it is impossible to ensure precise control of frequency. These guard bands represent wasted frequency space. Again, in CDMA they are not needed at all.

### Smooth Handoff

In the mobile environment perhaps the key problem is "handoff" where one user is passed from one cell to another. In an FDM system this is performed by switching frequency. In CDMA, all you do is pass the key (random sequence generator) to the next cell and you can get a very smooth handoff.

At this time existing radio LANs do not allow for fully mobile operation. When a station is moved it makes a new connection with a new base station. However, there are many applications in factories (large plant areas) and warehouses which need continuous connection to the system. Any system which aims to provide this will require a method for smooth handoff.

### Requirement for Power Control

As mentioned earlier (the near-far problem), DSSS receivers can't distinguish a signal if its strength is more than about 20 dB below other similar signals. Thus if many transmitters are simultaneously active a transmitter close to the receiver (near) will blanket out a signal from a transmitter which is further away.

The answer to this is controlling the transmit power of all the stations so that they have roughly equal signal strength at the receiver. It should be noted that this implies a "base station to user" topology, since in an any-to-any topology power control cannot solve the problem.

### Easier System Management

With FDM and TDM systems users must have frequencies and/or time slots assigned to them through some central administration process. All you need with CDMA is for communicating stations to have the same key.

## 14.5 Frequency Hopping (FH)

In a Frequency Hopping spread spectrum system, the available bandwidth is divided up into a number of narrowband[3] channels. The transmitter and the receiver "hop" from one channel to another using a predetermined (pseudo-random) hopping sequence. The time spent in each channel is called a "chip". The rate at which hopping is performed is called the "chipping rate". This is illustrated in Figure 14-6 on page 14-14.

3 They actually have to be "narrower" (than the available frequency band) rather than "narrowband" as such. That is, it is possible (and very reasonable) to frequency hop among a number of DSSS channels.

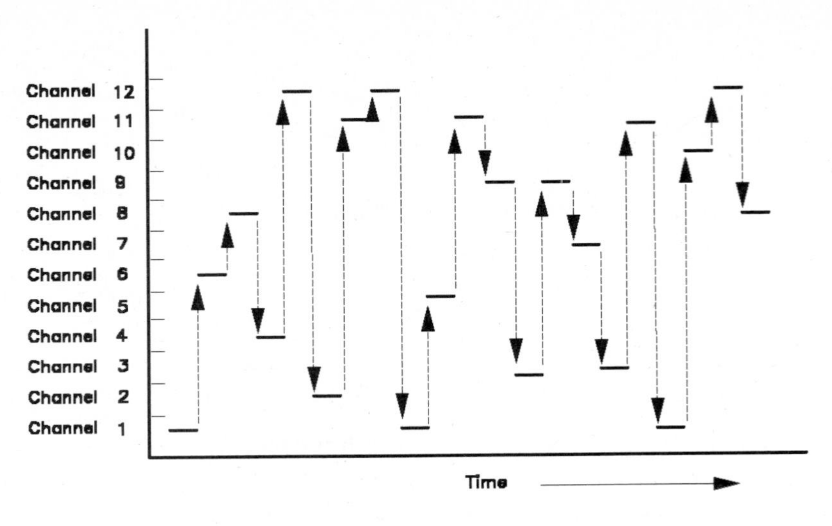


*Figure 14-6. Frequency Hopping*

**Fast Frequency Hopping**

A Fast Frequency Hopping system is one where frequency hopping takes place faster than the data (bit) rate. FFH demonstrates exactly the capacity gain suggested by the Shannon-Hartly law.

Unfortunately, while FFH systems work well at low data rates they are difficult and expensive to implement at data rates of 1 Mbps and above; thus, while they are theoretically important, there are no high-speed (user data rate above 1 Mbps) FFH systems available.

**Slow Frequency Hopping**

Slow Frequency Hopping is where hopping takes place at a lower rate than the user data (bit) rate. To be considered an SFH system (from a regulatory point of view) hopping must take place at least once every 400 ms and it must statistically cover all of the available channels.

There are many advantages to SFH. However, the capacity gain achieved by other spectrum spreading methods is *not* demonstrated in SFH systems.

When encoding data for transmission over an SFH system the same requirements apply as for regular narrowband transmission. That is, the data stream must contain frequent transitions and should average the same amount of time each symbol state. These characteristics are usually inherent in the data encoding scheme. If the encoded data is not in this form then it is necessary to randomize (scramble) the data before transmission and to descramble it on reception.

### 14.5.1 CDMA in FH Systems

Sharing the wideband channel between multiple FH systems is possible and can be considered a form of CDMA. With two or more systems hopping over the same bandwidth collisions do occur. When there is a collision, data is corrupted and lost.

In an FFH system (say 10-100 hops per bit) then corrupted chips will have little effect on the user data. However, in an SFH system user data will be lost and higher layer error recoveries will be needed. One way of avoiding the problem in the SFH environment is to arrange the hopping patterns so that each system uses a *different* set of channels so that collisions cannot occur.

## 14.6 DSSS and SFH Systems Compared

There is some discussion in the industry over which system of spread spectrum operation is the most cost effective. The technology is not at all mature yet and researchers are still trying to settle the matter but there are some early indications.

1. In a paper presented to the IEEE, Chen and Wu (1992) report a performance comparison between the two systems. The study uses two kinds of mathematical channel models and studied two speeds of operation. Systems were compared *without* equalization or error correction techniques being applied.

   Their conclusion was that at speeds of 1 Mbps the SFH system was superior to DSSS in almost every respect and significantly so in most. At speeds of 10 Mbps their conclusion is the opposite. That is, that DSSS is better, again under most simulated conditions.

   As manufacturers bring more systems to market, experience will show the difference.

2. An assessment of manufacturing cost shows that SFH "should" cost less to manufacture and operate at lower power than DSSS. (This all depends on the system design.)

   It should be noted that there are many ways to implement either system. For example, you can have a DSSS system which uses only a very short pseudo-random sequence. This saves significant cost in the adapter but limits the potential for CDMA operation and removes much of the security advantage.

3. An SFH system can easily avoid local sources of strong narrowband interference. All it needs to do is to modify the hopping pattern to avoid the particular frequency band. The ISM bands have many uses and sources of narrowband interference are relatively common. While, in general, a narrowband interferer will not bother DSSS, a strong local interferer (such as a nearby microwave system) will. An SFH system can detect and avoid the frequency bands involved.

4. Laboratory tests of a DSSS-based LAN system collocated with an SFH-based system have shown that the SFH system is more robust. That is, the SFH system was not affected by the DSSS system but the DSSS system ceased to function! This was caused by the signal level of the SFH system being too high for the DSSS one (because the two systems were interspersed in the same room).

## 14.7 Building a Radio LAN System

There are many possible radio LAN topologies and three of them are illustrated in the following:

**Direct User-to-User Transmission**

This is where there is no base station and traffic is directly transmitted from user to user.

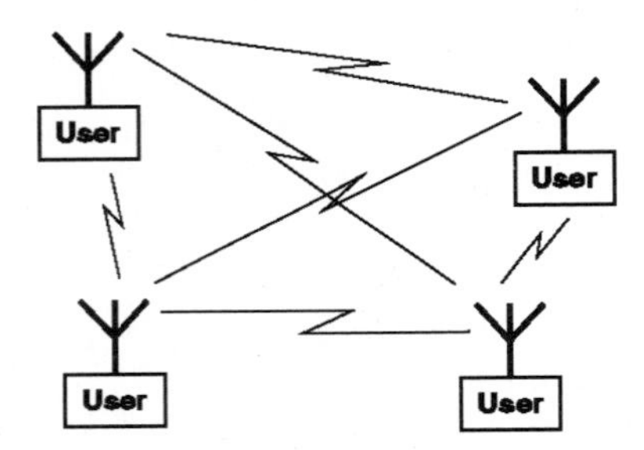


*Figure 14-7. Radio LAN Topologies - An "Ad-Hoc" Structure*

This mode of operation is considered essential because many users will want to set up ad-hoc connections between small numbers of stations on an as-needed basis. LANs such as these might be set up, used and dispersed again within the space of an hour.

Such a system could use multiple channels (FDM or CDMA) between pairs of users or a single channel with TDM or CSMA operation to share the available capacity between users.

**Use of a Base Station**

When a base station is used, all transmissions from workstations are routed to or from the base station. The base station performs the function of a bridge (optionally) connecting the radio LAN segment to a wired LAN.

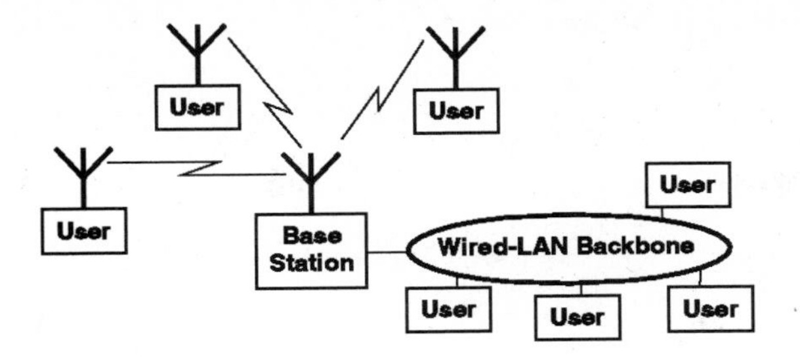


*Figure 14-8. Radio LAN Topologies - Use of a Base Station*

## Connection to a Wired LAN

Most often a radio LAN will require a connection to a wired LAN. In this case the base station should perform the function of a bridge connecting the radio LAN segment to the wired LAN segment.

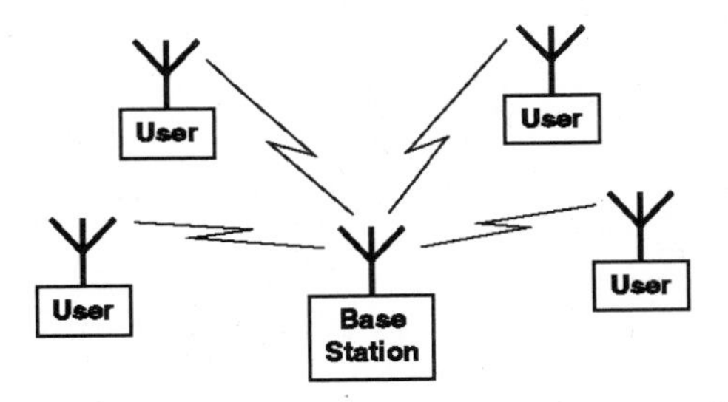


*Figure 14-9. Radio LAN Topologies - Connection to a Wired LAN*

In future LANs it will be possible to have multiple base stations connected together by a wired LAN with a mobile user moving around and being passed from one base station to another much like a cellular telephone user. There are many applications in large plant environments where this would be a very useful function. Currently there are no radio LAN products on the market which will do this.

### 14.7.1.1 Topologies Compared

*Table 14-2. Comparison of Peer-to-Peer versus Base-to-Remote Operation*

| | Peer-to-Peer | Base-to-Remote |
|---|---|---|
| Coverage | Unpredictable (Hidden Terminals) | Predictable (Base to Remote) |
| Area Covered | Transmission Range = Network Diameter | Transmission Range = Network Radius |
| Access Points (to Network) | Multiple | 1 per Cell |
| Security | Single Level (Network O/S Only) | Multi-Level Base, MAC and Physical Control |
| Management | Unpredictable (Hidden Terminals) | Predictable (Mgmt function through Base) |
| Expansion | Limited - Difficult | Multi-Cell Design |
| Future Upgrades | Manual Distribution | Automated (through Base) |

In comparing a user-to-user (ad hoc) configuration to a base station configuration the following points should be considered:

1. In the user-to-user configuration the maximum size of the LAN is a circle of *diameter* equal to the maximum transmission range. In the base station approach the maximum size of the LAN is a circle of *radius* equal to the maximum range of the transmission. Thus the base station approach allows a single radio LAN to be geographically much larger than the user-to-user approach (all else being equal).

2. If the traffic pattern is genuinely peer-to-peer and evenly distributed the user-to-user approach offers much greater capacity and efficiency. (If you go through a base station the data must be transmitted over the air twice - halving the system capacity.)

   However, in practical LANs this is almost never the case. Communication is usually from workstation to server or from workstation to gateway. In the radio case where there is a connection to a wired LAN, a significant proportion of the traffic will probably need to go between the radio users and wired LAN users.

   Thus systems with a base station will usually be a better approach. A good system might put the base station and the bridging function in the same machine as the most used server.

## 14.7.2 Cellular Systems

The big problem with radio systems is that the electromagnetic spectrum is shared by everyone and in consequence is a scarce resource. The cellular concept arose through the need to get significant increases in capacity from that resource.

If a restricted amount of bandwidth is available for a particular function it doesn't matter much how you multiplex it into channels (FDM, TDM or CDMA); there will be a finite number of channels available for that function. If a large geographic area is covered by high-power equipment then the capacity of the total system is just the number of channels available.

The large area can be broken up into smaller areas using lower power (short range) transmitters. Many transmitters can then use the same frequency (channel), provided they are far enough apart so that they don't interfere with one another. Everyone is familiar with this since radio stations in different cities transmit on the same frequencies and rely on the distance between stations to prevent interference. This gives a significant capacity increase for the whole system. The penalty is that each user can only communicate directly with close by stations - if a user needs to communicate over a longer distance then a method of connecting hub (base) stations within each cell must be provided.

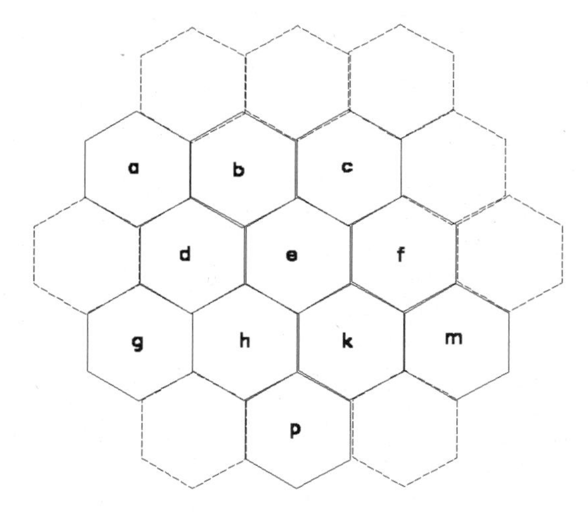


***Figure 14-10.*** *Cell Structure*

Figure 14-10 shows the notional construction of a cellular radio system. The problem here is that the boundaries in reality are fuzzy following geography rather than lines on a diagram. The concept here is as follows:

- Users within a cell are allocated a channel or set of channels to use and operate at sufficient power only to reach other users (or a base station) within the same cell.
- Because transmissions within one cell will still have significant strength in adjacent cells, the channels (frequencies) allocated to users in adjacent cells must be different. This is because of the uncertain nature of the boundary between cells. In addition, a user located near a boundary would experience equal strength interfering signals if the same frequency was re-used.

One of the most important design problems is that a user in one cell can be physically close to a user in a neighboring cell.

- If there is a base station within a cell and users communicate only with the base station, then the transmit power used only has to be sufficient to get between any user and the base station.

  If the system calls for direct user-to-user communication then the transmit power must be great enough to allow good signal strength for a distance of the diameter of a cell.

  Thus, in a base station to user configuration we can re-use channels much sooner than we could in a user-to-user configuration. In the figure, in a base station configuration the same frequencies could be re-used in cells p, m, e, g, and a. If this were a user-to-user system frequency re-use would be limited to cells that were farther apart such as cells m and b or p and a.

- Cellular systems work because of the very rapid decrease in signal strength as distance from the transmitter is increased. In free space signal strength declines as the square of the distance from the transmitter. Where the antennas are "close to the ground" signal strength declines with the fourth power of distance!

In practical cellular radio (telephone) systems there is a capacity trade-off. The smaller the cells the greater the capacity of the total system but the greater the cost, since these systems have a base station in every cell.

In other kinds of systems there may be no wired backbone and the cellular structure is only used as a means of increasing capacity. (Of course in this case, communication is limited to users within individual cells.)

## 14.7.3 Radio LAN Systems Considerations

### 14.7.3.1 Collocated but Unrelated Radio LANs

One important requirement for a radio LAN system is the need to allow multiple *unrelated* LANs (of the same type) to be located in the same area. This requires a system for channel sharing and LAN administration that allows each independent LAN to be set up and operated without the need to consider other (similar) LANs in the same space.

### 14.7.3.2 Countering Multi-Path Effects

As mentioned above, multi-path effects are the most serious problem for the indoor radio environment. The following are some of the general approaches used to counter them:

**Antenna Diversity**

Antenna diversity can mitigate both ISI and Rayleigh fading effects. There are many different ways of approaching this:

1. Multiple Directional Antennas

   An example of this is the Motorola "Altair" radio LAN system, which uses a six-segment antenna. Antenna segments are arranged in a circle at an angle of 60 degrees from each other. Each antenna segment is highly directional; thus, signals coming from different directions (reflections, etc.) are received on different antenna segments. As signals are received the system selects the antenna segment receiving the strongest signal and uses that signal alone. This severely limits the number of possible paths. Moreover, surviving paths will have lengths that are not too different from one another. This provides an excellent solution to the ISI problem but does not do a lot for fading. Notice however that the Altair system is a narrowband microwave system (1.6 cm wavelength) and at that wavelength Rayleigh fading is not as significant as it is at longer wavelengths.

2. Multiple Antennas

   Other systems use multiple dipole antennas separated from one another by more than half a wavelength. Signals are added together before detection and this does provide a measure of protection against fading (but not against ISI).

3. Multiple Coordinated Receivers

   Two antennas are situated exactly 1/4 of a wavelength apart. Each antenna services a different receiver circuit. The signals are then combined in such a way as to minimize multipath effects.

4. Polarization Diversity

   Because the signal polarization changes as reflections occur, a good counter to fading is to provide both horizontal and vertically polarized antennas acting together. The signal is transmitted and received in both polarizations.

**Data Rate**

The ISI problem is most severe when the delay spread covers more than one data bit time. The easy way to avoid this is to limit the data rate to less than the inverse of the delay spread. However, if the objective is to operate at LAN speeds (above 1 Mbps) then this will not always be practical.

**Spread Spectrum Techniques**

As discussed above, spread spectrum techniques provide a good measure of protection against ISI and fading. Moreover, spread spectrum is mandatory in the ISM bands. Thus in the indoor radio situation spread spectrum is a preferred method of controlling the multipath effects.

### Frequency Diversity

Fading in a narrowband system can be combatted by transmitting the signal on two different frequencies with sufficient separation for the channels to have different fading characteristics. When the signals are received, the station just picks the strongest.

You could call this "half-baked spread spectrum" since all it is doing is spreading the spectrum through an ad-hoc method.

### Adaptive Equalization

Adaptive equalization is a very good way of countering the ISI form of multipath interference. It is, however, relatively expensive to implement at high speed.

There is some disagreement among specialists as to under which circumstances (if any) adaptive equalization is needed. However, to our knowledge, *no current radio LAN system uses adaptive equalization.*

## 14.7.4 Media Access (MAC) Protocols

At the present time all of the available radio LAN systems are proprietary. This is because there is no available standard as yet. The IEEE LAN standardization committee has commenced an effort to develop such a standard. This will be known as IEEE 802.11. As yet there is no draft standard but there are a number of technical proposals before the committee. The following description is of an IBM contribution (proposal) to the IEEE 802.11 committee (Document IEEE 802.11/92-39).

The task of the MAC protocol[4] is to control which station is allowed to use the medium (transmit on a particular channel) at a particular time. It does not define the overall operation of the LAN system. (For example, in this case the MAC must allow for mobile stations but cannot prescribe how stations are handed off when a cell boundary is crossed.)

The proposed MAC supports the following LAN functions:

1. Slow Frequency Hopped communications system - but it will also operate with a DSSS system
2. Transmission rate between 1 and 20 Mbps
3. Support for broadcast and multicast operation

---

[4] Many of the features of the radio LAN environment are similar to features of passive optical networks. A discussion of MAC protocols in the passive optical network environment is presented in 16.2.3, "Access Protocols" on page 16-9.

4. Asynchronous frame delivery
5. Asynchronous (time bounded) frame delivery
6. Multiple, collocated LANs
7. Operation with a base station
8. Ad-hoc operation without a base station
9. Direct station-to-station transmission under control of the base station

### 14.7.4.1 Characteristics

The proposed MAC protocol has the following characteristics:

1. A single channel is used for each LAN segment. A channel may be either a unique frequency (narrowband system), a CDMA derived channel or an SFH hopping pattern. Multiple separate LANs or LAN segments may be collocated by using separate channels.
2. A base station (BS) schedules access. The system can operate without a base station in which case one of the mobiles performs the functions of the base station. All mobiles contain the basic base station functions.
3. A hybrid or reservation based protocol and random access protocols are used.

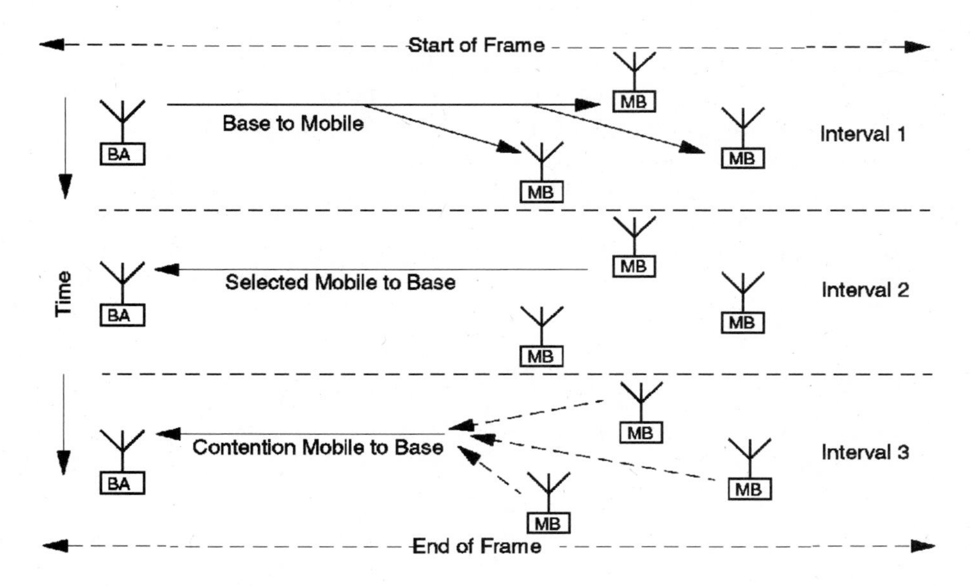


*Figure 14-11. MAC Operation - Concept*

### 14.7.4.2 Operation

An overview of the method of operation is shown in Figure 14-11 on page 14-23. Operation proceeds as follows:

**The Frame**

Different from the usual conception of a TDM frame, MAC frames are a concept in *time only*. That is, a frame is not a synchronous stream of bits but rather an interval of time. The length of a frame is variable and controlled by the base station.

**Frame Structure**

The frame is structured into three intervals:

1. In Interval 1 the base station sends data to mobiles (in MB).
2. In Interval 2 mobiles that have been scheduled for transmission by the base station may transmit.
3. In Interval 3 mobiles may contend for access to the air. This period can use either ordinary contention (Aloha) or CSMA type protocols.

The length of the frame can be varied but a typical length is thought to be around 50,000 bits.

**Slots**

For allocation purposes the length of each interval is expressed in numbers of slots. When time is allocated to a particular mobile it is done in numbers of slots. The size of a slot is yet to be determined but a figure of 500 bits is used in the performance studies.

**Data Framing**

Data blocks sent to air use HDLC framing to delimit their beginning and end and also to provide transparency.

**Base Station Control**

At the beginning of the frame *and* at the beginning of each interval the base station transmits a header to inform all stations of the characteristics of the next interval. Operation proceeds as follows:

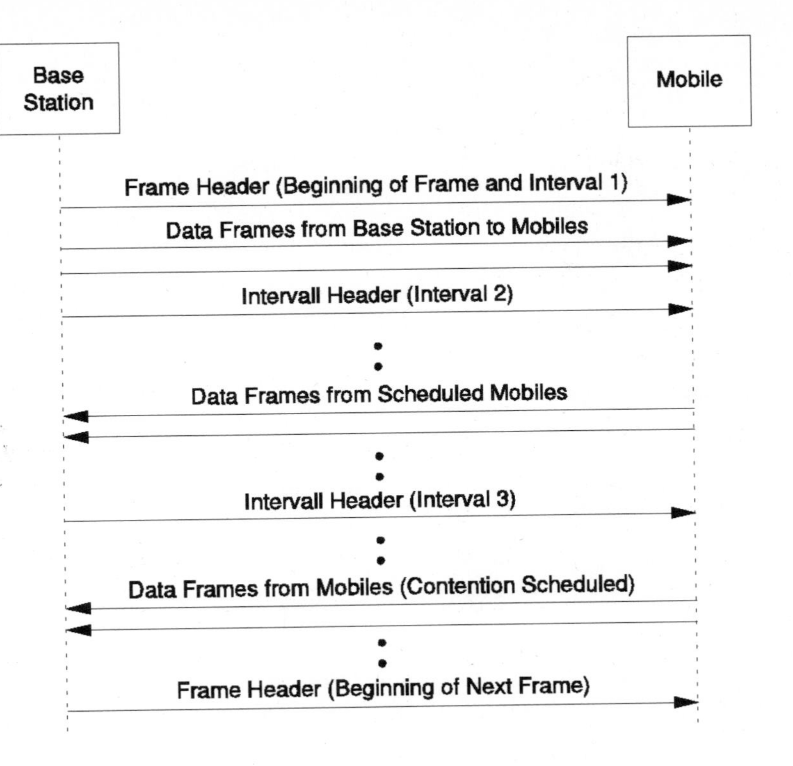


***Figure 14-12.*** *Radio LAN Operation*

Notice that there is a time delay whenever the direction of transmission changes.

### Interval 1 Header (also the Start of Frame)

The frame header doubles as the header for Interval 1 and contains the following information:

- Network ID
- Access Point ID
- Frequency to be used for next hop (if SFH operation)
- Remaining length of this hop
- Length of Interval 1
- Length of Interval 2
- Length of Interval 3
- Length of each interval header
- List of receiving stations

**Interval 2 Header**

This contains the following:

- Length of Interval 2
- Length of Interval 3
- A number representing the number of mobile stations that are allowed to transmit in this interval
- A list of user numbers paired with a number of slots

  Each entry in the list represents a mobile station and the allocated number of slots it is allowed to transmit in this interval. Mobiles transmit in the same order as the list.

**Interval 3 Header**

This contains only the length of the interval. Mobiles use contention to decide which one is to send.

**Registration with Base Station**

When a mobile is switched on it makes a request for registration with the base station during the next Interval 3.

**Reservation Requests**

Mobiles send reservation requests during Interval 3. The request can be for some immediate capacity or for regular assignment.

**Destination of Transmission**

Frames transmitted by a mobile are prepended by a header containing the origin and destination addresses, etc. This header also contains a flag to indicate whether the frame should be received by the base station or whether it is to be directly received by another mobile.

## 14.8 Radio LAN Systems

Described above have been two aspects of a radio LAN communication system, the physical transmission and the MAC. Of course, to build a usable system you need much more than this.

1. A management scheme is needed to control which stations are allowed to become members of a particular LAN.
2. Network management is needed so that errors can be found and fixed quickly and so that time people spend in administrative tasks is minimized.
3. If the users are to be mobile, then you need to build a cellular structure. Within each cell there is a base station (access point) and the base stations are interconnected by a wired LAN infrastructure (distribution system). The objective is to allow continuous

and transparent operation for users who are moving around. This means that a user must be able to continue a session (connection) to a server *without* interruption as the user moves between access points.

For this to occur, the access points must communicate with each other and there must be some method to determine when handoff is to occur, to which cell the user is to be handed and to synchronize the necessary system changes in order to do it smoothly.

At the present time, while there are several radio LAN products on the market, we are not aware of any one that enables full transparent mobility as described above. Of course the theoretical problem has been extensively studied in relation to cellular telephone networks.

# Chapter 15. The Frontiers of LAN Research

It is widely accepted in the research and standards communities that current LAN and MAN technologies are not adequate for speeds in the 1 Gbps and above range. FDDI LANs become less efficient as the geographic size, number of stations, or link speed increase, because only one station is allowed to transmit onto the LAN at any one time (where potentially many could do so). DQDB exploits concurrent access but suffers from the fairness problem, which becomes greater as the geographic size and link speeds are increased. In addition DQDB requires that a station should be able to receive data blocks from many senders "simultaneously". At very high link speeds, this becomes both difficult and costly to implement.

Researchers throughout the world are developing many proposals for LAN protocols to operate at speeds above 1 Gbps. Morten Skov (1989)[1] asserts that more than 50 such protocols have been reported in the literature. This chapter deals with two prototype LAN systems developed by IBM Research which are designed to operate in the very high-speed environment. Although both systems have been built in prototype form and publicly demonstrated it must be emphasized that *these are experimental prototypes only.* They were built to gain a better understanding of the principles and problems of operation at speeds above 1 Gbps. Information about them is included here for educational purposes only.

## 15.1 MetaRing

MetaRing is an *experimental* high-speed LAN protocol designed to improve the functioning of token passing rings at very high speeds. It was developed by IBM Research at Yorktown Heights, New York.

In most LAN architectures (TRN, FDDI, CSMA/CD, etc.), only one device can be transmitting onto the LAN at any one time. LANs with dual rings or buses can sometimes support two simultaneous devices, but that is the limit.[2] In the very high-speed LAN environment where the geographical extension of a single frame becomes small compared to the LAN size, we have the opportunity to do significantly better than this, improving the throughput of the LAN many times.

1 *Implementation of Physical and Media Access Protocols for High Speed Communication.*

2 The term LAN here is used to mean "LAN segment". A LAN consisting of multiple segments connected by bridges or routers can of course have one (or two) device(s) transmitting simultaneously on each LAN segment.

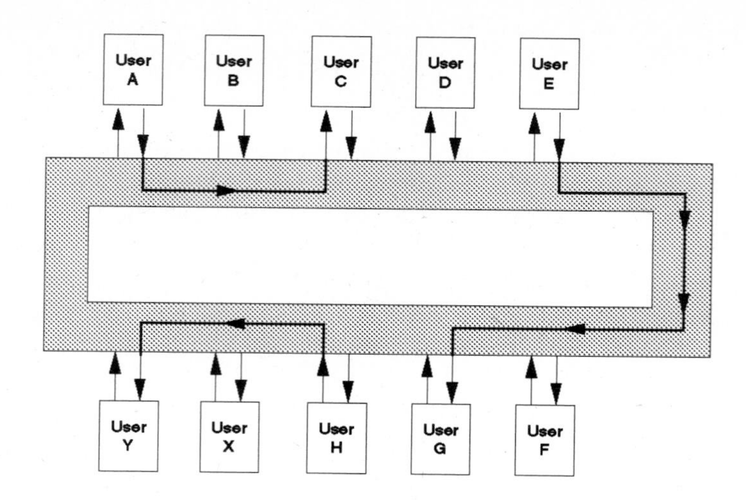


***Figure 15-1.*** *Multiple Simultaneous Communications on a Ring Topology*

Figure 15-1 shows a hypothetical ring LAN with user A sending to user C, user E sending to user G and user H sending to user Y. If this kind of operation were possible then the total throughput of the LAN would be improved significantly (in the hypothetical example, by 300%). Of course, when user A sends to user Y then only one user may transmit.

Looking at the problem of achieving this on a token ring (including FDDI) a number of observations can be made:

- At 4 Mpbs a single bit on a wire is about fifty meters long. Since with TRN protocols there is only a 2-bit buffer in each ring attachment, in most LANs, the beginning part of the frame is being received and discarded by the sending node before the end of the frame is transmitted! The conceptual picture of a frame on a LAN looking like a railway train on its track gives totally the wrong impression.

  Even at 16 Mbps a single bit is still 16 meters long. This means that at the usual token-ring speeds there is not much "storage effect" available on the LAN itself for internode buffering.

- Perhaps the desired result could be achieved by using many (more than one) active tokens. But if this technique was used then the tokens would tend to catch up with one another and group together in a very short time - negating the benefit of having more than one.

- Even if there were multiple tokens if two stations started sending at one time then there could be collisions - a frame arriving at a node while that node is itself transmitting.

One solution is to use a slotted bus technique with fixed length slots. Once a "free" slot is detected the node may confidently transmit into that slot without danger of collision. This is done in for example, in DQDB. But there are other problems here. If you want to send a single block into consecutive slots, the same problem recurs unless there is some other protocol in operation to ensure that sufficient empty slots will arrive consecutively. (See the description of CRMA in this chapter.)

The approach taken with MetaRing is called buffer insertion:

- The idea of having a token is to remove the possibility of collisions. If there are multiple tokens then there is the possibility of collision which must be handled. Therefore a token is not much use in this environment and therefore MetaRing does not use a token.

- If one node starts transmitting while another (downstream) node is transmitting then when the data from upstream reaches the downstream node a collision will occur unless something is done to prevent it.

  The MetaRing solution here is for each node (attached device) to have a large (larger than the longest possible frame) elastic buffer on its receive side. If data arrives from upstream while the node is transmitting then the upstream data is received into the insertion buffer. As soon as the node finishes its own transmission, data from the insertion buffer is immediately sent onto the LAN without waiting for the whole frame to be received. Data received when the node is not sending is sent through the insertion buffer with minimal delay.

  > Because the transmit clock is independent from the clock speed of the received data a buffer is needed to prevent overruns if the receive data stream is faster than the transmit one. The insertion buffer performs this function for data passed through the node. Underruns are not a problem since the transmitter will send idles if data arrives too slowly.

  This technique usually results in unacceptably long latency delays around the ring. This however can be overcome by using very high LAN speeds (100 Mbps and above).

The basic structure of a MetaRing node is shown in Figure 15-2 on page 15-4.

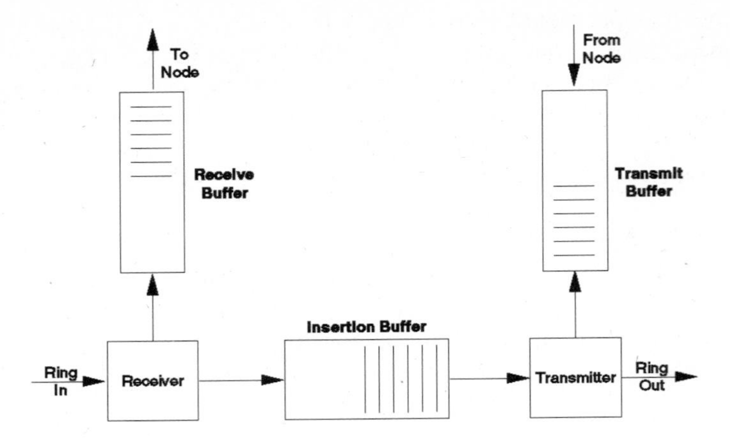


***Figure 15-2.*** *Buffer Insertion*

The first operational rule is:

- *If* nothing is currently being received into the insertion buffer *and* the insertion buffer is empty, *then* the node may transmit.

**An analogy**

MetaRing operation is like the operation of an English traffic roundabout (some of which are more than 200 meters in diameter and have six or more entrance roads). Traffic on the roundabout has priority over traffic entering but once a car starts to enter then traffic already on the roundabout must slow up and make room. Under medium load conditions this works very well.

But, as any connoisseur of English traffic roundabouts will be quick to point out, if one entering road has very heavy traffic then traffic on other entrances can be locked out for considerable periods of time.

This can be solved by the installation of traffic lights at each entrance to the roundabout.

- When a node receives anything from upstream it checks the address in the frame header to determine if it is the destination of the message. If the frame is addressed to this node then the data is directed into the node's receive buffer and does not go into the insertion buffer. (Of course, broadcasts go into both buffers.)

This is a good principle, provided the following conditions are true:

- The insertion buffer is large enough to accommodate the longest allowable frame.
- The ring speed is such that the additional buffering does not cause a problem with the additional insertion buffer delays.

According to Cidon and Ofek[3] simulation studies suggest a worst case total delay of one millisecond on a 100 megabit per second ring. (This depends on the number of active stations and the maximum frame size.)

Looking again at Figure 15-1 on page 15-2, if any user starts transmitting around the ring to a close upstream neighbor (an extreme example would be User B sending to User A) then this user could "hog" the ring and lock all other devices out until it ran out of data (exactly what happens on English traffic roundabouts in peak hour). A means of ensuring "fairness" is needed.

## 15.1.1 Fairness

MetaRing uses a counter-rotating control signal to allocate ring capacity to requesting nodes. This control signal is called a SAT (short for SATisfy). A SAT is not like a token *and* it travels in the opposite direction to the data. In order for the SAT to travel in the opposite direction to the data, a path is needed for it to travel on.

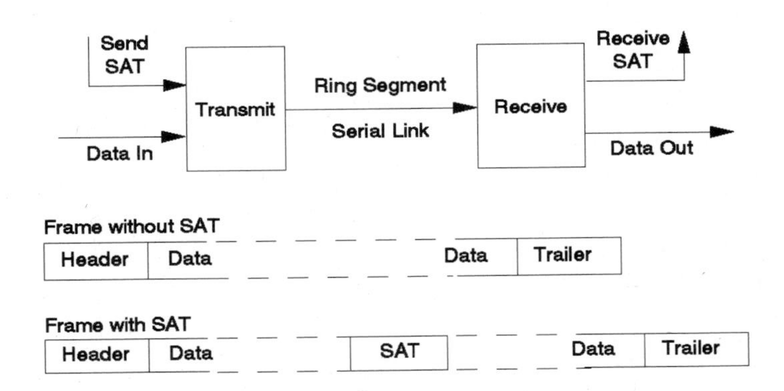


***Figure 15-3.*** *The SAT Control Signal*

In MetaRing there are *two* rings which rotate in opposite directions - just like FDDI without a token. Both rings are used for data transport (different from FDDI where only one of the two rings is used for data - the other is a standby). The SAT on one ring allocates access rights for the other ring. Both rings operate in exactly the same way. There are two SATs, one on each ring, and each SAT allocates capacity for access to *the other* ring.

But if the SAT has to queue behind the data in all those potentially long insertion buffers then the SAT would be limited in effectiveness. SATs are sent around the ring pre-

3 *MetaRing - A Full-Duplex Ring with Fairness and Spatial Reuse*

empting data transmission as they go! When a SAT is to be sent, data transmission is suspended, the SAT is sent, and then data transmission is resumed.

Because the SAT can preempt data transmission it travels around the ring at maximal speed (with only link delays and minor buffering in each node).

When a SAT is received by a node the node is given a predefined quota of data it may send onto the other ring.

- A node is given permission to send a frame (or a quota of frames) when it receives a SAT.
- If it has nothing to send or if it has sent its quota since the last SAT was received then the SAT is forwarded.
- If not (meaning the node does have data to send but the ring has been busy all the time since the last SAT arrived), then the SAT is held until the node has sent a frame (quota of frames).

More formally:

**The SATisfied Condition**

The node is SATisfied if a quota of data has been sent between two successive visits of the SAT message or if its output queue is empty.

**The SAT Algorithm**

When the SAT message is received, do the following:

- If the node is SATisfied then forward the SAT.
- Else hold until SATisfied and then forward the SAT.

After forwarding the SAT the node obtains its next quota of frames.

The SAT algorithm results in fair access.

- Each rotation of the SAT message gives the subset of busy nodes permission to transmit the same amount of data.
- The SAT algorithm is deadlock free.

### 15.1.2 Priorities

A priority mechanism is implemented by assigning a priority number to the SAT. When a SAT has a priority number a receiving node may only send frames with that priority or a higher one.

When a node has priority traffic to send it may increase the priority number (when it forwards the SAT) to ensure that its priority traffic is given preference. Other nodes may increase the priority number further if they have still higher priority traffic. When the node that increased the priority number detects that there is no more priority traffic, then it must decrease the priority number in the SAT to what it was before that node increased it.

## 15.1.3 Control Signaling

The communication of the SAT signal around the ring is only a special case of control signaling. There are more control signals than the SAT only.

Control signaling is achieved by using a redundant serial codeword in the transmission code. MetaRing uses the same physical layer encoding as FDDI (this 4/5 encoding is discussed in 13.6.5, "Physical Layer Protocol" on page 13-39).

Each group of four data bits is actually sent as five bits. This leaves a number of five-bit combinations that may be used to signal special conditions.

As noted above (for the SAT) and illustrated in Figure 15-4, control messages preempt data transmission with no loss in efficiency.

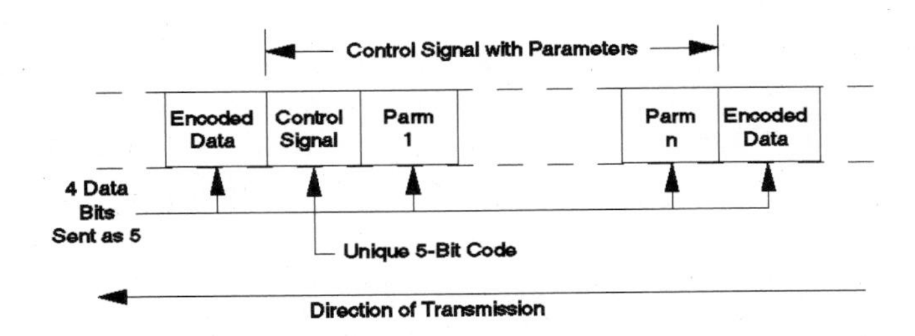


*Figure 15-4. Control Signal Format*

Control messages may travel on either ring. Some control messages (such as the SAT) travel in the opposite direction to the function they control. Others travel in the same direction as the controlled function.

## 15.1.4 Ring Monitor Functions

The functions required to maintain the ring are similar to those functions required in FDDI and token-ring. There must be a ring monitor function to handle:

- Setting up the rings
- Creating SATs and handling error conditions such as lost or multiple SATs
- Re-configuration after a break in either ring

## 15.1.5 Addressing

When the ring is initialized, nodes are allocated a temporary address called a Physical Access Name. Physical access names are really just the sequence of nodes on the ring (1, 2, 3, etc.). Each node must keep a table relating the physical access name of each node on the ring to the node's physical (unchanging) address. When a new node enters the ring a reinitalization process takes place and all physical access names are reassigned.

The physical access name is used partly to determine which ring should be used to send data to another node. There is a selective copy ability in addition to the usual broadcast and point-to-point addressing modes. These are implemented using the physical access names.

## 15.1.6 Fault Tolerance

Since MetaRing uses dual counter-rotating rings they may be wrapped onto one another should a break occur. This is just like the method in FDDI.

A protocol inconsistency arises in that the SAT messages normally travel in the opposite direction to the ring they control. When the rings are wrapped, they become one ring (although one that passes through each node twice). There is a means included in the protocol that takes account of the situation of connecting the two rings as one and the resulting condition of possible multiple SATs and lost SATs.

The wrapping mechanism is so designed that any arbitrary disconnected section of a MetaRing may continue to operate as a disconnected ring.

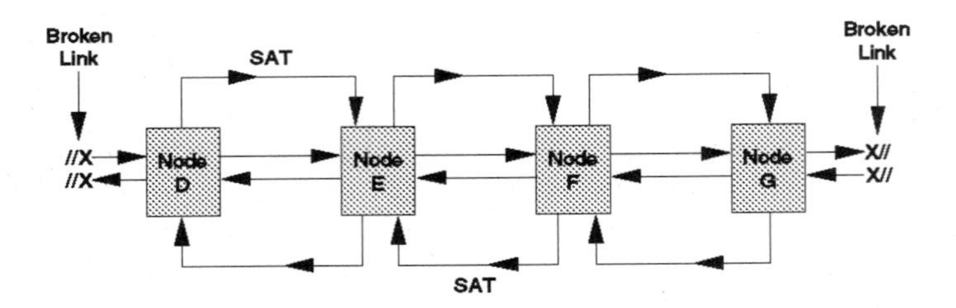


***Figure 15-5. MetaRing Operation on a Disconnected Ring Section.*** Protocols operate correctly (and maintain their fairness property) over a disconnected section of the full-duplex ring.

## 15.1.7 Throughput

In practical LAN situations (in LANs with a large number of nodes), a high percentage of the LAN traffic is local in scope. That is, most LAN traffic is within a work group. Also, people typically site servers close to the work group being served (a print server will usually be close enough for a person to walk over and pick up the printout).

This locality of reference characteristic enables MetaRing LANs to be very efficient indeed. Throughput of many times that of FDDI at the same speed is achievable. In a uniform traffic situation a throughput improvement of eight times can be achieved. Because both rings are used for data traffic, even in the worst case throughput will be twice that of FDDI.

### 15.1.8 Slotted Mode

In some system implementations there is a concern with variable ring latency. There is a mode in MetaRing which is designed to eliminate the insertion buffer at each node by formatting the ring into fixed-length slots.

When this happens one node performs the function of slot generator and there is a busy/empty bit in the beginning of each slot. A node may send into an empty slot subject to the fact that the SAT protocol still operates normally. This reduces ring latency at the cost of losing the capability to send complete frames longer than the fixed slot size in a contiguous manner.

### 15.1.9 Synchronous and Isochronous Traffic

There is also provision in MetaRing for the transport of isochronous traffic such as there is in FDDI-II. After a connection is set up by a monitor, isochronous bandwidth is available with a periodic rate of 125 μsec. It can consist of single or several multiplexed channels, potentially with different bit rates. Isochronous streams bypass insertion buffers and preempt all other transmissions. Specific isochronous start and end delimiters allow network stations to recognize this type of traffic.

Traffic with a real-time (guaranteed-bandwidth) requirement (in FDDI terminology, "synchronous" traffic) is managed by using a mechanism very similar to the timed-token method used in FDDI. See 13.6.2, "Access Protocol Operation" on page 13-34.

A control message (called ASYNC-EN) similar in function to the SAT, also travelling in the opposite direction to the flow of data, is used to control the integration of asynchronous and synchronous traffic.

### 15.1.10 Practical MetaRing

In its experimental implementation MetaRing uses dual, counter-rotating, 100 Mbps (optical) rings (the same as FDDI).

### 15.1.11 Advantages of MetaRing

**Operates Efficiently at Any Speed**

Traditional token-rings (including FDDI) decrease in efficiency as the ring speed is increased. MetaRing will operate efficiently at speeds well into the gigabit per second range.

**Not Particularly Sensitive to Ring Length**

In both FDDI and token-ring, as the ring length increases (both in terms of physical length and in number of attached devices) throughput efficiency decreases substantially. MetaRing throughput efficiency is not affected by ring length. This is because the SAT allocates capacity before it is used and then passes on. It is not like a token that is held during transmission of a block.

**Significantly Improved Throughput**

Again, compared to token-ring or FDDI, MetaRing can achieve very high overall throughput. This comes from the ability for many devices to transmit onto the ring at the same time. The amount of gain is highly dependent on the "locality of reference" but is generally many times higher than an FDDI ring of the same speed.

**Same Cost as FDDI**

An engineering evaluation shows that the circuit complexity needed to implement MetaRing is comparable to that of FDDI. However, you need more storage on the interface chip than is required in FDDI.

A MetaRing chip set can be constructed for much the same cost as an FDDI chip set.

Since the throughput is much greater than FDDI at much the same cost, the cost performance is much better.

## 15.2 Cyclic Reservation Multiple Access (CRMA)

CRMA is an experimental LAN protocol implemented as a prototype by IBM Zurich Research Laboratory. The prototype was demonstrated (using a link speed of 1.13 Gbps on single-mode optical fiber) at the Telecom '91 exhibition in Geneva. The demonstration included prototype connections to IBM PS/2 systems, IBM RS/6000 workstations, IBM 3172 Interconnect Controllers and connection to FDDI rings.

The advantages of CRMA are:

- It will operate with fairness over metropolitan distances (hundreds of kilometers).

- It does not degrade in efficiency as link speed is increased.
- Although data is sent in cells, blocks of user data are sent in a contiguous stream of cells, so receivers don't need multiple reassembly buffers as, for example, are required in DQDB.

A CRMA network is configured as either a "folded bus" or a "dual bus".

## 15.2.1 Bus Structure

The folded bus configuration is shown in Figure 15-6.

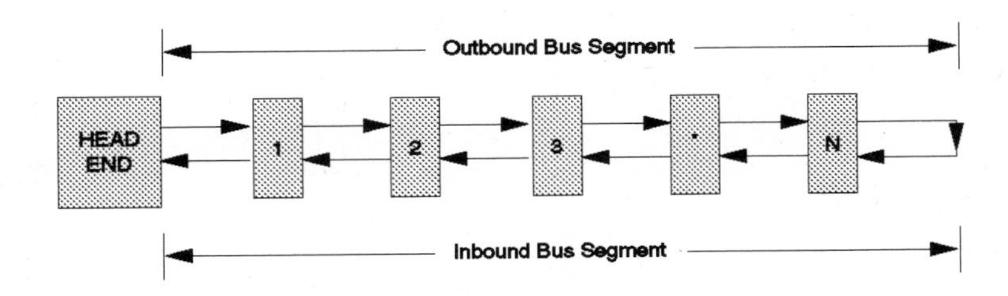


***Figure 15-6.*** *CRMA Folded Bus Configuration*

The bus itself is unidirectional but passes through each node twice (once in each direction). Nodes transmit data on the "outbound bus segment" (that part of the bus traveling *away* from the head-end). They receive data on the "inbound bus segment" (that is, where the data flow is toward the head-end. (This is one advantage of the folded bus configuration, that the nodes do not need to know the position of other nodes on the bus in order to send data to them.) As will be seen later, nodes receive control information on the outbound bus segment as well as transmitting on that segment.

In practical systems the head-end function (and the tail-end too) would be incorporated into every node so that the network would be configured as a physical loop. Only one node at any time would perform the role of head-end (and also of the tail-end). Then, if a break occurs anywhere in the bus it may be reconfigured around the break. A node on one side of the break would become the new head-end and a node on the other side of the break the new tail-end. This technique would enable the bus to continue operation after a single break. DQDB networks use this same principle as described in 13.9.10, "Fault Tolerance" on page 13-67.

## 15.2.2 Slotted Format

Like DQDB, CRMA uses a slotted bus structure. The slot format is conventional and is shown below:

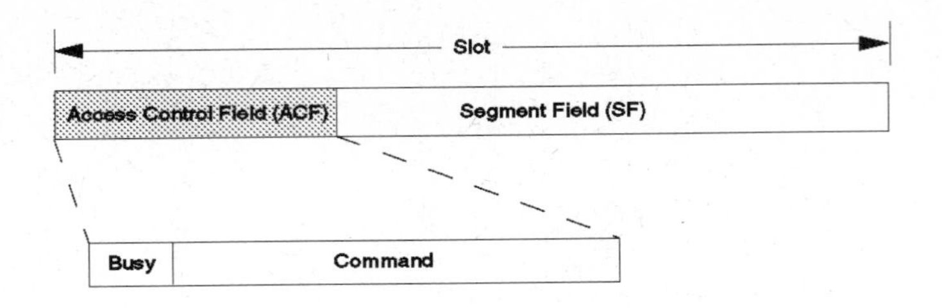


*Figure 15-7. CRMA Slot Format*

## 15.2.3 The Global Queue

In order to understand CRMA it is necessary to consider the concept of a global queue. As described in 13.1.2, "Access Control" on page 13-4, many users (or nodes) on the LAN generate data blocks at different times. It is reasonable to consider these blocks, as they are generated, as forming a global queue for the single resource of the LAN. Because the queue is distributed geographically we can't know the true state of this queue at any particular instant in time. If we conceive of "fairness" to mean FIFO operation then there is the logical problem for the LAN protocol of how to control which node is allowed to send data next.

CRMA solves this problem by appointing a single node (the head-end node) to:

1. Keep track of the global queue size as it builds up.
2. Control a time reference so that attached nodes can know their positions in the queue.
3. Control when nodes are allowed to transmit.

## 15.2.4 The RESERVE Command

The head-end of the bus controls the whole protocol. At intervals,[4] it sends out a special slot with a command in it called a "RESERVE". This command contains two important things:

1. A cycle number that is used by the node to determine its place in the queue
2. A counter field that keeps track of how much data has become available for transmission since the last RESERVE command

---

4 The size of the interval is a tuneable value. It is normally predetermined but may be modified by the head-end depending on traffic conditions on the bus.

When the RESERVE command arrives at a node the slot count in the command is increased by the amount of data (number of slots) that has become available for transmission at this node *since the last RESERVE command.*

Notice that the RESERVE command doesn't give any node permission to send anything. When it returns to the head-end node it contains a count of the amount of data (expressed in slots) that has become available for transmission since the last RESERVE command. The RESERVE command returns to the head-end node in the minimum time of one network latency delay (outbound and inbound bus) - because (unlike a token) it cannot be held by any node. The attaching nodes just add to the counter, they can't delay the slot.

### 15.2.5 The Cycle

Permission to send data is allocated in "cycles". The head-end node sends a START command including the cycle number. When a node receives the START command it has permission to send into the next n available slots. The number of slots the node may send "n" is the number it requested on the previous RESERVE command with the same cycle number.

The START command travels around the bus and each node in turn may send the amount of data that it requested for this cycle.

The head-end node then keeps a queue of cycles that it will allocate in the future. With each cycle number it keeps the number of slots needed for the cycle and also keeps track of the total number of slots for all outstanding cycles.

When the head-end node begins a cycle it generates a START command followed by exactly the number of empty slots needed for that cycle. When it has finished generating one cycle it will then send a START command for the next cycle immediately.

This whole process results in a much better FIFO ordering in the sending of data than does, for example, a token controlled process. In addition it removes the throughput inefficiency of the token principle caused by the latency delays between when a node finishes sending and when another node may start. Under conditions of load, every slot time on the LAN is usable.

The process requires cooperation between the head-end node and the other nodes on the LAN. The head-end node *never knows* any detail about individual nodes. All it sees is the total amount of data requested by all nodes for each cycle.

### 15.2.6 Operation of the Node

When a node receives a RESERVE command, it checks to see if any new data is available to send. If so, it adds the number of slots required to contain that data to the count field within the RESERVE command. It also remembers that it "made a reservation" to send this number of slots in this particular cycle. So the node must keep a record of cycle numbers and the number of slots it requested for each cycle.

For example, in Figure 13-3 on page 13-5 data arrives (or is generated by the node) at each node at different times. If this was a CRMA LAN a RESERVE command sent out at time 1 (let's call it cycle 12) would tell the head-end node the total amount of data that was available at nodes (users) A and E. But user A would keep a record that it requested a number of slots in cycle 12 (so would user E). A RESERVE command sent out at time 2 (call it cycle 13) would only show the amount of data that had arrived at node D (since cycle 12). At time 3 (or cycle 14) the head-end would hear about still more data, this time from nodes B and C.

Let us assume that the bus was busy with previously queued data until after the RESERVE for cycle 14 had returned to the head-end. At this time then, nodes A and E have reservations for cycle 12, node D has a reservation for cycle 13 and nodes B and C have reservations for cycle 14. The head-end node knows only the amount of data that has been reserved in each cycle - not the order of the queue.

The head-end then issues a START command for cycle 12. The START command will occupy a slot and will be followed by the total number of empty slots requested by all reservations for cycle 12. The START command contains a cycle number. When a node receives this command, it has permission to send data into the next empty slot. It is allowed to send into as many empty slots as it reserved for cycle 12 in the previous RESERVE command. Notice that nodes B, C and D all have data waiting but are not allowed to send until START commands are received with a cycle number matching the reservation they made in a previous RESERVE command.

As soon as the head-end has finished generating the correct number of empty slots for cycle 12 it will immediately issue a START command for cycle 13. Notice that when the data is sent on the bus it is sent in the order in which reservations were made. This gives a much better FIFO characteristic than token-controlled access.

In the meantime, at fixed intervals, the head-end continues to issue RESERVE commands. (Slots containing a RESERVE command may appear anywhere - they don't have to wait for the end of a cycle.)

Of course there are limits. Each node can be allocated a maximum number of slots that it can RESERVE on any one cycle. (This is to stop a node from "hogging" the bus.) But when a node sends a block (frame) of data, it sends that data into contiguous slots. This means that a node *must* be able to RESERVE sufficient slots for the maximum sized frame that it can send.

### 15.2.7 Limiting the Access Delay

The above mechanism will guarantee FIFO operation of the global queue at very high utilizations. But is FIFO operation always appropriate? In a congested situation several high-capacity nodes could make reservations of the maximum allowance on every RESERVE cycle. If another node now has data to send then it will have to wait until all the previously reserved data has been sent. In heavy load situations this could result in very long access delays. We are now saying that FIFO is *not* always the best strategy.

CRMA has two additional commands - REJECT and CONFIRM. These commands are used to implement a "backpressure" mechanism which limits the size of the forward global queue so that access delay can be bounded (contained within some limits).

The basic CRMA protocol described above is modified. The RESERVE command no longer implies certainty. The RESERVE command is a request from the nodes and must be accepted by the head-end. When the head-end sees the return of a RESERVE command it may CONFIRM the cycle (that is, accept the reservation), REJECT the cycle (and all previous cycles that have not been confirmed), or START the cycle (if there are no cycles queued ahead).

This means that each node must now maintain three queues:

- A queue of data (by cycle number) for which confirmation has been received.
- A queue of data (again by cycle number) for which reservations have been made, but as yet no confirmation has been received.
- A queue of data for which a reservation has not yet been made.

The head-end node has a predefined limit on the allowed length of the global reservation queue. When a RESERVE returns to the head-end node it looks to see how many slots have been reserved.

- If the total number of slots reserved exceeds the limit, then the head-end confirms the reservations just received (sends a CONFIRM with the same cycle number as that of the RESERVE just received) but then issues a REJECT command to terminate any outstanding RESERVE commands. The head-end will then suppress issuing further RESERVE commands until the number of reserved slots drops below the limit.
- If the number does not exceed the limit (but there are other cycles pending), the head-end issues the CONFIRM command. After a predetermined time interval, the head-end will issue another RESERVE command.

## 15.2.8 Dual Bus Configuration

CRMA can use a dual bus configuration as shown in Figure 15-8.

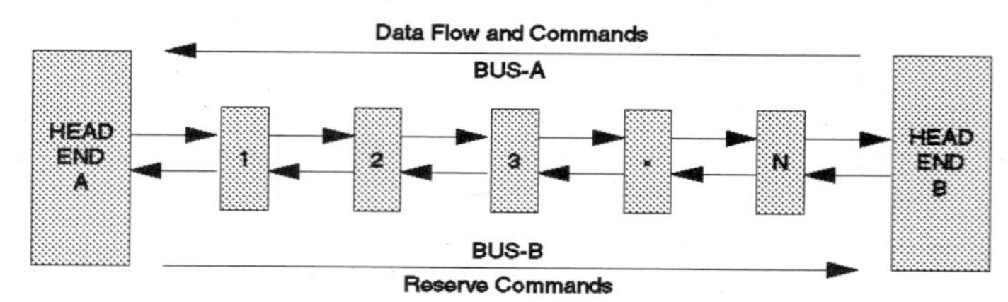


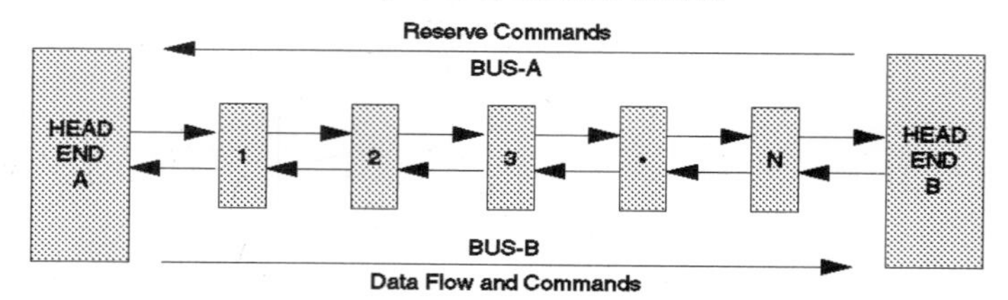


***Figure 15-8.*** *CRMA Dual Bus Configuration.* The system is logically two separate parts. Data flow on one bus is controlled (allocated) by RESERVE commands on the other bus.

The advantage of the dual bus configuration is that it can double the potential throughput. However, all the functions of the single bus configuration must be doubled (which adds significant cost to the adapter). In addition, the nodes must know the location on the bus of all other nodes. (For example, referring to the diagram, if Node 3 wants to send to Node 1 then it must use Bus B; if it wants to send to node N then it must use Bus A.) To do this there must be an information exchange protocol so that each node can discover the location (upstream or downstream) of each other node that it may send to (in order to determine which bus to send on). The upstream or downstream location may change when the bus is reconfigured so that a node location table must be built whenever the bus is initialized (or reconfigured).

As illustrated, operation can be thought of as taking place in two independent halves - the protocol is completely symmetric. Considering only data transport on Bus A:

- RESERVE commands are sent out by head-end B on Bus B.
- CONFIRM, START and REJECT commands are sent out on Bus A by head-end A.
- Head-end A generates the cycles on Bus A.

- The only modification of the protocol is caused by the fact that the head-end node generating the RESERVEs cannot know the state of the global queue. In the folded bus case, when a RESERVE is returned such that the amount of data requested pushes the outstanding total requests for data above the limit, the head-end rejects any RESERVEs that may be in progress and stops issuing RESERVEs until the amount of reserved slots falls below the limit again.

  In the dual bus case it can't stop the reservation process because the head-end node generating the RESERVEs does not know the status of the applicable global queue (that's at the other end of the bus). So, when head-end A rejects a RESERVE (and all RESERVEs currently in progress), head-end B immediately reissues a RESERVE with the same cycle number as the rejected one. When this RESERVE arrives at the other head-end, it may be confirmed or cancelled depending on the current status of the global queue.

Operation for data transport on Bus B is exactly symmetric.

### 15.2.9 Priorities

A priority scheme can be implemented by associating each cycle number with a priority. That is, there might be a cycle 2 for priority 1 and a cycle 2 for priority 2. RESERVEs would be issued separately for each priority at very different rates. This could lead to cycle 2,110 at priority 1 interrupting cycle 3,125 at priority 2. There is no necessary link between cycle numbers at each priority.

The priorities would operate with high priorities preempting the lower ones. Thus, a priority 1 START command (and the slots associated with it) could be issued in the middle of a sequence of vacant slots being generated for priority 2. So, the whole protocol is repeated at each priority level and higher priorities preempt lower ones.

### 15.2.10 Characteristics

As a result of the method of operation, CRMA exhibits the following characteristics:

- Efficiency. Cycles may be scheduled with no time gaps between them so there is no time wasted on the LAN looking for a device that has data to send next.
- Speed insensitivity. The protocol results in high bus utilizations even at very high data rates (Gbps).
- Because of its slotted structure the protocol is easily extendable to handle isochronous traffic. In this case the head-end node would generate premarked slots for isochronous traffic at predetermined intervals. These slots would be ignored by the CRMA data transfer protocol. (This is the way isochronous traffic is handled in DQDB.)

The protocol is especially suitable for Gbps LANs and MANs that are geographically long and have a large number of attached nodes. For short LANs with a small number of nodes there would seem to be little advantage over a token passing approach. In long LANs at very high speed there is a significant advantage.

## 15.3 CRMA-II

Cyclic Reservation Multiple Access - II (CRMA-II) represents the frontier of on-going LAN and MAN research. Although not implemented, the protocol has been extensively studied and simulated. It was developed as a result of the experience gained from the CRMA and MetaRing prototype projects.[5]

It should be noted that CRMA-II (like CRMA and MetaRing) is a Medium Access Control (MAC) protocol. There are many other functions that must occur on a real LAN or MAN that are not part of a MAC protocol. These are primarily management functions such as error recovery, monitoring, initialization and the like.

### 15.3.1 Objective

CRMA-II uses many detailed features of the existing LAN/MAN protocols already discussed, especially CRMA and MetaRing. Each of these had characteristics which were very desirable and other characteristics which needed to be improved. The objective of CRMA-II is to adopt the best features of these protocols so as to arrive at the best possible result.

**Cyclic Reservation**

The cyclic reservation principle of CRMA has proven excellent at high utilizations. Access delay for low utilization nodes has a strict upper bound and fairness of access is extremely good. But:

1. CRMA is less good at very low utilizations. The minimal access delay on a lightly loaded bus is the waiting time for a RESERVE and a START command - which corresponds to one network round-trip delay.
2. There is no reuse of slots on the bus once data has been received at the destination. On a bus with many active nodes, there is considerable potential for re-use of slots which increases the capacity of the LAN significantly.

**Buffer Insertion**

Buffer insertion (MetaRing) on the other hand is an excellent principle at low and medium utilizations - it gives low access delay and maximal reuse of LAN capacity. At high utilizations, however, some precautions must be taken:

5 CRMA-II is the result of work performed at the IBM Research Division, Zurich, Switzerland. A list of journal articles and conference papers relating to CRMA-II may be found in the list of related publications.

1. A "hog" node can completely prevent its immediate downstream neighbors from transmitting. (This was effectively solved in MetaRing by the use of the SAT protocol.)
2. At very high utilizations ring latency can become dominant if many nodes have data in their insertion buffers.
3. Access delay while minimal at low loadings can also become significant at high LAN utilizations.

CRMA-II uses the cyclic reservation technique of CRMA which is mainly active at high utilizations combined with the buffer insertion principle to allow for immediate access at low utilizations whilst still preserving slot contiguity in frame transmission. Operation takes place in both modes simultaneously at all times but naturally shifts from being predominantly one mode to the other. In this way CRMA-II gains the best aspects of both protocols. CRMA-II is less complex than CRMA.

## 15.3.2 Principles of CRMA-II

Perhaps the first principle of CRMA-II is generality. Most individual mechanisms of CRMA have been extended and generalized so that they can be considered independent of their original context.

### 15.3.2.1 Topology

CRMA-II is able to use ring, bus or folded bus topologies. The protocol is designed to allow the building of a common set of interface chips that can be used for any of the three topologies.

### 15.3.2.2 Physical Layer Coding

CRMA-II (as with MetaRing and CRMA) proposes an "8 out of 10" (8B/10B) coding scheme similar in principle to the 4B/5B code used in FDDI (see 13.6.5.2, "Data Encoding" on page 13-41). This means that every 8-bit group is coded into 10 bits on the optical medium. Only bit combinations that have a mixture of one bits and zero bits are allowed. This means that no string of longer than three consecutive bits is allowed to be either all ones or all zeros. This is done for three reasons:

1. It provides frequent transitions in the code to allow a receiver PLL to derive accurate timing from the incoming bit stream. (See 2.1.6.1, "Phase Locked Loops (PLLs)" on page 2-11.)
2. It allows some valid (sufficient transitions) combinations that do not have a corresponding data value. These are used for delimiters and synchronization.
3. It minimizes the amount of high-speed circuitry necessary to implement an adapter.

In CRMA-II this principle (of encoding groups of bits on the medium) is generalized. To simplify hardware, so-called Atomic Data Units (ADUs) are introduced. Although the line coding is 8B/10B, the protocol is arranged such that the smallest unit of data that may be coded or decoded is either 16 or 32 data bits (that is, 20 or 40 bits on the medium). These units are called ADUs (Atomic Data Units). (32-bit ADUs are deemed appropriate for 2.4 Gbps operation.) No coding or decoding operation takes place in CRMA-II on anything smaller than the 16 or 32-bit ADU *except* synchronization. The synchronization sequence is a unique 8B/10B code that forms the first eight data bits of a delimiter ADU.

This is done because as the speed of the medium increases into the multi-gigabit range (5 Gbps is a practical speed today) the logic speed of available circuitry cannot keep up. Very fast logic (Gallium Arsenide technology) is very costly and not very dense. Slower logic comes in many shapes and sizes but recently a combination of "bipolar" technology and the common CMOS technology (called "BiCMOS") which allows reasonably high speeds at containable cost has become available.

By using ADUs, the circuitry that handles the bit stream in serial form must operate at the speed of the medium and therefore it must continue to use expensive technology (such as GaAs). But as soon as a 40-bit group is received it can then be processed in parallel (as a 32-bit data group) at 1/40th of the medium speed using significantly lower-cost circuit technology.

This involves almost no loss of efficiency in coding.

#### 15.3.2.3 Slots

Data in CRMA-II is transferred in a slotted format to allow for capacity allocation and scheduling.

The principle involved is very similar to that used in DQDB or CRMA, but there is a basic difference. In other LAN/MAN slotted systems a slot is a fixed entity identified by a delimiter (such as a code violation) followed by a fixed number of bits and immediately followed by another slot. That is, on the medium slots are synchronously coupled with one another. In CRMA-II a slot is fixed in size but special variable length frames carrying scheduling information are inserted as needed *between* slots. This means that slots are loosely coupled with one another.

A slot is delimited by a START ADU and an END ADU. The first eight bits of the start ADU is a synchronization character. The format for 32-bit ADUs is shown in Figure 15-9 on page 15-21.

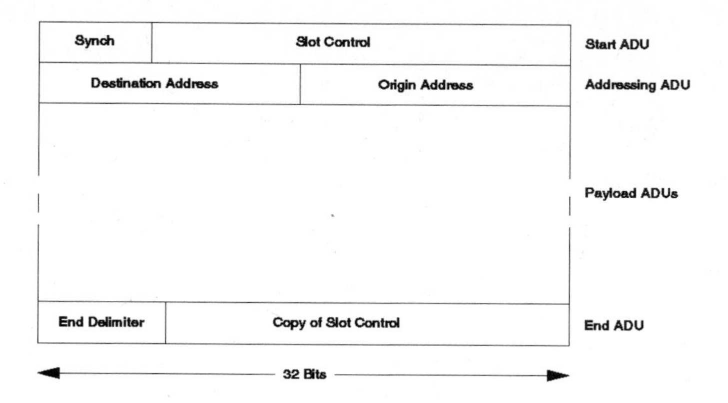


*Figure 15-9. CRMA-II Slot Format*

MAC commands which travel between the "scheduler" and the nodes *no longer "piggyback" in the slot headers of data slots.* They are carried as special (varying length entities) *between* regular data slots.

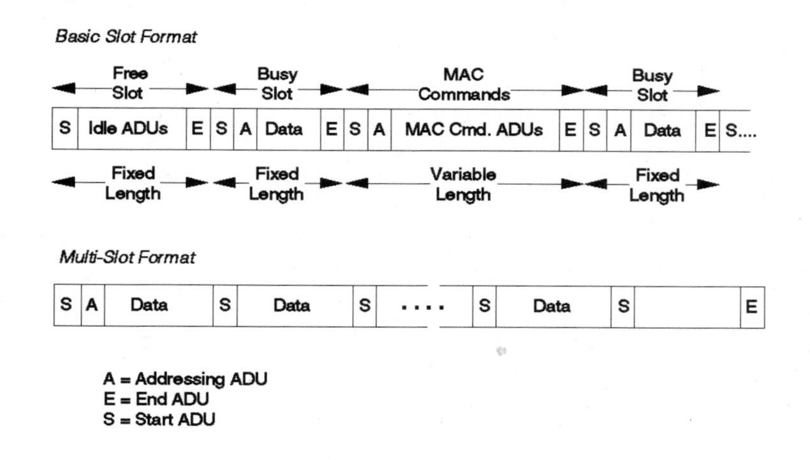


*Figure 15-10. CRMA-II Slot Formats*

When a node sends data over multiple slots the basic slot marking is maintained but much of the slot overhead is avoided by having only one END ADU (for the whole frame) and only one addressing ADU at the start of the frame. See Figure 15-10.

### 15.3.2.4 The Scheduler

The functions performed by the "head-end" node in CRMA are generalized into a capacity scheduling function in CRMA-II. The scheduler allocates capacity individually, on a node-by-node basis in response to requests made by the nodes during a reservation cycle. This differs from CRMA where the head-end node does not know about individual node demands - it only knows about the total capacity requested in each cycle. This is required to control fairness in the presence of slot reuse.

Information is exchanged with individual nodes by MAC commands of variable length (see Figure 15-10 on page 15-21). The scheduler sends out a RESERVE command as a special start/end ADU pair. Individual nodes that want to send data insert their requests (individually) between the Start/End ADU pair. When the frame returns to the scheduler, it contains an ADU from each node requesting a capacity allocation. The scheduler then responds by sending a CONFIRM command (delimited by a Start/End ADU pair) containing an individual response ADU for each node that made requests. In this way each requesting node is given an individual capacity allocation for this cycle.

In a ring network the scheduler function would normally be part of a generalized monitor function. In a ring network a monitor is necessary to detect and purge errored (permanently busy) slots, etc.

### 15.3.2.5 Capacity Allocation Concept

The principles behind the allocation of capacity are:

1. Slot re-use. After a slot has been delivered to a destination, this slot becomes available for immediate reuse either by the destination node itself or by any other node.

2. Immediate access to unreserved slots. At periods of light loading, the necessary wait to receive a RESERVE followed by a CONFIRM could cause an unnecessary delay. If a slot is not currently being controlled by the scheduler and is "free" it can be used by any node that it passes.

Thus there are two types of slots "Reserved" and "Gratis". A Reserved slot is one that has been allocated by the scheduler. A Gratis slot is one that is not currently under the control of the scheduler. Slots dynamically change from Reserved to Gratis status and back again.

A Reserved slot may only be used by a node that has been granted a capacity allocation through a CONFIRM command from the scheduler. (Whenever the scheduler sends a group of CONFIRMs it immediately begins marking enough slots Reserved to satisfy the amount of capacity it just confirmed.)

A slot that contains data is always marked as Busy/Gratis even if it was previously Reserved. When the data is received by the destination (or back at the originator if it was a broadcast) the slot is marked Free/Gratis. In this state it may be claimed and re-used by any node receiving it.

#### 15.3.2.6 The Cyclic Reservation Protocol

Although CRMA-II will work in bus, folded bus, and ring topologies, the protocol is most general in ring operation and therefore it is best studied in the ring configuration. The scheduler function may be active in any node on a ring but only in the head-end node of a bus.

The cyclic reservation protocol is similar to that of CRMA.

- The scheduler sends out a RESERVE command but, different from CRMA, every node that wants to make a reservation inserts its own request into the variable-length RESERVE command which increases with each insertion.
- RESERVE requests contain the number of requested slots and the number of slot transmissions done by this node since the last reservation cycle.
- It is important to note that the scheduler does not know the identity of each requesting node. No information is kept by the scheduler about previous cycles or about previous requests from individual nodes. The scheduling decision is made based solely on information returned in the RESERVE command.
- The scheduler then decides how much data (how many slots) will be allowed to each node on this cycle.
- The scheduler then sends a CONFIRM command which contains an individual response to each requesting node. (The CONFIRM is a block of responses each one corresponding to a request made on the ALLOCATE. All outstanding ALLOCATE requests are replied to in the same CONFIRM.)
- Immediately after sending the CONFIRM command, the scheduler begins marking slots as reserved.

    In a ring topology this means marking Gratis slots. In a bus topology it means generating them.

- This cyclic reservation protocol is quite different from CRMA in that there is only one cycle in progress at any one time, so that no cycle number is needed and there is no need to correlate cycle start commands with previously made requests.
- When the CONFIRM is received by a node, it records the number received as its "confirmation count". This means that the node is now allowed to use this number of Free/Reserved slots as they arrive. The CONFIRM command shrinks (gets shorter) with each information removal.

#### 15.3.2.7 The Scheduling Algorithm

The scheduling algorithm is quite intelligent. At periods of high loading some nodes may want to use much more than "fairness" would dictate. Because any node may use a Free/Gratis slot at any time these high throughput nodes could continue to use LAN capacity even when the scheduler wants to slow them down a bit.

This is prevented by the scheduler sending either a reserved slot allocation or a "DEFERRED Allocation" to each node.

A node with a deferred allocation may access only after it has let pass the indicated number of Free/Gratis slots.

This occurs only at times of extremely high loading.

#### 15.3.2.8 Cycles

As described above individual reservation cycles are run one at a time with no reservation in advance for future cycles. The single cycle concept simplifies the reservation-based fairness control significantly because only two commands (RESERVE, CONFIRM) are alternatively on the medium. This makes the protocol extremely robust and enables the system to recover from command failures without any additional command.

When one cycle finishes (when the scheduler has marked the allocated total number of slots as reserved) the next cycle is started by issuing the RESERVE command to collect requests from the nodes. The reservation cycle itself starts when the RESERVE command has returned (after having circulated on the LAN) and the scheduler has allocated the reservations.

All this produces a significant gap between two reservation cycles (that is between the end of slot marking and the start of the next cycle). This however does not mean that the system loses throughput. On the contrary, transmissions continue to take place in Free/Gratis slots and since access to these slots is less restricted (only when a node must defer) system throughput must be higher than for the case of back-to-back cycles. In fact, slots are only marked as reserved to correct unfairness and to guarantee a low bounded access delay.

#### 15.3.2.9 Addressing

The system uses "short" addresses. A single ADU contains both destination and origin LAN addresses. This means that the full LAN/MAN address isn't used for sending data. During the initialization procedure a set of local addresses are allocated. Each node keeps a table relating the real (long form) LAN address and the shortened addresses needed for send/receive operation.

#### 15.3.2.10 Data Transfer

- When a node has been granted an allocation, this means that the node may use the allocated number of Free/Reserved slots. (A Free/Reserved slot is one that has been allocated by the scheduler but as yet has not been used by any node.) There are two ways in which a node may use a Free/Reserved slot. It may send data in that slot or it may use the slot to empty its insertion buffer (this subject is treated later).
- When a node puts data into a Free/Reserved slot it changes the slot status to Busy/Gratis. (Busy because it has data in it, Gratis because it has been used and therefore is no longer under allocation control of the scheduler.)
- When the Busy/Gratis slot is received by its destination, the data is copied and the slot marked Free/Gratis.
- A Free/Gratis slot is always available for use by any node receiving it (including the node that marked it Free/Gratis). So this slot may be immediately re-used.

In operation, at very low loads, most slots will be Free/Gratis and may be used immediately by any node wanting to send. As the load builds up, the scheduler will begin getting allocation requests from nodes. The scheduler will begin marking Free/Gratis slots to Free/Reserved as they pass by in order to make sure that requesting nodes can get the allocated capacity.

If the scheduler were to mark only Free/Gratis slots there would be an apparent problem here. Then, what if a node immediately before the scheduler on the ring decides to use all the passing Free/Gratis slots thus preventing the scheduler from getting any slots to reserve? Therefore the scheduler does not only mark Free/Gratis slots to Free/Reserved it also marks passing Busy/Gratis slots (these are slots containing data) to the Busy/Reserved status. When a Busy/Reserved slot is received by a node, the Busy status is changed to Free resulting in the creation of a Free/Reserved slot that may be used by a node having a capacity allocation. So, ultimately the scheduler has caused the creation of the correct number of Free/Reserved slots. Thus when the scheduler allocates x slots it satisfies the allocation by immediately marking passing Gratis slots (either Busy or Free) to the reserved status.

When operation is examined two characteristics should be noted:

1. Some Free/Reserved slots will pass by the scheduler. This is fine and is a result of a Busy/Gratis slot being marked Busy/Reserved on its last trip past the scheduler and then later being marked Free by a receiving node.
2. The slot contiguity property, as given in CRMA requires an additional mechanism as described below. In CRMA, frames of data are sent in a contiguous stream (or block) of cells. Successive cells are used to transmit a frame until the end of that frame. Between the first and last cells of a frame of data *no* other data is allowed.

In CRMA-II slot re-use causes the fragmentation of blocks of cells to the point where there is no way of guaranteeing any contiguous stream of free cells. This means that a node cannot know when there will be (or if there will be) a stream of consecutive cells in which to send a frame of any particular size.

### 15.3.2.11 ATM "Mode" of Data Transfer

If we wish to use the protocol as a basis for a distributed ATM (see 9.1, "Asynchronous Transfer Mode (ATM)" on page 9-3) switch then nothing more is needed. The cell format would be:

- Start ADU.
- Address ADU (contains origin and destination short addresses).
- ATM cell (48 bytes of data with 5 bytes of header) in 14 ADUs. For ease of processing you might put the ATM header in the first two ADUs and the ATM data segment in the following 12 ADUs.
- End ADU.

Since the whole ATM concept is based on the principle of the asynchronous multiplexing of separate cells then the property of slot contiguity for frame transmission is not relevant.

### 15.3.2.12 Buffer Insertion

If we wish to use CRMA-II as a traditional LAN or MAN architecture the ability to send a frame of data into contiguous slots is very valuable. Without this ability a receiving node must maintain multiple frame reassembly buffers (and logic to reassemble different frames) so that it may receive from many senders "simultaneously". At the speeds involved, this is quite complex and expensive to do.

CRMA-II meets this objective by introducing the buffer insertion principle discussed above (see 15.1, "MetaRing" on page 15-1).

In order to use this principle the node has a buffer large enough to accommodate the maximum sized frame *between* its receiver and its transmitter. This is shown below:

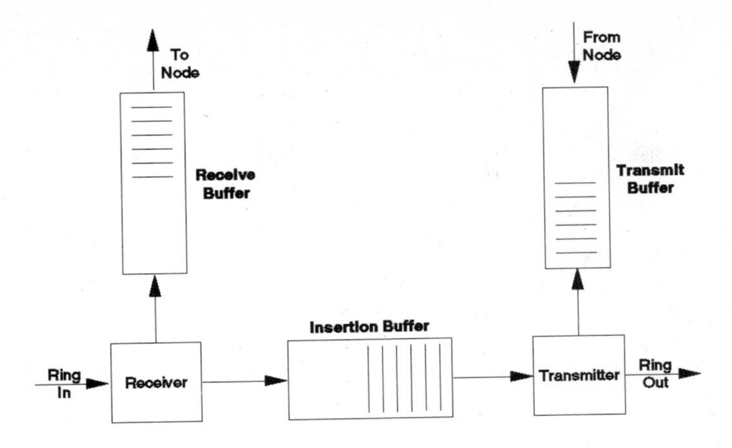


*Figure 15-11. Principle of Buffer Insertion*

The principle is basically the same as that described for MetaRing but with a few differences:

- In MetaRing the rule is that a node may start sending provided there is nothing being received from the ring *and* there is nothing in the insertion buffer.

  Because of the slotted transmission structure, the rule for sending in CRMA-II is that when a Free/Gratis slot (or a Free/Reserved slot if the node has reservations) is detected on the ring (or bus) segment *and* there is nothing in the insertion buffer, the node may commence sending.

- Data is sent as a contiguous frame but with interspersed Start ADUs at slot boundaries. This is illustrated in Figure 15-10 on page 15-21.

  When the data is received at the destination node the destination node reformats the multi-slot into a stream of single Free slots.

- While a node is transmitting a frame in this way, slots continue to arrive on its inbound side. If a Free/Gratis slot arrives then it is discarded. If a Free/Reserved slot arrives *and* the node has reservations then this slot also may be discarded (the node must of course decrement its allocation of reserved slots in this case).

- When Busy slots arrive (and/or Free/Reserved slots if the node does not have an allocation) they are held in the insertion buffer until the node finishes its transmission.

At the end of transmission of the frame, data is sent onto the ring from the insertion buffer and new slots arriving are entered into it. The insertion buffer also performs the function of elastic buffer to accommodate differences in the clock speeds at various nodes. The node is not allowed to send again until its insertion buffer becomes empty.

As operation continues:

- Incoming data from the medium is delayed because of the data queued ahead of it in the insertion buffer.
- When a Free/Gratis slot arrives it is discarded and since a slot full of data is now being transmitted from the insertion buffer this empties the insertion buffer of a slot full of data.
- In a busy ring, the node may find that the insertion buffer will not empty quickly enough by just waiting for Free/Gratis slots. In this case the node will request an allocation the next time the scheduler sends out a RESERVE command. If the node has more data to send it will request slots from the scheduler sufficient to both empty its insertion buffer and to send its next frame.
- When the node receives a CONFIRM command containing a slot allocation it will begin treating Free/Reserved slots in the same way as Free/Gratis slots and discarding them. This process empties the insertion buffer.
- Once the insertion buffer is empty, data passing through the node from upstream is no longer delayed.
- The node is allowed to send again as soon as it receives a Free/Gratis slot or (if it has an allocation) a Free/Reserved slot.

### 15.3.3 Summary

CRMA-II is designed to provide optimal fairness under varying load conditions on a very fast LAN or MAN. (The principle will work over a very wide range of speeds but the objective is to operate well at 2.4 Gbps per second.)

1. The buffer insertion protocol is used to provide almost instant access at low loadings and to allow for the sending of a frame of user data as a stream of contiguous slots.
2. The reservation protocol allows fairness in operation (and in particular low access delays) at from medium to very high utilizations.
3. Operation is such that both protocols operate at all times but one will tend to dominate the other depending on load conditions.
4. It exhibits the same properties as discussed for MetaRing with respect to efficient operation at any speed, throughputs well beyond the medium speed due to slot reuse, insensitivity to ring length and the number of nodes, as well as support of asynchronous, synchronous and isochronous traffic.

# Chapter 16. Lightwave Networks

The optical networks so far described (FDDI, DQDB, MetaRing, SDH) all share a common feature. Logically they could be implemented just as easily on copper wire. In other words, fiber has been used as a substitute for copper wire (although with many advantages, including speed).

Around the world there is a significant amount of research going on aimed at producing a generation of "Lightwave Networks" which would operate quite differently from the systems we have today. This is because it is widely believed that in the five-year future there will be a demand for networks with large numbers of workstations (thousands) each of which could generate a sustained data rate of perhaps 1 Gbps.

***To our knowledge, there are no commercial WDM network products yet available. However, among researchers it is widely believed that effective WDM networks could be built today.***

It was mentioned earlier (4.1.2.2, "Transmission Capacity" on page 4-11) that the potential data carrying capacity of fiber is enormous - at least ten thousand times today's 2 Gbps practical limit. The aim is to make use of this to build networks with capacities of two or three orders of magnitude greater than we have today.

This is not as easy to do as it sounds.

1. We can't increase the transmission rate because the electronics needed just won't go that fast. Today's practical maximum speed is around 2 Gbps (up to 10 in the lab). In addition, as transmission speeds get faster, the cost of the necessary electronics increases exponentially.

2. Fiber cabling is quite restrictive when it comes to constructing a multi-user LAN or MAN.

   - If the fiber is to be used as a bus then taps need to be made in order for a station to receive or transmit. On the receive side, a splitter is inserted in the fiber and half the light directed to the station and the other half goes on to the next station. This means the bus loses half its light (3 dB) at every receive station.

     This is quite different from electrical transmission where a tap can be inserted for a single station with only trivial loss of signal.

   - Fiber is basically a unidirectional medium so we can't have a true (bi-directional) bus structure.

   - When data is to be sent from a station onto the fiber, another device (a passive combiner) must be inserted to combine the signal already on the fiber with the incoming signal from the station. Of course, some light is lost when this is done.

These problems don't so much represent "limitations" but rather are characteristics of the fiber medium that must be considered when designing a totally optical system.

### 16.1.1 Objectives

The way in which we approach building a lightwave network is critically dependent on the job the network has to perform and the environment in which it must operate. There are a number of different environments for which lightwave networks look promising but the technical design for one environment can be very different from the technical design of a lightwave network in a different environment. These environments can be roughly classified as follows:

**Local Communications**

This is the interconnection of computers and computer devices in close proximity to one another. It also includes the interconnection of the "internals" of the computer itself. This means the connection of the processor to its memory for example. Or more likely, the interconnection of multiple processing elements with multiple memories.

A current example of the use of fiber to replace a computer I/O channel is the IBM "ESCON" channel. This device is an enormous advance of its electronic predecessor but it only uses fiber as a transmission medium - all of the switching is electronic. This was discussed in Chapter 10, "High-Speed Circuit-Switching Systems" on page 10-1.

**Local Area Networks and Metropolitan Area Networks**

Most research in lightwave networks is concentrated in the LAN and MAN area. This is partly because of worldwide legal and administrative restrictions surrounding the construction of private wide area networks. Another reason is that it is widely believed that the requirement for gigabit speeds at the workstation is primarily for communication within a single work group.

**Wide Area Networks**

This is a completely different type of environment to the local one. There is an enormous amount of work going on in applying fiber optics to wide area communication. Indeed, in many countries optical fiber is now the primary means of wide area communication. However, most of the work is centered on using fiber for transmission replacing traditional wire but not changing the basic design of systems.

**Local Distribution Networks**

This is the "fiber to the home" environment. The objective is to replace existing cable television and telephone distribution systems with a wideband system capable of carrying the above traffic but also able to carry new services. These services could be things like interactive video entertainment or just the ability to "dial a movie," that is, to see any movie on demand at any time *without* needing to rent a tape.

Of course there are issues in design of a network which reach well beyond the technical parameters. For example, one of the first lessons learned by the early implementers of MAN networks has been that users are not willing to allow their data to transit any other company's premises. So a MAN network using WDM would be commercially unacceptable if the multiplexed WDM stream was delivered to every end user.

### 16.1.2 Sharing the Fiber

There are four principal ways in which the fiber can be shared among multiple users. These are the same ways that we are used to in the electrical world.

**Block Multiplexing**

This is the technique of existing electronic LANs. (See A.1.6, ""Block" Multiplexing" on page A-6.) It's not a very good idea here because it doesn't satisfy our objectives. The medium is used as a single channel which, of course, is limited to electronic speeds.

However, within another multiplex structure (such as WDM) this technique can be used very effectively to sub-multiplex single channels. The CSMA technique has been used in a number of experimental networks to enable sharing of a control channel.

**Code Division Multiple Access (CDMA)**

This technique allows multiple users to share the same channel by transmitting different types of signal *at the same wavelength*. The principles are described (in relation to radio communication) in 14.4.2, "Code Division Multiple Access (CDMA)" on page 14-11. Those same principles apply also in the optical domain. However, the limitation of transmitters and receivers to electronic speeds means that the chip rate would be about 2 Gbps at a maximum. The data rate available for individual channels would be significantly lower than this. In the context of purely optical networks it seems that CDMA may be useful as a sub-multiplexing technique.

**Time Division Multiplexing**

TDM techniques do work nicely on a fiber. But again, TDM uses a single channel which is accessed (although at different times) by many devices. This means that each device must be able to transmit and receive at the full speed of the channel. This brings us back to the same problem of the speed of the electronics. You can have one channel only and it is limited by electronic speed. TDM does, however, reduce the electronics cost a bit by enabling the device to use less high-speed electronics than it otherwise would.

TDM techniques (especially the "ALOHA" techniques) can be used on individual channels within a group which is multiplexed by WDM. In this case TDM becomes a sub-multiplexing technique within a WDM system.

### Wavelength Division Multiplexing (WDM)

Wavelength Division Multiplexing is just another way of saying Frequency Division Multiplexing.[1] When dealing with the very high frequencies of light it is much more convenient to talk about wavelength rather than frequency. Of course, these are the same thing expressed differently:

$$Wavelength = \frac{\text{speed of light}}{frequency}$$

The principles of FDM are described in A.1.1, "Frequency Division Multiplexing" on page A-1.

Many independent "channels" are derived on the medium by sending separate signals at different wavelengths. Provided they are kept somewhat apart they do not interfere with one another (or rather there isn't enough interference to bother us too much). Device A can send to device B using wavelength $\lambda_1$ at the same time as device C is sending to device D using wavelength $\lambda_2$. The beauty here is that each communication can take place at full electronic speed quite independently of the other.

This means that the data rate being operated on the fiber is (number of channels) × (data rate of each individual channel). In this way we can get much greater data rates on the fiber than electronic circuits will allow.

In this discussion we are considering the building of a single logical network. This means that all stations use the same modulation techniques, speeds, etc. Each channel is operated in the same way.

However, it should be pointed out that a major advantage of WDM is the insensitivity to modulation technique and speed between different channels. Different channels can operate at different speeds with different (even analog) modulation techniques. A network that allows many different kinds of users (using different modulation techniques and transmission speeds) using an overall "virtual circuit" approach may well find practical application in MAN networks of the future.

So it should not be surprising that the bulk of research on lightwave networks is being done on WDM systems.

---

[1] In the world of optical communications, it has been usual to talk about the wavelength of a signal or a device without reference to frequency. However, when you get to very narrow linewidth lasers and coherent detection systems, these are normally expressed in MHz or GHz.

## 16.2 WDM for LANs and MANs

### 16.2.1 Network Topology

The objective of the network topology design is to provide a path from the transmitter of any station to the receiver of any other (any-to-any connectivity). This would seem to be simple but the unique characteristics of fiber and the use of the WDM technique combine to place a number of restrictions on the kinds of network topologies which are possible.

**Ring Topologies**

These are not appropriate for the types of WDM system under discussion. (This is not because of the optical nature of the network but because multiple independent signals are sharing the same medium - it would be equally true in the electrical world using FDM multiplexing.)

The problem is removing an old signal from the ring. In order to remove a single channel from the ring and replace it with a different one, the station would need to receive *all* the channels on the ring and repeat the ones its wasn't concerned with. This could be done either electrically or with a wavelength selective filter. Unless the old signal is removed, any new signal put on the fiber at a given wavelength just mixes with what's already there and you get garbage.

Tapping the fiber such that a single wavelength (and only that wavelength) is removed from the ring and directed to an attached station could perhaps be done with wavelength selective filters. However, in most proposed systems, these filters would need to be tuneable and their presence would significantly complicate the system's design.

**Folded Buses**

A folded bus system is shown in Figure 16-1.

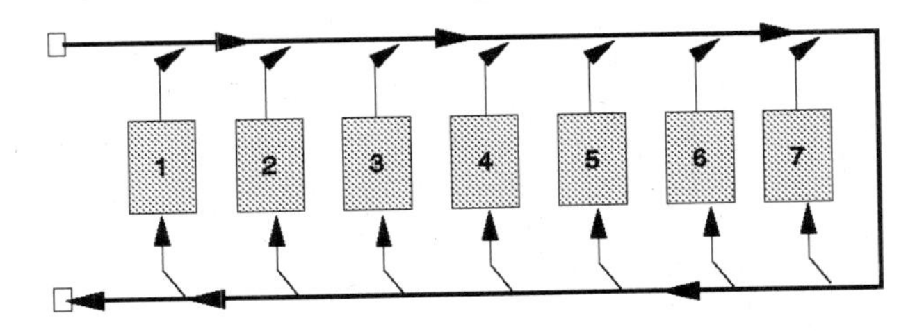


***Figure 16-1.*** *Folded Bus Configuration.* Stations (1 to 7) transmit on different wavelengths each onto the top part of the bus where the signals mix. Taps on the return section deliver the mixed signal (although with varying strength) to each node.

These will work but require amplifiers at frequent intervals down the bus.

The problem is that as the fiber is tapped at each station the signal is split and half carries on along the bus and half goes to the attached station. In Figure 16-1 on page 16-5, station 7 will get half the signal and then station 6 will get half of that (1/4 of the original signal). Station 5 will get half of that (1/8) of the original signal until station 1 will get 1/128th of the original signal.

If there are n stations on the bus the signal degrades to $\frac{1}{2^n}$ of what it was originally (where n = the number of stations).

It is possible to build splitters that direct a smaller proportion of the signal to the attached station but this is difficult and introduces other problems.

### Passive (Reflective) Stars

This configuration is illustrated in Figure 16-2.

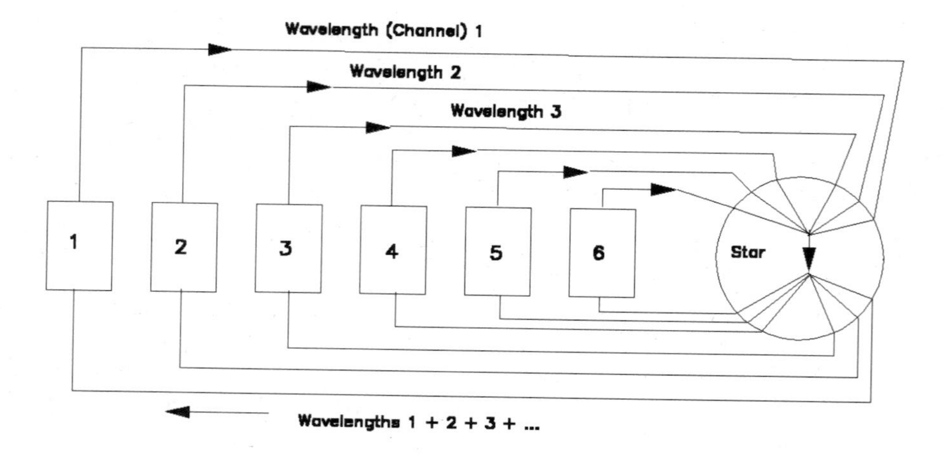


*Figure 16-2. Reflective Star Configuration.* On the transmit side, a separate fiber connects each station to the input side of the star. The signals are mixed and then split. Separate fibers deliver the mixed signal (all channels) to each station.

These have been used in several experimental systems because they can support many more stations without amplification than can bus networks.

As shown in the figure, separate fibers are connected from each station to the star. This device is really a combiner followed by a splitter. All incoming signals are combined onto a single fiber and then this is split to direct 1/n part of the combined signal back to each station. That is, the output signal is reduced by $10\log_{10}N$ - where N equals the number of stations. Of course, a topology like this can handle significantly more stations than can the bus topology described above.

A feature of the topology is that the star is a passive (non-powered) device - a characteristic considered very important for reliability.

Nevertheless, any fiber LAN or MAN topology will require amplifiers if a meaningful number of devices is to be handled.

## Tree Structures

Tree structures such as that shown in Figure 16-3 are also possible.

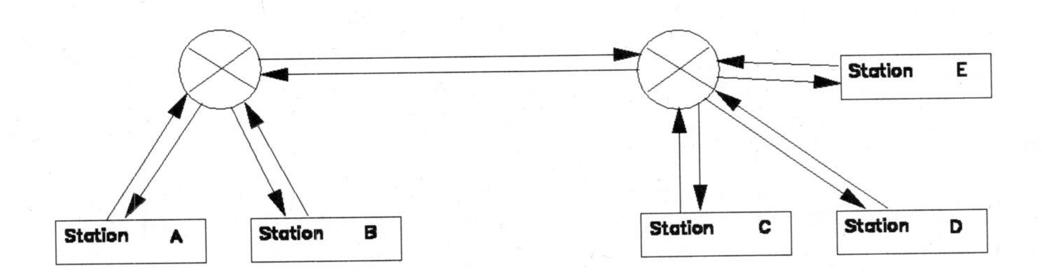


***Figure 16-3.** Tree Configuration.* Stations transmit on different wavelengths to a small local reflective star or coupler. Loops in the structure are not allowed.

In general a number of couplers or stars can be interconnected such that anything sent by one station will be received by all stations. This can be very effective in a distributed topology where a number of "hubs" interconnect a few stations each and are connected together to form a larger LAN structure.

As always there are a few problems:

- The relative signal strength of different transmitting stations will be very different (perhaps 20 dB or so) at the receiver. Some proposed access protocols rely on a transmitting station being able to receive its own signal in order to detect collisions. Of course a tree topology allows this. But collisions could be quite hard to detect if the colliding station is a long way away in the network.
- There can't be any loops in the structure. If multiple paths exist between stations in the network, the signal will go on all paths. When such a signal is received it will collide with itself and become garbage at the receiver.

It can be seen that the topology design is quite complex and is critical to the success of any optical networking scheme.

## 16.2.2 Transmission System Design

Building tuneable transmitters and receivers is quite difficult to do. This is mentioned in 4.1.3, "Light Sources" on page 4-14. The important parameters are:

- The speed at which transmitters and receivers are able to tune to the required frequency.
- The stability with which a frequency is maintained.
- The tuneable range.
- The linewidth[2] of the transmitter and the selectivity of the receiver.
- Of course the above all interact to determine how close channels may be packed together. The closer together they are, the more you can have within a given tuning range and the faster the tuning will be.

### 16.2.2.1 Stabilizing Frequencies

The biggest problem in WDM system design is stabilizing the frequencies. Lasers are subject to very significant variation with temperature and a number of lesser factors. This affects coherent detectors and some filters (because they are driven by lasers). Temperature control is critical.

> Even the data stream is important. Lasers have a problem very similar to "baseline wander" in electronic systems. If you send a lot of pulses one after another then the temperature in the laser cavity increases and so does the frequency (by amounts like 50 GHz).

Another problem is that a typical laser pulse exhibits a profound "chirp" (rapid increase in frequency immediately after the beginning of the pulse followed by a decline).

In single channel systems with incoherent receivers this doesn't matter a lot. Even in the case of coherent receivers, if there is only one channel then the receiver can "track" the frequency of the transmitter.

In WDM systems you want to place the wavelengths as close together as possible but channels can't be allowed to wander into one another.

There are many proposed approaches to this problem:

1. Create a "comb" of reference frequencies:
    - Construct a special Fabry-Perot laser with a large number of modes.

---

2 Optical transmitters (both LEDs and lasers) produce a band of wavelengths spread over a range. This is termed the "spectral linewidth". See the discussion in 4.1.3, "Light Sources" on page 4-14.

- Lock this laser on to an atomic frequency reference (this has been done in the lab).
- Use the wavelengths produced as a "comb" of wavelengths to stabilize another laser (transmitter or local oscillator).

2. Build a network with all of the tuneable components in a central location (hub) along with the reflective star. In this configuration a single multimode laser could be used to produce a comb for all variable transmitters, receivers and filters in the system. In this case the atomic clock reference is unnecessary as all frequencies will drift together. Individual workstations would have fixed transmitters and receivers.
3. Transmit a frequency reference somewhere a bit separate from the comb of channels. Each station would then have a special receiver for this channel and this could be used to stabilize all other devices in the system.

All of these alternatives are costly - but some more than others.

### 16.2.3 Access Protocols

If there are a number of stations connected to a common medium and two of them want to communicate, all we have to do is select a mutually agreed wavelength/s (channel/s) for them to use and communication is immediately possible (provided no other station is using the selected channel/s).

**Note:** In any communication between two stations (A and B) there are always two channels involved - one for each direction (A-to-B and B-to-A).

In the simple case, we could allocate a channel to a group of devices with a pencil and paper - by system definition. This would mean that these devices were able to use the nominated channel/s all of the time but they would be unable to communicate with other devices on the network. This might sound silly but it is not at all! A carrier organization (PTT) might well connect a MAN type structure around a city area and allocate channels to various customers on a fixed basis. This is a very practical structure but avoids the issue.

Our objective in creating a "Lightwave Network" is to provide any-to-any connectivity for all attached stations. But then there is the question of how do we want it to operate.

1. Do we want it to operate like a traditional LAN with single blocks of data individually addressed on a block-by-block basis?
2. Or are we happy with a "virtual circuit" approach where pairs of stations are given a channel for a period of time of a few seconds (or milliseconds)?

Most WDM access protocols require either transmitters or receivers (or both) to tune to a particular channel before data transfer can take place. This can be a significant length of time (compared with the transmit time for a single block). A virtual circuit approach can tolerate a relatively long delay in circuit establishment but offers instant access for data blocks after the first.

A connectionless (traditional LAN) approach means that you have the same delay for every block transmitted. Of course, a virtual circuit approach is very inefficient if a channel is occupied for a long period of time with only occasional data transfer. In this case, it would be better to use a connectionless system and be able to share the channel capacity.

When station A wants to send data to station B then they have to find a vacant channel and both tune to it before station A can commence sending. The central problem for the access protocol is: "How do we arrange for stations wanting to communicate to use the same channel (wavelength)?" This is not a trivial problem! First, the stations must have some ability to vary their operating wavelength (switch from channel to channel). We could have:

- Each station allocated to a fixed transmitting channel and all stations able to tune their receivers to any channel at will.
- Each station could be allocated a fixed receiving frequency and a tuneable transmitter.
- Both transmitter and receiver could be tuneable.
- Stations could have multiple (say two or three) receivers and/or transmitters.

**Fixed Receivers - Tuneable Transmitters**

An obvious method of operation would be to have receivers fixed to a dedicated channel (one station per channel) and each station would have a tuneable transmitter. In operation, all a station would have to do to send to another station would be to tune to its channel and transmit.

But there is then the possibility of two or more stations trying to transmit to the same destination at the same time and collisions occurring.

**Fixed Transmitters - Tunable Receivers**

In this system each station transmits on its own fixed channel and receivers must tune to this channel in order to receive the data. This is often called the "broadcast and select" principle. There are two problems here:

- How does a station know to which channel to tune its receiver? It has to know (somehow) that a particular station wants to send it data.
- If station A wants to send to station B, there would always be a free channel (because station A has a dedicated transmit channel) but station B's receiver could be busy receiving something from station G somewhere else in the network. This is sometimes called "receiver collision".

This is, in fact, a very promising principle. There are several proposed access protocols that aim to solve the above problems. See 16.3.2.2, "IBM "Rainbow-1"" on page 16-18.

There is another benefit here. All receivers (or a subset) could tune to the same channel. This allows for a broadcast ability. But this may not be practical because of the need to get all receivers listening to the same channel at the same time - some may already be busy receiving something different.

**Both Transmitter and Receiver Tuneable**

Of course, this is by far the ideal system if only you could make it work. In systems where either a receiver or transmitter is dedicated to a particular channel you are limited to a maximum number of stations equal to the number of channels in the system. (Of course, it is possible to put multiple stations on the same channel but then there are new problems of conflict.)

From a usage efficiency point of view, tuning both the transmitter and receiver is by far the best. This is because we can potentially have many more stations than channels and all stations contend for the same pool of capacity. (Of course, we may not always care about usage efficiency in an environment where capacity is almost endless!)

This is not a silly idea at all. A network of perhaps 1000 stations might be easily supported on a system offering only (say) 100 channels. Twenty channels packed closely together would allow the use of a very narrow tuning range and hence very fast tuning.

But in this configuration, now both stations must have a mechanism for deciding which channel they will use. Another point is that if there are more stations than channels then there is the possibility of "blocking" (a station wanting to transmit when there is no free channel) - and this possibility must be provided for - the problem is not so much the possibility of blocking but the additional complexity in system protocols needed to handle the situation.

***An access protocol is the mechanism used to determine just which channel should be used by each new communication.***

The biggest problem for the access protocol is exactly the same for all high-speed LAN/MAN protocols. *Although the speed of data transmission has increased by many orders of magnitude, the speed of light in a fiber and of electricity in a wire (at about 5 µsec per km) hasn't changed.* Propagation delays are exactly the same as they are for traditional LANs, so propagation delays become relatively much longer than block transmission times and therefore very significant in terms of efficiency. Of course the problem increases significantly with distance. It has the most effect on systems:

1. Which have any protocol exchange for pretransmission coordination? (because each round-trip between sender and receiver incurs two propagation delays.)

2. Which use CSMA/CD protocols? (because the probability of collision increases with propagation delay.)

In general terms there are a number of options:

**Controlling Station**

The simplest method available is to have a station somewhere on the LAN responsible for allocating channels to stations on a demand basis.

A typical system of this kind would have two control channels (one for each direction - to or from the controlling station). When a station wants to send some data it asks the control station for a channel and the control station allocates one from its knowledge of the pool of free channels - it also knows if the intended receiver is currently busy with some other communication. It then sends a control packet to the requester and to the intended destination allocating the channel. When communication is complete one of the stations needs to notify the control station that the channel is free.

This kind of system is simple and easy to implement but it has a number of problems.

1. While the allocation of channels can be near to optimal, it takes a long time to complete. A few hundred µsec as a minimum. At a speed of one Gbps a frame of 1000 bits takes only one µsec to transmit. Thus it would be a very inefficient protocol for traditional LAN (connectionless, packet) type of operation (but quite good for a virtual circuit environment).

2. The control station represents a single point of failure and therefore would need to be duplicated and even then would detract from the reliability of the system.

3. The cost of the control station adds a significant "entry cost" to the system. (Users who want to start with only a few stations are forced to buy a control station.)

4. If the control function is decentralized (for example, put into every adapter) it adds cost to each adapter.

**Control Channel**

Many proposed systems coordinate their transmissions by using a dedicated control channel which is shared among all attached stations. The protocols used on this control channel are not difficult because the load will be very low. CSMA/CD has been suggested as has Aloha and Slotted Aloha mechanisms.

This can be used to distribute the control function among the stations. The main problem is that any coordination before transmission takes time. This time, added to the transmit time of every block can severely degrade the efficiency of the system.

An interesting proposed protocol using a control channel is described in 16.3.1.2, "Coordination on a Control Channel" on page 16-15.

**Dynamic Allocation**

This class of systems uses neither a control channel nor a centralized station to coordinate transmissions. Most of the proposed and experimental systems described below use this approach.

# 16.3 Some Possible Systems Approaches

## 16.3.1 Centralized WDM Circuit Switch

A WDM circuit-switching system is illustrated in Figure 16-4. This performs the same logical switching function as the electronic circuit-switching system described in Chapter 10, "High-Speed Circuit-Switching Systems" on page 10-1 without the need for the expensive electronic switch.

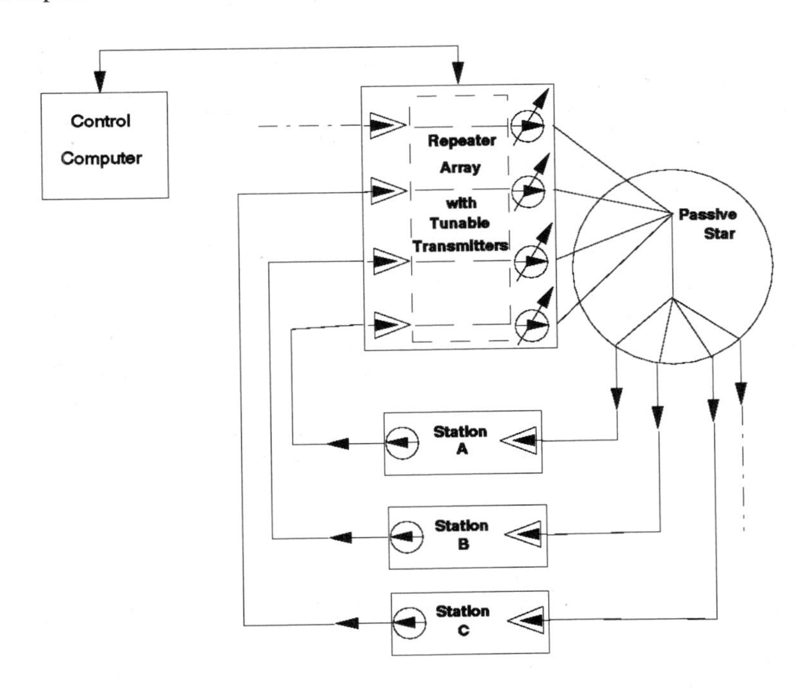


*Figure 16-4. Wavelength Switching System*

Each station transmits on a dedicated fiber (on a fixed wavelength) to the switch. Each station receives on a different wavelength. (So the maximum number of stations is determined by the number of available channels.) The switch receives the optical signal and re-transmits it on the wavelength of the intended receiver. The "star" mixes the signals from the switch so that each receiver sees all the signals.

The logical connection of a transmitter in a station to a receiver in another station is performed by wavelength tuning. The system is constructed as follows:

- Each station has a fixed wavelength transmitter and a fixed wavelength receiver. Wavelength used in this section of the system is irrelevant. All stations could use the same wavelength to transmit.
- The signal is received by an array of electronic repeaters where the transmitter at each repeater is tuneable.
- Each station receives on a unique wavelength (also fixed).
- When Station C is to send to Station A then the transmitter in the switch (corresponding to Station A) is tuned to the wavelength of the receiver in Station C.

This is a circuit-switched system.

- When a station is not communicating with another station its transmissions are received by the control computer.
- To make a connection a station places a "call request" with the control computer.
- If the destination station is available the control station will exchange a message with it to confirm that it will accept this connection.
- If all is OK then the control computer will tell the requesting station that a connection will be made.
- The control computer will then connect the two stations by tuning the wavelengths of both stations to point to each other.

The major disadvantage with this approach is the relatively long circuit establishment time (it requires program intervention in a controlling computer) but the electronic switch it replaces has exactly the same problem.

It is obvious that placing a tuneable transmitter within each station would eliminate the need for the tuneable repeater array. But the centralized switch approach has some significant advantages:

1. Very simple centralized control. There is no problem with "collisions".
2. All the transmitters can be controlled from the same frequency reference. This means that potentially the channels could be more densely packed. However, receivers would still require stabilization in some way.

3. A major advantage of this configuration is that (at very high speeds) it should be significantly lower in cost than a fully electronic crosspoint switch.

#### 16.3.1.1 Multichannel CSMA/CD

In this proposal the network would be configured exactly as in Figure 16-2 on page 16-6.

- In this proposal each station is equipped with:
  - One tuneable transmitter
  - One tuneable receiver
  - One fixed receiver
- Each station receives data *only* on its *fixed* receiver.
- The tuneable receiver is used for collision detection on the station's transmit channel. (This helps significantly in cost since both tuneable elements are always tuned to the same frequency.)
- When a station wants to transmit it tunes both its transmitter and its tuneable receiver to the channel on which the other station receives.

  It then operates a (more or less standard) CSMA/CD protocol.

  It listens to see if there is any data on its intended transmit channel. If there is none, it will transmit. While it is transmitting it monitors the receive channel to detect possible collisions. If there was a collision, the transmitter backs off for a random amount of time before retry.
- This system will work over the star or bus topologies but may have problems with the tree structure. In order to detect collisions the signal received from its own transmitter must not be too strong so as to swamp the colliding station's signal.

The system is simple and offers very fast packet switching access time. It also has the advantage of being able to have multiple stations on each channel. Statistically this is not as good as having a fully tuneable transmitter and receiver system because two devices on the same channel may conflict when there are plenty of other channels which are not currently busy. But it offers other advantages in access speed and the absence of any need for pretransmission coordination.

#### 16.3.1.2 Coordination on a Control Channel

There are many proposals for using a control channel to coordinate transmissions presented in the literature. Most of these have proposed either a TDM (slotted) or a CSMA approach to administration of the control channel itself.

An extreme solution might be for each station to have a fixed transmitter and receiver (tuned to the control channel) and tuneable ones for the data. Every station would keep track of the channels in use and when a station wanted to send, it would tell the receiver (and all other stations) that it was about to use channel x. It would then notify other stations when the channel was free. Although the chance of collision could be minimized by having each transmitter select the next channel to use based on a (different) random number there is still some chance of collision and such a system would be quite costly.

***An example of such a system is given below:***

- The network topology could be any of the three possibilities (star, bus, or tree) described above.
- Each station would have both receiver and transmitter tuneable.
- When a station wants to send to another, it does the following:
  1. Selects a channel with no signal on it (by using its receiver to scan).
  2. Tunes its transmitter to the control channel and sends a control packet to tell the receiver that a packet will be following on the (nominated) channel. The transmission channel number is included in the control packet.
  3. Tunes its transmitter to the nominated channel.
  4. Waits until the receiver can be assumed to have tuned and stabilized.
  5. Sends the packet.
- Of course, this is not a particularly good protocol:
  - There is a lot of time taken up in receiver and transmitter tuning.
  - There is the possibility of collision on the control channel and the intended receiver never receiving the control packet.
  - There is a significant probability of collision on the data channel.
  - The receiver might not be listening to the control channel at all - it might be busy receiving something else.

Even though there are significant problems, there are many proposed improvements to the above and these improved protocols are serious contenders for systems in the future.

### 16.3.2 Experimental Systems

WDM networks are a very recent development. With the first papers appearing in the literature in 1985, most of the initial research was done by three organizations:

- AT&T Bell Laboratories
- Bell Communications Research (Bellcore)
- British Telecom Research Laboratories

These experiments varied from bench testing of partial systems to the building of demonstration and prototype systems. Understandably, most of this early research was oriented towards wide area communications systems.

A few years later, other organizations (including IBM) were able to build on this early work in projects to explore the use of WDM technology in the LAN environment.

#### 16.3.2.1 Lambdanet

Lambdanet is an experimental WDM system designed to explore a number of different possible uses.

The network topology is a broadcast star as shown in Figure 16-2 on page 16-6 and discussed above.

- The experimental configuration used 18 stations.
- A 16x16 star coupler was used and extended to 18 connections by attachment of two smaller coupling devices.
- The network itself is totally passive except for the attached stations.
- Each station transmits on a fixed unique frequency.
- The thing that makes Lambdanet different from other proposed architectures is that *nothing is tuneable*. Each station separates the received signal (all 18 wavelengths) using a diffraction grating and then feeds each separate signal to a separate receiver! Thus a Lambdanet station receives all transmissions and decides which ones to process electronically.

The technical characteristics of the system were as follows:

- Lasers were the Distributed Feedback (DFB) type.
- Wavelengths were from 1527 to 1561 nm with a 2 nm channel separation.
- Receivers were commercial (InGaAs) APD receivers.
- "Regular" (non-dispersion shifted) single-mode fiber was used.
- Two data rates were experimented with - 1.5 Gbps and 2 Gbps.

Applications thought suitable for this technology include:

- Providing Exchange (Central Office) to Exchange multiplexed bearers for:
  1. Traditional PTT services such as telephone and synchronous data (such as "T1 links"). This could be done by traditional TDM techniques applied to the WDM channels.
  2. Constructing private "virtual" data networks for individual organizations. This could be done also by TDM sharing of the WDM links.

- One-way video distribution. This would become particularly important in a "fiber to the home environment".

### 16.3.2.2 IBM "Rainbow-1"

Rainbow-1 is a prototype WDM LAN system developed by IBM Research.[3] It was publicly demonstrated at the TELECOM-91 exhibition in Geneva in October 1991.

The system consists of a passive "reflective star" connected to 32 IBM PS/2 computers. The electronic and optical components are built on two standard Micro Channel cards - this gives them the ability to be used in other products that use the Micro Channel such as the IBM 3172, the IBM RS/6000 and some models of the IBM 4300 processor series). As many as 32 simultaneous 200 Mbps data channels can operate simultaneously.

The system design is illustrated in Figure 16-5.

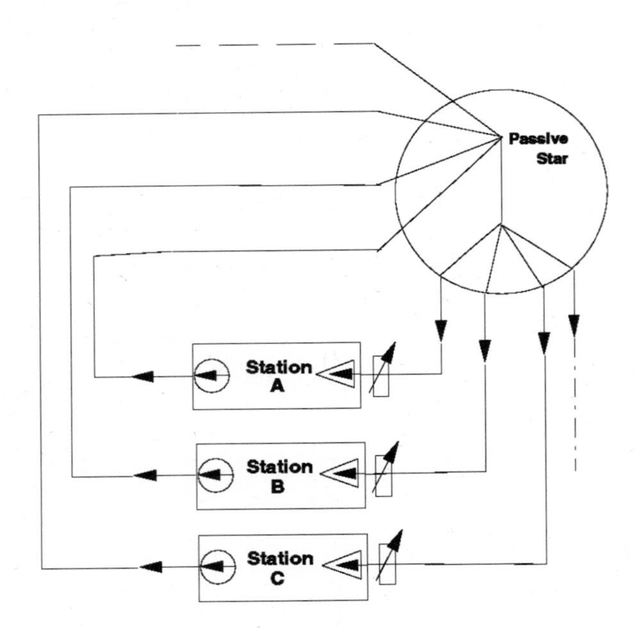


*Figure 16-5. Rainbow-1 System Design.* The design features a passive network with fixed transmitters and tuneable receivers. The receivers are actually fixed incoherent detectors preceded by tuneable Fabry-Perot filters.

---

[3] Rainbow is a research project, *not* a product. IBM cannot make any comment on what uses, if any, may be made of the Rainbow technology in future IBM products.

## Overview

- Each station is equipped with a fixed frequency transmitter and a tuneable receiver.
- Each station is allocated a unique wavelength from a band of wavelengths from 1505 to 1545 nm.
- The tuneable receivers are actually fixed frequency incoherent detectors each of which is preceded by a Fabry-Perot tuneable filter with a tuning range of 50 nm. The tuning rate is about 10 μsec per nm which gives an average time to locate a channel as 250 μsec.
- Simple OOK[4] modulation is used. It is noted, however, that the system needs some form of coding that provides sufficient transitions in the data for the receiver PLL to synchronize.
- Data rate is 200 Mbps over standard 8-micron single-mode fiber.

***The system operates as follows:***

- When station A wants to establish a connection with station B, it does the following:
  1. Begins sending a setup request to station B. Note this is sent on its own (station A's) dedicated transmit wavelength. This is a continuous repetition of the same (very short) message and synchronization.
  2. Tunes its receiver to the wavelength of station B's transmitter.
- If station B is busy doing something else (such as receiving data from another station), station A will continue sending the setup request.
- When station B is not communicating with another station it continuously scans across the range of all wavelengths looking for a setup request addressed to itself.
- When station B receives a setup request addressed to itself it locks its receiver on to the signal from station A and immediately sends a confirmation to the other station. It is able to do this since its transmitter is not tuneable and station A must already be waiting for a response.
- Both stations are then able to exchange data freely until they agree to disconnect. At this point both stations begin scanning all channels again looking for the next setup request.

Due to the timings involved (up to one millisecond to make a connection) it will be seen that this is a "short hold mode" circuit-switching system rather than a packet switch.

---

4 On-off keying

**Details**

- The system was built with commercially available optical and electronic components.
- The transmitter lasers had an unmodulated linewidth of less than 350 MHz. These were modulated in such a way as to reduce the chirp problem but the major factor in the control of chirp was the relatively wide channel spacings.

**Conclusion:** The system works well. A summary of the lessons learned may be found in the paper by Paul E. Green (1992). Rainbow is a research prototype and it is expected that the project will continue. The ultimate aim is to prove the feasibility of a 1000 station WDM LAN/MAN operating at 1 Gbps.

#### 16.3.2.3 IBM "Rainbow-2"

Rainbow-2 is the next generation of experimental LAN system from Rainbow-1. It was developed during 1993 and 1994 and is currently working in the laboratory. In principle, it is the same as Rainbow-1; however, in practice it is quite different.

- Rainbow-1 was a LAN system oriented to interconnecting user workstations. Rainbow-2 is intended to provide supercomputer interconnection and access.
- Rainbow-1 was implemented on a PS/2 adapter card where Rainbow-2 is an external box. This external box implements many functions for offloading processing from the host computer.
- The optical principles and protocols of the two projects are very similar but Rainbow-2 begins to explore systems aspects of how to take advantage of the enormous bandwidth now available.
- The Rainbow-2 project connects 32 stations at a speed of 1 Gbps per station over metropolitan area distances (max 15 km).

More information can be found in Green (1994).

### 16.3.3 Multihop Lightwave Systems

The idea of using a large number of very simple switches configured logically as an array is almost as old as data communication itself. The switches in proposed systems range from very simple circuit switch devices with two inputs, two outputs and minimal buffering to quite complex fast packet switches with many attached links.

Although these schemes have had some success as centralized switch fabrics, they have never been adopted for use in WAN or LAN applications for a number of reasons:

- A large number of separate link connections are required. If these have to be physically separate, the configuration becomes very difficult to manage.

- Because a packet of data is received and retransmitted by a number of nodes between sender and receiver there is an additional "staging delay" which is significant if link speeds are low.
- Analog link error rates in the WAN environment meant that stage-by-stage error recovery was desirable - something which adds complexity and is a cause of congestion.

The advent of fiber optics has removed many of the potential disadvantages and researchers have taken new interest in this approach.

**The Concept:** The concept is illustrated in Figure 16-6.

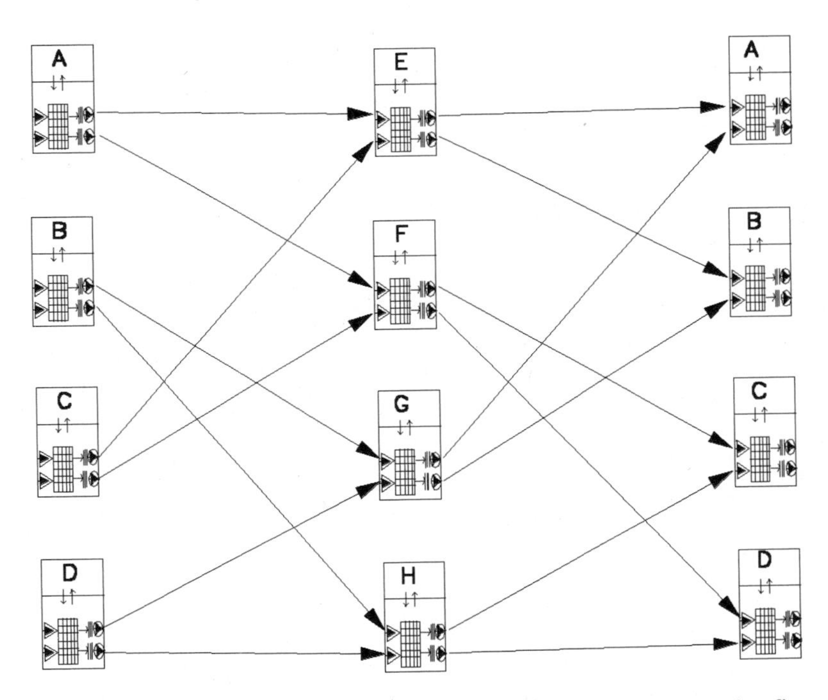


*Figure 16-6. Multihop Optical Network - Logical View.* Note that the first and last columns are the same stations (A to D).

- An individual node consists of a switching element which has at least two input links and at least two output links. (These links may be logical or physical.) The device may also be a user workstation in which case the switching function will have internal links to the workstation code.

- Links between nodes are dedicated, point-to-point links. That is, a node may send on any of its transmitters at any time and the destination node is expected to receive the data.
- In the network diagram (Figure 16-6 on page 16-21) it should be noted that the first and last columns of stations are the *same* stations - this was done to make the diagram more easily readable. In this (trivial) network there are eight stations.
- If station B has data to send to station H, then it may do so at any time, directly.
- If station B has data to send to station A then it must send the data to station G and that station will send the data on to its destination. If station B has data to send to station E then the path is longer (B to H to C to E).

## Node Structure

The structure of a single station is shown in Figure 16-7. The idea is to make it extremely simple, totally implemented in hardware and able to handle the full link speed (perhaps 2 Gbps). It should also be low in cost.

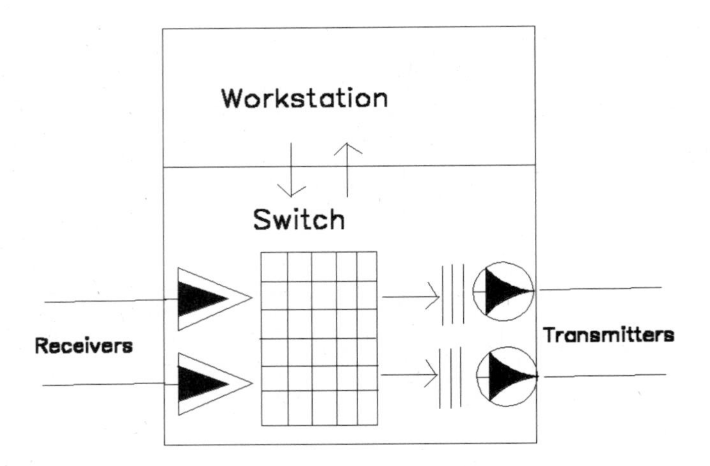


*Figure 16-7. Multihop Optical Network - Individual Workstation*

A node here is a simple 3x3 packet switch. Each data block is received in full, the destination address examined and then passed to the appropriate output queue. Queueing at the output side is suggested to improve the performance in a congestion situation.

## Network Capacity

The capacity of a network with this design is very high. All links may be active simultaneously. Therefore the network capacity is:

$$\text{network bandwidth} = \frac{\text{number of links} \times \text{link speed}}{\text{average number of hops}}$$

Since data packets may be sent one after another on all links with no separation or tuning delay the bandwidth efficiency (compared to other WDM architectures) is extremely high.

**Network Addressing Structure**

When a packet is received, it must be routed to the appropriate output port very quickly. There is no time to perform complex address calculation or database lookup.

There are many schemes to do this. Automatic Network Routing (ANR), described in 11.2.2, "Automatic Network Routing (ANR)" on page 11-18 is one appropriate technique. Another proposal is to arrange the nodes (as per the figure) such that the destination address is just a binary number. When a frame arrives at a node the first bit (or bits) of the destination address are used to route the packet and then the bits are stripped away. This is the basis of so-called "Banyan" networks.

**Congestion Control**

Since there is nothing in the network to prevent most of the stations transmitting to the same destination at once, congestion is a problem and must be controlled.

The best ways to control congestion in a network like this are a combination of input rate control and packet discard techniques. These are described in 6.1, "Control of Congestion" on page 6-6.

**Physical Topology**

Of course, the links shown in the figure are *not* intended to be physical links. They are channels in a WDM network.

The physical topology could be any of the WDM topologies shown in Figure 16-1 on page 16-5, Figure 16-2 on page 16-6 or Figure 16-3 on page 16-7.

**Scalability**

Such networks can be very easily scaled up in size. When you do, the number of required hops does increase but that doesn't pose too much of a problem.

**Performance**

Various studies have shown that multihop networks can be equivalent to or better than the single-hop networks discussed above. This is because, although there are many stages in the data transfer, there is no tuning delay required before sending a packet.

**Management**

Management is critical to the operation of this kind of network. When a new node is added to the network or when an operational node becomes unavailable all nodes must update their routing tables. This has to happen very fast in order to avoid disruption to end users.

This is not a difficult job but it is made somewhat more complex by the fact that links are unidirectional and don't have a return path.

There are two environments where this principle is suggested:

1. In the LAN environment. Here workstations would be connected to a WDM bus as discussed above. In principle, you don't need tuneable transmitters and receivers (just ones fixed to the wavelengths they need). However, in practice some tuneability is needed in order to reconfigure as stations are removed and added.
2. As the internal architecture for a centralized packet switch. The architecture is a very good candidate as a very high throughput ATM switch.

   End users and trunks are attached to the switch on point-to-point optical link connections (or SDH-derived channels). Input/output trunks are connected to switching elements *instead* of the "workstation" as shown in Figure 16-7 on page 16-22.

   Internally the switch would use a WDM architecture and would be much easier to build because all of the tuneable optics are within the centralized switch and could be synchronized from a single timing and frequency reference.

However, if the architecture is for a centralized node, why do we need WDM at all? Links between switching elements are fixed for long periods of time. Why not just connect the modules together through a fiber patch panel? (This somehow takes away the aesthetic appeal but it probably halves the cost!)

If you really want to reduce the cost, why not do all the internal connections electrically and save the cost of optical transceivers?

Time will tell, but multihop networks are a real and serious contender for many network switching roles in the future.

### 16.3.4 Wavelength Selective Networks

The concept of a wavelength selective network is illustrated in Figure 16-8 on page 16-25. Each wavelength is treated as a (unidirectional) circuit. Wavelength selective networks have been proposed which use either active or passive switching elements. That is, the switching nodes in the figure could be perhaps mechanically tuned to configure circuits through them or dynamically tuned by using tuneable filters, etc.

Wavelengths may be reused in different parts of the network. This is an important feature. Notice that each fiber illustrated is unidirectional. Potentially, the only restriction is that each wavelength must be unique on each fiber. The same wavelength may be used for different purposes on different interconnecting fibers. Thus if wavelength "3" is used for the connection from Workstation 1 to Workstation 3 (in the figure) then it would be possible for the same wavelength to be used for the connection from Workstation 2 to Workstation 4. All this depends on the internal design of the switching nodes - different designs may impose restrictions but in principle there is very little limitation in the reuse of wavelengths in different parts of the network. This is an advantage over reflective star-based networks where all wavelengths must be unique.

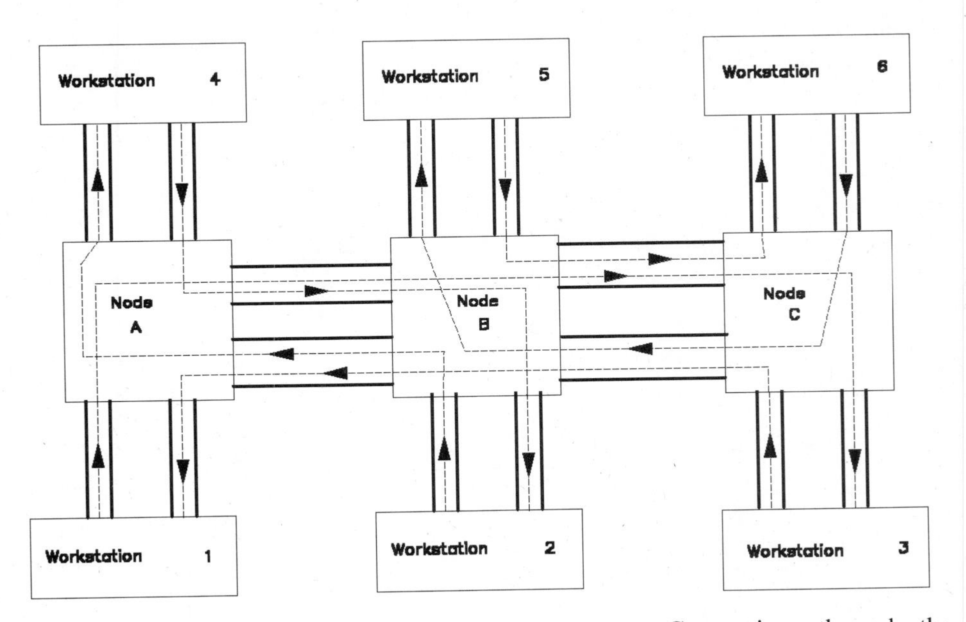


***Figure 16-8. Wavelength Selective Network - Concept.*** Connections through the network are formed by routing individual wavelengths.

The principles involved here look superficially like the ones we know well from electronic networking systems such as ATM. However, the optical case is significantly more difficult than the electronic one. The problem is that we cannot change the wavelength of a single channel (by passive optical means) within the network. The transmitting and receiving stations must use the same wavelength. This is not a problem for the workstations themselves but is a very significant problem for the network.

In traditional networks (such as ATM) the subchannel (in ATM the VPI/VCI) changes at every switching node. Because we cannot do this with optical signals the problem of allocation of wavelengths becomes very difficult in any kind of complex network.

## 16.4 MuxMaster - A WDM WAN Research Prototype

MuxMaster[5] is an experimental IBM device that allows the user to multiplex up to 10 full-duplex information streams over a single fiber (NOT a pair) for distances of up to 70 km. This research was motivated by the desire to explore the immediate commercial possibilities of WDM technology.

The need for MuxMaster arises primarily from users with two or more large sites in the same city (such as a large mainframe complex and a backup site). “Dark Fiber” is available in the U.S. (and to a very limited extent in some other countries) but it costs around $150 per month per mile per strand. A typical mainframe interconnection might require six Excon channels using two fibers each for a total of 12 fibers. MuxMaster allows for carrying all of the traffic on a single fiber strand (with provision to back up the system on a second, single strand).

An experimental system was installed at a customer site in the U.S. in 1994. It is believed to be the very first production use of dense WDM optical multiplexing.

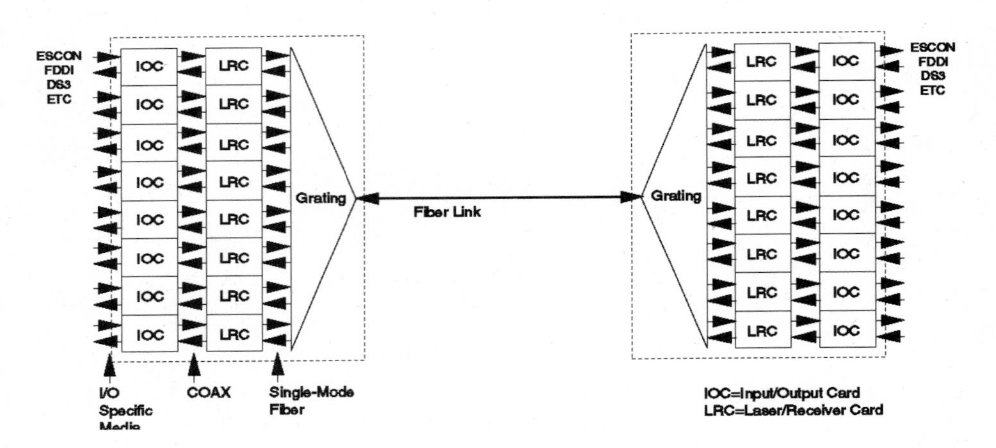


*Figure 16-9. MuxMaster Principle.* Multiple optical wavelengths are carried on a single fiber point-to-point between two locations.

The principle used in MuxMaster is shown in Figure 16-9.

5 MuxMaster is a research project NOT a product. IBM can make no comment on the possible use of this technology in future products.

- I/O specific modules are used to interface to particular protocols such as ESCON and FDDI.
- What the IOC does depends on the attaching protocol. If the attaching system is using FDDI or ESCON, for example, IOC processing is very simple indeed. Pulses that arrive on an FDDI interface are converted to electronic pulses and then used to drive the laser transmitter. There is no need to change the encoding at all - the fiber link becomes a simple repeater. More complex protocols, such as ones intended to operate on copper connections require more complex processing (they have to be decoded and then re-encoded in a protocol suitable for fiber).
- Pulses are fed from the IOC to the LRC (Laser/Receiver Card) and directly drive the transmitting laser.
- Each laser is tuned to a different wavelength, so the system uses 20 different optical wavelengths. This provides up to 10 full-duplex channels each of which is quite independent and runs at data rates of up to 1 Gbps.
- The maximum link distance allowed is 70 km but this depends on the fastest single channel rate in use. A channel speed of 200 Mbps requires that the maximum link distance be reduced to 50 km.
- Each MuxMaster node is managed by a RISC processor which implements a Simple Network Management Protocol (SNMP) agent.

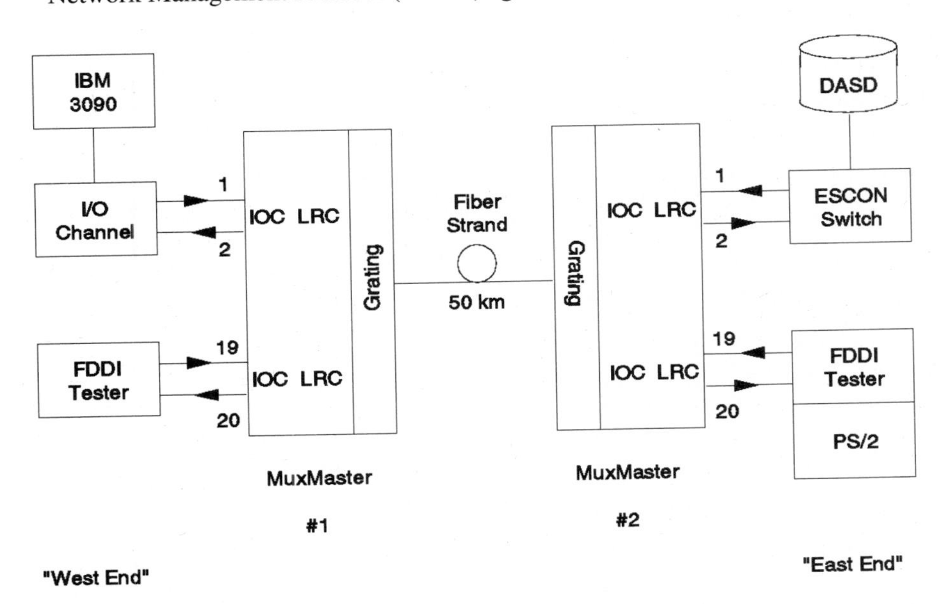


*Figure 16-10. MuxMaster Field Demonstration*

Figure 16-10 shows the configuration used in the first operational field trial. Another simple possibility is the use of MuxMaster to interconnect LANs through bridges. This is shown in Figure 16-11 on page 16-28.

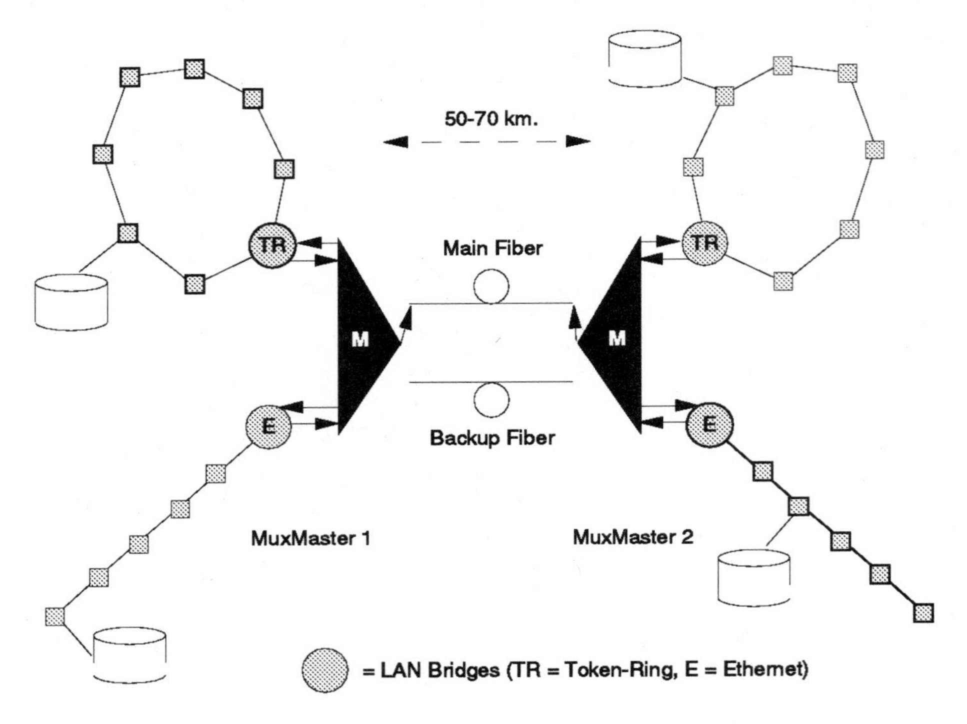


***Figure 16-11.*** *MuxMaster System.* A simple application in the interconnection of LANs

The first implementations of MuxMaster are simple point-to-point multiplexing which are aimed at saving the cost of having multiple fibers. But there is an interesting possibility of interconnecting many of them into a network such as is shown in Figure 16-12 on page 16-29.

This suggests the possibility of a type of network midway between today's electronic networks and tomorrow's all optical ones.

- In today's world, optical fibers are just used as "optical wire" where an optical fiber replaces an electric wire for long-distance interconnection and nothing much else changes. ATM and SDH networks fall into this category.
- In the future we expect to have wide area networks with fully optical routing from end-to-end but this seems some years away. This was discussed earlier in 16.3.4, "Wavelength Selective Networks" on page 16-24.

- Connecting MuxMasters into a network configuration gives a compromise solution which could be implemented today. That is, we construct a multiple-wavelength optical network *but use electronic switching at the nodes.* This gives many of the advantages (especially the increased bandwidth) of the fully optical approach in a technique that can be implemented today.

This compromise solution could in fact be quite attractive if specially designed opto-electronic components were used for the crosspoints. IBM research is exploring this kind of architecture (see Green 1994).

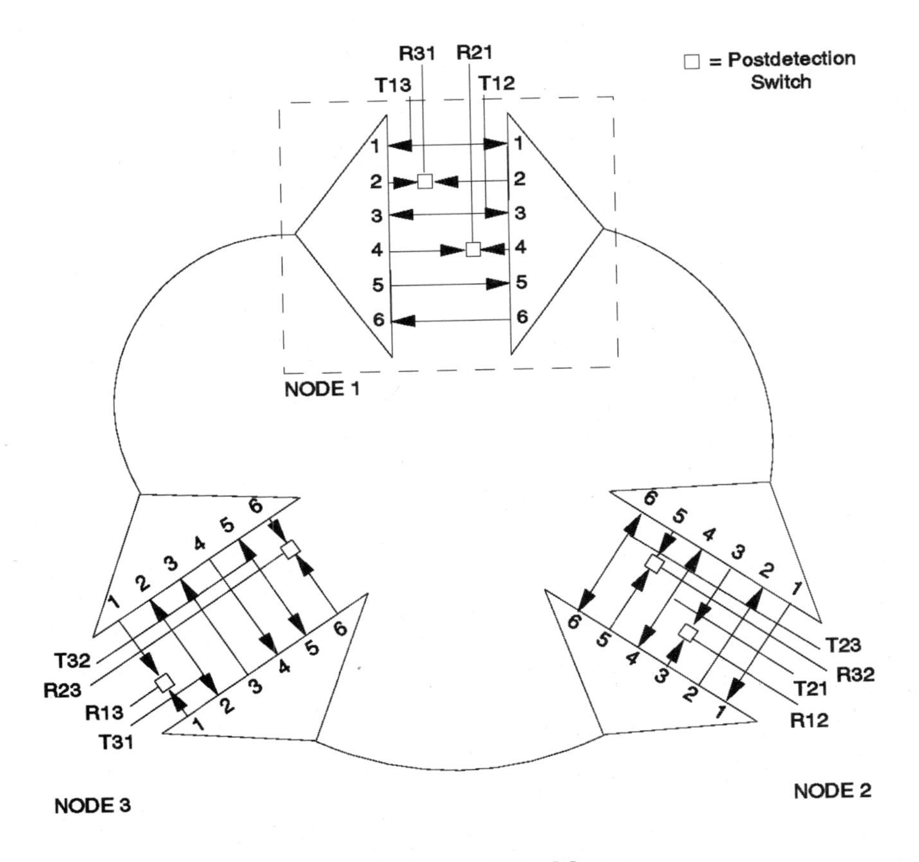


***Figure 16-12.*** *RingMaster Network.* Ring of MuxMasters.

The figure shows a simple ring configuration. Other configurations (of arbitrary complexity) are possible but then there is a significant problem in network control and path allocation, etc.

# Chapter 17. LAN Hub Development

One of the supreme ironies in the development of communications systems is the current direction of LAN hub development. Before the advent of LANs the predominant method of connecting computing devices together in a local environment was with a packet switch. LANs brought high-speed any-to-any connectivity to peer devices within a local area. LAN hubs have now developed to the point where it looks like they are evolving back into local packet switches. It is possible (though perhaps unlikely) that LANs will be completely replaced by hub-based packet switches - perhaps by the year 2000!

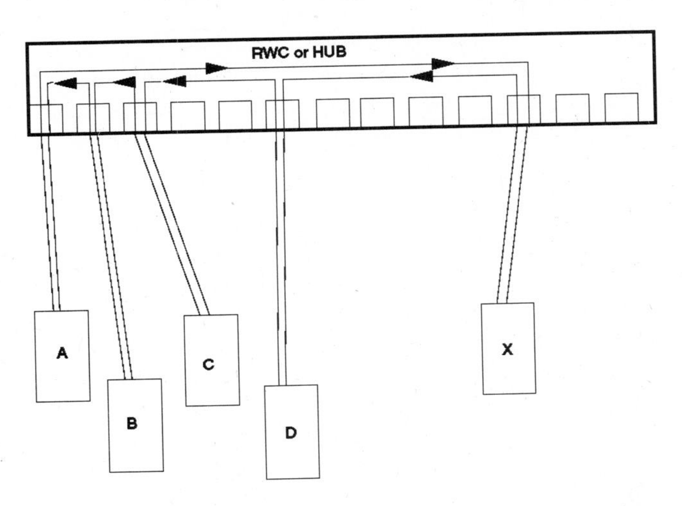


*Figure 17-1. Ring Wiring Concentrator - Logical View.* Wiring is point-to-point from each station to the WRC. The ring (or bus) structure of the LAN is constructed by wiring within the WRC.

### 17.1.1.1 The Early LANs

The early LANs[1] were built using bi-directional buses and were cabled from device to device directly. Wiring was very simple and in the environment of the time perfectly adequate.

Over time several problems with these early LAN systems emerged.

---

1 Just how LANs developed in the late 1960s and 1970s is fascinating but outside the scope of this book. For our purposes let us accept that the first serious production LAN system was Ethernet.

- "Broadband" (modulated carrier) systems over coaxial cable did not allow much flexibility in cabling. Devices had to be placed at nodes on the cable and the whole cable needed to be tuned to an exact length (multiple of the wavelength). When new devices were added or old ones deleted the cable had to be re-tuned (because of the loading effect of attaching cable stubs).
- With small numbers of devices in a restricted area, bus cabling did not (and does not) prove too much of a problem. However, as LAN sizes grew, severe management problems arose due to extreme difficulty in locating cable faults and malfunctioning devices.

#### 17.1.1.2 Token-Ring (1982)

When the token-ring system was developed the previous experience with CSMA/CD LAN management was well recognized. However, a token-ring has a problem that a CSMA/CD LAN does not. If it is wired as a loop from station to station, it ceases to function when a single device is powered off or if the LAN is broken.

The solution to these problems was the use of "star ring" wiring and the use of a Ring Wiring Concentrator (RWC). Star ring wiring is shown in Figure 17-1 on page 17-1.

The RWC is a passive (non-powered) device which simply connects wires together *except* that it has a bypass relay which switches a device out of the ring when that device is powered off. When a TRN adapter card is powered on, it places a DC (direct current) voltage on to the ring connection "underneath" (on the same wires as) the data. This DC voltage is used to hold a relay open in the RWC which connects the device to the ring. When the device is powered off (or the wire is severed) the relay closes immediately and ring continuity is maintained. (The DC has no other effect on the system as the signal is inductively coupled to the adapters in the workstation.)

Over time however, other requirements emerged.

- LANs needed to be connected together for several reasons:
  1. To increase the number of accessible devices (there is a maximum number of stations that you can attach to any LAN segment).
  2. To increase LAN throughput (if you divide a single LAN into two and connect them together with a bridge then you double the throughput).
  3. To interconnect geographically separate LAN segments. This is especially true in the Ethernet environment because the performance of the whole LAN degrades with LAN length (see 13.2.2, "CSMA/CD Performance" on page 13-12).

  To answer these requirements, first bridges and then routers were developed. These are separate devices connected to the LAN.

- In large LANs, fault finding within attached devices themselves is complex, the more so because users often do not have a high level of technical skill (why should they?). LAN Network Management devices were developed to ease this task. Once again, the LNM is a separate workstation on one LAN segment.

#### 17.1.1.3 Unshielded Twisted Pair Cable

In the late 1980s the desire to save cost by using existing UTP cable infrastructure bore fruit in the form of the "10BaseT"[2] system for Ethernet and 16 Mbps token-ring over UTP.

The problem with both these systems is the inherent limitations imposed by the use of UTP (especially the lower grade Telephone Twisted Pair). Attenuation in the cable severely limits the distance you can send. In addition, reactive components in the cable distort the signal.

To get adequate distance over UTP both TRN and Ethernet require a signal regenerator or repeater at the RWC to refresh and reshape the signal.

*When you put power into the RWC and then regenerate the signal it becomes a hub.*

#### 17.1.1.4 Smart Hubs

Once a hub is present in the LAN it becomes a natural point to centralize LAN administration and interconnection functions. Thus the "smart hub" developed.

**Improved Network Management**

When you integrate a network management device into the hub you gain much more than convenience. There is great potential for increased management function, such as:

- Security control
- Improved finding of ring faults
- Dynamic reconfiguration

In addition, cost is saved because the management device can share the same covers and power supply as the hub.

**Heterogeneous LAN Types**

Intelligent hubs typically connect a number of different LAN architectures (Ethernet, TRN, FDDI, etc.). This allows for the easy construction of arbitrary LAN segments as needed (provided the cable types are compatible). Of course,

2 10BaseT = 10 Mbps, baseband, (unshielded) twisted pair.

simultaneous LAN management for all connected segments and LAN types is provided.

**Interconnection of LAN Segments (Repeater Function)**

LANs are often interconnected over distance with simple optical fiber repeaters. Typically two hubs are connected together with a pair of fibers and the interconnected LAN segments function as one.

**Bridges and Routers**

The natural place to centralize bridge and router functions is in the hub. The whole can (at least potentially) be managed as a single coherent unit and there are significant cost savings in common power supplies (you can now afford to use very highly reliable, duplexed supplies) and common mechanical construction.

#### 17.1.1.5 But Why Have a LAN at All?

**Functions**

When you look logically at the intelligent hub as described above, its functions are strikingly similar to the functions of a packet switch (such as an IBM 3745). In fact the logical functions performed are the same.

There are significant differences however:

1. Hubs connect to each LAN device in a point-to-point fashion but the data switching is external to the hub (on the LAN).
2. LANs usually have a much higher data rate than is traditional for a packet switch.

**Throughput**

Using instantaneous data rates as a measure of throughput can be very misleading. On a LAN the absolute maximum throughput is the maximum data rate (actual throughput is usually a lot less). On a packet switch, the throughput is the *sum* of the throughputs of all the attached links divided by two. Packet switch attached links are normally full-duplex where LANs are half-duplex in operation. This is also true of fast circuit switching approaches (see Chapter 10, "High-Speed Circuit-Switching Systems" on page 10-1).

Throughput measures must *always* be considered with care. Throughput depends on the load offered to the system. Often, traffic patterns are asymmetric (such as in host-to-terminal or server-to-client). A fully peer-to-peer packet-switching architecture may not be much better than a LAN (at the same speed) if all traffic is from a single server to many clients - a common situation.

### Packet Switching as an Alternative Local Network

What if we could build a low-cost very fast packet switch into the hub. Connections from the hub to the workstations would be point-to-point. LAN throughput could be increased dramatically. Most of the cost of a packet switch is in the link terminations (attachments). If you have an intelligent hub, you have already paid for these link terminations - so the cost of changing a hub to a packet switch is not as high as might be expected.

With relatively balanced traffic, a moderate-speed packet-switching system can have a greater throughput than a very-high-speed (and costly) LAN. If this is true then why do we need very-high-speed LANs? A packet-switched architecture built into the hub using simple 10BaseT Ethernet links for connection could have a significantly higher throughput than a 100 Mbps FDDI LAN, and it could cost much much less.

The trick here is to use a simple switching architecture such as the one described in 6.12, "High-Speed Packet and Cell Switching Architectures" on page 6-41. The cost benefit comes because circuitry becomes exponentially more costly as speed increases - partly because circuit packing density decreases as speed increases (you can get much less logic on a high-speed "bi-polar" chip than you can get on good old CMOS). 10 Mbps Ethernet adapter cards are available for around $100 US. FDDI (even on copper) costs $1000 minimum. Of course, this cost applies both to the hub end of the connection and to the workstation end (so you double the cost).

### User Demand

Over the past few years many organizations have seen a fairly substantial increase in the loading on their LANs. A typical response to this has been to make LAN segments (especially Ethernet segments) much smaller. When a load problem comes along users have been breaking overloaded LANs up into a number of bridged segments. Of course, if you continue this process until there is only one station on each attached link to the hub then the bridge has logically become a packet switch!

### System Architecture

Cost-effective small packet switches can be built which will perform the LAN function. There are many alternatives available and many things to consider.

- What should the access protocol (from the station to the switch) be, Ethernet or ATM or something else?

    1. Ethernet adapter cards are very low in cost, the protocol will work very well on a point-to-point connection and users have massive investments in Ethernet software.

2. On the other hand, all LAN protocols depend very heavily on the ability to broadcast reliably. This is complex to provide in a packet switch and causes significant increased need for buffers and logic. In addition, because LAN protocols are connectionless, the switch has to look at each destination address to determine the routing. (Connection-oriented ATM is much simpler to route and therefore faster and lower in cost).

3. ATM is a much better protocol than Ethernet for the switch; it is compatible with planned PTT WAN standards and works over many media and at many speeds. If the PTTs offer a wide area ATM service, the connection could be seamless.

4. ATM, however, is a connection-oriented system. LAN protocols are connectionless. The use of LAN-like protocols over ATM requires significant additional software in each workstation adapter card (and perhaps in the workstation itself). There is also increased load on the workstation adapter card in splitting the data frame into cells for transmission and in cell reassembly on reception.

   There are other logical problems. For example, when a station in an ATM system receives a stream of cells it is possible (indeed probable) that cells from many different origins (other stations) will arrive intermixed with one another. A frame of user data when received is not contiguous. Thus the receiving adapter must contain significant additional buffers and logic to reassemble many data frames concurrently.

- How should the switch work internally? There are many possible architectures.

There are many potential combinations of LAN access with ATM switching (the intelligence can go either in the workstation or in the hub).

In 1993 at least one manufacturer (NET) currently markets an ATM-based LAN switch. This device uses unique adapter cards and the access protocol is ATM. It provides virtual LAN function to the workstation and is cost competitive with FDDI and hubs. Other suppliers are offering "turbocharged 10BaseT hubs" which are the kind of packet switch envisaged above. Moreover, at least one of these is optimized for asymmetric traffic by allowing 100 Mbps connections to servers and 10 Mbps connections for ordinary workstations. (Who said the mainframe was dead?)

Time will tell, but we could be witnessing the beginning of the end of the LAN.

# Appendix A. Review of Basic Principles

The objective of a network is to provide connections between end users using shared facilities (lines, nodes, etc.).

There are several general techniques available for the sharing of a facility between different data connections and/or voice circuits. These are general techniques and apply (although with different levels of efficiency) to each element of the system separately, so they are described here first.

## A.1 Available Techniques

### A.1.1 Frequency Division Multiplexing

This technique is exactly the same as is used for radio or television broadcasting. A sender is allocated a range of frequencies between which a signal may be sent and information may be encoded on that signal using a range of "modulation techniques". The receiver must be able not only to receive that frequency but also to decode the modulation technique used. On a cable, or on a microwave carrier, the available band of frequencies is limited but the principle is still the same. The amount of information that can be carried within a frequency "band" is directly proportional to the width of that band and is also dependent on the modulation technique used. There are theoretical limits that cannot be avoided such that every frequency "band" has a finite limit. Because of the necessary imprecision of the equipment involved, there are "buffer" zones (guard bands) allowed between bands so that one band will not interfere with either of the adjacent ones. The size of these buffer zones is also determined by the modulation technique (you need a lot less for Frequency Modulation (FM) than for Amplitude Modulation (AM)) and by the precision (and hence cost) of the equipment involved.

Frequency division multiplexing has, in the past, found use in telephone systems for carrying multiple calls over (say) a microwave link. It is also the basis of cable TV systems where many TV signals (each with a bandwidth of 4 or 7 MHz) are multiplexed over a single coaxial cable. It is also used in some types of computer local area networks (LANs).

Frequency division multiplexing is also sometimes called "broadband multiplexing".

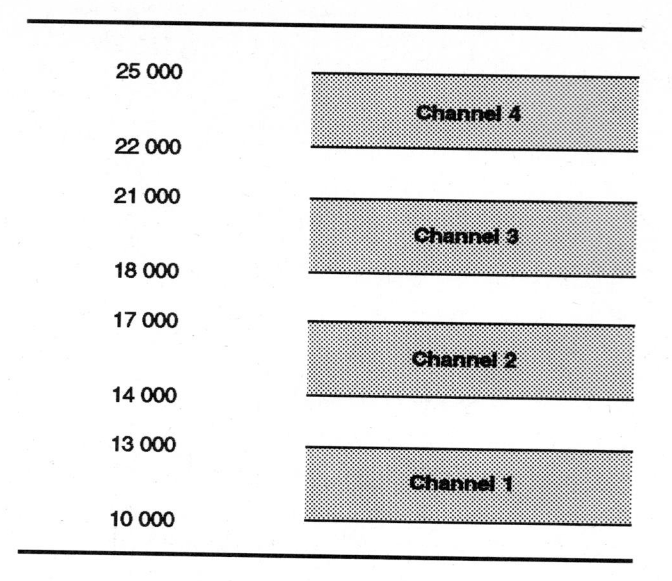


*Figure A-1. The Concept of Frequency Division Multiplexing.* The physical carrier provides a range of frequencies called a "spectrum", within which many channels are able to coexist. Notice the necessary "buffer zones" between frequency bands.

## A.1.2 Time Division Multiplexing

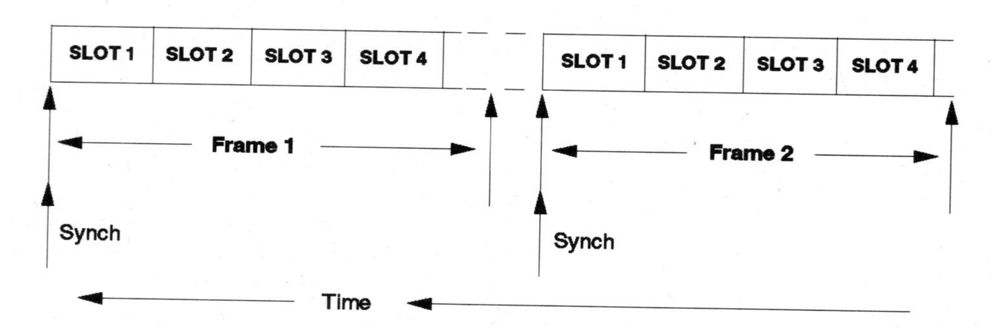


*Figure A-2. Time Division Multiplexing Principles*

Consider the diagram above. "Frames" are transmitted over a single high-speed channel. Within each frame there are many slots. A low-speed channel is allocated one (or more) slots within a high-speed frame. Thus a 2048000 bps channel can be subdivided into 32 subchannels of 64000 bps. The start of each frame is signaled by some coding which allows the sender and the receiver to agree on where the beginning of the frame is. This synchronization coding is sometimes a special (unique) bit stream (as when SDLC or BSC traditional data transmission is used) but with digital transmission is usually signaled by some special state in the underlying PCM coding. (The common one is called a "code violation".)

Attaching equipment is able to insert data into any slot and to take data from any slot. Thus while the medium can run at a very high speed, each attachment operates at a much lower data rate.

### A.1.3 Packetization

This technique involves the breaking of incoming bit streams (voice or data) into short "packets". Different techniques use variable or fixed length packets. Packets have an identifier appended to the front of them which identifies the circuit or channel to which they belong.[1] In the TDM example above, a time slot was allocated for a low-speed channel within every frame even if there was no data to be sent. In the packet technique blocks are sent only when a full block is available and "empty" packets are not sent. Thus utilization of the high-speed link can be dramatically improved.

Thus if a voice channel (without compression) is regarded as 64KB of data and a TDM approach gives 32 channels, then using packetization the number of channels that can be handled will dramatically increase. If, on an average, each (one-way) channel is only operational for half of the time (as in voice conversation) then perhaps 64 voice channels could be available. However, now there will be statistical variations and there will be a finite probability that all 64 channels will want the same direction at once. In this case some data will be lost but the probability is very small. The probability of 33 channels wanting to operate in the same direction simultaneously is quite high however. It is a matter for statisticians to decide how many channels can be safely allocated without too much chance of losing information (overrun). This will depend on the width of the carrier and the number of channels. The larger the number of channels the smaller the variation and the greater the safe utilization. This is a similar situation to the queueing models of data communication but the characteristics are quite different. A good starting assumption is that the channel can be utilized to perhaps 70% of its capacity safely, (in a 2 Mbps circuit). In a 140 Mbps circuit (PCM fiber channel), the 2000 telephone calls will have a much more even distribution and, therefore, efficiency could perhaps approach 90%. That is, perhaps 3500 calls could be handled. (Other things, such as routing headers and the requirement for uniform transit times will probably reduce this somewhat.)

---

[1] Alternatively, they could have a routing header which identifies the source and destination of the packet.

## A.1.4 Sub-Multiplexing

It is quite possible, indeed usual, for multiplexors to be "cascaded" as suggested in Figure A-3. A "high order" multiplexor is used to derive a number of lower speed channels that then are further reduced by other (lower order) multiplexors. This may then be reduced even further by lower and lower order multiplexors.

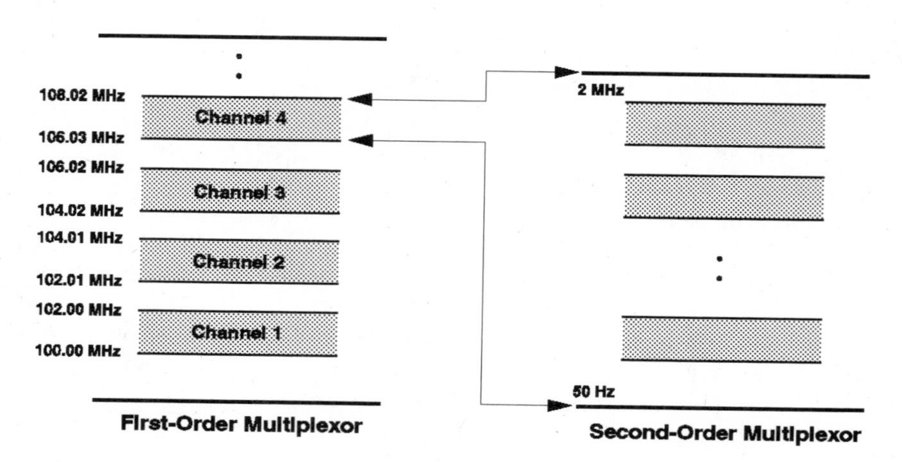


*Figure A-3. Sub-Multiplexing Concept.* Frequency division technique used within frequency division derived channel.

Since a derived channel is just like the original channel only "narrower", then different multiplexing techniques can be used within one another. For example, it is possible for a wideband microwave channel to be frequency divided into a number of slower channels, and then for one lower speed channel to be further divided by the frequency technique, another to be shared using the TDM digital technique, and yet another to be shared using the packet technique. There are limitations, however. For example, a digital channel cannot be shared using frequency division multiplexing and a TDM technique would not be a very attractive way of subdividing a packet technique. Still, mixtures of techniques can be used relatively freely.

The hierarchies of multiplexors used in different parts of the world are shown in Table A-1 on page A-5.

*Table A-1. PCM Hierarchies*

| | North American | | Japanese | | CCITT-CEPT | |
|---|---|---|---|---|---|---|
| **Order** | **Bit Rate (Mbps)** | **No. of Chan** | **Bit Rate (Mbps)** | **No. of Chan** | **Bit Rate (Mbps)** | **No. of Chan** |
| Single Channel | 64 Kbps | 1 | 64 Kbps | 1 | 64 Kbps | 1 |
| First Order | 1.544 | 24 | 1.544 | 24 | 2.048 | 30 |
| Second Order | 6.312 | 96 | 6.312 | 96 | 8.448 | 120 |
| Third Order | 44.736 | 672 | 32.064 | 480 | 34.368 | 480 |
| Fourth Order | 274.176 | 4032 | 97.728 | 1440 | 139.264 | 1920 |
| Fifth Order | | | 397.200 | 5760 | 564.992 | 7680 |

## A.1.5 Statistical Multiplexing

Statistical multiplexing is the generic name for any method that aims to use channel capacity (and send information) only when there is information to send. This is in contrast to the techniques of allocating a channel and then not caring whether that channel is used or not. Packetization is one form of statistical multiplexing.

The technique offers savings for voice in that the gaps in speech and the "half-duplex" characteristic of speech can potentially be exploited for other conversations. Likewise, the gaps in traditional data traffic can be exploited. There are multiplexors available that allocate a large number of voice channels over a smaller number of real channels by this technique. Listening to any one of the voice channels would provide the listener with intermixed phrases and sentences from different conversations on the one real voice channel. In data communications, the use of "statmuxes" that derive (for example) six or eight slow (2400 bps) channels from a "standard" 9600 bps line are in common use.

All of these have problems in that they require some technique to recognize "silence", that is, to determine what not to send. In voice, a delay buffer is needed so that when a word is spoken following a silence the need for a channel is recognized and the channel made available WITHOUT chopping off the beginning of the word.

In the past this technique has been used to improve utilization of expensive undersea telephone cables but is not in common use for other situations because of the cost and the impact on quality caused by the additional delays and the interposition of yet another piece of equipment which degrades the signal quality.

### A.1.6 "Block" Multiplexing

Block multiplexing is the usual method of operation of data networks. It is one form of statistical multiplexing.

A single channel is used to transmit "blocks" of varying lengths depending on the logical characteristics of the data to be transmitted and the physical characteristics of the devices involved. Often maximum limits are imposed on block lengths (though sometimes not). Blocks are usually queued for the link according to various criteria such as priority, length or message type. In IBM's Systems Network Architecture (SNA), this method is used on all links but different characteristics apply to different kinds of links. For example, on links between IBM 3725s block lengths can be very long (4000 bytes or more) and on links between 3725s and controllers, blocks are "segmented" (broken up) to fit into the I/O buffers of the receiving device.

Some types of local area network also use this technique.

## A.2 Characteristics of Multiplexing Techniques

**Frequency Division Multiplexing**

- This is an analog technique and applies to the kind of "interexchange carrier" systems still in use by many telephone companies (although it is rapidly being replaced by digital TDM techniques).
- Subchannels are separated from each other by "buffer zones" which are really wasted frequency space or wasted capacity, although necessary.
- The analog equipment needed to make this work is extremely sensitive to "tuning" of frequencies and to the stability of filters.
- This equipment is also very expensive because of its analog nature and its sensitivity to tuning, etc., and requires a large amount of labor to install and maintain.[2] It also requires retuning and maintenance whenever the physical channel changes (for example, is rerouted or repaired, etc.).
- Also, it is usual to use two channels per conversation, one in either direction. A reasonable estimate of "good" channel use by this technique (for voice traffic) is 10%.

---

2 Another factor contributing to the expense is that it is difficult to apply large scale integration techniques to analog systems. Analog equipment tends to have many more separate components than comparable digital systems (digital ones have more circuits but many are packed together into a single component). This leads to a higher cost for the analog alternative.

- However, the equipment is extremely modular and a failure in one element most often does not affect the operation of the remainder of the system.

**Time Division Multiplexing**

- This method is quite simple and can be built in single chip hardware logic.
- Therefore, the hardware is low in cost (compared to other techniques).
- It will operate at very high speeds.
- While it gives sharing and channelization of the link, it does not take into account, for example, the fact that telephone traffic is logically half-duplex (only one person talks at once) and though a channel is provided in each direction only one is in use at any one time. Nor does it take advantage of "gaps" in speech. There are intelligent multiplexing techniques (called statistical multiplexors) which do this. For these reasons, "good" utilization for telephone traffic is considered to be around 40%. This is a lot better than the analog frequency division technique.

**Packetization**

- The equipment required for packetization is MUCH more complex and expensive.
- Operation at very high speeds increases the complexity of the required equipment.
- Use of the packetization technique results in very much improved (optimal) use of the trunk. This is because when there is a silence no packet is transmitted. There are overheads inherent in the addressing technique which must be used to route and to identify the packet but nevertheless, an efficiency of 80% can perhaps be approached if the carrier is wide enough to permit a large number of simultaneous calls.
- In 1995 this technique is NOT operational in any "telco" voice system. However, this technique is the basis of ATM (Asynchronous Transfer Mode) and it is widely believed that this technique will ultimately replace TDM techniques as the basis of worldwide voice and data public communication networks.

  Packetization is a normal method for operation of data networks and is in wide use, (there is an important cost/performance trade-off discussed under "Block Multiplexing").

**Block Multiplexing**

This can be considered a special case of packetization (in the sense of variable-length packets). Alternatively, packetization can be considered a special case of block multiplexing with fixed-length blocks. In the data processing industry, the use of variable-length blocks is usual. In the data networks constructed by telephone companies (generically called X.25 networks because of the "standard" they use to interface to their users), packetization is the normal method.

In a network where data integrity is of supreme importance, a block must be fully received by an intermediate node BEFORE it is sent on to the next node.[3] Since the whole block must be received before it is sent on, the longer the block, the longer the delay in the intermediate node. If there are many nodes through which the data must pass, then the delay for each node adds to the total delay for the network transit. So the shorter the block, the more quickly it can be sent through a network. Thus if there are 2000 bytes to be sent, the transit time will be much faster if this is sent as ten, 200-byte "packets".

There is another problem with widely varying block lengths. Queueing delays for links become uneven and parallel link groups tend to operate erratically. (In SNA for example, "Transmission Group" (TG) operation could be greatly degraded by the presence of widely varying block lengths.) Another problem is that varying block lengths create erratic demands on buffer pool utilization in switching nodes.

It would seem sensible, therefore, to keep data block lengths to a minimum in all networks. However, there is a very important characteristic of computer equipment that must be taken into account. Processing a block (switching or sending or receiving) takes almost exactly the same amount of computer processing regardless of the length of the block. This applies to computer mainframes, switching nodes, terminal controllers etc.[4] So, in the example of a 2,000-byte block, the processing time in each involved processor (including the sender and receiver) will be multiplied by 10 if blocks are sent 200 bytes at a time.

Since the amount of processing involved is a cost factor, it will cost a lot more for processing hardware if short blocks or packets are sent. Hence the EDP industry tradition of sending variable, long blocks.

When considering voice transit, where network transit delay and uniformity of response are paramount, it would seem that mixing voice into such a data system would not be feasible.

---

3 Whether the routing header in the beginning of the block is correct is not determined until the end of the block has been received and the Frame Check Sequence (FCS) is checked. So the block cannot be sent on until it is checked.

4 In the IBM 3725, for example, switching an intermediate block takes (total including link control) around 3,200 instructions. Getting data into or out of the processor takes on the order of 100 nanoseconds per byte. So for INN (Intermediate Network Node - meaning between two 3725s) operation a 3725 can "switch" somewhere around 350-400, 200-byte blocks per second (70% utilization) and maybe 360 to 410 blocks per second if blocks are 100 bytes. (These figures are approximate and depend heavily on environmental conditions.)

However, the above applies to traditional systems where the block is "long" in time as well as in bytes. That is, the link speed is low compared to the length of the block. With high link speeds (for example, 4 Mbps on a local area network), block lengths that were considered "long" in the past become short enough not to be a problem (for example, 5000 bytes take 10 milliseconds at 4 Mbps).

Also, new equipment designs will, in the future, allow vastly reduced cost in the switching node so the cost of short packets may be less of a problem.

### Sub-Multiplexing

This technique is popular because it allows for great flexibility and for modularity of equipment. For example, a first order TDM multiplexor might break up a 140 Mbps fiber circuit into 64 2-Mbps channels. Some of these can then be further multiplexed into 30 (64 Kbps) voice channels or perhaps several 2 Mbps channels combined to provide a television circuit. The derived 64 Kbps voice channels can perhaps then be broken up further by (third order) multiplexors to provide many 4,800 or 9,600 bps data channels. The equipment modularity introduced also assists in reliability and serviceability management.

The ability to mix techniques is also very important. (There are some limits here; frequency division multiplexing cannot be used within a digital channel, for example.) A wideband analog carrier can be frequency multiplexed into several high-speed digital channels and then one of these could use packet mode techniques for carrying data and others could use TDM techniques for carrying voice traffic.

# Appendix B. Transmitting Information by Modulating a Carrier

In Chapter 2, “A Review of Digital Transmission Technology” on page 2-1 techniques for sending data as voltage (or current) changes directly on a wire were discussed. In many situations, however, information cannot be sent directly but must be carried as variations in another signal. Radio communication is perhaps the most common example of using a modulated carrier to convey information but the use of modems to carry digital information through the analog telephone network is also very common. This is often called “wideband”, “broadband” or ”passband” modulation (these terms mean roughly the same thing).

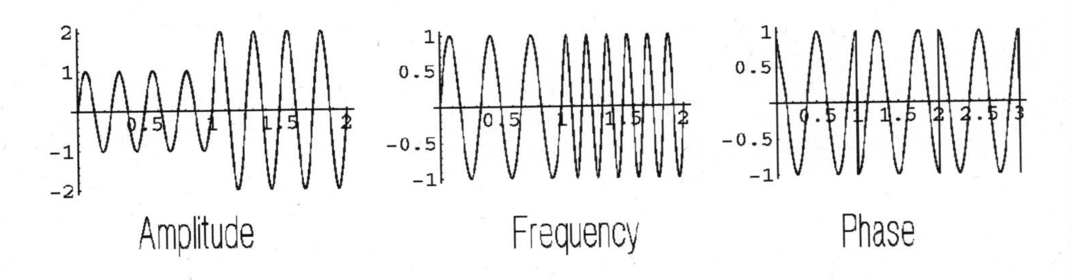


*Figure B-1. Three Primary Modulation Techniques*

A carrier signal is almost always a sinusoid wave of a particular frequency. Information is carried by introducing variations in this carrier signal. Figure B-1 illustrates the three ways of modulating a sinusoidal wave.

**Amplitude Modulation (AM)**

This is the simplest form of modulation and was the first to be used in practice. The strength of the signal (loudness or amplitude) is systematically changed according to the information to be transmitted.

**Frequency Modulation (FM)**

In FM the frequency of the carrier is varied.

**Phase Modulation (PM)**

In PM, systematic changes in the phase of the carrier are used.

There are hundreds of variations on just how a modulated signal is created in practice and how it is received. Many systems operate as shown in Figure B-2 on page B-2.

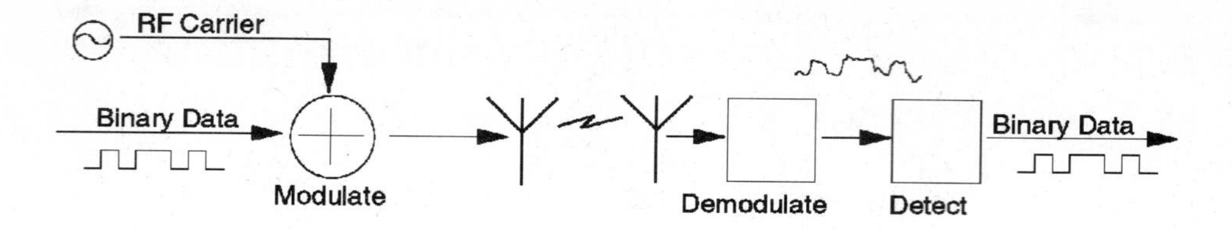


*Figure B-2. Transmission and Reception of a Modulated Signal*

1. A baseband binary data stream is created representing the bits to be sent.
2. A sinusoidal carrier signal is generated (at RF this is usually a crystal controlled oscillator).
3. The digital signal is then used to modulate the carrier signal and the resultant signal is sent to the antenna.
4. In the receiver, the signal is first filtered (to separate it from all other radio signals around) and then the carrier is removed.
5. The result is a baseband signal containing distortion and noise which has then to be processed by a detector in order to recover the original bit stream.

#### B.1.1.1 Sidebands

When a sinusoidal carrier signal is generated it varies by only a very small amount. That is, the range of frequencies over which the carrier is spread is very narrow. When such a signal is modulated, it seems reasonable that the frequency spread (at least for AM and PM techniques) should remain unchanged. *Sadly, it doesn't work quite this way.* Modulation of a carrier *always* produces a signal such as that shown in Figure B-3.

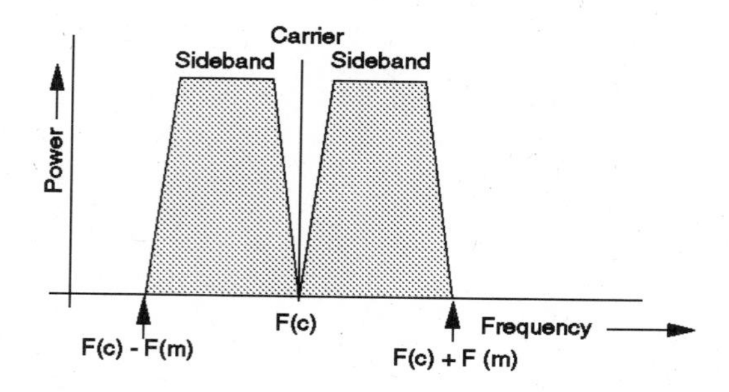


*Figure B-3. Sidebands*

You get a spread of frequencies equal to twice the maximum frequency of the modulating signal. What you get is a carrier signal (*carrying no information*) surrounded by two "sidebands" (above and below). Each sideband uses a frequency spread of exactly the maximum modulating frequency. All of the modulation information is carried in the sidebands - the carrier contains no information (it is nevertheless quite useful to have in some systems).

Some transmission systems suppress transmission of the carrier (it is pointless to waste power sending something that contains no information) and others suppress both the carrier and one sideband (Single Sideband - SSB Transmission).

It is important to note that sidebands are generated for all three modulation schemes. They are different in the sense that the precise form of the sidebands is different for each different modulating technique.

#### B.1.1.2 Bandwidth

The above leads us to the concept of bandwidth. A signal doesn't use just one frequency. It uses a band of frequencies equal in width (from lowest to highest) to twice the maximum frequency of the modulating signal. (If SSB transmission is used, the bandwidth occupied is just the maximum frequency of the modulating signal.)

### B.1.2 Digital Modulation Methods

There are hundreds of methods of digital modulation. When digital information is used to modulate a sinusoidal carrier, changes in characteristics of the signal are used to carry information rather than changes in voltage or current.

Most of the methods discussed in Chapter 2, "A Review of Digital Transmission Technology" on page 2-1 for baseband transmission can be used as methods of modulating a carrier. However, carrier modulation is used predominantly in environments where bandwidth is very limited and baseband techniques are most often used in situations where bandwidth is not the primary concern.[1] This leads to significant differences in the approach used in the two environments.

#### B.1.2.1 On-Off Keying (OOK)

OOK is the simplest method of modulating a carrier. You turn the carrier on for a 1 bit and off for a 0 bit. In principle this is exactly the same as early Morse code radio.

OOK is not often used as a modulation technique for radio transmissions. This is partly because the receiver tends to lose track of the signal during the gaps (0 bits) but mostly because it requires a very wide bandwidth for a given data rate. Other transmission techniques are significantly better.

---

1 There are many exceptions here, such as the use of spread spectrum techniques in some radio environments and the use of baseband techniques to get the maximum throughput from a telephone subscriber loop circuit.

As explained earlier in 4.1.6.1, “On-Off Keying (OOK)” on page 4-23, OOK is the primary method used in optical fiber communication.

### B.1.2.2 Shift Keying (ASK, FSK, PSK, etc.)

xSK techniques involve having two carrier states. Modulation is achieved by keying between the two states. In principle one state represents a zero bit and the other a 1 bit - although it is common to use techniques like NRZI to encode the data first.[2]

The common variants of this are:

- Amplitude Shift Keying (ASK)
- Frequency Shift Keying (FSK)
- Phase Shift Keying (PSK)

Such signals are very simple to generate and to receive and hence necessary equipment is inexpensive but they do not offer optimal performance in a bandlimited environment. However, some variations on these techniques are in very wide use. The most common 1200 bps modem uses FSK. In spread spectrum radio systems (where by definition we are not too worried about bandwidth restrictions) BPSK (BiPolar Phase Shift Keying) is commonly used.

### B.1.2.3 Bandwidth

If you examine the composition of a square wave (or stream of pulses with square corners) you find that it is composed of a number of sinusoidal waves of different frequencies and phases. A square wave (stream of pulses) can be represented as follows:

$$\cos(2\pi \times t) - \frac{1}{3}\cos(2\pi \times 3t) + \frac{1}{5}\cos(2\pi \times 5t) - \frac{1}{7}\cos(2\pi \times 7t) + \ldots + \frac{1}{13}\cos(2\pi \times 13t) + \ldots$$

In the equation t = time and represents the frequency of this component. Only the odd numbered harmonics are present in a square wave. Notice that this is an infinite series.

The point here is that a square wave with repetition frequency of 1 kHz has sinusoidal components strong enough to matter up to about 9 kHz. This means that to faithfully reproduce a square wave signal through carrier modulation requires the use of quite a

2 The word “keying” in general implies that the carrier is shifted between states in an abrupt (even brutal) manner. That is, there is no synchronization between the shifting of the carrier and its phase.

wide bandwidth.[3] When digitally modulating a carrier it is common to "shape" the modulating pulses in such a way that the required bandwidth usage is minimized.

### B.1.2.4 Timing Recovery

As shown in Figure B-2 on page B-2 what we get after demodulation when the signal is received is a baseband signal. An important problem for the receiver is to decide what is a bit and what is not - that is, we must recover not only the variations in the signal but also the timing. It is important that the data encoding system used provide frequent state changes so that the receiver can accurately determine the transitions between states. This was discussed at some length in 2.1.1, "Non-Return to Zero (NRZ) Coding" on page 2-4 and following.

### B.1.2.5 Scrambling

If we transmit the same symbol repetitively in many situations there will be a problem with keeping the signal within its allocated frequency band. This applies in both radio and voiceband telephone environments. If we use an encoding scheme that provides frequent transitions and is DC balanced then this is normally sufficient. If not, we need to use a "scrambler" to change the data into a form suitable for transmission (and a descrambler in the receiver).

### B.1.2.6 Many Bits per Symbol

Perhaps the most popular (and obvious) way of limiting the bandwidth required for a given data rate is to use one signal state to represent more than one bit. We could have (say) eight different amplitude (or phase or frequency) states and then each state could represent 3 bits. If we had 16 states then we could potentially represent 4 bits. The rate at which we switch between states (the number of state changes per second) is called the baud rate. Each discrete signaling state is commonly called a "symbol".

If we send a succession of different states at a rate of (say) 1000 per second, then the bandwidth used depends on just what the sequence is. However, the worst case is when we change from one extreme to another on alternate symbols. When this is the case we have a square wave of 500 Hz. (Remember that in this case 500 Hz will not be enough bandwidth because we need to carry some harmonics.)

The complicating factor here is noise. If it were not for noise a fairly simple receiver could discriminate between a very large number of states and we could get very large numbers of bits per symbol. Unfortunately, noise and distortion in the channel prevents this. In some environments the effects of noise can be mitigated by using more transmitter power (or a shorter distance) but most times this is not possible. In practice, noise

---

[3] Of course this is also true when using a baseband medium. The medium must have capacity to pass quite a wide bandwidth if it is to pass square pulses accurately.

sets a maximum limit on the number of usable states regardless of the complexity of the receiver.

**A baudy story**

The term "baud" when referring to the speed of data transmission is more often misused than used correctly. *The baud rate is the signaling rate. That is, it is the rate of state changes of the modulating signal (the symbol rate).* Thus if you have three bits per symbol and the baud rate is 2000 then bit rate is 6000 bps.

It is common to see advertisements and even articles in the technical press referring to voiceband modems as "9600 baud" when they mean 9600 bps. *There is no voiceband modem on the market with a baud rate higher than 2600* (in fact you couldn't have one since the telephone voice channel has a bandwidth of 3400 Hz). Fast voiceband modems currently use QAM with 6 bits per symbol and achieve a bit rate of 14400 bps using a signaling rate of 2400 baud.

### B.1.2.7 Quadrature Amplitude Modulation (QAM)

Phase
Amplitude

In order to send as many bits as we can within a restricted bandwidth many techniques modulate more than one variable (dimension) simultaneously. This is the concept behind QAM. QAM is the predominant modulation technique in high-speed data modems and microwave radio systems.

In QAM multiple states of amplitude and phase are used together. It is usual to show this as a "quadrature" illustrated above. Note that the position of the axes bisects the number of states. This is just for illustration - there is no such thing as a negative amplitude. In the example shown (more correctly called QAM-16) there are now 16 states and thus 4 bits can be represented. In higher quality channels QAM-64 (representing 6 bits) and QAM-256 (representing 8 bits) are sometimes used.

One of the big advantages of QAM is that the amplitude and phase of a signal can be represented as a complex number and processed using Fourier techniques. (This is the heart of the "DMT"modulation technique discussed in 3.2, "Discrete Multitone Transmission (DMT)" on page 3-5.)

### B.1.2.8 Trellis Coding

Trellis coding (and Vitterbi decoding) are commonly used in conjunction with QAM systems. The concept is quite simple although the implementation is sometimes very complex.

When a QAM symbol is received, the receiver will measure its phase and amplitude. Due to the effects of noise, these measured values seldom match the points on the quadrature exactly and a QAM receiver typically selects the nearest point and decides that this is the symbol received. But what if this received value was in error because noise changed it? In regular QAM this is just an error. Trellis coding is a way of avoiding a substantial proportion of these errors.

The concept is that the transmitter only sends a limited sequence of symbols. If a particular symbol has just been transmitted then the next symbol *must* be from a subset (not all) of the possible symbols. Of course this reduces the number of bits you can represent with a particular quadrature. Typically, in a 16-state quadrature, only eight states will be valid at any point in time (which eight depends on the last one sent). This means that you can represent only 3 bits rather than 4.

This relies on the concept of a sequence of line states. If you start out transmitting a particular line state then the next state must be one of eight states. When you transmit that state then the next one must be one of eight also. Therefore if you start at a particular line state there are 64 possible combinations for the next two states transmitted. What the receiver does is correlate the sequence of line states received with all the possible sequences of states. This works as follows:

1. When the receiver detects a line state, it does not immediately decide which symbol has been received. Instead it allocates a "weight" (the mean squared distance) between the detected point and all surrounding points.
2. As time progresses the receiver adds up the weights of all possible paths (this is an enormous processing problem since the number of possible paths grows exponentially).
3. After a number of symbol times a particular path is chosen to be correct, based on the minimum total weight accumulated along all the possible paths.
4. The sequence of symbols is then decoded into a sequence of bits.

The important characteristic here is that it is the sequence of line states that is important and not any individual received line state. This gives very good rejection of AWGN (Additive White Gaussian Noise) and many other types of noise as well.

Vitterbi decoding is the process usually used in conjunction with Trellis coding. It is simply a way of performing the path calculation such that the number of possible paths stays within the ability of a signal processor to handle the computation.

Depending on the number of points in the constellation, Trellis coding can show a gain in signal-to-noise terms of 4 to 6 dB.

# Appendix C. Queueing Theory

An understanding of the principles of queueing theory is basic to the understanding of computer networks and so a brief discussion is included here for reference.

When the earliest interactive (or "online") computer systems were built, the designers often did not understand that queueing theory would dictate the behavior of these new systems. Some serious and very costly mistakes were made because the way communications systems actually behave is *the opposite of what normal intuition would suggest.* That said, queueing theory can be applied to any situation where many users wish to obtain service from a finite resource in a serial fashion. Such situations as people queueing for the checkout at a supermarket or motor cars queueing at an intersection are much the same as data messages queueing for the use of a link within a data switching device.

Consider the diagram below:

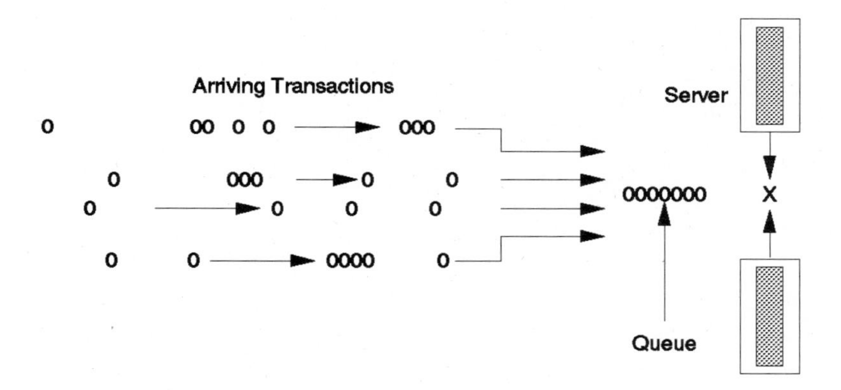


***Figure C-1.*** *Schematic of a Single Server Queue*

Imagine that this is a queue of people at a supermarket checkout. Most people would expect that if the average time it takes for the checkout clerk to serve one customer were two minutes, then the rate at which customers will be served would be 30 customers per hour. At this point the checkout clerk would be busy all the time (100% utilized). It also seems reasonable to expect that if the number of people who arrive to join the queue is about 30 per hour then the length of the queue should be one or two and the time spent waiting for service would be quite short. Nothing could be further from the truth! In the case just described (over time) the queue will become very long indeed. In theory the length of the queue in this situation will approach infinity!

The graph in Figure C-2 on page C-2 shows queue length as a function of server utilization for single server queues.

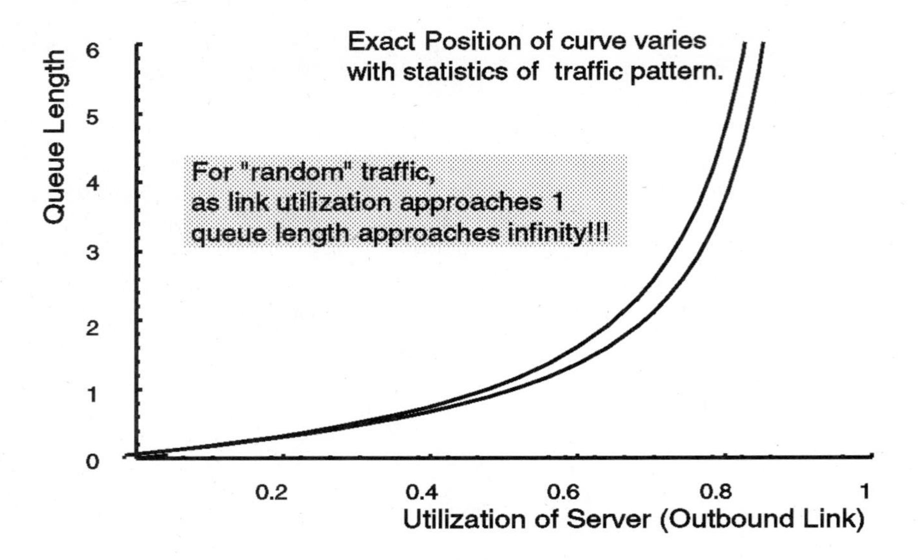


***Figure C-2.** Behavior of a Hypothetical Single Server Queue.* The curves show queue length as a function of server utilization. As utilization approaches 1 the length of the queue and hence the waiting time approaches infinity.

In order to discuss the way queues behave there are some technical terms that must be understood.

**Service Time** is the time taken by the checkout clerk to process a particular person. This will be different for each person depending on the number of items to be processed.

**Average Service Time** is the average over time of a number of people processed by the checkout.

**Arrival Rate** is the rate (people per hour) at which people arrive and join the queue.

**Queue Length** is the number of people waiting in the queue at a particular time.

**Average Queue Length** is the average length of the queue over a given period of time.

**Server** is the job of the checkout clerk.

**Utilization of the Server** is the percentage of time that the server is busy.

This is the average service time multiplied by the arrival rate divided by the length of time in question. The utilization value is something between zero and one but is often expressed as a percentage.

## C.1.1 Fundamentals

In order to describe the behavior of a queue mathematically we need the following information:

**Input Traffic**

- Arrival Rate

  The average (over some specified period of time) rate at which transactions (messages, people, etc.) arrive at a facility requiring service.

  This is represented by the parameter $\lambda$.

- Distribution of Arrivals

  Quoting an average arrival rate or an average service time tells us nothing unless we know something about the overall pattern which these things follow. In some systems, transactions may arrive at exactly regular intervals. In other systems arrivals may occur in bursts. In most interactive data communications systems transactions arrive for processing in a completely random way.

  The usual distribution of arrivals used in a data communication system is called a Poisson distribution. This distribution describes random arrivals from an infinite population independent of past events.

**The Waiting Queue**

- The Queueing Time

  The total time spent by a transaction in the queue (including the service time) is called the queueing time.

  $T_Q$ = mean (average) queueing time

- The Waiting Time

  The time spent waiting in the queue *not* including the service time is called the waiting time.

  $T_W$ = mean (average) waiting time

- Number of Transactions in the Queue

  The length of the queue expressed in terms of the number of waiting transactions is called $L_W$.

**The Service Facility**

- Mean Service Time

  This is the average time it takes to process a transaction and is denoted by $T_S$.

- Server Utilization

  This is the fraction of time the server is busy. It is symbolized by $\rho$. Busy time is (obviously) just the arrival rate multiplied by the average service time.

  $\rho = \lambda \times T_S$.

As $\lambda$, the rate of arrivals, increases then so does the utilization of the server, the queue length and the average time spent waiting in the queue. At $\rho = 1$, the server becomes saturated, working 100% of the time. Therefore the maximum input rate to a single server queue is:

$\lambda$ maximum $= 1/T_S = \mu$ (mean service rate)

The utilization coefficient is:

$\rho = \lambda/\mu$

Many of the numbers above are averages (means). If the arrivals are random then there will be a deviation around the mean values. For example, the 90th percentile is that value of time below which the random variable under study occurs 90% of the time. Specific values for the 90th and 95th percentiles for Poisson distributed arrivals are:

90th percentile = 2.3 × (mean value)

95th percentile = 3 × (mean value)

**The golden rule**

For most queueing situations where arrivals approximate a random distribution queue size, the average delay increases exponentially with the utilization rate. This is illustrated in Figure C-2 on page C-2.

## C.1.2 Distributions

There are two things under discussion that are governed to some degree by uncertainty:

1. The pattern of arrivals
2. The time it takes to service a given transaction

Both of these distributions may be exactly regular or completely random or anything in between. Notice that the distribution of arrivals and the distribution of service times are quite independent of one another.[1]

The "in between" distributions are called "Erlang distributions with parameter m", or just "Erlang-m". The "Erlang parameter" is a measure of randomness. In Figure C-2 on page C-2 the different curves apply to different service time distributions. Arrivals are assumed to be random.

In typical data communications systems interactive data traffic arrives with a fully random (Poisson) distribution. For batch traffic, unless it is controlled, the traffic will arrive at the maximum rate of the link. Voice traffic typically originates at the rate of one byte every 125 μsec. This is one 32-byte packet every 4 milliseconds. Unless there is compression and/or removal of silences, the voice traffic will travel through the network at exactly one (32-byte) packet every 4 milliseconds.

In a typical data communications application, service time is the time taken to send the transaction (frame) on a link and will vary in direct proportion to the length of the frame. If we are considering time taken to process a transaction (switch the block) in a packet switching computer typically this is the same amount of time regardless of the length of the block.

## C.1.3 Some Formulae

The following are some simple formulae which can be used to analyse typical queueing situations. These are for exponential arrival and exponential service distributions.

### C.1.3.1 Queue Size and Length

The mean queue size, including the transaction currently being serviced is:

$$L_q = \frac{\rho}{1 - \rho}$$

The mean length of the queue is:

$$L_w = \frac{\rho^2}{1 - \rho}$$

[1] This is not quite true. The rate of arrival of frames at a switching node is dependent on their length and the link speed. The longer they are, the lower the rate of arrival. For the purpose of discussion this effect can be ignored.

Then note that the queue length is shorter than the mean queue size by the quantity $\rho$; that is, the difference is, on the average, less than one transaction:

$$L_q = L_w + \rho$$

### C.1.3.2 Queueing Time

The mean queueing time is:

$$T_q = \frac{T_s}{1 - \rho}$$

Queueing time 90th percentile = $2.3T_q$.

Queueing time 95th percentile = $3T_q$.

Mean waiting time:

$$T_w = \frac{\rho \times T_s}{1 - \rho}$$

## C.1.4 Practical Systems

In a data communications processor (switch) there may be many queues. There is a queue (although a logically distributed one) for the processor resource. There are queues of data waiting for transmission on each outbound link. There may be many internal queues (such as for the I/O channel) depending on the structure of the processor.

The general rule is that no resource should be loaded more than 60% because of the effect of the waiting time on system responses. This is still a good rule if transactions arrive at truly random rates, are time sensitive and there are no congestion control mechanisms in place to control things. But there are a number of situations in which much higher utilizations are practical.

**Regularity of Input Distribution and Service Time Distribution**

If transactions arrive at a processing system (for example) at *exactly* one millisecond intervals *and* if processing takes *exactly* one millisecond then the facility will be utilized 100% and there will be no queue. It all hinges on the word "exact".

If the distribution of arrivals and of service times is truly random then the "exponential" curve in Figure C-2 on page C-2 will hold true.

If arrivals are regular and service times are exponentially distributed then the "constant" curve in the figure is appropriate.

In summary, for a particular system, the less randomness involved the higher the safe level of utilization.

### Traffic Priorities

Traffic prioritization is *very little use* unless there are congestion control mechanisms in place to allocate resources according to priority and to regulate low priority traffic.

In an SNA network for example, the extensive priority mechanisms can allow an internode link to be loaded in excess of 95% without significant degradation of the interactive traffic.

But the interactive traffic (the random traffic) itself had better not exceed about 60% utilization of any facility. What happens is that interactive traffic uses the system as though the batch traffic were not there (well, almost). Control protocols allocate spare capacity to non-time-critical batch traffic.

### The Law of Large Numbers

Consider a queue of data for a 9600 bps intermediate node (INN) link in an SNA network. The sizes of frames carried on the link could vary from 29-byte control frames up to 4,000-byte blocks.[2]

The transmission time required to send a 4,000-byte block is a bit less than 4 seconds. For the 29-byte block it is about 35 milliseconds. Perhaps, for the sake of example, the average block length might be 400 bytes and take a transmission time of about .4 of a second.

If you select say 10 frames from the link at random then the average of the selected frames will be different from the true average over, say, one million frames. (There is a chance that all 10 frames will be 4,000 bytes long - or 29 bytes long). If you keep selecting samples of 10 frames each then the averages of these samples will be distributed about the true average with some variation (variance). If you select a sample of 100 frames then the chance is much better that it will be close to the true average. If you select a sample of 1000 frames then the chance is better still. The point here is *as the selected sample gets larger then the probability that its mean is close to the true mean of the population from which the sample is taken increases.*

Now consider a queue for a real link. If there are two (4000-byte) blocks waiting, then this represents around eight seconds of transmission time. If there are two (29-byte) blocks waiting then there is only about 65 milliseconds of transmission time. The example is deliberately extreme. It is obvious that

[2] SNA does not packetize or segment data for transport on INN links. However, the maximum length of blocks entering the network can be controlled.

transit delays through the link in question will be highly erratic. (A good case for breaking the data up into short packets perhaps). In this situation it would be dangerous to plan for a link utilisation of more than an average 30% because of the extreme variation that is possible in the service time (transmission time).

A faster link can handle more traffic. This means that there can be more blocks handled over any given time interval. This has the statistical effect that the selected sample of the population is larger and thus the likelihood of an atypical average is decreased.[3]

For example, if the link speed is 2 Mbps, a 4,000-byte block now takes 16 milliseconds and the 29-byte block takes about 120 microseconds. At 60% utilization we can process about forty, 4000 byte blocks per second or perhaps 5000 29-byte control messages. If the average block length is 400 then the number of blocks per second for 60% utilization is about 400. In this situation a group of 400 blocks will come very close to the average. The fact that some blocks are 4000 and others are 29 will have very little effect on the average. There will be very little variation.

Imagine what happens at 100 Mbps!

This then is the effect: As the link speed increases the number of frames per second increases (unless we increase the block size). As the frame rate increases then the possible variation in a given sample of traffic (say one second) decreases. As the variance decreases one is able to use increasing link utilisations with safety. That is to say *the faster the link the higher the safe level of utilization.*

### High Speed in Itself

In practical networks of the past (with 9600 bps links) a planned queueing delay for a link of say .4 of a second was considered acceptable. In a modern-high speed network we are perhaps able to accept a queueing delay of 50 milliseconds. The link speed has increased by 1000 times but our delay objective has only become ten times more stringent.

This means that in the past, to achieve our .4 second delay objective, we could only plan on a queue length of perhaps 1 or 2, which means a link utilization of about 60%. With a very high-speed link we may be able to plan for a queue length of 60 to 100. Because of the stability associated with the very large number of frames per second, *a link utilization of 80% may be approached in some cases.*

---

[3] Another way of saying this is that if we sum n sources of bursty traffic then the total rate exhibits less burstiness as a result. As the number (n) of sources increases, the ratio of the standard deviation to the mean of a summed rate approaches zero.

## C.1.5 Practical Situations

In a practical networking situation there are number of points to note:

**Time Interval**

The time interval over which an average is expressed is absolutely critical. Traffic varies over time and expressions of arrival rates in "messages per hour" often do not help very much. On the other hand, extremely high peaks in message traffic over very short periods (say ten seconds) can be easily handled by buffering in the network.

Experience with conventional SNA networks suggests that an appropriate length of time over which to calculate peak message or transaction rates is five to ten minutes.

It is also important to realise that systems take a long time to reach a steady state after startup.

**Arrival Patterns**

Arrival patterns will not always be as the formulae assume. In any data communications system the population size of terminals is finite. In the case of interactive traffic there can only be a maximum of one transaction (perhaps many messages) per terminal in the system at any one time. Often a terminal device has a maximum rate at which transactions may be entered (for example, a bank cash dispenser). This could be because of mechanical functions that must be performed or because of necessary actions the human operator (like talking to a customer).

**Service Time Distribution**

This is almost always not random. In a communications node the time taken to transmit on a link is typically a linear function of the length of the data. The processor time taken by the node processor to receive the data on one link and enqueue it for another usually doesn't vary very much. Processing a transaction in a mainframe processor is usually reasonably constant *for each type of transaction* but things like disk access times tend to be random.

**Multiple Servers**

Instead of a single processor to handle transactions one could have a multiprocessor. Between nodes one can have parallel links. In this case we have a "multiserver queue". Statistics textbooks have many curves for the multiserver case but the principles are exactly the same as for a single server. In general, the curve shifts a bit to the right (meaning that slightly higher utilisations may be achieved). An important additional effect is that the queueing time becomes more uniform (less variance).

This is the situation such as in some banks where a single queue is used to supply multiple tellers. If one teller gets a customer requiring extensive time to service, the person in the queue immediately behind is serviced by the next free teller. If there were separate queues then this customer would have to wait much longer.

# Appendix D. Getting the Language into Synch

When describing the timing relationship between two things there are a number of words that must be understood. Unfortunately, these words are commonly used in different contexts with quite different meanings.

In this document the strict engineering definitions have been used except where otherwise noted such as in the description of FDDI. See 13.6, "Fiber Distributed Data Interface (FDDI)" on page 13-31. When reading other documents it is necessary to try to understand exactly what the author means by the various terms.

In *Communications Engineering*, when one bit stream is being compared with another, the following terms are often used:

**Synchronous**

This literally means "locked together". When two bit streams are said to be synchronous it is meant that they are controlled by the same clock and are in the same phase.

**Asynchronous**

Any two events that are not tied together exactly in time are said to be asynchronous.

**Isochronous**

Literally "in the same time". An isochronous bit stream is one that goes at a constant rate. The term isochronous is often used colloquially to mean "digitally encoded voice". The term is not often used in the world of data communications but is a common term in the voice communications and engineering context.

**Anisochronous**

Literally, "not equal". Used in the communications engineering context to mean bit streams of unequal rates (this causes a problem in time division multiplexing systems).

**Mesochronous**

The Greek prefix "meso" means "middle". If two isochronous bit streams have no precisely controlled relationship, but have exactly the same bit rate, they are called mesochronous.

If two bit streams start at some point of origin as synchronous streams and arrive at some destination by different routes or networking schemes they will be mesochronous at the point of arrival.

**Plesiochronous**

Literally "nearly the same". If two bit streams have nominally the same bit rate, but are controlled by different clocks, they will have bit rates that are nearly the same but not quite.

**Heterochronous**

If two bit streams have nominally different bit rates they are said to be heterochronous.

In data communications the common terms are "synchronous" and "asynchronous". Their meaning is usually determined by context.

The word "synchronous" when applied to a stream of bits *in itself* means that all the bits in the stream bear a strict timing relationship with one another. The same term can also be applied to a stream of characters.

The word "asynchronous" is usually used to mean *a data stream where the characters are not synchronized with one another but the bits within each character are.*

**This is the case of typical ASCII terminal operation.**

Each character consists of a start bit and a stop bit surrounding seven or eight data bits. Each data bit has a precise timing relationship with each other data bit within the character but characters are transmitted as they are typed and have no particular relationship with one another at all.

A synchronous link protocol such as SDLC (Synchronous Data Link Control) operates on blocks of data that are expected to be synchronous within themselves but there is no strict timing relationship between blocks of data.

Sometimes these concepts get mixed up as when SDLC data link protocol is used to transmit data over an asynchronous circuit or when ASCII protocols are used to send data through a synchronous channel.

In the FDDI standard the term synchronous is used in a completely different way: It means data traffic that has some real-time or "guaranteed bandwidth" requirement.

All of the above terms describe a timing relationship between two things. When using these terms, it is essential that we know just what things are being related and in what aspect they are being compared. Care is essential.

# Appendix E. Abbreviations

**AAL** ATM Adaptation Layer
**ACF** Access Control Field (DQDB)
**AC** Alternate Current
**ADPCM** Adaptive Differential Pulse Code Modulation
**ADSL** Asymmetric Digital Subscriber Line
**AL** Access Link
**AM** Amplitude Modulation
**AMI** Alternate Mark Inversion
**ANR** Automatic Network Routing
**ANSI** American National Standards Institute
**APD** Avalanche Photodiode
**ASCII** American (National) Standard Code for Information Interchange
**ASK** Amplitude Shift Keying
**ATM** Asynchronous Transfer Mode
**BECN** Backward Explicit Congestion Notification
**BER** Bit Error Rate
**bps** bits per second
**BRI** Basic Rate Interface
**B-ISDN** Broadband ISDN
**CAU** Controlled Access Unit
**CBR** Constant Bit Rate
**CCITT** Comite Consultatif International Telegraphique et Telephonique (International Telegraph and Telephone Consultative Committee)
**CDMA** Code Division Multiple Access
**CMIP** Common Management Information Protocol (ISO)
**CMIS** Common Management Information Service (ISO)
**CMOS** Complimentary Metal Oxide Semiconductor
**CMT** Configuration Management
**CPE** Customer Premises Equipment
**CPN** Customer Premises Network
**CRC** Cyclic Redundancy Check
**CSMA/CD** Carrier Sense Multiple Access with Collision Detection
**dB** decibel
**DC** Direct Current
**DFT** Distributed Function Terminal
**DLC** Data Link Control
**DLCI** Data Link Connection Identifier
**DPG** Dedicated Packet Group (FDDI)
**DQDB** Distributed Queue Dual Bus
**DSAP** Destination Service Access Point
**DSSS** Direct Sequence Spread Spectrum
**DTE** Data Terminal Equipment
**EBCDIC** Extended Binary Coded Decimal Interchange Code
**EIA** Electronic Industries Association
**EMC** Electromagnetic Compatibility
**FCC** Federal Communications Commission
**FCS** Frame Check Sequence
**FDDI** Fiber Distributed Data Interface
**FDM** Frequency Division Multiplexing

**FECN** Forward Explicit Congestion Notification
**FEXT** Far End Crosstalk
**FFH** Fast Frequency Hopping
**FM** Frequency Modulation
**FR** Frame Relay
**FSK** Frequency Shift Keying
**GFC** Generic Flow Control
**HDB3** High Density Bipolar Three Zeros
**HDLC** High-Level data Link Control
**HDSL** High Bit-Rate Digital Subscriber Line
**HDTV** High Definition Television
**IEEE** Institute of Electrical and Electronic Engineers
**ILD** Injection Laser Diode
**IMPDU** Initial MAC Protocol Data Unit (DQDB)
**INN** Intermediate Network Node
**IO** input/output
**IP** Internet Protocol
**ISDN** Integrated Services Digital Network
**ISI** Inter-Symbol Interference
**ISM** Industrial Scientific and Medical
**ISO** International Organization for Standardization
**IWS** Intelligent Workstation
**Kbps** kilobits per second (thousands of bits per second)
**LAB** Latency Adjustment Buffer
**LAM** Lobe Access Unit
**LAN** local area network
**LAPB** Link Access Procedure Balanced (X.25)
**LAPD** Link Access Procedure for the D_Channel (ISDN)
**LASER** Light Amplification by the Stimulated Emission of Radiation
**LE** Local Exchange
**LED** Light Emitting Diode
**LLC** Logical Link Control
**LMI** Local Management Interface (Frame Relay)
**LPDU** Logical Link Control Protocol Data Unit
**LSAP** Logical Link Control Service Access Point
**LT** Line Termination
**LU** logical unit (SNA)
**MAC** Medium Access Control
**MAN** metropolitan area metwork
**MAP** Manufacturing Automation Protocol
**MB** megabytes
**Mbps** megabits per second (million bits per second)
**MFI** MainFrame Interactive
**MMS** Manufacturing Messaging Services
**NADN** Nearest Active Downstream Neighbor
**NAUN** Nearest Active Upstream Neighbor
**NEXT** Near End Crosstalk
**NNI** Network Node interface
**NRZ** Non Return to Zero
**NRZI** Non Return to Zero Inverted
**NT** Network Termination
**NTRI** NCP Token-Ring Interface
**OC-n** Optical Carrier level n
**OSI** Open Systems Interconnection
**PABX** Private Automatic Branch Exchange
**PBX** Private Branch Exchange
**PC** Personal Computer
**PCM** Pulse Code Modulation
**PDM** Polarisation Division Multiplexing
**PDU** Protocol Data Unit
**PHY** Physical Layer

| | |
|---|---|
| **PLL** | Phase Locked Loop |
| **PM** | Phase Modulation |
| **PMD** | Physical Medium Dependent |
| **PON** | Passive Optical Network |
| **POH** | Path Overhead |
| **PRI** | Primary Rate Interface (ISDN) |
| **PRM** | Protocol Reference Model |
| **PSK** | Phase Shift Keying |
| **PTT** | Post, Telegraph and Telephone (Company) |
| **QAM** | Quadrature Amplitude Modulation |
| **QOS** | Quality of Service |
| **RAM** | random access memory |
| **RF** | Radio Frequency |
| **RFC** | Request For Comment |
| **RI** | Routing Information |
| **RR** | Receive Ready |
| **RWC** | Ring Wiring Concentrator |
| **SABME** | Set Asynchronous Balanced Mode Extended (Command) |
| **SAP** | Service Access Point |
| **SAR** | Segmentation and Reassembly |
| **SAW** | Surface Acoustic Wave |
| **SDDI** | Shielded (Twisted Pair) (F) DDI |
| **SDH** | Synchronous Digital Hierarchy |
| **SDM** | Space Division Multiplexing |
| **SFH** | Slow Frequency Hopping |
| **SDLC** | Synchronous Data Link Control |
| **SIP** | SMDS Interface Protocol |
| **SMDS** | Switched Multi-Megabit Data Service |
| **SMT** | Station Management |
| **STS** | Synchronous Transport Signal |
| **STM** | Synchronous Transport Module |
| **SNA** | Systems Network Architecture |
| **SNI** | Subscriber-Network Interface (SMDS) |
| **SNI** | SNA Network Interconnection (SNA) |
| **SOH** | Section Overhead |
| **SPE** | Synchronous Payload Envelope (Sonet/SDH) |
| **SPN** | Subscriber Premises Network |
| **SRPI** | Server/Requester Programming Interface |
| **SS** | Spread Spectrum |
| **SSAP** | Source Service Access Point |
| **STM** | Synchronous Transfer mode |
| **STP** | Shielded Twisted Pair |
| **TA** | Terminal Adapter |
| **TCP/IP** | Transmission Control Protocol/Internet Protocol |
| **TDM** | Time Division Multiplexing |
| **TE** | Terminal Equipment |
| **THT** | Token Holding Timer (FDDI) |
| **TIC** | Token-Ring Interface Coupler |
| **TR** | token-ring |
| **TRA** | Token-Ring Adapter |
| **TRM** | Token-Ring Multiplexor |
| **TRN** | token-ring network |
| **TRSS** | Token-Ring SubSystem |
| **TRT** | Token Rotation Timer (FDDI) |
| **TTP** | Telephone Twisted Pair (Wiring) |
| **TTP** | Timed Token Protocol (FDDI) |
| **TTRT** | Target Token Rotation Time |
| **UA** | Unnumbered Acknowledgement |
| **UNI** | User to Network Interface |
| **UTP** | Unshielded Twisted Pair |
| **VAD** | Voice Activity Detector |

**VBR** Variable Bit Rate

**VC** Virtual Circuit (X.25)
Virtual Connection (Frame Relay)
Virtual Channel (ATM)

**VCI** Virtual Channel Identifier (ATM,DQDB)

**VP** Virtual Path

**VPI** Virtual Path Identifier

**WAN** wide area metwork

**WDM** Wavelength Division Multiplexing

**XC** Cross Connect

**XID** Exchange Identification

# Bibliography

The following publications contain more information on related topics.

## General References


**Digital Telephony and Network Integration** Bernhard E. Keiser and Eugene Strange
Van Nostrand Reinhold Company Limited, New York. 1985.

**Megabit Data Communications** John T.Powers, Jr. and Henry H. Stair II. Prentice-Hall Inc., New Jersey. 1990.

**Metropolitan Area Networks: Concepts, Standards and Services.** Gary C. Kessler and David A. Train
McGraw-Hill Inc. New York. 1991.


## Digital Signaling Technology


**A Tutorial on Two-Wire Digital Transmission in the Loop Plant** Syed V. Ahamed, Peter P Bohn and N. L. Gottfried. IEEE Transactions on Communications, Vol. Com-29, No 11, November 1981.

**Line Codes for Digital Subscriber Lines** Joseph W. Lechleider. IEEE Communications Magazine, September 1989.

**Digital Subscriber Line Technology Facilitates a Graceful Transition from Copper to Fiber** David L Waring, Joseph W Lechleider and To Russell Hsing. IEEE Communications Magazine, March 1991.

**Study of the Feasibility and Advisability of Digital Subscriber Lines Operating at rates substantially in excess of the Basic Access Rate.** ANSII Committee T1E1.4, Technical Report 91-002R4.

**A Technical Report on High-Bit-Rate Digital Subscriber Lines (HDSL)** ANSII Committee T1E1.4, Technical Report 92-002R1.

**A Discrete Multitone Transceiver System for HDSL Applications.** Jacky S.Chow, Jerry C. Tu and John M. Cioffi. IEEE Journal on Selected Areas in Communication. August 1991.

**High Bit Rate Digital Subscriber Lines: A Review of HDSL Progress** Joseph W. Lechleider IEEE Journal on Selected Areas in Communication. August 1991.

**Multicarrier Modulation for Data Transmission: An Idea Whose Time Has Come.** John A. C. Bingham IEEE Communications Magazine, May 1990.

**A Multicarrier Primer** John Cioffi.

ANSII Committee T1E1.4, Contribution 91-157.

**Frequency Domain Data Transmission using Reduced Computational Complexity Algorithms** A. Peled and A. Ruiz. International Conference on Acoustics, Speech and Signal Processing. Denver, April 1980.

**The HDSL Environment** Jean-Jaques Werner. IEEE Journal on Selected areas in Communications, Vol 9, No 6, August 1991.


## Optical Networks

**Fiber Optic Networks** Paul E. Green Prentice Hall Inc. New Jersey, 1993.

**Terabit Lightwave Networks: The Multihop Approach** A.S. Acampora, M.J. Karol, M.G. Hluchyj AT&T Technical Journal, Vol.66, No.6, Nov-Dec. 1987, pp.21-34

**High-Capacity Lightwave Local Area Networks** P.S. Henry IEEE Communications Magazine, Vol.27, No.10, Oct. 1989, pp.20-26

**An Overview of Lightwave Packet Networks** A.S. Acampora, M.J. Karol IEEE Network, Vol.3, No.1, Jan. 1989, pp.29-41

**An All-Optical Computer Network: Lessons Learned** P.E. Green, Jr IEEE Network, Vol.6, No.2, March 1992, pp.56-60

**Toward Customer-Useable All-Optical Networks** Paul E. Green, Jr IEEE Communications Magazine, December 1994, pp.44-49

**WDM-Based Local Lightwave Networks. Part I: Single-Hop Systems** B. Mukherjee IEEE Network, Vol.6, No.3, May 1992, pp.12-27

**WDM-Based Local Lightwave Networks. Part II: Multihop Systems** B. Mukherjee IEEE Network, Vol.6, No.4, July 1992, pp.20-32

**Multi-Wavelength Lightwave Networks** R. Ramaswami IBM Research Report RC 17837 (3/25/92)

**Wavelength Domain Optical Network Techniques** G.R. Hill IEEE Proceedings, Vol.78, No.1, Jan. 1990, pp.121-132

**Broadband Photonic Switching using Guided Wave Fabrics** Narinder K. Ailawadi, Rod C. Alferness, Glen D Bergland and Richard A. Thompson IEEE LTS, May 1991.

**Toward the Development of Laser Safety Standards for Fiber-Optic Communication Systems** R.C. Petersen and D.H.Sliney, Applied Optics, Vol 25, No 7. April 1986.


## Radio LANs


**Medium Access Protocol for Wireless LANs (An Update)** K.S. Natarajan, C.C. Huang and D.F. Bantz. Submission to IEEE P802.11/92-39 (1992)

**Performance Comparison Between DSSS and SFH Transmission in Indoor Multipath Fading Channels** Kwang-Cheng Chen and Tsung-Cheng Wu. Submission to IEEE P802.11 (July 1992)

**Spread Spectrum for Mobile Communications** Raymond L. Pickholtz, Laurence B. Milstein and Donald L Schilling. IEEE Transactions on Vehicular Technology, Vol 40, No 2, May 1991

**Overview of Cellular CDMA** William C.Y. Lee. IEEE Transactions on Vehicular Technology, Vol 40, No 2, May 1991

**An ISM Band Spread Spectrum LAN: WaveLAN** Bruce Tuch. IEEE Workshop on Wireless LANs Worcester, MA. May 1991

**Radio Propagation and Anti-Multipath Techniques in the WIN Environment** James E. Mitzlaff. IEEE Network, November 1991

**Theory of Spread Spectrum Communication - A Tutorial** Raymond L. Pickholtz, Donald L. Schlling and Laurence B. Milstein. IEEE Transactions on Communications, May 1982

**Handover and Channel Assignment in Mobile Cellular Networks** Sirin Tekinay and Bijan Jabbari. IEEE Communications Magazine, November 1991

**On the Capacity of a Cellular CDMA System** Klein S. Gilhousen et. al. IEEE Transactions on Vehicular Technology, Vol 40, No 2, May 1991

**Broadband CDMA for Personal Communications Systems** Donald L. Schilling et. al. IEEE Communications Magazine, November 1991

## ISDN

**ISDN Data Link Control - Architecture Reference** IBM Order Number SC31-6826.

**ISDN Circuit Switched Signalin Control - Architecture Reference** IBM Order Number SC31-6827.

## Sonet/SDH

**Sonet - Now It's the Standard Optical Network** Ralph Ballart and Yau-Chau Ching. IEEE Communications Magazine, March 1989.

**CCITT Recommendations G.707, G.708 and G.709** CCITT Blue Book 1988 - Synchronous Digital Hierarchy

## Asynchronous Transfer Mode (ATM)

**Broadband ISDN and Asynchronous Transfer Mode (ATM)** by Steven E. Minzer. IEEE Communications Magazine, September 1989.

**Layered ATM Systems and Architectural Concepts for Subscribers' Premises Networks** by Jan P. Vorstermans and Andre P. De Vleeschouwer. IEEE Journal of Selected Areas in Communications, Vol 6, No 9, December 1988.

**Broad-Band ATM network Architecture Based on Virtual Paths** Ken-Ichi Sato, Satoru Ohta and Ikuo Tokizawa. IEEE Transactions on Communications, August 1990.

**Voice Packetization and Compression in Broadband ATM Networks** Kotikalapudi Sriram, R. Scott McKinney and Mostafa Hasheim Sherif. IEEE J. on Selected Areas in Communications, April 1991.

**Virtual Path and Link Capacity Design for ATM Networks** Youichi Sato and Ken-Ichi Sato. IEEE Journal on Selected Areas in Communications, January 1991.

**Draft Recommendations I.113, I.121, I.150, I.211, I.327, I.311, I.361, I.413, I.432 and I.610.** CCITT Study Group 18. Geneva, January 1990.

## Token Ring

**IBM Token-Ring Network Technology** IBM Order Number GA27-3732.

**IBM Multisegment LAN Design Guidelines** IBM Order Number GG24-3398.

## FDDI

**FDDI Concepts and Products** IBM ITSO Raleigh Center (1992) IBM Order Number GG24-3865.

**Performance Analysis of FDDI Token Ring Networks: Effect of Parameters and Guidelines for Setting TTRT** Raj Jain. IEEE LTS Magazine. May 1991.

## DQDB

**Introduction to Switched Multi-Megabit Data Service (SMDS), An Early Broadband Service** Christine F. Hemrick and Lawrence J. Lang. Proceedings of the International Switching Symposium, Session A3, Stockholm, June 1990.

**The IEEE 802.6 Physical Layer Convergence Procedures** Richard Brandwein, Tracy Cox and James Dahl. IEEE LCS Magazine, May 1989.

**New Proposal Extends the Reach of Metro Area Nets** John L. Hullett. Data Communications Magazine, February 1988.

**Distributed Queue Dual Bus (DQDB) Subnetwork of a Metropolitan Area Network (MAN)** IEEE 802.6 Working Group. Unapproved draft, October 1st 1990.

## MetaRing

**MetaRing - A Full-Duplex Ring with Fairness and Spatial Reuse** Israel Cidon and Yoram Ofek. IEEE Infocom 90, San Fransisco, CA. June 1990.

**Integration of Connection and Connectionless Traffic on the Metaring** Yoram Ofek. IEEE Workshop on Metropolitan Area Networks, 1990.

## CRMA and CRMA-II

**Cyclic-Reservation Multiple-Access Scheme for Gbit/s LANs and MANs based on Dual-Bus Configuration** M. Mehdi Nassehi. EFOC/LAN 90.

**CRMA: An Access Scheme for High Speed LANs and MANs** M. Mehdi Nassehi. Supercomm/ICC '90, Atlanta, Georgia. April 1990.

**CRMA-II: A Gbit/s MAC Protocol for Ring and Bus Networks with Immediate Access Capability** H.R. van As, W. W. Lemppenau, P. Zafiropulo and E. A. Zurfluh EFOC/LAN 91.

**Performance of a Gbps Reservation Based Ring with Fairness** H.R Van As and P. Zafiropolo ANSI X3T9.5 FDDI Standardization Meeting Fort Lauderdale Oct 91.

**DQMA and CRMA: New Access Schemes for Gbit/s LANs and MANs** Hans R Muller, M Mehdi Nassehi, Johnny W. Wong, Erwin Zurfluh, Werner Bux and Pitro Zafiropulo. Proceedings of IEE Infocom '90, San Fransisco, June 1990.

**Configuration Control for Bus Networks** Peter Heinzmann, Hans Müller and Ken Wilson. Proc. 15th Annual Conf. on Local Computer Networks, Minneapolis, MN. October 1990.

## Fast Packet Switching

**Paris: An Approach to Integrated High-Speed Private Networks** Israel Cidon and Inder S. Gopal. International Journal of Digital and Analog Cabled Systems., Vol. 1., 1988, pp 77-85.

**The PlaNET/Orbit High Speed Network** I. Gopal, P.M. Gopal, R. Guerin, J. Janniello and M. Kaplan. Where was this published?

**Bandwidth Managenent and Congestion Control in plaNET** Israel Cidon, Inder Gopal and Roch Guerin. IEEE Communications Magazine, October 1991.

**An Overview of the Aurora Gigabit Testbed** David D. Clark et. al. Proceedings of Infocomm'92

**A Taxonomy of Broadband Integrated Switching Architectures** George E. Daddis, Jr., and H. C. Torng. IEEE Communications Magazine. May 1989.

**ATM Technology for Corporate Networks** Peter Newman. IEEE Communications Magazine. April 1992.

## Circuit Switched Systems (IBM ESCON)

**Enterprise Systems Connection (ESCON) Architecture - System Overview.** S.A Calta, J.A. deVeer, E. Loizides and R.N. Strangwayes. IBM Journal of Research and Development. Vol 36, No 4. July 1992.

**Enterprise Systems Connection (ESCON) Architecture.** J.C. Elliott and M.W. Sachs. IBM Journal of Research and Development. Vol 36, No 4. July 1992.

## Protocol Issues

**Implementation of Physical and Media Access Protocols for High-Speed Networks** by Morten Skov. IEEE Communications Magazine, June 1989.

**Routing and Flow Control in High-Speed Wide-Area Networks** by Nicholas F. Maxemchuk and Magda El Zarki. Proceedings of the IEEE, Vol 78, No.1, January 1990.

**XTP Protocol Definition Revision 3.4,** Protocol Engines Incorporated, 1900 State St., Suite D, Santa Barbara, California 93101, 1989.

**The Xpress Transfer Protocol (XTP) - A Tutorial** by Robert M Sanders. Computer Science Report No. TR-89-10, Department of Computer Science, University of Virginia.

**A Survey of Light-Weight Transport Protocols for High-Speed Networks** by Willibald Doeringer, Doug Dykeman, Matthias Kaisersworth, Bernd Meister, Harry Rudin and Robin Williamson. IEEE Transactions on Communications, 38-11, (1990).

**Control Mechanisms for High Speed Networks** by Israel Cidon and Inder S. Gopal. ICC '90.

**Real-Time Packet Switching: A Performance Analysis** by Israel Cidon, Inder Gopal, George Grover and Moshe Sidi. IEEE Journal of Selected Areas in Communications, Vol. 6. No. 9, December 1988.

**Congestion Control for High Speed Packet Networks** by Krishna Bala, Israel Cidon and Khosrow Sohraby. Infocom 90.

**A Blind Voice Packet Synchronization Strategy** by Joong Ma and Inder Gopal. IBM Research Report. RC 13893. 1988.

**Linear Broadcast Routing** Ching-Tsun Chou and Inder S. Gopal. Journal of Algorithms 10, 490-517 (1989).

**Packet Video and Its Integration into the Network Architecture** Gunnar Karlsson and Martin Vetterli. IEEE J. on Selected areas in Communication, June 1989.

## Surveys

**Multimedia in a Network Environment** IBM ITSO Boca Raton Center. IBM Order Number GG24-3947

**Multimedia Networking Performance Requirements** James D. Russell. Proceedings of TriComm'93. Plenum Press, New York.

**Rationale, Directions and Issues Surrounding High Speed Networks** Imrich Chlamtac and William R. Franta. Proceedings of the IEEE, Vol. 78, No. 1. January 1990.

# Glossary

## A

**access control byte**. In the IBM Token-Ring Network, the byte following the start delimiter of a token or frame that is used to control access to the ring.

**access priority**. The maximum priority that a token can have for the adapter to use it for transmission.

**access unit**. A unit that allows multiple attaching devices access to a token-ring network at a central point such as a wiring closet or in an open work area.

- *Access unit* refers to either IBM 8228s or IBM 8230s.
- *Multistation access unit* refers specifically to IBM 8228s.
- *Controlled access unit* refers specifically to IBM 8230s.

**active monitor**. A function in a single adapter on a token-ring network that initiates the transmission of tokens and provides token error recovery facilities. Any active adapter on the ring has the ability to provide the active monitor function if the current active monitor fails.

**adapter**. In a LAN, within a communicating device, a circuit card that, with its associated software and/or microcode, enables the device to communicate over the network.

**adapter address**. Twelve hexadecimal digits that identify a LAN adapter.

**adjusted ring length (ARL)**. In a multiple-wiring-closet ring, the sum of all wiring closet-to-wiring closet cables in the main ring path less the length of the shortest of those cables.

**all-routes broadcast frame**. A frame that has bits in the routing information field set to indicate that the frame is to be sent to all LAN segments in the network (across all bridges, even if multiple paths allow multiple copies of the frame to arrive at some LAN segments). The destination address is not examined and plays no role in bridge routing.

**all-stations broadcast frame**. A frame whose destination address bits are set to all ones. All stations on any LAN segment on which the frame appears will copy it. The routing information, not the destination address, determines which LAN segments the frame appears on. All-stations broadcasting is independent of all-routes broadcasting; the two can be done simultaneously or one at a time.

**application program interface (API)**. The formally defined programming language interface that is between an IBM system control program or a licensed program and the user of the program.

**attenuation**. A decrease in magnitude of current, voltage, or electrical or optical power of a signal in transmission between points. It may be expressed in decibels or nepers.

**automatic single-route broadcast**. A function used by some IBM bridge programs to determine the correct settings for, and set the bridge single-route broadcast configuration parameters dynamically, without operator intervention. As bridges enter and leave the network, the parameter settings may need to change to maintain a single path between any two LAN segments for single-route broadcast messages. See also *single-route broadcast*.

## B

**backbone LAN segment**. In a LAN multiple segment configuration, a centrally located LAN segment to which other LAN segments are connected by means of bridges. In a hierarchical network, the LAN segment that is at the highest level of the hierarchy.

**backup path**. In an IBM Token-Ring Network, an alternative path for signal flow through access units and their main ring path cabling. The backup path allows recovery of the operational portion of the network while problem determination procedures are being performed.

**bandwidth**. In analog communications this is difference, expressed in hertz, between the highest and the lowest frequencies of a range of frequencies. For example, analog transmission by recognizable voice telephone requires a bandwidth of about 3000 hertz (3 kHz).

In digital communications this is often used to mean the total available bit rate of a digital channel. At other times it can mean the symbol rate (baud rate) of a digital channel.

**baseband**. (1) A frequency band that uses the complete bandwidth of a transmission medium. Contrast with *broadband*, *carrierband*. (2) A method of data transmission that encodes, modulates, and impresses information on the transmission medium without shifting or altering the frequency of the information signal.

**baseband local area network**. A local area network in which information is encoded, multiplexed, and transmitted without modulation of a carrier.

**beaconing**. An error-indicating function of token-ring adapters that assists in locating a problem causing a hard error on a token-ring network.

**bridge**. (1) An attaching device that connects two LAN segments to allow the transfer of information from one LAN segment to the other. A bridge may connect the LAN segments directly by network adapters and software in a single device, or may connect network adapters in two separate devices through software and use of a telecommunications link between the two adapters. (2) A functional unit that connects two LANs that use the same logical link control (LLC) procedures but may use the same or different medium access control (MAC) procedures. Contrast with *gateway* and *router*.

**bridge ID**. The bridge label combined with the adapter address of the adapter connecting the bridge to the LAN segment with the lowest LAN segment number; it is used by the automatic single-route broadcast function in IBM bridge programs.

**bridge label**. A 2-byte hexadecimal number that the user can assign to each bridge. See *bridge ID*.

**bridge number**. The bridge identifier that the user specifies in the bridge program configuration file. The bridge number distinguishes among parallel bridges. Parallel bridges connect the same two LAN segments.

**broadband**. (1) A frequency band between any two non-zone frequencies. (2) A frequency band divisible into several narrower bands so that different kinds of transmissions such as voice, video, and data transmission can occur at the same time. Synonymous with *wideband*. Contrast with *baseband*, *carrierband*.

**broadband local area network (LAN)**. A local area network (LAN) in which information is encoded, multiplexed, and transmitted through modulation of a carrier.

**broadcast**. Simultaneous transmission of data to more than one destination.

**bus**. (1) In a processor, a physical facility on which data is transferred to all destinations, but from which only addressed destinations may read in accordance with appropriate conventions. (2) A network configuration in which nodes are interconnected through a bidirectional transmission medium. (3) One or more conductors used for transmitting signals or power.

**bus network**. A network configuration that provides a bidirectional transmission facility to which all nodes are attached. A sending node transmits in both directions to the ends of the bus. All nodes in the path examine and may copy the message as it passes.

## C

**cable loss**. The amount of radio frequency (RF) signal attenuation caused by a cable. See *attenuation*.

**carrier**. A wave or pulse train that may be varied by a signal bearing information to be transmitted over a communication system.

**carrierband**. A frequency band in which the modulated signal is superimposed on a carrier signal (as differentiated from baseband), but only one channel is present on the medium (as differentiated from broadband). Contrast with *baseband, broadband.*

**carrier sense**. In a local area network, an ongoing activity of a data station to detect whether another station is transmitting.

**carrier sense multiple access with collision avoidance (CSMA/CA) network**. A bus network in which the medium access control protocol requires carrier sense, and in which a station always starts transmission by sending a jam signal. If there is no collision with jam signals from other stations, it begins sending data; otherwise, it stops transmission and then tries again later.

**carrier sense multiple access with collision detection (CSMA/CD) network**. A bus network in which the medium access control protocol requires carrier sense, and in which exception conditions caused by collision are solved by retransmission.

**coaxial (coax) cable**. A cable consisting of one conductor, usually a small copper tube or wire, within and insulated from another conductor of a larger diameter, usually copper tubing or copper braid.

**coaxial tap**. A physical connection to a coaxial cable.

**communication network management (CNM)**. The process of designing, installing, operating, and managing distribution of information and control among users of communication systems.

**controller**. A unit that controls input/output operations for one or more devices.

**crosstalk**. The disturbance caused in a circuit by an unwanted transfer of energy from another circuit.

**cyclic redundancy check (CRC)**. Synonym for *frame check sequence (FCS).*

## D

**datagram**. A particular type of information encapsulation at the network layer of the adapter protocol. No explicit acknowledgment for the information is sent by the receiver. Instead, transmission relies on the "best effort" of the link layer.

**data link control (DLC) layer**. (1) In SNA or Open Systems Interconnection (OSI), the layer that schedules data transfer over a link between two nodes and performs error control for the link. Examples of DLC are synchronous data link control (SDLC) for serial-by-bit connection and DLC for the

System/370 channel. (2) See *logical link control (LLC) sublayer*, *medium access control (MAC) sublayer*. **Note:** The DLC layer is usually independent of the physical transport mechanism and ensures the integrity of data that reach the higher layers.

**designated bridge**. In a LAN using automatic single-route broadcast, a bridge that forwards single-route broadcast frames. See also *root bridge*, *standby bridge*.

**destination**. Any point or location, such as a node, station, or particular terminal, to which information is to be sent.

**destination address**. A field in the medium access control (MAC) frame that identifies the physical location to which information is to be sent. Contrast with *source address*.

**destination service access point (DSAP)**. The service access point for which a logical link control protocol data unit (LPDU) is intended.

**destination service access point (DSAP) address**. The address of the link service access point (LSAP) for which a link protocol data unit (LPDU) is intended. Also, a field in the LPDU.

**differential Manchester encoding**. A transmission encoding scheme in which each bit is encoded as a two-segment signal with a signal transition (polarity change) at either the bit time or half-bit time. Transition at a bit time represents a 0. No transition at a bit time indicates a 1.

**Note:** This coding scheme allows simpler receive/transmit and timing recovery circuitry and a smaller delay per station than achieved with block codes. It also allows the two wires of a twisted pair to be interchanged without causing data errors.

**downstream physical unit (DSPU)**. A controller or a workstation downstream from a gateway that is attached to a host.

## E

**Early Token Release (ETR)**. In token-ring and Fiber Distributed Data Interface (FDDI) networks, a function that allows a transmitting adapter to release a new token as soon as it has completed frame transmission, whether or not the frame header has returned to that adapter.

**EBCDIC**. Extended binary-coded decimal interchange code. A coded character set consisting of 8-bit coded characters.

**electromagnetic interference (EMI)**. A disturbance in the transmission of data on a network resulting from the magnetism created by a current of electricity.

**Ethernet network**. A baseband LAN with a bus topology in which messages are broadcast on a coaxial cable using a carrier sense multiple access/collision detection (CSMA/CD) transmission method.

## F

**Federal Communications Commission (FCC)**. A board of commissioners appointed by the President under the Communications Act of 1934, having the power to regulate all interstate and foreign communications by wire and radio originating in the United States.

**Fiber Distributed Data Interface (FDDI)**. A high-performance, general-purpose, multi-station network designed for efficient operation with a peak data transfer rate of 100 Mbps. It uses token-ring architecture with optical fiber as the transmission medium over distances of several kilometers.

**filtered frames**. Frames that arrive at a bridge adapter but are not forwarded across the bridge, because of criteria specified in a filter program used with the bridge program.

**frame**. The unit of transmission in some LANs, including the IBM Token-Ring Network and the IBM PC Network. It includes delimiters, control characters, information, and checking characters. On a token-ring network, a frame is created from a token when the token has data appended to it. On a token bus network (IBM PC Network), all frames including the token frame contain a preamble, start delimiter, control address, optional data and checking characters, end delimiter, and are followed by a minimum silence period.

**frame check sequence (FCS)**. (1) A system of error checking performed at both the sending and receiving station after a block check character has been accumulated. (2) A numeric value derived from the bits in a message that is used to check for any bit errors in transmission. (3) A redundancy check in which the check key is generated by a cyclic algorithm. Synonymous with *cyclic redundancy check (CRC)*.

**frequency pair**. In the broadband IBM PC Network, the two frequencies or channels used by an adapter: one to transmit data to the network, and one to receive data from the network.

**functional address**. In IBM network adapters, a special kind of group address in which the address is bit-significant, each "on" bit representing a function performed by the station (such as "Active Monitor," "Ring Error Monitor," "LAN Error Monitor," or "Configuration Report Server").

# G

**gateway**. A device and its associated software that interconnect networks or systems of different architectures. The connection is usually made above the reference model network layer. Contrast with *bridge* and *router*.

**group address**. In a LAN, a locally administered address assigned to two or more adapters to allow the adapters to copy the same frame. Contrast *locally administered address* with *universally administered address*.

**group SAP**. A single address assigned to a group of service access points (SAPs). See also *group address*.

# H

**hard error**. An error condition on a network that requires that the source of the error be removed or that the network be reconfigured before the network can resume reliable operation. See also *beaconing*. Contrast with *soft error*.

**header**. The portion of a message that contains control information for the message such as one or more destination fields, name of the originating station, input sequence number, character string indicating the type of message, and priority level for the message.

**"hello" message**. A message used by the automatic single-route broadcast function of IBM bridge programs to detect what bridges enter and leave the network and to cause single-route broadcast parameters to be reset accordingly. The root bridge sends a "hello" message on the network every 2 seconds.

**hertz (Hz)**. A unit of frequency equal to one cycle per second.

**hierarchical network**. A multiple-segment network configuration providing only one path through intermediate segments between source segments and destination segments. Contrast with *mesh network*.

**hop count**. The number of bridges through which a frame has passed on the way to its destination.

**Note:** Hop count applies to all broadcast frames except single-route broadcast frames.

**hop count limit**. The maximum number of bridges through which a frame may pass on the way to its destination.

## I

**idles**. Signals sent along a ring network when neither frames nor tokens are being transmitted.

**impedance**. The combined effect of resistance, inductance, and capacitance on a signal at a particular frequency.

**individual address**. An address that identifies a particular network adapter on a LAN. See also *locally administered address* and *universally administered address*.

**International Organization for Standardization (ISO)**. An organization of national standards bodies from various countries established to promote development of standards to facilitate international exchange of goods and services, and develop cooperation in intellectual, scientific, technological, and economic activity.

## J

**jitter**. Undesirable variations in the arrival time of a transmitted digital signal.

## L

**LAN adapter**. The circuit card within a communicating device (such as a personal computer) that, together with its associated software, enables the device to be attached to a LAN.

**LAN multicast**. The sending of a transmission frame intended to be accepted by a group of selected data stations on the same LAN.

**LAN segment**. (1) Any portion of a LAN (for example, a single bus or ring) that can operate independently but is connected to other parts of the establishment network via bridges. (2) An entire ring or bus network without bridges. See *ring segment*.

**LAN segment number**. The identifier that uniquely distinguishes a LAN segment in a multi-segment LAN.

**latency**. The time interval between the instant at which an instruction control unit initiates a call for data and the instant at which the actual transfer of data begins. Synonymous with *waiting time*. See also *ring latency*.

**layer**. (1) One of the seven levels of the Open Systems Interconnection reference model. (2) In open systems architecture, a collection of related functions that comprise one level of hierarchy of functions. Each layer specifies its own functions and assumes that lower level functions are provided. (3) In SNA, a grouping of related functions that are logically separate from the functions of other layers. Implementation of the functions in one layer can be changed without affecting functions in other layers.

**limited broadcast**. Synonym for *single-route broadcast*.

**link**. (1) The logical connection between nodes including the end-to-end link control procedures. (2) The combination of physical media, protocols, and programming that connects devices on a network. (3) In computer programming, the part of a program, in some cases a single instruction or an address, that passes control and parameters between separate portions of the computer program. (4) To interconnect items of data or portions of one or more computer programs. (5) In SNA, the combination of the link connection and link stations joining network nodes.

**link station**. (1) A specific place in a service access point (SAP) that enables an adapter to communicate with another adapter. (2) A protocol machine in a node that manages the elements of procedure required for the exchange of data traffic with another communicating link station. (3) A logical point within a SAP that enables an adapter to establish connection-oriented communication with another adapter. (4) In SNA, the combination of hardware and software that allows a node to attach to and provide control for a link.

**lobe**. In the IBM Token-Ring Network, the section of cable (which may consist of several cable segments) that connects an attaching device to an access unit.

**local area network (LAN)**. A computer network located on a user's premises within a limited geographical area.

**Note:** Communication within a local area network is not subject to external regulations; however, communication across the LAN boundary may be subject to some form of regulation.

**local bridge function**. Function of an IBM bridge program that allows a single bridge computer to connect two LAN segments (without using a telecommunication link). Contrast with *remote bridge function*.

**locally administered address**. An adapter address that the user can assign to override the universally administered address. Contrast with *universally administered address*.

**logical connection**. In a network, devices that can communicate or work with one another because they share the same protocol. See also *physical connection*.

**logical link control protocol (LLC protocol)**. In a local area network, the protocol that governs the exchange of frames between data stations independently of how the transmission medium is shared.

**logical link control protocol data unit (LPDU)**. The unit of information exchanged between network layer entities in different nodes. The LPDU consists of the destination service access point (DSAP) and source service access point (SSAP) address fields, the control field, and the information field (if present).

**logical link control (LLC) sublayer**. One of two sublayers of the ISO Open Systems Interconnection data link layer (which corresponds to the SNA data link control layer), proposed for LANs by the IEEE Project 802 Committee on Local Area Networks and the European Computer Manufacturers Association (ECMA). It includes those functions unique to the particular link control procedures that are associated with the attached node and are independent of the medium; this allows different logical link protocols to coexist on the same network without interfering with each other. The LLC sublayer uses services provided by the medium access control (MAC) sublayer and provides services to the network layer.

**logical unit (LU)**. In SNA, a port through which an end user accesses the SNA network in order to communicate with another end user and through which the end user accesses the functions provided by system services control points (SSCPs). An LU can support at least two sessions, one with an SSCP and one with another LU, and may be capable of supporting many sessions with other logical units.

**LU type 6.2**. A type of logical unit that supports sessions between two application programs in a distributed data processing environment using the SNA general data stream, which is a structured-field data stream, between two type 5 nodes, a type 5 node and a type 2.1 node, and two type 2.1 nodes.

# M

**MAC frame**. Frames used to carry information to maintain the ring protocol and for exchange of management information.

**MAC protocol**. (1) In a local area network, the protocol that governs communication on the transmission medium without concern for the physical characteristics of the medium, but taking into account the topological aspects of the network, in order to enable the exchange of data between data stations. See also *logical link control protocol (LLC protocol)*. (2) The LAN protocol sublayer of data link control (DLC) protocol that includes functions for adapter address recognition, copying of message units from the physical network, and message unit format recognition, error detection, and routing within the processor.

**MAC segment**. An individual LAN communicating through the medium access control (MAC) layer within this network.

**main ring path**. In the IBM Token-Ring Network, the part of the ring made up of access units, repeaters, converters, and the cables connecting them. See also *backup path*.

**Manchester encoding**. See *differential Manchester encoding*.

**Manufacturing Automation Protocol (MAP)**. A broadband LAN with a bus topology that passes tokens from adapter to adapter on a coaxial cable.

**medium access control frame**. See *MAC frame*.

**medium access control (MAC) protocol**. In a local area network, the part of the protocol that governs communication on the transmission medium without concern for the physical characteristics of the medium, but taking into account the topological aspects of the network, in order to enable the exchange of data between data stations.

**medium access control sublayer (MAC sublayer)**. In a local area network, the part of the data link layer that applies medium access control and supports topology-dependent functions. The MAC sublayer uses the services of the physical layer to provide services to the logical link control sublayer and all higher layers.

**mesh network**. A multiple-segment network configuration providing more than one path through intermediate LAN segments between source and destination LAN segments. Contrast with *hierarchical network*.

**Micro Channel**. The architecture used by IBM Personal System/2 computers, Models 50 and above. This term is used to distinguish these computers from personal computers using a PC I/O channel, such as an IBM PC, XT, or an IBM Personal System/2 computer, Model 25 or 30.

# N

**NetView**. A host-based IBM licensed program that provides communication network management (CNM) or communications and systems management (C&SM) services.

**Network Basic Input/Output System (NetBIOS)**. A message interface used on LANs to provide message, print server, and file server functions. The IBM NetBIOS application program interface (API) provides a programming interface to the LAN so that an application program can have LAN communication without knowledge and responsibility of the data link control (DLC) interface.

**network layer**. (1) In the Open Systems Interconnection reference model, the layer that provides for the entities in the transport layer the means for routing and switching blocks of data through the network between the open systems in which those entities reside. (2) The layer that provides services to establish a path between systems with a predictable quality of service. See *Open Systems Interconnection (OSI)*.

**network management**. The conceptual control element of a station that interfaces with all of the architectural layers of that station and is responsible for the resetting and setting of control parameters, obtaining reports of error conditions, and determining if the station should be connected to or disconnected from the network.

**noise**. (1) A disturbance that affects a signal and that can distort the information carried by the signal. (2) Random variations of one or more characteristics of any entity, such as voltage, current, or data. (3) Loosely, any disturbance tending to interfere with normal operation of a device or system.

**non-broadcast frame**. A frame containing a specific destination address and that may contain routing information specifying which bridges are to forward it. A bridge will forward a non-broadcast frame only if that bridge is included in the frame's routing information.

# O

**observing link**. The reporting link (or authorization level) between a bridge and a network management program that authorizes the network management program to perform all network management functions except those restricted to the controlling link. (The restricted functions include removing adapters from a ring, changing certain bridge configuration parameters, and enabling or disabling certain bridge functions.)

**Open Systems Interconnection (OSI)**. (1) The interconnection of open systems in accordance with specific ISO standards. (2) The use of standardized procedures to enable the interconnection of data processing systems.

**Note:** OSI architecture establishes a framework for coordinating the development of current and future standards for the interconnection of computer systems. Network functions are divided into seven layers. Each layer represents a group of related data processing and communication functions that can be carried out in a standard way to support different applications.

**Open Systems Interconnection (OSI) architecture**. Network architecture that adheres to a particular set of ISO standards that relates to Open Systems Interconnection.

**Open Systems Interconnection (OSI) reference model**. A model that represents the hierarchical arrangement of the seven layers described by the Open Systems Interconnection architecture.

# P

**packet**. In data communication, a sequence of binary digits, including data and control signals, that is transmitted and switched as a composite whole. Synonymous with *data frame*.

**parallel bridge**. One of the two or more bridges that connect the same two LAN segments in a network.

**path**. (1) In a network, any route between any two nodes. (2) The route traversed by the information exchanged between two attaching devices in a network.

**path cost**. A value, maintained by each IBM bridge program that uses the automatic single-route bridge function, that indicates to the automatic single-route bridge function the relative length of the path between the root bridge and a designated or standby bridge.

**PC Network**. An IBM broadband or baseband LAN with a bus topology in which messages are broadcast from PC Network adapter to PC Network adapter.

**physical connection**. The ability of two connectors to mate and make electrical contact. In a network, devices that are physically connected can communicate only if they share the same protocol. See also *logical connection*.

**physical layer**. In the Open Systems Interconnection reference model, the layer that provides the mechanical, electrical, functional, and procedural means to establish, maintain, and release physical connections over the transmission medium.

**physical unit (PU)**. In SNA, the component that manages and monitors the resources of a node, such as attached links and adjacent link stations, as requested by a system services control point (SSCP) via an SSCP-SSCP session.

**port**. (1) An access point for data entry or exit. (2) A connector on a device to which cables for other devices such as display stations and printers are attached. Synonymous with *socket*.

**primary adapter**. In a personal computer that is used on a LAN and that supports installation of two network adapters, the adapter that uses standard (or default) mapping between adapter-shared RAM, adapter ROM, and designated computer memory segments. The primary adapter is usually designated as adapter 0 in configuration parameters. Contrast with *alternate adapter*.

**primary path**. In the IBM Token-Ring Network, the normal flow of signals through access units and the main ring path cabling.

**protocol**. (1) A set of semantic and syntactic rules that determines the behavior of functional units in achieving communication.(2) In SNA, the meanings of and the sequencing rules for requests and responses used for managing the network, transferring data, and synchronizing the states of network components. (3) A specification for the format and relative timing of information exchanged between communicating parties.

# R

**random access memory (RAM)**. A computer's or adapter's volatile storage area into which data may be entered and retrieved in a nonsequential manner.

**read-only memory (ROM)**. A computer's or adapter's storage area whose contents cannot be modified by the user except under special circumstances.

**remote bridge function**. The function of some IBM bridge programs that allows two bridge computers to use a telecommunications link to connect two LAN segments. Contrast with *local bridge function*.

**repeater**. In a network, a device that amplifies or regenerates data signals in order to extend the distance between attaching devices.

**ring error monitor (REM)**. A function that compiles error statistics reported by adapters on a network, analyzes the statistics to determine probable error cause, sends reports to network manager programs, and updates network status conditions. It assists in fault isolation and correction.

**Request for Comment (RFC)**. The Internet Protocol suite is evolving through the mechanism of Request for Comments (RFC). Research ideas and new protocols (mostly application protocols) are brought to the attention of the internet community in the form of an RFC. Some protocols are so useful that they are recommended to be implemented in all future implementations of TCP/IP; that is, they become recommended protocols. Each RFC has a status attribute to indicate the acceptance and stage of evolution this idea has in the TCP/IP protocol suite. Software developers use RFCs as a reference to write TCP/IP software.

**ring in (RI)**. In an IBM Token-Ring Network, the receive or input receptacle on an access unit or repeater.

**ring latency**. In an IBM Token-Ring Network, the time, measured in bit times at the data transmission rate, required for a signal to propagate once around the ring. Ring latency includes the signal propagation delay through the ring medium, including drop cables, plus the sum of propagation delays through each data station connected to the Token-Ring Network.

**ring network**. A network configuration in which a series of attaching devices is connected by unidirectional transmission links to form a closed path. A ring of an IBM Token-Ring Network is referred to as a LAN segment or as a Token-Ring Network segment.

**ring out (RO)**. In an IBM Token-Ring Network, the transmit or output receptacle on an access unit or repeater.

**ring segment**. A ring segment is any section of a ring that can be isolated (by unplugging connectors) from the rest of the ring. A segment can consist of a single lobe, the cable between access units, or a combination of cables, lobes, and/or access units. See *cable segment*, *LAN segment*.

**root bridge**. In a LAN containing IBM bridges that use automatic single-route broadcast, the bridge that sends the "hello" message on the network every 2 seconds. Automatic single-route broadcast uses the message to detect when bridges enter and leave the network, and to change single-route broadcast parameters accordingly. See also *designated bridge*, *standby bridge*.

**router**. An attaching device that connects two LAN segments, which use similar or different architectures, at the reference model network layer. Contrast with *bridge* and *gateway*.

**routing**. (1) The assignment of the path by which a message will reach its destination. (2) The forwarding of a message unit along a particular path through a network, as determined by the parameters carried in the message unit, such as the destination network address in a transmission header.

## S

**segment**. See *LAN segment, ring segment.*

**server**. (1) A device, program, or code module on a network dedicated to providing a specific service to a network. (2) On a LAN, a data station that provides facilities to other data stations. Examples are a file server, print server, and mail server.

**service access point (SAP)**. (1) A logical point made available by an adapter where information can be received and transmitted. A single SAP can have many links terminating in it. (2) In Open Systems Interconnection (OSI) architecture, the logical point at which an n + 1-layer entity acquires the services of the n-layer. For LANs, the n-layer is assumed to be data link control (DLC). A single SAP can have many links terminating in it. These link "endpoints" are represented in DLC by link stations.

**session**. (1) A connection between two application programs that allows them to communicate. (2) In SNA, a logical connection between two network addressable units that can be activated, tailored to provide various protocols, and deactivated as requested. (3) The data transport connection resulting from a call or link between two devices. (4) The period of time during which a user of a node can communicate with an interactive system, usually the elapsed time between log on and log off. (5) In network architecture, an association of facilities necessary for establishing, maintaining, and releasing connections for communication between stations.

**single-route broadcast**. The forwarding of specially designated broadcast frames only by bridges which have single-route broadcast enabled. If the network is configured correctly, a single-route broadcast frame will have exactly one copy delivered to every LAN segment in the network. Synonymous with *limited broadcast*. See also *automatic single-route broadcast.*

**socket**. Synonym for *port* .

**soft error**. An intermittent error on a network that causes data to have to be transmitted more than once to be received. A soft error affects the network's performance but does not, by itself, affect the network's overall reliability. If the number of soft errors becomes excessive, reliability is affected. Contrast with *hard error*.

**source address**. A field in the medium access control (MAC) frame that identifies the location from which information is sent. Contrast with *destination address*.

**source service access point (SSAP)**. The service access point (SAP) from which a logical link control protocol data unit (LPDU) is originated.

**source service access point (SSAP) address**. The address of the link service access point (LSAP) from which a link protocol data unit (LPDU) is originated. Also, a field in the LPDU.

**standby bridge**. In a LAN using automatic single-route broadcast, a bridge that does not forward single-route broadcast frames. A standby bridge is a parallel bridge or is in a parallel path between two LAN segments. See also *designated bridge, root bridge*.

**station**. (1) A communication device attached to a network. The term used most often in LANs is an *attaching device* or *workstation*. (2) An input or output point of a system that uses telecommunication facilities; for example, one or more systems, computers, terminals, devices, and associated programs at a particular location that can send or receive data over a telecommunication line.

**subsystem**. A secondary or subordinate system, or programming support, usually capable of operating independently of or asynchronously with a controlling system.

**symbolic name**. In a LAN, a name that may be used instead of an adapter or bridge address to identify an adapter location.

# T

**telephone twisted pair**. One or more twisted pairs of copper wire in the unshielded voice-grade cable commonly used to connect a telephone to its wall jack. Also referred to as "unshielded twisted pair"

**throughput**. (1) A measure of the amount of work performed by a computer system over a given period of time, for example, number of jobs per day. (2) A measure of the amount of information transmitted over a network in a given period of time. For example, a network's data transfer rate is usually measured in bits per second.

**token**. A sequence of bits passed from one device to another on the token-ring network that signifies permission to transmit over the network. It consists of a starting delimiter, an access control field, and an end delimiter. The access control field contains a bit that indicates to a receiving device that the token is ready to accept information. If a device has data to send along the network, it appends the data to the token. When data is appended, the token then becomes a frame. See *frame*.

**token-bus network**. A bus network in which a token-passing procedure is used.

**token-passing**. In a token-ring network, the process by which a node captures a token; inserts a message, addresses, and control information; changes the bit pattern of the token to the bit pattern of a frame; transmits the frame; removes the frame from the ring when it has made a complete circuit; generates another token; and transmits the token on the ring where it can be captured by the next node that is ready to transmit.

**token-ring**. A network with a ring topology that passes tokens from one attaching device (node) to another. A node that is ready to send can capture a token and insert data for transmission.

**token-ring network**. (1) A ring network that allows unidirectional data transmission between data stations by a token-passing procedure over one transmission medium so that the transmitted data returns to and is removed by the transmitting station. The IBM Token-Ring Network is a baseband LAN with a star-wired ring topology that passes tokens from network adapter to network adapter.(2) A network that uses a ring topology, in which tokens are passed in a sequence from node to node. A node that is ready to send can capture the token and insert data for transmission. (3) A group of interconnected token rings.

**topology**. The physical or logical arrangement of nodes in a computer network. Examples include ring topology and bus topology.

**transceiver**. Any device that can transmit and receive traffic.

**translator**. In broadband networks, an active device for converting an inbound channel to a higher frequency outbound channel. The conversion is done by removing the inbound carrier, adding the outbound carrier, and amplifying the signal. (A translator amplifies inbound errors and noise distortion.)

**Transmission Control Protocol/Internet Protocol (TCP/IP)**. A set of protocols that allow cooperating computers to share resources across a heterogeneous network.

**twisted pair**. A transmission medium that consists of two insulated conductors twisted together to reduce noise.

## U

**uninterruptible power supply (UPS).** A buffer between utility power or other power source and a load that requires uninterrupted, precise power. It is usually battery powered.

**universally administered address.** The address permanently encoded in an adapter at the time of manufacture. All universally administered addresses are unique. Contrast with *locally administered address*.

**unnumbered acknowledgment.** A data link control (DLC) command used in establishing a link and in answering receipt of logical link control (LLC) frames.

**unshielded twisted pair (UTP).** See *telephone twisted pair*.

# Index

## Numerics



## A



## B

# C

# D



# E

# F



# G

## M



## N

## O



## P

## Q



## R



## S

# T

## U



## V

## W



## X